Lecture Notes in Computer Science 10876

Commenced Publication in 1973
Founding and Former Series Editors:
Gerhard Goos, Juris Hartmanis, and Jan van Leeuwen

More information about this series at http://www.springer.com/series/7407

Rio Yokota · Michèle Weiland
David Keyes · Carsten Trinitis (Eds.)

High Performance Computing

33rd International Conference, ISC High Performance 2018
Frankfurt, Germany, June 24–28, 2018
Proceedings

 Springer

Editors
Rio Yokota (iD)
Tokyo Institute of Technology
Tokyo
Japan

Michèle Weiland
University of Edinburgh
Edinburgh
UK

David Keyes
King Abdullah University of Science
and Technology
Thuwal
Saudi Arabia

Carsten Trinitis
Technische Universität München
Garching bei München
Germany

ISSN 0302-9743   ISSN 1611-3349   (electronic)
Lecture Notes in Computer Science
ISBN 978-3-319-92039-9   ISBN 978-3-319-92040-5   (eBook)
https://doi.org/10.1007/978-3-319-92040-5

Library of Congress Control Number: 2018944377

LNCS Sublibrary: SL1 – Theoretical Computer Science and General Issues

Printed on acid-free paper

This Springer imprint is published by the registered company Springer International Publishing AG
part of Springer Nature
The registered company address is: Gewerbestrasse 11, 6330 Cham, Switzerland

Preface

ISC High Performance, formerly known as the International Supercomputing Conference, was founded in 1986 as the Supercomputer Seminar. Originally organized by Dr. Hans Meuer, Professor of Computer Science at the University of Mannheim and former director of its computer center, the seminar brought together a group of 81 scientists and industrial partners who shared an interest in high-performance computing. Since then, the annual conference has become a major international event within the HPC community and, accompanying its growth in size over the years, the conference has moved from Mannheim via Heidelberg, Dresden, Hamburg, and Leipzig to Frankfurt. With a 25% increase in the number of research papers submitted to the 2018 meeting over 2017, we project further monotonic growth in overall attendees, which reached 3,253 registrants in 2017. Their expertise will make ISC High Performance 2018 a powerful and memorable event.

H-P-C's on a glorious pace;
I-S-C stays on top of the race.
The talks from frontrunners
Will appeal to all comers
And make Frankfurt the happenin' place!

Beginning in 2007, the scientific component of the conference was strengthened with selected talks on research results arising within or relevant to the HPC community. These research paper sessions began as a separate day preceding the conference, and slides and accompanying papers were made available via the conference website. The research paper sessions have since evolved into an integral part of the conference, and the scientific presentations now take place over a period of three days and culminate in this archival proceedings.

For ISC High Performance 2018, the call for participation was issued in Fall 2017, inviting researchers and developers to submit original recent work to the Program Committee. In all, 81 papers were received from authors all over the world. The research papers Program Committee consisted of 83 members selected from 16 countries. Furthermore, 41 external expert reviewers from the community were invited to help with specific papers. After initial reviews were in place, a rebuttal process gave authors an opportunity to respond to reviewers' questions and help clarify issues the reviewers might have. To come to a final consensus on the papers for the program and these proceedings, a face-to-face meeting was held in Frankfurt, where each paper was discussed. Finally, the committee selected 20 papers for shepherding for publication, and for presentation in the research paper sessions.

Artificial Intelligence and Machine Learning was introduced as a track in 2018 and attracted papers touching the intersection of AI and HPC. In some of these, ML is employed for predicting performance that is difficult to model analytically, but for which lots of data exist, such as data center workflows. In other papers, HPC comes to the aid of ML, where single-node memory or performance is insufficient.

As exascale designs are now projected to exceed the originally hoped for maximum power of 20 MW, the energy efficiency of HPC systems and their components was a theme that ran through the technical program. Throw in the challenges of heterogeneity and variability in processing and memory systems, and the increasingly awkward latencies of I/O and messaging, and one has the ingredients for a technical feast. We believe that this volume will appeal across a broad range of specializations.

For the past several years, the ISC High Performance conference has presented an ISC-sponsored award to encourage outstanding research and to honor the overall best research paper submitted to the conference. Two years ago, this annual award was renamed the *Hans Meuer Award* in memory of the late Dr. Hans Meuer, General Chair of the ISC conference from 1986 through 2014, and a co-founder of the TOP500 benchmark project. From all research papers submitted, the research papers Program Committee nominated two papers as finalists for the award and, based on the final presentations during the conference, elected the best paper.

Two award committees selected papers considered to be of exceptional quality and worthy of special recognition:

– The Hans Meuer Award honors the overall best research paper submitted to the conference. The two finalists for this award were:

  "Compiler-Assisted Source-to-Source Skeletonization of Application Models for System Simulation" by Joseph Kenny, Samuel Knight, Sébastien Rumley, and Jeremiah Wilke
  "Chebyshev Filter Diagonalization on Modern Manycore Processors and GPGPUs" by Alan Bishop, Dominik Ernst, Holger Fehske, Georg Hager, Moritz Kreutzer, and Gerhard Wellein.

– The Gauss Centre for Supercomputing sponsors the Gauss Award. This award is assigned to the most outstanding paper in the field of scalable supercomputing and went to:

  "On the Accuracy and Usefulness of Analytic Energy Models for Contemporary Multicore Processors" by Johannes Hofmann, Georg Hager, and Dietmar Fey.

We would like to express our gratitude to all our colleagues for submitting papers to the ISC scientific sessions, as well as to the members of the Program Committee for organizing this year's attractive program.

As a haiku announcing the research papers program put it:
Collective wisdom
Is exponentiated,
Not merely added.

June 2018

Rio Yokota
Michèle Weiland
David Keyes
Carsten Trinitis

Organization

Research Papers Program Committee

Reseach Paper Chair and Deputy Chair

David Keyes   KAUST, Saudi Arabia
Carsten Trinitis   Technical University of Munich, Germany

Architectures and Networks

Holger Fröning   University of Heidelberg, Germany
Pedro Garcia   University of Castilla-La Mancha, Spain
Georgios Goumas   National Technical University of Athens, Greece
Wolfgang Karl   Karlsruhe Institute of Technology, Germany
Sébastien Rumley   Columbia University, USA
Martin Schulz (Track Chair)   Technical University of Munich, Germany
Federico Silla   Technical University of Valencia, Spain
Peter Ziegenhein   The Institute of Cancer Research, UK

Artificial Intelligence and Machine Learning

Christoph Angerer   NVIDIA, USA
Gonzalo Hernandez   USACH, Chile
Janis Keuper   Fraunhofer ITWM, Germany
Romeo Kienzler   IBM, Switzerland
Chuan Lu   Aberystwyth University, UK
Lukas Lukas   Universitas Katolik Indonesia Atma Jaya, Indonesia
Hayk Shoukourian   Leibniz Supercomputing Centre, Germany
Michael Steyer   Intel Corporation, Germany
Johan Suykens   KU Leuven, Belgium
Marcel Tilly   Microsoft, USA
Yu Wang (Track Chair)   Leibniz Supercomputing Centre, Germany
Edward Zimmermann   NONMONOTONIC Networks, Germany

Data, Storage, and Visualization

Timo Bremer (Track Chair)   Lawrence Livermore National Laboratory, USA
Mahdi Bohlouli   Institute of Web Science and Technologies,
                                 University of Koblenz, Germany
Matthieu Dorier   Argonne National Laboratory, USA
Steffen Frey   University of Stuttgart, Germany
Hideyuki Kawashima   University of Tsukuba, Japan
Jay Lofstead   Sandia National Laboratory, USA
Valerio Pascucci   University of Utah, USA

John Patchett   Los Alamos National Laboratory, USA
Shinji Sumimoto   Fujitsu, Japan
Ryousei Takano   AIST, Japan
Osamu Tatebe   University of Tsukuba, Japan
Venkatram Vishwanath   Argonne National Laboratory, USA

HPC Algorithms

Ilkay Altintas   San Diego Supercomputing Center, USA
Yuefan Deng   Stony Brook University, USA
Harald Köstler   FAU Erlangen-Nuremberg, Germany
Miriam Mehl   University of Stuttgart, Germany
Marek Michalewicz   ICM, University of Warsaw, Poland
Kengo Nakajima   The University of Tokyo, Japan
Philipp Neumann   German Climate Computing Center, Germany
  (Track Chair)
Lena Oden   Forschungszentrum Jülich, Germany
Daniel Ruprecht   University of Leeds, UK
Ana Lucia Varbanescu   University of Amsterdam, The Netherlands
Tobias Weinzierl   University of Durham, UK

HPC Applications

Vassil Dimitrov   University of Calgary, Canada
Hubertus Franke   IBM Research, USA
Guido Juckeland   HZDR, Germany
Gokcen Kestor   Oak Ridge National Laboratory, USA
Scott Klasky   Oak Ridge National Laboratory, USA
Axel Klawonn   Universität zu Köln, Germany
Miquel Moretó   Universitat Politècnica de Catalunya, Spain
Gabriel Noaje   NVIDIA, Singapore
Miquel Pericas   Chalmers University of Technology, Sweden
Michela Taufer   University of Delaware, USA
Antonio Tumeo   Pacific Northwest National Laboratory, USA
  (Track Chair)

Performance Modeling and Measurement

Christos Antonopoulos   University of Thessaly, Greece
Suren Byna   Lawrence Berkeley National Lab, USA
Yuefan Deng   Stony Brook University, USA
Jan Eitzinger   Erlangen Regional Computing Center, Germany
Allen Malony   University of Oregon, USA
Marek Michalewicz   ICM, University of Warsaw, Poland
Dimitrios Nikolopoulos   Queen's University Belfast, UK
Fabrice Rastello   Inria, Grenoble, France
Saday Sadayappan   Ohio State University, USA
  (Track Chair)

Aravind Sukumaran-Rajam   Ohio State University, USA
Josef Weidendorfer   Leibniz Supercomputing Centre/Technical University
                             of Munich, Germany

Programming Models and Systems Software

Ilkay Altintas   San Diego Supercomputing Center, USA
Alexandru Calotoiu   Technical University of Darmstadt, Germany
Bradford L. Chamberlain   Cray Inc., USA
Clemens Grelck   University of Amsterdam, The Netherlands
Christian Lengauer   Universität Passau, FIM, Germany
Simon McIntosh-Smith   University of Bristol, UK
Miriam Mehl   University of Stuttgart, Germany
Richard Membarth   DFKI & Saarland University, Germany
Marek Michalewicz   ICM, University of Warsaw, Poland
Lawrence Mitchell   Imperial College London, UK
Bernd Mohr   Juelich Supercomputing Centre, Germany
Antoniu Pop   The University of Manchester, UK
Sven-Bodo Scholz   Heriot-Watt University, UK
  (Track Chair)
Alex Shafarenko   University of Hertfordshire, UK
Hans Vandierendonck   Queen's University Belfast, UK
Tobias Weinzierl   University of Durham, UK

PhD Forum Program Committee

Hans-Joachim Bungartz   Technical University of Munich, Germany
Florina Ciorba   University of Basel, Switzerland
  (Deputy Chair)
Ewa Deelman   USC Information Sciences Institute, USA
Gracia Ester Martin Garzón   Almería University, Spain
Georgios Goumas   National Technical University of Athens, Greece
Alexandru Iosup   Vrije Universiteit Amsterdam and Technical University
                             of Delft, The Netherlands
Lois McInnes   Argonne National Laboratory, USA
Miriam Mehl   University of Stuttgart, Germany
Bernd Mohr   Juelich Supercomputing Centre, Germany
Raymond Namyst   University of Bordeaux, Inria, France
Rizos Sakellariou   The University of Manchester, UK
Olaf Schenk   Università della Svizzera Italiana, Switzerland
Martin Schulz   Technical University of Munich, Germany
Srishti Srivastava   University of Southern Indiana, USA
Bettina Schnor   University of Potsdam, Germany
Gerhard Wellein (Chair)   FAU Erlangen-Nuremberg, Germany

Research Posters Program Committee

Sunita Chandrasekaran (Deputy Chair)	University of Delaware, USA
James H. Cownie	Intel, UK
Saber Feki	KAUST, Saudi Arabia
Andy Herdman	AWE, UK
Guido Juckeland	HZDR, Germany
Andreas Knuepfer	Technical University Dresden, Germany
Julian Kunkel	Deutsches Klimarechenzentrum, Germany
John Leidel	Texas Tech University, USA
Naoya Maruyama	Lawrence Livermore National Laboratory, USA
Simon McIntosh-Smith	University of Bristol, UK
Matthias Müller (Chair)	RWTH Aachen University, Germany
Hitoshi Murai	RIKEN, Japan
Sameer Shende	University of Oregon, USA
Dirk Schmidl	Atos, Germany
Emmanuelle Saillard	Inria, France
Rich Vuduc	Georgia Institute of Technology, USA
Felix Wolf	Technical University Darmstadt, Germany

Project Posters Program Committee

Alvaro Aguilera	Technische Universität Dresden, Germany
Valeria Bartsch	Fraunhofer, Germany
Thomas Bönisch	High-Performance Computing Center Stuttgart, Germany
Matt Bryson	University of California, Santa Cruz, USA
Anja Gerbes	FIAS, Germany
Weicheng Huang	National Center for High-Performance Computing, Taiwan
Nabeeh Jumah	University of Hamburg, Germany
Oleksiy Koshulko	Glushkov Institute of Cybernetics of NASU, Russia
Julian Kunkel (Chair)	Deutsches Klimarechenzentrum, Germany
Glenn K. Lockwood	Lawrence Berkeley National Laboratory, USA
George S. Markomanolis	KAUST, Saudi Arabia
Alexander Moskovsky	RSC Group, Russia
Philipp Neumann	German Climate Computing Center, Germany
Ying Qian	East China Normal University, China
Yuichi Tsujita	RIKEN AICS, Japan
Ekaterina Tutlyaeva (Deputy Chair)	RSC Group, Russia
Rio Yokota	Tokyo Institute of Technology, Japan

Tutorials Committee

Damian Alvarez Mallon	Forschungszentrum Jülich, Germany
Rosa M. Badia (Chair)	Barcelona Supercomputing Center, Spain
Pavan Balaji	Argonne National Laboratory, USA
Alejandro Duran	Intel, Spain
Fernanda Foertter	Oak Ridge National Laboratory, USA
Dario Garcia	Barcelona Supercomputing Center, Spain
Ganesh Gopalakrishnan	University of Utah, USA
Gregory L. Lee	Lawrence Livermore National Laboratory, USA
Christian Perez	Inria, France
Enrique Quintana	Universidad Jaime I, Spain
William Sawyer	Swiss National Supercomputing Centre, Switzerland
Martin Schulz	Technical University of Munich, Germany
Eric Stotzer	Texas Instruments, USA
Domenico Talia	Universitá della Calabria, Italy
Michèle Weiland	EPCC, The University of Edinburgh, UK
Sandra Wienke (Deputy Chair)	RWTH Aachen University, Germany

BoFs Committee

David Bader	Georgia Institute of Technology, USA
Claudia Blaas-Schenner	Technical University of Vienna, Austria
Sunita Chandrasekaran	University of Delaware, USA
Dona Crawford	Lawrence Livermore National Laboratory, USA
Anne C. Elster	Norwegian University of Science and Technology, Norway
Nahid Emad	University of Versailles, France
Gerard Gorman	Imperial College London, UK
José Gracia	University of Stuttgart, HLRS, Germany
Georg Hager (Chair)	University Erlangen-Nuremberg, Germany
Harald Köstler	FAU Erlangen-Nuremberg, Germany
Oana Marin	Argonne National Laboratory, USA
Simon McIntosh-Smith (Deputy Chair)	University of Bristol, UK
Lawrence Mitchell	Imperial College London, UK
Marie-Christine Sawley	Intel, France
Masha Sosonkina	Old Dominion University, USA
Hinnerk Stüben	Universität Hamburg, Germany
Vladimir Voevodin	Moscow State University, Russia
Jan Wender	Atos BDS science+computing AG, Germany
Andreas Wierse	SICOS BW GmbH, Germany
Xingfu Wu	Argonne National Laboratory, USA
Roman Wyrzykowski	Czestochowa University of Technology, Poland

Workshop Committee

Sadaf Alam (Deputy Chair)	Swiss National Supercomputing Centre, Switzerland
Rosa M. Badia	Barcelona Supercomputing Center, Spain
François Bodin	IRISA, France
Bronis R. de Supinski	Lawrence Livermore National Laboratory, USA
Bilel Hadri	KAUST, Saudi Arabia
Heike Jagode	University of Tennessee, USA
Simon McIntosh-Smith	University of Bristol, UK
Bernd Mohr	Juelich Supercomputing Centre, Germany
Diana Moise	Cray, Switzerland
John Shalf (Chair)	Lawrence Berkeley National Laboratory, USA
Michela Taufer	University of Delaware, USA
Carsten Trinitis	Technical University of Munich, Germany
Antonio Tumeo	Pacific Northwest National Laboratory, USA
Didem Unat	Koç Universitesi, Turkey
Michèle Weiland (Workshop Proceedings Deputy Chair)	EPCC, The University of Edinburgh, UK
Rio Yokota (Workshop Proceedings Chair)	Tokyo Institute of Technology, Japan

Contents

Exascale Networks

Parallel Algorithms

Resource Management and Energy Efficiency

Heterogeneity-Aware Resource Allocation in HPC Systems

Alessio Netti[1(✉)], Cristian Galleguillos[1,2], Zeynep Kiziltan[1], Alina Sîrbu[3,4], and Ozalp Babaoglu[1]

[1] Department of Computer Science and Engineering,
University of Bologna, Bologna, Italy
{`alessio.netti,zeynep.kiziltan,ozalp.babaoglu`}`@unibo.it`
[2] Escuela de Ing. Informática, Pontificia Universidad Católica de Valparaíso,
Valparaíso, Chile
`cristian.galleguillos.m@mail.pucv.cl`
[3] Department of Computer Science, University of Pisa, Pisa, Italy
`alina.sirbu@unipi.it`
[4] Science Division, New York University Abu Dhabi,
Abu Dhabi, United Arab Emirates

Abstract. In their march towards exascale performance, HPC systems are becoming increasingly more heterogeneous in an effort to keep power consumption at bay. Exploiting accelerators such as GPUs and MICs together with traditional processors to their fullest requires heterogeneous HPC systems to employ intelligent job dispatchers that go beyond the capabilities of those that have been developed for homogeneous systems. In this paper, we propose three new heterogeneity-aware resource allocation algorithms suitable for building job dispatchers for any HPC system. We use real workload traces extracted from the Eurora HPC system to analyze the performance of our allocators when they are coupled with different schedulers. Our experimental results show that significant improvements can be obtained in job response times and system throughput over solutions developed for homogeneous systems. Our study also helps to characterize the operating conditions in which heterogeneity-aware resource allocation becomes crucial for heterogeneous HPC systems.

1 Introduction

Motivation. Modern scientific discovery is increasingly being driven by computation and High-Performance Computing (HPC) systems have come to play a fundamental role as "instruments" not unlike the microscopes and telescopes of the previous century [20]. Despite the enormous progress that has been achieved in processor technologies, we are still far from considering many important problems "solvable" using a computational approach. These problems include turbulence of fluids in finite domains, combustion hydrodynamics, computational biology, natural language understanding and modeling of the human brain [1].

© Springer International Publishing AG, part of Springer Nature 2018
R. Yokota et al. (Eds.): ISC High Performance 2018, LNCS 10876, pp. 3–21, 2018.
https://doi.org/10.1007/978-3-319-92040-5_1

Future HPC systems will achieve the performance required to solve these problems through a combination of faster processors and massive parallelism. Yet, a homogeneous parallelism employing millions of processor cores will result in power requirements that are unsustainable. Thus, the parallelism has to be heterogeneous, employing specialized energy-efficient accelerator units such as GPUs and MICs in addition to the traditional CPUs. In fact, among the top 100 HPCs of the latest Top500 List[1] (updated on 06-2017), almost 30% are based on GPUs and/or MICs.

Traditionally, HPC systems have been used to run compute-intensive jobs requiring days or even weeks to complete their massive computations. There is an increasing trend where HPC systems are being used to run "big data workloads" consisting of many shorter jobs performing data analytics as data is being streamed from a monitored system [16,17]. The ability to build predictive models from streamed data opens up the possibility for acting on the predictions in real time [15]. Turning this scenario into an effective "on-line control" mechanism requires intelligent strategies to achieve elevated levels of system performance with high throughput and low response times so that the predictive models built from data analytics correspond to recent, rather than a distant, past states of the monitored system.

The potential to fully exploit the raw computing potential of an HPC system and deliver it to applications (jobs) is conditional on intelligent system software making informed decisions to efficiently manage system resources. Among these decisions, those made by a *dispatcher* regarding job executions are particularly important for ensuring high levels of system performance. In an HPC system, the *scheduler* component of a dispatcher selects which jobs to run next among those currently in the wait queue; whereas the *allocator* component decides which resources to allocate for running them. While the scheduling aspect of dispatching has received considerable attention in the literature [5], the allocation problem has been studied to a lesser extent. Intelligent allocation is particularly important in heterogeneous systems where poor decisions can lead to poor resource usage and consequently poor performance of critical applications [13].

Related Work. Resource allocation strategies used in many popular HPC workload management systems [14,22] can be characterized as variations of well-known memory allocation heuristics such as *First-Fit* (FF) and *Best-Fit* (BF) [19]. In memory allocation, FF chooses the first block of memory that is large enough to satisfy the request. In an analogous manner, an FF resource allocator chooses the first resource among a list of available resources that satisfies a job's request. FF is primarily focused on satisfying a single job request without any regard for global considerations of resource usage. A BF allocator, on the other hand, chooses a resource, among a list of available resources, that is able to satisfy the job's request while leaving the smallest possible unused capacity.

These simple heuristics can be improved in several ways in an effort to utilize resources more intelligently so as to improve job response times and system

---

[1] https://www.top500.org/.

throughput. In [3], a "lookahead" capability is added to BF, taking into account the needs of other jobs in the queue. Specifically, resources are allocated to the current job in a manner such that, if possible, enough resources remain available for the largest job (requiring the largest amount of resources) in the queue. A similar idea can be applied to scheduling where a *backfilling scheduler* [18] selects short, low-resource jobs to fill the gaps in resource usage left over after scheduling larger jobs, even if the short jobs are not next in the queue. Large jobs that cannot be scheduled are blocked and resources are reserved for them. Instead of considering just one job at a time during the backfilling phase, multiple jobs can be considered together so that resource usage is improved [18]. In [12], resource allocation takes into account saturation of shared resources, such as memory bandwidth, that can cause some jobs to take longer to complete. To make a suitable allocation that does not reduce system throughput, penalties based on memory bandwidth saturation are included in the FF allocation heuristic.

The main shortcoming of the allocation strategies described above is that they were designed for a single resource type such as a CPU and do not consider characteristics inherent to heterogeneous systems, including different resource types or different configurations of the same resource type. This limitation can lead to unbalanced usage and fragmentation of heterogeneous resources, and cause undesirable delays. For instance, in [4], a dispatcher is presented for the heterogeneous HPC system *Eurora* [7] that has GPU co-processors in half of its nodes and MIC co-processors in the other half. For allocation, however, the dispatcher uses the simple BF heuristic, sorting the nodes by the total number of available computing resources, making no distinction between CPUs, GPUs or MICs. Consequently, with many jobs requesting just CPUs as processing resources, a simple allocation of computing resources will result in unnecessary delays for jobs that require GPUs or MICs in addition to CPUs.

In [23] multiple resources (CPU, bandwidth, memory) are considered and bottleneck resources are identified to obtain fair resource allocation to users. However, they do not consider systems with resources that are available only on a subset of all the nodes, such as the GPUs and MICs that characterize the systems we are analyzing. To the best of our knowledge, no previous work focusing on resource allocation for heterogeneous HPC systems exists.

Contributions. In this paper, we present several resource allocation algorithms for heterogeneous systems that adopt different strategies for minimizing wastage of critical resources, and consequently, minimizing job delays. The algorithms are based on simple heuristics that exhibit good performance with low compu-tational overhead, and are general enough to be applied to any heterogeneous HPC system where critical resources need to be managed efficiently. We eval-uate our allocators when combined with a suite of different schedulers using a workload trace collected from the Eurora HPC system. Our experimental results show that significant improvements can be obtained in job response times and system throughput compared to standard solutions like FF and BF. Our study also helps to characterize the operating conditions in which heterogeneity-aware resource allocation becomes crucial for heterogeneous HPC systems.

Table 1. Frequency and average duration of all jobs and the three classes CPU-based, MIC-based and GPU-based in the Eurora workload.

Job class	Share	Count	Average duration [hh:mm:ss]
All	100%	372320	00:16:08
CPU-based	22.8%	85046	00:47:36
MIC-based	0.7%	2500	00:56:28
GPU-based	76.4%	284774	00:06:23

Organization. The rest of the paper is organized as follows. The next Section briefly describes the Eurora HPC system, its workload datasets, and the scheduling algorithms we used in conjunction with our allocators for dispatching purposes. In Sect. 3 we introduce our allocation algorithms, while Sect. 4 presents our experimental evaluation results. Section 5 concludes the paper.

2   HPC System, Data and Job Dispatching

2.1   Eurora and the Workload Dataset

We evaluate our allocation strategies using workload data collected from the Eurora HPC system [7]. Eurora is a hybrid installation hosted at Cineca[2], the largest datacenter in Italy, that uses a combination of CPUs, GPUs and MICs to achieve very high energy efficiency. The system consists of 64 nodes, each equipped with two octa-core CPUs (Intel Xeon E5) and two accelerators. Half of the nodes have two GPUs as accelerators (Nvidia Tesla Kepler), while the other half have two MICs (Intel Xeon Phi Knights Corner). The resulting system is highly heterogeneous, making allocation of resources to jobs nontrivial.

The HPC workload, consisting of almost 400,000 jobs that were run on Eurora during the time period April 2014–August 2015, has been recorded as a trace and made available by Cineca. For our study, we classify the jobs in the workload based on their duration as *short* (under 1 h), *medium* (between 1 and 5 h) and *long* (over 5 h). Of all the jobs, 93.14% are short, 6.10% are medium and 0.75% are long. Hence, the workload is quite varied from this point of view. We further divide jobs into three classes based on the computing resources that they require: *CPU-based* jobs use CPUs only, while *MIC-based* and *GPU-based* jobs use MIC or GPU accelerators, respectively, in addition to CPUs. Table 1 shows statistics for each job class in the workload. We observe that GPU-based jobs are the most numerous, followed by CPU-based jobs, while MIC-based jobs are relatively few. In terms of duration, we observe that CPU-based jobs are on average longer than GPU-based jobs, consuming significantly more resources. This heterogeneity of job classes increases the difficulty of allocation decisions. Since CPU-based jobs are longer, they may keep nodes that have accelerators busy

---

[2] https://www.cineca.it/.

for longer periods, during which their accelerators are not available for other jobs. Given that GPU-based jobs are the most frequent, this can cause bottlenecks to form in the system, motivating the development of heterogeneity-aware allocation algorithms to be described in the following sections.

2.2 Scheduling Algorithms in Job Dispatching

In an HPC system, allocation goes hand in hand with scheduling in order to perform job dispatching. To test our allocation algorithms, we combined them with four state-of-the-art scheduling algorithms: *Shortest Job First* (SJF), *Easy Back-filling* (EBF), *Priority Rule-Based* (PRB), and *Constraint Programming Hybrid* (CPH). All these algorithms have been previously applied to Eurora workload data in [11], where it was shown that accurate prediction of job duration can improve scheduling performance. In the rest of this section we describe briefly the schedulers employed.

SJF. At scheduling time, the SJF scheduler selects the shortest job among all jobs in the queue to be scheduled first. The job is then passed to the allocator to be granted the required resources. A predicted job duration is used as the job length to establish an order.

EBF. This scheduling algorithm considers jobs in order of their arrival [21]. If there aren't enough available resources in the system for a given job that has been selected for scheduling, the job is blocked, and a reservation is made for it. A reservation consists of a starting time (computed using the predicted duration of running jobs) when enough resources are expected to become available to start the blocked job. A set of resources, as determined by the allocator, is also associated with the reservation and will be used for the blocked job at reservation time. While the blocked job waits for its reserved resources to become available, the algorithm will schedule shorter jobs that are expected to terminate before the starting time of the reservation (again based on predicted duration), using currently unused resources.

PRB. This algorithm sorts the set of jobs to be scheduled according to a priority rule, running those with higher priority first [6]. In our work, we use priority rules based on jobs' urgency in leaving the queue, as introduced by Borghesi et al. in [4]. To determine if a job could wait in the queue, the ratio between the current waiting time and the expected waiting time of the job is calculated. The expected waiting time is computed from data as the average waiting time over a certain queue. As a tie breaker, the "job demand" is used, which is the job's combined resource requirements multiplied by the predicted job duration.

CPH. One of the drawbacks of the aforementioned heuristic schedulers is the limited exploration of the solution space. Recent results show that methods based on *constraint programming* (CP) are able of outperforming traditional PRB methods [2]. To increase scalability, Borghesi et al. introduce a hybrid scheduler called *CPH* [4] combining CP and a heuristic algorithm, which we use in this paper. CPH is composed of two phases. In the first phase jobs are scheduled using CP, minimizing the total job waiting time. At this stage, each resource type is considered as a unique resource — CPU availability corresponds to the sum of the available CPUs of all the computing nodes, memory availability corresponds to the sum of the memory availability of all the computing nodes, and so on. Due to the problem's complexity, the search is bound by a time limit; the best solution found within the limit is the scheduling decision. The preliminary schedule generated in the first stage may contain some inconsistencies because of considering the available resources as a whole. The second phase performs resource allocation according to a heuristic in which any inconsistencies are removed. The specific heuristic being used depends on the allocator component of the dispatcher. If a job can be mapped to a node then it will be dispatched, otherwise it will be postponed.

2.3   Job Duration Prediction in Job Dispatching

An issue in simulating job dispatching strategies regards what information contained in the workload can be used when making decisions. A specific case is that of job durations. Since the workload data contains exact job durations, it is tempting to use them in order to make dispatching decisions. However, in a real system, exact job durations are not known in advance, so dispatching decisions cannot be based on this knowledge. Here, we take this into account and use instead *predicted* job durations, based on a very simple heuristic that was proposed in [11] and exploits time locality of job durations for individual users that was observed in the Eurora workload dataset. Specifically, it has been observed that consecutive jobs by the same user tend to have similar durations, especially when they have the same profile (job name, resources requested, queue, etc.). From time to time, a switch to a different duration is observed, which could happen, for example, when the user changes input datasets or the algorithm itself. Using this observation, the authors devise a set of rules to apply in order to predict job durations. They record job profiles for users, and their last durations. When a new job arrives in the system, they look for a job with the same or similar profile, and consider its duration to be also the duration of the new job. If no past profile is similar enough, the predicted duration is the default wall-time of the queue where the job is submitted. In case a match is found, the predicted duration is capped by the maximum wall-time of the queue. Both default and maximum wall-time values of the queues are part of the configuration of the dispatcher.

The mean absolute error (MAE) of this heuristic prediction with respect to the real job duration on the Eurora workload dataset is shown to be 40 min [11]. In the absence of any prediction, users supply dispatchers their own job duration estimation, which is typically the maximum wall-time of the queue. In the absence of even this information, the dispatchers use the default wall-time of the queue. We will refer to this as the wall-time approach. The MAE of the wall-time approach on the Eurora workload is 225 min [11], which is dramatically worse than that of the proposed prediction technique. The heuristic prediction therefore shows an improvement of 82% over the wall-time approach. We shall note that the time locality of job durations for individual users is not specific to the Eurora workload. It can also be observed in other workload datasets to which the same heuristic prediction can be applied. An example is the Gaia workload dataset[3] of the University of Luxemburg. We calculated that the MAE of the wall-time approach is 2918 min, while it is 220 min with our heuristic prediction, showing an improvement of 93%. The notable improvement over the Eurora dataset can be explained by the fact that the maximum wall-time values in Gaia are higher than those of Eurora.

3   Allocation Algorithms

Here we describe the allocation algorithms that we designed and implemented for heterogeneous HPC systems. We assume that a job is composed of multiple job units (such as MPI processes), each having the same resource requirement. All the algorithms are based on the *all-requested-computers-available* principle [21]: when an allocator is invoked for job j, nodes in the system are searched sequentially according to a specific order, and the largest number of *job units* of job j are allocated while traversing the nodes. The allocation process ends when either all job units have been allocated, in which case the allocation succeeds, or the list of nodes is exhausted, in which case the allocation fails. The jobs are ordered as specified by the scheduler, while the ordering criteria for the nodes is specific to the allocator. Our algorithms provide custom criteria for node ordering, resulting in allocation strategies with different strengths. The algorithms are generic and provide configuration parameters, hence they do not rely on any specific system architecture and can be tuned suitably for any heterogeneous system in consideration. In the following, we call a resource type *critical* if careless usage of the respective nodes may cause bottlenecks in the system.

Balanced Heuristic. The main focus of this algorithm is to avoid the fragmentation of *user-defined critical resource types*, like accelerators, by *limiting* and *balancing* the use of the respective nodes. The limiting effect is achieved by pushing the nodes with critical resources towards the end of the list of available nodes. In this way, by selecting nodes from the beginning of the list, jobs that do not need critical resources will not block such resources. The *balancing* effect is achieved by *interleaving* nodes having different types of critical resources, thus not favoring any of them.

By default, the critical resource types for Eurora are MIC and GPU, but they can be modified by the user based on the system architecture. The algorithm works in two phases. First, all nodes in the system are collected in *bins*: there is a bin for each critical resource type, and nodes are assigned to a specific bin according to which of those they currently have available. If they do not have any, they will be assigned to a special *nul* bin; conversely, they will be assigned to the bin for which they have the maximum availability, if multiple critical resources

---

[3] http://www.cs.huji.ac.il/labs/parallel/workload/l_unilu_gaia/index.html.

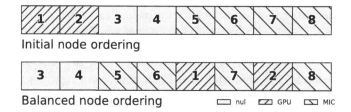

Fig. 1. An example of BALANCED node ordering on a small system with 8 nodes, each labeled with an ID and colored according to its corresponding bin.

are present (note that in Eurora, a node has only one type of critical resource). The bins are then combined in a final node list, which is built as follows: nodes belonging to the *nul* bin, which do not have any critical resource, are placed at the head. The rest of the list is built incrementally by picking a node from the *currently largest* bin until they are all empty. An example of BALANCED node ordering in a small system with 8 nodes can be seen in Fig. 1.

This type of reasoning is expected to be beneficial in an architecture like Eurora, where two continuous blocks of nodes have either GPU or MIC resources and are thus prone to unbalanced node usage. The BALANCED allocator does not consider the distribution of the resource requirements of jobs submitted to the system, and assumes that all critical resource types are used uniformly. This design choice ignores that some resources can become critical at runtime when the distribution is heavily skewed towards a specific resource type, but at the same time it increases the algorithm's robustness against sudden bursts of jobs requiring that specific resource. While BALANCED can be used in any system by suitably defining the critical resource types that must be protected, it is most effective on systems that are known to possess multiple critical resource types.

Weighted Heuristic. This algorithm is more general than BALANCED as it is able to detect the critical resources at runtime, as opposed to them being statically defined by the user, and focuses on avoiding their wastage. It is based on the popular BF heuristic, which at each allocation time sorts the nodes in non-decreasing order with respect to the total amount of available resources. BF can easily waste some resources as it does not distinguish between different resource types. WEIGHTED is instead aware of heterogeneous resources and adds lookahead features to allocation to increase the chance of success. For each job during allocation, it sorts the nodes in non-decreasing order of their ranking. A node is ranked based on the criticality of its resource types and their availability after a potential allocation. Consequently, nodes with highly critical resource types and nodes which will be providing high availability after allocation are pushed towards the end of the list, in order to be protected against jobs that do not need such resources, similar to what BALANCED does with nodes containing user-defined critical resources.

More formally, for a job allocation, after the number of job units that fit on a certain node is calculated, the *impact* of the allocation is defined for each resource type to be the amount of resources still available in the node after such allocation. We thus have, for each node i and for each resource type $k \in r$, an impact value $imp_{i,k}$. The impact serves to measure the resource wastage after allocation in the presence of multiple resource types. The ranking R_i of a node i is then computed by summing the $imp_{i,k}$ of each resource type k available on node i weighted by w_k:

$$R_i = \sum_{k \in r} w_k * imp_{i,k} \qquad w_k = \frac{\overline{req_k} * load_k}{cap_k} \qquad (1)$$

A weight w_k is computed at the system level and quantifies the level of criticality of a certain resource type k using three parameters as in Eq. 1. The first parameter $\overline{req_k}$ is the average amount requested for k by jobs in the queue. A highly requested resource type is considered critical. This average is computed over all jobs in the queue, weighted by the jobs' duration prediction. Considering the job duration as well in the average is mostly a fairness consideration, since most of our schedulers, like SJF, tend to favor shorter jobs. The second parameter $load_k$ is the *load ratio* for k, which is the ratio between the amount of resources used at a certain time and the total resource capacity of the system for k, assuming that resources assigned to jobs are always used fully [8]. A high load ratio means low availability, which makes the resource type critical. The $load_k$ parameter, however, does not consider the total capacity cap_k which can influence the criticality of k. We therefore use cap_k as a normalization factor.

With multiple factors assessing the criticality of resource types, WEIGHTED is expected to perform well in many scenarios. WEIGHTED is thus more flexible than BALANCED, even though it does not possess its interleaving capability.

Priority-Weighted Heuristic. The WEIGHTED and BALANCED allocators are expected to be most effective in different scenarios, with BALANCED performing better in the presence of bursts of jobs requiring critical resources, and vice versa. PRIORITY-WEIGHTED is a hybrid strategy, trying to combine the strengths of both allocators in order to obtain optimal performance. This algorithm extends WEIGHTED, by adding a new multiplicative parameter p_k to w_k. Specifically, p_k acts as a bounded *priority value*, used only for user-defined critical resource types like in BALANCED. For the other resource types, it is assumed to be always equal to 1. Such a priority value is calculated at runtime in a simple way: starting with the value 1, every time the allocation for a job requiring a critical resource type k fails, its priority value p_k is increased by 1. Conversely, when the allocation succeeds, p_k is decreased by 1. If a job requires multiple critical resource types, all the related p_k values are affected. The bound of p_k is user-defined and is set to 10 by default.

This solution allows us to take into account the runtime criticality of resources (like in WEIGHTED) and to protect user-defined critical resources (like in BALANCED) in a rather dynamic way by adjusting to the system's behavior. Various other solutions were tried for p_k, such as the average number of allocation failures per job or per allocation time, or the number of jobs in the queue for which allocation has previously failed. Out of all of these, our priority mechanism emerged to be the best technique, despite its simplicity.

4   Experimental Results

In this section, we present the experimental results obtained by using the Eurora workload dataset described in Sect. 2.1. All the data available for the Eurora system has been considered in the experiments. Due to space limitations, we cannot report tests performed on other systems.

4.1   Experimental Setup

Simulation of the Eurora system along with job submission and job dispatching were carried out using the open-source AccaSim HPC Simulator [10]. A total of 20 dispatchers were employed, which were obtained by combining the 4 scheduling algorithms (SJF, EBF, PRB, CPH) described in Sect. 2 together with 5 allocation algorithms: the three described in Sect. 3 (B, W, P-W) together with First-Fit (FF) and Best-Fit (BF). FF and BF are included solely for the purpose of comparison. Interpreted in the context of Eurora, FF searches the nodes with available resources in a static order, while BF sorts the nodes in non-decreasing order of the amount of available resources. The experiments were performed on a dedicated server with a 16-core Intel Xeon CPU and 8 GB of RAM, running Linux Ubuntu 16.04. All the dispatchers along with their source code in Python are available on the AccaSim website.[4]

In the experiments, we evaluate dispatchers in terms of their impact on job response times and system throughput, characterized by two metrics. The first is the *job slowdown*, a common indicator for evaluating job scheduling algorithms [9], which quantifies the effect of a dispatching method on the jobs themselves and is directly perceived also by the HPC users. The slowdown of a job j is a normalized response time and is defined as $slowdown_j = (T_{w,j} + T_{r,j})/T_{r,j}$, where $T_{w,j}$ and $T_{r,j}$ are the waiting time and duration of job j, respectively. A job waiting more than its duration has a higher slowdown than a job waiting less than its duration. The second metric is the *queue size*, which counts the number of queued jobs at a certain dispatching time. This metric is a measure of the effects of dispatching on the computing system itself. The lower these two metrics are, the better job response times and system throughput are.

We also compared the dispatchers in terms of their resource utilization. The metric we adopt for this purpose is the popular *system load ratio* [8] which considers the ratio between the amount of used resources in the HPC system at a certain time and its total resource capacity, assuming that resources assigned to jobs are always used fully.

---

[4] http://accasim.readthedocs.io/en/latest/.

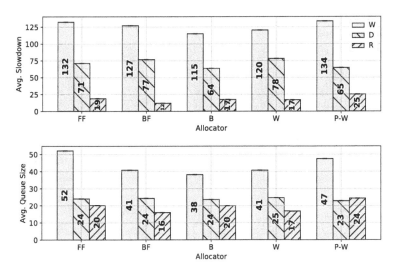

Fig. 2. Average slowdown and queue size results over the entire workload dataset using the CPH scheduler and five different allocators with wall-time (W), data-driven (D) and real duration (R) predictions for job durations.

4.2   Results over the Entire Workload Dataset

We first discuss the results obtained over the entire workload dataset. All the dispatchers are run using three different job duration predictions: wall-time (W), the data-driven prediction heuristic presented in Sect. 2 (D), and real duration (R). The purpose here is to assess the importance of using data-driven prediction for response time and throughput of a dispatcher, with respect to crude prediction (wall-time) and best prediction (real duration). Due to lack of space, we here present only the results related to the CPH scheduler, as it is the best performing among all and is highly representative of the behavior of the schedulers in conjunction with the allocators in question.

Figure 2 shows the average slowdown over all jobs and average queue size values over all dispatching times of the CPH scheduler for all available allocators. We make two observations. First, across all allocators, the data-driven job duration prediction has notable impact on job response times and system throughput, leading to results better than using the wall-time. Therefore, in the next sections we only present results using the data-driven job duration prediction for all jobs. Second, we do not note substantial performance variations among the various allocators. We believe that this could be due to certain time periods in our workload where the corresponding data does not possess significant characteristics for our study. For instance, there could be time periods in which few jobs are submitted to the system, keeping it in a low utilization state, or conversely periods in which large amounts of jobs are submitted, overloading it. In either case, an allocator is not expected to enhance the job response times and system throughput considerably.

Table 2. Average slowdown (s) and queue size (q) results for the April 2015 (a) and April 2014 (b) datasets.

Scheduler	Allocator										Best gain %			
	FF		BF		B		W		P-W		FF		BF	
	s	q	s	q	s	q	s	q	s	q	s	q	s	q
CPH	10	4	10	4	**7**	**4**	8	4	**7**	**4**	30%	0%	30%	0%
SJF	16	5	16	5	**10**	**5**	**10**	**5**	**10**	**5**	37%	0%	37%	0%
EBF	28	5	28	5	**18**	**4**	20	4	20	4	35%	20%	35%	20%
PRB	28	5	28	5	**21**	**4**	22	4	22	4	25%	20%	25%	20%

(a) April 2015 dataset.

Scheduler	Allocator										Best gain %			
	FF		BF		B		W		P-W		FF		BF	
	s	q	s	q	s	q	s	q	s	q	s	q	s	q
CPH	251	57	271	55	**238**	**63**	315	82	254	70	5%	-10%	12%	-12%
SJF	1269	230	1270	229	1266	233	1276	218	**1253**	**216**	1%	6%	1%	6%
PRB	1852	615	2023	640	**1778**	**594**	1829	627	1910	599	4%	3%	12%	7%
EBF	3004	697	2563	702	**2197**	**619**	2378	686	2313	674	26%	11%	14%	12%

(b) April 2014 dataset.

4.3   Results over Specific Time Periods

We now use only the data-driven prediction of job duration. We then restrict our study to shorter time periods in the workload, such as months, to be able to understand the operating conditions in which we can benefit from the new allocators. For this purpose, we extracted the results of the jobs that were submitted during a certain month after running the experiments once on the entire workload. Thus, the months never start in an idle state but carry on from the previous month, like in a real scenario.

Here we present some insights derived by analyzing data from four particular months. These months are not only interesting due to their peak job submissions, they are also representative in the sense that their job submission patterns and the corresponding experimental results are found in other months as well (not shown in the paper due to space reasons).

Tables 2 and 3 give the average slowdown (s) and queue size (q) of every dispatcher (composed by a scheduler in the first column and an allocator in the next 5 columns). For each scheduler, the best allocator result is indicated in bold, in addition to the best gain obtained in percentage by the new allocators compared to FF and BF. Figures 3 and 4 demonstrate instead job duration distributions, for each job class as in Sect. 2.1, as well as job submission patterns in terms of the total CPU core hours of the submitted jobs in every 30-min time window of a day. Sudden spikes in the job submission patterns are caused by the arrival of jobs that either have a high duration or require a large amount of resources. We do not consider the distributions of the amount of resources requested by jobs, as no significant differences across months have been observed.

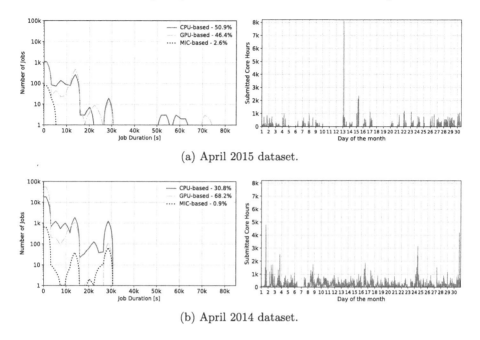

(a) April 2015 dataset.

(b) April 2014 dataset.

Fig. 3. Job duration distributions (left) and job submission patterns (right) for the April 2015 (a) and April 2014 (b) datasets.

Allocation with Moderate Gains. We start with the workloads related to April 2015 and April 2014 where the new allocators bring about relatively moderate gains in response times and throughput with respect to FF and BF. This can be immediately witnessed in Table 2. For the April 2015 dataset, while the slowdown values are reduced between 20% to 37%, the queue size remains the same with the two best-performing schedulers, CPH and SJF. In the case of the April 2014 dataset, the gains in slowdown are between 1% and 26%, while the queue size increases slightly with the best performing scheduler, CPH. Hence, in all cases we witness an improvement in slowdown, however queue size values improve only when not using the CPH scheduler.

Analyzing the characteristics of the workload in Fig. 3, we can understand the reason for having only moderate improvements. The April 2015 dataset contains 3,740 jobs with few of them long (duration >5 h), while the majority are short (duration <1 h) or medium ($1\leq$ duration ≤5 h). We would therefore expect low slowdown and queue size values without the need of dedicated allocators. Around half of the jobs in the workload require only CPU and memory, which do not need heterogeneity-aware allocators. Moreover, the system is rarely put under pressure, reducing the importance of complex dispatching algorithms. The only exception is in the sudden burst towards the middle of the month, in which over 8,000 core hours worth of jobs are submitted to the system in a very short time. This, however, overloads a small-scale HPC system like Eurora and is hardly managed by any of the dispatchers.

Table 3. Average slowdown (s) and queue size (q) results for the September 2014 (a) and August 2014 (b) datasets.

Scheduler	Allocator										Best gain %			
	FF		BF		B		W		P-W		FF		BF	
	s	q	s	q	s	q	s	q	s	q	s	q	s	q
CPH	41	27	42	28	11	11	10	10	**8**	**8**	80%	70%	81%	71%
SJF	34	28	29	23	19	20	23	19	**14**	**14**	58%	50%	50%	39%
PRB	43	24	47	27	**30**	**16**	36	16	40	20	30%	33%	36%	40%
EBF	51	33	48	34	39	19	**37**	**20**	53	37	27%	39%	22%	41%

(a) September 2014 dataset.

Scheduler	Allocator										Best gain %			
	FF		BF		B		W		P-W		FF		BF	
	s	q	s	q	s	q	s	q	s	q	s	q	s	q
CPH	8	7	7	6	11	7	**4**	**4**	7	6	50%	42%	42%	33%
PRB	20	13	22	14	14	10	8	6	**5**	**3**	75%	76%	77%	78%
EBF	22	15	26	16	21	15	**14**	**10**	18	13	36%	33%	46%	37%
SJF	26	17	32	22	18	14	18	13	**15**	**11**	42%	35%	53%	50%

(b) August 2014 dataset.

April 2014 is instead a big dataset of 85,245 jobs, with many more medium and long jobs compared to the April 2015 dataset. We would expect here high slowdown and queue size values even with dedicated allocators. The share of jobs requiring only CPU and memory resources is 30.8%, which is still high compared to the 22.8% share for the entire workload, reducing the contribution of allocators specifically designed for heterogeneous systems. In addition, job pressure on the system is always high, with frequent bursts that amount to more than 1,000 core hours. The main problem in this month seems to be the 5,000-h burst at its beginning: due to the large size of the workload, the early position of the burst results in a cascade effect, severely delaying all subsequent jobs.

Allocation with High Gains. We now discuss the datasets related to September 2014 and August 2014 for which significant improvements in response times and throughput are observed, as can be seen in Table 3. The gains in slowdown and queue size reach up to 81% and 71% in the September 2014 dataset, and up to 77% and 78% in the August 2014 dataset, respectively.

September 2014 is a big dataset of 77,786 jobs, while the August 2014 dataset has medium size with 47,967 jobs. The two datasets, however, share common traits that help understand the relevant results. As can be seen in Fig. 4, both datasets contain a high number of short and medium jobs. The number of long jobs is neither low, as in the case of the April 2015 dataset, nor too high as in the case of the April 2014 dataset. In addition, unlike the April 2015 and April 2014 datasets, GPU-based jobs constitute the vast majority of the workload. All these mean that we can expect considerable improvements in slowdown and queue size values with allocators for heterogeneous systems. Finally, from Fig. 4 we can see

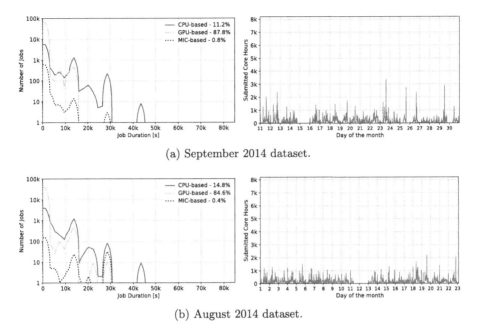

(a) September 2014 dataset.

(b) August 2014 dataset.

Fig. 4. Job duration distributions (left) and job submission patterns (right) for the September 2014 (a) and August 2014 (b) datasets.

that the September 2014 and August 2014 datasets are very bursty, much like the April 2014 one. Yet in the case of the September 2014 and August 2014 datasets, the bursts are much tamer in intensity, corresponding to the normal day-night usage cycles present in the HPC system. Moreover, unlike the April 2015 dataset, the system is often put under pressure, but such pressure is not as high as in the April 2014 dataset.

Comparison of Allocators. So far we have only studied the impact of the new allocators B, W and P-W in response times and throughput with respect to FF and BF in an heterogeneous system, but we did not contrast them. To do this, we show in Fig. 5 job submission patterns in the selected datasets, this time only for GPU-based jobs. These plots do not show the job pressure on the system, which we already illustrated in Figs. 3 and 4, but rather demonstrate the distribution of the jobs requiring accelerator resources over the workloads' time spans. Such resources are peculiar to heterogeneous systems and it is interesting to see when the new allocators behave differently in the presence of jobs requiring them. We are omitting the distributions for the April 2015 dataset due to its small size and the small variance in the behavior among the various allocators.

Intuitively, one may expect the W and P-W allocators to perform better than B since they take into account several resource criticality parameters and can adapt to different workload characteristics. However, as explained in Sect. 3, the

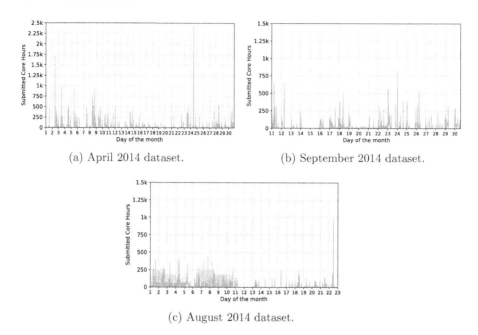

(a) April 2014 dataset.

(b) September 2014 dataset.

(c) August 2014 dataset.

Fig. 5. Submission patterns of jobs requiring GPUs for the April 2014 (a), September 2014 (b) and August 2014 (c) datasets.

B allocator is more robust than W against sudden bursts of jobs requiring critical resources, accelerators in this case, due to its simple nature: B always tries to limit the use of nodes equipped with critical resources, even if they are not actively needed or they are scarcely used by jobs, resulting in a fairly consistent behavior. This is reflected in our results. As seen in Table 2, B is consistently the best performer for the April 2014 dataset which contains several big bursts of GPU-based jobs (Fig. 5a). In the September 2014 dataset, some bursts of GPU-based jobs are still present, though less intense compared to those of the April 2014 dataset (Fig. 5b). In this case, as shown in Table 3, the W or P-W allocator performs better than B except when used with the PRB scheduler. In the August 2014 dataset instead, where W and P-W are consistently the best performers, GPU-based jobs are evenly distributed over most days of the month, with very few bursts (Fig. 5c).

Overall, B is more suited for extreme scenarios where critical resources must be protected at all costs and at all times. Otherwise, W and P-W are the best allocators. The gain offered by P-W over W is less clear. This can be attributed to the fact that P-W is primarily an hybridization strategy between B and W, and it can be better or worse than its constituting components depending on the workload characteristics and the type of scheduler.

4.4   Resource Utilization

We conclude our evaluation with the resource utilization results. In our analysis, we first looked at the distribution of the fraction of used resources, as a function of the fraction of used nodes in the system for all time points, separately for each resource type and combined for all resource types. The results obtained over the entire workload, as well on the four individual months are mainly homogeneous across all dispatchers and therefore are omitted here. This is still good news because we can see that the new allocators can improve response times and throughout without degrading resource utilization with respect to FF and BF, resulting in the best overall compromise between system performance and resource utilization. It is worth mentioning however a particular case when considering the GPU resources for the September 2014 dataset. Looking at the average distribution over all the nodes and all time points, referred to as system load ratio previously, the best-performing scheduler CPH has an improvement of 5.95% when resources are allocated with W instead of BF. Similar improvements are observed when CPH is used with B or P-W. This result may suggest that heterogeneity-aware allocators can lead to better usage of critical resources.

5   Conclusions

We have presented three allocation algorithms suitable for heterogeneous HPC systems aimed at intelligent management of critical, accelerator-like resources. The algorithms are general enough to be applied to any heterogeneous HPC system where critical resources need to be managed efficiently, they are based on simple heuristics that exhibit good performance with low computational overhead, and they can easily be integrated in live queueing systems (like PBS or SLURM) as they do not rely on features beyond those found in common heuristics (like Best-Fit). In order to assess their effectiveness, we modeled the Eurora HPC system with the AccaSim simulator driven by a real workload trace extracted from the same system. We conducted extensive evaluation of our allocators by coupling them with different scheduling algorithms and job duration predictors. We observed up to 81% improvements in average job response times and 78% in system throughput, compared to common solutions like First-Fit and Best-Fit. Also, all of the state-of-the-art schedulers we considered together with our allocators significantly benefited from our algorithms, while no degradation in resource utilization was observed compared to First-Fit and Best-Fit, thus confirming our algorithms as effective alternatives to them.

Although our study is based on a particular HPC system (Eurora) and its workload, our results help us to characterize the operating conditions in which heterogeneity-aware resource allocation becomes crucial for heterogeneous HPC systems in general. A system may go through different workload types, ranging from light loads with a small number of jobs requesting few critical resources, to heavy loads with a high number of jobs requesting large amounts of critical resources; and the majority of the jobs in the workload may range from being short, occupying critical resources for short periods, to long, blocking the critical resources for long periods of time. In addition, job submission patterns may fluctuate, keeping the system under different amounts of pressure, ranging from rare to heavy. We observed that protecting the critical resources is most useful when (i) the workload contains a significant amount of long jobs requiring critical resources, without dominating the workload; (ii) the system is under pressure consistently without sudden peaks in job submission patterns.

As future work, we plan to test our allocation algorithms on data from different heterogeneous architectures. We are also interested in the performance on a wider set of operating conditions, which can be tested also by employing a synthetic workload generator. The algorithms can also be improved further. For instance, allocating nodes fully may cause saturation of shared resources such as memory, which could result in decreased system performance. We plan to take this into account and allocate resources in a way that avoids saturation, something which we do not consider at the moment.

Acknowledgements. We thank Dr. A. Bartolini, Prof. L. Benini, Prof. M. Milano, Dr. M. Lombardi and the SCAI group at Cineca for providing access to the Eurora data. We also thank the IT Center of the University of Pisa (Centro Interdipartimentale di Servizi e Ricerca) for providing access to computing resources for simulations. A. Netti has been supported by a research fellowship from the *Oprecomp-Open Transprecision Computing* project. C. Galleguillos has been supported by Postgraduate Grant PUCV 2017. A. Sîrbu has been partially funded by the EU project *SoBigData Research Infrastructure—Big Data and Social Mining Ecosystem* (grant agreement 654024).

References

1. Ashby, S., Beckman, P., Chen, J., Colella, P., Collins, B., Crawford, D., et al.: The opportunities and challenges of exascale computing. Summary Report of the Advanced Scientific Computing Advisory Committee (ASCAC) Subcommittee, pp. 1–77 (2010)
2. Bartolini, A., Borghesi, A., Bridi, T., Lombardi, M., Milano, M.: Proactive workload dispatching on the EURORA supercomputer. In: O'Sullivan, B. (ed.) CP 2014. LNCS, vol. 8656, pp. 765–780. Springer, Cham (2014). https://doi.org/10.1007/978-3-319-10428-7_55
3. Bhattacharya, S., Tsai, W.: Lookahead processor allocation in mesh-connected massively parallel multicomputer. In: Proceedings of IPPS 1994, pp. 868–875. IEEE (1994)
4. Borghesi, A., Collina, F., Lombardi, M., Milano, M., Benini, L.: Power capping in high performance computing systems. In: Pesant, G. (ed.) CP 2015. LNCS, vol. 9255, pp. 524–540. Springer, Cham (2015). https://doi.org/10.1007/978-3-319-23219-5_37
5. Bridi, T., Bartolini, A., Lombardi, M., Milano, M., Benini, L.: A constraint programming scheduler for heterogeneous high-performance computing machines. IEEE Trans. Parallel Distrib. Syst. **27**(10), 2781–2794 (2016)
6. Buddhakulsomsiri, J., Kim, D.S.: Priority rule-based heuristic for multi-mode resource-constrained project scheduling problems with resource vacations and activity splitting. Eur. J. Oper. Res. **178**(2), 374–390 (2007)

7. Cavazzoni, C.: Eurora: a European architecture toward exascale. In: Future HPC Systems: The Challenges of Power-Constrained Performance. ACM (2012)
8. Emeras, J., Ruiz, C., Vincent, J.-M., Richard, O.: Analysis of the jobs resource utilization on a production system. In: Desai, N., Cirne, W. (eds.) JSSPP 2013. LNCS, vol. 8429, pp. 1–21. Springer, Heidelberg (2014). https://doi.org/10.1007/978-3-662-43779-7_1
9. Feitelson, D.G.: Metrics for parallel job scheduling and their convergence. In: Feitelson, D.G., Rudolph, L. (eds.) JSSPP 2001. LNCS, vol. 2221, pp. 188–205. Springer, Heidelberg (2001). https://doi.org/10.1007/3-540-45540-X_11
10. Galleguillos, C., Kiziltan, Z., Netti, A.: AccaSim: an HPC simulator for workload management. In: Mocskos, E., Nesmachnow, S. (eds.) CARLA 2017. CCIS, vol. 796, pp. 169–184. Springer, Cham (2018). https://doi.org/10.1007/978-3-319-73353-1_12
11. Galleguillos, C., Sîrbu, A., Kiziltan, Z., Babaoglu, O., Borghesi, A., Bridi, T.: Data-driven job dispatching in HPC systems. In: Nicosia, G., Pardalos, P., Giuffrida, G., Umeton, R. (eds.) MOD 2017. LNCS, vol. 10710, pp. 449–461. Springer, Cham (2018). https://doi.org/10.1007/978-3-319-72926-8_37
12. Guim, F., Rodero, I., Corbalan, J.: The resource usage aware backfilling. In: Frachtenberg, E., Schwiegelshohn, U. (eds.) JSSPP 2009. LNCS, vol. 5798, pp. 59–79. Springer, Heidelberg (2009). https://doi.org/10.1007/978-3-642-04633-9_4
13. Guim, F., Rodero, I., Corbalan, J., Parashar, M.: Enabling GPU and many-core systems in heterogeneous HPC environments using memory considerations. In: Proceedings of HPCC 2010, pp. 146–155. IEEE (2010)
14. Henderson, R.L.: Job scheduling under the portable batch system. In: Feitelson, D.G., Rudolph, L. (eds.) JSSPP 1995. LNCS, vol. 949, pp. 279–294. Springer, Heidelberg (1995). https://doi.org/10.1007/3-540-60153-8_34
15. Hentenryck, P.V., Bent, R.: Online Stochastic Combinatorial Optimization. The MIT Press, Cambridge (2009)
16. Wasi-ur Rahman, M., Islam, N.S., Lu, X., Panda, D.K.D.: A comprehensive study of mapreduce over lustre for intermediate data placement and shuffle strategies on HPC clusters. IEEE Trans. Parallel Distrib. Syst. **28**(3), 633–646 (2017)
17. Reuther, A., Byun, C., Arcand, W., Bestor, D., Bergeron, B., Hubbell, M., et al.: Scalable system scheduling for HPC and big data. arXiv:1705.03102 (2017)
18. Shmueli, E., Feitelson, D.G.: Backfilling with lookahead to optimize the packing of parallel jobs. J. Parallel Distrib. Comput. **65**(9), 1090–1107 (2005)
19. Silberschatz, A., Galvin, P.B., Gagne, G.: Operating System Concepts, 9th edn. Wiley, Hoboken (2014)
20. Villa, O., Johnson, D.R., Oconnor, M., Bolotin, E., Nellans, D., Luitjens, J., et al.: Scaling the power wall: a path to exascale. In: Proceedings of SC 2014, pp. 830–841. IEEE (2014)
21. Wong, A.K.L., Goscinski, A.M.: Evaluating the EASY-backfill job scheduling of static workloads on clusters. In: Proceedings of CLUSTER 2007, pp. 64–73. IEEE (2007)
22. Yoo, A.B., Jette, M.A., Grondona, M.: SLURM: Simple Linux Utility for Resource Management. In: Feitelson, D., Rudolph, L., Schwiegelshohn, U. (eds.) JSSPP 2003. LNCS, vol. 2862, pp. 44–60. Springer, Heidelberg (2003). https://doi.org/10.1007/10968987_3
23. Zeldes, Y., Feitelson, D.G.: On-line fair allocations based on bottlenecks and global priorities. In: Proceedings of ICPE 2013, pp. 229–240. ACM (2013)

On the Accuracy and Usefulness
of Analytic Energy Models
for Contemporary Multicore Processors

Johannes Hofmann[1(✉)], Georg Hager[2], and Dietmar Fey[1]

[1] Computer Architecture, University of Erlangen-Nuremberg,
91058 Erlangen, Germany
{johannes.hofmann,dietmar.fey}@fau.de
[2] Erlangen Regional Computing Center (RRZE), 91058 Erlangen, Germany
georg.hager@fau.de

Abstract. This paper presents refinements to the execution-cache-memory performance model and a previously published power model for multicore processors. The combination of both enables a very accurate prediction of performance and energy consumption of contemporary multicore processors as a function of relevant parameters such as number of active cores as well as core and Uncore frequencies. Model validation is performed on Intel Sandy Bridge-EP, Broadwell-EP, and AMD Epyc processors. Production-related variations in chip quality are demonstrated through a statistical analysis of the fit parameters obtained on one hundred Broadwell-EP CPUs of the same model. Insights from the models are used to explain the performance- and energy-related behavior of the processors for scalable as well as saturating (i.e., memory-bound) codes. In the process we demonstrate the models' capability to identify optimal operating points with respect to highest performance, lowest energy-to-solution, and lowest energy-delay product and identify a set of best practices for energy-efficient execution.

Keywords: Performance modeling · Power modeling
Energy modeling

1 Introduction

The usefulness of analytic performance and power models for modern processors is undisputed. Here, "analytic" means a simplified description of the interactions between software and hardware, simple enough to identify relevant performance and energy issues but also elaborate enough to be realistic at least in some important scenarios. There is a large gray area between the extremes of modeling procedures: Purely analytic, also called *first-principles* or *white-box* models, try to start from known technical details of the hardware and how the software executes, without additional empirical input such as measured quantities or parameterized fit functions. The other end of the spectrum is set by

© Springer International Publishing AG, part of Springer Nature 2018
R. Yokota et al. (Eds.): ISC High Performance 2018, LNCS 10876, pp. 22–43, 2018.
https://doi.org/10.1007/978-3-319-92040-5_2

black-box models that can be constructed from almost zero knowledge; measured runtime, hardware performance metrics, power dissipation, etc., are used to identify crucial influence factors for the metrics to be modeled. One can then use the "trained" system to predict properties of arbitrary code, or play with parameters to explore design spaces. In either case, the predictive power of the model enables insight beyond what we would get by just running the code on the hardware at hand.

Models that are at least partially analytic have several advantages, including:

- *Identification of universality*: If an analytic model is accurate in several different situations (e.g., processors, codes, ...), even if the actual parameters are different, this is an indication of universal behavior. Example: The "energy-frequency convexity rule" [2] states that, if the performance is linear in the clock frequency, the function describing the energy to solution versus the core clock speed has a minimum.
- *Identification of governing mechanisms*: If a model is built upon a certain assumption, and the model makes "good" predictions (qualitatively or quantitatively), this is a strong indication (though not a proof) that the assumption was correct. Example: The roofline model can be quite accurate on multi- and manycore CPUs, which substantiates the basic assumption that data transfers and execution overlap.
- *Insight via model failure*: If an analytic model is "off," i.e., does not agree with measurements, this means that its inherent assumptions must be challenged. This is especially interesting if the model works for some parameter ranges but not for all of them. Example: The roofline model sometimes fails to produce accurate performance predictions near the roofline knee or for sequential code. If one drops the assumption of full overlap between execution and data transfers, one arrives at the ECM model, which is more accurate in these situations.

The power dissipation and energy consumption of HPC systems has become a major concern. Developing a good understanding of the mechanisms behind it and how code can be executed in the most energy-efficient way is thus of great interest to the community. Navigating the parameter space of core count, clock frequencies, and (possibly) supply voltage will surely be insufficient to meet the challenges of future top-tier parallel computers is terms of power; however, running the hardware at energy-efficient operating points definitely contributes to a reduction in operating costs of HPC clusters. Moreover, there is a trend to employ power capping in order to enable a more accurate tailoring of the power supply to the needs of the machine, thereby saving a lot of expenses in the infrastructure. Under such conditions, letting code run "cooler" and knowing the energy vs. performance trade-offs will directly yield more science (i.e., useful core hours) per dollar.

This paper is concerned with core- and chip-level performance and power models for Intel and AMD server CPUs. These models are precise enough to yield quantitative predictions of energy consumption. In terms of performance we rely on the execution-cache-memory (ECM) performance model [5,13] (of which the well-known roofline model is a special case), which can deliver single-core and chip-level runtime estimates for loop-based code on multicore CPUs. A simple multicore power model [5] serves as a starting point for energy modeling. Both models are rather qualitative in nature; although the ECM model is precise on the single core, it is over-optimistic once the memory bandwidth starts to saturate. The original power model is very approximate and can only track the rough energy consumption behavior of the processor. In this work we refine both models to a point where the prediction accuracy for performance and power dissipation, and thus also for energy consumption, becomes unprecedented. This comes at the price of making the models more "gray-box"-like in the above terminology, i.e., they need more empirical input and fit parameters. However, the actual choice of functional dependencies is still motivated by white-box thinking.

This paper is organized as follows: The remainder of this section describes related work and lists our new contributions. In Sect. 2 we describe the hardware and software setup and our measurement methodology. Section 3 refines the ECM performance model to yield more accurate predictions for code near the bandwidth saturation point. In Sect. 4 we extend the simple multicore power model by refining it for better baseline power prediction and adapt it to the new processors with dual clock frequency domains (core and Uncore). Section 5 combines the two models and validates the predicted energy consumption. Motivated by the results we give some guidelines for energy optimization in Sect. 6 and conclude the paper with an outlook to future work in Sect. 7.

1.1 Related Work

Energy and performance models on the chip level have received intense interest in the past decade. The roofline model [15] is still the starting point for most code analysis activities, but it lacks accuracy and predictive power on the single core and for saturation behavior. The ECM model [5,13] requires less phenomenological input but encompasses more details of the underlying architecture than roofline, yielding better results on the single core. In contrast to the original ECM model we allow for latency penalty contributions that depend on the memory bus utilization, making the model accurate across the whole scaling curve.

Energy-performance trade-offs have been studied since the power envelope of processors became a major concern, but were only treated phenomenologically [3,12]. Rauber et al. [10] show using a simple heuristic model that the typical energy minimum versus clock speed observed for scalable code can be derived analytically. However, they do not have a useful performance model and do not take saturation patterns due to memory bandwidth exhaustion into account. Khabi et al. [9] study the energy consumption of simple, scalable compute kernels using a similar underlying power model, but they also lack a performance prediction. The energy model introduced by Hager et al. [5] includes performance saturation but is only qualitative and thus allows only rough estimates of energy consumption, due to the combined shortcomings of the underlying ECM and power models.

The consequences of manufacturing variations among processors of the same type were studied by several authors [8,14], and we do not add to their wisdom here; our contribution in this area is to show the relation between fitting parameters for a specific specimen and the "batch," yielding insight about the usefulness of a particular set of parameters.

1.2   Contribution

This paper makes the following contributions: We refine the ECM performance model to accurately describe the saturation behavior of memory-bound loops across cores. A previously published multicore power model is extended to include dual clock domains (core and Uncore) as well as frequency- and core-dependent baseline power (see Table 1 for a comparison with previous models). The achieved accuracy in predicting runtime, power, and energy (using both models combined) with respect to core frequency, Uncore frequency, and number of active cores is unprecedented. As a result the model can be used to identify the optimum operating point with respect to performance, energy-efficiency, and energy-delay product (EDP) in minutes compared to weeks required by empirical means.[1] This is demonstrated with AMD Epyc, Intel Xeon Sandy Bridge, and Intel Broadwell CPUs. We also identify which of the power model parameters depend on the code and which do not. A statistical analysis of the variation of power parameters due to production spread is given for a batch of Intel "Broadwell" 10-core CPUs, setting the limits for the generality of the power model fit parameters. Finally, based on the energy modeling results, we identify best practices for energy-efficient, best-performance, and lowest-EDP execution of scalable (DGEMM) and saturating (STREAM) code, with special emphasis on the Uncore clock of the Broadwell CPU, which we identify as a crucial parameter in energy-aware computing.

Table 1. Comparison of the capabilities of different power models.

	Nature of estimate	Considered parameters			Applicability	
		f_{core}	f_{Uncore}	n	Scalable	Saturating
Rauber et al. [11]	Quantitative	✓	—	—	✓	—
Khabi et al. [9]	Quantitative	✓	—	—	✓	—
Hager et al. [5]	Qualitative	✓	—	✓	✓	—
Proposed model	Quantitative	✓	✓	✓	✓	✓

---

[1] Consider, e.g., the 18-core Broadwell-EP chip, which offers 17 different Uncore and 12 different CPU core frequencies, for which a total of 3672 measurements (each with a non-negligible runtime to reach operating temperature equilibrium) are required. In contrast, setting up the model requires only four, six, and nine measurements on the AMD Epyc, Intel Sandy Bridge-EP, and Broadwell-EP processors, respectively.

2 Testbed and Methodology

All measurements were performed on one socket of standard two-socket AMD Epyc and Intel Xeon servers. A summary of key specifications of the testbed processors is shown in Table 2. The Sandy Bridge-EP (SNB) and Broadwell-EP (BDW) chips were selected for their relevance in scientific computing. Along with their "relatives," the Ivy Bridge-EP (IVB) and Haswell-EP (HSW) microarchitectures, they make up more than 85% of the systems in the latest TOP500 list published in November 2017. In addition, the AMD Zen (EPYC) microarchitecture was selected because it has some potential to become relevant to HPC in the future and to validate that the models also work on non-Intel hardware.

Table 2. Key specification of test bed machines.

Microarchitecture	Sandy Bridge-EP (SNB)	Broadwell-EP (BDW)	Zen (EPYC)
Chip model	Xeon E5-2680	E5-2697 v4	Epyc 7451
TDP	130 W	145 W	180 W
Supported core freqs	1.2–2.7 GHz	1.2–2.3 GHz	1.2–2.3 GHz
Supported Uncore freqs	1.2–2.7 GHz	1.2–2.8 GHz	unknown
Cores/Threads	8/16	18/36	24/48
L1 cache capacity	8 × 32 kB	18 × 32 kB	24 × 32 kB
L2 cache capacity	8 × 256 kB	18 × 256 kB	24 × 512 kB
L3 cache capacity	20 MB (8 × 2.5 MB)	45 MB (18 × 2.5 MB)	64 MB (8 × 8 MB)
Memory configuration	4 ch. DDR3-1600	4 ch. DDR4-2400	8 ch. DDR4-2666
Theor. Mem. Bandwidth	51.2 GB/s	76.8 GB/s	170.6 GB/s

Apart from obvious advances over processor generations such as the increased core count or microarchitectural improvements concerning SIMD ISA extensions, major frequency-related changes were made on the HSW/BDW microarchitectures. In contrast to the EPYC microarchitecture, which appears to have a fixed Uncore[2] clock, on the older SNB/IVB microarchitectures the chip's Uncore was clocked at the same frequency as CPU cores. On Haswell/Broadwell chips, separate clock domains are provided for CPU cores and the Uncore. As will be demonstrated, the capability to run cores and the Uncore at different clock speeds proves to be a distinguishing feature of the newer designs that has significant impact on energy-efficient operation.

The Haswell/Broadwell processors provide a feature called *Uncore frequency scaling* that allows chips to dynamically set the Uncore frequency based on the workload. When this feature is disabled, the Uncore frequency is fixed at the maximum supported setting. Although not officially documented, a means to

---

[2] The term Uncore refers to all parts of the chip that are not part of the core design, such as, e.g., shared last-level cache, ring interconnect, and memory controllers.

manually set the Uncore frequency via a model specific register is supported by all HSW, BDW, and Skylake processors; starting with version 4.3.0, the `likwid-setFrequencies` tool from the LIKWID tool suite[3] provides a convenient way to manually set the Uncore frequency.

Since previous investigations of the running average power limit (RAPL) interface indicate that the energy data provided by it is of high quality [4], all power-related empirical data was collected via RAPL using `likwid-perfctr` (also from the LIKWID tool suite). Representatives from the classes of scalable and saturating applications for which performance and energy behavior was investigated were DGEMM (from Intel's MKL, version 16.0.1) and the STREAM triad pattern (executed in `likwid-bench`, again from the LIKWID tool suite), respectively. Variance of empirical performance and power data was addressed by taking each measurement ten times; afterwards, the coefficient of variation[4] was used to assess variance, which in no case was higher than 2%. This indicated that variance was not a problem.

3   Refined ECM Performance Model

The ECM model takes into account predictions of single-threaded in-core execution time and data transfers through the complete cache hierarchy. These predictions can be put together in different ways, depending on the CPU architecture. On all recent Intel server microarchitectures it turns out that the model yields the best predictions if one assumes no (temporal) overlap of data transfers through the cache hierarchy and between the L1 cache and registers, while in-core execution (such as arithmetic) shows full overlap. Scalability is assumed to be perfect until a bandwidth bottleneck is hit. A full account of the ECM model would exceed the scope of this paper, so we refer to [13] for a recent discussion.

One of the known shortcomings of the ECM model is that it is rather optimistic near the saturation point [5,13], i.e., it overestimates performance when the memory interface is nearly saturated. There are several possible explanations for this effect. For example, it is documented that Intel's hardware prefetching mechanism reduces the prefetch distance when the memory bus is near saturation [1], which leads to larger latencies for individual accesses, causing an additional latency contribution to the data access time in the model. Thus the assumption that the scaling is linear with unchanged data delay contributions across all cores until the bandwidth bottleneck is exhausted cannot be upheld in this simple form. Based on this insight we make the following additional assumptions about performance saturation:

– Let $u(n)$ be the utilization of the memory interface with n active cores, i.e., the fraction of time in which the memory bus is actively transferring data. The plain ECM model predicts

---

[3] http://tiny.cc/LIKWID.
[4] The coefficient of variation is used to measure the *relative* variance of a sample. It is defined as the ratio of the standard deviation σ to the mean μ of a sample.

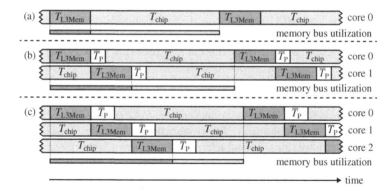

Fig. 1. Visualization of memory bandwidth saturation under the refined ECM model. The white boxes show the average latency penalty $\bar{T}_P$, which grows with with the utilization $u(n)$.

$$u(1) = \frac{T_{\text{L3Mem}}}{T_{\text{ECM}}} = \frac{T_{\text{L3Mem}}}{T_{\text{L3Mem}} + T_{\text{chip}}} \tag{1}$$

Here, T_{L3Mem} is the runtime contribution of L3-memory data transfers, and T_{chip} quantifies the data delay up to and including the L3 cache (see Fig. 1(a)). No change to the model is necessary at this level.

- For $n > 1$, the probability that a memory request initiated by a core hits a busy memory bus is proportional to the utilization of the bus caused by the $n - 1$ remaining cores. If this happens, the core picks up an additional average latency penalty $\bar{T}_P$ (see Figs. 1(b) and (c)) that is proportional to $(n - 1)u(n - 1)$:[5]

$$\bar{T}_P(n) = (n - 1)u(n - 1)p_0. \tag{2}$$

Here, p_0 is a free parameter that has to be fitted to the data. Hence, we get a recursive formula for predicting the utilization:

$$u(n) = \min\left(1, \frac{nT_{\text{L3Mem}}}{T_{\text{ECM}} + \bar{T}_P}\right) = \min\left(1, \frac{nT_{\text{L3Mem}}}{T_{\text{ECM}} + (n - 1)u(n - 1)p_0}\right). \tag{3}$$

The penalty increases with the number of cores and with the utilization, so it has the effect of delaying the bandwidth saturation.

- The expected performance at n cores is then $\pi(n) = u(n)\pi_{\text{BW}}$, where π_{BW} is the bandwidth-bound performance limit as given, e.g., by the roofline model. If $u(n) < 1$ for all $n \leq n_{\text{cores}}$, where n_{cores} is the number of available cores connected to the memory interface (i.e., in the ccNUMA domain), the code cannot saturate the memory bandwidth.

---

[5] For n active cores, the probability of a core's memory access encountering a busy bus is $u(n - 1)$; when the bus is busy, the penalty p_0, which increases with the number of cores, is applied.

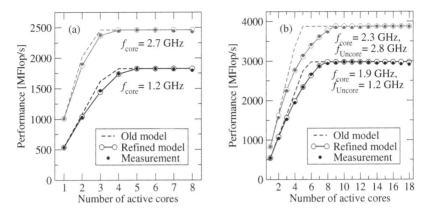

Fig. 2. Comparison of original and refined ECM model multi-core estimates to empirical performance data on (a) SNB ($p_0 = 7.8$ cy) and (b) BDW ($p_0 = 5.2$ cy) for the STREAM benchmark with a 16 GB data set size.

One input for the ECM model is the saturated memory bandwidth, which is typically determined by a streaming benchmark. There is no straightforward way to derive the memory bandwidth from core and Uncore clock frequencies, so we have to measure its dependence on these parameters. Figure 3(a) shows memory bandwidth versus (Un)core clock frequency on BDW and SNB, respectively. The measured bandwidth at a particular clock setting is then used together with the known memory traffic to determine T_{L3Mem}.

In Fig. 2 we show comparisons between the original scaling assumption (dashed lines) and our improved version (solid lines, open circles) together with measured performance data (solid circles) on the SNB and BDW chips. The agreement between the new model and the measurement is striking. It is unclear and left to future work whether and how p_0 depends on the code, e.g., the number of concurrent streams or the potential cache reuse. Note that the single-core ECM model is unchanged and does not require a latency correction.

Since there is no closed formula for the ECM-based runtime and performance predictions due to the recursive nature of the utilization ratio (3), setting up the model becomes more complicated. We provide a python script for download that implements the improved multi-core model (and also the power model described in the following section) at http://tiny.cc/hbpmpy. The single-core model can either be constructed manually or via the open-source Kerncraft tool [6], which can automatically derive the ECM and roofline models from C source and architectural information.

The ECM performance model can be applied to the AMD Epyc architecture, but its machine model is significantly different from Intel CPUs due to the presence of strongly overlapping components and the peculiar structure of the L3 cache. A thorough analysis is left for future work.

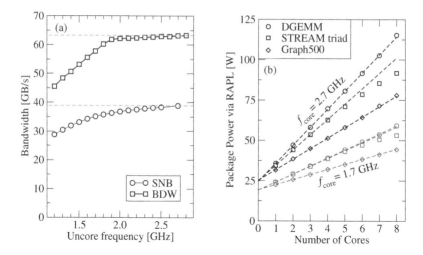

Fig. 3. (a) Maximum memory bandwidth (measured with STREAM) versus (Un)core clock frequency on SNB and BDW. (b) Package power consumption for DGEMM ($N = 20{,}000$), STREAM triad (16 GB data set size), and Graph500 (scale 24, edge factor 16) subject to active core count and CPU core frequency on SNB.

4   Refined Power Model

In [5] a simple power dissipation model for multicore CPUs was proposed, which assumed a baseline (static) and a dynamic power component, with only the latter being dependent on the number of active cores: $P = P_{\text{static}} + nP_{\text{dyn}}$, with $P_{\text{dyn}} = P_1 f + P_2 f^2$. Several interesting conclusions can be drawn from this, but the agreement of the model with actual power measurements remains unsatisfactory: The decrease of dynamic per-core power in the saturated performance regime, per-core static power, and the dependence of static power on the core frequency (via the automatically adjusted supply voltage) are all neglected. Together with the inaccuracies of the original ECM performance model, predictions of energy consumption become qualitative at best [16]. Moreover, since the introduction of the Uncore clock domain with the Intel Haswell processor, a single clock speed f became inadequate. An improved power model can be constructed, however, by adjusting some assumptions:

– There is a baseline ("static") power component for the whole chip (i.e., independent of the number of active cores) that is not constant but depends on the clock speed of the Uncore:[6]

$$P_{\text{base}}(f_{\text{Uncore}}) = W_0^{\text{base}} + W_1^{\text{base}} f_{\text{Uncore}} + W_2^{\text{base}} f_{\text{Uncore}}^2. \qquad (4)$$

---

[6] On Sandy and Ivy Bridge processors the Uncore is clocked at the same frequency as the CPU cores and can thus only be set indirectly.

– As long as there is no bandwidth bottleneck there is a power component per active core, comprising static and dynamic power contributions:

$$P_{\text{core}}(f_{\text{core}},n) = \left(W_0^{\text{core}} + W_1^{\text{core}} f_{\text{core}} + W_2^{\text{core}} f_{\text{core}}^2\right) \varepsilon(n)^\alpha. \qquad (5)$$

In the presence of a bandwidth bottleneck, performance stagnates but power increases (albeit more slowly than in the scalable case) as the number of active cores goes up. We accommodate this behavior by using a damping factor $\varepsilon(n)^\alpha$, where $\varepsilon(n)$ is the parallel efficiency at n cores and α is a fitting parameter.

The complete power model for n active cores is then

$$P_{\text{chip}} = P_{\text{base}}(f_{\text{Uncore}}) + nP_{\text{core}}(f_{\text{core}},n). \qquad (6)$$

The model fixes all deficiencies of the original formulation, but this comes at the price of a significant number of fitting parameters. The choice of a quadratic polynomial for the f dependence is to some extent arbitrary; it turns out that a cubic term does not improve the accuracy, nor does an exponential form such as $\beta + \gamma f^\delta$. Thus we stick to the quadratic form in the following. Note that there is a connection between the model parameters and "microscopic" energy parameters such as the energy per cache line transfer, per floating-point instruction, etc., which we do not use here since they also result from fitting procedures; they also cannot predict the power dissipation of running code with sufficient accuracy.

The model parameters W_*^* and α have to be determined by fitting procedures, running code with different characteristics. In Fig. 3(b) we show how P_{base} is determined by extrapolating the measured power consumption towards zero cores at different clock frequencies on SNB (there is only one clock domain on

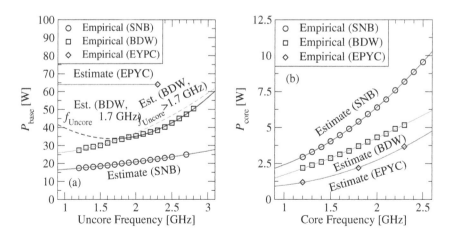

Fig. 4. (a) P_{base} and (b) P_{core} parameters derived from empirical data for different CPU core/Uncore frequencies on SNB, BDW, and EPYC. The P_{core} fit was done for the DGEMM benchmark; STREAM yields different fitting parameters (see Table 3).

this architecture). The STREAM triad, a DGEMM, and the Graph500 benchmark were chosen because they have very different requirements towards the hardware. In case of STREAM we ignore data points beyond saturation (more precisely, for parallel efficiency smaller than 90%) in order to get sensible results. The extrapolation shows that the baseline power is independent of the code characteristics, which is surprising since the Uncore includes the L3 cache, whose power consumption is expected to be a function of data transfer activity. Its variation with the clock speed can be used to determine the three parameters W_*^{base}, as shown in Fig. 4(a) for all three architectures. In this figure, each data point (circles, squares, and diamonds) is an extrapolated baseline power measurement for a different (Un)core frequency. On the EPYC CPU the Uncore frequency is fixed, resulting in a constant baseline power. Lacking event counters to determine the exact Uncore frequency, the measured baseline power of 64 W was plotted at the nominal CPU core frequency of 2.3 GHz. We have also verified that this value is independent of the core clock. On the BDW CPU, the measurements exhibit a peculiar change of trend as the frequency falls below 1.7 GHz; a different set of fit parameters is needed in this regime. We can only speculate that the chip employs more aggressive power saving techniques at low f_{Uncore}.

As for the core power parameters W_*^{core}, they do depend on the code as can already be inferred from the data in Fig. 3(b). In Fig. 4(b) we show the quality of the fitting procedure for DGEMM. The parameter α, which quantifies the influence of parallel efficiency reduction on dynamic core power in the saturated regime of STREAM, can be determined as well. Table 3 shows all fit parameters.

Table 3. Fitted parameters for the power model (4)–(6), using the STREAM and DGEMM benchmarks. Note that these numbers are fit parameters only; their physical relevance should not be overstressed.

	Microarchitecture	SNB	BDW	EPYC
	α	0.4	0.5	0.4
	W_0^{base} [W]	14.62	$27.2^a/70.8^b$	64.0
	W_1^{base} [W/GHz]	1.07	$-6.45^a/-44.1^b$	0
	W_2^{base} [W/GHz^2]	1.02	$5.71^a/13.1^b$	0
DGEMM	W_0^{core} [W]	1.42	-0.11	1.69
	W_1^{core} [W/GHz]	-0.52	-1.46	-1.81
	W_2^{core} [W/GHz^2]	1.51	1.47	1.16
STREAM	W_0^{core} [W]	1.33	0.45	-0.32
	W_1^{core} [W/GHz]	0.80	2.95	3.46
	W_2^{core} [W/GHz^2]	1.22	-0.24	-0.40

$^a f_{\text{Uncore}} \leq 1.7\,\text{GHz}$ $^b f_{\text{Uncore}} > 1.7\,\text{GHz}$

5   Energy Model and Validation

Putting together performance (π) and power (P_{chip}) estimates, we can now give predictions for energy consumption. Guidelines for energy-efficient execution as derived from this data will be given in Sect. 6 below. We normalize the energy to the work, quantifying the energy cost per work unit:

$$E = \frac{P_{\mathrm{chip}}(f_{\mathrm{core}}, f_{\mathrm{Uncore}}, n)}{\pi(f_{\mathrm{core}}, f_{\mathrm{Uncore}}, n)} \tag{7}$$

In our case this quantity has a unit of J/flop. Unfortunately, this model is too intricate to deliver general analytic predictions of minimum energy or EDP and the required operating points to attain them. Some simple cases, however, can be tackled. On a CPU with only one clock speed domain (such as SNB), where $f_{\mathrm{core}} = f_{\mathrm{Uncore}} = f$, and assuming that the code runtime is proportional to the inverse clock frequency, one can differentiate (7) with respect to f and set it to zero in order to get the frequency for minimum energy consumption. This yields

$$f_{\mathrm{opt}} = \sqrt{\frac{W_0^{\mathrm{base}} + nW_0^{\mathrm{core}}}{W_2^{\mathrm{base}} + nW_2^{\mathrm{core}}}}, \tag{8}$$

which simplifies to the expression derived in [5] if we set $W_0^{\mathrm{core}} = W_2^{\mathrm{base}} = 0$. The optimal frequency is large when the static power components dominate, which is plausible ("race to idle").

We have chosen the SNB, BDW, and EPYC processors for our study because they are representatives of server CPU microarchitectures that exhibit significantly different power consumption properties. The DGEMM and STREAM benchmarks are used for validation; it should be emphasized that almost all parameters in the energy and power models (apart from the base power) are code-dependent, so our validation makes no claim of generality other than that it is suitable for codes with substantially different characteristics. For STREAM we constructed the refined ECM model as described in Sect. 3, while for DGEMM we assumed a performance of 95% of peak, which is quite accurate on all platforms.

To discuss performance and power behavior we use use scatter plots that show (normalized or absolute) energy consumption versus code performance,[7] with some parameter varying along the data set. This can be, e.g., the number of active cores, a clock frequency, a loop nest tile size, or any other parameter that affects energy or runtime. In the plots, lines of constant energy cost are horizontal, lines of constant performance are vertical (e.g., a roofline limit is a hard barrier), and lines of constant EDP are lines through the origin whose slope is proportional to the EDP (assuming constant amount of work).

Figure 5 compares model predictions (open circles) and measurements (dots) for DGEMM on the three platforms, with varying number of active cores along the data sets. In case of SNB (Fig. 5(a)), each of the three data sets is for a different core frequency (and hence implicitly different Uncore frequency). To

---

[7] Wall clock time can also be used, which essentially mirrors the plot about the y axis.

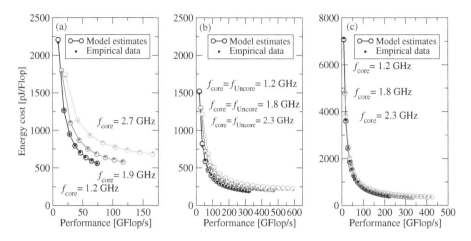

Fig. 5. Scatter plots relating performance and energy cost for DGEMM with from Intel's MKL on the (a) Sandy Bridge-EP processor for $N = 40,000$, (b) Broadwell-EP processor for $N = 60,000$, and (c) Epyc processor for $N = 60,000$ using different CPU core counts as well as CPU core and Uncore frequencies on the Broadwell-EP processor.

mimic the SNB behavior on BDW (Fig. 5(b)), we have set the core and Uncore frequencies to the same value. On EPYC (Fig. 5(c)), the Uncore frequency is fixed so only the core frequency is varied. The accuracy of the energy model is impressive, and much improved over previous work. As predicted by the model, lowest energy for constant clock frequency is always achieved with all cores. The clock frequency for minimum energy cost at a given number of cores depends on both parameters: the more cores, the lower the optimal frequency due to the waning influence of the base power. The spread in energy cost across the parameter range is naturally larger on BDW and EPYC with their large core counts (18 and 24 vs. 8). At full chip, all architectures show lowest EDP at the fastest clock speed. To quantify the model's quality, Fig. 6 shows a heat map of the model error with respect to core count and core frequency at fixed Uncore clock on BDW. The error is never larger than 4%; if one excludes the regions of small core counts and small core frequencies, which are not very relevant for practical applications anyway, then the maximum error falls below 2% and is typically smaller than 1%. Relative errors are even smaller on the SNB and EPYC processors, whose power saving capabilities are not as advanced as those of the BDW chip.

It is well known that manufacturing variations cause significant fluctuation across chips of the same type in terms of power dissipation [7,8]. This poses problems, e.g., when power capping is enforced because power variations then translate into performance variations [8], but it can also be leveraged for saving energy by intelligent scheduling [14]. For modeling purposes it is interesting to analyze the variation of fitted power model parameters in order to see how generic these values are. Figures 7 and 8 show histograms of W_*^{base} and W_*^{core} for

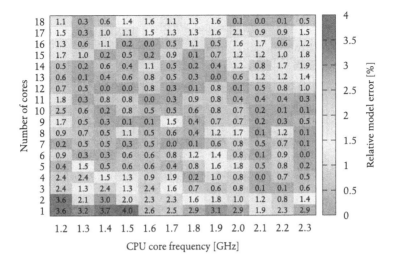

Fig. 6. Relative model error for DGEMM on the Broadwell-EP processor for different core counts and CPU core frequencies. The Uncore clock speed was set to the maximum (2.8 GHz).

DGEMM, including Gaussian fits for 100 chips of a cluster[8] based on dual-socket nodes with Intel Xeon Broadwell E5-2630v4 CPUs (10 cores). The data clearly shows that the accuracy of the power dissipation model can only be achieved for a particular specimen; however, the general insights are unchanged. It cannot be ruled out that some of the variation is caused by changes in environmental conditions across the nodes and CPUs. For example, the typical front-to-back airflow in many cluster node designs leads to one of the chips getting warmer. The (weak) bi-modal distribution of W_0^{base} may be a consequence of this. We have also observed that chips with a particularly high value of one parameter (e.g., W_2^{base}) are not necessarily "hot" specimen, because other parameters can be average or even smaller. These observations underpin our claim that one should not put too much physical interpretation into the power model fit parameters but rather take them as they are and try to reach qualitative conclusions, although the predictions for an individual chip are accurate.

Figure 9 compares the predictions and measurements for the STREAM triad with the same frequency settings as in Fig. 5. The saturation bandwidth, which limits the performance to the right in the plot, was taken from the data in Fig. 3(a). The SNB and BDW CPUs display the typical bandwidth saturation pattern exhibited by Intel processors. It can be attributed to the fact that data transfers in the cache/memory hierarchy do not overlap on these processors. The EPYC CPU does not have this shortcoming, so a single core is sufficient to saturate memory bandwidth inside a ccNUMA domain. Lacking saturation behavior, the plot instead shows the scaling across the chip's four ccNUMA

---

[8] https://www.anleitungen.rrze.fau.de/hpc/meggie-cluster/.

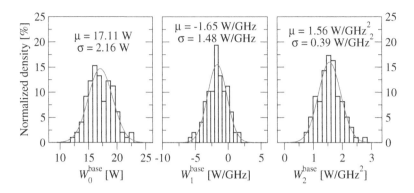

Fig. 7. Histograms of W_*^{base} for DGEMM among 100 Xeon Broadwell E5-2630v4 chips. The sum of all probabilities was normalized to one.

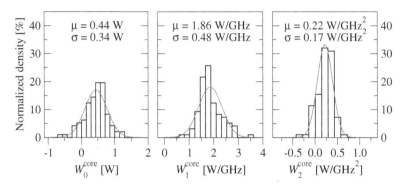

Fig. 8. Histograms of W_*^{core} for DGEMM among 100 Xeon Broadwell E5-2630v4 chips. The sum of all probabilities was normalized to one.

domains (corresponding to the four "Zeppelin" building blocks). For all processors the prediction accuracy is not worse than for DGEMM, despite the fact that the model is now much more complicated due to the saturating performance on SNB and BDW and the accompanying drop in parallel efficiency beyond the saturation point. A major difference between the SNB and BDW processors strikes the eye: The waste in energy for core counts beyond saturation is considerably smaller on BDW (although it is still about 20–25%), and the saturation point is almost independent of the clock speed. Only the refined ECM model can predict this accurately; in the original model, the saturation point depends very strongly on the frequency. At saturation, the energy consumption varies only weakly with the clock speed, which makes finding the saturation point the paramount energy optimization strategy. In contrast, on SNB one has to find the saturation point *and* choose the right frequency for the global energy minimum. If the EDP is the target metric, finding the optimal operating point is more difficult. For both chips it coincides with the saturation point at a frequency that is somewhere half-way between minimum and maximum.

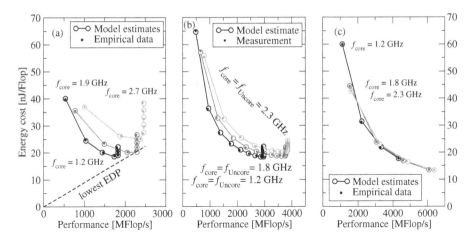

Fig. 9. Scatter plots relating performance and energy cost for the STREAM triad using a 4 GB data set for different CPU core counts as well as CPU core and Uncore frequencies on the (a) Sandy Bridge-EP, (b) Broadwell-EP, and (c) Epyc processors. On BDW, core and Uncore clock frequencies were set to the same value for this experiment.

In summary, our power model yields meaningful estimates of high quality with an error below 1% for relevant operating points (i.e., away from saturation and using more than a single core). In contrast to the work in [7], where the power/performance behavior was only observed empirically, we have presented an analytic model based on simplifying assumptions that can accurately describe the observed behavior.

6 Consequences for Energy Optimization

It is satisfying that our refined ECM and power models are accurate enough to describe the energy consumption of scalable and bandwidth-saturating code with unprecedented quality on three quite different multicore architectures. However, in order to go beyond an exercise in curve fitting, we have to derive guidelines for the efficient execution of code that are independent of the specific fit parameters determined for a given chip specimen. As usual, we differentiate between scalable and saturating code, exemplified by DGEMM and the STREAM triad, respectively.

6.1 Scalable Code

Figure 10(a) shows a scatter plot with two data sets (four and eight cores, respectively) and the core frequency as a parameter for the SNB processor running DGEMM. The highest performance, lowest energy, and lowest EDP observed are marked with dashed lines. From the energy model and our measurements we expect minimum energy for full-chip execution at a clock speed which is determined by the ratio of the baseline power and the f^2 component of dynamic power (see (8)). For the chip at hand, this minimum is at $f_{opt} \approx 1.4\,\mathrm{GHz}$ with all cores and at $f_{opt} \approx 1.7\,\mathrm{GHz}$ with only four cores. The global performance maximum (and EDP minimum) is at the highest core clock speed using all cores, as predicted by the model. Hence, on this chip, where the Uncore and core frequencies are the same by design, there is only a choice between highest performance (and, at the same time, lowest EDP) or lowest energy consumption. The latter is achieved at a rather low clock speed setting using all cores. About 21% of energy can be saved by choosing f_{opt}, albeit at the price of a 50% performance loss.

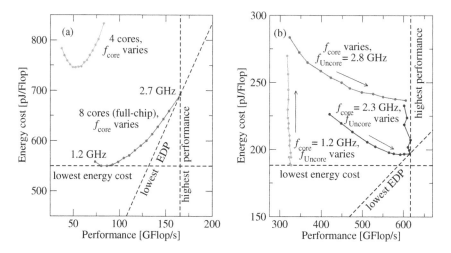

Fig. 10. (a) Scatter plot relating performance and energy cost for DGEMM from Intel's MKL for $N = 40{,}000$ running on four (half-chip) respectively eight (full-chip) cores of the Sandy Bridge-EP processor clocked at different CPU core frequencies, i.e., the core frequency varies along the curves. The energy minimum is exactly at the optimal frequency predicted by (8). (b) Scatter plot relating performance and energy cost for DGEMM from Intel's MKL for $N = 60{,}000$ running on all cores of the Broadwell-EP processor clocked at different CPU core frequencies and fixed, maximum Uncore clock (along the red curve) and at fixed maximum (blue curve) and minimum (green curve) core frequency with varying Uncore speed. Black arrows indicate the direction of rising (Un)core clock frequency. (Color figure online)

The situation is more intricate on BDW, where the Uncore clock speed has a strong impact on the power consumption as well as on the performance even of DGEMM. Figure 10(b) shows energy-performance scatter plots for different operating modes: Along the red curve the core clock speed is varied at maximum Uncore clock. This is also the mode in which most production clusters are run today since the automatic Uncore frequency scaling of the BDW processor favors high Uncore frequencies. In this case the energy-optimal core frequency is beyond the accessible range on this chip, which is why the lowest-energy (and highest-performance) "naive" operating point is at the largest f_{core}. Starting at this point one can now reduce the Uncore clock frequency at constant, maximum core clock (2.3 GHz) until the slow Uncore clock speed starts to impact the DGEMM performance (blue curve) due to the slowdown of the L3 cache. At $f_{\text{Uncore}} = 2.1$ GHz we arrive at the global performance maximum and EDP minimum, saving about 17% of energy compared to the naive operating point. At even lower f_{Uncore} the performance starts to degrade, ultimately leading to a rise in energy cost. The question arises whether one could save even more energy by accepting a performance degradation, just as on the SNB CPU. The green curve shows the extreme case where the core clock speed is at the minimum of 1.2 GHz. Here the Uncore frequency cannot be lowered to a point where it impacts the performance, which thus stays constant, but the energy consumption goes down significantly. However, the additional energy saving is only about 5% compared to the case of maximum performance at optimal Uncore frequency. This does not justify the almost 50% performance loss.

In conclusion, the BDW CPU shows a qualitatively different performance/energy trade-off due to its large and power-hungry Uncore. The Uncore clock speed is the dominating parameter here. It is advisable to set the core clock speed to a maximum and then lower the Uncore clock until performance starts to degrade. This is also the point where the global EDP minimum is reached. For codes that are insensitive to the Uncore (e.g., with purely core-bound performance characteristics), it should be operated at the lowest possible Uncore frequency setting.

We do not elaborate on the EPYC CPU here because it is strongly dominated by its constant baseline power. The qualitative behavior per Zeppelin die is no different from SNB. Using the values from Table 3 one can use (8) to derive optimal core frequency settings for minimal energy to solution: At 6 cores we get $f_{\text{opt}} \approx 3.3$ GHz, while at 24 cores we get $f_{\text{opt}} \approx 1.9$ GHz. Indeed, minimum energy is attained at 2.3 and 1.8 GHz, respectively.

6.2 Saturating Code

A performance saturation point marks an abrupt change in the energy behavior. The number of cores required to saturate depends on the clock speed(s) of the chip, so it cannot be assumed that the minimum energy point is always reached at the same number of cores (as was the case for saturating behavior).

Figure 11(a) shows data for the STREAM triad code and three different clock speeds (1.3, 1.8, and 2.7 GHz) on SNB. The number of cores varies from one to eight along the curves. On this CPU the lowest-energy and highest-performance operating points are quite distinct; the saturation point with respect to core count can be clearly identified by the lowest EDP (per core frequency) and coincides with the highest-performance point with good accuracy. Hence, there is a simple trade-off between performance and energy, with a performance loss of 25% for 28% of energy savings (only considering the saturation points). As mentioned before, using the whole chip is wasteful, especially at a fast clock speed.

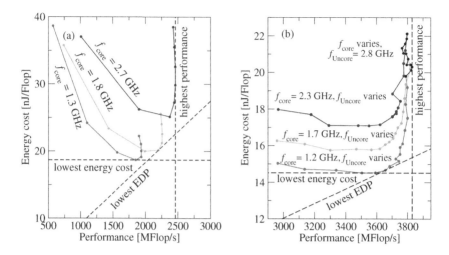

Fig. 11. Performance vs. energy cost for the STREAM triad with a 4 GB data set using various core counts as well as core and Uncore frequencies. (a) SNB at three clock frequencies with varying number of cores along the curves. (b) BDW at three core frequencies (red/green/blue) and varying Uncore clock speed along the curves. Black: fixed Uncore frequency (at maximum), varying core clock speed along curve. The number of cores at each data point on BDW was determined by minimizing the EDP vs. cores at fixed clock speeds. (Color figure online)

We expect the Uncore clock speed to be important on BDW. In Fig. 11(b) we thus show in red, green, and blue the plots for three different core clock speeds (1.2, 1.7, and 2.3 GHz) with the Uncore clock as the parameter along the curves. At each point, the number of cores was determined by the minimum EDP vs. active cores at fixed frequencies. As indicated in Fig. 3(a), there is a minimum Uncore frequency required to saturate the memory interface; Fig. 11(b) shows that it is largely independent of the core clock. In other words, there is an f_{core}-independent $f_{Uncore} \approx 2$ GHz that leads to (almost) maximum performance. f_{core} can then be set very low (1.2 GHz) for optimal energy and EDP without a significant performance loss. Again, a sensible setting of the Uncore frequency is the best way to save energy on BDW. The black data set shows a typical operating mode in practice, where the Uncore clock is set very high (or left to the Uncore frequency scaling) and the core clock is varied. Even with sensible concurrency throttling, the energy cost only varies by about 10%, whereas optimal parameters allow for additional savings between 27% and 33%. Since the AMD CPU shows no saturation pattern, its energy model for STREAM is not qualitatively different from the model for DGEMM on EPYC.

7   Summary and Outlook

By refining known ECM performance and power models we have constructed an analytic energy model for Intel multicore CPUs that can predict the energy consumption and runtime of scalable and saturating loop code with high accuracy. The power model parameters show significant manufacturing variation among CPU specimen. The Uncore frequency on the latest Intel x86 designs was identified as a major factor in energy optimization, even more important than the core frequency, for scalable and saturating code alike. Overall, energy savings of 20–50% are possible depending on the CPU and code type by choosing the optimal operating point in terms of clock speed(s) and number of active cores. If the energy-delay product (EDP) is the target metric, the scatter plot delivers a simple yet sufficiently accurate method to determine the point of lowest EDP. We have also applied the power model to an AMD Epyc 24-core CPU. It was found that its power dissipation is strongly dominated by a frequency-independent baseline, making energy optimization much easier. The ECM performance model can also be applied to this system but requires significant modifications of the machine model, which would go beyond the scope of this paper and is thus left for future work.

In light of the advantages of analytic modeling described in the introduction, our work could identify universality and governing mechanisms: We have shown that a general, quadratic power dissipation model *per clock frequency domain* is sufficiently accurate across multiple architectures, and that load-dependent latency penalties can describe bandwidth saturation very well. These insights would not have been possible by merely measuring power and performance for all relevant parameters.

Our work can be extended in several directions. The refined ECM model should be tested against a variety of codes to check the generality of the recursive latency penalty. We have ignored the "Turbo Mode" feature of the Intel and AMD CPUs, but our models should be able to encompass Turbo Mode if the dynamic clock frequency variation (depending mainly on the number of active cores) is properly taken into account. A related problem, the reduction of the base clock speed when using AVX SIMD instructions on the latest Intel CPUs, could be handled in the same way. An analysis of the new Intel Skylake-SP server CPU for its performance and power properties is currently ongoing. It would furthermore be desirable to identify more cases where the energy model (7) can yield simple analytic results. Finally, it should be useful to ease the construction of our improved analytic performance and energy models by extending tools such as Kerncraft [6].

References

1. Intel 64 and IA-32 Architectures Optimization Reference Manual. Intel Press, June 2016. http://www.intel.com/content/dam/www/public/us/en/documents/manuals/64-ia-32-architectures-optimization-manual.pdf
2. De Vogeleer, K., Memmi, G., Jouvelot, P., Coelho, F.: The energy/frequency convexity rule: modeling and experimental validation on mobile devices. In: Wyrzykowski, R., Dongarra, J., Karczewski, K., Waśniewski, J. (eds.) PPAM 2013. LNCS, vol. 8384, pp. 793–803. Springer, Heidelberg (2014). https://doi.org/10.1007/978-3-642-55224-3_74

3. Freeh, V.W., Lowenthal, D.K., Pan, F., Kappiah, N., Springer, R., Rountree, B.L., Femal, M.E.: Analyzing the energy-time trade-off in high-performance computing applications. IEEE Trans. Parallel Distrib. Syst. **18**(6), 835–848 (2007). https://doi.org/10.1109/TPDS.2007.1026

4. Hackenberg, D., Schöne, R., Ilsche, T., Molka, D., Schuchart, J., Geyer, R.: An energy efficiency feature survey of the Intel Haswell processor. In: 2015 IEEE International Parallel and Distributed Processing Symposium Workshop, pp. 896–904, May 2015

5. Hager, G., Treibig, J., Habich, J., Wellein, G.: Exploring performance and power properties of modern multicore chips via simple machine models. Concurr. Comput. Pract. Exper. (2013). https://doi.org/10.1002/cpe.3180

6. Hammer, J., Eitzinger, J., Hager, G., Wellein, G.: Kerncraft: a tool for analytic performance modeling of loop kernels. In: Niethammer, C., Gracia, J., Hilbrich, T., Knüpfer, A., Resch, M.M., Nagel, W.E. (eds.) Tools for High Performance Computing 2016, pp. 1–22. Springer, Cham (2017). https://doi.org/10.1007/978-3-319-56702-0_1

7. Hofmann, J., Hager, G., Wellein, G., Fey, D.: An analysis of core- and chip-level architectural features in four generations of intel server processors. In: Kunkel, J.M., Yokota, R., Balaji, P., Keyes, D. (eds.) ISC 2017. LNCS, vol. 10266, pp. 294–314. Springer, Cham (2017). https://doi.org/10.1007/978-3-319-58667-0_16

8. Inadomi, Y., Patki, T., Inoue, K., Aoyagi, M., Rountree, B., Schulz, M., Lowenthal, D., Wada, Y., Fukazawa, K., Ueda, M., Kondo, M., Miyoshi, I.: Analyzing and mitigating the impact of manufacturing variability in power-constrained supercomputing. In: Proceedings of the International Conference for High Performance Computing, Networking, Storage and Analysis, SC 2015, pp. 78:1–78:12. ACM, New York (2015). http://doi.acm.org/10.1145/2807591.2807638

9. Khabi, D., Küster, U.: Power consumption of kernel operations. In: Resch, M.M., Bez, W., Focht, E., Kobayashi, H., Kovalenko, Y. (eds.) Sustained Simulation Performance 2013, pp. 27–45. Springer, Cham (2013). https://doi.org/10.1007/978-3-319-01439-5_3

10. Rauber, T., Rünger, G.: Towards an energy model for modular parallel scientific applications. In: 2012 IEEE International Conference on Green Computing and Communications, pp. 523–532, November 2012

11. Rauber, T., Rünger, G., Schwind, M., Xu, H., Melzner, S.: Energy measurement, modeling, and prediction for processors with frequency scaling. J. Supercomput. **70**(3), 1451–1476 (2014). https://doi.org/10.1007/s11227-014-1236-4

12. Song, S., Su, C., Rountree, B., Cameron, K.W.: A simplified and accurate model of power-performance efficiency on emergent GPU architectures. In: 2013 IEEE 27th International Symposium on Parallel and Distributed Processing, pp. 673–686, May 2013

13. Stengel, H., Treibig, J., Hager, G., Wellein, G.: Quantifying performance bottlenecks of stencil computations using the Execution-Cache-Memory model. In: Proceedings of the 29th ACM International Conference on Supercomputing, ICS 2015. ACM, New York (2015). http://doi.acm.org/10.1145/2751205.2751240

14. Wilde, T., Auweter, A., Shoukourian, H., Bode, A.: Taking advantage of node power variation in homogenous HPC systems to save energy. In: Kunkel, J.M., Ludwig, T. (eds.) ISC High Performance 2015. LNCS, vol. 9137, pp. 376–393. Springer, Cham (2015). https://doi.org/10.1007/978-3-319-20119-1_27

15. Williams, S., Waterman, A., Patterson, D.: Roofline: An insightful visual performance model for multicore architectures. Commun. ACM **52**(4), 65–76 (2009). http://doi.acm.org/10.1145/1498765.1498785
16. Wittmann, M., Hager, G., Zeiser, T., Treibig, J., Wellein, G.: Chip-level and multi-node analysis of energy-optimized lattice Boltzmann CFD simulations. Concurr. Comput. Pract. Exper. **28**(7), 2295–2315 (2016). https://doi.org/10.1002/cpe.3489

Bayesian Optimization of HPC Systems for Energy Efficiency

Takashi Miyazaki[1(✉)], Issei Sato[2], and Nobuyuki Shimizu[1]

[1] Yahoo Japan Corporation, Tokyo, Japan
takmiyaz@yahoo-corp.jp, nobushim@yahoo-corp.jp
[2] The University of Tokyo, Tokyo, Japan
sato@k.u-tokyo.ac.jp

Abstract. Energy efficiency is a crucial factor in developing large super-computers and cost-effective datacenters. However, tuning a system for energy efficiency is difficult because the power and performance are con-flicting demands. We applied Bayesian optimization (BO) to tune a graphics processing unit (GPU) cluster system for the benchmark used in the Green500 list, a popular energy-efficiency ranking of supercomput-ers. The resulting benchmark score enabled our system, named "kukai", to earn second place in the Green500 list in June 2017, showing that BO is a useful tool. By determining the search space with minimal knowl-edge and preliminary experiments beforehand, BO could automatically find a sufficiently good configuration. Thus, BO could eliminate labori-ous manual tuning work and reduce the occupancy time of the system for benchmarking. Because BO is a general-purpose method, it may also be useful for tuning any practical applications in addition to Green500 benchmarks.

Keywords: Bayesian optimization · Energy efficiency
Automatic parameter tuning

1   Introduction

In the field of high performance computing (HPC), various supercomputer rank-ings have been compiled to promote the development of HPC technologies. Specifically, the TOP500 and Green500 lists are widely known rankings of super-computers in terms of their numerical computation performance and energy effi-ciency of their computations, respectively. However, obtaining the optimal result for a system often requires time-consuming work by experienced HPC experts. Furthermore, the whole system, which is a precious computing resource, is used for a long period to tune parameters for a benchmark. In particular, the energy-efficiency score used to determine the Green500 ranking has conflicting require-ments for higher numerical computation performance at the same time as lower power consumption, making it difficult even for experts to tune parameters for the benchmark due to its counter-intuitiveness.

© Springer International Publishing AG, part of Springer Nature 2018
R. Yokota et al. (Eds.): ISC High Performance 2018, LNCS 10876, pp. 44–62, 2018.
https://doi.org/10.1007/978-3-319-92040-5_3

One approach to address these challenges is to automatically tune parameters for a target benchmark. However, automatic parameter-tuning in the HPC setting includes the following difficulties. A single execution of benchmarking a supercomputer system often takes hours, so a parameter-tuning method must be able to handle the large cost (long execution time) to obtain a single measurement of an objective value. Furthermore, because only one target system exists, the parameter space cannot be searched in parallel. To cope with these difficulties, we propose applying Bayesian optimization (BO), which is considered a suitable black-box optimization method for such a problem setting [1]. BO is typically formulated by a Gaussian process (GP) [2], which leads to a nonparametric data-driven modeling and flexible representation of black-box functions. To summarize, our motivation is to reduce the tedious part of the tuning process by BO and let human experts focus on more insightful work.

We measured the Green500 score of our supercomputer system by taking advantage of automatic benchmark-parameter tuning using BO. We submitted the resulting score of our system, named "kukai", in June 2017 and obtained a good result in the Green500 ranking[1]: second place with a small difference in score from the highest ranked system. In this paper, we report on our experiences and findings of the Green500 measurement based on more extensive experiments conducted after the Green500 submission using a subset of the system.

The key contribution of the paper is twofold. First, we report how BO can be successfully applied to the tuning of an HPC system for energy efficiency in practice. Second, we show that BO can reach the maximum score found by exhaustive grid search within significantly fewer trials than the grid search.

The rest of the paper is organized as follows: In Sect. 2, we provide related work to this study. We give an overview of BO in Sect. 3, describe our system and how we implemented the auto-tuning system in Sect. 4, describe the search space, i.e., parameters to be auto-tuned, and the search algorithm in Sect. 5, explain our experimental results in Sect. 6, and discuss what can be learned from the results in Sect. 7. Finally, we conclude the paper in Sect. 8.

2   Related Work

Because the complexity of computer systems is increasing, the automatic tuning of system configurations and operating software parameters has evoked strong interest. Using machine-learning techniques for automatic tuning of parameters is considered particularly effective when the system is complicated, so the performance model is difficult to predict. We focus on research into the automatic tuning of HPC systems and cloud computing systems using black-box optimization and discuss their relationship with the work conducted in this study.

2.1   OpenTuner

Ansel et al. developed OpenTuner [3], an automatic tuning framework that supports ensembles of multiple search techniques, such as differential evolution [4].

---

[1] https://www.top500.org/green500/lists/2017/06/.

They searched for the optimal parameters for HPL [5], one of the most popular benchmarks for HPC systems, on a single machine with OpenTuner using minimal knowledge of machine specifications and obtained better performance than the processor vendor's implementation.

In contrast to the above single machine setting [3], we ran HPL on 80 nodes of a system consisting of central processing units (CPUs) and graphics processing units (GPUs), not a single machine. In a large-scale system, the execution time of the benchmark becomes long, so an efficient search is necessary. We exploited the knowledge about the HPL parameter tuning that has been accumulated so far in the HPC field. Then, we tuned the difficult parameters such that even human experts had to rely on trial and error, using BO. As a result, our system achieved a high ranking in the Green500 list, showing that BO works in a practical setting.

2.2   Structured Bayesian Optimization

Dalibard et al. [6] proposed a structured BO method, which integrates the developer's knowledge about the behavior of a system as a probabilistic model. This method is very efficient in terms of the number of samples and converges rapidly. The authors showed that it could successfully tune the garbage collection parameters of Cassandra database software and the scheduling of distributed neural network training using Tensorflow [7].

However, because the structural probabilistic model is hardcoded, the probabilistic-model program needs to be modified when the configuration of the system changes or when a mistake occurs in modeling. In contrast, we use a GP without domain knowledge and simply restrict the search space; it can be adjusted relatively easily on the spot even in situations that are not assumed in advance.

3   Bayesian Optimization

We focus on the problem of optimizing a nonlinear function $f(\boldsymbol{x})$ over a compact set $\mathcal{X} \subset \mathbb{R}^d$.

$$\boldsymbol{x}^* = \operatorname*{argmax}_{\boldsymbol{x} \in \mathcal{X}} f(\boldsymbol{x}). \tag{1}$$

BO is a method for optimizing the financially, computationally, or physically expensive black-box functions, the derivatives and convexity properties of which are unknown [1,8]. We start with explaining the GP, which is a basic component of BO, to model a statistical property of black-box functions.

3.1   Gaussian Process

A Gaussian distribution is a distribution over real random vectors fully specified by a mean vector $\boldsymbol{\mu} \in \mathbb{R}^k$ and covariance matrix $\Sigma \in \mathbb{R}^{k \times k}$. Note that n-dimensional vector $\boldsymbol{y}_{1:n} = (y_1, y_2, \ldots, y_n)$ follows a Gaussian distribution as

$$\boldsymbol{y}_{1:n} \sim \mathcal{N}(\boldsymbol{\mu}, \Sigma). \tag{2}$$

The GP is a distribution over functions $f : \mathcal{X} \to \mathbb{R}$, completely specified by a mean function $m : \mathcal{X} \to \mathbb{R}$ and kernel function $k : \mathcal{X} \times \mathcal{X} \to \mathbb{R}^+$. We define

$$m(\boldsymbol{x}_{1:n}) = (m(\boldsymbol{x}_1), m(\boldsymbol{x}_2), \dots, m(\boldsymbol{x}_n))^\top, \tag{3}$$

$$K = \begin{bmatrix} k(\boldsymbol{x}_1, \boldsymbol{x}_1) & k(\boldsymbol{x}_1, \boldsymbol{x}_2) & \cdots & k(\boldsymbol{x}_1, \boldsymbol{x}_n) \\ k(\boldsymbol{x}_2, \boldsymbol{x}_1) & k(\boldsymbol{x}_2, \boldsymbol{x}_2) & \cdots & k(\boldsymbol{x}_2, \boldsymbol{x}_n) \\ \vdots & \vdots & \ddots & \vdots \\ k(\boldsymbol{x}_n, \boldsymbol{x}_1) & k(\boldsymbol{x}_n, \boldsymbol{x}_2) & \cdots & k(\boldsymbol{x}_n, \boldsymbol{x}_n) \end{bmatrix}, \tag{4}$$

where $\boldsymbol{x}_{1:n} = (\boldsymbol{x}_1, \boldsymbol{x}_2, \dots, \boldsymbol{x}_n)$.

Let $f_{1:n} = (f(\boldsymbol{x}_1), f(\boldsymbol{x}_2), \dots, f(\boldsymbol{x}_n))$ be an n-dimensional vector of function values evaluated at n points $\boldsymbol{x}_i \in \mathcal{X}$. Note that $f_{1:n}$ is a random variable. If for any positive integer n and finite subset $\{\boldsymbol{x}_1, \dots, \boldsymbol{x}_n\} \subset \mathcal{X}$,

$$f_{1:n} \sim \mathcal{N}(m(\boldsymbol{x}_{1:n}), K), \tag{5}$$

then it is defined that function $f(\cdot)$ follows a GP, which is expressed as

$$f \sim \mathcal{GP}(f|m, k). \tag{6}$$

By modeling f as a function distributed from a GP, nearby locations have close associated values, where "nearby" is defined by the kernel of the GP. The smoothness of f is also controlled by the kernel.

With BO, f is typically assumed to be drawn from a GP, and observations $\mathcal{D}_{1:n} = \{\boldsymbol{x}_i, y_i\}_{i=1}^n$ are generated by

$$y_i = f(\boldsymbol{x}_i) + \epsilon_i, \quad \epsilon \sim \mathcal{N}(0, \rho^2). \tag{7}$$

The convenient properties of the GP allow us to compute marginal and conditional means and variances in closed form [2]. That is, the predictive distribution with mean μ and variance σ under the GP can be calculated as

$$p(y_*|\boldsymbol{x}_*, \mathcal{D}_{1:n}, m, k) = \mathcal{N}(y_*|\mu(\boldsymbol{x}_*; \mathcal{D}_{1:n}, m, k), \sigma^2(\boldsymbol{x}_*; \mathcal{D}_{1:n}, m, k)), \tag{8}$$

where

$$\mu(\boldsymbol{x}_*; \mathcal{D}_{1:n}, m, k) = \boldsymbol{k}(\boldsymbol{x}_*)^\top (K + \rho^2 I)^{-1}(\boldsymbol{y}_{1:n} - m(\boldsymbol{x}_{1:n})), \tag{9}$$

$$\sigma^2(\boldsymbol{x}_*; \mathcal{D}_{1:n}, m, k) = k(\boldsymbol{x}_*, \boldsymbol{x}_*) - \boldsymbol{k}(\boldsymbol{x}_*)^\top (K + \rho^2 I)^{-1} \boldsymbol{k}(\boldsymbol{x}_*), \tag{10}$$

$$\boldsymbol{k}(\boldsymbol{x}_*) = (k(\boldsymbol{x}_*, \boldsymbol{x}_1), k(\boldsymbol{x}_*, \boldsymbol{x}_2), \dots, k(\boldsymbol{x}_*, \boldsymbol{x}_n))^\top. \tag{11}$$

The squared exponential kernel is often used:

$$k^{\text{SE}}(\boldsymbol{x}, \boldsymbol{x}') = \theta_0 \exp \left\{ -\frac{1}{2} \sum_{d=1}^D \frac{(x_d - x'_d)^2}{\theta^2} \right\}. \tag{12}$$

After choosing the form of the kernel function, we must also manage the kernel parameters that govern its behavior. Snoek et al. [9] developed a fully Bayesian treatment of the kernel parameters based on slice sampling developed by Murray and Adams [10]. However, this approach typically requires a higher number of BO trials. Therefore, we used $\rho = 0.001$, $\theta_0 = 1$, and $\theta = 0.5$ in our experiments, which were empirically determined in our preliminary experiments. We also used $m(\cdot) = 0$, which is a common setting in the GP and indicates that the behavior is governed by only a kernel function.

3.2   Nonparametric Data-Driven Property of Gaussian Process

The GP has a flexible ability to model black-box functions. When we make new predictions, we use the predictive mean function $\mu(\boldsymbol{x}_*; \mathcal{D}_{1:n}, m, k) = \mathbb{E}_{p(y_* | \boldsymbol{x}_*, \mathcal{D}_{1:n}, m, k)}[y_*]$ in (8). We can rewrite the predictive mean function μ in Eq. (9) as

$$\mu(\boldsymbol{x}_*; \mathcal{D}_{1:n}, m, k) = \sum_{i=1}^{n} w_i k(x_i, x_*), \tag{13}$$

where $(w_1, w_2, \ldots, w_n)^\top = (K + \rho^2 \boldsymbol{I})^{-1} (\boldsymbol{y}_{1:n} - m(\boldsymbol{x}_{1:n}))$. This formulation means that every output y_i is weighted to make new predictions y_* by the kernel-induced similarity between its associated input $\boldsymbol{x}_i$ and to-be-predicted point x_*. This results in a simple weighted sum to make predictions for new points. The prediction only depends on the kernel k and observed data $\mathcal{D}_{1:n}$, which means that the GP regression is equivalent to a nonparametric regression model using basis functions k. This is why the GP is referred to as a nonparametric Bayesian model and is suitable for data-driven modeling of black-box functions.

3.3   Acquisition Function

Finding the maximum of f is achieved by generating successive queries $\boldsymbol{x}_1, \boldsymbol{x}_2, \ldots \in \mathcal{X}$. We use the posterior mean and uncertainty of f to find the next query to observe. The common approach to find the next query is to solve the alternative optimization problem, the objective function of which is relatively inexpensive to optimize.

We select the next query by finding the maximum of an *acquisition function*, $a(\boldsymbol{x})$, over a bounded domain in $\mathcal{X}$ instead of finding the maximum point of the objective function $f(\boldsymbol{x})$. The acquisition function is typically formulated by the posterior mean and uncertainty to balance exploration and exploitation. That is, we select the next query $\boldsymbol{x}_{n+1}$ by

$$\boldsymbol{x}_{n+1} = \underset{\boldsymbol{x}}{\operatorname{argmax}}\, a(\boldsymbol{x}; \mathcal{D}_{1:n}, m, k). \tag{14}$$

Several acquisition functions have been proposed. Močkus et al. [1] proposed expected improvement (EI):

$$a^{\mathrm{EI}}(\boldsymbol{x}; \mathcal{D}_{1:n}, m, k) = \mathbb{E}_{\mathcal{GP}(f | \mathcal{D}_{1:n}, m, k)} \left[f(\boldsymbol{x}) - \max f(\boldsymbol{x}_{1:n}) \right], \tag{15}$$

where $\max f(\boldsymbol{x}_{1:n}) = \max_i f(\boldsymbol{x}_i)$ and $\mathbb{E}_{\mathcal{GP}(f|\mathcal{D}_{1:n},m,k)}[\cdot]$ is the expectation over the GP posterior $\mathcal{GP}(f|\mathcal{D}_{1:n},m,k)$.

Srinivas et al. [11] proposed GP-based upper confidence bound (GP-UCB):

$$a^{\text{GP-UCB}}(\boldsymbol{x};\mathcal{D}_{1:n},m,k) = \mu(\boldsymbol{x};\mathcal{D}_{1:n},m,k) + \beta\sigma(\boldsymbol{x};\mathcal{D}_{1:n},m,k), \qquad (16)$$

where β is a parameter to balance exploration and exploitation.

Contal et al. [12] proposed GP mutual information (GP-MI):

$$a^{\text{GP-MI}}(\boldsymbol{x};\mathcal{D}_{1:n},m,k) = \mu(\boldsymbol{x};\mathcal{D}_{1:n},m,k) + \beta(\sqrt{\nu_n(\boldsymbol{x};m,k)} - \sqrt{\nu_{n-1}(\boldsymbol{x};m,k)}),$$

$$(17)$$

$$\nu_n(\boldsymbol{x};m,k) = \sigma^2(\boldsymbol{x};\mathcal{D}_{1:n},m,k) + \sum_{t=1}^{n-1} \sigma^2(\boldsymbol{x};\mathcal{D}_{1:t},m,k). \qquad (18)$$

In this study, we used GP-MI because it outperformed EI and GP-UCB on synthetic and real tasks and has a better theoretical guarantee [12], where parameter β of GP-MI is theoretically determined in terms of regret minimization.

4   System Setup for Auto-tuning

4.1   GPU Cluster System

We developed a GPU cluster system with 80 compute nodes and submitted a benchmark result to the TOP500/Green500. Each node in the cluster has one Intel Xeon E5-2650Lv4 processor (1.7 GHz, 14 cores) with 128-GB DDR4 memory and two NVIDIA Tesla P100 PCIe GPUs. Thus, the entire system has 80 Xeon processors and 160 GPUs in total. All nodes are connected with Mellanox FDR InfiniBand. In this paper, we report on the experimental results using a slightly smaller subset (64 nodes) of the cluster system.

We followed the instructions [13] for measuring power consumption during execution of the benchmark. Power was measured for 16 out of 64 nodes and 1 out of 4 network switches, and the total power was calculated by multiplying the scaling factor to the measured power.

We used HPL benchmark software [5] optimized for the Tesla P100 GPU provided by NVIDIA. We ran HPL on Linux with OpenMPI 1.10.7, CUDA 8.0, and Intel MKL 2017, and GPUDirect RDMA was enabled for better performance.

4.2   Implementation of Auto-tuning Method

The overview of our system used for auto-tuning experiments is shown in Fig. 1. We developed a few programs to control experiments which are consist of multiple trials of running the HPL program with different configurations. When running an experiment, we ran the optimizer on one node, and the optimizer invoked the benchmark driver many times with different hyperparameter values.

The benchmark driver simply executes the HPL program in an isolated directory with the specified hyperparameters, collects the information to calculate the objective value (energy efficiency in this study), then returns the calculated objective value to the optimizer. The HPL program runs in a distributed manner over nodes of the cluster using message passing interface (MPI). In the management node, we run the power measurement logger, which continuously records the measured power values to the power-measurement log file. This log file is used by the benchmark driver to calculate the energy-efficiency score.

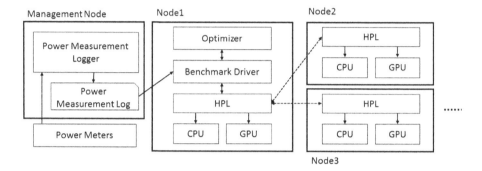

Fig. 1. System overview

The optimizer program executes BO for hyperparameter searches. We implemented the algorithm of BO described in Sect. 3 ourselves, but off-the-shelf software packages implementing similar algorithms can be obtained, such as spearmint [14], BayesOpt [15], and GPyOpt [16]. The optimizer can suspend an experiment at any time and resume it by reading the execution history file. This feature is useful when problems occur during experiments or when we need to further improve past experimental results.

The benchmark driver executes HPL and collects the log output from HPL and the power-measurement logger. From the optimizer point of view, the benchmark driver behaves as an objective function, which takes a set of hyperparameter values as inputs and outputs the resulting score of the benchmark as an objective value. Thus, the benchmark driver hides the details of HPL executions and power measurements, and this structure effectively separates the responsibility of each program. Figure 2 shows the flow chart of the coarse-grained behavior of the benchmark driver.

5   Search Space and Algorithm

5.1   Search Space

In this subsection, we explain how we determine the search space of our experiments. Table 1 lists the major possible parameters in our experimental settings.

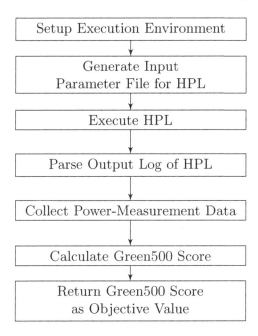

Fig. 2. Flow chart of benchmark driver

GPU_CLK and CPU_CLK are the clock frequencies of the GPU and CPU, and the other parameters from N to SWAP are the input parameters of the HPL benchmark software [5]. We determined the hyperparameters to be searched and their ranges in accordance with the literature [17] and preliminary experiments. We also referred to the tuning guide, which is provided by NVIDIA with the GPU optimized HPL.

The most fundamental parameters of HPL are N and NB. Parameter N specifies the size of the matrix to be solved, and NB specifies the size of the block dividing the matrix. In the HPL optimized for the GPU, the optimal N is within a certain range determined by the memory size of the GPU, and a suitable NB can be 128 multiplied by a small integer. However, the best combination of these parameters is determined through trial and error, so we use N and NB for search parameters. For N, we discretized the candidate values so that they are a multiple of 256.

Parameters P and Q are also important parameters that affect performance and determine the allocation of divided matrix blocks for each processor (GPU in this case). In our system, performance is extremely degraded, regardless of the value of other parameters, except for a few combinations of P and Q values. Therefore, by choosing the best combination of P and Q values in advance, we do not include P and Q for the search space of BO.

GPU_CLK greatly affects the energy efficiency of the benchmark. Higher energy efficiency can be obtained by decreasing GPU_CLK, but this also lowers

Table 1. Tuning parameters

Parameter	Range/Choices	Transformation	Description
N	Positive integer	linear	Matrix size
NB	1–N	linear	Block size
P, Q	P·Q = #Processes		Process grid size
NBMIN	1–NB	discrete	Recursive stopping condition
NDIV	Positive integer		# of Panels in recursions
PFACT	3 choices		# of Panel factorizations
RFACT	3 choices		# of Recursive panel factorizations
BCAST	6 choices	discrete	Broadcast type
DEPTH	Positive integer		Lookahead depth
SWAP	3 choices		Swapping algorithm
GPU_CLK	544–1,328	discrete	GPU clock frequency (MHz)
CPU_CLK	1,200–1,700	discrete	CPU clock frequency (MHz)

the Rmax substantially. For this reason, we added GPU_CLK to the search space while specifying a higher value for the lower bound.

Many other parameters can be used for finely controlling the behavior of the HPL benchmark. For each one, we measured benchmarks independently and decided to add the parameters of NBMIN and BCAST, which affected performance more than the other parameters. Because BCAST selects one of six broadcast communication methods, it cannot be mapped continuously to one dimension. We can generally use one-hot encoding, which means that each value of a nominal parameter is mapped to a distinct dimension. However, this tends to increase the dimension of the search space, often degrading the efficiency of the parameter search significantly. In this case, we could select two methods showing particularly high performance and assign them to the minimum and maximum values of one dimension of the search space. Finally, we decided to use five parameters: N, NB, NBMIN, BCAST, and GPU_CLK.

These five parameters are exactly what we used for Green500 submission, but we found that CPU_CLK sometimes affects the energy efficiency more than we first expected. CPU_CLK has a relatively smaller effect on energy efficiency than other parameters, but it is not small enough to be ignored, in particular, when optimally tuned. Thus, we also conducted experiments with a set of parameters with CPU_CLK instead of NBMIN. Concretely, the search parameters were: N, NB, BCAST, CPU_CLK, and GPU_CLK. We also changed the range of some parameters. The case in which the search parameters do not contain CPU_CLK is called Case I, and the other is called Case II.

To summarize, we chose five parameters with a restricted range or choices for the search space of BO, as indicated in the third column in Table 1. This search space contained 36,864 points in Case I and 291,840 points in Case II. In our setting, the HPL benchmark was typically executed in about five minutes, so a grid search over the entire search space would take more than four months in the former case and nearly three years in the latter. Because our system is relatively small, the single run of HPL benchmark required little time. In larger systems, it takes longer to complete the entire search space.

5.2   Search Algorithm Based on Latin Hypercube Sampling

The acquisition function is easy to evaluate. However, finding the global maximum solution of the acquisition function is difficult. Therefore, we generate candidate settings and query the next setting that maximizes the acquisition function. We use Latin hypercube sampling to generate candidate settings. Latin hypercube sampling is a statistical method for generating a sample inspired by a Latin square experimental design [18]. Latin hypercube sampling prevents the sample points from clumping together in a sample space; this problem can occur with purely random points. Because the sample points are spread out over the entire space, Latin hypercube sampling reduces the simulation's statistical variance associated with the finite sample size.

We have to consider one problem in using Latin hypercube sampling for generating candidate settings. Samples obtained by Latin hypercube sampling are just those over a hypercube. However, candidate settings have certain constraints. For example, some parameters take integer values, while Latin hypercube sampling generates samples over hypercube $[0, 1]^d \subset \mathbb{R}^d$. Therefore, we have to transform samples from Latin hypercube sampling into hyperparameter space. We use the transformation defined by

$$h_i = \begin{cases} \text{floor}((u_i - l_i + 1) \cdot x_i + l_i) & \text{(linear case)} \\ v_i^{(s_i)} & \text{(discrete case)} \end{cases}, \tag{19}$$

$$s_i = \text{floor}(i \cdot n_i), \tag{20}$$

where h_i denotes parameters i, x_i is a candidate setting generated by Latin hypercube sampling, u_i and l_i denote parameters for the upper and lower bound of hyperparameters i, $v_i^{(s_i)}$ denotes the value array for parameters i at index s_i, s_i denotes the index for the value array for parameters i, n_i denotes the number of elements in the value array for parameters i, and $\text{floor}(x) = \max\{z \in \mathbb{Z} \mid z \leq x\}$. We assume that the values of $v_i^{(s_i)}$ are arranged monotonically along s_i for each i.

6   Experimental Results

We conducted two lines of experiments. For Case I, we conducted experiments whose conditions were similar to those of which we submitted the energy efficiency score to the past Green500 list. For Case II, we also conducted experiments with five parameters containing GPU_CLK and CPU_CLK. These experimental conditions were more difficult even for human experts due to the complex and irregular dependence on these parameters, so using BO was considered to be more helpful.

6.1   Case I: Experiments Using Search Parameters Without CPU_CLK

We conducted ten BO experiments with five search parameters: N, NB, BCAST, NBMIN, and GPU_CLK. In each experiment, the first three trials of benchmarks were executed with randomly determined parameters. For the other 16 trials, the BO algorithm determined the next parameter values on the basis of the history of the parameters and the measured values. Figure 3 shows the cumulative maximum values of energy efficiency over the trials (including trials with random parameter selection) during the ten experiments. The style of each line indicates a different experiment. As the BO algorithm sought better energy efficiency, the cumulative maximum value of energy efficiency at each trial gradually increased. The average and standard deviation of the best values of energy efficiency obtained in each experiment were 14.18 ± 0.17 GFlops/W, comparable to those of the top ranked systems in recent Green500 lists. In particular, the overall best energy efficiency of 14.36 GFlops/W was obtained for the following configuration: N = 525,312, NB = 384, NBMIN = 8, BCAST = 3, and GPU_CLK = 1,189. Figure 8 in the Appendix shows the individual traces of energy efficiency (the solid lines) and cumulative best energy efficiency (the dashed lines) over the trials in the ten experiments. While the peak performances we found in this setting were lower, one may observe that BO tended to find good parameters earlier in its searches compared to the searches in Case II. As we noted in Sect. 5.1, we believe that this is due to smaller search space available to BO. This is the experimental setting similar to our submission to the past Green500 list.

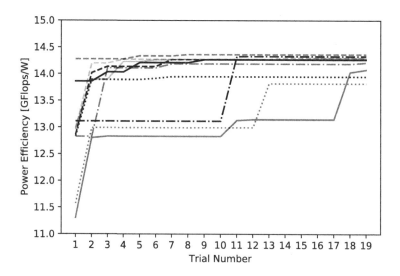

Fig. 3. Cumulative maximum energy efficiency for ten experiments (Case I)

6.2   Case II: Experiments Using Search Parameters with CPU_CLK

In Case I, our experimental setting tended to be narrowly focused but extensive with a larger number of experiments. Because BO found good configurations early in their searches, the results allowed us to be more confident in applying BO to a larger search space with a limited number of experiments.

To achieve the full potential of BO, we conducted three BO experiments with search parameters containing CPU_CLK. Specifically, the parameters used were: N, NB, BCAST, GPU_CLK, and CPU_CLK. In each experiment, the first three trials used randomly determined parameters and the successive 32 trials used the parameters provided from BO.

Figure 4 shows the cumulative maximum values of energy efficiency over trials during the three experiments, including trials with random parameter selection (the solid lines). The figure also shows the best value obtained from a grid search (GS) experiment (the dashed line). The search range of this GS experiment was almost identical with the BO experiments, but the candidate parameter values decreased because it took a significantly longer time to search all possible parameter values of the BO experiments. Although the number of candidate points was much larger than in Case I, the final scores converged to a relatively close value and exceeded 15.0 GFlops/W. While we cannot expect BO to obtain the best configuration without more trials, these final scores we obtained within 35 trials were close to the best value obtained from the GS experiment.

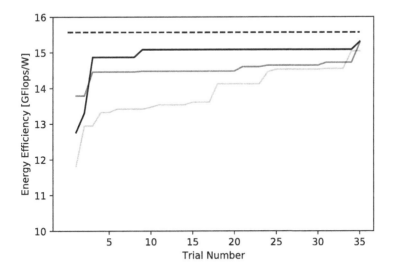

Fig. 4. Cumulative maximum energy efficiency for three experiments (Case II)

Table 2 shows some of the actual parameter values and resulting scores obtained during the experiments. The top six rows show the configurations with high energy-efficiency scores, and the bottom six rows show the configurations with high Rmax scores. For both energy efficiency and Rmax, we selected the five highest configurations from the BO experiments and the single highest configuration from the GS experiments. As can be seen from this table, the way Rmax and energy efficiency depend on the parameters greatly differ. For example, NB is likely optimal at the value of 384 for energy efficiency but has no simple relationship to Rmax.

Table 2. Actual parameter values that exhibit highest energy efficiency and Rmax scores

Method	N	NB	BCAST	GPU_CLK	CPU_CLK	Energy efficiency	Rmax
BO	483,328	384	1	1,101	1,300	15.30	336.1
	485,376	384	3	1,126	1,600	15.27	362.0
	486,656	384	1	1,113	1,200	15.08	330.3
	483,840	384	1	1,126	1,300	15.06	338.9
	486,656	384	1	1,151	1,600	15.04	369.2
GS	524,288	384	3	1,101	1,500	15.58	366.6
BO	515,840	128	3	1,303	1,700	11.82	397.6
	495,616	384	3	1,303	1,700	12.89	396.0
	522,496	256	3	1,328	1,500	12.57	395.6
	505,088	256	3	1,290	1,600	13.17	394.8
	552,704	256	3	1,278	1,700	12.77	392.4
GS	524,288	256	3	1,328	1,700	12.40	414.2

Figures 5 and 6 show how the Rmax values and energy-efficiency score depend on GPU_CLK and CPU_CLK obtained from the three BO experiments. As shown in Fig. 5, the highest Rmax values were concentrated in the area where both GPU_CLK and CPU_CLK were high. Thus, determining the performance in terms of Rmax is straightforward. However, Fig. 6 indicates that the highest energy-efficiency score scattered almost throughout the entire range of CPU_CLK.

We analyzed the overall measurement results from the BO and GS experiments. In Table 3, we summarize the relationships between the parameters and three metrics: Rmax, power, and energy efficiency. In the table, 'L' or 'H' means that a lower or higher parameter value was better for the metrics, 'M' means that the parameter values near the median value of the allowed range were better, and 'X' means that no simple relationships were evident. The results suggest that NB = 384 works best for energy efficiency and that the lower the GPU_CLK, the better the result. It is difficult to predict these relationships only from the specifications of the system in advance. Even knowing the relationships, it is necessary to adjust sensitive parameters by trial and error to obtain the best value. Thus, BO is considered useful to reduce laborious and time-consuming work to find the optimal configuration.

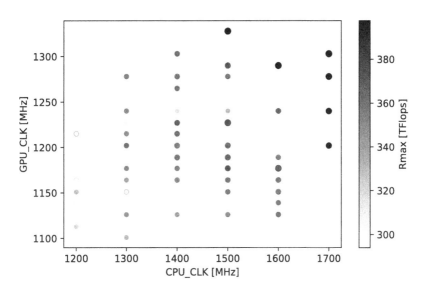

Fig. 5. Rmax, CPU_CLK, and GPU_CLK (Case II)

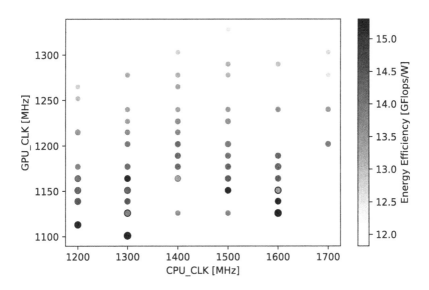

Fig. 6. Energy efficiency, CPU_CLK, and GPU_CLK (Case II)

Table 3. Qualitative relationships between parameters and metric values

Parameter	Rmax	Power	Energy efficiency
N	M	L,H	L,M
NB	X	L	384
BCAST	3	X	X
GPU_CLK	H	L	L
CPU_CLK	H	L	X

Figure 7 shows the frequency of values for each parameter that BO tuned. Consistent with the trend in the parameter providing high energy efficiency shown in Table 3, BO frequently searched the smaller values of N and GPU_CLK, the broad range of CPU_CLK, and NB = 256 and 384.

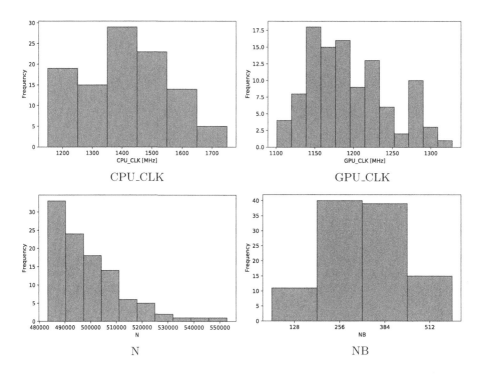

CPU_CLK   GPU_CLK

N   NB

Fig. 7. Frequency of parameter values tuned using BO (Case II)

7   Discussion

As described in Sect. 6, BO could reach near the best value of the GS experiment within 35 trials under our experimental conditions. In addition, the Green500 score for using BO was very close to the score of the top system in the official Green500 ranking.

Although BO worked successfully for our first attempt to enter Green500, some problems need to be considered. One is guaranteeing the minimum required performance of Rmax during optimization. According to the ranking rules of Green500, a system must not be lower than 500th place in the TOP500 ranking to be included in Green500. As the Rmax measurement is used for this ranking, we must maintain the minimum performance level of Rmax to ensure the system ranks in the TOP500. To cope with this challenge, we used a very high value for the lower limit of the search range of GPU_CLK, especially in Case I, because a lower GPU_CLK may reduce Rmax to an unacceptably low value if it is set too low. Ideally, BO should simultaneously optimize both energy efficiency and Rmax as objective functions or optimize energy efficiency with constraints such that Rmax remains above a certain value. This is important for not only ranking benchmarks but also real applications because it makes no sense to pursue greater energy efficiency if the performance plummets.

The other challenge is handling parameters, the possible values of which are from nominal categories. The only parameter that had this property among the selected search parameters was BCAST. We were able to select two effective values from among six values of BCAST and obtained satisfactory results. In general, however, choosing appropriate values from three or more nominal categories is likely to be essential in optimizing benchmarks.

In this study, we reported an application of BO in tuning the energy-efficiency benchmark, but the performance and energy efficiency of real applications also need to be tuned. The relationship between parameters and performance in real applications may be more complicated, but BO is expected to be successfully applied to real applications, as shown in this study, unless the dimensionality of the parameters is so high that BO fails to work effectively.

8   Conclusion

We demonstrated that BO is useful for efficiently determining the energy-efficient configuration of high-performance computing systems. Combining some domain knowledge and a few preliminary experiments, we could successfully reduce the search space, and BO eliminated laborious manual tuning work in a practical setting. Though we showed that BO is an easy-to-use tool for benchmark tuning, future work remains, for example, a more principled method of determining the search space and handling multiple constraints/objectives. By resolving these issues and further improving, we expect BO to become a popular tool for tuning various HPC systems.

Acknowledgements. We would like to thank Sunao Torii, Kenichi Inaba, Ryo Sakamoto, Yuki Yamaura and Michiya Hagimoto for their technical contributions, in particular, for their extensive expertise in liquid immersion cooling, system configuration, and power measurement. Without them, we would be unable to achieve second place in the Green500 ranking.

A   Individual Traces of Energy Efficiency over Trials in Each Experiment (Case I)

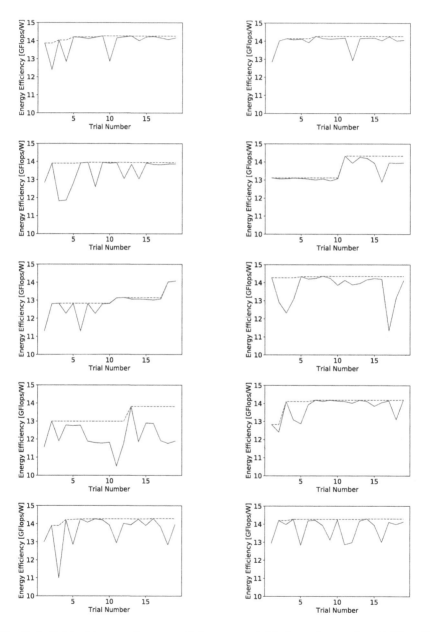

Fig. 8. Individual traces of energy efficiency over trials in each experiment (Case I)

References

1. Močkus, J., Tiesis, V., Zilinskas, A.: The application of bayesian methods for seeking the extremum. Towar. Glob. Optim. **2**, 117–129 (1978)
2. Rasmussen, C.E.: Gaussian Processes for Machine Learning (2006)
3. Ansel, J., Kamil, S., Veeramachaneni, K., Ragan-Kelley, J., Bosboom, J., O'Reilly, U.M., Amarasinghe, S.: Opentuner: an extensible framework for program auto-tuning. In: International Conference on Parallel Architectures and Compilation Techniques, Edmonton, Canada, August 2014
4. Storn, R., Price, K.: Differential evolution – a simple and efficient heuristic for global optimization over continuous spaces. J. Glob. Optim. **11**(4), 341–359 (1997)
5. Dongarra, J.J., Luszczek, P., Petitet, A.: The linpack benchmark: past, present and future. Concurr. Comput. Pract. Exp. **15**(9), 803–820 (2003)
6. Dalibard, V., Schaarschmidt, M., Yoneki, E.: Boat: building auto-tuners with structured Bayesian optimization. In: Proceedings of the 26th International Conference on World Wide Web, WWW 2017, Republic and Canton of Geneva, Switzerland, International World Wide Web Conferences Steering Committee, pp. 479–488 (2017)
7. Abadi, M., Barham, P., Chen, J., Chen, Z., Davis, A., Dean, J., Devin, M., Ghemawat, S., Irving, G., Isard, M., Kudlur, M., Levenberg, J., Monga, R., Moore, S., Murray, D.G., Steiner, B., Tucker, P., Vasudevan, V., Warden, P., Wicke, M., Yu, Y., Zheng, X.: Tensorflow: a system for large-scale machine learning. In: 12th USENIX Symposium on Operating Systems Design and Implementation (OSDI 16), pp. 265–283 (2016)
8. Kushner, H.J.: A new method of locating the maximum point of an arbitrary multipeak curve in the presence of noise. J. Fluids Eng. **86**(1), 97–106 (1964)
9. Snoek, J., Larochelle, H., Adams, R.P.: Practical Bayesian optimization of machine learning algorithms. In: Neural Information Processing Systems, pp. 2951–2959 (2012)
10. Murray, I., Adams, R.P.: Slice sampling covariance hyperparameters of latent Gaussian models. In: Advances in Neural Information Processing Systems, vol. 23, pp. 1732–1740 (2010)
11. Srinivas, N., Krause, A., Kakade, S.M., Seeger, M.: Gaussian process optimization in the bandit setting: no regret and experimental design. arXiv preprint arXiv:0912.3995 (2009)
12. Contal, E., Perchet, V., Vayatis, N.: Gaussian process optimization with mutual information. In: Proceedings of the 31th International Conference on Machine Learning, pp. 253–261 (2014)
13. EEHPC Working Group: Energy Efficient High Performance Computing Power Measurement Methodology (2015). https://www.top500.org/static/media/uploads/methodology-2.0rc1.pdf
14. Snoek, J., Larochelle, H., Adams, R.P.: Practical Bayesian optimization of machine learning algorithms. In: Pereira, F., Burges, C.J.C., Bottou, L., Weinberger, K.Q. (eds.) Advances in Neural Information Processing Systems, vol. 25, pp. 2951–2959. Curran Associates, Inc. (2012)
15. Martinez-Cantin, R.: Bayesopt: a Bayesian optimization library for nonlinear optimization, experimental design and bandits. J. Mach. Learn. Res. **15**, 3915–3919 (2014)
16. The GPyOpt authors: GPyOpt: a Bayesian optimization framework in python (2016). http://github.com/SheffieldML/GPyOpt

17. Petitet, A., Whaley, R.C., Dongarra, J., Cleary, A.: HPL tuning. http://www.netlib.org/benchmark/hpl/tuning.html
18. Stein, M.: Large sample properties of simulations using Latin hypercube sampling. Technometrics **29**, 143–151 (1987)

DTF: An I/O Arbitration Framework for Multi-component Data Processing Workflows

Tatiana V. Martsinkevich[1(✉)], Balazs Gerofi[1], Guo-Yuan Lien[1],
Seiya Nishizawa[1], Wei-keng Liao[2], Takemasa Miyoshi[1], Hirofumi Tomita[1],
Yutaka Ishikawa[1], and Alok Choudhary[2]

[1] RIKEN AICS, Tokyo, Japan
tatiana.mar@riken.jp
[2] Northwestern University, Chicago, USA

Abstract. Multi-component workflows, where one component performs a particular transformation with the data and passes it on to the next component, is a common way of performing complex computations. Using components as building blocks we can apply sophisticated data processing algorithms to large volumes of data. Because the components may be developed independently, they often use file I/O and the Parallel File System to pass data. However, as the data volume increases, file I/O quickly becomes the bottleneck in such workflows. In this work, we propose an I/O arbitration framework called DTF to alleviate this problem by silently replacing file I/O with direct data transfer between the components. DTF treats file I/O calls as I/O requests and performs I/O request matching to perform data movement. Currently, the framework works with PnetCDF-based multi-component workflows. It requires minimal modifications to applications and allows the user to easily control I/O flow via the framework's configuration file.

Keywords: Multi-component workflow · Workflow coupling
I/O performance · I/O arbitration

1 Introduction

In the past several years, the steady growth of computational power that newly built High Performance Computing (HPC) systems can deliver allowed humanity to tackle more complex scientific problems and advance data-driven sciences.

Rather than using the conventional monolithic design, many applications running in these systems are multi-component workflows in which components work together to achieve a common goal. Each component performs a particular task, such as building different physics models or running a model with different parameters as it is done in ensemble simulation programs. The result of the computation is then passed to the next component for further processing. A workflow may also include components for data analytics, in-situ visualization

© Springer International Publishing AG, part of Springer Nature 2018
R. Yokota et al. (Eds.): ISC High Performance 2018, LNCS 10876, pp. 63–80, 2018.
https://doi.org/10.1007/978-3-319-92040-5_4

and so on. Components may be either loosely coupled, i.e., by using files to pass data, or they can use a coupling software.

Such work pipelining allows to build powerful complex programs that perform sophisticated data processing. The module-based approach can also facilitate the development of new programs as they can be built fast by combining components from previously developed workflows. Many recent research works focus on tuning HPC systems so that they could run multi-component workflows more efficiently [1,2]. The I/O bottleneck in such applications is one of the issues that receives a lot of attention. The faster the component receives the data from the previous component, the sooner it can start processing it. However, for workflows coupled through files, file I/O can become a bottleneck, especially when they pass large amounts of data.

A motivating real-world application example for this work is an application called SCALE-LETKF [3]. SCALE-LETKF is a real-time severe weather prediction application that combines weather simulation with assimilation of weather radar observations. It consists of two components (Fig. 1) — SCALE and LETKF — that are developed independently. SCALE is a numerical weather prediction application based on the ensemble simulation; LETKF performs data assimilation of real-world observation data together with simulation results produced by SCALE.

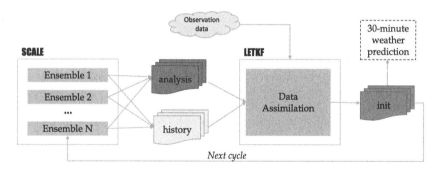

Fig. 1. SCALE-LETKF

In each iteration, SCALE writes the simulation result to the Parallel File System (PFS) using the Parallel NetCDF [4] API. The files are subsequently read by LETKF. After LETKF finishes assimilating the observation data, the output is written to files which become the input for SCALE in the next iteration. One of the results from every iteration is also used to predict weather for the next 30 min on separate compute nodes.

A particular feature of SCALE-LETKF is that it has a strict timeliness requirement. The target execution scenario is to assimilate the observations arriving at an interval of 30 s. Therefore, one full iteration of SCALE-LETKF, including the computations and I/O, must finish within this time period. However, this requirement quickly becomes hard to fulfill once the amount of file I/O grows too big.

One way to overcome this would be to switch from file I/O to some coupling software. However, this would require rewriting the I/O kernels in both components using the API of the coupler as such a software usually requires. This can be a daunting task for a software as large and complex as SCALE-LETKF.

In this work, we propose a framework called Data Transfer Framework (DTF) that silently bypasses file I/O by sending the data directly over network and requires minimal modifications to application source code. Current implementation of DTF assumes that the workflow components use PnetCDF API for file I/O. The framework uses the Message Passing Interface (MPI) [5] library to transfer the data. Applications like SCALE-LETKF can benefit from DTF because it allows the developers of the application to easily switch from file I/O to direct data transfer without having to rewrite the I/O code.

The main contributions of this work are:

- We propose a simple data transfer framework called DTF that can be used to silently replace PnetCDF-based file I/O with direct data transfer;
- Unlike many existing coupling solutions, DTF requires only minimal modifications to the application and does not require modifications of PnetCDF calls themselves;
- DTF automatically detects what data should be transferred to what processes transparently for the user, hence, it can be plugged into workflows fast and with minimal efforts and there is no need to provide a description of I/O patterns across components;
- Using a benchmark program, we show that the DTF exhibits stable performance under different I/O loads. A test run of DTF with the real-world workflow application (SCALE-LETKF) shows that the DTF can help multi-component workflows achieve real-time requirements.

The rest of this paper is organized as follows. In Sect. 2 we present in detail the design of our data transfer framework and discuss its implementation in Sect. 3. We present the results of the performance evaluation of the framework in Sect. 4. In Sect. 5 we overview existing solutions proposed to facilitate the data movement between the components in multi-component workflows. Finally, we conclude with Sect. 6.

2   Data Transfer Framework

DTF can be used in workflows in which the components use the PnetCDF library for file I/O. In this section, we first present some basic concepts of the (P)netCDF data format that had a direct influence on the design of the DTF. We then present the general overview of the framework and, finally, discuss in detail how the data transfer is performed.

We note that from now on we will call the component that writes the file and the component that reads it as the writer and the reader components, respectively.

2.1   Parallel NetCDF Semantics

Network Common Data Form [6] is a self-describing portable data format that supports handling of array-oriented scientific data. The NetCDF library provides users with an API that allows them to create files conforming to this data format and to define, store and retrieve the data. Parallel NetCDF (PnetCDF) is, as the name suggests, a parallel implementation of the NetCDF library. PnetCDF utilizes the parallel MPI-IO under the hood which allows multiple processes to share the file.

Before performing I/O, the user must first define the structure of the file, that is, define variables, their attributes, variable dimensions and dimension lengths.

Once the structure of the file is defined, the user may call PnetCDF's API to read or write variables. In a typical PnetCDF call, the user must specify the file id and variable id, which were assigned by PnetCDF during the definition phase, specify the start coordinate and block size in each dimension for multi-dimensional variables, and pass the input or output user buffer.

Similarly to MPI, PnetCDF has blocking and non-blocking API. In non-blocking I/O, the user first posts I/O requests and then calls a wait function to force the actual I/O. The purpose of non-blocking calls is to allow processes to aggregate several smaller file I/O requests into a larger request to improve the I/O throughput.

2.2   General Overview of DTF

DTF aims to provide users of multi-component workflows with a tool that would allow them to quickly switch from file I/O to direct data transfer without needing to cardinally change the source code of the components.

First, the user must provide a simple configuration file that describes the file dependency in the workflow (example in Fig. 4). It only needs to list the files that create a direct dependency between two components, i.e. if the components are coupled through this file. The DTF intercepts PnetCDF calls in the program and, if the file for which the call was made is listed in the configuration file as subject to the data transfer, the DTF handles the call accordingly. Otherwise, PnetCDF call is executed normally.

In order to transfer the data from one component to another, we treat every PnetCDF read or write call as an *I/O request*. The data transfer is performed via what we call *the I/O request matching*. First, designated processes, called *I/O request matchers*, collect all read and write requests for a given file. Then, each matcher finds out who holds the requested piece of data by matching each read request against one or several write requests. Finally, the matcher instructs the processes who have the data to send it to the corresponding process who requested it. All the inter-process communication happens using MPI. We note that here we differentiate between the PnetCDF non-blocking I/O requests and the DTF I/O requests, and we always assume the latter unless stated otherwise.

The I/O patterns of the component that writes to the file and the component that reads from it may be drastically different, however, dynamic I/O request matching makes DTF flexible and allows it to handle any kind of I/O patterns transparently for the user.

2.3   I/O Request Matching

When the writer component creates a file, matchers that will be handling the I/O request matching are chosen among its processes. The number of matchers can be configured by the user or else a default value is set.

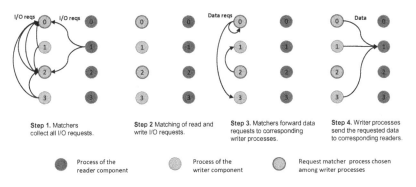

Step 1. Matchers collect all I/O requests.

Step 2 Matching of read and write I/O requests.

Step 3. Matchers forward data requests to corresponding writer processes.

Step 4. Writer processes send the requested data to corresponding readers.

Process of the reader component

Process of the writer component

Request matcher process chosen among writer processes

Fig. 2. I/O request matching. Request matchers are marked with a red shape outline. For simplicity, only one reader process is showed to have read I/O requests. (Color figure online)

When a process calls a read or write PnetCDF function for a file intended for data transfer, the DTF intercepts this call and, instead of performing file I/O, it internally creates an I/O request that stores the call metadata. Additionally, the process may buffer the user data if the DTF is configured to do so. The metadata consists of:

- varid - the PnetCDF variable id;
- rw flag - read or write request;
- datatype - in case this datatype does not match with the datatype used when the variable was defined, type conversion will take place;
- start - corner coordinate of the array block;
- count - length of the block in each dimension;
- buffer - pointer to the user buffer.

The request matching process can be divided in four steps (Fig. 2). First, all the processes of the reader and writer component send all their I/O requests posted so far to corresponding matching processes (Step 1). Then, a matching process takes the next read I/O request and, based on the corner coordinate start of the requested array block and the block size count, searches for matching write requests (Step 2). The I/O pattern of the reader and writer components are not necessarily identical, therefore, one read request may be matched with several write requests, each of them - for a sub-block of the requested array block. Once a match is found, the matcher sends a message to the writer process holding the requested portion of data and asks it to send this data to the corresponding reader process (Step 3). Finally, when a writer process receives a data request from the matcher, it finds the requested data in the memory, copies it to the send buffer along with the metadata and sends it to the reader (Step 4). When the reader receives the message, it parses the metadata and unpacks the data to the user buffer.

For better performance, the requests are distributed among the matching processes and each matcher is in charge of matching requests for a particular sub-block of a multi-dimensional variable. The size of the sub-block is determined by dividing the length of the variable in the lowest (zeroth) dimension by the number of matching processes. If there is a request that overlaps blocks handled by different matchers, such a request will be split into several requests for sub-blocks, and each matcher will match the corresponding part. There is a trade-off in this approach: On one hand, the matching happens in a distributed fashion, on the other hand, if there are too many matchers the request may end up being split too many times resulting in more communication between readers and writers. Therefore, it is recommended to do some test runs of the workflow with different number of matchers to find a reasonable configuration for DTF.

3   Implementation

The Data Transfer Framework is implemented as a library providing API to user programs. To let the DTF intercept PnetCDF calls, we also modified the PnetCDF-1.7.0 library. The modifications were relatively small and consisted of around 50 lines of code.

We use the MPI library to transfer the data. To establish the communication between processes in the reader and writer components, we use the standard MPI API for creating an inter-communicator during the DTF initialization stage in both components. This implies that the two components coupled through a file must run concurrently.

Current version of the DTF implements a synchronous data transfer, meaning that all the processes in the two components stop their computations to perform the data transfer and resume only when all the data requested by the reader has been received. Generally, it is preferable to transfer the data to the reader as soon as it becomes available on the writer's side so that the reader could proceed with computations. However, because the I/O patterns of the two components may differ significantly, it is hard to automatically determine when it is safe to start the matching process. Therefore, we require that the user signals to the DTF when to perform a request matching for a given file by explicitly invoking a special API function in both components.

To enable the data transfer, the user needs to modify the source code of all the components of the workflow by adding API to initialize, finalize the DTF, as well as explicitly invoke the data transfer. However, we believe that

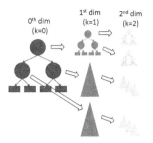

[INFO]
ncomp=2 ! number of components
comp_name="rdr" ! component name
comp_name="wrt"
ioreq_distrib_mode="range" !divide by dim length
buffer_data=0
[FILE]
filename="restart.nc"
writer="wrt" !component that writes to the file
reader="rdr" !component that reads from the file
iomode="memory" !enable direct transfer

Fig. 3. An example layout of a k-d tree to arrange sub-blocks of a 3-dimensional variable.

Fig. 4. DTF configuration file

these modifications are rather minimal compared to what traditional coupling software usually requires.

3.1 Handling of I/O Requests

Depending on the scale of the execution and the I/O pattern, matching processes sometimes may have to handle thousands of I/O requests. Using a suitable data structure to arrange the requests in such a way that matching read and write requests can be found fast is important.

Unless the variable is a scalar, an I/O request is issued for a multi-dimensional block of data. Such k-dimensional block can be represented as a set of k intervals. We use an augmented k-dimensional interval tree [7] to arrange these blocks in such a way that would allow us to find a block that overlaps with a quired block (read I/O request) in a reasonable amount of time. Figure 3 shows an example layout of a tree that stores write requests for a 3-dimensional variable. A tree on each level ($k = 0,1,2$) arranges intervals of the variable sub-blocks for which a write request was issued in the corresponding dimension. Each node of the tree links to the tree in the $k + 1$ dimension.

Read requests are stored as a linked list sorted by the rank of the reader. Every time new requests metadata arrives, the matcher updates the request database and tries to match as many read requests for a given rank as possible.

3.2 User API

The three main API functions provided by the DTF are the following:

- dtf_init(config_file, component_name) - initializes the DTF. The user must specify the path to the DTF configuration file and state the name of the current component which should match one of the component names in the configuration file;
- dtf_finalize() - finalizes the DTF;
- dtf_transfer(filename) - invokes the data transfer for file *filename*;

All the API functions are collective: `dtf_init()` and `dtf_finalize()` must be invoked by all processes in both components, while `dtf_transfer()` must be invoked only by processes that share the file.

During the initialization, based on the DTF configuration file, each component finds out all other components with whom it has an I/O dependency and establishes a separate MPI inter-communicator for every such dependency. All the further inter-component communication happens via this inter-communicator.

A `dtf_transfer()` call should be added after corresponding PnetCDF read-/write calls in the source code of both, reader and writer components. The call will not complete until the reader receives the data for all the read I/O requests posted before `dtf_transfer()` was invoked, therefore, it is user's responsibility to ensure that the components call the function in the correct place in the code, that is, that the writer does not start matching I/O until all the write calls for the data that will be requested in the current transfer phase have been posted as well. `dtf_transfer()` function can be invoked arbitrary number of times but this number should be the same for both components. We note that, because this function acts like a synchronizer between the reader and writer components, the recommended practice is to invoke it just once after all the I/O calls and before the file is closed.

By default, the DTF does not buffer the user data internally. Therefore, the user should ensure that the content of the user buffer is not modified between the moment the write PnetCDF call was made until the moment the data transfer starts. Otherwise, data buffering can be enabled in the DTF configuration file. In this case, all the data buffered on the writer's side will be deleted when a corresponding transfer function is completed.

3.3   Example Program

A simplified example of a writer and reader components is presented Figs. 5a and b, as well as their common DTF configuration file (Fig. 4). To enable the direct data transfer it was enough to add three lines of code to each component — to initialize, finalize the library and to invoke the data transfer — and provide a simple configuration file.

4   Evaluation

We first demonstrate the performance of DTF using the S3D-IO[1] benchmark program. Next, we show how the DTF performs with a real world workflow application—SCALE-LETKF.

S3D-IO [8] is the I/O kernel of the S3D combustion simulation code developed at Sandia National Laboratory. In the benchmark, a checkpoint file is written at regular intervals. The checkpoint consists of four variables—two three-dimensional and two four-dimensional—representing mass, velocity, pressure,

---

[1] Available at http://cucis.ece.northwestern.edu/projects/PnetCDF/#Benchmarks.

```
/* Initialize DTF*/
dtf_init(dtf_inifile, "wrt");
/* Create file*/
ncmpi_create("restart.nc",...);
<...>
 /* Write some data*/
ncmpi_put_vara_float(...);
/* Write some more data*/
ncmpi_put_vara_float(...);
/* Perform I/O request matching*/
dtf_transfer("restart.nc");
/* Close the file*/
ncmpi_close(...);
/* Finalize DTF*/
dtf_finalize();
```

```
/* Initialize DTF*/
dtf_init(dtf_inifile, "rdr");
/* Open the file*/
ncmpi_open("restart.nc",...);
<...>
/* Read all data at once*/
ncmpi_get_vara_float(...);
/* Perform I/O request matching*/
dtf_transfer("restart.nc");
/* Close the file*/
ncmpi_close(...);
/* Finalize DTF*/
dtf_finalize();
```

(a) Component writing to file   (b) Component reading from file

Fig. 5. Sample code using the DTF API

and temperature. All four variables share the lowest three spatial dimensions X, Y and Z which are partitioned among the processes in block fashion. The value of the fourth dimension is fixed.

We imitate a multi-component execution in S3D-IO by running concurrently two instances of the benchmark: Processes of the first instance write to a shared file, processes in the second instance read from it. Each test is executed at least eight times and an average value of the measured parameter is computed. To determine the number of matchers necessary to get the best performance for data transfer, we first execute several tests of S3D-IO varying the number of matching processes and use the result in the subsequent tests.

In the tests with the direct data transfer, the I/O time was measured in the following manner. On the reader side, it is the time from the moment the reader calls the data transfer function to the moment all its processes received all the data they had requested. On the writer's side, the I/O time is the time between the data transfer function and the moment the writer receives a notification from the reader indicating that it had got all the requested data. The I/O time also includes the time to register the metadata of the PnetCDF I/O calls and to buffer the data, if this option is enabled. In all our test cases it so happens that the writer component always invokes the transfer function before the reader and, therefore, sometimes it has to wait for the reader to catch up. Hence, by data transfer time we hereafter assume the I/O time of the writer component unless stated otherwise as it represents the lowest baseline. The runtime of the workflow is measured from the moment two components create an MPI inter-communicator inside the dtf_init() function and the moment it is destroyed in dtf_finalize() as these two functions work as a synchronization mechanism between the reader and writer components.

All the experiments were executed on K computer [9]. Each node has an 8-core 2.0 GHz SPARC64 VIIIfx CPU equipped with 16 GB of memory. Nodes are connected by a 6D mesh/torus network called Tofu [10] with $5\,GB/s \times 2$ bandwidth in each link. Compute nodes in K computer have access to a local per-node file system as well as a global shared file system based on Lustre file system.

4.1   S3D-IO Benchmark

Choosing the Number of Matching Processes. To get the best performance, it is recommended that the user chooses the number of matching processes that will perform I/O matching instead of using the default configuration of one matcher per 64 processes. This number is application-dependent. The load on a matching process is determined by the number of read and write I/O requests the process has to match. For example, if all reader and writer processes perform I/O symmetrically and the size of the variable in the zeroth dimension divides by the number of matchers, the number of I/O requests one matcher will have to match roughly equals the number of I/O requests one process generates multiplied by the number of processes in both components.

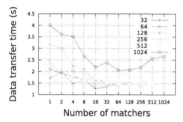

Fig. 6. Data transfer time for various test sizes and number of matching processes per component.

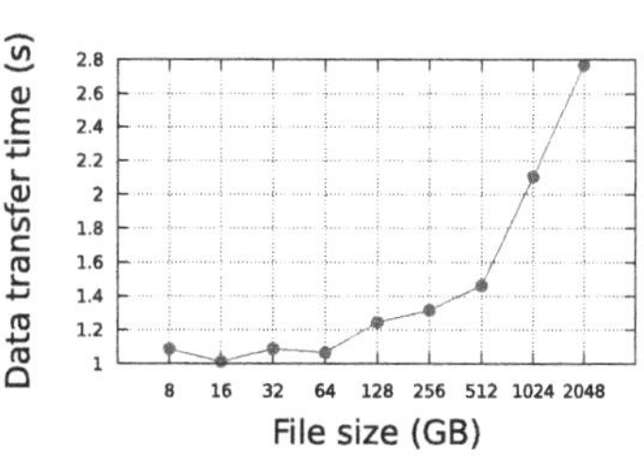

Fig. 7. DTF performance for various file sizes.

Depending on the I/O pattern, increasing the number of matchers does not always decrease the number of I/O requests per matcher, but it generally improves the throughput of data transfer. The reason is that rather than waiting for one matching process to match requests for one block of a multi-dimensional array, multiple processes can match sub-blocks of it in parallel. Consequently, the reader may start receiving the data earlier.

To find an optimal number of matchers, we run tests of different sizes—from 32 processes per component up to 1024—with a problem size such that each process reads or writes 1 GB of data. In each test we then vary the number of matchers and measure the time to transfer the data. The results in Fig. 6 show that increasing the number of matchers up to some point improves the transfer time and then the performance starts decreasing. The reason for this is that an I/O request for a block of data may be split into several requests for sub-blocks between multiple matchers and, if the number of matchers is too big, the request is over-split and it takes more smaller messages to deliver all the data to the reader. Based on this result, for our further tests we use the following setting: for tests with up to 256 processes in one component, each writer process functions as a matcher, for tests with 512 processes per component—four processes in one work-group, i.e. 128 matchers in total. Finally, for tests with 1024 processes per component the work-group size is 16, i.e. there are 64 matchers in total.

Scalability. We first demonstrate how the DTF scales compared to file I/O (PnetCDF) by measuring the read and write bandwidth for weak and strong scaling tests. In this test, processes write to a shared file using non-blocking PnetCDF calls. To measure the I/O bandwidth, we divide the total file size by the respective read or write I/O time. The results for the strong and weak scaling are presented on Figs. 8 and 9. The X axis denotes the number of processes in one component. We point out that the Y-axis is logarithmic in these plots. Figures 8a and 9a show the total execution time of the coupled workflow.

In all tests each process executes a PnetCDF read or write function four times—one per variable, i.e. each process generates four I/O requests.

In the strong scaling test, we fix the file size to 256 GB and vary the number of processes in one component. We note that, due to the node memory in K computer limited to 16 GB, the results in Fig. 8 start from the test with 32 processes per component. In the weak scaling tests, we fix the size of the data written or read by one process to 256 MB, thus, in the test with one process per component the file size is 256 MB, in the test with 1024 processes—256 GB.

As we see, DTF significantly outperforms file I/O in all tests. We also notice that the read bandwidth in all tests with the direct data transfer is always higher than the write bandwidth. We compute the bandwidth by dividing the size of the transferred data by the measured transfer time in the respective component. Thus, the reason for the different bandwidth is the timing when the matching starts in the reader component relatively to the writer component and is specific to our chosen test cases. As mentioned before, in our experiments the writer always entered the data transfer phase before the reader, hence, it sometimes had to wait for the reader. For this reason, from the writer's point of view, the transfer took longer than from the reader's point of view, hence, the write bandwidth is lower.

The bandwidth using the data transfer does flatten eventually in the strong scaling test (Fig. 8b and c), because the size of the data sent by one process decreases and the overhead of doing the request matching and issuing data requests starts to dominate the transfer time. In the weak scaling tests in Fig. 9 the data transfer time grows slower as the amount of data to transfer by one process stays the same and the overhead of the I/O request matching is relatively small. Hence, the total I/O bandwidth increases faster than in the strong scalability test.

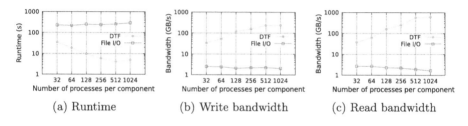

(a) Runtime   (b) Write bandwidth   (c) Read bandwidth

Fig. 8. Strong scaling of S3D-IO. Y-axis is in logarithmic scale in all plots.

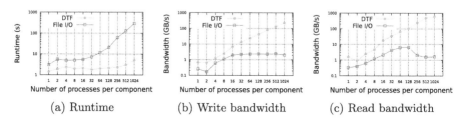

(a) Runtime   (b) Write bandwidth   (c) Read bandwidth

Fig. 9. Weak scaling of S3D-IO. Y-axis is in logarithmic scale in all plots.

DTF Performance Under I/O Load. Other major factors that impact the data transfer time apart from the number of matching processes are the size of data to transfer and the total number of I/O requests to be matched. To measure the former we perform data transfer for files of various sizes while the number of I/O requests per matcher stays the same. To evaluate the impact of the number of I/O requests, we fix the file size to 256 GB and increase the number of I/O requests a matcher process matches by manipulating how the I/O requests are distributed among matchers. By default, the size of the variable sub-block for which a matcher process matches read and write requests is defined by dividing the variable in the zeroth dimension by the number of matchers. An I/O request is split in the zeroth dimension based on this stripe size and distributed among the matchers in a round robin fashion. In this experiment, we vary the value of the stripe size which effectively changes the number of I/O requests each matcher has to handle.

In both experiments there are 1024 processes per component and there is one matcher per 16 processes. We also note that two out of four variables in S3D-IO have the zero dimension length fixed to 11 and 3, respectively. This is smaller than the number of matchers (64) and results in asymmetrical distribution of work among matchers. For this reason, in the two experiments, on top of the average number of I/O requests per matcher, a small group of matchers has to match approximately 4,000 more I/O requests.

Figure 7 shows the results of the first experiment. The file size was gradually increased from 8 GB to 2 TB. Each matcher process matched on average 576 requests in every test. We measured the time for actual matching of read and write requests—it took only around 2% of the whole data transfer time, thus, we conclude that most of the time was spent on packing and sending the data to reader processes. Thanks to the fast torus network in K computer, sending 2 TB of data over network took less than 3 s.

In the second experiment (Table 1) the file size is fixed, i.e. in every test each process transfers the same amount of data. The matching processes handled from 576 to 16,832 I/O requests, plus the additional requests for some matchers due to the imbalance. We expect that in this experiment it is the request matching process that will have the biggest impact on the data transfer time as the number of requests grow. However, according to the Table 1, the actual request matching took on average no more than 2–3% of the data transfer time and only in the test with 16,832 requests per matcher the matching took around 5% of the data transfer.

Table 1. DTF performance for different number of I/O requests

Average number of I/O requests per matcher	Data transfer time (s)	Time to match read and write requests (s)
576	1.799	0.041
1,088	1.498	0.031
2,144	2.107	0.046
4,224	2.061	0.045
8,448	2.108	0.058
16,832	1.777	0.085

Moreover, we observe that despite the growing number of I/O requests per matcher, the time to perform the data transfer actually decreases in some cases. One explanation for this could be that, when we decrease the stripe size by which the I/O requests are distributed, one matcher becomes in charge of several smaller sub-blocks located at a distance from each other along the zeroth dimension, rather than just one contiguous big sub-block. And this striping may accidentally align better with the I/O pattern of the program, so the matcher ends up matching requests for the data that was written by it. Then, instead of having to forward a data request to another writer process, the matcher immediately can send the data to the reader.

Overall, we conclude that the DTF shows stable performance under increased load of the amount of data that needs to be transferred as well as the load on the matching processes.

4.2 SCALE-LETKF

Finally, we demonstrate how DTF performs with a real-world multi-component application—SCALE-LETKF.

First of all, we explain the I/O pattern of SCALE-LETKF. At the end of one iteration, each ensemble in SCALE outputs the results to two files: a history file and a restart file. At the beginning of its cycle computation, each LETKF ensemble reads the data from the respective history and restart files. LETKF only requires a part of the data in the history file for its computations, i.e. it does not read the whole file. The data transfer function is invoked once per each of the two files. The tests are performed with one iteration because currently SCALE-LETKF does not support the multi-cycle execution.

In the chosen test case LETKF assimilates the data from a Phased Array Weather Radar [11] with a resolution of 500 m. The number of processes participating in one ensemble simulation is fixed to nine processes in all tests, the total number of processes per component is nine multiplied by the number of ensembles. The DTF is configured so that every process in the ensemble acts as a matcher. Additionally, the data buffering is enabled in DTF because the I/O in SCALE happens in several stages and the user buffers are overwritten by the time the data transfer function is called.

The size of the history and restart file in one ensemble is constant, we change the total amount of I/O by varying the number of ensembles from 25 to 100. Table 2 contains the information about the amount of data written and read in each configuration. In all tests, every ensemble process in SCALE writes 363 MB of data, out of which LETKF process requires only about one quarter. A SCALE process generates 255 write requests, LETKF process—31 read request.

Table 2. Cumulative I/O amount in SCALE-LETKF

Number of ensembles	Total write size (GB)	Total read size (GB)
25	79.78	18.97
50	159.56	37.94
75	239.35	56.91
100	319.13	75.88
Per process	363 MB	86.3 MB

Figure 10 shows the execution results of all configurations. Because SCALE-LETKF has a strict timeliness requirement, we focus on the time it took to perform the I/O rather than bandwidth. Additionally, we plot the standard deviation of I/O time between the processes because each ensemble performs I/O independently from each other.

The results show that the DTF helps to improve the total execution time of SCALE-LETKF (Fig. 10a) by cutting on the I/O time. In the largest execution with 100 ensembles, the I/O time was improved by a factor of 3.7 for SCALE and 10 for LETKF. This improvement is rather modest compared to what we observed in tests with S3D-IO mostly because SCALE-LETKF, along with its I/O kernel, is a much more complex application compared to the benchmark.

Apart from the I/O time, we also noticed that, when using the data transfer, the standard deviation decreases significantly compared to when file I/O is

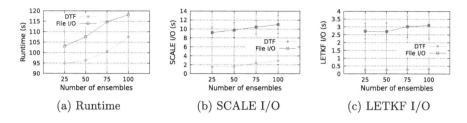

(a) Runtime   (b) SCALE I/O   (c) LETKF I/O

Fig. 10. SCALE-LETKF performance with DTF and file I/O.

used. This has a positive effect on the overall execution, because after LETKF has received all the data it performs global communication over all ensemble processes and smaller deviation in I/O time means that there should be less waiting for processes in other ensembles.

Finally, we note that SCALE-LETKF is still in the stage of development and the most recent version does not meet the target time requirement of 30 s per iteration as can be seen in Fig. 10a. However, we believe that our framework can be of great use to SCALE-LETKF and similar applications and it can help them achieve the execution goal by cutting on I/O time.

5   Related Work

A number of works has addressed the data movement problem, the file I/O bottleneck in particular, in multi-component workflows. Different coupling toolkits have been designed for such workflows [12], especially in Earth sciences [13–15] applications. Such toolkits often provide not only the data movement feature but also allow to perform various data processing during the coupling phase, such as data interpolation or changing the grid size.

For example, DART [16] is a software layer for asynchronous data streaming, it uses dedicated nodes for I/O offloading and asynchronously transferring the data from compute nodes to I/O nodes, visualization software, coupling software, etc. The ADIOS [17] I/O library is built on top of DART and provides additional data processing functionality. However, both, DART and ADIOS require to use a special API for I/O. In additional, ADIOS uses its own non-standard data format for files.

Other coupling approaches include implementing a virtual shared address space accessible by all the components [18], or using dedicated staging nodes to transfer the data from compute job to post-process analysis software during the runtime [19]. In [20], the authors propose a toolkit utilizing the type-based publisher/subscriber paradigm to couple HPC applications with their analytics services. The toolkit uses a somewhat similar concept to inter-component data transferring as proposed in this work, however, they rely on the ADIOS library underneath which the coupling toolkit was built which includes the description of the I/O pattern of the components. Additionally, in our work the matching process is simpler in a way that it takes fewer steps to perform the data transfer.

Providing support to multi-component executions on a system-level is another approach to facilitating the inter-component interaction [21,22]. Current HPC systems usually do not allow overlapping of resources allocated for one executable file. Thus, each component in a multi-component workflow ends up executing on a separate set of nodes and, consequently, the problem of data movement between the components arises. But, for example, in cloud computing, several virtual machines can run on the same node and communicate with each other via shared memory or virtual networking. It has been previously proposed to use virtualization techniques in HPC as well. For example, in [21], the authors show that such virtualization can be used in an HPC environment to allow more efficient execution of multi-component workflows with minimal costs. However, the virtualization is not yet widely adopted in HPC systems.

The main difference of our solution with the I/O library approaches like ADIOS is that such libraries usually provide their own I/O API and underneath that API they can switch between different standard I/O libraries or even perform direct data coupling at user's will. It is assumed that the programmer of the application used this special API during the development stage. In case the application originally used a different I/O library, the I/O kernel must be rewritten. But this may sometimes require a lot of effort, especially when component applications were developed by a third party. Our goal was to provide a simple framework that would allow to switch from file I/O to data transfer with minimal efforts and without having to rewrite the I/O kernels of the workflow components. The DTF operates underneath the PnetCDF library which is a popular I/O library. And while it does not provide as wide functionality as some more advanced coupling libraries, for cases where a user wants to compose a workflow consisting of applications developed relatively independently but all using PnetCDF for I/O, the DTF can work as a quick plug-in solution for faster coupling. The closest solution that we are aware of is the I/O Arbitration Framework (FARB) proposed in [23]. However, the framework was implemented for applications using NetCDF I/O library, that is, it assumes the file-per-process I/O pattern and a process-to-process mapping of data movement. Moreover, during the coupling stage in FARB, contents of the whole file were transferred to the other component's processes regardless of whether the process actually required the whole data or not. In our work, we determine at runtime what data needs to be transferred and only send this data.

6 Conclusion

Multi-component workflows that consist of tasks collaborating with each other to perform computations are becoming a common type of applications running in HPC environments. However, because the current HPC systems are often designed with monolithic applications in mind, it is necessary to determine the main obstacles that prevent multi-component workflows from running at maximum performance in these systems and find solutions. One of the most important issues is the data movement between the components and a number of solutions have been proposed to date.

In this work we proposed one such solution—a data transfer framework called DTF to speed up the data movement between the components in workflows that use PnetCDF API for file I/O. The DTF intercepts the PnetCDF calls and bypasses the file system by sending the data directly to the corresponding processes that require it. It automatically detects what data should be sent to which processes in the other component through a process of I/O request matching.

The DTF requires minimal efforts to start using it in a workflow: There is no need to modify the original PnetCDF calls, rewrite the code using some special API or provide the description of the I/O pattern of the components. The DTF only requires that the user compiles the components using our modified version of the PnetCDF library, provides a simple configuration file listing the files that need to be transferred and adds a few lines to the components' source code in order to enable the data transfer.

Through extensive testing we demonstrated that the DTF shows stable performance under different conditions. However, we believe there is a room for improving the load balancing of the I/O request matching, in particular, the way I/O requests are distributed among the matching processes.

Additionally, due to the fact that the current version of SCALE-LETKF does not support a multi-cycle execution, evaluation of the DTF in such an execution setting is also left for the future work. However, the results we obtained so far are promising and should help SCALE-LETKF to achieve its real-timeliness requirement.

References

1. LANL, NERSC, S.: APEX Workflows. White Paper (2016)
2. Deelman, E., Peterka, T., Altintas, I., Carothers, C.D., van Dam, K.K., Moreland, K., Parashar, M., Ramakrishnan, L., Taufer, M., Vetter, J.: The future of scientific workflows. Int. J. High Perform. Comput. Appl. (2017). https://doi.org/10.1177/1094342017704893
3. Miyoshi, T., Lien, G.Y., Satoh, S., Ushio, T., Bessho, K., Tomita, H., Nishizawa, S., Yoshida, R., Adachi, S.A., Liao, J., Gerofi, B., Ishikawa, Y., Kunii, M., Ruiz, J., Maejima, Y., Otsuka, S., Otsuka, M., Okamoto, K., Seko, H.: Big data assimilation; toward post-petascale severe weather prediction: an overview and progress. Proc. IEEE **104**(11), 2155–2179 (2016)
4. Argonne National Laboratory and Northwestern University: Parallel NetCDF (Software). http://cucis.ece.northwestern.edu/projects/PnetCDF/
5. Message Passing Interface Forum: MPI: A Message-Passing Interface Standard, Version 3.1 (1995). www.mpi-forum.org/docs/
6. UNIDATA: Network Common Data Form. http://www.unidata.ucar.edu/software/netcdf/
7. Mehta, D.P., Sahni, S.: Handbook of Data Structures and Applications. Chapman & Hall/CRC, Boca Raton (2004)
8. Liao, W.k., Choudhary, A.: Dynamically adapting file domain partitioning methods for collective I/O based on underlying parallel file system locking protocols. In: Proceedings of the 2008 ACM/IEEE Conference on Supercomputing, SC 2008. IEEE Press, Piscataway (2008)

9. Kurokawa, M.: The K computer: 10 peta-flops supercomputer. In: The 10th International Conference on Optical Internet (COIN 2012) (2012)

10. Ajima, Y., Sumimoto, S., Shimizu, T.: Tofu: a 6D mesh/torus interconnect for exascale computers. Computer **42**(11), 36–40 (2009)

11. Ushio, T., Wu, T., Yoshida, S.: Review of recent progress in lightning and thunderstorm detection techniques in Asia. Atmos. Res. **154**, 89–102 (2015)

12. Dorier, M., Dreher, M., Peterka, T., Wozniak, J.M., Antoniu, G., Raffin, B.: Lessons learned from building in situ coupling frameworks. In: Proceedings of the First Workshop on In Situ Infrastructures for Enabling Extreme-Scale Analysis and Visualization. ACM, New York (2015)

13. Valcke, S., Balaji, V., Craig, A., DeLuca, C., Dunlap, R., Ford, R.W., Jacob, R., Larson, J., O'Kuinghttons, R., Riley, G.D., Vertenstein, M.: Coupling technologies for earth system modelling. Geosci. Model Dev. **5**(6), 1589–1596 (2012)

14. Larson, J., Jacob, R., Ong, E.: The model coupling toolkit: a new Fortran90 toolkit for building multiphysics parallel coupled models. Int. J. Perform. Comput. Appl. **19**(3), 277–292 (2005)

15. Valcke, S.: The OASIS3 coupler: a European climate modeling community software. Geosci. Model Dev. **6**, 373–388 (2013)

16. Docan, C., Parashar, M., Klasky, S.: Enabling high-speed asynchronous data extraction and transfer using DART. Concurr. Comput. Pract. Exp. **22**(9), 1181–1204 (2010)

17. Lofstead, J., Zheng, F., Klasky, S., Schwan, K.: Adaptable, metadata rich IO methods for portable high performance IO. In: 2009 IEEE International Symposium on Parallel Distributed Processing, pp. 1–10, May 2009

18. Docan, C., Parashar, M., Klasky, S.: Dataspaces: an interaction and coordination framework for coupled simulation workflows. In: Proceedings of the 19th ACM International Symposium on High Performance Distributed Computing, HPDC 2010. ACM (2010)

19. Vishwanath, V., Hereld, M., Papka, M.E.: Toward simulation-time data analysis and I/O acceleration on leadership-class systems. In: 2011 IEEE Symposium on Large Data Analysis and Visualization, October 2011

20. Dayal, J., Bratcher, D., Eisenhauer, G., Schwan, K., Wolf, M., Zhang, X., Abbasi, H., Klasky, S., Podhorszki, N.: Flexpath: type-based publish, subscribe system for large-scale science analytics. In: 14th IEEE/ACM International Symposium on Cluster, Cloud and Grid Computing 2014, pp. 246–255 (2014)

21. Kocoloski, B., Lange, J., Abbasi, H., Bernholdt, D.E., Jones, T.R., Dayal, J., Evans, N., Lang, M., Lofstead, J., Pedretti, K., Bridges, P.G.: System-level support for composition of applications. In: Proceedings of the 5th International Workshop on Runtime and Operating Systems for Supercomputers, ROSS 2015. ACM, New York (2015)

22. Kocoloski, B., Lange, J.: Xemem: Efficient shared memory for composed applications on multi-OS/R exascale systems. In: Proceedings of the 24th International Symposium on High-Performance Parallel and Distributed Computing, HPDC 2015. ACM, New York (2015)

23. Liao, J., Gerofi, B., Lien, G.-Y., Nishizawa, S., Miyoshi, T., Tomita, H., Ishikawa, Y.: Toward a general I/O arbitration framework for netCDF based big data processing. In: Dutot, P.-F., Trystram, D. (eds.) Euro-Par 2016. LNCS, vol. 9833, pp. 293–305. Springer, Cham (2016). https://doi.org/10.1007/978-3-319-43659-3_22

Classifying Jobs and Predicting Applications in HPC Systems

Keiji Yamamoto$^{(\boxtimes)}$, Yuichi Tsujita, and Atsuya Uno

RIKEN, Kobe, Hyogo, Japan
keiji.yamamoto@riken.jp

Abstract. Next-generation supercomputers are expected to consume tens of MW of electric power. The power is expected to instantaneously fluctuate between several MW to tens of MW during their execution. This fluctuation can cause voltage drops in regional power grids and affect the operation of chillers and generators in the computer's facility. Predicting such fluctuations in advance can aid the safe operation of power grids and facility. Because abrupt fluctuations and a high average of consumed power are application-specific features, it is important to identify an application before job execution. This paper provides a methodology for classifying executed jobs into applications. By this method, various statistics for each application such as the number of executions, runtime, resource usage, and power consumption can be examined. To estimate the power consumed because of job execution, we propose a method to predict application characteristics using submitted job scripts. We demonstrate that 328 kinds of applications are executed in 273,121 jobs and that the application can be predicted with an accuracy of approximately 92%.

Keywords: Job analytics · Tracking · Monitoring
Administration tools

1 Introduction

The HPC system is entering an era of the exascale (10^{18} FLOPS[1]), and administrators must seriously consider gaining an understanding of the operations of the exascale system. A critical issue is power consumption. A next-generation supercomputer is expected to consume tens of MW of electric power. As of November 2017, a supercomputer consumes 17.8 MW of electricity [6]. Power fluctuations instantaneously change from an order of several MW to tens of MW during job execution. Because such fluctuations cause voltage drops in regional power grids, the grids are required to be controlled within a facility. Chillers and generators must also be operated in accordance with the fluctuations, but such equipment cannot handle rapid fluctuations because of various operational

---

[1] Floating-point Operations Per Second.

© Springer International Publishing AG, part of Springer Nature 2018
R. Yokota et al. (Eds.): ISC High Performance 2018, LNCS 10876, pp. 81–99, 2018.
https://doi.org/10.1007/978-3-319-92040-5_5

constraints. Predicting such fluctuations in advance can aid in the safe operation of the power grids and the facilities. Because abrupt fluctuations and a high average of power consumption are considered application-specific features, it is important to identify an application before job execution.

Leadership-class supercomputers are generally shared by many projects and users. Various applications are used for various projects, such as those on molecular dynamics, earthquake simulation, and machine learning. For the convenience of the users of supercomputers, frequently used software, such as applications and libraries, are pre installed in the system. Users can use preinstalled software and those that have been compiled and installed using the source code by them. In addition, users also have an option of developing and using their own applications. However, administrators do not possess sufficient knowledge about the number of executions and the amount resources consumed for each application because there is no mechanism for tracking applications.

The power characteristics of such computers are often application-specific. If we understand the application that is used by the job before execution, we can predict its power consumption using the power characteristics of the application that has been executed in the past. Among the jobs that have been executed so far, we need to identify the corresponding application and predict the subsequent application of the job to be executed.

In this paper, we propose a methodology for classifying executed jobs into applications and for predicting applications using job scripts. A job comprises executable files (i.e., applications). Features that are extracted from executable files are used to classify the file into various groups, known as application classes. Using the results of the classifications, various statistics for each application such as the number of executions, resource usage, performance, language, and compiler version can be examined. According to our classification method, executed jobs and application classes are associated with each other. Therefore, application classes can be predicted from job information prior to execution. If we use job scripts as job information, the prediction method employed will be similar to the general supervised learning method using application classes and job scripts. Considering a job script to be a text makes it a popular text classification problem.

The application class can be determined at the time of job submission. Therefore, past power consumption and runtime of the application class can be determined prior to job execution. This information is considered critical for the operation of next-generation supercomputers and is useful for job scheduling, considering the power efficiency and facility operation.

We demonstrate that 328 kinds of applications were executed on the K computer [21] between September 2016 and March 2017 and that the application class can be predicted from the job script with an accuracy of approximately 92%. The main contributions of our proposed method are summarized as follows:

- Classifying an executed job into its application class using the feature of the executable file

– Predicting the application class from a job script at the time of job submission

The rest of the paper is organized as follows: Sect. 2 provides the research background and introduces our operation of the supercomputer. Section 3 describes the method of classifying executed jobs into application classes using features extracted from executable files. Section 4 describes the method of predicting application classes from job scripts. Section 5 reports the summary of performance and characteristics of each application class. Related work is discussed in Sect. 6. Finally, we summarize our research and describe future issues in Sect. 7.

2   Background

The K computer comprises 82,944 compute nodes and consumes between 10 and 15 MW of power. There are two 5MW generators, which are used for active-standby configuration. We used electricity supplied by the generators and the electric power company. When executing high-power jobs, we used both generators because of the contractual upper limit on the amount of electricity consumed set by the electric power company. Because the generators were operated manually, we could not execute high-power jobs without prior notice. If a high-power job was executed without notice and the electricity exceeded the upper limit, the high-power job was terminated by an emergency job stopping system that monitors power consumption.

Figure 1 depicts power consumption for three days when power fluctuations of 5 MW occurred. In this situation, the operational staff had prior knowledge that a high-power job would be executed and that the job could be executed using both generators.

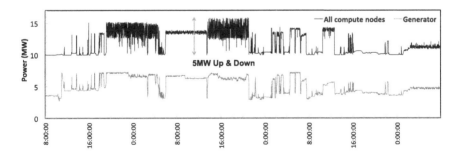

Fig. 1. Power consumption of compute nodes

The exascale system is expected require tens of MW of electric power. This power is considered to fluctuate in range from several MW to tens of MW. For future exascale operation, we intend to automate the classification of high-power jobs and the operation of generators. It is critical to estimate the power consumption of jobs. Because the power characteristics of jobs are often dependent on applications, the power consumption is estimated based on the application. In addition, it is necessary to specify the application that is used by the job before execution. Therefore, we intend to estimate the application at the time of job submission and to predict the power consumption using the execution history of the application.

3   Classifying Jobs

Generally, a job comprises executable files (i.e., applications) and is executed as an MPI program in HPC systems. Our objective is to identify the applications that are contained in the corresponding job. Therefore, we initially describe a method of extracting the features of the executable file from the corresponding jobs. The features of the executable file are as follows:

- the size of the executable file
- the name of the executable file
- the hash of the executable file
- information contained within the executable file itself

There are some methods for collecting these features from the job. We considered two methods: One is to provide a wrapper command to launch the MPI program. A parallel MPI program is launched using a parallel job launcher, such as mpirun or mpiexec. The wrapper command of the launcher is used to extract features. The other is to use LD_PRELOAD of the environment variable on Linux. The library is set in LD_PRELOAD and will be loaded before any other library. Thus, the function calls of the executable files can be hooked and their features can be extracted using the hook functions.

A wrapper can access only the features of the MPI program, whereas LD_PRELOAD also extracts features of programs other than the MPI program. In our environment, MPI applications are used at almost all instances, and the wrapper can be implemented with ease. Therefore, the features are collected using a wrapper program. The extraction process is performed in the background, and this process has little effect on the execution time of the job. In addition, the processing time is hidden by the initialization process of the MPI. These features are saved to files during job execution and are stored in the database by periodic processing after job completion.

Table 1 shows the information that was extracted from executable files. Although our system collects these features, we use only hashes and the symbols outputted nm command. In the succeeding section, we describe the application classification method based on the hashes and symbols of the executable files.

3.1   Classifying Jobs Using Hashes and Symbols

Even if there are different users or projects, if the hashes of the executable files are the same, they are considered to use the same executable file, i.e., application. In this study, we first classify the executable file using hashes. Many users

Table 1. Features extracted from executable files

Command	Description
nm	List symbols from object files
ident	Identify RCS keyword strings in files
strings	List strings of printable characters in files
ldd	Print shared library dependencies

execute jobs by changing the data that is provided for the applications. If a pre installed software is used by a job, the application can be identified using hash matching. In this method, the hashes of all the pre installed software are obtained in advance, which are compared with the hashes that are obtained from the executable files for the corresponding jobs. However, this method can not be used for applications that are compiled by users.

The symbols that are extracted using the nm command include function and variable names. If the symbol sets of the two executable files are observed to be identical, they can be considered as the same application. Therefore, we can determine the number of types of applications by classifying the executable files using symbol sets. Further, we use only function names to perform classification because the compiler inserts arbitrary symbols for the variable name.

Usually, applications that are observed to be the same may have different symbol sets. This is because the versions of the applications may be different, and symbols (or new functions) are added.

Small applications with only one **main function** are considered identical applications even if the content of **main function** is different. Because there are few HPC applications that have only **main function**, these applications are considered as one.

In the method described so far, we compare the hashes or symbol sets with the perfect match. Therefore, if one function is added to an application, this application is considered as a new application. From the viewpoint of classifying applications, we intend to neglect minor differences in symbol sets. In the succeeding section, we describe a classification method using the similarities of various symbol sets.

3.2 Classifying Jobs Using Similar Symbols

In the previous section, only when the two symbol sets are perfectly matched, they were considered as the same application. In this section, we describe a method for considering similar symbol sets to be the same application. The problem is to determine the ways of defining similarities among symbol sets. Further, we must also determine the degree of similarity that is required among these symbol sets to considered the same application.

Figure 2 depicts the classification process of the executable files. Symbols are extracted from the executable files using the nm command, and the feature

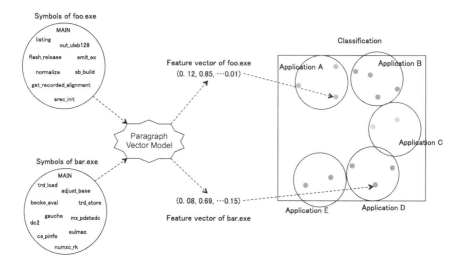

Fig. 2. Classification process of executable file

vectors are generated using this symbol set. The paragraph vector model [12] is used to vectorize symbols. Every executable file is represented as a point in feature space. If the distance between the points is observed to be small, there is a high probability that they are the same application. Further, cosine similarity is used as the distance and is given by the following equation:

$$cosine\ similarity = \frac{\boldsymbol{A} \cdot \boldsymbol{B}}{|\boldsymbol{A}||\boldsymbol{B}|} = \frac{\sum_{i=1}^{n} A_i B_i}{\sqrt{\sum_{i=1}^{n} A_i^2} \cdot \sqrt{\sum_{i=1}^{n} B_i^2}} \qquad (1)$$

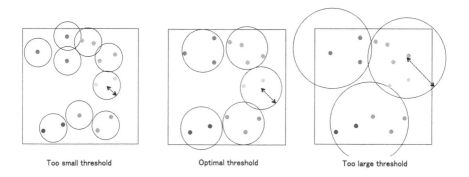

Fig. 3. Difference of classification results at various thresholds (Color figure online)

The higher the degree of similarity between the two vectors, the closer the value of this expression is to 1. The problem is to determine the degree of similarity at which various applications would be considered as the same.

Figure 3 illustrates that a big threshold of similarity can cause problems because different applications would be considered as the same. This threshold has almost the same meaning as the height of the tree in the hierarchical clustering method. If the similarity threshold is set small, the same original application would be classified into multiple applications. In this case, because one class contains one application, we do not encounter any problems. However, the number of application classes increases. It is essential to set a threshold that is as large as possible and reduce the number of classes.

In the Fig. 3, the application is colored and the optimal value of the threshold can be estimated. Generally, such colors are not attached to the application. Thus, we cannot estimate the optimal value. To obtain the optimal threshold, we consider coloring the application, as depicted in Fig. 3.

An application includes several symbols. Special symbols that only exist in the designated application are referred to as unique symbols in this paper. If the unique symbols for each application are determined, the executable files can be classified into applications in the presence of the unique symbols. However, the unique symbols of all applications cannot be found because we do not understand the types of applications in the first place. Therefore, we identify specific applications using the unique symbols and examine the optimal threshold.

3.3 Evaluation of Classification Method

We classified 273,121 executable files that were executed between September 2016 and March 2017 on the K computer. The number of unique hashes and symbol sets was 42,625 and 6,077, respectively. Thus, the number of applications is at most 6,077. The presence of several unique hashes indicates that the users executed jobs by developing their own applications.

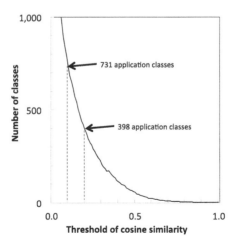

Fig. 4. The number of classes per threshold of cosine similarity

Next, we classified 6,077 executable files into application classes based on the similarity of symbols. Our classification method was implemented using the scikit-learn [15] and the gensim [16] libraries, which are used in several text mining projects. Figure 4 illustrates the number of application classes at various thresholds of similarity. As the threshold values increased, various applications were considered to be the same. Therefore, the number of classes observed was small. If the threshold was equal to 0, the number of classes was 6,077 because of perfect matches. If the thresholds were 0.1 and 0.2, the number of classes greatly reduced to 731 and 398, respectively.

To decide on an appropriate threshold value, we selected ten renowned applications and examined the unique symbols. These applications are depicted in Table 2. Because there are multiple executable files for each application, the number of symbols represent the value of an arbitrarily selected executable file. The value of the maximum threshold indicates that other applications are combined with the target application when the threshold is larger than this value.

Table 2. Well-known applications and their unique symbols

Application	# of symbols	Unique symbol	Max. threshold
HPCG	409	_Z13HPCG_Finalizev	0.16
VASP	4,733	vaspxml	0.20
LANS	149	sstkw_mod_	0.20
FrontFlowRed	1,655	module_array_fflow_	0.27
MODYLAS	751	init_md_check_	0.27
SIESTA	2,554	read_chemical_types_	0.38
GROMACS	8,480	_Z9gmx_mdruniPPc	0.35
LAMMPS	10,899	_ZN9LAMMPS_NS6LAMMPSD1Ev	0.40
CPMD	3,886	cpmd_	0.42
CP2K	11,595	print_cp2k_license_	0.48

In Table 2, the maximum threshold for each application is observed to vary substantially from 0.16 to 0.48. Because CP2K [10] has a large threshold, it is not very similar to other applications. HPCG [7] is observed to exhibit some similarities with other applications. HPCG uses the MPI wrapper library that is used in other applications. Therefore, the threshold was reduced because the symbol of this wrapper library became a symbol that could be shared with other applications. MODYLAS [2] includes 157 BLAS[2] functions. MODYLAS is classified in the same class as other applications using BLAS because approximately 20% functions of MODYLAS are BLAS library. VASP [11] includes approximately 1,600 FFTW[3] library symbols. FFTW is renowned and is also a pre installed library. Because several

---

[2] Basic Linear Algebra Subprograms.
[3] Fastest Fourier Transform library.

applications use FFTW, these applications and VASP were considered close to each other in the feature space. Using this result, the executable file can be safely classified into individual application classes with a threshold of approximately 0.16, and the number of application classes is 504.

3.4   Discussion

To summarize the evaluation, we classified executable files into 42,625 application classes by using the hash, into 6,077 classes by using the perfect match of symbols, and into 504 classes by using the similarity of symbols. We discuss methods to further improve the classification performance. From the results in the previous section, the classification performance was not considered as good because of the shared symbols, such as BLAS and FFTW.

By removing these symbols from the original symbol sets of executable files, the remaining symbols could well represent the characteristics of the application. Therefore, we classify jobs by using symbol sets that remove the shared symbols.

Generally, for text classification problems, shared symbols such as "A", "THE," and "THIS" are often eliminated based on the frequency of appearance. We cannot eliminate symbols based on the frequency of appearance because the frequency of appearance of symbols is dependent on the number of executions of applications. Therefore, we compare the symbol sets with different applications and consider the duplication of both to be the shared symbols. For example, when symbols of MODYLAS and VASP are compared, the common symbol is considered a shared symbol. Furthermore, when symbols of MODYLAS and GROMACS are compared, the same process is repeated. In particular, there is insufficient knowledge of the application. Therefore, we compare the symbols of the executable files having minor similarities.

The number of shared symbols that were extracted using this method was 103,305. When the shared symbols were excluded from the original symbol set of executable files, the average number of symbols reduced from 3,602 to 1,069. This means that the application contains many shared symbols that resemble noise for classification.

Table 3. Result of excluding shared symbols

Application	# of symbols	Max. threshold
HPCG	82	0.40
VASP	3,299	0.48
LANS	142	0.34
FrontFlowRed	1,603	0.44
MODYLAS	621	0.40

Table 3 displays the classification results when the shared symbols were excluded. These are five applications having a small threshold and are represented in Table 2. The value of the maximum threshold was much larger because the shared symbols were eliminated. The executable file can be safely classified into individual application classes having an approximate threshold of 0.34. The number of application classes of this particular threshold was 279. The application class has been reduced from 504 to 279 using this method.

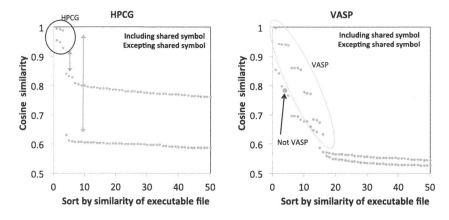

Fig. 5. Similarities between the target application and other executable files

Figure 5 depicts the similarities between the target application and other executable files. They are sorted in descending order of similarity. HPCG has three types of executable files, i.e., three hashes and three symbol sets. Regardless of the presence of shared symbols, HPCG was observed to be clearly separated from other executable files. By excluding the shared symbols, the classification performance increased, i.e., the allowable range of the threshold increased from 0.16 to 0.40. VASP contained 16 types of executable files, i.e., sixteen hashes. In the graph of VASP including shared symbols, the executable file of the fourth similarity is not VASP. Therefore, it was necessary to set the threshold to 0.2 for accurate classification. When the shared symbols were exempted, we observed that VASP and other executables were classified better. VASP was considered to contain five or six different versions (with similarities of: 1.0, 0.94, 0.86, 0.78, 0.68, and 0.63) from the viewpoint of similarities. If we classify VASP into a single class, the threshold ranges between 0.37 and 0.48. For example, if the threshold is 0.37, LANS can be classified with other applications. However, if the threshold is 0.3, LANS can be classified into a LANS-only class, but VASP would be classified into two classes.

The proposed classification method can be summarized as illustrated in Fig. 6. Considering adequate safety, we chose 0.3 to be the threshold, and the number of application classes was observed to be 328. Therefore, we observe that up to 328 kinds of applications were executed for seven months on the K computer.

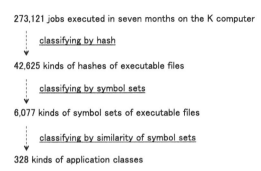

273,121 jobs executed in seven months on the K computer

classifying by hash

42,625 kinds of hashes of executable files

classifying by symbol sets

6,077 kinds of symbol sets of executable files

classifying by similarity of symbol sets

328 kinds of application classes

Fig. 6. The flow of the proposed classification method of the executable files

4   Predicting Application Class Using Job Scripts

In the previous section, the executed jobs were classified into application classes. In this section, we describe a method for predicting an application class at the time of job submission.

Predicting the application before job execution can help predict the job's behavior such as electric power consumption, I/O traffic, and runtime. Previous studies estimate these behaviors from the user, the project, the number of nodes, job scripts, and so on [14]. We intend to estimate such behaviors from the application class.

Information about the username, group name, and job script can be used during job submission. Many job-related features are included in the job script. Therefore, the application class is predicted using the contents of the job script. We have observed the jobs and application classes in the previous section. Further, we observe that this problem can be solved as a supervised classification problem.

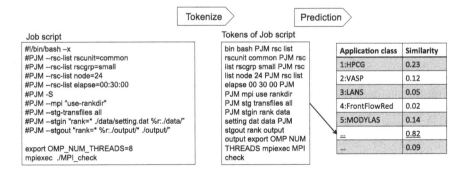

Fig. 7. The method for predicting an application class using a job script

Figure 7 provides an overview of the method for predicting an application class using a job script. This prediction method is similar to the general supervised learning method using job scripts and application classes. Considering a job script to be a text makes it a popular text classification problem.

4.1   Tokenize of Job Script

Job scripts are considered as text, and feature vectors representing job scripts are generated. The job script is divided into tokens by symbols such as [_, /, -]. A token comprises two or more letters or numbers. The token of "a.out" is [out] and the token of "elapse-limit=24:00:00" is [elapse, limit, 24, 00, 00]. The initial and the last 1,000 lines are applied to be the job script. This is because hundreds of thousands of lines (several tens of MB) of huge job scripts exist in our data set. Generally, the parameters of the scheduler are written at the head of the job script, whereas the actual processes of the job are written at the tail end of the job script. Lines beginning with "#" are comment lines, but they are not ignored because they may contain certain features. Lines starting with "#PJM" represent directives to the job scheduler. As in the existing research [14], it is possible to extract only the parameters using such directive lines. However, we select a method of extracting features using the entire contents of the job script.

4.2   Prediction Model

We use the paragraph vector model that has been described in the previous section to predict the application class from the tokens of job scripts. Job scripts may contain multiple applications. In this paper, to simplify the problem, it is assumed that one job script executes one application. When a single job script includes multiple applications, we consider multiple applications as a one series of application. In this case, we can apply the same prediction method.

4.3   Evaluation

We evaluated the accuracy of prediction using 215,957 job scripts which comprise the same dataset as described in the previous section. These job scripts have only one executable file. That is, the job script and its application class correspond one-to-one. We used a 10-fold cross validation, which is a method for evaluating machine learning algorithms.

Table 4 displays the predicted accuracy of the application class from the job script. The threshold of similarity indicates the threshold that was considered for the classification of the executable files in the previous section. As the threshold increases, the number of classes decreases. Therefore, prediction becomes easier. If the threshold is small, the number of classes is large, which necessitates accurate prediction. Accuracy was evaluated by modifying the threshold from 0.1 to 0.3 in increments of 0.05. The evaluation method used was a 10-fold cross validation. The results illustrate that any threshold can be predicted with an accuracy of >92%. Even when the threshold was observed to be small, the accuracy hardly changed. When predicting an application using a job script,

Table 4. Accuracy of application class

Threshold of similarity	# of classes	Accuracy
0.10	801	92.5%
0.15	632	92.1%
0.20	491	92.3%
0.25	398	93.5%
0.30	328	93.4%

the prediction accuracy did not change much regardless of the threshold value. When statistical processing is performed using classified application classes, the number of classes increases, whereas the number of executions of each class of applications decreases when the threshold is small. We concluded that it is better to increase the threshold until sufficient learning data can be collected.

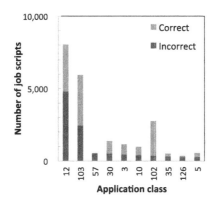

Fig. 8. Number of correct and incorrect predictions per application class

To analyze the incorrect predictions of 7%–8% that occur in the model, we created a prediction model using all the job scripts and predicted the application class for all of them. We calculated the number of correct and incorrect predictions for each application class. Figure 8 illustrates top ten application classes for incorrect predictions. The figure further depicts that there are numerous errors in the two classes that contain a large number of job scripts. Application class #12 was executed with 8,068 jobs. This class depicted 3,250 correct and 4,818 incorrect predictions. Further, Application class #103 was executed 5,969 times, and the prediction error was 2,470. In these two classes, 10,787 predictions failed, and this number was observed to correspond to 3.4% of all jobs.

Further analysis of classes #12 and #103 is depicted in Fig. 9. While predicting the application class using the class #12 job script, 138 kinds of classes were predicted excluding class #12, which was the correct class. The major job script

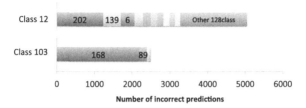

Fig. 9. Details of incorrect predictions per class

for application class #12 is illustrated in Fig. 10. This job script contained a few features. The directive lines that begin with PJM and the mpiexec commands were included in almost all job scripts. Although the name of the executable file is the only feature, this feature alone is considered insufficient for predicting the correct application class. Therefore, such featureless job scripts predict various incorrect application classes (Fig. 10).

```
#!/bin/bash −x
#
#PJM −−rsc−list "node=4"
#PJM −−rsc−list "elapse=01:00:00"
#PJM −−stg−transfiles all
#PJM −−mpi "use−rankdir"
#PJM −−stgin "rank=* ./sample %r:./"
#PJM −s
#

. /work/system/Env_base

mpiexec ./sample
```

Fig. 10. Typical job script of application class #12

Figure 9 depicts that the most incorrect predictions of application class #103 were class #168. Application classes #103 and #168 were actually different versions of the same application according to our judgment. The distance between the classes was observed to be greater than the threshold; therefore, they were classified as different application classes. However, their job scripts were almost the same; thus, the prediction results of classes #103 and #168 were combined. There was not much difference in job scripts between the classes. Therefore, it was difficult to accurately predict these differences.

Because the prediction accuracy can be calculated for each application class, in addition to the prediction result, its degree of reliability can also be obtained. Resolving incorrect predictions for poorly featured job scripts is a future work. In addition to job scripts, users, projects, names of job scripts, and job submission time may improve prediction accuracy.

5   Statistics of the Classified Application

In this section, we demonstrate a few statistics of 328 types of applications that were classified by our proposed method. Figure 11 depicts the resource usage of the top 200 applications. The top ten applications use 33% of the resources that were provided to the K computer. Additionally, the top 50 applications accounted for 76% of the provided resources. Several applications were observed to use most of the resources. If these applications are optimized, more computations can be performed using the resources that freed after this optimization. In addition, tuning the library that was used by these applications had a positive effect on improving the performance of the application. This ultimately led to the effective utilization of the computational resources.

Table 5 shows a summary of the top 10 applications of resource usage. The statistics of the application 1 is given as follows:

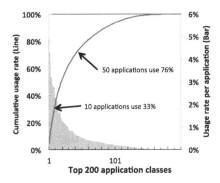

Fig. 11. Statistics of each application

Table 5. Statistics of the top 10 applications

Application	$Node \times Hour$	Counts	Projects	Nodes	FLOPS (%)	Power (W)
1	13,050,366	1,815	9	7,865	2.0	128.4
2	11,572,741	6,190	5	634	13.9	126.9
3	10,289,375	2,106	11	9,013	6.0	130.6
4	8,496,869	3,092	7	4,400	0.8	118.2
5	8,416,425	6,543	7	449	4.6	121.6
6	7,737,148	5,459	5	836	2.5	125.3
7	7,485,516	322	3	1,494	12.5	127.1
8	7,394,633	1,098	5	2,972	25.1	135.9
9	7,287,444	13,172	5	1,518	11.9	121.8
10	6,264,331	21,620	1	1,904	24.7	133.7

- Resource usage: approximately 13 M $Node \times Hour$
- The number of executions: 1,815
- The number of using projects: 9 projects
- The average number of nodes: 7,865
- The percentage of Peak FLOPS: 2.0%
- Average power per node: 128.4 W

The application name is not displayed in this table because our dataset contains private projects and applications. We observed that for a familiar application, the application name could be determined from the symbol information and the job script. Applications developed by the user were indicated by their application class ID because their name were unknown.

For example, applications #1 and #4 may be optimized from a perspective of FLOPS. The power consumption of application #4 is lower than that of other applications. The CPU and memory appear to not be fully operational because of the I/O wait.

For efficient operation of the facilities, it is useful to obtain electric power consumption at the time of job submission. It is necessary to predict the power consumption by deduction via data like the users, the projects, the queues, the number of nodes, and the limit of elapsed time.

6   Related Work

Various methods have been proposed for predicting job characteristics. Our approach is based on classification of jobs into applications and to predict the application. We compare our study with previous studies that have been conducted on similar subjects.

ALTD [9] and XALT [1] are infrastructural tools to collect job-level and link-time data of every job. XALT is designed to track the linkage and execution information for applications that are compiled and executed on the HPC system. XALT knows when the executable file was built, who built it, and when the file was executed. Our work can track executable files as well as XALT. However, we focus on classifying executable files into applications. In addition to tracking executable files, our classification method performs feature extraction, vectorization, and classification of executable files. An improved XALT [4] can further track external subroutine and function names of the object file. However, XALT can only collect symbols and does not perform classification like our work. psacct [20] is an application that monitors user and application activities widely used on Linux systems. psacct collects information about process creation time, elapsed time, average memory usage, command name, and so on, but not features of the executable file. Job schedulers such as TORQUE [18] and SLURM [22] can be used to monitor HPC systems; however, they can track only certain characteristics of jobs such as elapsed time, max memory usage and power consumption. They cannot perform tracking based on the application. Lu et al. [13] developed a tool to automatically extract compiler and library usage using signature-based detection, a common strategy employed by anti-virus software to search for known patterns of data within the executable files. We have also gathered such usage data which can be obtained for each application. But they cannot gathered it for each executable file.

A number of approaches have been proposed for predicting the power consumption [17,19] and runtime [5] of batch jobs. Borghesi et al. [3] tackled the prediction of power consumption of a job using the machine learning approach. The power consumption of a job was predicted using the following features: user, queue, requested duration, number of requested nodes, number of requested cores, and so on. Because the content of the job script was not used, the power consumption of jobs with the same characteristics and different job scripts could not be predicted. McKenna et al. [14] predicted runtime and I/O traffic using several machine learning techniques. They also used similar specific features that were obtained from the job script. However, they did not use the contents of the job script. Gaussier et al. [8] predicted the runtime of a job using the machine learning approach and improved backfilling scheduling. Their prediction also obtained a single value. However, power consumption comprises time series data. It is necessary to determine not only the average power consumption but also the fluctuations in power for the optimized operation of the exascale supercomputer. We can obtain the time series data of power consumption for each application because of the classification of jobs. Furthermore, we can also obtain the electricity statistics using the data.

A feature of our method involves the classification of jobs from the viewpoint of the application. Such classification has not been performed so far. In addition, because the application can be predicted at job submission, using those classifications will help estimate the power consumption, the runtime, etc.

7 Conclusion and Future Work

In this paper, we proposed a method for classifying jobs and predicting applications. Using features that were extracted from the executable file, we classified the executable file into application classes. Using the classification result, we can obtain statistical information such as resource usage, the number of executions, power consumption, language, and compiler version for each application. In our classification method, jobs and application classes were associated. Therefore, application classes could be predicted from job scripts during job submission. This prediction method is similar to the general supervised learning method using job scripts and application classes. Considering a job script to be a text makes it a popular text classification problem.

The application class can be determined at the time of job submission. Therefore, the power required and the runtime of the application class can be known prior to execution from past data. This information is considered to be critical for the operation of next-generation supercomputers and is useful for job scheduling, predicting the power efficiency, and optimized facility operation.

As future work, we plan to implement and evaluate the proposed method while using the K computer. Additionally, we propose to study the power prediction method of a job using application classes. In the future, we would like to summarize the usage of each application and try to improve the operations.

References

1. Agrawal, K., Fahey, M.R., McLay, R., James, D.: User environment tracking and problem detection with XALT. In: Proceedings of the First International Workshop on HPC User Support Tools, HUST 2014, pp. 32–40 (2014)
2. Andoh, Y., Yoshii, N., Fujimoto, K., Mizutani, K., Kojima, H., Yamada, A., Okazaki, S., Kawaguchi, K., Nagao, H., Iwahashi, K., Mizutani, F., Minami, K., Ichikawa, S., Komatsu, H., Ishizuki, S., Takeda, Y., Fukushima, M.: MODYLAS: a highly parallelized general-purpose molecular dynamics simulation program for large-scale systems with long-range forces calculated by fast multipole method (FMM) and highly scalable fine-grained new parallel processing algorithms. J. Chem. Theory Comput. **9**(7), 3201–3209 (2013)
3. Borghesi, A., Bartolini, A., Lombardi, M., Milano, M., Benini, L.: Predictive modeling for job power consumption in HPC systems. In: Kunkel, J.M., Balaji, P., Dongarra, J. (eds.) ISC High Performance 2016. LNCS, vol. 9697, pp. 181–199. Springer, Cham (2016). https://doi.org/10.1007/978-3-319-41321-1_10
4. Budiardja, R.D., Agrawal, K., Fahey, M., McLay, R., James, D.: Library function tracking with XALT. In: Proceedings of the XSEDE16 Conference on Diversity, Big Data, and Science at Scale, XSEDE 2016, pp. 30:1–30:7 (2016)
5. Chen, X., Lu, C.D., Pattabiraman, K.: Predicting job completion times using system logs in supercomputing clusters. In: 2013 43rd Annual IEEE/IFIP Conference on Dependable Systems and Networks Workshop (DSN-W), pp. 1–8, June 2013
6. Dongarra, J.: TOP500 Supercomputer Sites: Lists, November 2017. https://www.top500.org/lists/2017/11/
7. Dongarra, J., Heroux, M.A., Luszczek, P.: A new metric for ranking high-performance computing systems. Natl. Sci. Rev. **3**(1), 30–35 (2016)
8. Gaussier, E., Glesser, D., Reis, V., Trystram, D.: Improving backfilling by using machine learning to predict running times. In: Proceedings of the International Conference for High Performance Computing, Networking, Storage and Analysis, SC 2015, pp. 64:1–64:10 (2015)
9. Hadri, B., Fahey, M.: Mining software usage with the automatic library tracking database (ALTD). Procedia Comput. Sci. **18**(Supplement C), 1834–1843 (2013). International Conference on Computational Science
10. Hutter, J., Iannuzzi, M., Schiffmann, F., VandeVondele, J.: CP2K: atomistic simulations of condensed matter systems. Wiley Interdisc. Rev. Comput. Mol. Sci. **4**(1), 15–25 (2014)
11. Kresse, G., Hafner, J.: Ab initio molecular dynamics for liquid metals. Phys. Rev. B **47**, 558–561 (1993)
12. Le, Q., Mikolov, T.: Distributed representations of sentences and documents. In: Proceedings of the 31st International Conference on International Conference on Machine Learning, ICML 2014, vol. 32, pp. II-1188–II-1196 (2014)
13. Lu, C.D.: Automatically mining program build information via signature matching. In: Proceedings of the 11th ACM SIGPLAN-SIGSOFT Workshop on Program Analysis for Software Tools and Engineering, PASTE 2013, pp. 25–32 (2013)

14. McKenna, R., Herbein, S., Moody, A., Gamblin, T., Taufer, M.: Machine learning predictions of runtime and IO traffic on high-end clusters. In: 2016 IEEE International Conference on Cluster Computing, pp. 255–258 (2016)
15. Pedregosa, F., Varoquaux, G., Gramfort, A., Michel, V., Thirion, B., Grisel, O., Blondel, M., Prettenhofer, P., Weiss, R., Dubourg, V., Vanderplas, J., Passos, A., Cournapeau, D., Brucher, M., Perrot, M., Duchesnay, E.: Scikit-learn: machine learning in python. J. Mach. Learn. Res. **12**, 2825–2830 (2011)
16. Řehůřek, R., Sojka, P.: Software framework for topic modelling with large corpora. In: Proceedings of the LREC 2010 Workshop on New Challenges for NLP Frameworks, pp. 45–50, May 2010
17. Shoukourian, H., Wilde, T., Auweter, A., Bode, A.: Predicting the energy and power consumption of strong and weak scaling HPC applications. Supercomput. Front. Innov. **1**(2), 20–41 (2014)
18. Staples, G.: Torque resource manager. In: Proceedings of the 2006 ACM/IEEE Conference on Supercomputing, SC 2006 (2006)
19. Storlie, C., Sexton, J., Pakin, S., Lang, M., Reich, B., Rust, W.: Modeling and Predicting Power Consumption of High Performance Computing Jobs. ArXiv e-prints, December 2014
20. Tam, A.M.: Enabling process accounting on Linux HOWTO. http://www.tldp.org/HOWTO/text/Process-Accounting
21. Yamamoto, K., Uno, A., Murai, H., Tsukamoto, T., Shoji, F., Matsui, S., Sekizawa, R., Sueyasu, F., Uchiyama, H., Okamoto, M., Ohgushi, N., Takashina, K., Wakabayashi, D., Taguchi, Y., Yokokawa, M.: The k computer operations: experiences and statistics. Procedia Comput. Sci. **29**, 576–585. International Conference on Computational Science (2014)
22. Yoo, A.B., Jette, M.A., Grondona, M.: SLURM: simple linux utility for resource management. In: Feitelson, D., Rudolph, L., Schwiegelshohn, U. (eds.) JSSPP 2003. LNCS, vol. 2862, pp. 44–60. Springer, Heidelberg (2003). https://doi.org/10.1007/10968987_3

Performance Analysis and Tools

A Survey of Programming Tools for D-Wave Quantum-Annealing Processors

Scott Pakin[1]($\boxtimes$) (iD) and Steven P. Reinhardt[2]

[1] Computer, Computational and Statistical Sciences Division,
Los Alamos National Laboratory, Los Alamos, NM 87545, USA
pakin@lanl.gov
[2] D-Wave Systems Inc., Burnaby, BC V5G-4M9, Canada
sreinhardt@dwavesys.com

Abstract. The rapid growth in the realized performance of D-Wave Systems' annealing-based quantum processing units (QPUs) has sparked a surge in tools development to deliver the anticipated performance to application developers. In this survey we describe the tools that are available, their goals (e.g., performance or ease of use), the programming abstractions they expose, and their use for application development. The existing tools confirm the need for interfaces at a variety of points on the continuum between complexity and simplicity in using the QPU. Most of the current tools abstract the hardware's native topology but generally not using existing interfaces that are familiar to typical programmers. To date, only a small number of applications have been implemented for QPUs. Our survey finds that tools provide potentially great leverage to enable more applications as long as the tools expose the appropriate abstractions and deliver the anticipated performance.

1 Introduction

Since the first commercial delivery of a quantum-annealing-based processor, a 128-qubit D-Wave One™ system, to Lockheed Martin in 2011 [1], quantum-computing developers and researchers have made dramatic improvements in the performance obtained from such systems [2,3]. If the rate of improvement is sustained through a few more years, future quantum-annealing-based processing units (QPUs) will deliver performance on certain problems that will overwhelm the capability of any classical system. With this performance growth, many organizations that fundamentally depend on a computational advantage are considering when and how they will deploy the first QPUs that deliver differentiated performance. Those questions require insight into the types of applications that will likely benefit from those systems, but they also depend critically on the software interfaces and tools that will be available to program them.

This paper describes tools that are currently available as of early 2018 for programming QPUs. This leaves out some tools that have been described but are

© Springer International Publishing AG, part of Springer Nature 2018
R. Yokota et al. (Eds.): ISC High Performance 2018, LNCS 10876, pp. 103–122, 2018.
https://doi.org/10.1007/978-3-319-92040-5_6

not yet available for routine use. For each tool, we describe its goals, including its intended audience (e.g., expert vs. novice), its programming abstractions, its core algorithms and implementation to the extent that those are important to its users, applications that have been developed based on it—especially those developed by people other than the tool's developers—and how the tool is made available to potential users.

The remainder of this paper is structured as follows. Section 2 provides background information on the native quantum-annealing (QA) programming model, specifically that of QPUs produced by D-Wave Systems Inc. The paper describes each tool separately in Sect. 3, compares and contrasts the tools and types of tools in Sect. 4, presents examples of tool usage in Sect. 5, and finally draws some conclusions in Sect. 6.

2   Background

A D-Wave system natively solves a single problem, which is to minimize the energy of an Ising-model Hamiltonian:

$$\arg\min_{\sigma} \left(\sum_{i=1}^{N} h_i \sigma_i + \sum_{i=1}^{N-1} \sum_{j=i+1}^{N} J_{i,j} \sigma_i \sigma_j \right) \tag{1}$$

given $h_i \in \mathbb{R}$ and $J_{i,j} \in \mathbb{R}$ and solving for $\sigma_i \in \{-1, +1\}$. This is sometimes described as being in *polynomial form*. An equivalent expression, known as either a *quadratic unconstrained binary optimization* (QUBO) or an *unconstrained binary quadratic programming* (UBQP)[1] has an elegant algebraic representation:

$$\arg\min_{x} x^{\mathsf{T}} Q x \tag{2}$$

in which the $Q_{i,i} \in \mathbb{R}$ correspond to the h_i in Eq. 1, the $Q_{i,j} \in \mathbb{R}$ (with $i < j$) correspond to the $J_{i,j}$, and the $x_i \in \{0, 1\}$ correspond to the σ_i. A linear transformation maps between Eqs. 1 and 2. Throughout this paper we use the term "QUBO" generically to refer interchangeably to Eqs. 1 or 2.

Even this formulation is slightly abstracted, as (a) h_i and $J_{i,j}$ have limited range, precision, and accuracy, and (b) only a small subset of all possible $1 \leq i < j \leq N$ have an associated $J_{i,j}$ in the physical topology, which takes the form of a *Chimera* graph [5] (a degree-6 graph) in current D-Wave systems.

In fact, *no* sizable quantum computer provides all-to-all connectivity, much like interconnection networks in classical computing clusters. As a result, the problem graph must be *embedded* into the hardware graph, a process known to graph theorists as finding a *graph minor*—essentially a graph isomorphism that

---

[1] Note the possibility of confusion between this definition of unconstrained BQP and the definition of BQP as bounded-error quantum polynomial time [4], a computational complexity class. To avoid this confusion, we refer to the problem as a QUBO throughout this paper.

allows vertices to be replicated during the mapping. Alas, this problem is NP-hard so a need for efficient heuristics was called out by many early users [6–8]. To date, existing approaches include

- D-Wave Systems' minorminer [9] or improved *heuristic* embedder, which uses multiple heuristics to try to find a graph minor embedding; the Python-callable minorminer package has been open sourced; an implementation of the original heuristic embedder is included in the SAPI library (Sect. 3.1);
- D-Wave Systems' clique embedder [10,11], which precomputes the maximal-sized clique or biclique that can be embedded in the Chimera graph (which, for cliques, is known to be of size $\sqrt{2N}$ for N vertices) and embeds problem graphs into subsets of that maximum clique;
- NCSU and ORNL's virtual hardware embedder [12,13] introduces a virtual-hardware abstraction to simplify embedding algorithms and uses this to exploit bipartite structure in the problem graph for high-speed embedding;

with others known to be under development by the University of Southern California's Information Sciences Institute and D-Wave Systems.

The D-Wave processor exploits quantum effects—superpositioning, entanglement, and quantum tunneling—to rapidly find the σ that minimize Eq. 1. In terminology that is closer to the hardware, each σ_i is implemented with a *qubit* (quantum bit); each h_i is implemented with an *external field*; and each $J_{i,j}$ is implemented with a *coupler*. In current generation systems, one set of σ can be returned every QA cycle (1 µs). However, there is no guarantee that the values returned do in fact correspond to the true minimum. Consequently, it is typical to sample a large number (e.g., thousands) of possible σ in search of those that come close to minimizing Eq. 1.

The key programming challenge is to map an arbitrary problem into a list of h_i and $J_{i,j}$ values so that the problem's solution corresponds to the Boolean σ_i values that minimize Eq. 1. In the rest of this paper, we survey tools that help programmers express problems in this format.

3   Available Tools

Widely available QA tools are described in this section. They are roughly ordered from lowest level of abstraction, which equates to a small difference from the underlying D-Wave system interface, to highest level, which expresses a problem in an intermediate representation that makes sense to an application developer or subject-matter expert, with less resemblance to the underlying system interface.

3.1   SAPI (D-Wave Systems)

The Solver Application Programming Interface (SAPI) [14] was, until recently, the sole interface to a D-Wave system. Its primary goal is to expose the full power of a D-Wave QPU in a way that enables expert users and tool developers to extract the best performance. SAPI's main abstraction is an instance of a *quantum machine instruction* (QMI), which corresponds to the h and J coefficients in Eq. 1, and the QMI's accompanying solutions. SAPI exposes functions to establish a connection to a remote D-Wave system and query its characteristics, to embed a problem graph in the target QPU's hardware graph, to execute QMIs either synchronously or asynchronously and retrieve the resulting solutions, and to correct errors in those solutions via various post-processing techniques. The SAPI library also provides software simulators that mimic to varying extents the behavior of the QPU, enabling software development without immediate access to a QPU. SAPI interfaces are provided for the C/C++, Python®, and MATLAB® programming languages. In practice, many of the other software packages described here use SAPI at their lowest level for D-Wave system access.

SAPI includes several functions that provide higher-level functionality, such as a function that can reduce the size of a QUBO by, for example, recognizing that two variables will always have the same (or opposite) value and replacing every instance of one with the other (or its complement). A function for reducing higher-order interactions of more than two variables to interactions of just two variables (that can be directly represented in a QUBO) is valuable for mapping certain problem types to QUBOs.

SAPI has been the programming interface for essentially all benchmarking results published on D-Wave systems to date, including notably Denchev et al.'s [2], King et al.'s [3] and Andriyash et al.'s [15] results. It has also been used for many of the applications implemented to date, including satellite scheduling [16,17], database multi-query optimization [18], machine learning [19], circuit fault detection [20], and SAT filters [21]. SAPI client libraries are available in binary form to users who have access to a D-Wave system.

3.2   dwave-cloud-client (D-Wave Systems)

The minimal cloud client from D-Wave Systems [22] is an open-source implementation of a subset of the D-Wave Python SAPI client's functions. Its intent is to be an open-source building block for higher-level tools. Like SAPI, its main abstraction is the QMI. Currently it provides resource discovery and synchronous and asynchronous QMI execution on a D-Wave system via a cloud interface. Embedding and post-processing, among other features, are not yet implemented.

3.3   dw (D-Wave Systems)

The dw tool from D-Wave Systems [23] can be viewed as a command-line interface to SAPI. It was initially designed to help new users learn to program a D-Wave system independently from any particular programming language. The dw tool lets users build, execute, and view the results of a QMI, all from the Bash [24] prompt. dw supports a symbolic QUBO format that includes parameters, variables, and assertions. QUBOs defined in this format can be embedded directly into a simulator or D-Wave system or can be translated into qbsolv input, which provides additional useful abstractions (see Sect. 3.11).

dw integrates with a client-based visualization tool, Quantum Apprentice (Sect. 3.4), which allows one to view, edit, and save QMIs visually. dw is provided in binary form to D-Wave users as part of D-Wave's qOp package.

3.4 Quantum Apprentice (D-Wave Systems)

Quantum Apprentice is a graphical tool designed more for acquainting users with low-level D-Wave QPU behavior than for serious application development. It is written as a spreadsheet that may be processed by Microsoft Excel™ or LibreOffice®. The first three sheets let users enter h_i and $J_{i,j}$ values for versions of Eq. 1 with $N = \{2, 3, 4\}$. Each sheet shows all possible values of the σ variables, with those that minimize Eq. 1 highlighted. This helps users visually determine if a small subproblem is logically correct.

The remaining sheets present, respectively, a view of the user's program loaded onto a Chimera graph and color-coded to distinguish different h and J values; the QMI as an editable list of coefficients; a current solution as a list of σ_i values; and a command interface that lets users save, load, and execute QMIs on either the hardware or a simulator.

Figure 1 is a screenshot of the first of those, illustrating a simulated 128-qubit D-Wave system. Node and edge colors indicate the corresponding h and J coefficients, from highly negative (blue) to highly positive (red). Although it is not practical to develop a large program node-by-node and edge-by-edge in a GUI, Quantum Apprentice is useful both for pedagogy and for experimentation with manual layout of regularly structured problems. Quantum Apprentice is provided as a spreadsheet to D-Wave users as part of D-Wave's qOp package.

3.5 QC Ware Platform (QC Ware)

QC Ware Platform is a Python library that supports application development by providing both simplified access to a QPU and fine-grained, SAPI-level control. Consistent with that approach, its primary method is callable simply by specifying a few arguments, or callable with numerous processor-specific controls.

In addition to QMI execution, the QC Ware Platform software provides functionality to convert constrained-optimization problems to a QUBO. The QC Ware Platform materials describe several examples implemented using the software, including job-shop scheduling. QC Ware Platform is available as a binary Python package from QC Ware [25].

3.6 QDK (1QBit)

The Quantum-Ready™ software development kit (QDK) from 1QB Information Technologies (1QBit™) is a Python library that addresses computationally difficult combinatorial optimization problems. The focus is on enabling application

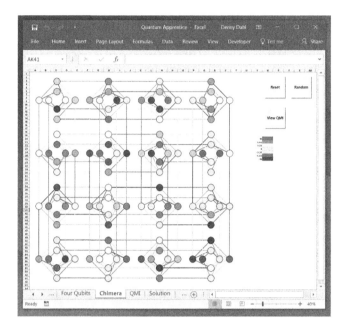

Fig. 1. Quantum Apprentice's "Chimera" sheet (Color figure online)

development, starting from converting an original problem into QUBO form, then solving the QUBO and mapping the result back to the original problem.

The primary object types are the *polynomial function* (reduced to quadratic form before solution) and the *solver* (used to find the solution that minimizes the function). The QDK offers a rich set of options for some system-specific steps, such as embedding, assigning chain strength,[2] and correcting broken chains.[3] A higher-level algorithm layer implements a variety of graph algorithms, including graph similarity, quasi-k-clique, and clique cover. Applications developed using QDK include financial portfolio optimization [26] and drug discovery [27]. QDK is available as a binary Python package from 1QBit [28] (registration required).

3.7   QxLib (QxBranch)

QxLib from QxBranch [29] is a Python library that is intended to foster rapid prototyping and experimentation in solving problems on QPUs. A key strategy for achieving this is exposing layered software abstractions that make it easy to map computational problems. The main concepts are symbolic and numerical representations of QUBOs, for which symbolic representations can

---

[2] *Chain strength* is the relative strength of couplings between qubits corresponding to the *same* problem variable to couplings between qubits corresponding to *different* problem variables.

[3] A chain is considered *broken* if its qubits, which correspond to the same problem variable, are assigned different values.

be reduced to numerical QUBOs. The QxLib software has a Python interface with performance-critical components implemented in C++; functions accessing a D-Wave system call SAPI. Contact QxBranch for QxLib access.

3.8   XACC (ORNL)

The eXtreme-Scale ACCelerator Programming (XACC) software from Oak Ridge National Laboratory [30] is a programming framework that treats quantum processing units (QPUs), of both quantum-annealing and gate-model architectures, as accelerators to classical systems. XACC is intended as a heterogeneous CPU-QPU programming model analogous to the OpenCL™ specification's heterogeneous CPU-GPU (graphics processing unit) programming model [31].

Like OpenCL, the main concepts are the creation of computational *kernels* targeting accelerators and the execution of those kernels. Kernels may be expressed in quantum programming languages appropriate for the architecture being targeted, e.g., QUBOs or higher-order binary optimization problems for QA-based QPUs. The current XACC software integrates with the Rigetti Quantum Virtual Machine™ (QVM) and Quil compiler [32] and the Scaffold compiler [33], which all target gate-model QPUs. XACC also integrates with the virtual-hardware embedder (Sect. 2) and SAPI (Sect. 3.1) for D-Wave execution. An application of financial portfolio optimization has been developed using XACC [34]. XACC is available as open-source software [35].

3.9   bqpsolvers (LANL)

bqpsolvers from Los Alamos National Laboratory [36] comprises a set of tools with the goal of unifying program development for different *Ising processing units* (IPUs).[4] Current physical examples of IPUs include QPUs, neuromorphic processors, and CMOS annealers, among others.

The main abstraction in bqpsolvers is the QUBO. bqpsolvers provides several solvers for QUBOs. Inputs and outputs are uniformly expressed in bqpjson, a JSON format for QUBOs. A helper tool, D-WIG (D-Wave Instance Generator), generates QUBO problems from a set of parameterized problem classes. bqpsolvers is available as open-source software [37].

3.10   QMASM (LANL)

QMASM (quantum macro assembler), from Los Alamos National Laboratory [38], is a tool that automates some tedious aspects of creating a QMI for a D-Wave system while limiting the classical processing required to prepare a QMI. By analogy to a classical macro assembler, its expected audience is programmers comfortable with a low-level interface.

---

[4] Section 2 mentions the difference between the Ising-model Hamiltonian and the QUBO. For consistency with the rest of this paper we use QUBO terminology here.

The central concept in QMASM is the expression of small subproblems as macros that can be repeatedly instantiated and combined to represent large, complex problems. QMASM supports qubits referred to by symbolic names, coupler and external-field values that can be expressed unconstrained by any hardware restrictions, and the definition and instantiation of macros. Supplied examples show how to use QMASM to solve circuit-satisfiability problems, implement sorting networks (which can also be used as permutation generators), and find shortest paths. QMASM is available as open-source software [39].

3.11   qbsolv (D-Wave Systems)

The qbsolv [40] tool enables users to solve QUBOs that are larger and/or more densely connected than the target D-Wave system. The programming abstraction that qbsolv exposes is a QUBO of arbitrary size and connectivity. The qbsolv algorithm decomposes large QUBOs into smaller ones that can fit on the underlying system, then combines the individual solutions into a solution to the original, large QUBO. This capability makes qbsolv useful both directly to application developers and indirectly as a back end for higher-level tools.

The qbsolv tool includes a tabu solver [41], which can be run either purely classically or in a hybrid quantum-classical mode. Because qbsolv's tabu solver is so fast, it can serve as a performance benchmark against which other QUBO solvers, including D-Wave systems, can be compared.

Several groups have developed applications with qbsolv, including graph partitioning [42], non-negative/binary matrix factorization [43], community detection [44], traffic-flow optimization [45], refinery scheduling [46], and cluster analysis [47]. qbsolv is available as open-source software [48].

3.12   ThreeQ (LANL)

ThreeQ [49], from Los Alamos National Laboratory, is a Julia [50] module influenced by JuMP [51] that is intended to enable developers to program QPUs more easily. The main programming abstraction is the QUBO, to which programs can add terms using the full flexibility of Julia. The constructed QUBO can then be solved on a D-Wave system using either SAPI, dw, or qbsolv.

The developers provide examples of solving systems of linear equations and linear least-squared problems, factoring integers, performing PDE-constrained optimization, four-coloring maps, and running hydrologic inverse analysis. They have also published a new non-negative/binary matrix factorization method that uses ThreeQ [43]. ThreeQ is available as open-source software [52].

3.13   ToQ (D-Wave Systems)

The ToQ tool (pronounced "two Q") from D-Wave Systems [23] enables subject-matter experts to express constraint-satisfaction problems for a D-Wave system at a conceptual level with which they are already comfortable. The primary concept is a collection of assertions that together express the problem. The assertions can be on named binary or integer variables. Each assertion is individually evaluated classically, then the set of individual assertions is combined into a complete QUBO that can then be solved by any of several solvers. The many ToQ examples provided by its developers include a Sudoku game and the solution of a set of Diophantine equations. ToQ is provided in binary form to D-Wave customers and partners as part of D-Wave's qOp package.

3.14   D-Wave NetworkX (D-Wave Systems)

D-Wave NetworkX from D-Wave Systems [53] is an extension of the NetworkX graph-analytic package from LANL [54]. Its primary benefit for subject-matter experts is to extend NetworkX's graph abstraction for D-Wave execution. It also makes it easy to generate and visualize graphs corresponding to the current D-Wave Chimera hardware topology. The existing NP-hard kernels include graph coloring, minimum vertex cover, maximum independent set, (minimum) maximal matching, maximum cut, weighted maximum cut, and structural imbalance. A proto-application using the structural-imbalance kernel analyzes signed social networks to understand the growth of terrorist networks [55,56].

3.15   edif2qmasm (LANL)

edif2qmasm [57] is a tool from Los Alamos National Laboratory that converts programs written in Verilog™ [58], VHDL [59], or other hardware-description languages to QMASM format and from there to QUBOs for execution. The resulting QUBOs can exploit a quantum processor's ability to solve for program inputs as easily as for program outputs. One can use edif2qmasm to easily solve NP-complete and NP-hard problems by coding up a solution verifier and running the code "backward" from "the solution is valid" to a set of inputs that constitute a valid solution.

The main concept is a digital circuit, specified in the EDIF netlist format [60], which is typical output of hardware-synthesis tools such as the Yosys Open SYnthesis Suite [61]. Examples from the developer include integer multiplication/-factoring and map coloring. edif2qmasm is available as open-source software [57].

4   Discussion

Based on the tool descriptions presented in Sect. 3, this section discusses common themes across tools and possible directions for future tool development.

4.1   Characterizing Tools by Supported Features and Abstractions

Figure 2 characterizes the tools by a set of features, ranging from closest to the hardware (bottom) to most distinct from the hardware (top). Colors indicate the organization that produced the tool. Starting from the hardware up, the features are

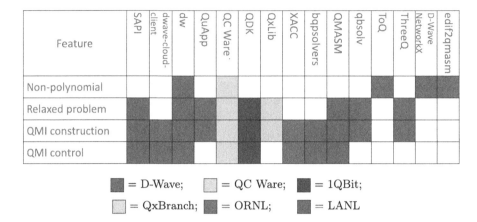

Fig. 2. Features of the tools described in this paper (Color figure online)

- **QMI control**—whether the tool enables a knowledgeable user to control the execution of a QMI in a system-specific way, such as controlling the annealing schedule on a per-qubit basis or introducing spin-reversal transformations;
- **QMI construction**—whether the tool enables explicit construction and execution of a QMI (i.e., defining a QUBO that takes the hardware's physical topology and coefficient ranges into account);
- **Relaxed problem**—whether the tool maintains the basic polynomial form of Eq. 1 but abstracts away one or more hardware details such as the number of qubits (N), the available qubits within the range $[1, N]$ (or even the fact that qubits are numbered), the valid values for the external fields (h_i), the valid values for the couplers ($J_{i,j}$), or the degree of the polynomial (2); and
- **Non-polynomial**—whether the tool accepts input that bears little or no resemblance to Eqs. 1 and 2, such as the constraint-satisfaction interface provided by QC Ware, the graph interface provided by D-Wave NetworkX, and the hardware-circuit interface provided by edif2qmasm.

4.2   QUBO-Creation/Execution Interfaces

Most of the tools discussed expose interfaces for creating and executing QUBOs, including SAPI, dwave-cloud-client, dw, QC Ware Platform, QDK, QxLib, bqp-solvers, QMASM, and ThreeQ. For these tools, the programmer is responsible for expressing a program in terms of coefficients to Eq. 1. However, there exists diversity even in this space. For example, SAPI, QDK, and QxLib all support reducing higher-order unconstrained binary optimization problems (HUBOs) to QUBOs, which comes at the cost of an increased number of terms required. As another example of diversity is QC Ware Platform's support of constrained-QUBO execution. Of the tools that provide an API, the vast majority bind to Python as the primary language.

In discussions with the developers of these tools, we learned that they chose to implement them primarily to use as building blocks for constructing higher-level tools. The low-level tools are generally not expected to be used directly by application developers. One could therefore conclude that a well-implemented open-source library with layers that vary the degree of program control would satisfy the needs of many higher-level tools. A common library with multiple language bindings would require fewer resources community-wide and simplify the environment for those building higher-level tools. The dwave-cloud-client tool developed by D-Wave is targeted for this role.

4.3 NetworkX as Common Interface for Graph Analysis

The recent open-source release of D-Wave NetworkX makes it simple for users of NetworkX, an existing graph-analytic library, to execute problems on a D-Wave system. Other developers have also created graph-analytic packages targeting D-Wave execution, notably 1QBit's QDK and LANL's graph-partitioning and community-detection work [42]. Making all D-Wave-targeted graph-analytic functions available via the NetworkX interface will benefit application developers. (We believe that such commonality could be achieved while preserving software vendors' ability to have proprietary libraries.)

4.4 General Optimization Problems

A primary concept for QDK, QxLib, and ThreeQ is the QUBO, which is a very limited expression of optimization problems (no higher-order terms, no constraints, only binary result variables). QC Ware Platform and ToQ, in contrast, support more general constraint specification, which is then reduced to a QUBO for execution. Going even further, many subject-matter experts use sophisticated optimization tools like AMPL [62], GAMS [63], MiniZinc [64], and Pyomo [65], which can express problems convertible to QUBO form and have the advantage of familiarity. It appears there is an opportunity to implement linkages between those higher-level tools and the existing QA tools. Such linkages would need to be carefully built with performance in mind, but the benefit of approaching users via well-known interfaces is considerable.

5 Tool Usage Examples

To give the reader a flavor of the various tools and their associated programming model, we devise a simple problem and discuss how it can be solved by a representative subset of the tools presented in Sect. 3. Our example problem, which we call the "threes" problem, can be stated as follows:

How can one configure five light switches, labeled A–E, such that exactly one of A, B, and C is on, exactly one of B, C, and D is on, and exactly one of C, D, and E is on?

With only five Boolean variables, this problem is trivial to solve by hand. (N.B.: there are three solutions.) However, it lets us examine the programming approach supported by the various tools.

For setting up the problem we follow the methodology laid out by Pakin [66], which comprises (1) characterizing solutions, (2) identifying repeated subproblems, (3) manually solving these subproblems in the reverse direction (values to coefficients), and (4) combining the simple problems into a complex full problem for D-Wave solution. The key subproblem is "one of three on". With known solutions for this subproblem—{off, off, on}, {off, on, off}, and {on, off, off}—we can solve Eq. 1 for the h and J coefficients. One possible solution, using -1 for "off" and $+1$ for "on", sets all coefficients to 1:

$$\mathcal{H}_{1\_of\_3}(\sigma_x, \sigma_y, \sigma_z) = \sigma_x + \sigma_y + \sigma_z + \sigma_x\sigma_y + \sigma_x\sigma_z + \sigma_y\sigma_z. \tag{3}$$

The reader can verify that $\mathcal{H}_{1\_of\_3}$ is minimized when exactly one of the three inputs is $+1$ and the rest are -1. See Pakin [66] for a discussion on how $\mathcal{H}_{1\_of\_3}$'s coefficients could have been derived.

The solution to our original problem can be expressed as a sum,

$$
\begin{aligned}
\mathcal{H}(\sigma_A, &\sigma_B, \sigma_C, \sigma_D, \sigma_E) \\
&= \mathcal{H}_{1\_of\_3}(\sigma_A, \sigma_B, \sigma_C) + \mathcal{H}_{1\_of\_3}(\sigma_B, \sigma_C, \sigma_D) + \mathcal{H}_{1\_of\_3}(\sigma_C, \sigma_D, \sigma_E) \\
&= \sigma_A + 2\sigma_B + 3\sigma_C + 2\sigma_D + \sigma_E + \sigma_A\sigma_B + \sigma_A\sigma_C + 2\sigma_B\sigma_C + \sigma_B\sigma_D \\
&\quad + 2\sigma_C\sigma_D + \sigma_C\sigma_E + \sigma_D\sigma_E,
\end{aligned}
\tag{4}
$$

of subproblem terms for which $\arg\min_\sigma \mathcal{H}$ is the solution being sought.

5.1   SAPI

SAPI provides the lowest-level D-Wave programming interface. Listing 1.1 shows how SAPI's Python bindings can be used to minimize $\mathcal{H}$ in Eq. 4. As a low-level API, problems must be made to fit onto the physical topology, which supports only a subset of the desired quadratic terms, and coefficients must be made to fit within an acceptable range. Although SAPI provides functions to help with these tasks, Listing 1.1 is based on a version of Eq. 4 manually mapped to the hardware-compatible expression,

$$
\begin{aligned}
\mathcal{H}_{\text{phys}} = {} &0.375\sigma_0 + 0.25\sigma_2 + 0.5\sigma_3 + 0.5\sigma_4 + 0.375\sigma_5 + 0.25\sigma_6 + 0.5\sigma_0\sigma_4 - \sigma_0\sigma_5 \\
&+ 0.25\sigma_0\sigma_6 + 0.25\sigma_2\sigma_4 + 0.25\sigma_2\sigma_5 + 0.25\sigma_3\sigma_4 + 0.5\sigma_3\sigma_5 + 0.25\sigma_3\sigma_6,
\end{aligned}
\tag{5}
$$

in which the σ subscripts correspond to physical qubit numbers. Line 16 of Listing 1.1 shows the logical-to-physical variable mapping. Note that σ_C is mapped to both σ_0 and σ_5 to help work around the topology's constraints.

Listing 1.1. SAPI solution to the "threes" problem (Python bindings)

```python
1   #! /usr/bin/env python
2
3   from dwave_sapi2.remote import RemoteConnection
4   from dwave_sapi2.core import solve_ising
5   import os
6
7   # Establish a remote connection to the D-Wave.
8   url = os.environ["DW_INTERNAL__HTTPLINK"]
9   proxy = os.environ["DW_INTERNAL__HTTPPROXY"]
10  token = os.environ["DW_INTERNAL__TOKEN"]
11  solver_name = os.environ["DW_INTERNAL__SOLVER"]
12  conn = RemoteConnection(url, token, proxy)
13  solver = conn.get_solver(solver_name)
14
15  # Construct the problem.
16  A = 6; B = 3; Cs = [0, 5]; D = 4; E = 2
17  hs = [0]*7
18  hs[A] = 0.25; hs[B] = 0.5; hs[Cs[0]] = 0.375; hs[Cs[1]] = 0.375; hs[D] = 0.5; hs[E]
        = 0.25
19  Js = {(A, Cs[0]): 0.25, (Cs[0], Cs[1]): -1.0, (A, B): 0.25, (Cs[0], D): 0.5, (E, Cs
        [1]): 0.25, (B, D): 0.25, (E, D): 0.25, (B, Cs[1]): 0.5}
20
21  # Solve the problem on the D-Wave.
22  answers = solve_ising(solver, hs, Js, num_reads=1000, answer_mode="
        histogram", annealing_time=20, postprocess="optimization")
23
24  # Output the answers.
25  soln_set = set()
26  for soln in answers["solutions"]:
27      soln_set.add(tuple([(soln[i]+1)//2 for i in [A, B, Cs[0], D, E]]))
28  for soln in sorted(soln_set):
29      print(soln)
```

5.2   QMASM

In its simplest form, a QMASM solution to the "threes" problem is merely a transcription of the coefficients shown in Eq. 4. For example, $3\sigma_C$ can be written as "C 3", and $2\sigma_A\sigma_B$ can be written as "A B 2". In fact, the QMASM code shown in Listing 1.2 is closer to the first part of Eq. 4 in that it lets QMASM accumulate the coefficient values from the three $\mathcal{H}_{1\_of\_3}$ terms.

Listing 1.2. Basic QMASM solution to the "threes" problem

```
1   A 1
2   B 1
3   C 1
4   A B 1
5   A C 1
6   B C 1
7
8   B 1
9   C 1
10  D 1
11  B C 1
12  B D 1
13  C D 1
14
15  C 1
16  D 1
17  E 1
18  C D 1
19  C E 1
20  D E 1
```

Listing 1.3. QMASM solution to the "threes" problem using macros

```
1   !begin_macro 1of3
2     x 1
3     y 1
4     z 1
5
6     x y 1
7     x z 1
8     y z 1
9   !end_macro 1of3
10
11  !use_macro 1of3 $ABC $BCD $CDE
12
13  $ABC.y = $BCD.x
14  $ABC.z = $BCD.y
15  $ABC.z = $CDE.x
16  $BCD.y = $CDE.x
17  $BCD.z = $CDE.y
18
19  A = $ABC.x
20  B = $ABC.y
21  C = $ABC.z
22  D = $BCD.z
23  E = $CDE.z
```

Listing 1.3 presents an alternative QMASM formulation that defines a `1of3` macro corresponding directly to Eq. 3, instantiates that macro three times (as `$ABC`, `$BCD`, and `$CDE`), and establishes variable equivalences across instantiations (e.g., that `C`, `$ABC.z`, `$BCD.y`, and `$CDE.x` should have equal values).

5.3 ToQ

The ToQ solution to the "threes" problem (Listing 1.4), is fundamentally different from the SAPI and QMASM solutions in that it is based on constraints rather than coefficients. Conveniently for "threes", ToQ includes `OneOf`, which requires exactly one of its arguments to be TRUE, as a built-in predicate. Listing 1.4 therefore follows fairly naturally from the problem statement. One catch is that ToQ performs a substantial amount of classical pre-processing for each `assert` clause in the process of constructing a QMI.

5.4 edif2qmasm

A typical edif2qmasm program is based on implementing an inverse problem and running it "backwards". Listing 1.5, which solves the "threes" problem, follows this design pattern. It presents Verilog code that accepts bits A, B, C, D, and E and returns a `valid` bit that indicates if the on/off pattern honors the problem-stated

Listing 1.4. ToQ solution to the "threes" problem

```
1  bool: @A, @B, @C, @D, @E
2  assert: OneOf(@A, @B, @C)
3  assert: OneOf(@B, @C, @D)
4  assert: OneOf(@C, @D, @E)
5  end:
```

Listing 1.5. edif2qmasm solution to the "threes" problem (using Verilog)

```
1  `define ONE_OF(X, Y, Z) ((X & !Y & !Z) | (!X & Y & !Z) | (!X & !Y & Z))
2
3  module threes (A, B, C, D, E, valid);
4     input A, B, C, D, E;
5     output valid;
6
7     assign valid = `ONE_OF(A, B, C) & `ONE_OF(B, C, D) & `ONE_OF(C,
         D, E);
8  endmodule
```

constraints. Once processed by edif2qmasm, the code is run by hard-wiring `valid` to TRUE and leaving the other variables unbound so that the D-Wave system will solve for them.

6 Conclusions

We observe the recent rapid rate of improvement in tools for QPUs. Of the 15 tools described in this paper, as of the summer of 2016, seven of them (QC Ware Platform, XACC, bqpsolvers, ThreeQ, edif2qmasm, dwave-cloud-client, and D-Wave NetworkX) were not available to users, and an eighth (qbsolv) was not available in its current open-source version. We should not confuse activity with accomplishment, but much of this extensive activity appears productive. We believe that this outburst is akin to the Cambrian explosion, a time when relative stasis was disrupted by a short period of rapid biological diversification [67]. In the case of QA tools, one clear cause is the increasing availability and performance of QA hardware. We should expect continued rapid evolution of QA tools and programming methods at least until applications start to deliver differentiated performance, at which time users will expect some stability to enable exploiting that performance.

We also look to aspects of a mature QA tools environment that we lack today. First is fast and space-efficient embedding algorithms for mapping (relatively dense) problem graphs onto (sparse) hardware graphs. A second aspect is connections between today's relatively low-level tools and more desirable higher-level interfaces such as AMPL, JuMP, and MiniZinc, which subject-matter experts are using today to solve problems that may be well-suited for QPUs. The QA community's inexperience with tools for QPUs means we poorly understand the best methods for converting problems to the QUBO form implemented natively by today's commercial QPUs. We expect that methods will first arise by manual trial and error for a small number of problem types and then be codified into tools such that the conversion can be computer-aided if not automated. The range of convertible problem types will also grow over time.

In classical computing, not every problem is suitable for executing on a GPU. There may be insufficient data parallelism or too little computational intensity, for instance. Likewise, not every problem is suitable for executing on a QPU. Figure 3 illustrates some of the reasons: out of all problems, only a subset can be expressed in terms of Eq. 1. Of those, some require vastly more variables than contemporary QPU hardware provides. (It is not practical to run a billion-variable problem when only thousands of qubits are available in hardware.) Finally, many problems that fit in today's relatively small quantum computers are easy to solve classically; there would be little point in migrating such problems to a QPU. However, looking to the future, as QPUs increase in qubit counts and connectivity, the inner two regions of Fig. 3 should grow proportionally, implying a greater set of problems that QPUs can potentially accelerate.

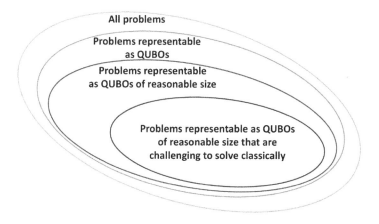

Fig. 3. Venn diagram illustrating the class of problems worth executing on a QPU

Despite QPU hardware and tools being largely in their infancy, the rapid progress in tool development over the last year bodes well for future tools that will effectively deliver the anticipated performance of quantum processing units to a great number of applications.

Acknowledgments. Thanks to the developers of the tools for helping us understand them: Timothy Goodrich of North Carolina State University for the virtual-hardware embedder; Denny Dahl of D-Wave Systems for dw, Quantum Apprentice, and the screenshot of Quantum Apprentice in action (Fig. 1); Matt Johnson, Peter McMahon, and David Hyde of QC Ware for QC Ware Platform; Andrew Fursman of 1QBit for QDK; Mark Hodson and John Kelly of QxBranch for QxLib; Alex McCaskey,

Keith Britt, and Kathleen Hamilton of Oak Ridge National Laboratory for XACC; Carleton Coffrin and Dan O'Malley of Los Alamos National Laboratory for bqpsolvers and ThreeQ, respectively.

Los Alamos National Laboratory is operated by Los Alamos National Security LLC for the US Department of Energy under contract DE-AC52-06NA25396.

Any use of trade names or trademarks herein is purely nominative and is not meant to suggest an endorsement or association between any person and the authors (or the authors' employers).

References

1. Lockheed Martin Corporation: Quantum, August 2011. http://www.lockheedmartin.com/us/what-we-do/emerging/quantum.html
2. Denchev, V.S., Boixo, S., Isakov, S.V., Ding, N., Babbush, R., Smelyanskiy, V., Martinis, J., Neven, H.: What is the computational value of finite-range tunneling? Phys. Rev. X **6**(3), 031015 (2016)
3. King, A.D., Hoskinson, E., Lanting, T., Andriyash, E., Amin, M.H.: Degeneracy, degree, and heavy tails in quantum annealing. Phys. Rev. A **93**(5), 052320 (2016)
4. Wikipedia: BQP, August 2017. https://en.wikipedia.org/wiki/BQP
5. Bunyk, P.I., Hoskinson, E.M., Johnson, M.W., Tolkacheva, E., Altomare, F., Berkley, A.J., Harris, R., Hilton, J.P., Lanting, T., Przybysz, A.J., Whittaker, J.: Architectural considerations in the design of a superconducting quantum annealing processor. IEEE Trans. Appl. Supercond. **24**(4), 1–10 (2014)
6. Anthony, A.: Has the age of quantum computing arrived?, December 2016. https://www.theguardian.com/technology/2016/may/22/age-of-quantum-computing-d-wave
7. NASA Quantum Artificial Intelligence Laboratory (QuAIL), December 2016. https://ti.arc.nasa.gov/tech/dash/physics/quail/
8. Grant, E.: D-Wave adiabatic quantum computer, October 2016. http://web.eecs.utk.edu/courses/fall2016/cosc594/presentations/D-Wave.pdf
9. Boothby, K.: D-Wave improved heuristic embedder, October 2017. https://github.com/dwavesystems/minorminer
10. Boothby, T., King, A.D., Roy, A.: Fast clique minor generation in chimera qubit connectivity graphs. Quantum Inf. Process. **15**(1), 495–508 (2016)
11. Boothby, K.: D-Wave clique embedder, October 2017. https://github.com/dwavesystems/chimera-embedding
12. Goodrich, T.D., Sullivan, B.D., Humble, T.S.: Optimizing adiabatic quantum program compilation using a graph-theoretic framework. arXiv preprint arXiv:1704.01996 (2017)
13. Goodrich, T.D.: AQC virtual embedding, October 2017. https://github.com/TheoryInPractice/aqc-virtual-embedding
14. D-Wave Systems Inc.: Burnaby, British Columbia, Canada: Developer Guide for C (2017)
15. Andriyash, E., Bian, Z., Chudak, F., Drew-Brook, M., King, A.D., Macready, W.G., Roy, A.: Boosting integer factoring performance via quantum annealing offsets, December 2016. https://www.dwavesys.com/sites/default/files/14-1002A_B_tr_Boosting_integer_factorization_via_quantum_annealing_offsets.pdf
16. Rieffel, E.G., Venturelli, D., O'Gorman, B., Do, M.B., Prystay, E.M., Smelyanskiy, V.N.: A case study in programming a quantum annealer for hard operational planning problems. Quantum Inf. Process. **14**(1), 1–36 (2015)

17. Stollenwerk, T., Basermann, A.: Experiences with scheduling problems on adiabatic quantum computers. In: Proceedings of the 1st International Workshop on Post-Moore Era Supercomputing (PMES), Future Technologies Group Technical report FTGTR-2016-11, pp. 45–46 (2016)
18. Trummer, I., Koch, C.: Multiple query optimization on the D-Wave 2X adiabatic quantum computer. Proc. VLDB Endow. **9**(9), 648–659 (2016)
19. Adachi, S.H., Henderson, M.P.: Application of quantum annealing to training of deep neural networks. arXiv preprint arXiv:1510.06356 (2015)
20. Perdomo-Ortiz, A., Fluegemann, J., Narasimhan, S., Biswas, R., Smelyanskiy, V.N.: A quantum annealing approach for fault detection and diagnosis of graph-based systems. Eur. Phys. J. Spec. Topics **224**(1), 131–148 (2015)
21. Douglass, A., King, A.D., Raymond, J.: Constructing SAT filters with a quantum annealer. In: Heule, M., Weaver, S. (eds.) SAT 2015. LNCS, vol. 9340, pp. 104–120. Springer, Cham (2015). https://doi.org/10.1007/978-3-319-24318-4_9
22. Douglass, A.: dwave-cloud-client, March 2017. https://github.com/dwavesystems/dwave-cloud-client
23. Booth, M., Dahl, E., Furtney, M., Reinhardt, S.P.: Abstractions considered helpful: a tools architecture for quantum annealers. In: 2016 IEEE High Performance Extreme Computing Conference (HPEC), pp. 1–2. IEEE (2016)
24. Ramey, C.: Bash, the Bourne-again shell. In: Proceedings of The Romanian Open Systems Conference & Exhibition (ROSE 1994), The Romanian UNIX User's Group (GURU), 3–5 November 1994
25. QC Ware: QC Ware Platform, October 2017. https://platform.qcware.com
26. Rosenberg, G., Haghnegahdar, P., Goddard, P., Carr, P., Wu, K., de Prado, M.L.: Solving the optimal trading trajectory problem using a quantum annealer. IEEE J. Sel. Topics Sig. Process. **10**(6), 1053–1060 (2016)
27. Accenture: Biogen, 1QBit and Accenture: Pioneering Quantum Computing in R&D, August 2016. https://www.accenture.com/us-en/success-biogen-quantum-computing-advance-drug-discovery
28. 1QBit: 1QBit Quantum Development Kit, October 2017. https://qdk.1qbit.com
29. Hodson, M., Fletcher, D., Padilha, D., Cook, T.: Rapid prototyping with symbolic computation: fast development of quantum annealing solutions. In: 2016 IEEE High Performance Extreme Computing Conference (HPEC), pp. 1–5. IEEE (2016)
30. McCaskey, A.: XACC–eXtreme-scale ACCelerator programming framework, October 2016. https://github.com/ORNL-QCI/xacc
31. Munshi, A.: The OpenCL specification. In: 2009 IEEE Hot Chips 21 Symposium (HCS), pp. 1–314. IEEE (2009)
32. Smith, R.S., Curtis, M.J., Zeng, W.J.: A practical quantum instruction set architecture. arXiv preprint arXiv:1608.03355 (2016)
33. JavadiAbhari, A., Patil, S., Kudrow, D., Heckey, J., Lvov, A., Chong, F.T., Martonosi, M.: ScaffCC: scalable compilation and analysis of quantum programs. Parallel Comput. **45**, 2–17 (2015)
34. Elsokkary, N., Khan, F.S., La Torre, D., Humble, T.S., Gottlieb, J.: Financial portfolio management using adiabatic quantum optimization: the case of Abu Dhabi securities exchange. In: 2017 IEEE High Performance Extreme Computing Conference (HPEC), pp. 1–4. IEEE (2017)
35. McCaskey, A.: Eclipse XACC: Hardware Agnostic Quantum Programming, May 2018. https://github.com/eclipse/xacc
36. Coffrin, C., Nagarajan, H., Bent, R.: Ising processing units: potential and challenges for discrete optimization. arXiv preprint arXiv:1707.00355 (2017)

37. Coffrin, C.: BQPSOLVERS, BQPJSON, and DWIG, May 2018. https://github.com/lanl-ansi/bqpsolvers, https://github.com/lanl-ansi/bqpjson, https://github.com/lanl-ansi/dwig
38. Pakin, S.: A quantum macro assembler. In: Proceedings of the 20th Annual IEEE High Performance Extreme Computing Conference (HPEC 2016), Waltham, Massachusetts, USA, IEEE, 13–15 September 2016
39. Pakin, S.: Quantum macro assembler (QMASM), October 2017. https://github.com/lanl/qmasm
40. Booth, M., Reinhardt, S.P., Roy, A.: Partitioning optimization problems for hybrid classical/quantum execution, August 2017. https://github.com/dwavesystems/qbsolv/blob/master/qbsolv_techReport.pdf
41. Glover, F.: Tabu search-part I. ORSA J. Comput. **1**(3), 190–206 (1989)
42. Mniszewski, S.M., Negre, C.F., Ushijima-Mwesigwa, H.M.: Graph partitioning using the D-Wave for electronic structure problems. Technical report LA-UR-16-27873, Los Alamos National Laboratory (2016)
43. O'Malley, D., Vesselinov, V.V., Alexandrov, B.S., Alexandrov, L.B.: Nonnegative/binary matrix factorization with a D-Wave quantum annealer. arXiv preprint arXiv:1704.01605 (2017)
44. Ushijima-Mwesigwa, H., Negre, C.F.A., Mniszewski, S.M.: Graph partitioning using quantum annealing on the D-Wave system. arXiv preprint arXiv:1705.03082 (2017)
45. Neukart, F., Compostella, G., Seidel, C., Von Dollen, D., Yarkoni, S., Parney, B.: Optimizing traffic flow using quantum annealing and classical machine learning. arXiv preprint arXiv:1708.01625 (2017)
46. Ossorio-Castillo, J.: Solving energy-related scheduling problems with column generation and an adiabatic quantum computer, Tokyo, Japan, 26–29 July 2017
47. Dulny, J.S.: Quantum annealing enabled cluster analysis, Tokyo, Japan, 26–29 July 2017
48. Booth, M., Douglass, A., et al.: QUBO solver (qbsolv), October 2017. https://github.com/dwavesystems/qbsolv
49. O'Malley, D., Vesselinov, V.V.: ToQ.jl: a high-level programming language for D-Wave machines based on Julia. In: 2016 IEEE High Performance Extreme Computing Conference (HPEC), pp. 1–7. IEEE (2016)
50. Bezanson, J., Edelman, A., Karpinski, S., Shah, V.B.: Julia: a fresh approach to numerical computing. SIAM Rev. **59**(1), 65–98 (2017)
51. Lubin, M., Dunning, I.: Computing in operations research using Julia. INFORMS J. Comput. **27**(2), 238–248 (2015)
52. O'Malley, D.: ThreeQ, October 2017. https://github.com/lanl/ThreeQ.jl
53. Condello, A.: D-Wave NetworkX, October 2017. https://github.com/dwavesystems/dwave_networkx
54. Hagberg, A.A., Schult, D.A., Swart, P.J.: Exploring network structure, dynamics, and function using NetworkX. In: Proceedings of the 7th Python in Science Conference (SciPy 2008), Pasadena, California, USA, pp. 11–15, August 2008
55. Ambrosiano, J.J., Roberts, R.M., Sims, B.H.: Using the D-Wave 2X quantum computer to explore the formation of global terrorist networks. Technical report LA-UR-17-23946, Los Alamos National Laboratory (2017)
56. Condello, A.: Structural imbalance demo, December 2017. https://github.com/dwavesystems/structural-imbalance-demo
57. Pakin, S.: edif2qmasm–run hardware descriptions on a quantum annealer, August 2017. https://github.com/lanl/edif2qmasm

58. Thomas, D., Moorby, P.: The Verilog Hardware Description Language. Springer Science & Business Media, New York (2008). https://doi.org/10.1007/978-0-387-85344-4
59. Ecker, W.: Using VHDL for HW/SW co-specification. In: Proceedings EURO-DAC 1993 European Design Automation Conference, 1993, with EURO-VHDL 1993, pp. 500–505. IEEE (1993)
60. Crawford, J.D.: EDIF: a mechanism for the exchange of design information. IEEE Des. Test Comput. **2**(1), 63–69 (1985)
61. Wolf, C., Glaser, J., Kepler, J.: Yosys–a free Verilog synthesis suite. In: Proceedings of the 21st Austrian Workshop on Microelectronics (Austrochip) (2013)
62. Fourer, R., Gay, D.M., Kernighan, B.W.: A modeling language for mathematical programming. Manag. Sci. **36**(5), 519–554 (1990)
63. Bussieck, M.R., Meeraus, A.: General Algebraic Modeling System (GAMS). Appl. Optim. **88**, 137–158 (2004)
64. Nethercote, N., Stuckey, P.J., Becket, R., Brand, S., Duck, G.J., Tack, G.: MiniZinc: towards a standard CP modelling language. In: Bessière, C. (ed.) CP 2007. LNCS, vol. 4741, pp. 529–543. Springer, Heidelberg (2007). https://doi.org/10.1007/978-3-540-74970-7_38
65. Hart, W.E., Watson, J.P., Woodruff, D.L.: Pyomo: modeling and solving mathematical programs in Python. Math. Program. Comput. **3**(3), 219–260 (2011)
66. Pakin, S.: Navigating a maze using a quantum annealer. In: Proceedings of the 2nd International Workshop on Post Moore's Era Supercomputing, Denver, Colorado, USA, pp. 30–36. ACM, 13 November 2017
67. Gould, S.J.: Wonderful Life: The Burgess Shale and the Nature of History. W. W. Norton & Company, New York (1990)

Compiler-Assisted Source-to-Source Skeletonization of Application Models for System Simulation

Jeremiah J. Wilke[1(✉)], Joseph P. Kenny[1], Samuel Knight[1], and Sebastien Rumley[2]

[1] Sandia National Laboratories, 7011 East Ave, Livermore, CA, USA
jjwilke@sandia.gov
[2] Lightwave Research Laboratory, Columbia University, New York City, USA

Abstract. Performance modeling of networks through simulation requires application endpoint models that inject traffic into the simulation models. Endpoint models today for system-scale studies consist mainly of post-mortem trace replay, but these off-line simulations may lack flexibility and scalability. On-line simulations running so-called skeleton applications run *reduced* versions of an application that generate traffic that is the same or similar to the full application. These skeleton apps have advantages for flexibility and scalability, but they often must be custom written for the simulator itself. Auto-skeletonization of existing application source code via compiler tools would provide endpoint models with minimal development effort. These source-to-source transformations have been only narrowly explored. We introduce a pragma language and corresponding Clang-driven source-to-source compiler that performs auto-skeletonization based on provided pragma annotations. We describe the compiler toolchain, validate the generated skeletons, and show scalability of the generated simulation models beyond 100 K endpoints for example MPI applications. Overall, we assert that our proposed auto-skeletonization approach and the flexible skeletons it produces can be an important tool in realizing balanced exascale interconnect designs.

1 Introduction

Simulations require application endpoint models to generate representative traffic or memory patterns. To achieve system scale, endpoint models need to be as lightweight as possible while still capturing the most important application features. Endpoint models can be generally classified as *off-line* or *on-line*. Off-line simulations replay post-mortem traces collected from an existing system [15]. The traffic pattern is therefore fixed or requires complicated extrapolation schemes to modify. On-line simulations instead run modified application codes to generate traffic in the simulator. These modified codes generally consist of either state machine models (motifs) [12] or skeleton applications [22].

© Springer International Publishing AG, part of Springer Nature 2018
R. Yokota et al. (Eds.): ISC High Performance 2018, LNCS 10876, pp. 123–143, 2018.
https://doi.org/10.1007/978-3-319-92040-5_7

Accurate conclusions about network provisioning critically depend on end-point models generating accurate traffic patterns appropriate to the problem and architecture. The pitfalls here are starkly illustrated by the historical performance progression for the top 3 systems in Fig. 1. Clearly, byte/flop ratios are decreasing as nodes accelerate more quickly than the network, making off-node data movement one of the critical performance challenges for exascale [17,20]. However, that trend has been somewhat balanced by the "surface area-to-volume" decreases in injected traffic for many applications (see below). While over some time periods performance was driven by number of nodes, recently increases have mainly been in individual node throughput. Realistic workloads for testing future machine designs should therefore be a mix of adjusting node quantity (more nodes, same problem size per node) and node throughput (same number of nodes, larger problem per node). Without assessing applications over a range of realistic inputs, erroneous conclusions about network provisioning and system design might be reached.

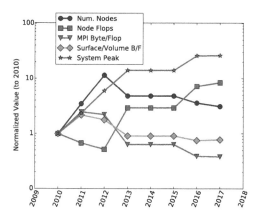

Fig. 1. Progression of top 3 systems since 2010 for total number of nodes, node peak throughput, byte/flop ratios, and system peak throughput. Surface/volume normalizes the Byte/Flop metric by accounting for the decrease in communication traffic relative to total throughput, in this case $(B/F)^{2/3}$

Today endpoint models consist mainly of post-mortem trace replay. These off-line simulations lack flexibility, and trace collection itself may not be scalable. The traces are also often valid only for the exact problem considered, i.e. executing a stencil code with grid N × N on a 1024 rank system. Characterizing an application should ideally cover scaling behavior for a range of application inputs. Trace extrapolation can approximate large-scale traces from small-scale runs in some cases [14], but is often limited to only "weak scaling" to produce a larger number of MPI ranks with the same problem per rank. This presents validation concerns and is not useful for tuning input parameters. In other trace extrapolations, compute delays are reduced by a constant factor to simulate hardware acceleration on next-generation hardware. This suffers from two drawbacks. First, it often assumes a uniform speedup of all compute kernels, which is unrealistic. Second, new hardware generations are usually characterized by larger nodes with more parallelism rather than simply faster cores. Byte/flop ratios for applications can vary widely with problem size. For Lulesh, e.g., doubling the problem size per node can decrease the off-node byte/flop ratio by 1.6.

On-line simulations, in contrast, can tune both scale and input parameters. On-line simulations, however, often rely on custom models written specifically for simulation, as done in state machine models [12]. Skeleton applications, in contrast, are regular source code with much of the computation replaced by delay models. For message-passing applications (MPI), skeletonization requires two steps. First, MPI calls are emitted to the simulator for modeling in place of a real network stack (Fig. 2). Second, expensive computation should be replaced by delay models. Manually eliminating expensive computation, however, currently requires significant human effort. Scalable skeletons also require removing large memory allocations that would otherwise exceed the capacity of the simulator's hardware.

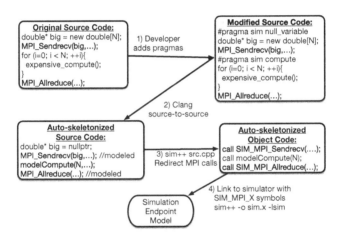

Fig. 2. Overview of skeletonization workflow for generating endpoint models from existing source code. (1) Pragmas are added to describe skeletonization, (2) compiler completes source-to-source transformation with skeleton source code, (3) code is compiled with compiler wrapper on top of Clang/GCC, (4) MPI symbols linked to simulator.

Auto-skeletonization via source-to-source transformation of existing application source code is highly desirable. A single application source code that is usable for both actual production runs and simulation improves (1) validation since the skeleton is directly derived from the real application, and (2) co-design since any changes made immediately transfer between simulation and actual production tests, (3) ease of use since input parameters and system scales can be flexibly tuned without re-collecting or extrapolating traces. Auto-skeletonization through source-to-source transformations has only been narrowly explored [22]. Distinguishing between computation blocks that can be safely elided and those that are required to reproduce the traffic pattern can be difficult or impossible at compile-time.

Instead of completely automatic skeletonization, we propose augmenting source code with skeletonization hints via pragmas. While pragma augmentation is not fully automatic (Fig. 2), developers with domain-specific knowledge can annotate existing apps in contrast to the tedious and error-prone task of manually skeletonizing. In addition, rather than making conservative assumptions or highly approximate guesses, a compiler can report specific line numbers where static analysis fails and hints are required. This creates an almost automatic workflow in which the compiler tells the domain experts exactly where pragmas are needed.

To achieve this workflow, we describe an approach for user-guided application skeletonization. We introduce a simple pragma language which provides hints to a skeletonizing compiler and demonstrate this approach with a toolchain based on Clang. We provide data-centric pragmas to eliminate expensive memory allocations and execution-centric pragmas to eliminate expensive computation. We demonstrate the approach for three applications (Lulesh, CoMD, and HPCG). We show scalability with simulations beyond 100 K endpoints using the Structural Simulation Toolkit (SST) to provide a parallel discrete event core. We further perform a performance study for each application that both validates the correctness of generated skeletons and demonstrates the flexibility of on-line simulations.

2   Related Work

2.1   Simulators

Numerous simulators have been developed with various accuracy/cost tradeoffs. On-line simulators usually emulate an API such as MPI [11] and link to application code, intercepting function calls to estimate elapsed time. SMPI is a notable example supporting on-line simulation [8]. Off-line simulators, such as Tracer/-CODES [15], use time differences between trace communication events to determine compute delay. Time-independent traces with architecture-independent hardware counters have been used [9,21] as well as application-specific task specifications [6]. Time-independent traces provide flexibility in changing trace replay behavior for different processor or memory architectures, but still capture a single, fixed problem. Xu explored auto-generating skeletons from traces [26] without requiring source code transformations.

For estimating communication time, simulators usually model individual hardware components or use a fixed analytic function to provide timings for the overall system. Analytic functions often use a simple delay model, and some formulas try to incorporate congestion [14]. Structural simulators simulate discrete events on each switch and link as messages traverse the network with varying degrees of accuracy. There are high levels of detail in Booksim [16], packet-level models in SST/macro [25] and CODES [15], and more coarse-grained models or flow models in BSIM [24] and SMPI [8].

2.2   MPI Source-to-Source

There are several studies that involve either source-to-source transformations of MPI codes or semi-automatic construction of communication skeletons. Guo et al. used source-to-source transformations of MPI codes to improve communication overlap [13]. Preissl et al. used the ROSE compiler to perform general performance optimizations [18]. Strout et al. performed data-flow analysis of MPI programs, although mainly in the context of automatic differentiation [23].

Sottile et al. explored source-to-source skeletonization of MPI codes using ROSE [22]. Skeletonization was guided mainly by configuration files with some supplementary pragmas. The tool performed a def-use analysis to delete all code that did not affect the parameters inside an MPI call. This skeletonization is brute force, deleting all code that does not affect MPI function parameters, but also conservative, preserving all code that affects MPI parameters no matter how expensive to execute. Compute modeling of removed code was not performed. The auto-skeletonization approach from Sottile et al. [22] followed a bottom-up procedure, deriving backwards all code that could affect MPI parameters. Our approach is top-down and data-centric, labeling large data structures that should not be allocated. It prioritizes expensive code and memory allocation removal over conserving MPI call parameters. The consequence is that the MPI parameters may not be exactly preserved, instead being estimated. While our approach requires more input, the compiler directs domain experts to the lines of code where hints are needed and provides a rich set of pragmas.

3   MPI Simulation

The Structural Simulation Toolkit (SST) [19] provides a discrete event simulation framework that includes element libraries designed for scalable modeling of large (potentially exascale) systems. Using SST, we aim to achieve scalable, flexible simulation through (1) lightweight endpoint models, (2) efficient network models, and (3) brute force parallelization.

The simulator *emulates* many virtual MPI processes running in a single physical process. The terms virtual and physical are critical here to distinguish between the simulated application code and the simulator code itself. Without skeletonization, our simulator components can act as an MPI emulator. The simulator provides a minimal MPI middleware implementing the needed semantics and API bindings. The C/C++ code compiled and linked with the `sim++` compiler wrapper can then execute as if running on a real platform. To achieve this, the simulator must emulate three memory regions used by physical processes:

- Heap memory
- Stack memory
- Global variables

On a real system, the kernel enforces memory separation between MPI ranks. Virtual MPI ranks, which are encapsulated by lightweight threads, must synthetically enforce memory separation. Virtual ranks can allocate from a common heap without the risk of sharing private data. Stacks require more work. Instead of each virtual MPI rank receiving its own kernel thread (pthread), they are explicitly-managed user-space threads (GNU pth, ucontext, fcontext). Control is transferred between application threads via context switching to simulate concurrent progress of MPI ranks. Global variables are the most difficult to manage. Source-to-source transformation must convert all global variables to user-space thread-local variables.

At some point, application ranks must transfer control to the simulator. This occurs when emulated bindings, e.g. a call to MPI_Send, are emitted to the simulator instead of an actual MPI implementation. This symbol interception requires both compile-time and link-time steps. The compiler wrapper includes a preprocessor which redirects MPI calls to simulator functions:

```
#define MPI_Send(...) SIM_MPI_Send(...)
```

The compiler then links against -lsim which provides the simulator's MPI bindings. Symbol interception can occur at any layer of a software stack (Fig. 3). While our simulation components provides a minimal MPI implementation, an existing MPI could run on a simulated uGNI or libfabrics layer.

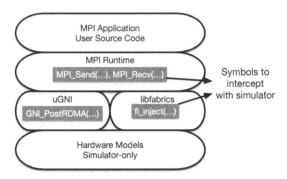

Fig. 3. Software stack with possible symbol interception points for the simulator.

Simulation time advances when the application enters an emulated binding. The thread blocks (context switches), the simulator predicts a time delay, inserts another event into the event queue, and returns control to the main simulator thread. After simulation time advances, the main thread context switches back to the application thread.

4   Source-to-Source Compiler

4.1   Overview

The auto-skeletonizing compiler has three tasks:

– Remove large memory allocations that would prevent scalable simulation
– Substitute compute-intensive kernels with an accurate delay estimate
– Redirect global variable accesses to thread-private memory

Global variable refactoring occurs automatically, but the remaining two require domain experts to insert pragmas.

4.2   Introductory Example

To illustrate the basic concept, consider the following code which exchanges messages, computes, and then exchanges messages again.

```
  ...
  MPI_Sendrecv(..., size, ...);
#pragma sst compute
  for (int i=0; i < N; ++i){
   //do work
  }
  MPI_Sendrecv(..., size, ...);
  ...
```

For scalable simulation, we wish to generate the correct traffic pattern with minimal complexity in the application endpoint model. The code should be modified in two ways. First, instead of executing the compute loop, a compute delay model should be inserted. Second, instead of actually exchanging data in the send/recv, a network model should estimate the communication delay based on the message size. The auto-skeletonizing source-to-source compiler accomplishes both of these things. It recognizes the pragma, decides to replace the computation, and estimates a delay model based on the number of operations performed inside the loop. It then replaces the MPI calls with calls into the simulator. The result is a lightweight endpoint model generating the correct traffic pattern. We now review the most important pragmas.

4.3   Data-Driven Pragmas

Marking large data structures that are not critical to control-flow as null types identifies large memory allocations to elide and provides hints to the compiler of compute blocks to avoid.

pragma sim null_variable. This pragma decorates a variable declaration. An example can be seen in CoMD:

```
#pragma sim null_variable
   int* nAtoms;
```

In most cases, all operations involving the null variable are replaced with compute delay models. However, there may be cases where the compiler may decide deleting an operation cannot be done automatically since it may affect control flow, e.g., if the variable is used inside an if-statement. When this occurs, a compiler error is thrown flagging where the ambiguity occurs. Another pragma must then be applied to the conditional to tell the compiler how to proceed. While the skeletonization process requires user intervention and iteration, the process is fully-guided by the compiler and therefore straightforward.

pragma sim null_type. This applies to C++ class variable declarations. Memory allocations are eliminated, but specific member functions used for tracking type size may be kept. Consider an example from Lulesh:

```
#pragma sim null_type sim::vector size resize empty
   std::vector<Real_t> m_x ;  /* coordinates */
```

Here we wish to indicate the vector is "null" and should not actually allocate memory or allow array accesses. However, we still wish to track the vector size and whether it is empty. The first argument to the pragma is a new type name that implements the "alias" functionality. For `std::vector`, the compiler automatically provides an alias `sim::vector`.

```
namespace sim {
class vector {
 public:
  void resize(unsigned long sz){
    size_ = sz;
  }
  unsigned long size() const {
    return size_;
  }
  template <class... Args> void emplace_back(Args... args){
    ++size_;
  }
  bool empty() const {
    return size_ == 0;
  }
 private:
  unsigned long  size_;
};
}
```

`std::vector` is substituted with the new type `sim::vector` in the code. In this case, even though the alias vector class provides more functions, we only allow `size`, `resize`, and `empty` to be called.

pragma sim branch_predict. This pragma replaces a branch condition. The `branch_predict` pragmas are necessary for predicates containing null variables. Although most uses of this pragma will substitute `true` or `false` as the replacement, any arbitrary C++ boolean expression can be used as the replacement.

4.4   Compute Pragmas

pragma sim compute/pragma omp parallel. These compute pragmas substitute the computations in a decorated scoping block with a basic delay model.

The compiler can also be configured to automatically use existing OpenMP pragmas as skeletonization hints. For the current work, static analysis of memory accesses and arithmetic operations generates a simple delay model for a coarse-grained processor model that generates a time estimate.

pragma sim loop_count. If the `sim compute` or `omp parallel` pragma is applied to an outer loop with one or more inner loops, the compute model static analysis might fail. This occurs when the inner loop control flow depends on the actual execution. Any variables declared or modified *inside* the compute block are not valid to use in the compute estimate. Only variables in scope at the beginning of the outer loop are valid.

When the static analysis fails, a corresponding compiler error is thrown. This usually requires giving a loop count hint. Consider an example from HPCG:

```
#pragma omp parallel for
  for (local_int_t i=0; i< localNumberOfRows; i++) {
    int cur_nnz = nonzerosInRow[i];
  #pragma sim loop_count 27
    for (int j=0; j<cur_nnz; j++) mtxIndL[i][j] = mtxIndG[i][j];
  }
```

The static analysis fails on `cur_nnz`. However, that value is almost always 27. Thus we can safely tell the compiler to just assume a given loop count.

pragma sim branch_predict. When `branch_predict` appears inside a marked compute block, the argument must be a value between 0 and 1 (or true/-false). The value informs the static analyzer of the proportion of branches taken. Because all program logic must be estimated in the skeleton, `branch_predict` must be used inside such a block when the branch condition is dependent on variables declared in the same scope. Consider an example from CoMD:

```
#pragma sim branch_predict areaFraction
  if(r2 <= rCut2 && r2 > 0.0){
```

Inside this compute block, computation depends on whether a particle distance is less than a cutoff. Based on the way CoMD constructs unit cells and halo regions, we can estimate the ratio of the particles (and therefore computations) that are expected within the cutoff.

4.5   Source-to-Source

No changes to an existing make system are required to auto-skeletonize. Installation of the element library installs compiler wrappers `simcc` and `sim++`. Figure 4 shows the compiler auto-skeletonization workflow that is performed automatically by the compiler wrappers. Remapping global variables requires static registration of special C++ variables, which requires merging a temporary C++ object file into the original target object file (see Fig. 4).

The source-to-source translation occurs through analysis of the Clang abstract syntax tree (AST). The AST is accessed by registering custom Clang

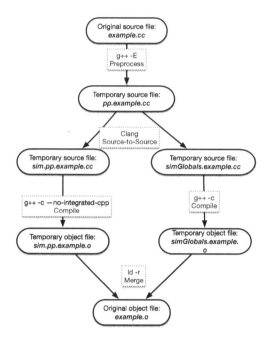

Fig. 4. Source-to-source transformation workflow. These steps occur automatically through the compiler wrapper. For C source files, g++ can be swapped with gcc. The underlying compiler is arbitrary and could be gcc or another compiler.

frontend actions with the AST visitor interface. New pragmas can be easily registered with the Clang preprocessor. The source-to-source can work on most C++ template code since the Clang frontend provides a visitable AST node for each implicitly instantiated template function. Type-dependent compute models can also be constructed for compute pragmas inside template code. This will be implemented in future versions of the source-to-source translator.

5   Methodology

Lulesh 2.0.3 was downloaded from the Lawrence co-design center [2]. CoMD reference version 1.1 was downloaded from the Mantevo project [3]. HPCG reference version 3.0 was download from the HPCG benchmark site [1]. The Clang 4.0 frontend was used for source-to-source transformations and skeleton compilation. Each application takes a basic set of 3–6 input parameters defining either the total problem size or the problem size per MPI rank. Lulesh is an explicit shock hydrodynamics code with communication dominated by nearest-neighbor halo exchanges. CoMD is a lattice-based molecular dynamics code with communication dominated by cell exchanges of neighboring atoms. HPCG is a conjugate-gradient solver with multigrid preconditioning.

An analytic delay model similar to LogP [14] was used for the network. The processor model also used a simple analytic delay model

$$\Delta T = \beta B + \gamma_f F + \gamma_i I. \tag{1}$$

Here B is the number of bytes used, F is the number of floating-point operations, and I is the number of integer operations. β is the inverse bandwidth in seconds/bytes and γ is the inverse frequency in seconds/operation for floating point and integer arithmetic.

Timings were collected on a Xeon E7-8870 at 2.4 GHz. STREAM benchmarks showed $\sim$6 GB/s of single-core memory throughput. For our processor delay model we therefore use $\beta = 0.16$ s/GB and $\gamma_i = \gamma_f = 0.42$ ns/Op.

6   Results and Discussion

6.1   Weak- and Strong-Scaling Spider Plots

The skeleton applications should behave as much as possible like the full application running on a real system. As a first validation we validate scaling of relative application runtime (rather than absolute time). Given a set of input parameters (as they would be given to the real application), compute and communication times should scale appropriately. For example, given a mesh size 2x larger and the same number of processors, Lulesh should take 2x longer to run. Similarly, given the same mesh and 2x the number of processors, Lulesh should run 2x faster. Using a simple processor model and a contention-free network model, we ensure that the skeleton apps generate correct weak and strong scaling behavior from weak and strong scaling inputs (see Appendix for the set of inputs used). Figure 5 shows spider plots for the skeleton applications with mixed weak and strong scaling curves. Given weak and strong scaling inputs, the simulator produces the correct behavior - ideal scaling in this case given the contention-free machine model. This demonstrates (1) the correctness of the skeletons since correct scaling behavior is seen and (2) flexibility of the skeletons to generate several traffic patterns for different application inputs and scales.

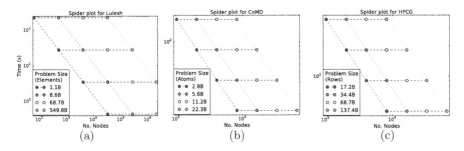

Fig. 5. Spider plot showing weak and strong scaling curves for simulated applications. Weak and strong scaling inputs to the skeleton application exactly generate the expected scaling behavior. Shown are (a) Lulesh up to 2M network endpoints, (b) CoMD up to 65 K network endpoints, and (c) HPCG up to 65 K network endpoints.

6.2   Traffic Pattern Validation

Beyond validating the timing behavior of the skeleton applications, we want to ensure that the generated traffic patterns are correct. Lulesh and HPCG exactly generate the correct number, size, and sequence of MPI messages (and thus generate no interesting figures). CoMD is more complicated. The skeleton application creates an approximate traffic pattern based on the average number of atoms per cell. No computation is ever performed on individual atoms. The exact CoMD traffic pattern is partially data-dependent, however. Certain border cells can have partial occupancy with fewer atoms than interior cells. With domain expertise, this variation in number of atoms communicated can be computed via tractable (but tedious) mathematical expressions rather than looping through all atoms. Using pragmas, the code computing the number of atoms to send can be replaced rather than completely elided. The approximations used in this work create a minor discrepancy between the exact traffic pattern and the skeleton traffic pattern (Fig. 6).

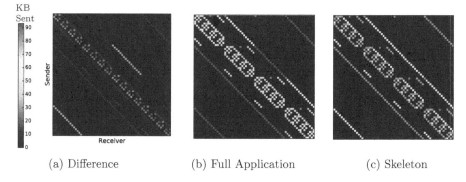

(a) Difference   (b) Full Application   (c) Skeleton

Fig. 6. Traffic matrix plots (spyplot) for CoMD showing the (a) difference between (b) full application and (c) skeleton application.

This discrepancy is critical in distinguishing our current approach from previous auto-skeletonization work [22]. In previous work, every MPI call had to be exactly preserved. The compiler worked bottom-up from each MPI call to decide what code was necessary. For CoMD, the traffic pattern depends on individual atom computations. A naive auto-skeletonizer would therefore preserve *every* line of code in the application. In our top-down approach, the large data structures containing atoms are marked null. This then generates compiler warnings or errors where computation depends on individual atoms. Approximations are then introduced with pragmas to estimate the number of atoms being exchanged. This generates an efficient skeleton with approximately correct MPI calls. Although some point-to-point sends are incorrect by 10–30% in Fig. 6, the traffic pattern as a whole is preserved. As discussed above, these estimates could be improved with more domain knowledge of the CoMD application.

6.3   Simulator Performance

Beyond validating that the simulator produces correct scaling and traffic results, we want to ensure that skeleton application is consuming minimal amounts of memory and executing quickly. Performance results for memory usage and timings are shown in Fig. 7. Even past 100 K endpoints, memory usage is only 20 GB total for all three applications considered. We note that the total memory usage for each skeleton app is almost the same. The dominant memory cost is actually the user-space thread stacks used by the simulator and not heap-allocated variables within the skeleton apps. Even for large runs (>100 K endpoints), the simulations finish within a few hours on a single core, showing that no significant computation is occurring within each application.

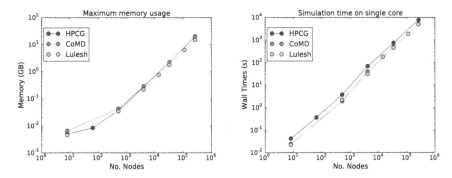

Fig. 7. Maximum memory usage (GB) and total simulation wall time for increasing scales of Lulesh, CoMD, and HPCG skeleton applications.

Another critical performance question for skeleton-driven simulation is the inherent scalability of the simulation itself as more physical cores are used to execute the simulation. Parallel discrete event simulation (PDES) is a notoriously challenging problem [10]. In particular, since the endpoint model is no longer a basic trace, optimistic PDES is much more challenging. Weak-scaling and strong-scaling performance of the simulator wall-clock time is shown in Fig. 8 for a conservative algorithm. The base case (64 cores; 32 K virtual ranks) executes in 12.9 s. This fails to perfectly weak scale, with the largest run (512 cores; 262 K virtual ranks) taking 19.4 s, but is still an effective scaling of 5.3X with 8X number of cores. For strong-scaling, e.g. working from the base case (64 cores; 262 K virtual ranks) results in speedups of 2.0, 2.8, and 3.8 for 2X, 4X, and 8X number of cores, respectively. Good speedups are obtained, although far from ideal. Still, very large (262 K virtual rank) simulations can be performed in reasonable times when scaled to greater than 500 simulator cores.

Finally, the choice of running skeletons rather than a state machine model requires context switching between distinct application threads as discussed in Sect. 3. Minimizing context switching overheads is therefore important for performance. We incorporated three different context switching libraries (GNU pth,

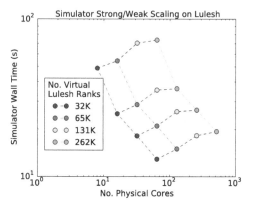

Fig. 8. Scaling of skeletons with parallel discrete event simulator for increasing number of simulation processes (physical ranks). Lulesh configuration is 5 iterations with weak-scaling $50 \times 50 \times 50$ box per rank.

fcontext, ucontext) and measured context switch overheads through a benchmark that switches 1000 times amongst 1000 user-space threads. The results are shown in Table 1 for two different systems. While pth and ucontext have sizable overheads, context switches are very fast with Boost fcontext. Context switching overheads are therefore negligible with respect to the cost of the simulator itself.

Table 1. Cost per context switch for different threading libraries on Linux (CentOS 7) and Mac OS X (10.11).

Threading	CentOS 7	Mac OS X 10.11
fcontext	83ns	54 ns
pth	560ns	$1.66\,\mu s$
ucontext	595ns	n/a

6.4   Number of Pragmas

To indicate the amount of work required to skeletonize each application, we count the number of each type of pragma used in Table 2. As previously discussed, in our top-down approach skeletonization begins with inserting `null_type` pragmas to label data structures that should not be allocated. The remaining skeletonization is fairly automatic, with the compiler noting exactly where additional hints are required. While this process is iterative and requires active input from an app developer, it drastically reduces the development and validation time required relative to manually generating skeleton or other on-line endpoint models. For CoMD and HPCG, the number of pragmas is not significantly more than the number of pre-existing `omp parallel` pragmas. Lulesh has more data structures, but the process is still very quick for someone with domain knowledge of the application. The whole process in general should be a few hours, not days or weeks to write an entirely new skeleton app.

Table 2. Number of pragmas in each of the considered example applications.

Pragma	Lulesh	CoMD	HPCG
null_type/null_variable	48	8	18
replace/init	70	19	14
compute	76	8	13
omp parallel	30	15	17
branch_predict	10	2	0
loop_count	0	18	2

6.5   Compute Model Accuracy

Although the main goal here is not to demonstrate an accurate compute model, we assess what accuracy can be obtained by simply counting source code operations and using the analytic delay estimate from (1). Figures 9, 10 and 11 compare actual timings to the estimates. Actual timings will be highly-compiler dependent and thus we show a min-max range for -O3 and -O0 optimizations.

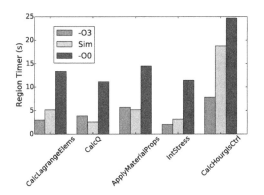

Fig. 9. Individual region timers for different kernels in Lulesh. The compute model is based only on counting floating point/integer operations in the source code. The simulated delay estimates are compared to two different levels of compiler optimization.

CoMD (Fig. 10) is dominated by a single compute kernel: `force`. The force kernel is dominated by compute rather than memory and the estimated delay is surprisingly accurate. For comparison, Fig. 10 shows timing estimates from a much smaller kernel. The velocity kernel is much more memory-bound, making

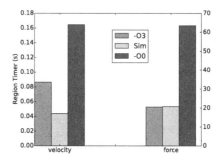

Fig. 10. Individual region timers for different kernels in CoMD. The compute model is based only on counting floating point/integer operations in the source code. The simulated delay estimates are compared to two different levels of compiler optimization.

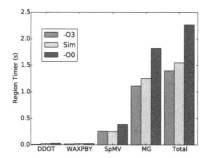

Fig. 11. Individual region timers for different kernels in HPCG. The compute model is based only on counting floating point/integer operations in the source code. The simulated delay estimates are compared to two different levels of compiler optimization.

it harder to estimate. In this case, the compiler actually undercounts the number of memory accesses leading to the discrepancy.

For HPCG (Fig. 11), the simulation slightly overestimates relative to O3 but is bracketed above by O0. Lulesh (Fig. 9) shows similar results to HPCG with O3 and O0 bracketing the simulation estimates. The simulation does underestimate certain Lulesh kernels even with O3. More study is required to determine if (1) the static analysis is undercounting operations or (2) the basic delay model fails to account for certain contention effects. For CalcQ (Fig. 9), the square root function is used extensively. Because the square root code is not available to the compiler, it cannot estimate the number of flops and omits them. This leads to the observed underestimate. Additional pragmas could be added with flop/byte estimates for such functions. Still, despite the limitations of our initial implementation, the auto-skeletonizing compiler is effective at generating realistic delay models and, correspondingly, realistic traffic injection.

6.6   Example Study with Lulesh

We perform an example study that would be difficult with traces, but is straight-forward with skeleton applications. In particular, we evaluate the performance and scaling of Lulesh executed in SMP mode (one MPI process per node parallelized with OpenMP) and MPI-only mode (one MPI process per core). For simplicity, we consider a node with 8 cores. The study shown in Fig. 12 requires both several different application scales as well as different application inputs. In particular, the SMP problem requires a $40 \times 40 \times 40$ grid for each MPI process while the MPI-only problem requires a $20 \times 20 \times 20$ grid per MPI process. For the example problem, at 512 cores (64 nodes) both approaches have similar performance, although the SMP approach is slightly faster. The performance gap increases as scale is increased to 32 K cores (4K nodes), although the effect is small for the relatively compute-bound Lulesh. Although beyond the scope of the current work, more detailed analysis would show the performance difference is due to contention on message injection and extra memory traffic from intranode MPI messages.

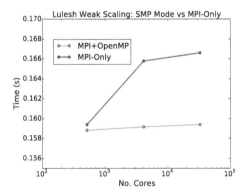

Fig. 12. Simulated runtimes for Lulesh application running $20 \times 20 \times 20$ grid per core either in SMP-mode (8 cores per MPI process) or MPI-only mode (1 core per process).

7   Future Work

The two most critical areas for improvement are compute model generation and skeletonization of more dynamic applications. While compute models are generated simply from source code operations (abstract syntax tree), more sophisticated models could be generated from either LLVM IR (intermediate representation) or even assembly. IR can be easily generated from the AST using LLVM code generators, allowing compute models for loops or other nodes in the AST to be based on IR [7]. More sophisticated static analysis, particularly for nested loops, might also involve polyhedral techniques to better estimate cache traffic or computational intensity [4].

Because arbitrary source code modifications at the site of a compute-intensive code region are possible, the source-to-source technique also potentially enables integration with detailed simulators such as gem5 [5]. To limit computational cost, a single MPI rank could be run via detailed simulation with the estimated times for compute-intensive regions being memoized and reused for all other MPI ranks. While this would involve potentially complicated instrumenting of the application source code, these modifications can be embedded in the source-to-source tool and easily reused rather than requiring ad-hoc simulator-specific instrumentation in the actual source code.

Dynamic applications, e.g. adaptive mesh refinement (AMR), pose new challenges to the skeletonization process. HPCG, Lulesh, and CoMD have semi-static traffic patterns which are dominated by the structure of the computation and not the values stored in the data structures. For an AMR code, the traffic pattern between refinements will similarly be "static" and compatible with skeletonization. For a library like BoxLib [27], the data structures defining the box sizes and nesting are modest in size compared to the actual element or field data contained within each box. The actual refinement computation must be replaced with an approximate model. Previous studies have used coarse-grained box traces [6]. In contrast to MPI communication traces, the box traces are flexible and can be immediately used for strong scaling studies. An alternative is to base box refinements on known properties of the input problem. For MiniAMR [3], refinement is driven by objects pushed through the mesh, which could be approximated by an analytic function yielding an inexpensive estimate of refinement.

8   Conclusions

This work presents a compiler-assisted approach to generating skeleton applications directly from existing application source code. Validation of the generated skeletons is demonstrated by analyzing weak and strong scaling behavior of the skeleton apps and comparing traffic patterns from skeletons to the parent application pattern. Having on-line skeleton models for system-level simulation improves validation, scalability, and flexibility of the simulation. This flexibility is critical for network-design studies, particularly in understanding the required balance between compute and network provisioning as problem scales and problem inputs change. Overall, the auto-skeletonizer's ease of use and the efficient execution of skeletons with the parallel simulator should make the presented tools useful for future network and system design.

Acknowledgment. This work was funded by Sandia National Laboratories, which is a multimission laboratory managed and operated by National Technology and Engineering Solutions of Sandia, LLC., a wholly owned subsidiary of Honeywell International, Inc., for the U.S. Department of Energy's (DOE) National Nuclear Security Administration (NNSA) under contract DE-NA-0003525.

A   Appendix

A.1   Strong scaling inputs

Lulesh. All simulations are equivalent to running the SLURM command `srun -n M -N M ./lulesh -s S -i 5` with 1 MPI rank per node and some number M of MPI ranks. The problem size S is per rank and per dimension, for a total problem size of S^3 per rank. Lulesh requires a cubic number of processors so each point in the strong scaling curve contains 8x processors from the previous point. For the first strong scaling curve (1.1B elements) in Figure 5, we ran:

```
srun −n 64      −N 64      ./lulesh −s 256 −i 5
srun −n 512     −N 512     ./lulesh −s 128 −i 5
srun −n 4096    −N 4096    ./lulesh −s 64  −i 5
srun −n 32768   −N 32768   ./lulesh −s 32  −i 5
```

CoMD. All simulations are equivalent to running the SLURM command `srun -n M -N M ./comd -e -i I -j J -k K -x X -y Y -z Z -N 5 -n 1` with 1 MPI rank per node and some number M of MPI ranks. Here I, J, K give the processor grid such that $M = I \times J \times K$. Here X, Y, Z give the total spatial dimensions in Angstrom for the problem, with the total number of atoms then determined by the default density parameter. $-N$ is the number of steps. For the first strong scaling curve (2.8B atoms) in Figure 5, we ran:

```
srun −n 1024 −N 1024 ./comd −e −i 8  −j 8  −k 16 −x 704 −y 704 −z 1408 −N 5
srun −n 2048 −N 2048 ./comd −e −i 16 −j 8  −k 16 −x 704 −y 704 −z 1408 −N 5
srun −n 4096 −N 4096 ./comd −e −i 16 −j 16 −k 16 −x 704 −y 704 −z 1408 −N 5
srun −n 8192 −N 8192 ./comd −e −i 16 −j 16 −k 32 −x 704 −y 704 −z 1408 −N 5
```

HPCG. All simulations are equivalent to running the SLURM command `srun -n M -N M ./hpcg --nx=X --ny=Y --nz=Z --rt=0` with 1 MPI rank per node and some number M of MPI ranks. Here X, Y, Z give the problem size per MPI rank. The rt parameter sets a special quick path mode in HPCG, which only executes the solve and skips a tuning phase. For the first strong scaling curve (17B rows) in Figure 5, we ran:

```
srun −n 1024 −N 1024 ./hpcg −−nx=256 −−ny=256 −−nz=256 −rt=0
srun −n 2048 −N 2048 ./hpcg −−nx=128 −−ny=256 −−nz=256 −rt=0
srun −n 4096 −N 4096 ./hpcg −−nx=128 −−ny=128 −−nz=256 −rt=0
srun −n 8192 −N 8192 ./hpcg −−nx=128 −−ny=128 −−nz=128 −rt=0
```

References

1. HPCG Benchmark. http://www.hpcg-benchmark.org/software/index.html
2. Livermore Unstructured Lagrangian Explicit Shock Hydrodynamics (LULESH). https://codesign.llnl.gov/lulesh.php
3. The Mantevo Project. https://mantevo.org/packages/
4. Bao, W., et al.: Static and dynamic frequency scaling on multicore cpus. ACM Trans. Archit. Code Optim. **13**(4), 51:1–51:26 (2016)

5. Binkert, N., et al.: The gem5 simulator. SIGARCH Comput. Archit. News **39**(2), 1–7 (2011)
6. Chan, C.P., et al.: Topology-aware performance optimization and modeling of adaptive mesh refinement codes for exascale. In: International Workshop on Communication Optimizations in HPC (COMHPC), pp. 17–28. IEEE (2016)
7. Chennupati, G., et al.: AMM: scalable memory reuse model to predict the performance of physics codes. In: 2017 IEEE International Conference on Cluster Computing (CLUSTER), pp. 649–650 (2017)
8. Degomme, A., Legrand, A., Markomanolis, G.S., Quinson, M., Stillwell, M., Suter, F.: Simulating MPI applications: the SMPI approach. IEEE Trans. Parallel Distrib. Syst. **28**, 2387–2400 (2017)
9. Desprez, F., Markomanolis, G., Quinson, M., Suter, F.: Assessing the performance of MPI applications through time-independent trace replay. In: PSTI 2011: Second International Workshop on Parallel Software Tools and Tool Infrastructures (2011)
10. Fujimoto, R.M.: Parallel discrete event simulation. Commun. ACM **33**, 30–53 (1990)
11. Gropp, W., Lusk, E.L., Skjellum, A.: Using MPI - 2nd Edition: Portable Parallel Programming with the Message Passing Interface. The MIT Press, Cambridge (1999)
12. Groves, T., et al.: (SAI) Stalled, Active and Idle: characterizing power and performance of large-scale dragonfly networks. In: 2016 IEEE International Conference on Cluster Computing (CLUSTER), pp. 50–59 (2016)
13. Guo, J., Yi, Q., Meng, J., Zhang, J., Balaji, P.: Compiler-assisted overlapping of communication and computation in MPI applications. In: 2016 IEEE International Conference on Cluster Computing (CLUSTER), pp. 60–69 (2016)
14. Hoefler, T., Schneider, T., Lumsdaine, A.: LogGOPSim: simulating large-scale applications in the LogGOPS model. In: HPDC 2010: 19th ACM International Symposium on High Performance Distributed Computing, pp. 597–604 (2010)
15. Jain, N., et al.: Evaluating HPC networks via simulation of parallel workloads. In: SC16: International Conference for High Performance Computing, Networking, Storage and Analysis, pp. 154–165 (2016)
16. Jiang, N., Becker, D.U., Michelogiannakis, G., Balfour, J.D., Towles, B., Shaw, D.E., Kim, J., Dally, W.J.: A detailed and flexible cycle-accurate Network-on-Chip simulator. In: ISPASS, pp. 86–96 (2013)
17. Minkenberg, C.: HPC networks: challenges and the role of optics. In: Optical Fiber Communications Conference and Exhibition (OFC), 2015, pp. 1–3. IEEE (2015)
18. Preissl, R., Schulz, M., Kranzlmüller, D., de Supinski, B.R., Quinlan, D.J.: Using MPI communication patterns to guide source code transformations. In: Bubak, M., van Albada, G.D., Dongarra, J., Sloot, P.M.A. (eds.) ICCS 2008, Part III. LNCS, vol. 5103, pp. 253–260. Springer, Heidelberg (2008). https://doi.org/10.1007/978-3-540-69389-5_29
19. Rodrigues, A., et al.: Improvements to the structural simulation toolkit. In: International Conference on Simulation Tools and Techniques, pp. 190–195 (2012)
20. Rumley, S., et al.: Optical interconnects for extreme scale computing systems. Parallel Comput. **64**, 65–80 (2017)
21. Snavely, A., et al.: A framework for performance modeling and prediction. In: SC 2002: International Conference for High Performance Computing, Networking, Storage and Analysis, pp. 1–17 (2002)
22. Sottile, M., et al.: Semi-automatic extraction of software skeletons for benchmarking large-scale parallel applications. In: PADS 2013: ACM SIGSIM Conference on Principles of Advanced Discrete Simulation, pp. 1–10 (2013)

23. Strout, M.M., Kreaseck, B., Hovland, P.D.: Data-flow analysis for MPI programs. In: ICPP 2006: International Conference on Parallel Processing, pp. 175–184 (2006)
24. Susukita, R., et al.: Performance prediction of large-scale parallel system and application using macro-level simulation. In: SC 2008: International Conference for High Performance Computing, Networking, Storage and Analysis (2008)
25. Wilke, J.J., Sargsyan, K., Kenny, J.P., Debusschere, B., Najm, H.N., Hendry, G.: Validation and Uncertainty assessment of extreme-scale HPC simulation through Bayesian inference. In: Wolf, F., Mohr, B., an Mey, D. (eds.) Euro-Par 2013. LNCS, vol. 8097, pp. 41–52. Springer, Heidelberg (2013). https://doi.org/10.1007/978-3-642-40047-6_7
26. Xu, Q.: Automatic Construction of Coordinated Performance Skeletons, p. 84 (2007)
27. Zhang, W., Almgren, A.S., Day, M., Nguyen, T., Shalf, J., Unat, D.: Boxlib with tiling: An AMR software framework. CoRR abs/1604.03570 (2016)

Zeno: A Straggler Diagnosis System for Distributed Computing Using Machine Learning

Huanxing Shen$^{(\boxtimes)}$ and Cong Li

Intel Corporation, Shanghai, People's Republic of China
{huanxing.shen,cong.li}@intel.com

Abstract. Modern distributed computing frameworks for cloud computing and high performance computing typically accelerate job performance by dividing a large job into small tasks for execution parallelism. Some tasks, however, may run far behind others, which jeopardize the job completion time. In this paper, we present *Zeno*, a novel system which automatically identifies and diagnoses stragglers for jobs by machine learning methods. First, the system identifies stragglers with an unsupervised clustering method which groups the tasks based on their execution time. It then uses a supervised rule learning algorithm to learn diagnosis rules inferring the stragglers with their resource assignment and usage data. *Zeno* is evaluated on traces from a Google's Borg system and an Alibaba's Fuxi system. The results demonstrate that our system is able to generate simple and easy-to-read rules with both valuable insights and decent performance in predicting stragglers.

Keywords: Distributed computing · Straggler diagnosis
Unsupervised clustering · Supervised rule induction

1 Introduction

In cloud computing and high performance computing, a large job is typically divided into many small tasks for parallel execution in a distributed environment (see, e.g., [8,22]). In ideal scenarios, maximum parallelism is achieved when all the tasks of a job (or a stage of a job if the job is composed of different heterogeneous stages) complete approximately at the same time. In reality, however, some tasks run considerably slower than the others, straggling the overall job completion time. Ananthanarayanan et al. [1] shows that without those *stragglers* in real-world production clusters, the average job completion time would have been improved by 47% in Facebook's trace, 29% in Bing's trace, and 36% in Yahoo's trace. Yadwadkar et al. [21] reports that 22–28% of the total tasks are stragglers in a replay of Facebook's and Cloudera's customers' Hadoop production cluster traces. It becomes a practical way for job owners to identify and diagnose those stragglers so that the performance in a future run can be improved.

© Springer International Publishing AG, part of Springer Nature 2018
R. Yokota et al. (Eds.): ISC High Performance 2018, LNCS 10876, pp. 144–162, 2018.
https://doi.org/10.1007/978-3-319-92040-5_8

There are many reasons for a task to become a straggler such as hardware differences, prioritized dynamic allocation of constrained resources to tasks running concurrently on the same server, uneven partition of workloads, data locality, etc. A diagnosis system to assist job owners to identify the potential causes of stragglers is not available. Traditionally a wide range of tools and APIs have been created by the performance analysis community to collect performance data. Various methods including, e.g., scalable displays of performance data, interactive visualization of performance data, etc., are proposed to analyze the far too large and too complex data (see, e.g., [5,6]). However, those methods still rely on significant manual analysis, which is labor-intensive, error-prone, and much more time-consuming.

In this paper, we present *Zeno*[1], a novel straggler diagnosis system which can automatically identify and diagnose stragglers for jobs in distributed computing. For a completed job, *Zeno* interacts with the job running framework and its cluster manager to retrieve the execution information, the resource allocation data, and the resource usage data of its tasks. Based on their execution time, an unsupervised clustering method is employed to group the tasks of the job into clusters, thereby identifying and labeling the stragglers among them. The task straggler labels, the resource allocation data, and the resource usage data are then put into a supervised rule induction algorithm. A simple and easy-to-read rule is learned as the diagnosis result discovering the interesting and valuable insight into why the tasks are slow. The job owner can translate the diagnosis result to actions for performance enhancement. For example, a diagnosis rule of '*if its assigned memory is less than γ, then the task will be slow*' provides the insight that the stragglers are caused by insufficient memory resource assignment. The job owner can understand the insight easily and allocate the right amount of memory to the tasks in the future execution to improve the job performance. A simple user interface is provided for users to view the analysis results.

Zeno is evaluated on real-world traces from a Google's Borg system [20] and an Alibaba's Fuxi system [23]. Preliminary experimental results indicate that *Zeno* is able to generate simple and easy-to-read rules. Not only can the rules discover valuable insights into why some tasks are slow but also they can predict stragglers with a decent performance on held-out sets of tasks within the same jobs.

Our contributions are three-fold. First, we propose a novel approach to straggler identification and diagnosis combining unsupervised clustering and supervised rule induction. Next, we implement *Zeno* which, to the best of our knowledge, is the first straggler diagnosis system for distributed computing. Last but not least, equipped with the new system we identify and diagnose the stragglers on two publicly-available cluster traces.

The rest of the paper is organized as follows. In Sect. 2 we present the new machine learning approach to straggler identification and diagnosis. The implementation of *Zeno* is described in Sect. 3. Section 4 presents the experimental results. Related work is reviewed in Sect. 5. Finally, we make a conclusion in Sect. 6.

---

[1] Zeno was the Greek philosopher who raised the paradox that the quickest runner can never succeed in overtaking a slow-moving tortoise.

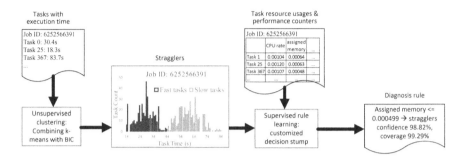

Fig. 1. Diagram of the machine learning approach.

2 Machine Learning Method for Straggler Diagnosis

We introduce a two-phase machine learning approach to identify and diagnose stragglers in the distributed computing framework. Figure 1 shows the diagram of our approach. First, stragglers are identified among the tasks in a job (or in a stage of a job) using an unsupervised clustering method. Second, a customized decision stump induction algorithm is designed to learn simple and easy-to-read rules for straggler inference. The two phases are described in detail in the following subsections.

2.1 Straggler Identification

The first phase of straggler identification takes the execution time of all the tasks in a job as the input and identifies a subset of the tasks as the stragglers.

The details of this algorithm are shown in Fig. 2. It employs the k-means homogeneous clustering method in conjunction with Bayesian information criterion for cluster number selection. Given a certain cluster number, the standard k-means clustering algorithm [14] runs on the one-dimensional data of the task execution time. After a random initialization of the cluster membership, the algorithm iterates between two steps. The first step estimates the cluster centroids using the current cluster membership. The second step resigns the tasks into the clusters based on their proximities with the centroids. Such an iterative process continues until no cluster membership reassignment happens in the iteration.

After that, Bayesian information criterion (BIC) [17] is calculated for the specific cluster number k. The first term of BIC,

$$-2\sum_{i=1}^{n}\log[p_{m(i)}\frac{1}{\sqrt{2\pi}\sigma_{m(i)}}e^{-\frac{(t^{(i)}-\bar{t}_{m(i)})^2}{2\sigma^2_{m(i)}}}],$$

gives the negative log-likelihood of generating all the execution time data from the clustering model. The generative model assumes that values in each of the clusters follow a normal distribution. Lower the negative log-likelihood, more probable the data is. The second term, $2k\log n$, gives the complexity of the

Input the n tasks with execution time $t^{(1)},...,t^{(n)}$
For $k = 1,...k_{max}$
    For task $i = 1,...,n$, randomly assign its cluster membership $m(i) \in \{1,...,k\}$
    Iterate till convergence (no cluster membership reassignment in step 2):
        Step 1: calculate the centroids of the clusters with the current members
$$\bar{t}_j = \frac{\sum_{i:m(i)=j} t^{(i)}}{\sum_{i:m(i)=j} 1}, j = 1,...k$$
        Step 2: reassign the tasks cluster membership
$$m(i) = \underset{j}{\arg\min} |t^{(i)} - \bar{t}_j|, i = 1,...,n$$
Calculate the probability of each cluster, the standard deviation of each cluster, and then Bayesian information criterion (BIC) of the clustering result:
$$p_j = \frac{\sum_{i:m(i)=j} 1}{n}, \sigma_j = \sqrt{\frac{\sum_{i:m(i)=j}(t^{(i)}-\bar{t}_j)^2}{\sum_{i:m(i)=j} 1}}, j = 1,...,k$$
$$BIC(k) = -2\sum_{i=1}^n \log[p_{m(i)}\frac{1}{\sqrt{2\pi}\sigma_{m(i)}} e^{-\frac{(t^{(i)}-\bar{t}_{m(i)})^2}{2\sigma_{m(i)}^2}}] + 2k \log n$$
Take the clustering result with the best k minimizing BIC
$$k^* = \underset{k}{\arg\min} BIC(k)$$
In the clustering result, if $\frac{\bar{t}_{k^*-1}}{\bar{t}_{k^*}} \leq 90\%$ and $\sum_{i:m(i)=k^*} 1 \leq 60\% \cdot n$, we label the tasks in the slowest cluster as the stragglers. Otherwise null is output indicating no straggler identified.

Fig. 2. Straggler identification using k-means clustering and Bayesian information criterion for cluster number selection.

model. The complexity of a model is measured approximately with its prior probability, where $2k$ is the total number of parameters involved in describing the k normal distributions. We choose the best cluster number with the lowest BIC value, which minimizes the joint objective of the negative log-likelihood and the model complexity.

Heuristic filtering is further performed in post-processing the corresponding clustering results. The two slowest clusters are examined. If the task number of the slowest cluster is lower than a predefined threshold and its mean execution time is considerably longer than that of the second slowest cluster, we label the tasks in the slowest cluster as stragglers. The first condition prevents us from labeling most of the tasks in a job as stragglers when only a small number of the tasks are fast. The second condition prevents us from labeling tasks as stragglers which are just a little bit slower.

2.2 Straggler Diagnosis

The second phase of straggler diagnosis is based on a supervised rule induction method which takes the straggler labels (that is, the output from the first phase of straggler identification), the resource allocation data, and the resource usage data of the tasks as the inputs. A rule to infer stragglers based on their resource allocation and usage is output as the learning result. It is expected that the

Input the task attributes $x^{(i)} = (x_1^{(i)}, ..., x_d^{(i)})$ and the straggler label $y^{(i)} \in \{1, -1\}$
  for each of the task $i = 1, ..., n$
For attribute $j = 1, ..., d$, enumerate all the atomic conditions $C_j = \{c_{j,1}, ..., c_{j,s}\}$,
  where each atomic condition $c_{j,q}$ is in the form of either '$x_j > \gamma$' or '$x_j \leq \gamma$'
For attribute pair $(j, k), j = 1, ..., d, k = j + 1, ..., d$, enumerate the
  combo of 2 atomic conditions $C_{j,k} = \{c_{j,q} \wedge c_{k,r} | c_{j,q} \in C_j, c_{k,r} \in C_k\} \cup$
  $\{c_{j,q} \vee c_{k,r} | c_{j,q} \in C_j, c_{k,r} \in C_k\}$
Generate the candidate condition set with both atomic conditions and 2-atomic-
  condition combos
$$C = \bigcup_{j=1,...d} [C_j \bigcup_{k=j+1,...d} C_{j,k}]$$
Search through the space C, where for a condition $c \in C$:
  Create a rule 'if c, then $y = 1$'
  For task $i = 1, .., n$:
    Use the rule and the task features to determine its straggler label $\widehat{y}^{(i)}$
    Calculate confidence (empirical precision), coverage (empirical recall), and
    empirical f-measure of the rule c with on the same dataset
$$p(c) = \widehat{P}(y^{(i)} = 1 | \widehat{y}^{(i)} = 1)$$
$$r(c) = \widehat{P}(\widehat{y}^{(i)} = 1 | y^{(i)} = 1)$$
$$f(c) = \frac{2p(c)r(c)}{p(c)+r(c)}$$
Find the rule in the search to maximize the empirical f-measure
$$c^* = \underset{c \in C}{\arg\min} f(c)$$
If $f(c^*) > \theta$, (an acceptance threshold, say, e.g., 70%), then output the rule 'if
c^*, then $y = 1$, else output null indicating a failure in automatically generating
diagnosis result.

Fig. 3. Customized decision stump induction algorithm for straggler diagnosis.

diagnosis rule is able to address why the tasks are slow. This rule helps the job
owner understand the probable causes of the stragglers and perform adjustments
accordingly. In this way, the job performance can be improved in the future run.

The diagnosis rule is customized from the decision stump classifier [11]. A
decision stump is a one-level decision tree that takes a single condition test on
the input attributes of a task and then determines whether the task is a straggler
or not based on the test result. Decision stumps can be easily re-written into
simple rules. The example below shows a rule when the condition test applies to
one attribute only (to which we refer as an 'atomic condition'):

'*If its assigned memory is no greater than γ, then the task is a straggler.
(Otherwise it is not a straggler.)*'

The condition test is further extended to combine two atomic conditions with
the 'and' or 'or' operator. When the condition test becomes a 2-atomic-condition
combo, a rule looks like the example below:

'*If its CPU rate is no greater than η and its canonical memory usage is
greater than λ, then the task is a straggler. (Otherwise it is not a straggler.)*'

The induction algorithm is shown in Fig. 3. For each task, its resource
allocation data and resource usage data are taken to create a feature vector

$x^{(i)} = (x_1^{(i)}, ..., x_d^{(i)})$. The straggler label, $y^{(i)} \in \{1, -1\}$, is the class label to be predicted by the decision stump classifier. Walking through all the attributes, all the atomic conditions are enumerated. 2-atomic-condition combos are then generated by connecting two of the atomic conditions using the 'and' and 'or' operators. The atomic conditions and the 2-atomic-condition combos form the entire search space, in which a heuristic grid search is then performed to induce a decision stump.

For a certain condition being searched, its utility is evaluated on the training set as follows. We first build a rule using the condition and then apply it to the training set to predict whether a task is a straggler or not. The rule's confidence (that is, its empirical precision $p(c)$) is calculated, which is the number of true positives versus that of both true positives and false positives. It gives the likelihood that a straggler identified by the rule is a true straggler on the training set. The rule's coverage (that is, its empirical recall $r(c)$) is also calculated, which is the number of true positives versus the number of both true positives and false negatives. It gives the likelihood that a true straggler is identified successfully by the rule on the training set. As a higher coverage usually results in lower confidence (and vice versa), the two metrics are combined with their harmonic average, the empirical f-measure $f(c)$. The rule with the best f-measure is selected. To control the output quality, only when the f-measure value exceeds a predefined threshold, the rule is accepted as the diagnosis result.

The information gain criterion [18], which is commonly used for decision tree induction, is not used here because in an unbalanced dataset it would more likely generate rules determining the non-stragglers with high confidence. In the scenario of straggler diagnosis, the various extent of label distribution imbalance exists.

Note that the rule is selected based on training data only. It does not guarantee its performance on an unseen set of tasks. However, simple classifiers are more likely to perform similarly on an unseen dataset as they do on the training samples drawn from the same probability distribution [3]. Our rules are simple in terms of using atomic conditions and 2-atomic-condition combos. Therefore it is expected that the rule performs well in explaining the stragglers for different runs of the same job even if they are not seen in the training data.

3   Implementation of *Zeno*

We build *Zeno* upon the proposed method to automatically identify and diagnose stragglers for cloud and high performance computing. Figure 4 shows its architecture which is divided into three parts, the job data preprocessor, the back-end service for straggler identification and diagnosis, and the web-based user interface.

Job Data Preprocessor: The job data preprocessor interacts with the cluster manager and job running frameworks to retrieve and preprocess task information for straggler identification and diagnosis. Adapters are developed to retrieve the data from different systems. An adapter discovers the task set of a job and

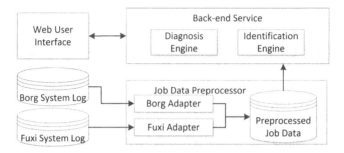

Fig. 4. Architecture of *Zeno*.

extracts the attributes for each of the tasks in the set from the corresponding system, including the task execution time, the resource allocation data, and the resource usage data. All the task data extracted for one job are compiled into a single file. Currently we have developed two non-intrusive adapters preprocessing the information from Borg system log and Fuxi system log respectively.

Straggler Identification and Diagnosis Service: The backbone of *Zeno* is the service to identify and diagnosis stragglers for the jobs. The straggler identification engine and the straggler diagnosis engine are implemented based on Sect. 2.

User Interface: Straggler identification and diagnosis results are presented to users through a web user interface. After the user selects a job, *Zeno* runs the analysis immediately and presents the results in two panels on a web page. Figure 5 shows an example. In the straggler identification panel, a histogram describes the distribution of execution time of the tasks, where stragglers and non-stragglers are labeled in different colors. It gives the user a high-level impression on how many tasks are identified as the straggler and to which extent they straggle the job performance. Detailed statistics of the non-stragglers and stragglers execution time are also provided. Figure 5(a) gives an example of the straggler identification panel. The straggler diagnosis panel shows the straggler diagnosis result. A simple and easy-to-read rule is highlighted along with its confidence and coverage. The histogram of task execution time is shown again, but the tasks are now labeled based on the prediction of the rule. Users are able to evaluate the empirical performance of the rules straightforwardly. The system also shows how the tasks are distributed with respect to the attributes involved in the rule. If the rule comes with a single condition, the task histogram with respect to the attribute is given. If the rule comes with a combo condition, a scatter plot of the tasks over the two attributes would show. In either case, straggler and non-straggler tasks are colored differently. Figure 5(b) is an example of the straggler diagnosis panel with a single condition rule.

Through the web user interface, users are able to understand the diagnosis result easily. Given the high-level knowledge extracted from a large amount of low-level data, they are able to translate the result into improvement actions.

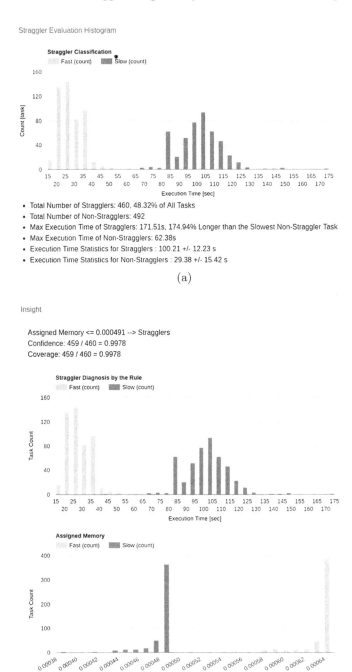

Fig. 5. A screenshot of *Zeno*: (a) the straggler identification panel and (b) the straggler diagnosis panel.

4   Experiments

We evaluate *Zeno* on two production cluster traces from a Google's Borg system [20] and an Alibaba's Fuxi system [23]. In the next several subsections, we first introduce the two datasets used in experiments. Results of straggler identification and diagnosis are then presented. After that four case studies are given. Finally, we perform an objective evaluation of the rule quality in terms of the straggler prediction performance on held-out sets of tasks within the same jobs.

4.1   Datasets

Google Cluster Trace: Borg [20] is a cluster management system running a large number of jobs from many different applications across clusters on tens of thousands of servers in Google. The system supports the concurrent execution of jobs, process-level isolation for tasks, and dynamic resource allocation. Each job running in Borg consists of a set of homogeneous tasks which execute the same binary, request the same resource, and start approximately at the same time. However, resources assigned for each task depends on its relative priority to other concurrent tasks on the same computing cell and its resource usage history.

A representative Borg workload is publicly available[2]. It is a one-month trace of a Google production cluster with more than 12000 servers. Job and task information are logged in the trace. For each task, its resource allocation and usage data are monitored every five minutes. The values, however, are scaled.

The trace is divided into 500 parts chronically. We use the first 50 parts for evaluation. Jobs with less than 50 tasks are excluded, as we focus our effort on jobs with a considerable extent of parallelism. After filtering, 3889 jobs are selected. We extract the start and end time for all the tasks in each of the jobs for straggler identification. In straggler diagnosis, we assemble the feature vector with the resource allocation and usage values of 'CPU rate', 'canonical memory usage', 'assigned memory'[3], 'unmapped page cache', 'total page cache', 'disk I/O time', and 'local disk space usage'[4]. Those values are averaged for each of the tasks across their lifetime.

Alibaba Cluster Trace: Fuxi [23] is a resource management and job scheduling system in Alibaba that handles batch processing workload. Though with a different set of terminologies, the distributed computing paradigm is similar to that of Borg: a 'task' in Fuxi system contains a set of 'instances' which execute exactly the same binary with the same resource request.

A trace containing the information of a 12-h run on a production cluster with more than 1000 machines is publicly available[5]. While the trace also contains

---

[2] https://github.com/google/cluster-data.

[3] The attribute is named as 'assigned memory usage' in the trace. However, according to [20] its semantic is the amount of memory assigned, not the amount used.

[4] Network utilization, unfortunately, is not available in the trace, which may probably impact the success rate of straggler diagnosis.

[5] https://github.com/alibaba/clusterdata.

Table 1. Experimental results on successful identification of stragglers.

Datasets	Number of jobs input	Number of jobs output	Success rate
Google trace	3887	2447	62.92%
Alibaba trace	5138	830	16.15%

services not managed by Fuxi, we extract the relevant information from Fuxi system in the trace for evaluation. The concepts of 'tasks' and 'instances' in Fuxi system are translated to jobs and tasks in our straggler diagnosis system. Similarly, we filter out the jobs with less than 50 tasks. 5138 jobs are resulted from the filtering process. Again the start time and end time for tasks in a job are used for straggler identification. The relevant part of the trace contains much less information on resource allocation and usage. During straggler diagnosis, the two attributes, 'average CPU' and 'average memory', are used to assemble the feature vector.

4.2   Straggler Identification and Diagnosis

We first perform the experiments of straggler identification. Table 1 shows the experimental results of straggler identification on the two datasets. For jobs with stragglers identified in the two traces, Fig. 6 shows the scatter plots correlating the percentage of stragglers within a job with the percentage of *additional* time spent by the stragglers versus the time spent by all the tasks (assuming that their start time is aligned).

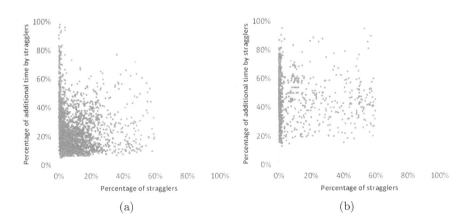

Fig. 6. Stragglers percentage (x-axis) versus percentage of additional time spent by the stragglers (y-axis) within individual jobs. (a) Results on Google cluster trace (b) Results on Alibaba cluster trace.

In the first phase of straggler identification, in Google cluster trace, more than 60% of the 3887 jobs are identified to have straggler tasks. In Alibaba cluster trace, about 16% of the 5138 jobs are identified to have straggler tasks. Although a preliminary examination suggests that jobs in the trace from Alibaba cluster seem to be impacted less by stragglers, we conjecture that it is because of the bias to short jobs in a shorter trace. It is very likely that some jobs impacted by stragglers do not finish in the 12 h so that their information is not included in the dataset. From the two scatter plots, we see quite a lot of data points scattered at the left side to the upper left corner of the figure. This indicates that quite a lot of jobs are impacted by a small portion of stragglers, sometimes to such a significant extent that more than 80% of the job execution time is devoted solely to stragglers.

We next perform the experiments of straggler diagnosis. Among 2447 jobs with stragglers identified in the trace from the Google's Borg cluster, 820 jobs with no less than 30 stragglers are chosen for diagnosis. This is because that smaller number of stragglers (positive samples) may not only pose difficulties to statistical machine learning method but also impact the objective evaluation performed in Sect. 4.4. On the much smaller dataset from Alibaba cluster, most jobs contain very few stragglers. As a result, we take all those jobs with stragglers identified for diagnosis. This challenges our straggler diagnosis to tackle with difficult cases of few outliers. Table 2 shows the experimental results of successful straggler diagnosis on the two datasets.

Table 2. Experimental results on successful diagnosis of stragglers.

Datasets	Number of jobs input	Number of jobs output	Success rate
Google trace	820	417	50.85%
Alibaba trace	830	580	69.88%

From the experimental results, we see that in the two datasets, when the rule acceptance threshold is 70% (θ in Fig. 3), more than half of the jobs are automatically diagnosed with simple and easy-to-read rules generated.

4.3   Case Study

We present four case studies of straggler diagnosis using *Zeno*.

Case 1: The first case comes from Alibaba cluster trace. Among all the 580 jobs which succeed in straggler diagnosis, 405 jobs (close to 70%) are diagnosed to be caused by low CPU usage with empirical f-measure no less than 90%. Figure 7(a) shows the screenshot of the diagnosis result for a typical job. Due to the space limitation, we only show the diagnosis panel in the case studies. Among all the 475 tasks in the job, 99% of them finish within 90 s while the remaining 1% straggler tasks do not complete until the 156th second. *Zeno* diagnoses that a task becomes a straggler if its CPU usage is less than a threshold, suggesting that the stragglers are not able to obtain enough CPU resource to run as fast as

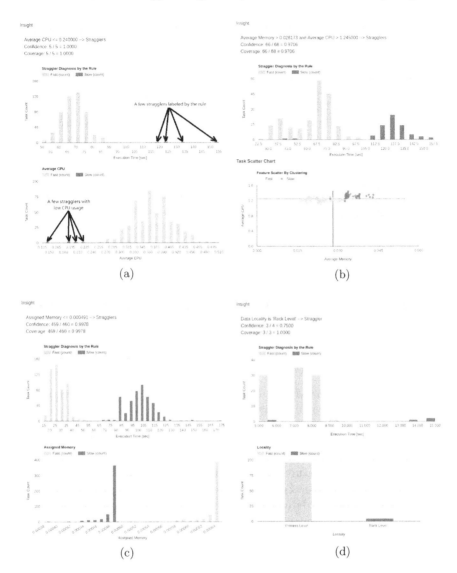

Fig. 7. System screenshots of the four case studies: (a) stragglers caused by low CPU usage; (b) stragglers caused by high resource usage of both CPU and memory; (c) stragglers caused by insufficient memory assignment; and (d) stragglers caused by data locality

the others. During a visit to Alibaba to present *Zeno*, we were told by Alibaba Cloud Team that the CPU resource of the batch jobs in its clusters is overly throttled in quite a few cases, thus confirming the explanation of the stragglers diagnosed by *Zeno*. In those cases, the job owners are able to get the hint that performance can be improved by fine-grain resource allocation and reservation.

Case 2: The second case study from Alibaba cluster trace is more complex. As shown in Fig. 7(b), about half of the tasks impede the completion of the job. Though the rule generated in straggler diagnosis incorrectly labels a very small portion of the tasks, it shows that most of the stragglers consume high CPU usage as well as high memory usage. In the scatter plot, most of the stragglers sit in the quadrant of high CPU and memory usage. The pattern strongly suggests that the uneven partition of the workload is the root cause for the stragglers. Similar cases are observed in some of the jobs in Google cluster trace as well. To mitigate the stragglers in the job or similar jobs, the job owner may consider explicit data partition or re-examine the partition if it has already been done.

Case 3: In Google cluster trace, we find a few cases of the stragglers caused by insufficient resource assignment. In a typical example shown in Fig. 7(c), the diagnosis rule states that insufficient memory assignment causes the stragglers, significantly impacting the completion of the job. It is further illustrated by the task histogram of 'assigned memory' used by the rule. In the histogram, two patterns of memory assignment are identical in shape but have distinct peak values. They are clearly labeled in different colors according to whether the tasks are stragglers or non-stragglers. We conjecture that the job is for in-memory processing so that an insufficient memory assignment results in the swap of the data being processed (see, e.g., [22]). To improve job performance, the job owner may co-work with the cluster administrators for an explicit reservation and assignment of enough memory for the tasks.

Case 4: The case is observed in our lab environment on a small cluster with 3 servers. A Spark [22] job, collaborative filtering based on alternative least squares for a movie recommendation system, runs on top of the Hadoop YARN [19] cluster manager with the default configuration. It reads the GroupLens dataset[6] from HDFS, a local distributed file system. Default Spark task attributes are used in *Zeno* as the task features. In one of the job stages which shows the final recommendation data frame, *Zeno* identifies the stragglers within the tasks of this stage and suggests that data locality is the cause of the stragglers[7]. Few 'rack level' tasks run far behind the other tasks with the data locality of 'process level'. By looking into the detail of this stage, we confirm that the 'rack level' straggler tasks read intermediate computing frame from other nodes while the 'process level' tasks read from the same executor instance. To improve job performance, the job owner needs to resolve the data locality issue, probably with a better task scheduling or with more data replicas.

Summary: The case studies here show the effectiveness of *Zeno* in identifying and diagnosing stragglers for jobs running in large scale production clusters. The diagnosis results discover valuable insights into why tasks become stragglers. Based on different insights discovered, performance improvement in future runs of the jobs relies on job owners (sometimes with the help from cluster

---

[6] https://grouplens.org/datasets/.

[7] The same conclusion can be reached if the network usage of the tasks (rather than the default Spark task attributes) is monitored and used for diagnosis.

administrators) to translate the diagnosis results to improvement actions, e.g., explicit data partition, explicit resource reservation in some forms of service level agreement, etc.

4.4   Rule Quality Evaluation

As we are not able to recover the full job information from the public trace, it is difficult to judge subjectively on whether those rules truly cast light on the causes of the stragglers. Instead, we use the objective metrics, the performance in predicting stragglers in a held-out set of tasks, to evaluate the quality of the rules automatically generated. The goal is to understand how well *Zeno*'s straggler diagnosis algorithm is able to correlate the task slow-down with an appropriate pre-condition in a specific job run. A good performance indicates that the rule is able to predict stragglers well on unseen data in the similar context including, e.g., the same job or similar jobs, the same or similar scheduling context.

We design our experiments as follows. For each of the jobs which are successful in automatic straggler diagnosis, we divide its tasks evenly into 20 mutually exclusive parts. We then rerun the rule induction algorithm for 20 times. Each time we take 19 of the 20 parts for rule induction and use the remaining part for straggler prediction. With the 20-fold cross-validation, we are able to retain a close-to-original dataset with a similar size for rule induction and at the same time utilize all the tasks in evaluating the performance of the rules. Rule quality evaluation is performed on Google dataset only, in which each of the jobs contains at least 30 stragglers so that each of the 20 parts contains at least one or two stragglers. Most jobs from Alibaba dataset contain very few stragglers. Therefore they are not eligible to be used for rule quality evaluation.

To rate the quality of the rules induced, we use the standard metrics of f-measure on test data, which is derived from precision and recall. Precision indicates how likely an identified straggler is a true straggler and recall indicates how likely a true straggler gets identified. As the harmonic average of precision and recall, f-measure balances the two metrics, penalizing the bias to either of the two. In computing the final evaluation score, we first calculate the f-measure for each job and then compute the average score across all the jobs with the same weight.

We first compare our method with several other rule-based classifiers:

1. a default rule stating that all the tasks are stragglers, which results in 100% recall along with a low precision;
2. decision stumps with atomic conditions only, but not 2-atomic-condition combos;
3. standard one-level decision trees, (that is, decision stumps using the traditional measurement, information gain, to select the test condition); and
4. two-level decision trees[8].

---

[8] In most cases, a two-level decision tree is equivalent to two rules in inferring stragglers, each with two test conditions connected with the 'and' operator. Note that in such cases, a two-level decision tree is more complex than the customized decision stump since two rules are involved.

Table 3. Performance of predicting stragglers using rules induced.

Method	Average f-measure
The default rule: any task is a straggler	30.92%
Decision stumps with atomic conditions	73.77%
One-level decision trees	65.70%
Two-level decision trees	76.14%
Customized decision stumps	**78.62%**

Table 4. Comparing with other classifiers which are not human-readable.

Method	Average f-measure
k-nearest neighbor classifiers	74.79%
Logistic regression with L_2 regularization	76.87%
Random forests	82.65%
Customized decision stumps	78.62%

Table 3 shows the straggler prediction performance of the customized decision stumps as well as the rules induced by the other baseline methods. As we see from the experimental results, the customized decision stumps achieve an average f-measure close to 80%, outperforming the other baselines.

Decision stumps using atomic conditions beat one-level decision trees. It indicates that using empirical f-measure as the criterion to select the best condition is more appropriate than using information gain. Decision stumps using both atomic conditions and 2-atomic-condition combos outperform that using only atomic conditions, indicating that it is rewarded to consider a slightly more complex condition.

Our decision stump approach is also compared with other machine learning algorithms[9] including k-nearest neighbors [2], logistic regression with L_2 regularization [15], and the random forest [4]. Classifiers resulted from these learning algorithms are not readable and cannot be understood from the human perspective.

We use the same experimental setting of 20-fold cross-validation with the same data split. Table 4 shows the experimental results from the comparative study. As we see from the table, in predicting the stragglers for the 417 jobs,

---

[9] We have also used the well-recognized state-of-the-art classifier, support vector machine [7]. We have used SVMLight (http://svmlight.joachims.org/) and LibSVM (https://www.csie.ntu.edu.tw/~cjlin/libsvm/), the two main-stream tools. We have tried the linear kernel and the radius basis function kernel. None of the combinations produces satisfactory results, probably due to the various extent of imbalanced and noisy nature across different jobs, which may require fine-tuning the soft margin parameter for each of the jobs. As a result, we do not report out the results in the paper.

the decision stumps induced by our method perform comparably well with the classifiers resulted from those commonly-used machine learning algorithms. Due to the robustness against noise in training data, random forests perform the best. However, they cannot be used as the straggler diagnosis results as the knowledge extracted by the random forests are not human-readable. This is a common problem shared by the non-rule-based learning algorithms including k-nearest neighbors, logistic regression, support vector machines, etc. By contrast, customized decision stumps induced by our learning algorithm are easy-to-read, and therefore are well-suited to be presented as the results of automatic straggler diagnosis.

Finally, we use more rigid thresholds for rule acceptance in rule induction. Instead of setting the parameter θ in Fig. 3 to the default value of 70%, we test two alternative values, 75%, and 80%.

Again, in the experiment we use the same setting of 20-fold cross-validation for rule quality evaluation. Table 5 shows the experimental results on the number of jobs successful diagnosed as well as the quality of the rules induced. As we see from the results, with more rigid thresholds, fewer jobs are successfully diagnosed. However, the performance of the rules gets improved. With the rigid threshold of 80%, our method is still able to diagnose a decent portion (more than 30%) of the jobs with the average f-measure close to 85%.

Table 5. Results using more rigid thresholds in rule acceptance: lower success rate but better performance in straggler prediction.

Thresholds	Number of jobs output	Success rate	Average f-measure
70%	417	50.85%	78.62%
75%	344	41.95%	81.11%
80%	247	30.12%	84.84%

5 Related Work

Cloud computing and high performance computing frameworks typically monitor task completion status and launch backup tasks for stragglers during job execution (see, e.g., [8,22]). However, they do not provide post analysis and do not help diagnose the stragglers to prevent them from happening in the future execution of the same job or similar jobs. When backup tasks are launched for stragglers, the job performance has already been impacted.

In traditional straggler identification performed either offline or online with intrusive monitoring, the typical criterion is to compare the task's execution time (or progress) with a threshold calculated based on the median value within all the tasks (see, e.g., [1,9]). However, the portion of the stragglers depends on how popular the cause manifests. Moreover, the extent that they impede the completion of a job depends on the severity of the cause. Using a predefined criterion based on the median value is not likely to fit different cases. The offline straggler identification approach proposed by us is able to accommodate different scenarios, e.g., in the case studies presented in Sect. 4.3, while a median-based threshold will fail at least in one of them. [16] proposes a dynamic threshold calculation for straggler identification. The work targets to optimize speculative execution with task replication based on the quality of services, task execution progress, and cluster resource usage. Its objective is completely different from ours.

Data-driven methods (see, e.g., [10,21]) are proposed to model task execution performance or categorize stragglers. Those methods target to improve automatic resource allocation. The models are not human-readable. Directly applying the methods in a complicated cloud or high performance computing environment is difficult due to various factors that a scheduler may consider. Furthermore, the problem of the uneven partition of workload and that of data locality cannot be addressed by automatic resource allocation with those methods. Given that the models are not human-readable, one cannot use the methods to identify those problems.

There are few studies on the post-execution diagnosis of stragglers. Garraghan et al. [9] diagnoses the root-causes of stragglers in a production cluster. However, the diagnosis is done manually with significant effort.

Offline analysis available in standard computing frameworks is limited. Those frameworks provide APIs to retrieve performance data and other runtime information for post analysis. There are also a wide range of tools for scalable display and interactive visualization of performance data to analyze the far too large and too complex data (see., e.g., [5,6]). While those tools rely on significant manual analysis which is labor-intensive, error-prone, and much more time-consuming, *Zeno* is automated. *Zeno* is also complementary to those tools in terms of extracting high-level knowledge from a large amount of low-level data.

Cluster managers, e.g., YARN [19], Quincy [12], Borg [20], have different focus. They provide resource isolation and allocation based on usages, job priorities, and fairness. They do not provide answers to which tasks are stragglers within a job or to why those tasks are slower. They help cluster administrators more in terms of cluster utilization efficiency while *Zeno* helps job owners more in terms of job execution efficiency.

6   Conclusion

In this paper we have presented *Zeno*, a straggler diagnosis system which automatically identifies and diagnoses straggler tasks for jobs running in a distributed environment. *Zeno* employs an unsupervised clustering method for straggler identification and uses a customized decision stump induction algorithm in straggler diagnosis. The rules generated by *Zeno* help users discover insights into why some tasks are slow and what can be done to improve the job performance. In future work, we plan to extend *Zeno* for real-time straggler analysis during task execution. Although the extension may close the loop of automatic performance improvement, our current focus relies on human as part of the loop.

Acknowledgements. We thank Tai Huang and Jia Bao for their valuable comments and suggestions on an early draft of the paper. We acknowledge the four anonymous reviewers for their valuable comments and criticisms. We thank Xing Zhao for her checking of the English of the paper. A previous description of the machine learning methods for straggler diagnosis appeared as a 6-page extended abstract on a workshop [13].

References

1. Ananthanarayanan, G., Ghodsi, A., Shenker, S., Stoica, I.: Effective straggler mitigation: attack of the clones. In: Proceedings of the 10th USENIX Conference on Networked Systems Design and Implementation (NSDI 2013), pp. 185–198 (2013)
2. Bailey, T., Jain, A.K.: A note on distance-weighted k-nearest neighbor rules. IEEE Trans. Syst. Man Cybern. **8**(4), 311–313 (1978)
3. Blumer, A., Ehrenfeucht, A., Haussler, D., Warmuth, M.: Occam's razor. Inf. Process. Lett. **24**(6), 377–380 (1987)
4. Breiman, L.: Random forests. Mach. Learn. **45**(1), 5–32 (2001)
5. Bremer, P.T., Mohr, B., Pascucci, V., Schulz, M. (eds.): Proceedings of the 2nd Workshop on Visual Performance Analysis (VPA 2015) (2015)
6. Bremer, P.T., Gimenez, J., Levine, J.A., Schulz, M. (eds.): Proceedings of the 3rd International Workshop on Visual Performance Analysis (VPA 2016) (2016)
7. Cortes, C., Vapnik, V.: Support-vector networks. Mach. Learn. **20**(3), 273–297 (1995)
8. Dean, J., Ghemawat, S.: Mapreduce: simplified data processing on large clusters. In: Proceedings of the 6th Symposium on Operating System Design and Implementation (OSDI 2004), pp. 137–150 (2004)
9. Garraghan, P., Ouyang, X., Yang, R., McKee, D., Xu, J.: Straggler root-cause and impact analysis for massive-scale virtualized cloud datacenters. IEEE Trans. Serv. Comput. (2017). https://ieeexplore.ieee.org/document/7572191/
10. Gupta, S., Fritz, C., Price, R., Hoover, R., de Kleer, J., Witteveen, C.: ThroughputScheduler: learning to schedule on heterogeneous Hadoop clusters. In: Proceedings of the 10th International Conference on Autonomic Computing (ICAC 2013), pp. 159–165 (2013)
11. Iba, W., Langley, P.: Induction of one-level decision trees. In: Proceedings of the 9th International Workshop on Machine Learning (ML 1992), pp. 233–240 (1992)
12. Isard, M., Prabhakaran, V., Currey, J., Wieder, U., Talwar, K., Goldberg, A.: Quincy: fair scheduling for distributed computing clusters. In: Proceedings of the ACM SIGOPS 22nd Symposium on Operating Systems Principles (SOSP 2009), pp. 261–276 (2009)
13. Li, C., Shen, H., Huang, T.: Learning to diagnose stragglers in distributed computing. In: Proceedings of the 9th Workshop on Many-Task Computing on Clouds, Grids, and Supercomputers (MTAGS 2016), pp. 1–6 (2016)
14. Lloyd, S.P.: Least squares quantization in PCM. IEEE Trans. Inf. Theory **28**(2), 129–137 (1982)
15. Ng, A.Y.: Feature selection, L_1 vs. L_2 regularization, and rotational invariance. In: Proceedings of the 21st International Conference on Machine Learning (ICML 2004) (2004)

16. Ouyang, X., Garraghan, P., McKee, D., Townend, P., Xu, J.: Straggler detection in parallel computing systems through dynamic threshold calculation. In: Proceedings of the 30th International Conference on Advanced Information Networking and Applications, (AINA 2016), pp. 414–421 (2000)
17. Pelleg, D., Moore, A.W.: X-means: Extending k-means with efficient estimation of the number of clusters. In: Proceedings of the 17th International Conference on Machine Learning (ICML 2000), pp. 727–734 (2000)
18. Quinlan, J.R.: Induction of decision trees. Mach. Learn. **1**(1), 81–106 (1986)
19. Vavilapalli, V.K., Murthy, A.C., Douglas, C., Agarwal, S., Konar, M., Evans, R., Graves, T., Lowe, J., Shah, H., Seth, S., Saha, B., Curino, C., O'Malley, O., Radia, S., Reed, B., Baldeschwieler, E.: Apache Hadoop YARN: yet another resource negotiator. In: Proceedings of the 4th Annual Symposium on Cloud Computing (SOCC 2013) (2013)
20. Verma, A., Pedrosa, L., Korupolu, M., Oppenheimer, D., Tune, E., Wilkes, J.: Large-scale cluster management at Google with Borg. In: Proceedings of the 10th European Conference on Computer Systems (EuroSys 2015) (2015)
21. Yadwadkar, N.J., Hariharan, B., Gonzalez, J.E., Katz, R.: Multi-task learning for straggler avoiding predictive job scheduling. J. Mach. Learn. Res. **17**(1), 3692–3728 (2016)
22. Zaharia, M., Chowdhury, M., Franklin, M.J., Shenker, S., Stoica, I.: Spark: cluster computing with working sets. In: Proceedings of the 2nd USENIX Workshop on Hot Topics in Cloud Computing (HotCloud 2010) (2010)
23. Zhang, Z., Li, C., Tao, Y., Yang, R., Tang, H., Xu, J.: Fuxi: a fault-tolerant resource management and job scheduling system at internet scale. Proc. VLDB Endow. **7**(13), 1393–1404 (2014)

Applicability of the ECM Performance Model to Explicit ODE Methods on Current Multi-core Processors

Johannes Seiferth[1](✉), Christie Alappat[2], Matthias Korch[1],
and Thomas Rauber[1]

[1] Department of Computer Science, University of Bayreuth, Bayreuth, Germany
johannes.seiferth@uni-bayreuth.de
[2] Erlangen Regional Computing Center (RRZE),
Friedrich-Alexander University of Erlangen-Nuremberg, Erlangen, Germany

Abstract. To support the portability of efficiency when bringing an application from scientific computing to a new HPC system, autotuning techniques are promising approaches. Ideally, these approaches are able to derive an efficient implementation for a specific HPC system by applying suitable program transformations. Often, a large number of implementations results, and the most efficient of these variants should be selected. In this article, we investigate performance modelling and prediction techniques which can support the selection process. These techniques may significantly reduce the selection effort, compared to extensive runtime tests. We apply the execution-cache-memory (ECM) performance model to numerical solution methods for ordinary differential equations (ODEs). In particular, we consider the question whether it is possible to obtain a performance prediction for the resulting implementation variants to support the variant selection. We investigate the accuracy of the prediction for different ODEs and different hardware platforms and show that the prediction is able to reliably select a set of fast variants and, thus, to limit the search space for possible later empirical tuning.

Keywords: Performance model · ECM model
Performance prediction · Variant selection · Multicore

1 Introduction

Applications from scientific computing typically need to be adapted to the characteristics of a specific HPC (high-performance computing) platform to achieve a high efficiency. A high efficiency typically requires the use of program optimization techniques, such as loop unrolling or loop tiling, for the compute-intensive inner kernels of the application. This involves the selection of suitable parameter values, such as loop unrolling factors or tile block sizes. The use of such techniques may significantly increase the overall efficiency, but typically requires a large effort from the application programmer, including a large number of

© Springer International Publishing AG, part of Springer Nature 2018
R. Yokota et al. (Eds.): ISC High Performance 2018, LNCS 10876, pp. 163–183, 2018.
https://doi.org/10.1007/978-3-319-92040-5_9

runtime tests with different implementation variants. Moreover, the best implementation variant selected for one HPC platform may not be the best implementation variant for a new HPC platform and to find a good implementation variant for the new platform may again require a large programming effort.

To support the selection of efficient implementation variants, offline and online autotuning techniques have been developed for different application areas. Offline approaches are suitable if the execution behaviour of the application mainly depends on the size of the input data and other properties of the input data only play a minor role. This is, e.g., the case for dense linear algebra problems, and many examples for offline approaches come from this area, including ATLAS [1] and PHiPAC [2]. Online approaches are required if properties of the input set play an important role for the execution behaviour, as it is, e.g., the case for sparse linear algebra problems or particle codes. Examples for online approaches are Active Harmony [3] and Periscope [4].

The challenge for autotuning is the selection of a suitable implementation variant from a potentially large number of possible variants. The implementation variants can be compared by runtime experiments, but this can be quite time consuming. An alternative is the use of performance prediction using analytical approaches. To be suitable, the performance prediction must be accurate enough to clearly distinguish the performance of the different implementation variants and to order the implementation variants such that the order analytically determined corresponds to the order which would result by runtime tests.

To explore whether such a performance modelling approach is suitable, we investigate the approach for a complex example from numerical analysis. In particular, we consider the usage of the execution-cache-memory (ECM) performance model and apply the model to compute performance predictions for explicit solution methods for ODE systems. These solution methods compute a numerical approximation for the solution by performing a series of time steps one after another [5]. Each time step consists of the computation of a fixed number of stage vectors which are then combined to the next approximation vector for the unknown solution. Overall, these methods exhibit a complex loop structure, which can be modified by loop transformations such as loop interchange, unrolling, or tiling, yielding a large set of implementation variants. It is not a priori clear, which of the resulting implementation variants leads to the smallest execution time on a given multi-core system. The performance behaviour of these implementation variants depends on the organization of the computations and the memory accesses within each time step, but also on the characteristics of the ODE system to be solved.

A performance modelling approach can be used in the offline phase to analytically estimate the execution time of different implementation variants and to build a set of candidate variants that can then be tested further in the online phase. As a representative class of explicit ODE methods, we use a class of iterated Runge-Kutta (iterated RK, IRK) methods, which possess a complex loop structure leading to a high number of possible implementation variants. To apply the tools available for the ECM model, we split the time-step code of the ODE solver into a number of kernels and assemble the overall prediction by putting together the predictions of the individual kernels. This yields for each variant a quantitative prediction of the time needed to execute a single time step. Taking into account that performance models always include an abstraction of the real hardware and introduce a prediction error, we do hope, however, that the model is accurate enough to allow a qualitative ranking of different implementation variants. Such a ranking information can be useful for an autotuning approach, e.g., by helping the autotuning driver during the online phase to decide which variants to test next or which variants to discard.

The contribution of this paper is (i) to apply the ECM model to a complex numerical method with complicated runtime behaviour, (ii) to perform a detailed experimental analysis to assess the accuracy of the prediction for different settings (ODE system and hardware architecture), (iii) to discuss the applicability in the context of autotuning. The rest of the paper is organized as follows: Sect. 2 discusses related work. Section 3 gives an overview of the ECM model. Section 4 describes the computational structure of the ODE solution method and Sect. 5 applies the ECM model. Section 6 describes the experimental evaluation and Sect. 7 concludes the paper.

2   Related Work

Many modelling approaches to estimate the optimal performance of codes and to validate the effectiveness of applied optimizations techniques exist. Roughly two categories can be distinguished: *black box* models that rely on statistical methods and machine learning to describe and predict performance behaviour based on observed data like hardware performance metrics [6,7], and *white box* models that use simplified machine models to describe the interaction of code and hardware [8,9]. In this paper, we focus on a white box model, the ECM model [10,11], which can provide a single-core performance and scaling prediction for loop kernels, and apply it to time-step-oriented explicit ODE methods.

The biggest challenge for autotuning is the selection of a suitable implementation variant or of a pool of suitable variants from a potentially large number of possible variants. Thus, optimizing that selection process is of vital importance for autotuning, for which many approaches have been proposed. The above mentioned modelling approaches can be used to filter out *slow* variants by giving performance estimations for variants without actually having to run the code. Next to the performance prediction through modelling, there are many other means to support the *quest* for the most suitable implementation variant by reducing the potentially large search space of possible variants. Search strategies like exhaustive sampling [2], line search [1], hill climbing [3] or evolutionary algorithms [4] can be used to selectively scan through the space of possible variants and evaluate promising variants. Further, heuristic-based search tree pruning methods [12,13] or machine learning techniques [14,15] can be used to reduce the search space.

There are many numerical methods for the solution of ODE IVPs. Next to the classical explicit and implicit RK and multi-step methods [5], a broad range of methods exploiting parallelism exists, e.g., iterated RK methods [16,17], waveform relaxation methods [18], and peer two-steep methods [19]. In this paper, we focus on a class of IRK methods, more precisely, a class of explicit predictor corrector (PC) methods of RK type. In this paper, we use this class as a representative example to investigate the applicability of the ECM model to the general class of time-step-oriented explicit ODE methods.

3   ECM Performance Model

The ECM performance model is an analytic performance model which predicts the number of CPU cycles required to execute a given number of loop iterations on a multi- or many-core chip. The estimation includes contributions from the in-core execution time T_{core} and the data transfer time T_{data}. T_{core} is defined as the time spent executing instructions in the core under the assumption that all data is in the L1 cache. T_{data} describes the time required to transfer all data from its location in the cache-memory hierarchy to the L1 cache. Further, the model assumes that single-core performance scales linearly with the cores until a shared bottleneck is saturated and names the core count necessary to saturate that bottleneck. This count is called the loop's *performance saturation point*.

Modern core designs consist of multiple execution units each dedicated to perform certain work: data transfer operations, arithmetic operations, etc. The model assumes that all instructions are scheduled independently to the ports of the units and that, thus, in-core execution time T_{core} is determined by the unit that takes the most cycles to execute its instructions. Besides, other architecture-specific constraints for T_{core} might apply, e.g. the four micro-op per cycle retirement limit for Intel Xeon cores. Data transfer times are initially modelled by the model as a function of bandwidth with latency effects neglected. The contributions of each level in the cache-memory hierarchy (T_{L1L2}, T_{L2L3}, T_{L3Mem}) are determined depending on the amount of transferred cache lines (CLs). T_{data} comprises all necessary data transfers in the memory hierarchy required to transfer data to the L1 cache and back. E.g., for data coming from the L3 cache and under the no-overlap hypotheses for data transfer, we get:

$$T_{\text{data}}^{\text{L3}} = T_{\text{L1L2}} + T_{\text{L2L3}}. \tag{1}$$

To obtain a prediction $T_{\text{ECM}}^{\text{level}}$ of the single core execution time, the in-core execution and data transfer times must be combined. Therefore, the ECM model determines which of the runtime contributions can overlap with each other. T_{OL} is the part of the core execution that overlaps with the data transfer time and T_{nOL} the part that does not. The in-core execution time T_{core} and the total cycle prediction for data from a particular memory level $T_{\text{ECM}}^{\text{level}}$ are defined as:

$$T_{\text{core}} = \max(T_{\text{OL}}, T_{\text{nOL}}), \tag{2}$$
$$T_{\text{ECM}}^{\text{level}} = \max(T_{\text{OL}}, T_{\text{nOL}} + T_{\text{data}}^{\text{level}}). \tag{3}$$

These predictions can be gained automatically using *kerncraft* [20], which is a loop kernel analysis and performance modelling toolkit capable of analysing loop kernels of particular codes (streaming, stencil or dense linear algebra) using predictions based on the ECM model and static code analysis. So far, *kerncraft* has been effectively applied to kernels having streaming and stencil patterns [20].

kerncraft provides its prediction by combining a parameter file describing machine characteristics and information from the loop kernel code (i.e. in-core execution cycles and data traffic between different memory hierarchies). Specific machine information (e.g. data transfer rates, cache sizes, ...) are obtained using simple benchmarks of the *likwid_bench* microbenchmarking framework [21], that are carried out once per target machine. For a given kernel, *kerncraft* automatically compiles and extracts assembly instructions which are then analyzed by the *Intel Architecture Code Analyzer* [22] to estimate the in-core execution cycles (T_{OL}, T_{nOL}). *kerncraft* provides two options to analyze the data traffic: (a) *SIM* mode (b) *LC* mode. *SIM* mode is a general mode that is applicable to all *kerncraft*-capable kernels. In this mode a cache-simulator is used to count accesses, misses and hits occurring within different cache hierarchies. The *LC* mode can only be used with relatively simple kernels and basically works on analytical models and layer condition estimates [11].

In this work, we apply *kerncraft* to a group of more complex loop kernels: explicit ODE methods. Compared to the kernels evaluated previously, our codes consist of not perfectly nested loops and may contain conditions (depending on the ODE to be solved). As this is not supported by the used version of *kerncraft* (0.6.4), simplifications of our codes were necessary. We limited us to simpler ODE systems (few boundary points, consistent access pattern(s) for inner points) and split our codes into several *kerncraft*-capable loop kernels. Further, we used *kerncraft*'s *SIM* mode to estimate the data traffic, since some of the kernels were too complex to be analyzed with the *LC* mode.

4   Application Example: ODE Solvers

In this paper, we consider IRK methods as a representative example of the general class of explicit ODE methods to investigate the applicability of the ECM model to this general class. Within each time step, the IRK methods exhibit a four-dimensional loop structure, which enables loop transformations, such as loop interchange, loop tiling, and loop unrolling. This leads to a potentially large number of possible implementation variants with potentially highly varying performance characteristics, depending on (a) the target hardware, (b) the ODE system to be solved, (c) the number of stages of the selected base ODE method, and (d) the selected compiler and its flags. Hence, a reliable performance model would be of great value to either directly select the best variant or to preselect a set of candidate variants for an autotuning procedure.

4.1   Computational Structure of IRK Methods

IRK methods are based on s-stage implicit RK methods [23] and belong to the class of one-step methods, i.e., in each time step t_κ, a new approximation $\boldsymbol{y}_{\kappa+1}$ is computed directly from the previous approximation $\boldsymbol{y}_\kappa$. An implicit RK method with coefficient matrix $A = (a_{ij}) \in \mathbb{R}^{s,s}$, weight vector $\boldsymbol{b} = (b_i) \in \mathbb{R}^s$, node vector $\boldsymbol{c} = (c_i) \in \mathbb{R}^s$, and order p is used as base method (*corrector method*). As initial approximation (*predictor*), we choose:

$$\boldsymbol{Y}_l^{(0)} = \boldsymbol{y}_\kappa, \quad l = 1, \ldots, s. \tag{4}$$

Then, the corrector method is applied a fixed number of $m = p - 1$ times:

$$k = 1, \ldots, m:$$

$$\boldsymbol{Y}_l^{(k)} = \boldsymbol{y}_\kappa + h_\kappa \sum_{i=1}^s a_{li} \boldsymbol{F}_i^{(k-1)}, \quad l = 1, \ldots, s \tag{5a}$$

$$\text{with } \boldsymbol{F}_i^{(k-1)} = \boldsymbol{f}(t_\kappa + c_i h_\kappa, \boldsymbol{Y}_i^{(k-1)}), \tag{5b}$$

where $\boldsymbol{f}$ is the given right-hand-side function (RHS) of the ODE system to be solved. The output approximation $\boldsymbol{y}_{\kappa+1}$ is then obtained by:

$$\boldsymbol{y}_{\kappa+1} = \boldsymbol{y}_\kappa + h_\kappa \sum_{i=1}^s b_i \boldsymbol{F}_i^{(m)}, \tag{6}$$

For efficient step size control, an error vector can be computed by:

$$\boldsymbol{e} = h_\kappa \sum_{i=1}^s b_i \left(\boldsymbol{F}_i^{(m)} - \boldsymbol{F}_i^{(m-1)} \right). \tag{7}$$

Based on the difference between the norm of $\boldsymbol{e}$ and a user-defined tolerance, time steps can be accepted or rejected, and the step size can be increased or decreased.

4.2   Selected Implementation Variants

The implementation of the computations in (5) leads to a nested four-dimensional loop structure which iterates over:

1. the corrector steps ($k = 1, \ldots, m$),
2. the argument vectors $\boldsymbol{Y}_l^{(k)}$ ($l = 1, \ldots, s$),
3. the summands of $\sum_{i=1}^s a_{li} \boldsymbol{F}_i^{(\kappa-1)}$ ($i = 1, \ldots, s$),
4. the system dimension ($j = 1, \ldots, n$).

For the development of generally applicable implementation variants, the evaluation of one component of the RHS function $f_j \left(t_\kappa + c_i h_\kappa, \boldsymbol{Y}_i^{(k-1)} \right)$ must be assumed to depend on all components of the argument vector $\boldsymbol{Y}_i^{(k-1)}$ from the previous corrector step. This requires the corrector steps to be computed one after another, i.e., the k-loop has to be the outermost loop. All other loops (l-, i-, and j-loop), however, are independent of each other and fully permutable. Thus, we can apply loop transformations such as interchange, fusion, fission and/or tiling. This also implies that IRK methods have the potential to exploit parallelism across the ODE system (j-loop) and the stages (l-loop and i-loop).

```
 1 barrier();
 2 for (l = 0; i < s; ++l) // Predictor step
 3   for (j = 0; first <= last; ++j) F[l][j] = f(j, ..., y);
 4 barrier();
 5 for (k = 0; k < m; ++k) { // Corrector steps
 6   Y = LC(F, y, A, h)
 7   barrier();
 8   for (l = 0; l < s; ++l)
 9     for (j = first; j <= last; ++j) F[l][j] = f(j, ..., Y[l]);
10   barrier(); }
11 for (i = 0; i < s; ++i) // Approximation
12   for (j = first; j <= last; ++j) dy[j] += b[i] * F[i][j];
13 for (j = first; j <= last; ++j) y[j] += h * dy[j]; // Update
```

Listing 1. Basic IRK implementation.

In this article, we consider OpenMP implementation variants written in C. All variants used focus on parallelism across the ODE system, i.e., the n equations of the ODE system are partitioned among all p threads using a blockwise distribution. Thus, each thread is assigned a block of $\approx n/p$ consecutive components. The independence of the stages is exploited, however, by reducing the number of global synchronizations (barriers) to only two per corrector step.

To explore the applicability of the ECM model, we apply the model to a specific base implementation (Listing 1). This implementation separates the linear combination of Eq. (5a) and the evaluations of the RHS functions (Eq. (5b)) into two phases and applies barrier operations to ensure that the two phases do not overlap. It uses two $s \times n$ matrices to store $F^{(k)}$ (F) and $Y^{(k)}$ (Y) and two n-vectors for the input/output approximation y (y) and the difference between the input and the output approximation $\boldsymbol{y}_{\kappa+1} - \boldsymbol{y}_{\kappa}$ (dy). In addition, one $s \times s$ matrix and two s-vectors are required for the coefficients A, $\boldsymbol{b}$, $\boldsymbol{c}$ of the corrector method. To simplify the analysis, step control is not yet considered.

As the l-loop, i-loop and j-loop are fully permutable, there are six possible implementations of the linear combination (LC(...)). Different loop permutations lead to variants with a high spatial locality and a high potential for SIMD vectorization by the compiler or to variants that enable temporal reuse of argument vector components in write operations corresponding to updates of the sum $\sum_{i=1}^{s} a_{li} \boldsymbol{F}_i^{(k-1)}$ in (5), but which also reduce the spatial locality.

5   Application of the ECM Model

We use the ECM model to derive runtime predictions θ_ϵ of the time required to execute a single time step of different variants $\epsilon \in [\text{Aijl, Ailj, Ajil, Ajli, Alij, Alji}]$ of the base implementation. In particular, we apply the *kerncraft* tool to obtain θ_ϵ. Therefore, ϵ is split into several smaller loop kernels that are then analysed with *kerncraft*.

The used version of *kerncraft* (0.6.4) does not support conditional statements inside loop kernels. Hence, we have to decide whether we limit the analysis to the inner points of the grid(s) of the ODE system used ignoring all boundary points or if we consider all points independently. The first approach could result in an underestimation of the prediction if the computation of the boundary points is much more expensive and the system size is not big enough to hide that. However, this approach is less time-consuming as less *kerncraft* runs are required to obtain θ_ϵ. Thus, it would be suitable for the online phase of an autotuning procedure. In contrast, the second approach might yield more accurate and reliable predictions, even for complex RHSs, but is only feasible in non time-sensitive contexts, e.g. the offline phase. A combination of both approaches is conceivable as well. In this paper, we focus on ODE systems applicable to the first approach.

5.1   Runtime Prediction

We predict the runtime θ_ϵ required to execute a single time step of an IRK implementation variant ϵ as:

$$\theta_\epsilon = \sum_\lambda \phi_\lambda + t_{sync}, \tag{8}$$

where ϕ_λ is the kernel runtime prediction of a particular loop kernel λ of ϵ. Term t_{sync} factors in the synchronization costs of the threads executed τ. The runtime prediction ϕ_λ of kernel λ is defined as:

$$\phi_\lambda = \frac{\zeta_\lambda}{f \cdot \min(\tau, \sigma_\lambda)}, \tag{9}$$

where f is the CPU frequency of the target machine, σ the saturation point of kernel λ and ζ_λ the kernel prediction of λ. The kernel prediction ζ_λ yields the number of cycles required to execute kernel λ:

$$\zeta_\lambda = \frac{\alpha_\lambda \beta_\lambda}{\delta}, \tag{10}$$

where α_λ is defined as the number of cycles required to execute one CL of data and, thus, corresponds to the result of the ECM model prediction (Eq. (3)). To obtain ζ_λ, α_λ is multiplied by the number of iterations executed β_λ and divided by the number of data elements δ fitting into one CL (e.g., eight doubles (each eight bytes) per CL on our target platforms). That division is necessary to take into consideration that α_λ is already per CL. As a simplification to our formula, we assume that δ yields the same value for all caches.

5.2   Variants ϵ of the Base Implementation

The runtime prediction θ_ϵ of a variant ϵ of the base implementation is obtained by assembling its single kernel runtime predictions ϕ_λ according to (9). Depending on the used permutation of the LC, five (jil, jli, lji) or six loop kernels (ijl, ilj, lij) are needed to model these variants. All variants differ in their *LC* kernel(s), but share the remaining kernels: *Pre, RHS, Appr, Upd*.

   In this section, we limit us to discussing variant *Alji*, whose loop kernels are described in Listings 2 to 5. The predictor step (lines 2–3 in Listing 1) is handled by kernel *Pre*, which executes a RHS-dependent number of operations in each loop iteration. In total, *Pre* comprises $\beta_{\text{Pre}} = s \cdot n$ loop iterations. The computation of the output approximation (lines 11–12) is covered by kernel *Appr* and comprises $\beta_{\text{Appr}} = s \cdot n$ iterations. The update of y (line 13) is captured by kernel *Upd*, which executes $\beta_{\text{Upd}} = n$ iterations. The k-loop over the corrector steps (lines 5–10) cannot be captured by a single kernel as its loop structure is not perfectly nested. Instead, multiple kernels need to be considered: *LC* (line 6), *RHS* (lines 8–9). Kernel *LC_lji* captures the LC required to determine the argument vector Y of the RHS function evaluation. The i-loop is unrolled and, thus, the kernel comprises only $\beta_{\text{LC\_lji}} = m \cdot s \cdot n$ iterations. Kernel *RHS* evaluates the RHS function. It executes $\beta_{\text{RHS}} = m \cdot s \cdot n$ iterations. By substituting the single kernel predictions ζ of *Alji* into our formula we get:

$$\theta_{\text{Alji}} = \frac{n}{f \cdot \delta} \Big(\frac{s \cdot \alpha_{\text{Pre}}}{\min(\tau, \sigma_{\text{Pre}})} + m \cdot s \big(\frac{\alpha_{\text{LC\_lji}}}{\min(\tau, \sigma_{\text{LC\_lji}})} + \frac{\alpha_{\text{RHS}}}{\min(\tau, \sigma_{\text{RHS}})} \big)$$
$$+ \frac{s \cdot \alpha_{\text{Appr}}}{\min(\tau, \sigma_{\text{Appr}})} + \frac{\alpha_{\text{Upd}}}{\min(\tau, \sigma_{\text{Upd}})} \Big) + t_{\text{sync}}. \tag{11}$$

Remark: When a non-perfectly nested loop is split into several kernels, a prediction error may be introduced, because the split loop structure may have a different reuse pattern. In the following experimental evaluation, we will show that this error is acceptable for our application.

```
1 for (l = 0; l < s; ++l)
2   for (j = 0; j < n; ++j) F[l][j] = f(..., y);
```

Listing 2. Loop kernel *Pre/RHS*.

```
1 for (l = 0; l < s; ++l)
2   for (j = 0; j < n; ++j) {
3     for (i = 0; i < s; ++i) Y[l][j] += A[l][i] * F[i][j]; // Unrolled
4     Y[l][j] = Y[l][j] * h + y[j]; }
```

Listing 3. Loop kernel *LC_lji*.

```
1 for (i = 0; i < s; ++i)
2   for (j = 0; j < n; ++j) dy[j] += b[i] * F[i][j];
```

Listing 4. Loop kernel *Appr*.

```
1 for (j = 0; j < n; ++j) y[j] += h * dy[j];
```

Listing 5. Loop kernel *Upd*.

6   Experimental Evaluation

In this section, we present an experimental evaluation of our prediction formula by applying it to the IRK implementation variants considered using different test problems and hardware platforms.

6.1 Experimental Setup

```
// Constants: N12
N12 * (y[j-N] + y[j-1] - 4 * y[j] + y[j+1] + y[j+N]);
```

Listing 6. Kernel code fragment of H2D.

```
// Constants: Uop, R, eta, Uthr, C
((Uop - y[j]) * R - (eta * ((y[j-1] - Uthr) * (y[j-1] - Uthr)
    - (y[j-1] - y[j] - Uthr) * (y[j-1] - y[j] - Uthr)))) / C;
```

Listing 7. Kernel code fragment of IC.

```
// Constants: dz, dz2, c
// z = (j + 1) * dz; t = (dz - 1.0) * (z - 1.0) / c;
// a = 2.0 * (z - 1.0) * t / c; b = t * t;
(a * y[j+1] - y[j-1]) / (2.0 * dz) + (y[j-1] - 2.0 * y[j] + y[j+1] * b / dz2)
    - k * y[j] * y[j+N]; // 1. PDE
- k * y[j+N] * y[j-1]; // 2. PDE
```

Listing 8. Kernel code fragments of MEDAKZO.

```
// Constants: diff
// x = y[j] ; a = y[j+N]; b = y[j+2N];
// u = (x - 0.7) * (x - 1.3); v = u / (u + 0.1);
-10000.0 * (b + x * (a + x * x)) + diff * (y[j+1] - 2.0 * x + y[j-1]); // 1. PDE
b + 0.07 * v + diff * (y[j+N+1] - 2.0 * a + y[j+N-1]); // 2. PDE
(1.0 - a * a) * b - a - 0.4 * x + 0.035 * v
    + diff * (y[j+2N+1] - 2.0 * b + y[j+2N-1]); // 3. PDE
```

Listing 9. Kernel code fragments of CUSP.

Test Problems. We consider four sparse ODE systems as test problems which exhibit different characteristics regarding their execution time (compute-bound, memory-bound, mixed behaviour) and are therefore suitable for the investigation of our prediction formula. Sparse ODE systems have the property that the runtime is less dominated by the evaluation of the RHS function (only few components need to be touched) and, thus, there is need for autotuning the LC. Most large and sparse ODE systems tend to have some regular access pattern and, thus, should be quite accurately predictable by our formula. Even if the prediction would not be as accurate for more complex sparse ODE systems, still the majority of the runtime will be spent in the LC, thus mitigating the less accurate prediction of the RHS. Listings 6 to 9 show the codes used to replace the RHS function f(...).

- **H2D** is the 2d heat equation and describes the distribution of heat in a given region over time. Its ODE system is derived from a PDE by a second order discretization on a $N \times N$ grid and has the dimension $n = N^2$. H2D is memory-bound due to the growth of its access distance N with increasing n. In the worst case, loading the required elements of $\boldsymbol{y}$ takes three single cache loads ($i - N$, $i - 1$ to $i + 1$, $i + N$).

Table 1. Overview of the target platforms considered.

Name	HSW	IVB
Microarch.	Haswell EP	Ivy-Bridge EP
CPU	Intel Xeon E5-2630 v3	Intel Xeon E5-2660 v2
Clock (GHz)	2.4 GHz	2.2 GHz
Cores(Thr.)	8(16)	10(20)
L1 cache	32 kB (data)	32 kB (data)
L2 cache	256 kB	256 kB
L3 cache	20 MB (shared)	25 MB (shared)
CL size	64 B	64 B
Instruction throughput per cycle		
LOAD/STORE	2/1	1/1/2
ADD/MUL/FMA	1/2/2	1/1/-

- **IC** is the electric circuit model of an inverter chain [24] and describes a traversing signal through a chain of N concatenated inverters. Its ODE system has the dimension $n = N$. IC is compute-bound due to the expensive DIV operation.
- **MEDAKZO** is the medical Akzo Nobel problem [25] and describes the penetration of radio-labeled antibodies into a tissue that has been infected by a tumor. Its ODE system is derived from two 1d PDEs by the method of lines and has the dimension $n = 2N$. The number of cycles required to evaluate the ODE components differs between components derived from the first (memory-bound) and second PDE (compute-bound). The implementation used first stores all N components of the first PDE followed, then all N components of the second by the second PDE's N components.
- **CUSP** combines Zeeman's "cusp catastrophe" model for the nerve impulse mechanism with the van der Pol oscillator [23]. Its ODE system is derived from three 1d PDEs and has the dimension $n = 3N$. The first PDE is memory-bound, while the other two PDEs are compute-bound. As for MEDAKZO, the implementation used stores all N components of the first PDE, then all N components of the second PDE, then all N components of the last PDE.

Hardware. The runtimes predicted by our formula are evaluated using runtime experiments on two different hardware platforms, which are described in Table 1.

- **HSW** is a Intel Xeon E5-2630 v3 2.4 GHz Haswell-EP processor with an experimentally measured load only bandwidth of 51 GB/s.
- **IVB** is a two-socket Intel Xeon E5-2660 v2 2.2 GHz IvyBridge-EP processor with ten cores per socket. The load only bandwidth per socket is 46 GB/s.

On both platforms the codes used in our experiments are compiled with the Intel C/C++ compiler and compiler flags `-O3`, `-xHost` and `-fno-alias` set.

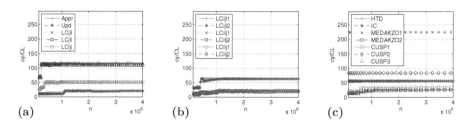

Fig. 1. Kernel predictions ζ of the loop kernels considered for varying n on HSW. (a), (b) Loop kernels *Appr*, *Upd*, *LC**. (c) Loop kernels of the RHS.

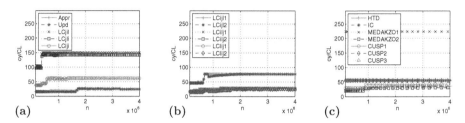

Fig. 2. Kernel predictions ζ of the loop kernels considered for varying n on IVB. (a), (b) Loop kernels *Appr*, *Upd*, *LC**. (c) Loop kernels of the RHS.

Test Configuration. We test our IRK implementation variants on a broad range of system dimensions $n = N^2$ ($N \in [400, 2000]$) using a *Radau IIA* method ($s = 4$ stages, order $p = 7$) that applies $m = 6$ corrector steps per time step.

6.2   Kernel Predictions ζ

In this section, we present the kernel predictions ζ obtained for the single loop kernels. These predictions ζ are required to assemble runtime predictions θ for combinations of different IRK implementations and test problems and are depicted for both target platforms in Figs. 1 and 2. These figures are set up as follows: (a) and (b) give predictions ζ for those loop kernels that do not contain a RHS function call `f(...)`. Specifically, this includes kernels *Appr* and *Upd* and the various LC kernels. For these kernels, ζ must be computed only once in an autotuning procedure that supports multiple test problems. (c) gives predictions ζ for the RHS kernels of the various test problems considered. Each of these figures shows the dimension n of the ODE system on the x axis and ζ in cycles per CL (cy/CL) on the y axis.

RHS-Independent Loop Kernels. Figure 1(a) gives kernel predictions ζ for *Appr* and *Upd* on HSW. A step shape is visible for both kernels, which indicates that both are bandwidth-bound. By comparing these steps with the cache limits given it can be observed that these steps approximately correspond to levels of HSW's memory hierarchy. E.g., all data of *Appr* fit into the L2 cache for small

n ($\lesssim 1.0 \cdot 10^4$), while the next step marks the range in which data is loaded from the L3 cache ($n \lesssim 4.0 \cdot 10^5$). For bigger n (some) data have to be fetched from memory and the memory bandwidth measured is taken into account as well. In this transition area it can be seen that the predictions fluctuate first. Depending on n and, thus, the amount of data fetched from memory the predicted data transfer time between the L3 cache and memory differs slightly. In Fig. 1(a) and (b) ζ is shown for the kernels of the LC. A step shape can be observed for all kernels and these steps also correspond to levels of HSW's memory hierarchy. Further, there are once more fluctuations in the transition area between the L3 cache and memory. All kernels are data-intensive on the complete range of n.

Figure 2 gives ζ for the RHS-independent kernels on IVB. All kernels again exhibit a step shape and the predictions fluctuate in the transition area. However, compared to HSW we obtain higher cy/CL values for all kernels. The main reason for this is that HSW has a higher memory and cache bandwidth than IVB. In addition, IVB's lower instruction throughput per cycle also contributes towards the fact. Further, the steps are shifted to the left due to IVB's larger L3 cache.

RHS-Dependent Loop Kernels. Figures (c) show ζ for the kernels of the different test problems on HSW (Fig. 1) and IVB (Fig. 2). The memory-bound kernels (*H2D*, *MEDAKZO2*, *CUSP1*) exhibit the step shape already seen in previous figures. However for the remaining compute-bound kernels, this characteristic curve progression is not observable, but rather a continuous course over n. In these kernels the constant share of T_{OL} dominates (3) for the range of n considered in our experiments and, thus, we obtain a constant ζ.

Reuse of Kernel Predictions. The ability to reuse already obtained kernel predictions ζ to give runtime predictions θ for new test problems or additional variants is an advantage of our prediction-based methodology compared to variant sampling. While variant sampling makes it necessary to run all newly added variants or when switching the test problem even requires to rerun all available variants, our methodology only has to provide ζ for changed or new kernels. These new ζ can then, together with the known ζ of the unchanged kernels, be used to assemble θ. E.g. when switching from H2D to IC a single *kerncraft* run to obtain ζ for IC's RHS kernel suffices, while sampling would need to rerun all six variants. Besides, prediction reuse can also be exploited when adding further variants. E.g. new variants could be derived by fusing kernels *Appr* and *Upd* (Listings 4 and 5) into a single kernel. With our methodology only an extra *kerncraft* run is needed to compute θ for these new variants.

Further, the step shape of memory-bound kernels allows to give kernel predictions for a step's complete range of n by a single *kerncraft* run. Therefore, only transition points between steps need to be identified. As these points correspond to levels of the memory hierarchy, this could be done using a kernel's working set sizes for the different levels of the memory hierarchy. For compute-bound kernels, a single *kerncraft* run suffices as the kernel prediction stays constant over n.

6.3   Quality of Runtime Prediction θ

We validate our runtime prediction θ by comparing runtimes predicted by our formula with actual runtimes measured on the target platforms. In particular, we benchmark the runtimes of the single loop kernels and use them to assemble a total runtime for each implementation variant considered as the sum of the products of the single kernel runtimes and the β values introduced by (10). We measure sequential runtimes ($\tau_{HSW} = \tau_{IVB} = 1$; $t_{sync} = 0$) with hyper-threading disabled and fixed clock speeds ($f_{HSW} = 2.4$ GHz; $f_{IVB} = 2.2$ GHz).

The obtained results are presented in Figs. 3, 4, 5, 6, 7, 8, 9 and 10. In (a) and (b), θ and the runtime composition of the kernels measured are shown, respectively. Both figures plot the system dimension n on the x axis and the normalized runtimes (time per step divided by n) on the y axis. Figure (c) shows the percentaged deviation of θ from the runtime measured.

HSW. Figure 3 depicts the quality of θ for test problem H2D on HSW. It can be observed that the ranking predicted (a) corresponds to the ranking measured (b). Implementation variants *Ajil*, *Ajli* are the most performant variants, followed by variants *Alji* and *Aijl*, with *Alij* and *Aijl* being the slowest. Except for some smaller n ($\lesssim 1.0 \cdot 10^6$), our predictions are in general too optimistic. Some deviations can be explained by fluctuations of the memory bandwidth. Our prediction formula uses a fixed predetermined bandwidth value, while this value fluctuates slightly in each run during kernel benchmarking. Further, deviations between single runs have to be factored in as well. This leads to a prediction error that is observable in (c). However, the deviations stay within a 25% range and are roughly constant for $n \gtrsim 2.0 \cdot 10^6$.

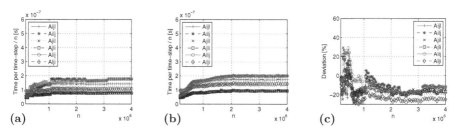

(a)   (b)   (c)

Fig. 3. Comparison of the runtime predicted with measured for varying n of H2D on HSW. (a) Predicted. (b) Measured (benchmarks). (c) Percentaged deviation.

The same ranking predicted as for H2D can be observed for IC (Fig. 4). The predictions are, however, more accurate. Besides *Aijl* and *Alij*, no variant is off more than 5% for $n \gtrsim 3.0 \cdot 10^6$. In general, the deviations stay within a 20% range for $n \gtrsim 0.5 \cdot 10^6$. Similar observations can be made for MEDAKZO (Fig. 5), where the deviations stay within a 15% range over the complete range of n. CUSP (Fig. 6) is the only test problem for which we obtain too pessimistic predictions. Yet, the ranking predicted still corresponds to the ranking measured and the predictions are not more off than for other test problems.

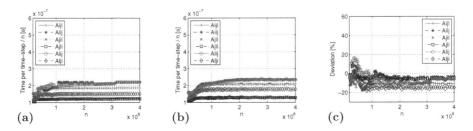

Fig. 4. Comparison of the runtime predicted with measured for varying n of IC on HSW. (a) Predicted. (b) Measured (benchmarks). (c) Percentaged deviation.

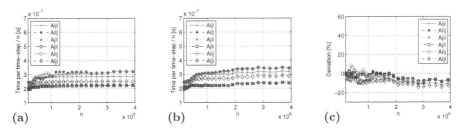

Fig. 5. Comparison of the runtime predicted with measured for varying n of MEDAKZO on HSW. (a) Predicted. (b) Measured (benchmarks). (c) Percentaged deviation.

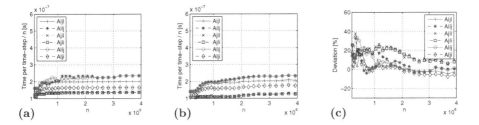

Fig. 6. Comparison of the runtime predicted with measured for varying n of CUSP on HSW. (a) Predicted. (b) Measured (benchmarks). (c) Percentaged deviation.

IVB. Figures 7, 8, 9 and 10 give the results on IVB. The same ranking predicted as on HSW can be observed. However, the prediction are in general no longer too optimistic for all variants. For H2D (Fig. 7) the predictions for variants *Alij*, *Ailj*, *Ajil*, *Ajli* are too pessimistic. Compared to the results on HSW, on IVB the predictions for H2D are more off. The deviations stay within a 20% range and are approximately constant for $n \gtrsim 2.0 \cdot 10^6$. Similar observations can be made for IC (Fig. 8), MEDAKZO (Fig. 9) and CUSP (Fig. 10). The deviation stays in a constant 20% range for $n \gtrsim 2.0 \cdot 10^6$ for IC. For the more complex test problems, our predictions are of similar quality (approximately 20% off).

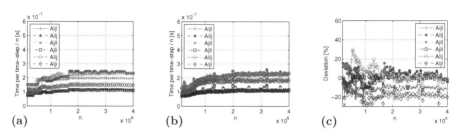

Fig. 7. Comparison of the runtime predicted with measured for varying n of H2D on IVB. (a) Predicted. (b) Measured (benchmarks). (c) Percentaged deviation.

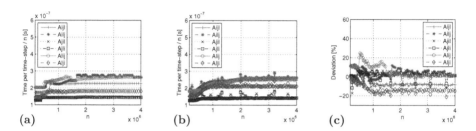

Fig. 8. Comparison of the runtime predicted with measured for varying n of IC on IVB. (a) Predicted. (b) Measured (benchmarks). (c) Percentaged deviation.

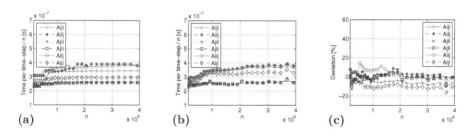

Fig. 9. Comparison of the runtime predicted with measured for varying n of MEDAKZO on IVB. (a) Predicted. (b) Measured (benchmarks). (c) Percentaged deviation.

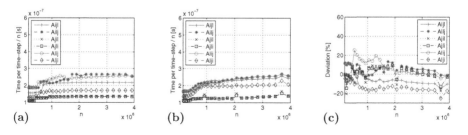

Fig. 10. Comparison of the runtime predicted with measured for varying n of CUSP on IVB. (a) Predicted. (b) Measured (benchmarks). (c) Percentaged deviation.

6.4 Quantitative Ranking of Implementation Variants

A *reliable* quantitative ranking of implementation variants can be an excellent instrument inside an autotuning approach to filter out *slow* variants during the offline phase without actually running them. However, an unreliable ranking might have the opposite effect and lead to the dismissal of performant variants or the time-consuming execution of slow variants during the online phase.

In this section we validate the quantitative ranking of variants obtained by the runtimes predicted. Therefore, we compare the runtimes predicted for the test problems given with runtimes of IRK implementation code. Measurements were done on a single socket of both target platforms using a fixed number of threads ($\tau_{HSW} = 8$; $\tau_{IVB} = 10$), fixed clock speeds ($f_{HSW} = 2.4$ GHz; $f_{IVB} = 2.2$ GHz) and hyper-threading disabled. Costs of the $2(m + 1)$ synchronizations barriers needed were benchmarked ($t_{sync\_HSW} = 9.0 \cdot 10^{-6}$ s, $t_{sync\_IVB} = 1.2 \cdot 10^{-5}$ s) on both platforms for the given number of threads.

Figures 11 and 12 show the runtime ratio of the best implementation variant to the other variants and to the obtained runtime predictions of those variants for the different test problems on both target platforms. The x axis plots the system dimensions n and the y axis the runtime ratio. A ratio >1 means that a variant is by that ratio slower than the best one, while a ratio <1 means that it is faster. Ideally, the order of the graphs of the runtimes predicted reflects the order of the graphs of the runtimes measured. If such a pattern can be observed for a combination of platform and problem we can conclude that our prediction formula gives a good quantitative ranking of the variants for that configuration.

HSW. Figure 11 gives the obtained quantitative rankings on HSW. Our prediction leads us to the correct order of variants for H2D (a) for $n \gtrsim 1.0 \cdot 10^6$ demonstrating that our quantitative ranking is applicable for that range of that configuration. However, we can not provide a reliable ranking for smaller n. The same observation can be made for IC (b), MEDAKZO (c) and CUSP (d) as well.

IVB. On IVB (Fig. 12) the same conclusions can be drawn. Our prediction can provide a reliable ranking for $n \gtrsim 1.0 \cdot 10^6$, while it fails to do so for smaller n.

Performance Loss. Figure 13 depicts the percentaged performance loss sustained by executing the predicted best variant instead of the experimentally evaluated best variant. These figures plot the system dimension n on the x axis and the percentaged performance loss on the y axis. Ideally, the performance loss is 0, i.e. our prediction selected the proper variant.

On HSW (a) the performance loss is marginal (about 1% maximum) for $n \gtrsim 2.0 \cdot 10^6$. Because runtimes and predictions of the two best variants are fairly close (Fig. 11), minor measurement inaccuracies in the small times measured can already lead to the selection of the *wrong* variant. These losses are, however, insignificant as both variants are practically equally performant. For smaller n, for which we can not provide a reliable ranking, the performance losses are considerably higher. Similar observations can be made on IVB. Here, the maximum performance loss for $n \gtrsim 1.5 \cdot 10^6$ is slightly higher than on HSW.

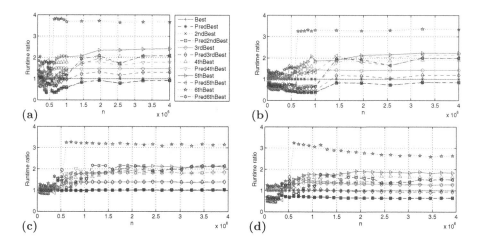

Fig. 11. Quantitative ranking of variants by the runtime ratio regarding the best variant for varying n on HSW. (a) H2D. (b) IC. (c) MEDAKZO. (d) CUSP.

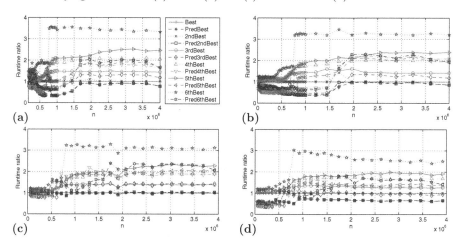

Fig. 12. Quantitative ranking of variants by the runtime ratio regarding the best variant for varying n on IVB. (a) H2D. (b) IC. (c) MEDAKZO. (d) CUSP.

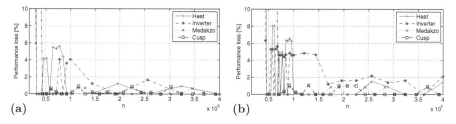

Fig. 13. Percentaged performance loss comparing the performance of the predicted best variant versus the experimentally evaluated best variant for varying n and different test problems. (a) HSW. (b) IVB.

7   Conclusion and Future Work

We have successfully applied the ECM model to a representative class of explicit ODE methods and, thus, have shown that the ECM model leads to qualitative good predictions for this kind of methods.

In particular, we have determined ECM model predictions for different implementation variants of IRK methods on different target platforms for a bandwidth-bound, a compute-bound and two mixed (bandwidth- and compute-bound) ODE systems. We have combined those predictions with a cost estimate of the synchronization mechanism of the variants and defined a formula that predicts the time required to execute a time step for a particular combination of variant, ODE system and target platform. Using the predicted times, we have been able to specify a performance ranking of the variants for each particular combination. Finally, we have validated our predictions by comparing our ranking with actual runtimes measured on different target platforms.

Our future work includes investigations of additional implementation variants of IRK methods. In particular, we want to apply our formula to more complex variants using loop tiling and pipeline-like loop structures with stepsize control. In addition, we plan to validate our predictions on additional target platforms (Intel Skylake and Intel Xeon Phi) and intend to study the accuracy of our predictions for more complex ODE systems.

Acknowledgments. This work is supported by the German Ministry of Science and Education (BMBF) under project number 01IH16012A. Discussions with Julian Hammer (RRZE) are gratefully acknowledged.

References

1. Whaley, R.C., Dongarra, J.J.: Automatically Tuned Linear Algebra Software. Technical report, University of Tennessee (1999)
2. Bilmes, J., Asanovic, K., Chin, C.W., Demmel, J.: Optimizing matrix multiply using PHiPAC: a portable high-performance, ANSI C coding methodology. In: Proceedings of the 11th International Conference on Supercomputing (ICS 1997), pp. 340–347. ACM (1997)
3. Tiwari, A., Hollingsworth, J.K.: Online adaptive code generation and tuning. In: Proceedings of the IEEE International Parallel & Distributed Processing Symposium, pp. 879–892. IEEE (2011)
4. Gerndt, M., César, E., Benkner, S. (eds.): Automatic Tuning of HPC Applications - The Periscope Tuning Framework. Shaker Verlag, Aachen (2015)
5. Hairer, E., Nørsett, S., Wanner, G.: Solving Ordinary Differential Equations I: Nonstiff Problems, 2nd edn. Springer, Heidelberg (2000). https://doi.org/10.1007/978-3-540-78862-1
6. Tikir, M.M., Hollingsworth, J.K.: Using hardware counters to automatically improve memory performance. In: Proceedings of the ACM/IEEE Conference on Supercomputing, SC 2004, p. 46. IEEE Computer Society (2004)

7. Tallent, N.R., Mellor-Crummey, J.M.: Effective performance measurement and analysis of multithreaded applications. In: Proceedings of the 14th ACM SIGPLAN Symposium on Principles and Practice Parallel Programming, PPoPP 2009, pp. 229–240. ACM (2009)
8. Williams, S., Waterman, A., Patterson, D.: Roofline: an insightful visual performance model for multicore architectures. Commun. ACM **52**(4), 65–76 (2009)
9. Tang, L., Hu, X.S., Barrett, R.F.: Perdome: a performance model for heterogeneous computing systems. In: Proceedings of the Symposium on High Performance Computing, HPC 2015, pp. 225–232. Society for Computer Simulation International (2015)
10. Treibig, J., Hager, G.: Introducing a performance model for bandwidth-limited loop kernels. In: Wyrzykowski, R., Dongarra, J., Karczewski, K., Wasniewski, J. (eds.) PPAM 2009. LNCS, vol. 6067, pp. 615–624. Springer, Heidelberg (2010). https://doi.org/10.1007/978-3-642-14390-8_64
11. Stengel, H., Treibig, J., Hager, G., Wellein, G.: Quantifying performance bottlenecks of stencil computations using the execution-cache-memory model. In: Proceedings of the 29th ACM International Conference on Supercomputing, ICS 2015, pp. 207–216. ACM (2015)
12. Luszczek, P., Gates, M., Kurzak, J., Danalis, A., Dongarra, J.: Search space generation and pruning system for autotuners. In: IEEE International Parallel Distributed Processing Symposium on Workshops, IPDPSW 2016, pp. 1545–1554, May 2016
13. Feng, W., Abdelrahman, T.S.: A sampling based strategy to automatic performance tuning of GPU programs. In: IEEE International Parallel Distributed Processing Symposium on Workshops, IPDPSW 2017, pp. 1342–1349. IEEE Computer Society, May 2017
14. Luo, Y., Tan, G., Mo, Z., Sun, N.: FAST: a fast stencil autotuning framework based on an optimal-solution space model. In: Proceedings of the 29th ACM International Conference on Supercomupting, ICS 2015, pp. 187–196. ACM, June 2015
15. Bei, Z., Yu, Z., Zhang, H., Xiong, W., Xu, C., Eeckhout, L., Feng, S.: RFHOC: a random-forest approach to auto-tuning Hadoop's configuration. IEE Trans. Parallel Distrib. Syst. **27**(5), 1470–1483 (2016)
16. Nørsett, S.P., Simonsen, H.H.: Aspects of parallel Runge-Kutta methods. In: Bellen, A., Gear, C.W., Russo, E. (eds.) Numerical Methods for Ordinary Differential Equations. LNM, vol. 1386, pp. 103–117. Springer, Heidelberg (1989). https://doi.org/10.1007/BFb0089234
17. van der Houwen, P.J., Sommeijer, B.P.: Parallel iteration of high-order Runge-Kutta methods with stepsize control. J. Comput. Appl. Math. **29**, 111–127 (1990)
18. Burrage, K.: Parallel and Sequential Methods for Ordinary Differential Equations. Oxford Science Publications, Oxford (1995)
19. Schmitt, B.A.: Peer methods with improved embedded sensitivities for parameter-dependent ODEs. J. Comput. Appl. Math. **256**, 242–253 (2014)
20. Hammer, J., Hager, G., Eitzinger, J., Wellein, G.: Automatic loop kernel analysis and performance modeling with kerncraft. In: Proceedings of the 6th International Workshop on Performance Modeling, Benchmarking, and Simulation High Performance Computing Systems, PMBS 2015, pp. 4:1–4:11. ACM (2015)
21. Treibig, J., Hager, G., Wellein, G.: LIKWID: a lightweight performance-oriented tool suite for x86 multicore environments. In: Proceedings of the 39th International Conference on Parallel Processing Workshops, ICPPW 2010, pp. 207–216. IEEE Computer Society (2010)
22. Israel, H., Gideon, S.: Intel architecture code analysis. https://software.intel.com/en-us/articles/intel-architecture-code-analyzer

23. Hairer, E., Wanner, G.: Solving Ordinary Differential Equations II: Stiff and Differential-Algebraic Problems, 2 rev. edn. Springer, Heidelberg (2002). https://doi.org/10.1007/978-3-642-05221-7
24. Bartel, A., Günther, M., Pulch, R., Rentrop, P.: Numerical techniques for different time scales in electric circuit simulation. In: Breuer, M., Durst, F., Zenger, C. (eds.) High Performance Scientific and Engineering Computing. LNCSE, vol. 21, pp. 343–360. Springer, Heidelberg (2002). https://doi.org/10.1007/978-3-642-55919-8_38
25. Mazzia, F., Magherini, C., Kierzenka, J.: Test Set for Initial Value Problem Solvers, Release 2.4, February 2008. https://archimede.dm.uniba.it/~testset/

Machine Learning Based Parallel I/O Predictive Modeling: A Case Study on Lustre File Systems

Sandeep Madireddy[✉], Prasanna Balaprakash, Philip Carns, Robert Latham, Robert Ross, Shane Snyder, and Stefan M. Wild

Mathematics and Computer Science Division, Argonne National Laboratory, 9700 South Cass Avenue, Lemont, IL 60439, USA
{smadireddy,pbalapra,carns,robl,rross,ssnyder,wild}@mcs.anl.gov

Abstract. Parallel I/O hardware and software infrastructure is a key contributor to performance variability for applications running on large-scale HPC systems. This variability confounds efforts to predict application performance for characterization, modeling, optimization, and job scheduling. We propose a modeling approach that improves predictive ability by explicitly treating the variability and by leveraging the sensitivity of application parameters on performance to group applications with similar characteristics. We develop a Gaussian process-based machine learning algorithm to model I/O performance and its variability as a function of application and file system characteristics. We demonstrate the effectiveness of the proposed approach using data collected from the Edison system at the National Energy Research Scientific Computing Center. The results show that the proposed sensitivity-based models are better at prediction when compared with application-partitioned or unpartitioned models. We highlight modeling techniques that are robust to the outliers that can occur in production parallel file systems. Using the developed metrics and modeling approach, we provide insights into the file system metrics that have a significant impact on I/O performance.

Keywords: I/O performance variability · Parallel file systems
Machine learning · Robust Gaussian process regression

1 Introduction

I/O performance variability is a critical concern on modern HPC platforms because it often leads to an overall decrease in system utilization and productivity. The ability to model I/O performance and its variability allows for more accurate prediction of application I/O performance at runtime as well as application- and system-level optimizations to proactively mitigate performance variability. I/O performance models could therefore be leveraged to make more efficient use of the I/O subsystem, a crucial shared resource on HPC systems. However, no well-established method exists for modeling I/O variability on HPC

© Springer International Publishing AG, part of Springer Nature 2018
R. Yokota et al. (Eds.): ISC High Performance 2018, LNCS 10876, pp. 184–204, 2018.
https://doi.org/10.1007/978-3-319-92040-5_10

platforms, in part because of the increasingly large-scale and complex (in terms of number of hardware and software components) I/O subsystem designs that such platforms employ.

Several approaches have been employed to address I/O performance modeling, ranging from analytical to empirical models, which lately have focused on machine learning-based approaches. Although several researchers have developed machine learning-based I/O performance models (see Sect. 5 for a summary), the critical issue of modeling performance variability has received little attention. In this paper, we develop a new modeling approach that explicitly treats I/O performance as a random variable, and we adapt a particular class of machine learning algorithms to model the I/O performance and its variability as a function of application and file system characteristics. We illustrate the effectiveness of our modeling and learning approaches with data obtained on a production Lustre file system over a five-month period. The key contributions of the paper are threefold. (1) We propose a sensitivity-based modeling approach that computes the sensitivity of application parameters on I/O performance and groups applications with similar characteristics automatically. (2) We tailor a Gaussian process model to predict I/O performance and its variability as a function of application and file system characteristics; our approach can effectively handle the outliers in the data without manual intervention and has higher predictive accuracy than out-of-the-box high-performing machine learning algorithms. (3) Using the developed model, we provide insights into the Lustre file system parameters that can explain I/O performance variability. We empirically show that the load on storage server CPUs, imbalance across the OSTs, and system-wide background reads and writes are the important factors contributing to I/O performance and its variability on an exemplar production system.

2   Modeling Methodology

The wide variety of application patterns and the significant variability in application performance evidenced on parallel file systems necessitate careful treatment of the predictive modeling of applications employing shared parallel file systems. To that end, we study three modeling approaches: global, application-based, and sensitivity-based.

In the **global modeling** approach, the I/O time ϕ on a given platform can be modeled as

$$\phi = f(\alpha, \zeta, \omega), \tag{1}$$

where α represents a set of observable parameters that describe application characteristics, ζ represents a set of observable parameters that describe file system and/or I/O characteristics, and ω represents unobservable parameters that remain unchanged and/or uncontrolled. The performance modeling problem is to find a function f that models the relationship between ϕ and the parameters (α, ζ). Given the unobservable nature of ω, we treat it as a (possibly multivariate) hidden random variable. The central idea behind this formulation is that for the same values of parameters in α and ζ, we can observe variability in ϕ; we attribute this variability to the hidden random variable ω and model its effect in f. Therefore, for a given input parameter values in (α, ζ), the function f should provide a prediction (as in any other typical modeling approaches) as well as *distributional information* (such as standard deviation, quantiles) that captures the variability in ϕ.

In the **application-based modeling** approach, for each application z we build a model as follows:

$$\phi_z = f_z(\alpha_z, \zeta_z, \omega), \tag{2}$$

where α_z and ζ_z are specific to a given application. The disadvantage of this approach is that a model built for one application may not be as generalizable to other applications.

In the **sensitivity-based modeling** approach, we build separate models based on the impact of the application parameters in α and file system parameters in ζ on ϕ. Formally, we have

$$\phi_s = f_s(\alpha_s, \zeta_s, \omega), \tag{3}$$

where $\alpha_s \subseteq \alpha$, $\zeta_s \subseteq \zeta$ denote a subset s of parameters that are selected based on some sensitivity of parameters in α, ζ on ϕ. The key idea behind this approach stems from the fact that a sensitivity-based subset results in a parameter-space and file system-space partition. Applications with similar characteristics will have similar sensitivity, and they are grouped in the same partition. In contrast to application-based modeling, the number of models does not grow with the number of applications, and a model built for a sensitivity-based subset can be generalized to another application that has similar characteristics.

The sensitivity computation is crucial to the effectiveness of the sensitivity-based models. We leverage the feature importance capability of extremely randomized trees regression (ETR), a high-performing supervised learning algorithm [12,13]. ETR builds a number of decision trees, each of which is built on a random subsample of training data. Each tree is built by recursively splitting the training data into subgroups on a subsample of training data. At any recursive step, the best split is given by the split on a parameter $p' \in (\alpha, \zeta)$ that gives the maximal reduction in output variance. These splits give rise to a tree where each parent node represents a split. Consequently, the most sensitive parameters are selected for the split in the beginning of the recursion because they produce the most variance in the output. The frequency of each parameter in the splits and the split depths are aggregated from each tree to compute the overall importance of the parameter p'.

A limitation of this approach is that when integer- or real-valued parameters emerge as the most sensitive parameters, the number of partitions can become large. Therefore, we partition only the categorical parameters; the regression models (introduced below) that build within each partition are chosen for their ability to efficiently handle sensitive numeric (i.e., noncategorical) variables.

These three modeling approaches have been motivated by the fact that I/O performance behavior of certain applications can be similar while the others can be drastically different. The global modeling approach represents the case where all application behave similarly and can be represented by using a single model. The application-based modeling approach represents the case where all applications behave differently and individual predictive models are required for each application. On the other hand, the sensitivity-based modeling approach aims to find an ideal grouping of the applications such that subset of similar applications can be represented using by a single model.

It would be interesting to consider the temporal aspect of data and use a time series-based modeling approach. However, our objective is to capture the I/O performance variability of an application (or application group) as a function of the system-wide traffic. Hence we use the modeling approaches described above. Moreover, the experiments carried out at different times (described in Sect. 3) are to capture a different system-wide traffic signature.

2.1   Gaussian Process Regression

The functional relationship described in each of the three modeling approaches can be obtained by using regression methods. Several machine learning approaches have been adopted in the literature for regression. They include the generalized linear model, support vector machines, and neural networks [4] that are designed to obtain the best function whose response matches with the experimental data, which then can be used for predictions. There are tree-based approaches such as the extremely randomized trees [12] and the eXtreme Gradient Boosting [6] which predicts the target value as an average of predictions from an ensemble of trees fit to experimental data. On the other hand, there are probabilistic methods that learn a probability distribution over possible functions where the main advantage is the principled manner of quantifying the uncertainty of knowledge about the true function based on the observed data. These methods also provide distributional estimates (e.g., probability intervals) that quantify the variability in the predictions. Gaussian process regression [4] is a popular probabilistic method widely used in literature, especially in domain where the prediction and its uncertainty are important. For this reason, we chose the Gaussian process (GP) regression as the method of preference in this work.

Gaussian processes are probability distributions over functions; see Fig. 1 for an illustration. GP regression uses training data to update a specified prior distribution in order to produce a posterior distribution from which functions can be drawn. To perform prediction at an input x, one uses the value of these functions at x to obtain a distribution (and therefore any statistic, such as mean or standard deviation).

GP regression uses a covariance form to assume that similar inputs will have similar ϕ values. In this way, training points that are near an arbitrary input x are informative about the prediction of $\phi(x)$. Because of its flexibility and generalizability, here we use a Matern family covariance function [30] parametrized by θ_f. Many popular covariance functions (e.g., exponential, Gaussian) can be derived as a special case of this family; we set the hyperparameter $\nu = 5/2$, which controls the smoothness of the resulting posterior functions.

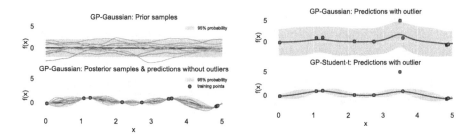

Fig. 1. Illustration of GP. First plot shows the function samples from a prior distribution (Gaussian distribution of mean and standard deviation of 0 and 1, respectively). Training forces the function samples to pass near the training data points, resulting in posterior distribution of functions and small prediction intervals near observed data. The third and fourth plots show the 95% probability interval for predictions using GP-Gaussian and Student-t in the presence of outliers.

To apply GPs to model the relationship between I/O time (ϕ) and the parameters (α, ζ) of application and file system, we reformulate Eq. 1 as

$$\phi = f(\alpha, \zeta) + \epsilon, \tag{4}$$

where ϵ represents a stochastic error term and $x = \{\alpha, \zeta\}$. Training is performed by making an assumption on the distributional form to represent ϵ in order to derive a likelihood function (parametrized by θ_l). A common choice for the distribution of ϵ (and hence the likelihood) is Gaussian, which has the benefit that the marginal likelihood (weighted average of likelihood over function distributions sampled from the prior) is available through closed-form analytical expressions. Consequently, a derivative-based mathematical optimization algorithm can be used to find the best values for the model parameters (θ_l, θ_f) that maximize the likelihood.

A limitation of the Gaussian likelihood is that it cannot effectively handle outliers (i.e., observations that deviate strongly from the rest) [11]. Such outliers occur often in I/O performance data due, for example, to failing hardware subcomponent, abnormal I/O traffic, and/or failed monitoring instrumentation. To overcome this limitation, we also consider a Student-t distribution, which has a higher probability content far away from the mean as compared to the Gaussian distribution [11].

The impact of outlier on the GP predictive distributions with Gaussian and Student-t likelihoods is illustrated in third and fourth plots in Fig. 1. The Student-t distribution is a probability distribution parametrized by a scale parameter σ, degrees of freedom (κ), and $\theta_l = \{\sigma, \kappa\}$. As $\kappa \to \infty$, the Student-t distribution approaches the Gaussian distribution. In contrast to a Gaussian distribution, the Student-t posterior distribution and the marginal likelihood distributions do not have a closed form. For this reason, we employ a variational inference method that transforms the problem of approximating the posterior into an optimization problem that seeks to minimize the Kullback-Leibler distance between the assumed distribution and the posterior [4,18]. The posterior predictive density in this case is estimated by using a weighted average of the likelihood distribution over a range of function distributions sampled from the variational distribution. This distribution cannot be computed analytically; hence a numerical integration procedure is used to evaluate it.

To calculate the median and credible intervals of this distribution, we adopt an importance nested Mont Carlo sampling-based algorithm MultiNest [10]. It is an iterative sampling algorithm that generates random samples from an arbitrary probability distribution for which direct sampling is often difficult, similar to the posterior predictive distribution in our case. These samples are used to estimate the sample median and credible intervals of predictions.

3   Data Collection and Modeling Parameters

The GP regression for various modeling approaches described in Sect. 2 requires training data. In this section, we describe the parameters in the set α, ζ and the (training) data collection methodology.

The data for this study were obtained on Edison, a Cray XC30 system at the National Energy Research Scientific Computing Center over a period of approximately five months (Feb 14 to July 11, 2017). Edison consists of 133,824 compute cores, 357 TB of memory, and a 7.56 PB disk storage on a Lustre file system. The storage is built by using Cray Sonexion 1600 Lustre appliances and consists of three file systems: Scratch 1 and 2 with 2.1 PB of storage and Scratch 3 with 3.2 PB of storage, which results in a maximum aggregate bandwidth of 168 GB/s. I/O monitoring data were continuously collected on Edison by using the methods described in [22], particularly those provided by the Darshan [28] and Lustre monitor tools (LMT) utilities. We note that the I/O monitoring data available on a given production HPC platform are dictated by capabilities provided by system vendors and facility operators and is not easily modified. Several researchers have recognized the need to integrate metrics from disparate components into a unified framework to facilitate analysis [3,22], but it is still a work in progress. Hence we utilize this particular method to collect data and then use the data to derive parameter values related to application-level I/O characteristics, system-wide file system activity, available file system capacity, and job scheduler activity.

All the application groups considered in this work involve either a standalone write or a read I/O. The timestamps corresponding to the start of the first write (read) I/O operation (T^s) and the end of the last write (read) I/O operation (T^e) for a given application are obtained from Darshan. We define the I/O time (ϕ) for an application z as $\phi_z = T_z^s - T_z^e$.

3.1   Application-Specific Parameters

Data related to two different benchmarks have been collected. They are IOR (Interleaved Or Random), a widely used I/O benchmark to measure the performance of a parallel file system [23], and HACC (Hardware Accelerated Cosmology Code), a cosmology application that generates checkpoints by using a POSIX file-per-process strategy [15].

The IOR benchmark is configured to run 8 instances (executed sequentially) that correspond to the combination of two possible options for each of the three configuration parameters shown in Table 1. The HACC benchmark uses a single motif (POSIX file-per-process), but we vary the operation type and file system options in the same manner as described for IOR. Each of the 12 total benchmark permutations is run on 128 nodes and 2,048 MPI processes, with the POSIX file-per-process instances producing 2,048 GiB of I/O and the MPI-IO instances producing 512 GiB of I/O. This configuration is similar to the one used by Lockwood et al. [22]. Each of these 12 instances is run multiple times over a five-month period. The summary statistics for their I/O time is shown in Table 2. We treat each instance as an application group; each is representative of a common production application workload on large-scale HPC systems.

Table 1. IOR benchmark configuration options

Configuration	Option 1	Option 2
I/O Motif	POSIX file per proc	MPI-IO shared file
I/O Operation	Reads	Writes
File system	Scratch 1	Scratch 2

Table 2. Application statistics

Application group	Data count	Mean	Std. dev	Application group	Data count	Mean	Std. dev
IOR-Read-Posix-Scratch1	66	60.70	30.54	IOR-Read-Posix-Scratch2	60	60.19	9.26
IOR-Read-MPIIO-Scratch1	69	55.30	30.70	IOR-Read-MPIIO-Scratch2	61	49.51	21.95
IOR-Write-Posix-Scratch1	74	67.42	6.35	IOR-Write-Posix-Scratch2	62	84.26	17.54
IOR-Write-MPIIO-Scratch1	56	61.27	70.34	IOR-Write-MPIIO-Scratch2	68	56.28	36.42
HACC-Read-Posix-Scratch1	88	57.60	6.37	HACC-Read-Posix-Scratch2	75	64.73	15.60
HACC-Write-Posix-Scratch1	74	67.50	6.54	HACC-Write-Posix-Scratch2	48	91.39	55.00

In this case, the application characteristics (categorical variables) represented by α_z are {I/O Motif, I/O Operation, Benchmark} and the file system characteristic represented by ζ_z is {File system}. Since α_z, and ζ_z are binary parameters, a particular application group has a constant value of α_z, ζ_z. For example, an IOR with file per process write I/O on scratch 1 can be represented as $\alpha_z = \{0, 1, 0\}$ and $\zeta_z = \{0\}$. Hence the application-based modeling approach needs to build 12 separate models.

3.2 File System-Specific Parameters

The data on the state of the file system are obtained from the Lustre Monitoring Tool (LMT). LMT data represent overall file system activity across time intervals without knowledge of which applications produced the I/O activity. LMT collects several counters related to the object storage servers (OSS) and meta data servers (MDS) at a 5-s granularity and reports them as a time series. The LMT measurement does not provide all information required for modeling. For example, total system-wide background read and write traffic data is not part of the LMT measurement and needs to be calculated by aggregating data from each storage server. Therefore, we define additional parameters and compute the corresponding values from the LMT measurement.

Let $T_1, \ldots, T_{n-1}$ be the LMT output time stamps between T^s and T^e for a particular application that belongs to an application group, and let Δ be the granularity of LMT measurement such that

$$T_0 \leq T^s < T_1 = T_0 + \Delta < \ldots < T_{n-1} < T^e \leq T_n.$$

For $i = 0, \ldots, n$ and $j = 1, \ldots, N_o$ (where N_o is the number of object storage targets (OSTs)), we let R_i^j and W_i^j denote, respectively, the system-wide read and write bandwidths seen by an OST j as reported by LMT at the end of interval i (i.e., at time T_i). We define the total system-wide background read and write volumes as

$$\psi_W = \Delta \sum_{j=1}^{N_o} \sum_{i=1}^{n} W_i^j - F_W, \quad \psi_R = \Delta \sum_{j=1}^{N_o} \sum_{i=1}^{n} R_i^j - F_R, \tag{5}$$

where F_W and F_R are, respectively, the aggregate data written and read by the application.

Each of the OSTs can potentially have a different contribution to the I/O performance depending on factors such as their fullness, incoming requests, and I/O scheduling policy. To characterize this variation in performance, we introduce a parameter called "lag time" (η), which is defined as the time from when the first OST drops below the threshold to the time when all the OSTs cease doing I/O above that threshold. Figure 2 shows the write bandwidth seen by all the OSTs and the corresponding lag time calculation for a particular application. We found that a threshold value of 0.1 GiB/s was appropriate for this purpose.

However, optimal threshold value in general could depend on the amount of background workload on the file system. This situation can be addressed by using tools such as *lltop*[1] that have the ability to associate the file system traffic with the application it originates from, thus increasing the reliability of the metric.

---

[1] https://github.com/jhammond/lltop.

A more informative metric would be the lag time relative to I/O time; hence we use "% lag time (η_{pct})".

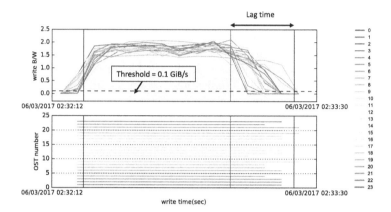

Fig. 2. Top: write bandwidth (GiB/s) as a function of time for each of the 24 OST during the runtime of a particular application. The shaded region indicates the time between the start and end of the application as reported by Darshan, and the vertical black lines indicate T^s and T^e. The horizontal dashed line indicates the threshold used to calculate the lag time. **Bottom**: The time for which each of the OST's write bandwidth is above the threshold.

Based on the thresholding, the amount of time spent by each OST doing I/O can be estimated. The OST that has the longest time (i.e., the slowest OST) is the one that defines the end of the write/read phase and hence directly affects the I/O time.

In addition, we leverage several other parameters from [22], which are described below:

Average OSS CPU Load (ν_{avg}^{C}), Maximum OSS CPU Load (ν_{max}^{C}) are given by:

$$\nu_{avg}^{C} = \frac{1}{nN_o} \sum_{j=1}^{N_o} \sum_{i=1}^{n} L_i^j, \quad \nu_{max}^{C} = \max_{i \in \{1, N_o\}, j \in \{1, n\}} L_i^j, \tag{6}$$

where L is the percentage of the time spent by the CPU cores on the individual object storage servers doing work observed at a 5-s granularity. The corresponding value for the metadata server average MDS CPU load (ν_{avg}^{M}) is defined similarly as ν_{avg}^{C}.

The fullness of an OST is known to be a contributing factor to I/O performance on Lustre file systems [22]. On Edison, the percentage fullness of each OST is recorded every fifteen minutes. The data obtained at the closest times-tamp preceding the start of the application (T^s) are used to calculate the average

% OST fullness (Γ_{avg}) and maximum % OST fullness (Γ_{max}):

$$\Gamma_{avg} = \frac{\sum_{j=1}^{N_o} D_{used}^j}{\sum_{j=1}^{N_o} D_{total}^j} \times 100, \quad \Gamma_{max} = \max_{j=1}^{N_o} \frac{D_{used}^j}{D_{total}^j} \times 100, \tag{7}$$

where D_{used}^j, D_{total}^j are the used and total disk volume, respectively, on OST j.

Several other parameters related to the metadata server were collected by using LMT and used in this study. These parameters were calculated as the aggregate over the "n" intervals in which a particular application was active. The parameters used are the number of file open operations (β_{opens}), number of file close operations (β_{closes}), number of "getattr" and "setattr" operations ($\beta_{getattr}$, $\beta_{setattr}$), number of unlink operations (β_{unlink}), number of rmdir operations (β_{rmdir}), number of rename operations (β_{rename}), and number of mkdir operations (β_{mkdir}).

The information from the job scheduler is used to identify the number of concurrent jobs that were active during the execution of a particular job of interest (N_{jobs}). Information on the different components of the OSS is also collected to make sure that there are no offline or failed-over components. The reported values at timestamp T_i for write/read bandwidth and/or CPU load is zero for a few time intervals. We discarded all jobs from our study that executed during these time intervals because they represent monitoring data loss rather than system behavior.

A subset of the file system-specific parameters is chosen for modeling by removing the parameters that provide redundant information. This analysis is done by calculating the Spearman correlation between the parameters and choosing only one among the set of parameters that have high correlation among them. The file system-specific parameters selected by using this procedure are Γ_{avg}, ν_{avg}^C, N_{jobs}, η_{pct}, ψ_W, ψ_R, ν_{avg}^M, β_{attrs}, β_{xattr}, β_{mkdirs}, β_{opens}, $\beta_{renames}$, β_{rmdirs}, and $\beta_{unlinks}$.

4   Results and Discussions

The data for different modeling approaches are obtained as follows. For the *global model*, the data from the 12 application groups are combined without the binary application parameters, which is then used to build one predictive model. The *application-based models*, consists of 12 predictive models, one for each application group. For the *sensitivity-based models*, we applied ETR on the full data to group the the categorical application and file system parameters. The resulting subgroups are shown in Fig. 3. The full data in the first level are split on the I/O motif (API) into the MPI-IO and POSIX subgroups. The corresponding box plots for the I/O time in these two groups are shown in Fig. 4. The plots show a significant difference between the I/O time between the subgroups. In the second level, the MPI-IO subgroup is not split further because none of the binary variables has high relative importance. However, the POSIX sub-group is further split into the POSIX-write and POSIX-read subgroups. In the third level,

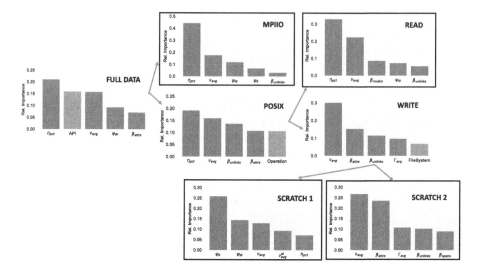

Fig. 3. Sensitivity-based modeling approach in which the data are hierarchically partitioned into subgroups based on the relative importances obtained by using extra trees regression at each level

while the POSIX-read subgroup is not split further, the POSIX-write is split on the file system into POSIX-write-scratch1 and POSIX-write-scratch2 subgroups. The partitioning approach does not progress to the next level because there are no binary variables with high importance in the subgroups at this level. In summary, the four subgroups of data obtained from ETR are MPI-IO,

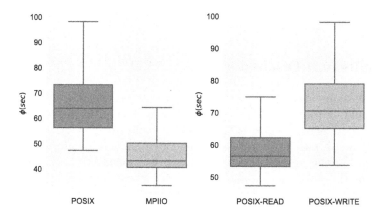

Fig. 4. Box plots for I/O time between the two subgroups obtained after splitting the data based on I/O motif (API) (left) and I/O operations (right). The plots show the median value, box with 25% and 75% quantile values as well as the whiskers that extend to 1.5 interquartile range. The outliers are not shown in the figure.

where all the application groups that were configured to run MPI-IO shared file I/O motif irrespective of other configurations or application choice; `POSIX-read`, where all the application groups that were configured to run the POSIX file-per-process I/O motif with a read I/O operation irrespective of other configurations or application choice; `POSIX-write-scratch1`, where all the application groups that were configured to run the POSIX file-per-process I/O motif with a write I/O operation which utilize the Scratch 1 file system irrespective of the application, and `POSIX-write-scratch2`, where all the application groups that were configured to run POSIX file-per-process I/O motif with a write I/O operation that utilizes the Scratch 2 file system irrespective of the application choice.

4.1   Evaluation Metrics

To evaluate the predictive accuracy of the three modeling approaches, we use k-fold cross validation. The data set is divided into k subsets; one of the subsets is used as the test set, and the other $k - 1$ subsets are put together to form a training set. We set k to 30 in order to have sufficient observations to perform statistical tests and calculate summary statistics. For each modeling approach, we compare GP with Student-t likelihood (GP-Student-t) with that of Gaussian likelihood (GP-Gaussian) in order to analyze the impact of outliers (using the implementation in GPFlow [26]). We include ETR [12] and XGBoost (XGB) regression [6] as candidates for high-performing machine learning algorithms and generalized linear regression (GLM) [4] as the baseline. An implementation of these approaches in Scikit-learn [27] was utilized for inference.

The predictive accuracy of each algorithm is evaluated using two metrics: mean squared error (MSE) and mean log posterior density (MLPD). MSE measures the mean of the squares of the errors between the target value and model prediction; thus a lower value of MSE indicates better predictive accuracy and MLPD measures the mean of the logarithm of all target value densities evaluated using the posterior predictive distribution of the model; thus a higher value of MLPD indicates better predictive accuracy. The MLPD metric is calculated for GP-Student-t, GP-Gaussian by using the posterior predictive distribution described in Sect. 2, while that for GLM is calculated by using the mean and variance of prediction evaluated after fitting the model. MLPD could not be calculated for the ETR and XGB algorithms, so they are omitted in the results discussed later in this section.

The predictive accuracy between any two algorithms was compared by using the Mann-Whitney U test [25]. This is a nonparametric statistical test used to test the hypothesis that the 30-fold cross validation results from one approach are larger (or smaller) than those in the other at a statistical significance level of 0.05.

4.2   Comparing Modeling Approaches

Table 3 shows the 5% and 95% quantiles of MSE and MLPD obtained from 30-fold cross validation. Results also include the case where the sensitivity-based

Table 3. Comparison of the predictive accuracy of the global, application-based, and sensitivity-based models using the median (5% quantile, 95% quantile) values of the MSE and MLPD error metrics obtained by using 30-fold cross-validation.

App Group	Measure	GLM	ETR	XGB	GP-Gaussian	GP-Student-T
Global	MSE	145.97(69.75,1740.88)	70.78(31.46,1538.52)	129.14(41.97,1616.71)	147.59(22.75,1885.64)	28.20(9.00,2688.67)
	MLPD	-3.91(-5.1,-3.54)	–	–	-3.69(-7.92,-3.24)	-3.11(-9.20,-2.97)
Application-based	MSE	265.13(86.26,4243.25)	75.41(15.76,1526.58)	76.04(23.15,2128.45)	70.17(14.35,1662.33)	28.26(7.19,1975.75)
	MLPD	-3.31(-4.43,-2.89)	–	–	-3.32(-121.39,-2.77)	-2.92(-10.80,-2.47)
Sensitivity-based	MSE	253.1(88.19,2673.41)	50.76(14.01,1182.13)	69.77(22.26,1361.53)	55.27 (20.71,858.42)	18.96(7.41,2096.71)
	MLPD	-3.69(-4.38,-3.3)	–	–	-3.21(-6.97,-2.84)	-2.81(-8.38,-2.55)
Sensitivity-based (no lagtime)	MSE	228.92(98.38,1773.37)	95.6(28.33,1280.67)	105.89(28.73,1461.78)	95.01(30.4,1161.2)	27.22(9.53,2267.73)
	MLPD	-3.72(-4.6,-3.39)	–	–	-3.61(-7.57,-3.13)	-3.05(-8.51,-2.77)

model is fit to the data in the subgroups but without including the lag time metric (η_{pct}) as an input parameter. This experiment is carried out because η_{pct} measures the imbalance between the OSTs, which is not a file system parameter that can be observed directly from monitoring tools and can only be calculated after the completion of a particular application run. Hence, we compare this with the other three modeling approaches in order to determine its utility.

From the median values of the MSE, for all the algorithms except GLM, we observe that the predictive accuracy for the sensitivity-based model is higher than that of the global and application-based models. The median of MSE using GP-Student-t for the sensitivity-based model is 18.96, while that of the global and application-based models are 28.20 and 28.26, respectively. The median of MLPD, shows a trend in predictive accuracy similar to that of MSE, with GP-Student-t having the best predictive accuracy among all algorithms.

For GLM, all three modeling approaches have poor performance. The predictive accuracy using median values of the MSE and MLPD of the sensitivity-based model without η_{pct} is better than the global model but worse than the sensitivity-based model with η_{pct} included. Although the accuracy degrades without η_{pct}, the sensitivity-based model obtains accuracy values that are better than those of the global model.

Table 4 shows the Mann-Whitney U Test results comparing the 30-fold CV results for the sensitivity-based model with the other two approaches. The results show that the predictive accuracy of sensitivity-based model is better than the global model using the MLPD metric for GP-Student-t but cannot be distinguished from the application-specific model at a statistical significance level of 0.05.

4.3 Comparing Learning Algorithms for Sensitivity-Based Models

Table 5 shows the median, 5%, and 95% quantiles of the two error metrics of the five different algorithms for the four subgroups MPI-IO, POSIX-read, POSIX-write-scratch1, and POSIX-write-scratch2. Table 6 shows the results of the statistical test.

We observe that GP-Student-t obtains medians of MSE and MLPD that are better than the others. For MPI-IO, the statistical test shows that the predictive

Table 4. Statistical significance using Mann-Whitney U test w.r.t sensitivity-based model (bold font indicates that the sensitivity-based model is significantly better than the respective models at a p-value of 0.05) for global and application-based models.

App Group	Measure	GLM	ETR	XGB	GP-Gaussian	GP-Student-t
Global model	MSE	9.42e−01	7.89e−02	**9.55e−03**	5.27e−02	1.89e−01
	MLPD	9.95E−01	–	–	9.99E−01	**2.91E−03**
Application-based	MSE	1.55e−01	2.645e−01	5.96e−01	5.38e−01	1.77e−01
	MLPD	**1.07E−03**	–	–	7.32E−01	5.84E−01

Table 5. Comparison of the predictive accuracy of the sensitivity-based models using the median (5% quantile, 95% quantile) values of the MSE and MLPD error metrics obtained using 30-fold cross-validation

App Group	Measure	GLM	ETR	XGB	GP-Gaussian	GP-Student-t
MPI-IO	MSE	383.07(105.08,1599.29)	98.46(17.58,2400.51)	191.16(31.77,1547.83)	89.88(25.72,2199.95)	21.67(4.00,5398.86)
	MLPD	-4.39(-5.11,-3.74)	–		-3.89(-9.12,-3.62)	-3.23(-8.39,-3.04)
POSIX-read	MSE	48.5(11.05,324.41)	15.16(3.35,601.74)	28.65(6.61,147.49)	9.79(3.31,121)	9.00(2.47,109.49)
	MLPD	-3.36(-4.3,-2.62)	–		-2.54(-4.6,-2.19)	-2.48(-4.65,-2.23)
POSIX-write-scratch1	MSE	14.72(1.96,221.43)	7.16(1.36,183.97)	13.34(2.72,173.41)	8.98(2.87,198.61)	8.32(2.54,209.74)
	MLPD	-2.76 (-4.11,-1.74)	–		-2.63(-7.67,-2.41)	-2.51(-5.86,-2.06)
POSIX-write-scratch2	MSE	184.68(48.55,10532)	43.87 (3.99,3449.99)	36.01(6.44,6116.55)	31.55(3.21,1311.98)	22.60(1.89,2514.48)
	MLPD	-4.03(-5.9,-3.36)	–		-3.71(-7.25,-2.76)	-3.09(-6.64,-2.66)

accuracy of GP-Student-t is significantly better than the other algorithms; for POSIX-read, it is significantly better than GLM, ETR, and XGB but indistinguishable from GP-Gaussian. For POSIX-write-scratch1, GP-Student-t cannot be distinguished from the rest; for POSIX-write-scratch2, GP-Student-t is significantly better than GLM but cannot be distinguished from the remaining three algorithms; for MPI-IO, GP-Student-t is significantly better than the others because this subgroup has a significant number of outliers. GP-Student-t is indistinguishable from the other algorithms for POSIX-write-scratch1 since

Table 6. Statistical significance using Mann-Whitney U test w.r.t GP-Student-t (bold font indicates that GP-Student-t is significantly better than the respective algorithm at a p-value of 0.05) for sensitivity-based models

App group	Measure	GLM	ETR	XGB	GP-Gaussian
MPI-IO	MSE	**1.79E−05**	**2.54E−03**	**1.13E−03**	**5.57E−04**
	MLPD	**1.33E−04**	–	–	**1.59E−04**
POSIX-read	MSE	**2.17E−05**	**4.27E−02**	**1.95E−02**	4.91E−01
	MLPD	**1.79E−05**	–	–	6.47E−01
POSIX-write-scratch1	MSE	1.93E−01	6.73E−01	1.93E−01	3.47E−01
	MLPD	4.43E−01	–	–	9.28E−02
POSIX-write-scratch2	MSE	**2.63E−05**	4.03E−01	2.05E−01	1.32E−01
	MLPD	**5.56E−04**	–	–	9.28E−02

this particular subgroup did not have any outliers. POSIX-read has a small number of outliers; hence the overall predictive accuracy is not significantly different from GP-Gaussian. In the case of MPI-IO, the 95% quantile value of MSE using GP-Student-t is larger than that of the other algorithms. An explanation for this is that GP-Student-t model identified a large number of outliers, in which case the error metric comparing the model prediction and the observed outliers is large. This drives the 95% quantile to larger values. A similar trend is shown by MLPD.

The GP-Student-t and GP-Gaussian models provide a probability distribution at every prediction point of interest; hence, distributional information can be calculated in addition to the point estimates (mean) at these prediction points. Figure 5 show the mean and 90% probability interval for each of the predictions as well as the comparison between the observed and predicted target values using the GP-Gaussian and the GP-Student-t algorithms, respectively, using the data from POSIX-read subgroup. For clarity, the results are shown only for subset of input parameters (that have the highest feature importances). The comparison of the prediction values and their uncertainties between GP-Gaussian and GP-Student-t (Fig. 5) show the robustness of the latter approach to the outliers in the data

4.4   Insights from Sensitivity-Based Model Using GP-Student-t

To provide insights on the impact of application and file system parameters on the I/O performance, we study their importances for each sensitivity-based subgroup. We built a predictive model for each subgroup, and analyzed the relative parameter importance for all 14 input features. The relative importances are obtained by comparing the inverse of the length scale hyperparameters (one for each parameter) in the covariance function. This is obtained after the GP-Student-t model is trained on the data [4].

The results are shown in Fig. 6(b). For the MPI-IO subgroup, the %lag time (η_{pct}) and system-wide background writes (ψ_W) emerge as the top two parameters; for POSIX-read and POSIX-write-scratch2, we observe average OSS CPU load (ν_{avg}^C) and %lag time (η_{pct}) as important parameters; For POSIX-write-scratch1, the important parameters are system-wide background reads (ψ_R) and average MDS CPU load (ν_{avg}^M).

We note that the average OSS CPU load (ν_{avg}^C) has high importance for POSIX-write-scratch1 but not for POSIX-write-scratch2. A possible reason is that there are two straggler OSTs on the scratch 2 file system that consistently end up as the ones that spend the longest time doing I/O (as shown in Fig. 6(a)). We also observe that the corresponding OSS CPUs experience maximum load at the same time. This behavior is nonexistent for the scratch 1 file system, where the OST behavior and the OSS CPU behavior are more balanced and hence the average OSS CPU load does not have high importance.

The system-wide background writes (Ψ_W) have the highest relative feature importance for MPI-IO, indicating that the background traffic is a major factor driving the I/O time variability.

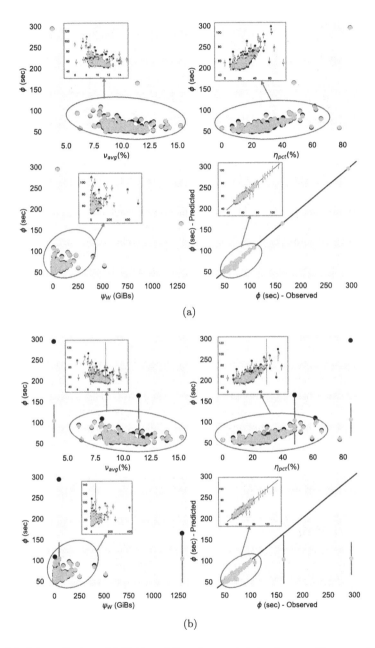

Fig. 5. Model prediction of I/O time (ϕ) and uncertainty shown with respect to average OSS CPU load (ν_{avg}), percentage lag time (η_{pct}), system-wide background writes (ψ_W), and observed I/O time for `POSIX-read` (a) using GP regression with Gaussian likelihood; (b) using GP regression with Student-t likelihood. GP-Gaussian suffers from outliers, but GP-Student-t identifies outliers and ignores them automatically.

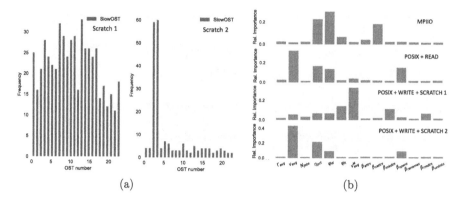

Fig. 6. (a) Histogram plot showing the frequency with which a particular OST ends up spending the longest time doing I/O when a POSIX file per process application is run on the Scratch 1 and Scratch 2 file systems; (b) relative feature importances for all the input parameters using Gaussian process regression with Student-t likelihood for `MPI-IO`, `POSIX-read`, `POSIX-write-scratch1`, and `POSIX-write-scratch2` models.

Overall, the average OSS CPU load (ν_{avg}^C), % lag time (η_{pct}), and system-wide background reads (Ψ_R) and writes (Ψ_W) emerge as important parameters. These factors are either the root causes or surrogate to another unmeasured factor. For example, %lag time is an indicator of the skewness in the OSTs, but exactly what factors caused this is unknown. Moreover, we observe that I/O time (ϕ) decreases with the increase in ν_{avg}^C, but the exact reason is not known (Fig. 5). However, the importances of the system-wide background reads and writes indicates that performance depends on other applications and interference.

We note that the relative importances and hence the most important features obtained here are specific to the sensitivity-based groups and the period in which the data was collected and hence can potentially be different for other sensitivity-groups/data combination.

5   Related Work

A common approach for I/O performance prediction is analytical modeling, where I/O experts use the system and application knowledge to develop predictive models. Lee and Katz [21] developed analytical models of disk arrays to approximate their utilization, response time, and throughput. Barker et al. [1] used analytical performance models for two applications to predict their performance for new storage system deployment. Kuo et al. [20] studied the I/O contention between applications run concurrently and developed analytical models for application runtime in the concurrent and standalone cases. Given the complexity of the state-of-the-art file systems, however, developing analytical models is often time consuming and insufficient to obtain expected predictive accuracy [7]. To address this gap, several researchers have focused on developing empirical and machine learning approaches for modeling the I/O performance. Kunkel et al. [19] used decision trees to build an I/O performance model and used it optimize ROMIO data sieving. Behzad et al. [2] developed a semi-empirical approach to model the performance of MPI-IO operations. Isaila et al. [17] combined analytical and machine learning approaches for modeling the performance of ROMIO collectives. Xie et al. [31] developed microbenchmarks to characterize storage system write performance, identified the most important input parameters, and developed machine learning-based models. In all these analytical and empirical approaches, however, the I/O performance is treated as a deterministic quantity, and the variability is not taken into account.

Yildiz et al. [32] investigated root causes of I/O interference and demonstrated that interference results from the interplay between several components in the I/O stack. Several approaches have been proposed to mitigate I/O performance variability. Dorier et al. [8], for example, proposed a middleware called Damaris, which attempts to reduce the I/O performance variability by offloading I/O to dedicated compute resources; the authors reported that this approach can achieve higher throughput compared with collective I/O and in turn successfully reduces the I/O variability. Son et al. [29] proposed to mitigate I/O performance variability by selecting an optimal set of storage servers to write data identified by runtime probing of the file system servers. Lofstead et al. [23] observed that I/O performance variability can also arise from inter application interference and proposed an approach that adaptively coordinates the inter application I/O to make a balanced use of the file system that potentially reduces variability. Dorier et al. [9] proposed a framework called CALCioM that aims to mitigate the I/O performance variability by enabling the applications to communicate with other concurrent applications to coordinate their I/O; the author demonstrated the potential of this approach to reduce contention between application and in turn reduce I/O performance variability. The I/O performance variability has also been reported and studied in the context of clustered storage system [14] and local storage stacks [5]

Inacio et al. [16] used statistical approaches to analyze the variance in I/O time. They found that the environment (system configuration) used to run the applications explained 71.02% of the performance variability, while stripe count and I/O strategy was the next major ones. However, their study did not involve any concurrent applications that cause I/O interference on a small test cluster. Supervised learning was used in our previous work [24] to analyze the relationship between application performance variability and system-wide I/O activity. All these works focus on analyzing the I/O performance variability. Here, we explicitly model and develop GP regression to capture the variability.

6   Conclusions

From the modeling perspective, we developed and studied three approaches to model the I/O performance as a function of observable parameters that describe the application and file system I/O characteristics. A particularity of the modeling approach is the explicit notion of I/O performance variability due to the presence of a multivariate random variable that describes unobservable I/O parameters.

We demonstrated that the sensitivity-based modeling approach, which leverages importance of application and file system parameters, offers significant improvements to accuracy compared with the global model. It also offers similar and in some cases better accuracy compared with the application-based model without the need for models to be generated for each application, thus making this approach more readily generalizable. From the algorithmic viewpoint, we developed robust Gaussian process regression-based predictive models that automatically reduce the effect of outliers in the data. We compared this approach with other commonly used machine learning approaches using two error metrics MSE and MLPD, which are based on point estimate and the entire probability distribution of predictions, respectively. We showed that the robust approach obtains better predictive accuracy especially in the presence of outliers.

The models developed by using the sensitivity-based approach and robust Gaussian process regression can be used to gain detailed insights into metrics that explain the I/O performance variability for each of the subgroups. This approach not only confirms that system-wide background traffic (reads and writes) are one of the major source of I/O performance variability but also provides a systematic approach to predict the I/O performance as a function of the background traffic and to quantify the uncertainty (obtain credible intervals) in the prediction. This information can assist system administrators in scheduling jobs informed by the system-wide background traffic load and can provide users with the time bounds on the expected runtime of their job. The end users can utilize this information directly: to dynamically schedule their application's checkpointing informed by the state of the file system. Application sub-groups can be scheduled/handled differently in order to optimize the I/O resources: applications with a low but constant I/O volume can be scheduled so that they do not contend with applications that produce short bursts of heavy I/O.

Although this approach is demonstrated only for a small set of applications and on a specific file system (Lustre) in this work, it can readily extended to other applications and file systems by identifying similar metrics on a different file system (as illustrated in [22]) and by creating more sensitivity-based subgroups as required.

We intend our future work to include (1) augmenting data with a diverse set of applications and I/O characteristics, run on multiple file systems, (2) developing a global model that has the robustness properties of the GP-Student-t and the predictive accuracy of sensitivity-based model, and (3) integrating the proposed approach with the I/O monitoring tools (Darshan, LMT, etc.) and providing real-time feedback.

Acknowledgment. This material is based upon work supported by the U.S. Department of Energy, Office of Science, Office of Advanced Scientific Computing Research, under Contract DE-AC02-06CH11357. This research used resources of the National Energy Research Scientific Computing Center, a DOE Office of Science User Facility supported by the Office of Science of the U.S. Department of Energy under Contract No. DE-AC02-05CH11231.

References

1. Barker, K.J., Davis, K., Kerbyson, D.J.: Performance modeling in action: performance prediction of a Cray XT4 system during upgrade. In: International Symposium on Parallel & Distributed Processing, pp. 1–8. IEEE (2009)
2. Behzad, B., Byna, S., Wild, S.M., Prabhat, M., Snir, M.: Improving parallel I/O autotuning with performance modeling. In: 23rd International Symposium on High-Performance Parallel and Distributed Computing, pp. 253–256. ACM (2014)
3. Betke, E., Kunkel, J.: Real-time I/O-monitoring of HPC applications with SIOX, elasticsearch, Grafana and FUSE. In: Kunkel, J.M., Yokota, R., Taufer, M., Shalf, J. (eds.) ISC High Performance 2017. LNCS, vol. 10524, pp. 174–186. Springer, Cham (2017). https://doi.org/10.1007/978-3-319-67630-2_15
4. Bishop, C.M.: Pattern Recognition and Machine Learning. Springer, New York (2006)
5. Cao, Z., Tarasov, V., Raman, H.P., Hildebrand, D., Zadok, E.: On the performance variation in modern storage stacks. In: FAST, pp. 329–344 (2017)
6. Chen, T., Guestrin, C.: XGBoost: a scalable tree boosting system. In: 22nd ACM SIGKDD International Conference on Knowledge Discovery and Data Mining, pp. 785–794. ACM (2016)
7. DOE-ASCR: storage systems and input/output to support extreme scale science. In: DOE Workshops on Storage Systems and Input/Output (2014)
8. Dorier, M., Antoniu, G., Cappello, F., Snir, M., Sisneros, R., Yildiz, O., Ibrahim, S., Peterka, T., Orf, L.: Damaris: addressing performance variability in data management for post-petascale simulations. ACM Trans. Parallel Comput. 3(3), 15:1–15:43 (2016)
9. Dorier, M., Antoniu, G., Ross, R., Kimpe, D., Ibrahim, S.: CALCioM: mitigating I/O interference in HPC systems through cross-application coordination. In: 28th International Parallel and Distributed Processing Symposium, pp. 155–164. IEEE (2014)
10. Feroz, F., Hobson, M., Cameron, E., Pettitt, A.: Importance nested sampling and the MultiNest algorithm. arXiv preprint arXiv:1306.2144 (2013)
11. Gelman, A., Carlin, J.B., Stern, H.S., Dunson, D.B., Vehtari, A., Rubin, D.B.: Bayesian Data Analysis, 2nd edn. CRC Press, Boca Raton (2014)
12. Geurts, P., Ernst, D., Wehenkel, L.: Extremely randomized trees. Mach. Learn. 63(1), 3–42 (2006)
13. Geurts, P., Louppe, G.: Learning to rank with extremely randomized trees. In: JMLR: Workshop and Conference Proceedings, vol. 14, pp. 49–61 (2011)
14. Gulati, A., Merchant, A., Varman, P.J.: mClock: handling throughput variability for hypervisor IO scheduling. In: 9th USENIX Conference on Operating Systems Design and Implementation, pp. 437–450. USENIX Association (2010)
15. Habib, S., Morozov, V., Finkel, H., Pope, A., Heitmann, K., Kumaran, K., Peterka, T., Insley, J., Daniel, D., Fasel, P., et al.: The universe at extreme scale: multi-petaflop sky simulation on the BG/Q. In: International Conference on High Performance Computing, Networking, Storage and Analysis, p. 4. IEEE (2012)
16. Inacio, E.C., Barbetta, P.A., Dantas, M.A.: A statistical analysis of the performance variability of read/write operations on parallel file systems. Procedia Comput. Sci. 108, 2393–2397 (2017)

17. Isaila, F., Balaprakash, P., Wild, S.M., Kimpe, D., Latham, R., Ross, R., Hovland, P.: Collective I/O tuning using analytical and machine learning models. In: International Conference on Cluster Computing, pp. 128–137. IEEE (2015)
18. Jordan, M.I., Ghahramani, Z., Jaakkola, T.S., Saul, L.K.: An introduction to variational methods for graphical models. Mach. Learn. **37**(2), 183–233 (1999)
19. Kunkel, J., Zimmer, M., Betke, E.: Predicting performance of non-contiguous I/O with machine learning. In: Kunkel, J.M., Ludwig, T. (eds.) ISC High Performance 2015. LNCS, vol. 9137, pp. 257–273. Springer, Cham (2015). https://doi.org/10.1007/978-3-319-20119-1_19
20. Kuo, C.S., Nomura, A., Matsuoka, S., Shah, A., Wolf, F., Zhukov, I.: Environment matters: how competition for I/O among applications degrades their performance. IPSJ SIG Technical report 2013-HPC-142(11), 1–7 (2013)
21. Lee, E.K., Katz, R.H.: An analytic performance model of disk arrays. In: ACM SIGMETRICS Performance Evaluation Review, vol. 21, pp. 98–109. ACM (1993)
22. Lockwood, G.K., Snyder, S., Yoo, W., Harms, K., Nault, Z., Byna, S., Carns, P., Wright, N.J.: UMAMI: a recipe for generating meaningful metrics through holistic I/O performance analysis. In: 2nd Joint International Workshop on Parallel Data Storage and Data Intensive Scalable Computing Systems (PDSW-DISCS 2017) (2017)
23. Lofstead, J., Zheng, F., Liu, Q., Klasky, S., Oldfield, R., Kordenbrock, T., Schwan, K., Wolf, M.: Managing variability in the IO performance of petascale storage systems. In: International Conference for High Performance Computing, Networking, Storage and Analysis, pp. 1–12. IEEE (2010)
24. Madireddy, S., Balaprakash, P., Carns, P., Latham, R., Ross, R., Snyder, S., Wild, S.M.: Analysis and correlation of application I/O performance and system-wide I/O activity. In: International Conference on Networking, Architecture, and Storage, pp. 1–10. IEEE (2017)
25. Mann, H.B., Whitney, D.R.: On a test of whether one of two random variables is stochastically larger than the other. Ann. Math. Stat. **18**, 50–60 (1947)
26. van der Matthews, A.G.D.G., Wilk, M., Nickson, T., Fujii, K., Boukouvalas, A., León-Villagrá, P., Ghahramani, Z., Hensman, J.: GPflow: a gaussian process library using TensorFlow. J. Mach. Learn. Res. **18**(40), 1–6 (2017)
27. Pedregosa, F., Varoquaux, G., Gramfort, A., Michel, V., Thirion, B., Grisel, O., Blondel, M., Prettenhofer, P., Weiss, R., Dubourg, V., et al.: Scikit-learn: machine learning in Python. J. Mach. Learn. Res. **12**, 2825–2830 (2011)
28. Snyder, S., Carns, P., Harms, K., Ross, R., Lockwood, G.K., Wright, N.J.: Modular HPC I/O characterization with Darshan. In: Workshop on Extreme-Scale Programming Tools (2016)
29. Son, S.W., Sehrish, S., Liao, W., Oldfield, R., Choudhary, A.: Reducing I/O variability using dynamic I/O path characterization in petascale storage systems. J. Supercomput. **73**(5), 2069–2097 (2017)
30. Stein, M.L.: Interpolation of Spatial Data: Some Theory for Kriging. Springer, New York (2012). https://doi.org/10.1007/978-1-4612-1494-6
31. Xie, B., Huang, Y., Chase, J.S., Choi, J.Y., Klasky, S., Lofstead, J., Oral, S.: Predicting output performance of a petascale supercomputer. In: 26th International Symposium on High-Performance Parallel and Distributed Computing, pp. 181–192. ACM, New York (2017)
32. Yildiz, O., Dorier, M., Ibrahim, S., Ross, R., Antoniu, G.: On the root causes of cross-application I/O interference in HPC storage systems. In: International Parallel and Distributed Processing Symposium, pp. 750–759. IEEE (2016)

Performance Optimization and Evaluation of Scalable Optoelectronics Application on Large Scale KNL Cluster

Yuta Hirokawa[1(✉)], Taisuke Boku[1,2], Mitsuharu Uemoto[2], Shunsuke A. Sato[3], and Kazuhiro Yabana[2]

[1] Graduate School of Systems and Information Engineering,
University of Tsukuba, Tsukuba, Japan
`hirokawa@hpcs.cs.tsukuba.ac.jp`
[2] Center for Computational Sciences, University of Tsukuba, Tsukuba, Japan
[3] Max Planck Institute for the Structure and Dynamics of Matter,
Hamburg, Germany

Abstract. "ARTED" is an advanced scientific code for electron dynamics simulation which has been ported to various large-scale parallel systems including the "K" Computer, the ex-fastest supercomputer in the world, and many other MPP and cluster systems.

In this paper, we describe ARTED's code optimization and performance evaluation applied to a large-scale cluster with Intel's latest many-core processor, KNL (Knights Landing), based on past research regarding porting ARTED to the KNC (Knights Corner) coprocessor. Code optimization for dominant computation has been thoroughly carried out in KNL to achieve the highest performance with detailed optimization such as memory access, vectorization for the AVX-512 instruction set, cache utilization, etc. For further tuning, we investigated various KNL-dedicated techniques such as combining MCDRAM/DDR4 memories and parallel vector summation.

After detailed performance tuning on each core to achieve up to 25% of theoretical peak in the kernel part with 3-D stencil computation, we evaluated the application performance on the full system (25 PFLOPS of theoretical peak) of the KNL cluster "Oakforest-PACS" which is the largest KNL-based cluster in the world using the Intel Omni-Path Architecture. It shows excellent weak scaling with a dominant Hamiltonian performance of up to 4 PFLOPS (16% efficiency of the system) in double precision irrespective of simulation size as well as reasonable strong scaling on material simulations requiring high degree of parallelism.

1 Introduction

The many-core architecture promises to be a new generation of high performance processors, providing a large number of cores on a chip to achieve an aggregated

© Springer International Publishing AG, part of Springer Nature 2018
R. Yokota et al. (Eds.): ISC High Performance 2018, LNCS 10876, pp. 205–225, 2018.
https://doi.org/10.1007/978-3-319-92040-5_11

performance with relatively simple control of each core rather than increasing the CPU clock frequency, and providing highly functional multiple cores to save on total power consumption of the chip to achieve a higher FLOPS-Watt ratio. Intel's Xeon Phi processor series is today's representative many-core processor and is the most currently promoted standalone self-bootable CPU using the KNL (Knights Landing) architecture based on the previous KNC (Knights Corner) coprocessor, which is implemented as an accelerator card. The performance of a KNL CPU is not solely based on the number of cores, but also by highly enhanced SIMD instructions and high bandwidth on-chip memory named MCDRAM. Therefore, when we port any scientific code, it is necessary to tune the originally developed code for the ordinary Xeon CPU to fit the architectural characteristics of KNL.

In December, 2016, the Joint Center for Advanced HPC (JCAHPC) [22], under cooperation with the University of Tsukuba and the University of Tokyo, started the full operation of the world largest-scale KNL cluster[1] called "Oakforest-PACS" with 8,208 nodes and a theoretical peak performance of 25 PFLOPS. The system ranked in sixth position of the TOP500 list on November 2016 in its first appearance, achieving a Linpack performance of 13.55 PFLOPS. Many-core architecture systems have entered a new era by utilizing the KNL CPU to provide a standalone system to replace ordinary commodity CPU clusters, especially for highly-computational and memory-bounded applications.

Studies have been conducted on the development of an electron dynamics simulation code, named "ARTED", for use in various large-scale parallel systems including the "K" Computer [20], which was the world's fastest supercomputer with a theoretical peak performance of 10 PFLOPS. The purpose of the application is to enhance research progress in optoelectronics, which is at the frontier of computational science. The application contributes to optical material sciences under international collaboration allowing atto-second (10^{-18} s) time-scale simulations for identifying the ultra-fast dynamics of an electron [17,18].

By implementing the application on the latest supercomputers, we expect that users will be able to study material sciences with high-resolution and fine-grained time-scale simulations. To achieve the much higher performance required for the next generation of material sciences, the ARTED code was optimized specifically for large-scale heterogeneous accelerated clusters with the KNC coprocessor [16].

As a novel contribution to the research fields for the application, our purpose in this paper is to achieve the best performance on a many-core based standalone cluster based on KNL. The remainder of this paper is structured as follows. First, we describe related work in Sect. 2, and then introduce the overview of our target code ARTED in Sect. 3. Section 4 introduces our target system Oakforest-PACS. Section 5 briefly introduces the application porting on KNL from a KNC-based system, and we evaluate the performance. After describing additional performance tuning for KNL in Sect. 6, its performance is evaluated and discussed

---

[1] There are several larger KNL-based MPPs such as the Cray XC40 series; however Oakforest-PACS is still the largest cluster.

on the full configuration of the Oakforest-PACS system in Sect. 7. Finally, we conclude the paper in Sect. 8.

2   Related Work

As an open source software based on ab-initio TDDFT (Time-Dependent Density Functional Theory), OCTPUS [3, 24] has been widely utilized. It incorporates parallelization by dividing the spatial region as well as the orbitals. Using OCTOPUS, calculations of a system composed of 4,096 compute nodes (16,384 processor cores) using BlueGene/P at the Rechenzentrum Garching Academie of the Max Planck Society, Germany, have been reported [3]. "GCEED" is another real-time real-space DFT code which has been reported using large-scale computations of up to 7,920 compute nodes (63,360 processor cores) on the K Computer [4]. As another challenge for a large-scale simulation, Sequoia BlueGene/Q at LLNL recorded an actual performance of approximately 8.75 PFLOPS using 98,304 compute nodes (1,572,864 processor cores) [5]. These studies present the performance of multi-core processors with up to 16 cores per node.

NERSC reported a performance evaluation with the KNL processor on 15 real applications [6]. The application performance bounds MCDRAM memory bandwidth by straightforward porting to KNL from Xeon codes. In several applications, OpenMP overhead degrades the performance, so they improved the OpenMP parallelized codes. TACC reported the performance evaluation of two mini-application suites and two real applications under KNL [7]. KNL provides a four-mesh network mode on a chip; however, they claimed that the performances differed slightly with different network modes. [8] evaluated 4-D stencil computation performance in the "Wilson-Dslash operator" of lattice quantum chromodynamics. The study achieved up to 505 GFLOPS performance under MCDRAM with four threads per core, and the kernel achieved 221 GB/s bandwidth. [9] proposed temporal wave-front tiling for stencil computation that is an extended algorithm of temporal blocking. They achieved approximately 800 GFLOPS for 3-D stencil computation under cache-mode with the proposed algorithm regardless of MCDRAM capacity limit.

The KNL stand-alone cluster system is 0.16 Byte/FLOP with the actual bandwidth of MCDRAM, while the K Computer provides well-balanced computing resources at 0.5 Byte/FLOP with the theoretical bandwidth of DRAM. Therefore, achievable performance under a many-core system is much lower than the traditional multi-core system. The KNL system achieved insufficient performance in the latest high-performance Linpack results [23] in spite of computing bottlenecks, where "Trinity" at LANL, "Cori" at LBNL, and Oakforest-PACS, achieved approximately 32%, 50%, and 54% efficiency of theoretical peak performance, respectively. As a novel contribution to the research fields for the application, our biggest challenge in this paper is to achieve the best performance for a world-class KNL system considering the large difference between theoretical and actual performance.

3   ARTED: Electron Dynamics Simulator

3.1   Overview

The ARTED simulator is a simulation program that describes electron dynamics in matters induced by a pulsed electric field based on ab-initio TDDFT. The program was developed at the Center for Computational Sciences, University of Tsukuba [1], has already been released as open-source software, and the entire implementation has been published at [25][2].

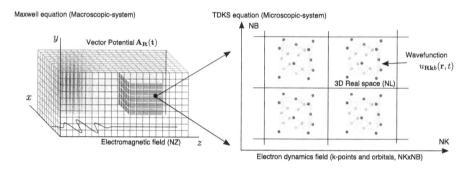

Fig. 1. ARTED computation fields (3-D Maxwell + 3-D TDKS equation)

ARTED targets light-matter interactions, in particular ultrafast phenomena induced by laser pulses that are one of the current topics in optical science. ARTED has two simulation modes: "single-cell" and "multi-scale". The single-cell mode treats electron dynamics in a unit cell of crystalline solids solving the TDKS (Time-Dependent Kohn-Sham) equation, a basic equation of TDDFT. This calculation may be carried out on small computer clusters. The multi-scale mode treats coupled dynamics of light electromagnetic fields and electron dynamics simultaneously. The former is described by Maxwell's equation while the latter is by the TDKS equation which requires large-scale parallel systems such as the K Computer. In this paper, we evaluate the performance of multi-scale simulations on a large-scale KNL cluster.

Figure 1 shows the multi-scale model and coordinate system. The electromagnetic fields of the pulsed light are described by a vector potential $\mathbf{A_R}(t)$ that satisfies Maxwell's equation,

$$\frac{1}{c^2}\frac{d^2}{dt^2}\mathbf{A_R}(t) + \nabla_\mathbf{R} \times \nabla_\mathbf{R} \times \mathbf{A_R}(t) = -\frac{4\pi e}{c}\mathbf{J_R}(\{u_{\mathbf{R}kb}\};t), \qquad (1)$$

where $\mathbf{J_R}(\{u_{\mathbf{R}kb}\};t)$ is the electric current that is calculated from the Bloch orbitals $u_{\mathbf{R}kb}(\mathbf{r},t)$ as described below. Maxwell's equation is solved using the

---

[2] Currently, an open-source optoelectronics application package named "SALMON" [26] is partly based on ARTED.

FDTD (Finite Difference Time-Domain) method, preparing a three-dimensional Cartesian grid system for the macroscopic coordinate $\mathbf{R}$, as shown in the left-part of Fig. 1.

In microscopic (less than nanometer) scale, electron dynamics is described by TDDFT. At each macroscopic grid point $\mathbf{R}$, we prepare Kohn-Sham (Bloch) orbitals, $u_{\mathbf{R}kb}(\mathbf{r}, t)$, which describe electron dynamics in a unit cell of a crystalline solid. As the typical optical wavelength is much longer than the typical spatial scale of electron dynamics, we assume that the electronic system at each macroscopic grid point $\mathbf{R}$ may be treated as infinitely periodic. The TDKS equation for Bloch orbitals $u_{\mathbf{R}kb}(\mathbf{r}, t)$ is given by

$$i\hbar\frac{\partial}{\partial t}u_{\mathbf{R}kb}(\mathbf{r}, t) = h_{\mathbf{R}}^{KS}(\mathbf{r}, t)u_{\mathbf{R}kb}(\mathbf{r}, t), \tag{2}$$

where the coordinate $\mathbf{r}$ describes microscopic motion of electrons in a unit cell, $\mathbf{k}$ is the crystalline wave number, and b is the orbital index. $h_{\mathbf{R}}^{KS}$ is the Kohn-Sham Hamiltonian operator given by

$$h_{\mathbf{R}}^{KS}(\mathbf{r}, t) = -\frac{\hbar^2}{2m}\left\{\nabla_{\mathbf{r}} + i\mathbf{k} + \frac{ie}{\hbar c}\mathbf{A}_{\mathbf{R}}(t)\right\}^2 + V_{\mathbf{R}}(\mathbf{r}, t). \tag{3}$$

We solve the TDKS equation using a three-dimensional Cartesian grid for $\mathbf{r}$, as shown in the right-part of Fig. 1. We solve Eqs. (1) and (2) simultaneously for a given initial condition where the electronic system at each $\mathbf{R}$ grid point is prepared in the ground state. An incident light wave, which is described by the vector potential $\mathbf{A}_{\mathbf{R}}(t)$, is set in a vacuum region at the initial time.

We call this scheme the Maxwell-TDDFT multi-scale simulation. Because microscopic electron dynamics calculations must be carried out at a number of macroscopic grid points $\mathbf{R}$ simultaneously, the calculation is large-scale even for a one-dimensional problem in coordinate $\mathbf{R}$. We here report on 2-D Maxwell and 3-D TDDFT simulations.

The computation of a single wave-space domain involves fitting to a single node for both performance and memory capacity. 3-D stencil computation is applied to every wave band, and a sufficient degree of parallelism is obtained in total. Actually, we do not apply domain decomposition for a 3-D stencil computation to avoid communication overhead in the halo region. A stencil computation arises by operating a Hamiltonian of the wave function. The number of time steps in the time-development loop is quite large, within the range of 10,000–100,000 steps depending on the required time-scale [2], and optimization of the stencil computation is the most crucial in this code. ARTED is a suitable application for large-scale parallel systems because the communication time scale is in microseconds while the computation time scale is in milliseconds, as described in Sect. 6.2

3.2 Implementation and Parallelization

ARTED has four parameters related to computational complexity: a macroscopic grid point, Bloch wave number $\mathbf{k}$, band number, and space lattice for representing the wave function of electrons. A wave function is represented by an array of (NZ, NK, NB, NLx, NLy, NLz). NZ denotes the number of macroscopic grid points, NK denotes the Bloch wave number k, NB denotes the size of the band, and (NLx, NLy, NLz) denote the size of the three-dimensional space lattice. The total size of a 3-D space is also denoted as NL ($=$NLx $\times$ NLy $\times$ NLz). The electron dynamics field (TDKS equation) is modeled by a three-dimensional array (NK, NB, NL). NZ indicates the size of the electromagnetic field (Maxwell equation), and it relates only to a weak scaling performance.

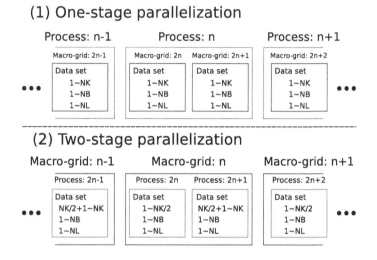

Fig. 2. Parallelization scheme

In multi-scale simulation, we consider how to parallelize the computation in a hybrid manner using MPI and OpenMP as shown in Fig. 2. If the size of the TDKS equation fits a single node resource (especially memory capacity and computation performance), we can select a simple parallelization scheme, that is, MPI distribution is applied to the Maxwell equation only. This scheme is called "one-stage parallelization" as shown in Fig. 2.-(1), and it computes the closed TDKS equation on a node and communication requires only the Maxwell equation. Otherwise, we should apply MPI distribution to both Maxwell and TDKS equations. This scheme is called "two-stage parallelization" as shown in Fig. 2.-(2), and computes a TDKS equation by multi-node using an MPI sub-communicator; therefore communication is required in both stages. A single node has a macroscopic grid point (a single TDKS equation) when executing with two-stage parallelization.

In one-stage parallelization, a node has one or more macroscopic grid points and it solves a large number of TDKS equations. In a TDKS equation with two-stage parallelization, only the Bloch wave number k (NK) is distributed to processes using MPI because this is the largest parameter for the computation domain; note that which of the two methods to use depends on the physical target material.

The domain with $NK/NP \times NB$ is then parallelized by OpenMP threads, where NP denotes the number of MPI processes. Each MPI process computes the space domain (NL) with the amount of $NK/NP \times NB$. The time-development on a stencil computation is then executed iteratively. Here, the most important aspect is that we do not apply domain decomposition on the space, which is the most popular parallelization in ordinary stencil computation. The space domain size (NL) is relatively small compared with the wave counts (NK and NB), and thus it is inefficient to distribute it to multiple threads or processes. As a result, there is no data exchange for a 3-D space lattice in the halo region. Each OpenMP thread computes a space lattice (NL) independently and sequentially. Hence, the degree of parallelism of stencil computation in an OpenMP thread is $NK/NP \times NB$. This hybrid parallelization minimizes the communication and synchronization overhead because we can compute the Bloch wave number and wave bands independently in a single time step. Therefore, we can focus on the optimization of the many-core processors for the sequential computation in a thread and for OpenMP thread scheduling.

A space lattice of the computation field is represented by a double-precision complex (double-complex) value, and it computes a 25-point stencil with a periodic boundary condition on the Hamiltonian computation. Here, the memory bandwidth requested is 2.68 Byte/FLOP without cache utilization. Therefore, the performance is strongly bounded by the memory bandwidth, and the cache hit ratio is critical for performance improvement.

4   Evaluation Environment: KNL Cluster Oakforest-PACS

The KNL cluster Oakforest-PACS appeared on the TOP500 List in November 2016 (first-time entry) where it was ranked No. 6 in the world and No. 1 in Japan [23]. It provides 25 PFLOPS of theoretical peak performance in double precision FP as well as 13.55 PFLOPS of Linpack performance, exceeding that of the K Computer, the former fastest Japanese supercomputer. It employs the KNL processor as the CPU of a computation node and is also equipped with Intel's Omni-Path Architecture as the interconnection network. On December 2016, the JCAHPC [22] cooperating with the University of Tsukuba and the University of Tokyo began the test-running phase with full system size, and official operations began on April 2017.

As a generic KNL-based PC cluster system, Oakforest-PACS is the largest system in the world. The system is implemented by Fujitsu Co. Ltd. with an originally designed mother board and high-density chassis. Each node is equipped with a single socket of the Intel Xeon Phi 7250 (KNL) with 3.05 TFLOPS of peak performance, and the number of nodes is 8,208. Table 1 lists the basic specifications of the system.

In this paper, we utilize up to 8,192 nodes, which correspond to 99.8% of the full system size. ARTED is one of the largest-scale real applications on

Table 1. Basic specification of Oakforest-PACS system

CPU	Intel Xeon Phi 7250 with 68 cores, 1.4 GHz base clock
# of nodes	8,208
Memory	16 GB of MCDRAM and 96 GB of DDR4-2400
Actual bandwidth	490+ GB/s of MCDRAM, 90+ GB/s of DDR4-2400
Chip configuration	Quadrant with Flat or Cache memory mode
Interconnect	Intel Omni-Path Architecture with 100 Gbps link
Network topology	Full bisection bandwidth of Fat-Tree
File system	Lustre with 26 PB by DDN SFA7700X, 500 GB/s bandwidth
File cache	Burst Buffer with 940 TB by DDN IME14K, 1,560 GB/s bandwidth
Cooling	Water colling for CPU and Air cooling for others
Power consumption	Max.: 4.2 MW (including cooling)
Operating system	CentOS 7 and McKernel (developed by RIKEN)

Oakforest-PACS so far. To exploit real scientific results through this challenge, we run multiple jobs on this system size, and the longest job execution time is approximately 8 h. The file I/O request of the ARTED code is quite small so we did not rely on the Burst Buffer feature.

We evaluate the performance with two materials using multi-scale simulation as shown in Table 2, computing different parallelization models. The data sets are provided from real simulation problems of the actual target materials, which are scientifically important. These simulations contribute to the laser processing of materials [19]; the interaction between an ultra-short pulse laser and a thin film of silicon or graphite. Regarding the performance evaluation, we choose the data sets that are possible to run only on the full-system Oakforest-PACS to

Table 2. Evaluated materials

	Graphite	Silicon
MPI procs/macro-grid	8	–
Macro-grids/MPI proc	–	1–4
Total # of macro-grid (NZ)	1,024	32,768
# of wave count (NK × NB)	$7,928 \times 16$	$8^3 \times 16$
Size of 3-D real-space (NL)	$26 \times 16 \times 16$	16^3

contribute to real computational material sciences. Graphite is computed using two-stage parallelization with 8 MPI processes per macroscopic grid point. One-stage parallelization is applied to the silicon simulation, and we evaluate 1–4 macroscopic grid points per MPI process.

5   Porting to KNL

A study on porting the ARTED code to the first-generation Intel Xeon Phi many-core coprocessor, KNC, is described in [16] as our previous study. In this section, we discuss this work briefly to clarify the study presented in this paper. Then we introduce additional tuning at the core-level followed by a performance comparison at the chip-level.

5.1   Summary of Tuning for KNC

A 25-point stencil computation was implemented using explicit vectorization of the C-language ("Explicit" vectorized) for the KNC accelerator processor after optimizing the automatic vectorization of the Fortran90 compiler ("Compiler" vectorized). In particular, the Z-dimension (unit-stride) memory access should be optimized to decrease the memory pressure. An `alignr` instruction (concatenated shift) is used for implementation of unit-stride memory access without `gather` because the instruction performance is very low in each processor [10]. This implementation updates four grid points to fit to the SIMD operation length. Our approach is optimized to a periodic boundary condition based on Intel's report [11]. Whereas [11] avoids a periodic boundary condition, [16] covers both situations (with and without such condition).

The index calculation for a periodic boundary condition requires an integer remainder operation, and performance is degraded by this operation because this instruction on Xeon Phi processors is extremely slow compared with the Xeon CPU. When a field size is a power of 2, we can replace this operation with a logical AND instruction. The KNC performance of a stencil computation with a remainder operation is only 65% of a logical AND for a masking operation. With Explicit vectorization, we apply a table lookup instead of a remainder operation to avoid limiting the size to a power of 2. This method is slower than a logical AND, but it is still faster than using a remainder operation.

5.2   Converting to AVX-512 from IMCI

Our code has already been vectorized with IMCI (Initial Many-Core Instruction) to achieve high performance on KNC. We will tune the code for higher performance on both KNC and KNL considering the execution latency, register utilization, etc. The computation environment such as L1 cache size and SIMD length is the same between KNC and KNL. Here we focus on the conversion of the IMCI vectorized code into the AVX-512 instruction set, which is provided with KNL, Skylake-SP, and later Intel CPUs. The instruction format, such as four arithmetic operations, is basically the same in both IMCI and AVX-512 except for shuffle, permute, and other special instructions. In the unaligned load instruction, whereas IMCI requires two instructions be sent between cache lines, AVX-512 only issues one instruction as like as AVX. Our implementation requires that a few instructions and operations be replaced for execution under AVX-512 with 5–10 lines of inline functions.

```
#ifdef __AVX512F__
/* Intrinsics for KNL and AVX-512 processors */
#define _mm512_storenrngo_pd _mm512_stream_pd
#elif __MIC__
/* Intrinsics for KNC */
inline __m512i _mm512_loadu_si512(int const* v) {
  __m512i w = _mm512_loadunpacklo_epi32(w, v + 0);
  return     _mm512_loadunpackhi_epi32(w, v + 16);
}
#endif
```

Fig. 3. Schematic of code conversion to AVX-512 from IMCI with preprocessor

These modifications can be made easily with preprocessor directives as shown in Fig. 3. This figure shows an example of replacing the non-temporal store instruction and unaligned load instruction with preprocessor directives. The __AVX512__ or __MIC__ macro symbol is defined by the compiler when compiling for AVX-512 provided processors or KNC, respectively. Our explicit vectorization code for KNL is implemented based on KNC-optimized code with applied preprocessor directives, and we further optimized it for KNL. An AVX-512 instruction set consists of several separate subsets and some generations of processors do not support all subsets. Our implementation only requires a common subset (named the AVX-512F instruction set), which is supported by all types of processors that include the AVX-512 feature.

In our target system, it is recommended to use 64 cores per node because Xeon Phi 7250 enables 34 Tiles (1 Tile = 1 pair of cores) out of 36 total Tiles for a total core count of 68 [14]. It is desirable to maintain four cores in reserve to support the operating system, interrupt handling, etc. Additionally, our target system is equipped with the tickless-kernel which provides no OS interruption to cores except for core 0. We think that execution with up to 64 cores is the best practice because of cache pollution of the L2 cache, which is shared by each Tile, and because a number with power of 2 is easy to understand and handle.

5.3   Additional Optimization and Performance Comparison

Table 3 shows the performance impact of hyper-threading technology under KNL for the single-cell simulation of silicon. We constantly set the number of OpenMP threads per KNL as 256 (four threads per core) which is always achievable to provide the best performance in our application based on pre-evaluations. KNC always takes 240 OpenMP threads (four threads per core with 60 cores) in the same manner. The entire computation (time-development part) has the low run-to-run deviation of less than 3% regardless of the number of compute nodes. Therefore, we show the fastest case of results in all performance evaluation.

Table 3. Performance impact of KNL hyper-threading

Threads/core	Total threads	Rel. performance
1	64	1.00
2	128	2.06
3	192	2.91
4	256	3.44

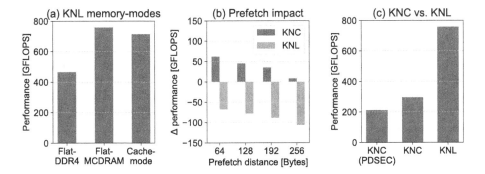

Fig. 4. Performance results of the stencil computation (fastest case)

Initially, we evaluate the stencil computation performance on KNL with various memory modes as shown in Fig. 4-(a) when executing the single-cell mode with silicon material. KNL provides three configurations for MCDRAM (high bandwidth, small capacity) and DDR4 memory (low bandwidth, large capacity): Flat-mode (separates as NUMA memory), Cache-mode (MCDRAM is the last-level cache) and Hybrid-mode (MCDRAM is divided into NUMA memory and last-level cache). For maximizing the memory bandwidth, we should combine MCDRAM and DDR4; however, controlling data placement is extremely complicated. If the data size per node is less than the MCDRAM capacity, we believe that it is the best to use MCDRAM only.

In Fig. 4-(a), the Flat-MCDRAM case allocates all of the application data to MCDRAM, whereas the Flat-DDR4 case uses only DDR4 memory and MCDRAM is not used in the application. When the data size fits to MCDRAM capacity, even cache-mode is expected to achieve a performance comparable with that of Flat-MCDRAM[3].

---

[3] This is not exactly correct, as MCDRAM is used for the direct-map cache in cache-mode, where line conflicts between different arrays may occur.

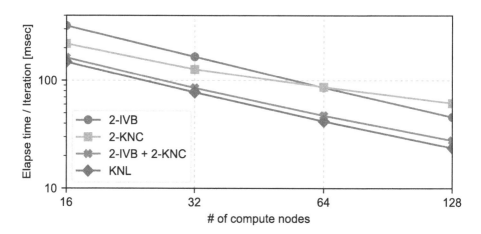

Fig. 5. Strong scaling evaluation to compare KNC and KNL (fastest case)

Each thread computes a Hamiltonian using thread-local working arrays. A thread copies the working set from global arrays on MCDRAM or DDR4 before computing the Hamiltonian, which we refer to as a "domain" hereafter. A domain is small enough to fit to the L2 cache size, so that the computation is always performed in the cache. Then the performance difference between Flat-MCDRAM and Flat-DDR4 is relatively low, where the impact is caused by the memory bandwidth available to move data to the L2 cache.

For the advanced optimization, we apply software prefetch instructions on KNC and KNL. Our implementation is optimized by a spatial locality, and the data in registers are fully utilized in the computation. Here, the software prefetch instructions are issued for the required data at the next iteration after issuing a load instruction during the current iteration. A stencil domain is aligned to a 64-byte block, which is identical to the cache line size, and the code always prefetches the next cache line. Figure 4-(b) shows the software prefetch impact described by the delta performance for the silicon material. The performance in KNL is degraded by a software prefetch, whereas the KNC performance is improved by up to 60 GFLOPS. In several cases, KNL does not require the manual insertion of the software prefetch owing to the improved hardware prefetcher, an advanced feature from KNC [8]. The computation data size of silicon is 64 KB per domain and may not spill out from the L2 cache on each Tile.

We compared the performance of the case with one KNC card and one KNL processor, corresponding to the single-node performance of the COMA cluster with KNC coprocessor card [16] and Oakforest-PACS. The COMA system consists of 393 nodes, and it equips two IVB (Ivy-Bridge) Xeon E5-2670v2 CPUs and two KNC 7110P cards as accelerators on each node [21].

Figure 4-(c) shows the stencil computation performance with KNC and KNL. "KNC (PDSEC)" represents the performance of our previous implementation [16] and KNC represents our additional tuning with software prefetching and instruction-level tuning, which is 1.39x faster than previous code. KNL achieves 2.56x the performance of a KNC card. Finally, KNL achieves a performance of 758.4 GFLOPS corresponding to 24.8% of theoretical peak, which implies a large degree of thread level parallelism and relatively low sequential execution. It should be noted that the theoretical peak performance of KNL is actually impossible to reach due to frequency control by the processor itself to maintain the TDP, where the AVX-512 instructions cannot always run with 100% speed. Therefore, a sustained performance at a quarter of theoretical peak performance is very high. Because we optimized the KNL version based on the KNC-optimized code, the optimization of KNC strongly assists further optimization on KNL.

Figure 5 shows the overall performance under strong scaling for the single-cell simulation of silicon. In this comparison, a wave function array parameter is set to (NK, NB, NL) = $(24^3, 16, 4096 = (16, 16, 16))$. We show the performance comparison with up to 128 nodes only due to the available resource limit of COMA, where two KNC cards are used. On COMA, we evaluated IVB-only (Xeon only), KNC-only (through Private mode execution of KNC), and Symmetric mode execution where IVB and KNC cooperate using MPI. KNL achieves a comparable or higher performance in the Symmetric mode of two KNCs and two IVBs, and the KNC-only execution is slower than IVB-only. While KNC requires high parallelism for the application, KNL can achieve acceptable performance even with relatively low parallelism. Therefore, KNL can more easily fit traditional CPU applications than KNC.

5.4   Performance Analysis

We estimated the achievable performance using KNC and KNL based on a memory bandwidth bottleneck. Figure 6 shows a roofline model analysis with L2 cache bandwidth [15], and a dot plot shows the actual performance of KNC or KNL, respectively. Our stencil computation is strongly impacted by the L2 cache bandwidth because the domain size per two cores fits the L2 cache capacity, where silicon size is 64 KB per domain. KNL follows the roofline model, whereas KNC reaches only 70% of estimated performance.

Table 4. Profiling result with Intel VTune

Vectorization	Memory	# of Thread	Perf. [GFLOPS]	Max BW [GB/s]	SIMD Inst./Cycle	Backend Bound [%]	L2 Hit Bound [%]	L2 Miss Bound [%]
Explicit	MCDRAM	64	458.1	273.5	0.454	45.6	15.0	8.7
		128	723.9		0.335	61.5	24.3	8.0
		192	744.8		0.222	74.3	22.1	7.7
		256	772.3		0.179	80.3	30.1	11.4
	DDR4	128	417.8	83.2	0.135	80.8	12.6	6.2
Compiler	MCDRAM	256	555.3	154.2	0.161	80.0	43.8	9.6
	DDR4	128	371.2	82.7	0.158	76.4	21.6	6.1

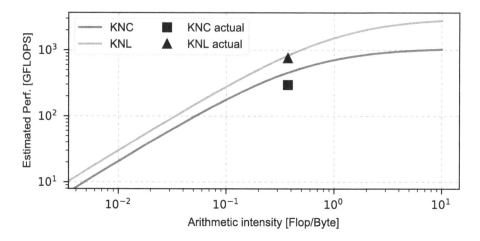

Fig. 6. Roofline analysis with L2 cache bandwidth

We profile the performance metrics under KNL with the Intel VTune profiler, as shown in Table 4. "Compiler" represents the performance of the vectorization by Intel's compiler. "Explicit" represents our explicit vectorization code based on the [16] implementation. Note that the profiling region does not match with the previous section. Hamiltonian operation includes the stencil computation and pseudo-potential (physical intuition) computation; therefore, we analyze the metrics without the physical intuition computation. An input data (stencil computation domain) size is set to 2 GB. The metrics are defined as follows:

Perf.
Computation performance. (FLOP count from the source code.)
Max BW
Maximum attained memory bandwidth.
SIMD Inst./Cycle
FPU utilization of the code.
Backend Bound
Instruction pipeline's stalled cycles.
L2 Hit Bound
Typically, L2 access latency in cycles.
L2 Miss Bound
Ratio of cycles spent handling L2 misses to all cycles.

Percentage metrics show the ratio of total execution cycles in analytical areas.

In MCDRAM memory mode, the explicit vectorization has higher SIMD execution (involving the FPUs) efficiency than the compiler vectorization; however, it does not affect the overall performance because the code is basically memory bandwidth bounded. Moreover, the explicit vectorization code attains 273.5 GB/s of bandwidth while the compiler vectorization attains only 154.2 GB/s.

L2 cache access is a considerable overhead in performance, whereas data reutilization improves performance more than the compiler vectorization. Another serious performance bottleneck is caused by the instruction pipeline stall when waiting for the completion of SIMD instructions. Hyper-threading achieves good performance of the application as shown in Table 3; however, "Backend Bound" (the number of instruction pipeline stalled cycles) becomes a dominant problem with increasing number of hyper-threads per core. We consider that this problem is caused by frequently issued SIMD operations by multiple threads that overload the physical FPU.

In conclusion, we confirmed that the most serious performance bottleneck in our implementation is caused by physical FPU overload although memory bandwidth also remains a performance problem. For additional improvement of the performance, the application requires reduction of the number of SIMD operations, the enhancement of cache reutilization, and L2 cache latency hiding.

6 Further Performance Tuning

6.1 Utilization of MCDRAM and DDR4 Memories

In Fig. 4-(a), we show the stencil computation performance on a KNL with various memory modes. The MCDRAM-only mode is the best for memory bandwidth bottlenecked applications, which maximizes the performance of real-world scientific applications. However, MCDRAM has a low 16 GB capacity on a chip, whereas DDR4 memory capacity is larger (96 GB per node). We should combine MCDRAM and DDR4 memories to fully utilize the computing resources on KNL clusters. As a simple strategy, application uses MCDRAM as a "scratch-pad cache", which is deemed as the user-handled cache-mode as follows. An application allocates all data to DDR4, and the working set data (the domain) are manually copied to MCDRAM before the computation. After completing the computation, results data in the working set are manually written back to DDR4. Explicit cache managing is a difficult problem for users because they should search for the best size of cache-block; however, the dominant computation part of our target application behaves the same as this strategy naturally using the original code.

Figure 7 shows the entire code performance when the data of a problem exceeds MCDRAM capacity. Flat-DDR4 and Flat-MCDRAM means that all data is allocated on DDR4 or MCDRAM, respectively. Flat-DDR4+MCDRAM combines DDR4 and MCDRAM to be used as main memory and a scratchpad cache, respectively. We can successfully expand the computation fields on the application to naturally move data between DDR4 and MCDRAM. Cache-mode performance is also nearly comparable with Flat-DDR4+MCDRAM because each thread computes a Hamiltonian under thread-local working memory (its domain) as described in the previous section. However, Flat-DDR4+MCDRAM performance slightly exceeds that of Cache-mode as shown in Fig. 4. We think this is because the nature of the direct-mapping feature of Cache-mode causes line conflicts.

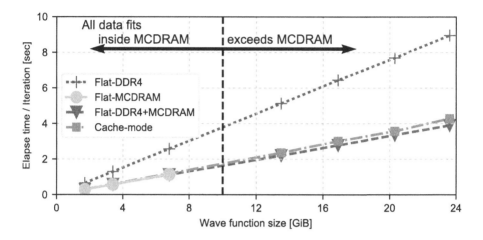

Fig. 7. Entire code performance of different memory modes (fastest case)

6.2 Parallel Vector Summation for Many-Core Processor

In the TDKS part, the code computes the electron current density for coupling using Maxwell's equation. It is performed by a vector summation using the following formula where Zu denotes the wave function:

$$il = 1, 2, \ldots, NL$$

$$rho_{il} = \sum_{ik=1}^{NK} \sum_{ib=1}^{NB} c_{ib,ik} |Zu_{il,ib,ik}|^2$$

The equation is the summation of the vectors with NL (real space domain length) over $NK \times NB$ times (the number of wave domains). Here, we consider the OpenMP parallelization strategies. The formula is very simple, but difficult to parallelize because of the dependency of the innermost loop (named "First-approach"). This parallelization causes expensive overhead by the implicit thread synchronization at the end of the innermost loop on a many-core processor, and it drastically degrades performance. From OpenMP 3.0, we can maximize the degree of parallelism combining *collapse* and *reduction* clauses (named "OpenMP-suitable"). If the *reduction* clause with a vector variable does not achieve enough performance, we can implement a manual summation into the OpenMP parallelized loop (named "Manual-summation"). In Manual-summation, we apply an algorithm based on traditional parallel binary-tree reduction [12], which is also effective on modern GPUs [13].

Figure 8 shows the performance results of vector summation with 32 KNL nodes, that is, the evaluation simulates the vector summation performance of the single-cell simulation where strong scaling is difficult to achieve. First-approach causes heavy overhead by the implicit synchronization in OpenMP. However, OpenMP-suitable achieves higher performance but saturates at 128 threads per

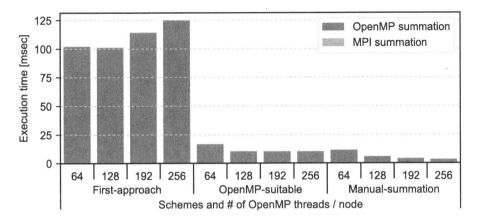

Fig. 8. Various implementation performances of parallel vector summation (fastest case)

node (2 threads per core). On the other hand, Manual-summation reduces the overhead up to 30x compared with First-approach. This result shows that the OpenMP *reduction* clause may not be optimized to a vector summation on a many-core processor. The MPI communication is negligible in the ARTED execution, so this vector summation in OpenMP parallelization is more important than MPI.

While tuning reduced the vector summation cost from the 100 to the 1 ms order, scaling of the entire code execution time is 10–100 ms per iteration, the same as First-approach, as described in the next section. This result implies that performance tuning is required in every detail of the entire code for efficient execution on a many-core processor.

7   Performance Evaluation and Discussion on the Full-System of Oakforest-PACS

Lastly, we evaluate the large-scale problem performance with the full-system of Oakforest-PACS. Table 5 shows the evaluated configuration. The application uses MCDRAM only, where DDR4 memory is used by system services such as the operating system. Our application perfectly achieves very good weak scaling, while strong scaling shows different results for silicon and graphite, as shown in Fig. 9. In the weak scaling results, the entire performance is scaled up to 4 PFLOPS with 16% of theoretical peak when executing on the full-size system with 8,192 nodes. We investigated why the performance degradation on strong scaling of graphite occurs and found that there is a 20 to 30% difference in the execution times of different computation nodes.

Figure 10 shows the variations between the fastest and slowest nodes for the same computation amount, where the breakdown shows that the Hamiltonian

Table 5. Evaluated configuration on Oakforest-PACS

# of MPI processes	1 process/node (up to 8,192 processes)
# of OpenMP threads	256 threads/process
Memory mode	Flat-mode with MCDRAM only

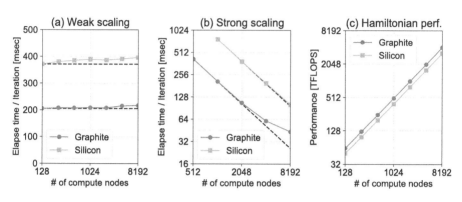

Fig. 9. Performance scaling results for the full-system of Oakforest-PACS (fastest case)

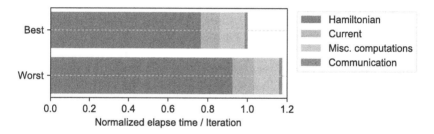

Fig. 10. Entire code breakdown with normalized elapsed time per iteration

computation time causes the dominant differences. Because all the computation nodes are synchronized at the `MPI_Allreduce` barrier, this performance difference seriously impacts the total performance of ARTED. Note that the computation load of all nodes is perfectly fair in our code.

We think that the root cause of this oddity exists in the Intel Turbo Boost mechanism for AVX-512 instructions. This technology adjusts the processor clock frequency dynamically to achieve the highest performance as long as the processor remains within its TDP limit under current temperature. It is known that when using KNL, it is difficult to remain within the TDP limit when AVX-512 instructions are operated continuously, which may reduce the clock frequency automatically according to the computation load and processor temperature. We observed that such a performance variant occurs randomly, regardless of the node location in Oakforest-PACS.

Such a dynamic frequency adjustment as that in Intel Turbo Boost is important to balance the performance and power consumption under temperature. It is especially important in many-core architectures because the number of target cores is quite large. However, our experiment makes it clear that a large scale parallel execution encounters such a problem on a non-algorithmic variant affecting the execution time for each node. It is difficult to avoid such a problem with fixed size task allocation applied to nodes as that which takes place with ARTED. The best way to avoid the issue may be by introducing dynamic load balancing; however, this may be considered in future work.

8   Conclusion

In this paper, we presented the performance of an electron dynamics simulation code, named "ARTED", as a real-scientific application on a large-scale KNL cluster, "Oakforest-PACS". Our purpose was to achieve high sustained performance on a many-core base cluster from the basic code tuned to KNC coprocessors.

We focused on how to port the application for KNL from KNC-based optimization and considered additional tuning for many-core processor dedicated techniques. As the most time-consuming part, the stencil code with Hamiltonian computation was successfully implemented on KNL with a minor change regarding the KNC-optimized version with 512-bit SIMD instructions. We achieved a performance of 758.4 GFLOPS per node for the 3-D stencil kernel, which corresponds to 24.8% of theoretical peak. This result indicates that the code tuning for KNC has had a positive impact on KNL.

For the performance evaluation on Oakforest-PACS, we used up to 8,192 nodes which correspond to 99.8% of the system. Our application achieved very good weak scaling on the dominant Hamiltonian computation, up to 4 PFLOPS with 16% of theoretical peak. The paper demonstrated that the application is scalable on a world-class KNL system using our performance tuning.

We also showed that there are differences among nodes where the computation time differs up to approximately 20%, even for the same amount of computation. We think that it is caused by the Turbo Boost mechanism and dynamic frequency control by the hardware to maintain the TDP. Such a problem is more serious on many-core processors than ordinary multi-core processors.

We hope our results contribute significantly to the optoelectronics sciences with KNL-adapted ARTED and the large-scale KNL cluster, Oakforest-PACS.

Acknowledgment. A part of this research was based on the Oakforest-PACS system operated at the JCAHPC in cooperation with the Information Technology Center at University of Tokyo and the Center for Computational Sciences at University of Tsukuba. The performance evaluation applied in this paper using the COMA system was supported in part by the interdisciplinary collaborative research program at the Center for Computational Sciences, University of Tsukuba. This work was also supported by CREST, JST (Grant No. JPMJCR16N5).

References

1. Sato, S.A., Yabana, K.: Maxwell + TDDFT multi-scale simulation for laser-matter interactions. J. Adv. Simulat. Sci. Eng. **1**(1), 98–110 (2014)
2. Yabana, K., Sugiyama, T., Shinohara, Y., et al.: Time-dependent density functional theory for strong electromagnetic fields in crystalline solids. Phys. Rev. B **85**(4), 11 (2012). https://doi.org/10.1103/PhysRevB.85.045134
3. Andrade, X., et al.: Time-dependent density-functional theory in massively parallel computer architectures: the OCTOPUS project. J. Phy. Condens. Matt. **24**, 233202 (2012)
4. Noda, M., Ishimura, K., Nobusada, K., et al.: Massively-parallel electron dynamics calculations in real-time and real-space: toward applications to nanostructures of more than ten-nanometers in size. J. Comput. Phys. **265**(14), 145–155 (2014)
5. Draeger, E.W., Andrade, X., Gunnels, J.A., et al.: Massively parallel first-principles simulation of electron dynamics in materials. In: 2016 IEEE International Parallel and Distributed Processing Symposium, p. 832 (2016)
6. Barnes, T., Cook, B., Deslippe, J., et al.: Evaluating and optimizing the NERSC workload on Knights Landing. In: Proceedings of the 7th International Workshop on PMBS 2016, pp. 43–53 (2016)
7. Rosales, C., Cazes, J., Milfeld, K., Gómez-Iglesias, A., Koesterke, L., Huang, L., Vienne, J.: A comparative study of application performance and scalability on the Intel Knights Landing processor. In: Taufer, M., Mohr, B., Kunkel, J.M. (eds.) ISC High Performance 2016. LNCS, vol. 9945, pp. 307–318. Springer, Cham (2016). https://doi.org/10.1007/978-3-319-46079-6_22
8. Joó, B., Kalamkar, D.D., Kurth, T., Vaidyanathan, K., Walden, A.: Optimizing Wilson-Dirac operator and linear solvers for Intel® KNL. In: Taufer, M., Mohr, B., Kunkel, J.M. (eds.) ISC High Performance 2016. LNCS, vol. 9945, pp. 415–427. Springer, Cham (2016). https://doi.org/10.1007/978-3-319-46079-6_30
9. Yount, C., Duran, A.:: Effective use of large high-bandwidth memory caches in HPC stencil computation via temporal wave-front tiling. In: Proceedings of the 7th International Workshop on PMBS 2016, pp. 65–75 (2016)
10. Hofmann, J., Treibig, J., Hager, G., Wellein, G.: Comparing the performance of different x86 SIMD instruction sets for a medical imaging application on modern multi- and manycore chips. In: Proceedings of WPMVP 2014, pp. 55–64 (2014)
11. Andreolli, C.: Eight Optimizations for 3-Dimensional Finite Difference (3DFD) Code with an Isotropic (ISO). https://software.intel.com/en-us/articles/eight-optimizations-for-3-dimensional-finite-difference-3dfd-code-with-an-isotropic-iso
12. Blelloch, G.E.: Prefix Sums and Their Applications, School of Computer Science, Carnegie Mellon University, CMU-CS-90-190, November 1990
13. Martin, P.J., Ayuso, L.F., Torres, R., Gavilanes, A.: Algorithmic strategies for optimizing the parallel reduction primitive in CUDA. In: 2012 International Conference on High Performance Computing and Simulation, pp. 511–519, July 2012
14. Sodani, A.: Knights Landing (KNL): 2nd generation intel Xeon Phi processor. IEEE Hot Chips **27**, 1–24 (2015)
15. Williams, S., Waterman, A., Patterson, D.: Roofline: an insightful visual performance model for multicore architectures. Commun. ACM **52**(4), 65–76 (2009)
16. Hirokawa, Y., Boku, T., Sato, S.A., Yabana, K.: Electron dynamics simulation with time-dependent density functional theory on large scale symmetric mode Xeon Phi cluster. In: The 17th IEEE International Workshop on PDSEC 2016 (2016)

17. Schultze, M., Ramasesha, K., Pemmaraju, C., et al.: Attosecond band-gap dynamics in Silicon. Science **346**(6215), 1348–1352 (2014)
18. Lucchini, M., Sato, S.A., Ludwig, A., et al.: Attosecond dynamical Franz-Keldysh effect in polycrystalline diamond. Science **353**(6302), 916–919 (2016)
19. Malinauskas, M., Zukauskas, A., Hasegawa, S., et al.: Ultrafast laser processing of materials: from science to industry. Light Sci. Appl. **5**, e16133 (2016)
20. RIKEN AICS. http://www.aics.riken.jp/en/
21. CCS, University of Tsukuba. http://www.ccs.tsukuba.ac.jp/eng/
22. Joint Center for Advanced HPC. http://jcahpc.jp/eng/
23. TOP500. http://www.top500.org/
24. OCTOPUS. http://octopus-code.org
25. Github: ARTED. https://github.com/ARTED/ARTED
26. SALMON. http://salmon-tddft.jp/

A Novel Multi-level Integrated Roofline Model Approach for Performance Characterization

Tuomas Koskela[1,5,6(✉)], Zakhar Matveev[3], Charlene Yang[1],
Adetokunbo Adedoyin[4], Roman Belenov[3], Philippe Thierry[3], Zhengji Zhao[1],
Rahulkumar Gayatri[1], Hongzhang Shan[2], Leonid Oliker[2], Jack Deslippe[1],
Ron Green[4], and Samuel Williams[2]

[1] NERSC, Lawrence Berkeley National Laboratory, Berkeley, CA 94720, USA
[2] CRD, Lawrence Berkeley National Laboratory, Berkeley, CA 94720, USA
[3] Intel Corporation, Santa Clara, USA
[4] Los Alamos National Laboratory, Los Alamos, USA
[5] University of Helsinki, Helsinki, Finland
`tuomas.koskela@helsinki.fi`
[6] University of Turku, Turku, Finland

Abstract. With energy-efficient architectures, including accelerators and many-core processors, gaining traction, application developers face the challenge of optimizing their applications for multiple hardware features including many-core parallelism, wide processing vector-units and on-chip high-bandwidth memory. In this paper, we discuss the development and utilization of a new application performance tool based on an extension of the classical roofline-model for simultaneously profiling multiple levels in the cache-memory hierarchy. This tool presents a powerful visual aid for the developer and can be used to frame the many-dimensional optimization problem in a tractable way. We show case studies of real scientific applications that have gained insights from the Integrated Roofline Model.

Keywords: Performance models
Application performance measurement · Roofline · Knights landing

1 Introduction

As HPC systems move towards exascale computing, the growing complexity in processor micro-architecture makes it more and more challenging to develop performance and energy-efficient applications. As an example, the Intel many-core Xeon Phi processor architecture has introduced a large number of relatively low-frequency cores per chip with additions of on-package high-bandwidth memory and wide vector units. It offers increased computing power for algorithms that can leverage high parallelism and vectorization, at a lower energy cost. Although optimizing (e.g. more parallelism) applications is beneficial on most platforms, a

© Springer International Publishing AG, part of Springer Nature 2018
R. Yokota et al. (Eds.): ISC High Performance 2018, LNCS 10876, pp. 226–245, 2018.
https://doi.org/10.1007/978-3-319-92040-5_12

metric is required to guide application developers in their performance optimization efforts so that applications can be optimized for the correct performance bounds. Guiding users through this optimization process is a challenge that many HPC facilities around the world are facing as they transition their communities to energy-efficient architectures.

As the Mission HPC facility for the United States Department of Energy's (DOE) Office of Science, the National Energy Research Scientific Computing Center (NERSC), located at Lawrence Berkeley National Lab, is addressing this challenge with its broad user community of over 6000 users from 600 projects spanning a wide range of computational science domains. NERSC recently deployed the Cori system — a Cray XC-30 system comprising over 9600 Xeon-Phi 7250 processors (code-named "Knights Landing" or KNL for short).

Each KNL processor includes 68 cores running at 1.4 GHz (1.2 GHz for AVX code) and capable of hosting four HyperThreads (272 HyperThreads per node). Each core has a private 32 KB L1 cache and two 512-bit wide vector processing units. Each pair of cores (called a "tile") shares a 1 MB L2 cache and each node has 96 GB of DDR4 memory and 16 GB of on-package high bandwidth (MCDRAM) memory.

Users are transitioning to this system from NERSC's Edison system that contains roughly 5000 nodes with a more traditional dual-socket Xeon (Ivy-Bridge) architecture. When transitioning from Edison to Cori, users are faced with a number of important changes: the "many-core" nature of Cori, the increased vector widths (512-bit) provided with the AVX-512 instruction set, and changes to the cache-memory hierarchy including the lack of an L3 cache but addition of an on-chip 16 GB fast-memory (MCDRAM) memory layer that can be configured as a transparent cache. In order to effectively optimize an application for KNL, users therefore need to know which of these hardware features should be targeted in order to reach the largest gains. And practically, they need to know when to stop: i.e. when they've reached the expected performance for their application on the architecture.

The Roofline model [1] is a visually-intuitive performance model used to bound the performance of applications running on multiple architectures. Rather than using percent-of-peak estimates, the Roofline model can be used to quantitatively compare the performance of an application to the performance bounds, or ceilings, set by the architecture of the compute platform. The Roofline model combines this information into a simple performance figure that can be used to determine both algorithmic and implementation limitations of an application.

The Roofline model characterizes an application's performance in gigaflops per second (GFLOPS) as a function of its arithmetic intensity (AI). AI is the ratio of floating-point operations performed to the bytes transferred from cache or memory during execution. This performance number can be compared against the bounds set by the peak compute performance and the cache/memory bandwidth of the system to determine what is limiting performance. The measurement of AI can be done in multiple ways, based on different levels of the memory hierarchy of modern computer systems. In literature, the Roofline model is often labeled by the level of memory its AI is measured from. The most well-known flavors of Roofline are the Cache-Aware Roofline Model (CARM) that measures the AI presented to the cache hierarchy [2,3] and the classical Roofline model that measures the DRAM AI (AI after filtering by the cache hierarchy) [1].

Over the past few years, the utility of the Roofline performance model for guiding and tracking application optimizations has been demonstrated [4]. However, these efforts have been limited in a couple of ways: gathering Roofline data was cumbersome and limited in practice to a few code regions manually designated by the programmer and, secondly, data from only one level of the cache-memory hierarchy is typically gathered, while many applications have complex dependencies on the entire hierarchy.

In this paper, we discuss the benefits of an Integrated Roofline Model (IRM) that collects the AI from all available levels of the memory hierarchy, and present a tool, Intel® Advisor, that automates the data collection and visualization in a user friendly fashion. The novelty of this work with regards to [2,3] is the new performance analysis method that uses memory traffic between all levels of the memory hierarchy simultaneously and the demonstration of a tool for automating the data collection. In CARM, one has a single AI (that is usually close to the L1 AI) and can estimate effective memory bandwidth by comparing observed performance to the L1, L2, ..., DRAM ceilings. Thus, if one observes performance between the L2 and L3 ceilings, one can conclude that the average memory bandwidth is somewhere between the L2 and L3 bandwidths. Unfortunately, CARM does not actually calculate the attained memory bandwidth at each level nor does it identify which level might be a performance bottleneck. To that end, we developed and implemented a hierarchical roofline formulation with a unique AI for each memory level and used a cache simulator to accurately calculate the data movement between each level of the memory hierarchy. With this information we can calculate at which level of the memory hierarchy the dominant data movement occurs and the degree to which bandwidth at that level is overprovisioned. An example that illustrates these improvements will be shown in Sect. 4.2. Integration of this technology into a performance tool has allowed it to be applied to full applications, linked to source and assembly, and visualized using the well-known Roofline formulation. It allows us to automatically determine whenever CPU or a given level of memory hierarchy are the primary bottlenecks in terms of throughput and expose it in a visually-intuitive manner.

The remainder of the paper is organized as follows: In Sect. 2 we discuss the implementation of the Integrated Roofline Model in the Intel Advisor tool. In Sect. 3, we show case studies of how real science application performance is characterized using the Integrated Roofline Model. In Sect. 4, we demonstrate two examples where the Integrated Roofline Model has been used to highlight the effects of optimizations on applications and to demonstrate application performance differences of the KNL and Intel Xeon (Haswell generation) architectures that are present in a smaller data-partition on Cori.

2 Intel Advisor Roofline: Underlying Design and Methodology

Three measurements from an application are needed for roofline analysis: the number of floating-point operations executed, the number of bytes transferred from memory and the execution time. In this section we discuss the measurements implemented in Intel Advisor to collect the data required to build the IRM [3,5,6].

In order to measure memory traffic and attribute it to the loops and functions of the application, we use binary instrumentation and cache simulation. We process all memory arguments of the executed instructions; the CARM traffic is obtained by adding their sizes, while feeding their sizes and addresses to the cache simulator provides the numbers for other levels of the memory hierarchy. The cache simulator is configured according to the actual hardware properties including individual caches, cache capacities, as well as core and socket counts.

The traffic for each memory level is defined as a number of bytes transferred between corresponding component and lower (closer to the CPU core) cache or the core itself. The only exception is L1 cache — where we count the total number of bytes accessed by CPU instructions instead, producing approximately the same arithmetic intensity as in the CARM. The difference is caused by the instructions that access memory by bypassing the cache subsystem, e.g., non-temporal stores used to store data not expected to be reused.

We attribute traffic to the instruction that caused it — and, afterwards, group it by loops and functions adding the numbers for corresponding instructions. For example, if a load causes a cache miss and in order to place the new line in cache it is required to evict the line modified earlier, storing it to the next level of the memory hierarchy, the store traffic is attributed to this load instruction. This may sound counter intuitive, but note that to correctly place the loop on the Roofline chart we need to measure the traffic generated while the loop was executing, thus even if it evicts cache lines modified by a preceding loop nest, corresponding store traffic should be taken into account.

Note that all transfers besides "L1 traffic" values are actually done in cache line units, which also affects the traffic. For example, if an instruction loads one byte and the load causes a cache miss and is eventually served by DRAM, we will measure one byte of L1 traffic, and the traffic defined by the cache line size (64 bytes on most modern CPUs) for all other caches and DRAM. This may lead to "L1" arithmetic intensity being larger than L2 or even DRAM, while the opposite is true for the code with good cache line reuse.

We also count the number of floating-point operations using binary instrumentation, analyzing floating-point instructions. For vector instructions, this enables us to accurately count the number of elements actually processed, i.e., properly account for masked vector instructions, noting that instructions can also involve several FLOPs (e.g. for FMA instructions). By implementing a time, traffic and FLOP measurement workflow in Intel Advisor it became possible to fully automate Roofline characterization not only for individual loops or functions, but for full applications.

The binary instrumentation by its nature causes significant overhead. The overhead varies based on the application (see Table 1). In general, the better the application is using the CPU resources, the higher is the influence of instrumentation and cache simulation logic. Particularly, the overhead is usually higher for the code with good cache locality because simulation code, besides consuming computational resources, evicts application data from the cache, increasing cache miss rate; if most accesses from the application are served by DRAM anyway, the impact is lower. The overhead is also affected by the other factors, such as the use of Hyper-Threading or thread synchronization pattern.

Note that in order to correctly measure the execution time of the program and individual loops, memory traffic estimation is done in a second analysis pass. So time is measured in first separate pass, using a low-overhead non intrusive time sampling technique, and therefore cache simulation overhead does not affect the execution time (seconds) and final FLOP/s measurements representativeness and accuracy.

Table 1. Cache simulation overhead for the applications in the paper

Name	XGC1	VASP	fwi2d	SW4	CoMD	GPP	BIGSTICK
Overhead	37×	21×	21×	23×	8×	9×	18×

Performance counters were used to validate the cache simulation results prior to this work. We used different compute kernels and benchmarks for validation and the discrepancy was found to be within 10% on average. We chose to use cache simulation, since, even though core (and offcore response matrix) counters can be used to measure read traffic from DRAM, writes to DRAM (caused by dirty lines evictions from LLC) are not measured. Note that although there is an OFFCORE_REQUEST bit corresponding to writebacks, it refers to writebacks from L2 to LLC. Counting writes from LLC to DRAM would require an additional OFFCORE_RESPONSE type. Furthermore, measuring traffic on loop/function boundaries requires source/binary instrumentation that may distort PMU measurements (especially for small inner loops). Also, in parallel code, it only makes sense on parallel region boundaries. Thus, it would not be possible to deep-dive inside the parallel regions and measure roofline data for inner loops or functions.

In this paper we use the following techniques available to analyze Roofline data generated by Intel Advisor. First, Intel Advisor's interactive GUI is utilized to explore Roofline charts directly (Fig. 2). Secondly, the Intel Advisor command line interface or Intel Advisor Python customization API ([7]) can be used to implement custom extension of Intel Advisor; this approach was used in this paper to generate custom Integrated Roofline charts shown in the article (e.g. see Fig. 1).

3   Application Characterization Case Studies

In this section, we show the utility of the roofline model for assessing the performance of scientific applications that routinely run on NERSC systems. Real-life scientific applications often feature complex algorithms that may be very difficult to analyze analytically. For demonstration of the integrated roofline method on a simple analytic benchmark, the reader is encouraged to refer to [8,9]. The applications analyzed in this paper are summarized in Table 2.

Table 2. General characteristics of the application evaluated in this paper. Note, "BW" stands for memory bandwidth

Name	XGC1	VASP	fwi2d	SW4	CoMD	GPP	BIGSTICK
Domain	Magnetic Fusion	Materials Science	Geo-physics	Geo-dynamics	Poly-crystalline Materials	Material Science	Nuclear Physics
Motif	PIC	DFT + CG	FD Stencils	FD Stencils	MD	DFT	CI
Release	upon request	paid	closed	open source	open source [10]	open source	upon request
MPI	✓	✓	✓	✓	✓		✓
OpenMP	✓	✓	✓	✓	✓	✓	✓
LOC	100 k	470 k	2 K	87 k	4 K	400	91 k
Perf. bound	Gather/ Scatter, Compute	BW, latency	BW	BW, Compute	BW	BW	BW

3.1   XGC1

XGC1 (X-point Gyrokinetic Code) [11] is a fusion plasma physics gyrokinetic particle-in-cell (PIC) code originally from Princeton Plasma Physics Laboratory (PPPL). It is one of the codes selected for the US exascale computing project (ECP). It is primarily used to study turbulence in the edge region of tokamak fusion plasmas — essential for the success of future fusion reactors.

The main unique feature of XGC1 is its use of unstructured meshes to simulate the whole tokamak volume. The mesh is decomposed over MPI ranks into poloidal planes that are connected via a field-following mapping. Within a poloidal plane, particles are decomposed over both MPI ranks and OpenMP threads. XGC1 uses kinetic ions and electrons, and uses a sub-cycling scheme for the electron motion that is the most time-consuming part of the simulation. In a typical production run on Cori, roughly 70–80% of the total CPU time is spent in the electron push kernel [12].

Within the electron push kernel, communication between threads is only needed roughly every 50 electron time steps. The electron push algorithm uses a 4th order Runge-Kutta scheme to integrate the gyrokinetic equation of motion [11]. The computation has a high flop to byte ratio, but CPU time is dominated by indirect memory accesses and latency from gather/scatter instructions due to the random motion of particles across the grid. This is a typical feature of PIC codes and is exacerbated in XGC1 by the unstructured mesh.

We run XGC1 on a single KNL node in quad-cache mode for an artificially small problem size, to make data collection with Advisor feasible. The mesh consists of 7500 nodes in a single axisymmetric plane and the number of particles is 25,000 per thread, 1.6 million total. We run the code for two ion time steps with 50 electron sub-cycles per time step, without collisions, using 16 MPI ranks and 4 OpenMP threads per rank. The Advisor data is collected on rank 0 only.

The five most time-consuming loops of XGC1 are shown on the Roofline chart in Fig. 1. All the loops shown are called from the electron push kernel, which dominates the ion push by a factor 50 in call volume. The loops all have good cache locality in the L2 cache, shown by a large increase in AI from LLC to L2, and the highest-performing loops also have good L1 locality, while the rest have only moderate L1 locality. The kernels clearly are not bandwidth bound, with the possible exception of bicub_mod:295 being bound by the L1 bandwidth. It also is worth noting that the DRAM traffic within these loops is too small to be measured by Advisor. That is, the loops are fully running from cache. The loops are vectorized and do not fall clearly into either bandwidth or compute bound regimes. Our hypothesis is that they are bound by cache throughput which is specific to the load instruction. This has been confirmed by instruction set analysis which shows gather/scatter instructions are generated in the loops. Our conclusion is the high-performing loops are bound by L1 instruction throughput and the lower-performing loops by L2 throughput. One could measure a memory bandwidth roofline for gather/scatter instructions to present the more realistic performance bound in the roofline model, this is planned for future work.

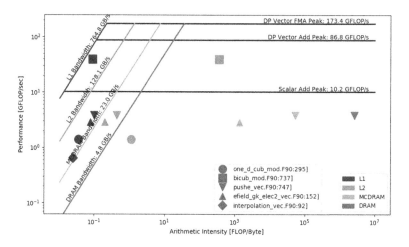

Fig. 1. XGC1 Roofline figure for Cori (KNL) in a quad-cache configuration. The symbols represent different loops and the colors of the markers represent AI's of the loops measured from different memory levels. The memory bandwidth ceilings are similarly colored. That is, points of a given color should be compared against the memory ceiling of the same color. Although `bicub_mod` attains near L1 roofline performance, most other kernels are well-below the L2 and scalar add rooflines. (Color figure online)

3.2   Fwi2d

Fwi2d (full waveform inversion) is a seismic imaging code from the Paris School of Mines (MinesParisTech) used to obtain subsurface images from low frequency wave velocity fields. This is critical for successful exploration and reservoir delineation in oil and gas exploration, but such algorithms can be used for civil engineering as well. FWI is a computationally-intensive process that requires propagating waves using time (or frequency) domain wave equation solvers. We consider here a second-order wave equation and we are using a time domain finite difference (TDFD) approach based on explicit finite difference schemes in time (4th order) and space (8th order) with a quasi-Newton (with L-BFGS algorithm) optimization scheme for the model parameters update. The stencil in use to compute the derivatives has an extremely strong impact on the flop per byte ratio, on the memory accesses, and finally on the implementation efficiency. Those algorithms are also known as time reversal techniques that need cross correlation of a forward propagating field and a backward propagating field. This method usually leads to heavy I/O to keep snapshots of the forward wavefields. In the present isotropic acoustic 2D implementation of FWI, we keep the snapshots in memory for simplicity. The main advantage of a 2D implementation is to quickly evaluate new features such as more complicated wave equations, new cost functions, finite-difference stencils or boundary conditions and evaluation of new memory hierarchies in the context of snapshot management. This technique is popular due to its simple stencil based implementation on a Cartesian grid and its natural parallelization in the shot domain, e.g. the parallelization is achieved through standard MPI seismic shot distribution and OpenMP for domain decomposition within the PDE loop.

In the example runs, we try to understand OpenMP scalability and the performance impact of absorbing boundary condition that potentially impact data alignment and vectorization. As presented on Figs. 2 and 3, we can analyze the data movement between memory levels for each loop. Since the number of FLOPs is the same between those levels, any move comes from a change in the number of bytes transferred. The amplitude of the horizontal movement of each dot is indicative of potential bottlenecks. For example, the triangles on Fig. 3 are very close for the L1, L2 and L3 levels (blue, green, yellow) and far to the right for the DRAM to LLC traffic (red triangle). This demonstrates that data resides in the cache and is not impacted by DRAM bandwidth. A look at the vectorization analysis will then give some recommendations on how to improve the performance (we ultimately want those triangles against the roofline). Another interesting behavior is visible with the blue and green diamonds of Fig. 3 where we do not have any data traffic between DRAM-LLC and LLC-L2 levels (no yellow or red diamonds). The increase in data movement between L1 and registers demonstrates a possible issue with vectorization and data alignment.

Using the multi-level Roofline view for all functions and loops is a nice companion to vectorization analysis in order to characterize a full application at the function/loop levels on a given platform or when moving from one machine to another generation. To illustrate this, we performed tests on a dual-socket

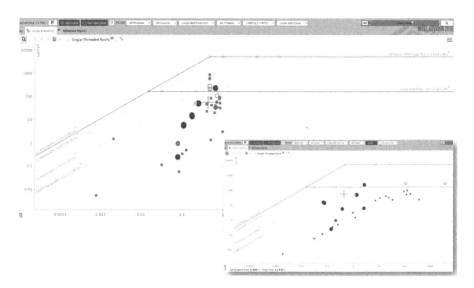

Fig. 2. fwi2d Intel Advisor 2018 "Roofline" view screen-shots. These two pictures represent the data traffic between L1 and register (top left) and between L1 and L2 (bottom right). As the number of FLOPs remains constant between the pictures, we can see that several functions/loops have the same volume of bytes transferred while some other points suffer from cache misses that strongly increase the data traffic.

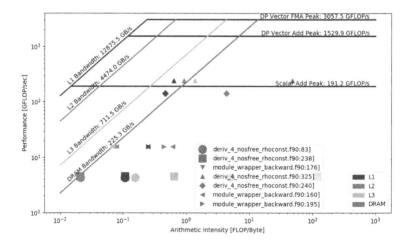

Fig. 3. Roofline for Fwi2d using 1 MPI rank of 40 OpenMP threads running on a dual socket Skylake server. Selected loops are from the stencil routines and boundary conditions. We can see, the data movement between memory levels is very different for each loop and each of the loops is not bounded by the same level, i.e. by the same bandwidth. This is one of the key features of the multi-level view. (Color figure online)

server using Intel® Xeon® Gold 6148 processors codenamed Skylake with 20 cores running at 2.4 GHz and 192 GB of DDR3–2667 DRAM, leading to a stream triad bandwidth of about 200 GB/s. This architecture is different from the KNL processor of the Cori system, corresponds to the latest Xeon architecture, and contains a number of enhancements (AVX512 instruction set and larger cache sizes). In some cases, applications may need to be optimized for the new cache hierarchy. In fwi2d this is reflected in the need to reshape the cache block sizes to fit L2 and benefit from its bandwidth. More details are available at [13].

3.3 VASP

The Vienna Ab-initio Simulation Package (VASP) [14,15] is a widely used materials science application, supporting a wide range of electronic structure methods, from Density Functional Theory (DFT) to many-body perturbation approaches (GW and ACFDT). VASP solves a set of eigenvalue and eigenfunction (wavefuntion) pairs for the many-body (electrons) Schrödinger equation iteratively within a planewave basis set (Fourier space). VASP computation consists of many independent 3D FFTs, matrix-matrix multiplications, matrix diagonalizations, and other linear algebra methods, such as Gram-Schmidt orthogonalization, Cholesky decomposition, and matrix inversion. Therefore VASP heavily depends on optimized mathematical libraries.

VASP was written in Fortran and parallelized with MPI. To exploit more energy-efficient processors like Intel KNL, the VASP developers have added OpenMP directives to the code recently to address increased on-node parallelism. In the hybrid MPI+OpenMP VASP code, the bands are distributed over MPI tasks, and the coefficients of the bands are distributed over OpenMP threads, either explicitly via OpenMP directives, or implicitly via the use of threaded libraries like FFTW or LAPACK/BLAS3. To exploit wider vector units, VASP employs OpenMP SIMD constructs using both explicit loop-level vectorization via `omp simd` and sub-routine/function vectorization through `omp declare simd`. To effectively vectorize the nested function calls and complex loop structures mixing scalar and vector code that compilers often fail to auto-vectorize, the code employs a combination of user-defined high-level vectors together with OpenMP SIMD loop vectorization. More details about the OpenMP implementation and SIMD optimizations in VASP can be found in [16].

Figure 4 shows the four most time consuming loops in the hybrid MPI+OpenMP VASP (code path: hybrid functional calculation with the damped iteration scheme) on the roofline chart for Cori KNL. VASP was run with four KNL nodes in quad-cache using 64 MPI tasks and 8 OpenMP threads per task (16 MPI tasks per node). Note, the performance data is collected on rank 0 and the flops are normalized to full node by simply multiplying the relevant values by the number of MPI tasks per node. The benchmark used is a 256-atom Silicon supershell with a vacancy. The hybrid MPI+OpenMP VASP (last commit 10/16/2017) was compiled with the Intel compiler (2018.0.128) and was linked to the MKL, ELPA (2016.05.004), and Cray MPICH (8.6.0) libraries.

Figure 4 shows that the performance of the most time consuming loops (each of them accounting for 4–6% of the total execution time) are well below the scalar add peak. Except the loop, apply_gfac_exchange_, being MCDRAM bandwidth bound, the dots for the rest of the loops are well below the corresponding level's memory bandwidths, indicating they are neither compute or bandwidth bound but likely latency bound. Advisor detected inefficient memory access patterns and assumed dependencies in these loops. The large separation between the MCDRAM and DRAM arithmetic intensities is indicative that the working set fits well in the MCDRAM cache. Note that the four most time consuming loops shown in the figure are not the ones that execute the most floating-point calculations. VASP executes most of the floating-point calculations via the BLAS and FFT routines in MKL whose performances, being closer to or above the double precision vector peak, result in a shorter execution times.

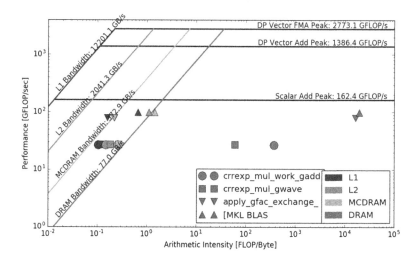

Fig. 4. VASP Roofline for KNL. The four most time consuming loops are shown in the chart. Except the loop, apply_gfac_exchange_, which appears to be the MCDRAM bandwithd bound, the rest of the loops are neither compute or bandwidth bound.

3.4 BIGSTICK

BIGSTICK [17] implements the parallel Configuration Interaction (CI) method (widely used to solve the nuclear many body problem) using Fortran 95 and MPI+OpenMP. Perhaps the greatest challenges in efficient implementation and execution of the CI method is its immense memory and data movement requirements. In CI, the non-relativistic many-body nuclear Schrödinger equation is cast as a very large sparse matrix eigen-problem with matrices whose dimension can exceed ten billion. With typical sparsity (between 1 and 100 nonzeros per million matrix elements) such large-scale sparse matrix eigen-problems place high demands on memory capacity and memory bandwidth. To reduce the memory pressure, BIGSTICK reconstructs nonzero matrix elements on the fly. As a results, the memory requirements, compared with the stored matrix approach, is reduced 10–100×. To further reduce memory requirements, BIGSTICK may be run in a hybrid MPI+OpenMP mode. Figure 5 shows the Roofline for BIGSTICK on KNL using 1 MPI process of 64 threads. The data set used is b10nmax4 (^{10}B), an ab initio calculation that has five protons and five neutrons (10B); the designation Nmax = 4 describes the model space and signifies the maximum excitation in units of harmonic oscillator energies. Generally speaking, two interrelated factors drive down both AI and performance — high-stride memory access patterns and a lack of vectorization. However, the large DRAM AI suggests the MCDRAM cache is effectively capturing the working set.

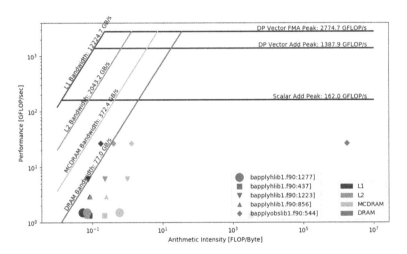

Fig. 5. Roofline for BIGSTICK on KNL for 1 MPI process with 64 OpenMP threads. The low performance is due to high stride data access without vectorization.

3.5 SW4

SW4 [18] is a block-structured, finite difference code that implements substantial capabilities for 3D seismic modeling. SW4 is parallelized with MPI and has performance kernels (SW4Lite) threaded with OpenMP.

Figure 6 shows the Roofline model for SW4 running with 8 processes of 8 threads on KNL in quad-cache. The performance of four of the kernels are directly tied to MCDRAM bandwidth, while the fifth, rhs4sg_rev, dominates the runtime, underperforms its MCDRAM limit, but exceeds the scalar FMA performance. L1, L2, and MCDRAM(LLC) AIs are widely separated indicating multiple levels of locality and reuse distances. Note, we do not show DRAM AI as the problem size completely fits in MCDRAM.

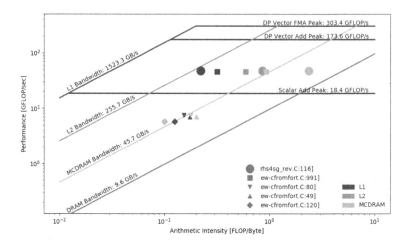

Fig. 6. SW4 running with 8 MPI ranks of 8 threads on KNL in quad-cache. Observe four kernels are strongly tied to MCDRAM(LLC) bandwidth.

The rhs4sg_rev and addsgdfort_indrev are the most time consuming routines in the project. Nearly 80% of the computation time is spent in these routines. From the Fig. 6, we can observe that both these routines are optimized efficiently and since there are sizable gaps between L1, L2 and LLC, it indicates that there is reuse in all three levels of cache. We do not show the DRAM data in Fig. 6, since the problem size shown fits completely in the MCDRAM.

4   Guided Optimization Case Studies

4.1   CoMD

CoMD [19–22], a proxy/mini application developed at Los Alamos National Laboratory (LANL), was designed to mimic the workloads of ddcMD [23] and Scalable Parallel Short-range Molecular Dynamics (SPaSM) [23] and is a material science application for performing molecular dynamics (MD) simulation on polycrystalline materials. MD algorithms are classified as N-body problems with an approximate complexity of $O(n^2)$ or lower. The two types of force calculations implemented in CoMD (typically the bottleneck of MD algorithms) is the Leonard Jones (LJ) and Embedded Atom Model (EAM). CoMD is implemented in C with MPI and OpenMP.

Initial observations showed that the LJ force kernel strongly dominates the run time. Therefore, for the purpose of demonstrating the viability of the Roofline approach, we will focus on the LJ force kernel.

Figure 7(left) shows out-of-the-box CoMD performance on KNL compared to a two-socket Haswell node (thread concurrencies greater than 64 indicate oversubscription). Data provided by Intel Advisor, Fig. 7(right), shows that the LJ kernel dominates the run time and has substantial L2 and MCDRAM data

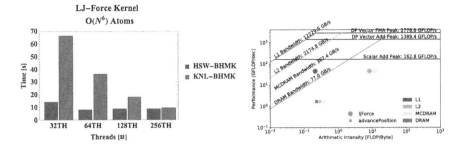

Fig. 7. (Left) Out-of-the-box CoMD LJ-Force on KNL generally underperforms Haswell (oversubscription beyond 64 threads). (Right) Roofline analysis of CoMD on KNL shows the LJ kernel dominates the run time and has high data locality. Note, HyperThreading on Haswell only supports 64 simultaneous threads.

locality. However, it clearly shows that there is a great deal of L1 data movement (much lower L1 AI). Advisor noted the lack of vectorized loops, unaligned data, and non-unit stride stores. Therefore, the conclusion from the roofline analysis was the performance is not bound by memory bandwidth, since good locality is achieved, and optimization efforts on KNL should focus on leveraging the vector instructions to reach higher compute ceilings.

After several optimization sessions with the goal of improving the data and thread level parallelism, Fig. 8 shows approximately 30% improvement in the LJ-force kernel performance on both KNL and HSW. The modernization effort in CoMD for the LJ-force kernel includes improving vectorization via simd clauses, branch hints for simd, simdized functions, alignment, compiler hints, and data structure transformations. However, the roofline performance figure indicates that work remains to bridge the remaining performance gaps.

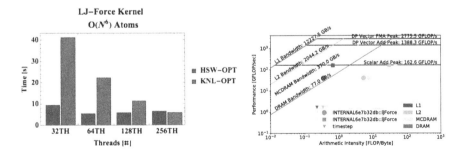

Fig. 8. (Left) Optimized CoMD LJ-Force on KNL and Haswell. (Right) Roofline analysis of optimized CoMD on KNL. Note, HyperThreading on Haswell only supports 64 simultaneous threads.

4.2   BerkeleyGW (GPP)

BerkeleyGW [24] is a material science application that predicts the excited-state properties of a wide range of materials. GPP [25] is a proxy code for BerkeleyGW, written in Fortran90 and parallelized with OpenMP. It calculates the electron self-energy using the common General Plasmon Pole (GPP) approximation [26]. The computation represents the work an individual MPI task would perform in a much larger calculation (typically spanning hundreds or thousands of nodes). The code implements several nested loops, where the innermost loop iterates over the longest dimension of arrays. For a small BerkeleyGW problem, with 512 electrons (bands) and 32,768 plane wave basis elements, the innermost loop, for example at line 303 in the code [25], must read/write 2 MB of data for each outer iteration. As this 2 MB working set doesn't fit into the L2 cache on either Haswell or KNL, a cache-blocking strategy is deployed.

Using 32 threads on the Cori/Haswell nodes and 64 threads on the Cori/KNL nodes (quad-cache), Fig. 9 shows that this core computational loop is MCDRAM-bound on KNL and L3-bound on Haswell, since there is essentially no difference between the LLC, L2 and L1 AI's. This means that data is being streamed from the LLC and there is no reuse of data in L1 or L2. Table 3 shows that when one applies cache blocking, the LLC AI improves by 3×, which is due to the fixed trip count of three for loop iw. Likewise, Fig. 9 shows significant separation appears between the L2 and LLC AI's after cache blocking - meaning reuse out of L2 has been achieved. The GFLOPS/s performance has improved by 16–18%, lower than 3×, because there are divide, shuffle and unpack instructions involved in the innermost loop.

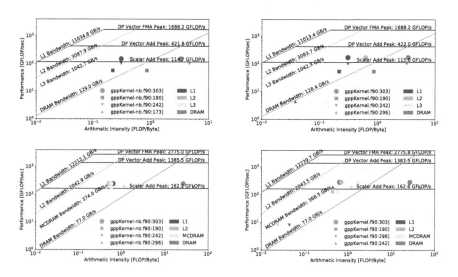

Fig. 9. Integrated Roofline for GPP on Haswell (top) and KNL (bottom) before (left) and after (right) cache blocking. Observe the lack of differentiation for L2 and L3 AI's in the left figures for loop at line 303.

Table 3. Integrated roofline AI and performance for GPP on Haswell and KNL with and without cache blocking. Observe the 3× increase in LLC AI.

gppKernel.f90:303	Haswell		KNL	
	Original	Cache blocked	Original	Cache blocked
L1+NTS AI	0.31	0.31	0.64	0.64
L2 AI	0.46	0.62	0.51	0.69
LLC AI	0.46	1.40	0.56	1.71
DRAM AI	3.31	3.44	26.45	26.83
GFLOPS/s	148.57	172.48	242.55	287.28

Tables 3 and 4 show that the (single) AI obtained from CARM is exactly the same as the L1 AI obtained in the Integrated Roofline Modeling (n.b., CARM GFlop/s is different as it was collected in a separate run that resulted in a slightly different run time). While the CARM Roofline approach, in Fig. 10, can show the upward movement of the performance through optimization, it fails to provide any information on which level of cache this optimization has affected, whereas in the Integrated Roofline (Fig. 9), the increase of LLC AI clearly indicates that data has been blocked to L2 and traffic between L2 and LLC has been reduced.

Table 4. CARM Roofline AI and performance for GPP on Haswell and KNL with and without cache blocking.

gppKernel.f90:303	Haswell		KNL	
	Original	Cache blocked	Original	Cache blocked
CARM AI	0.31	0.31	0.64	0.64
GFLOPS/s	147.60	169.83	250.88	290.03

5   Related Work

The literature is filled with many performance models and tools specialized for varying levels of detail and different bottlenecks. Whereas the Integrated Roofline presented in this paper includes all levels of the cache hierarchy, the original Roofline model [1] focused on only a single level at a time (e.g. DRAM). As accurately measuring data movement can be a hard problem (hence the cache model used in the Integrated Roofline), the Cache-Aware Roofline Model [2] transforms the problem by fixing arithmetic intensity at the L1 and infers locality based on the position of performance relative to bandwidth ceilings.

Whereas, Roofline presents an idealized machine that can perfectly overlap computation with L1, L2, and DRAM data movement, many real processors may

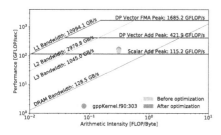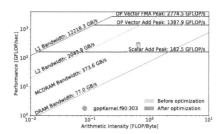

Fig. 10. CARM Roofline for GPP on Haswell (left) and KNL (right) before (cyan) and after (magenta) cache blocking. (Color figure online)

not be able to realize this. To that end, the Execution-Cache-Memory Model was developed [27] to more accurately capture how specific processor microarchitectures fail to perfectly overlap communication and computation.

Rather than modeling the cache hierarchy, tools like PAPI [28] and LIKWID [29] can directly read the hardware performance counters that record various compute and data movement events. Unfortunately, performance counter tools are only as good as the processor vendor's implementation of the underlying performance counters. Where the counters are inaccurate, incomplete (e.g. failing to incorporate masks when counting vector flops), or simply missing, tools will not provide the requisite data. Additionally, such tools often rely on coarse-grained sampling techniques that are error-prone on short loops or are otherwise challenged in attribution. The latter, attribution (i.e. which loop caused the data movement observed on a shared uncore counter), is a direct motivator for out cache simulator based approach. Nevertheless, performance counter sampling incurs minimal performance impact and thus enables full-application instrumentation at scale.

When performance falls out of the throughput-limited regime, overheads and inter-process communication can dominate an application's performance characteristics. To that end, depending on message size, messages per synchronization point, and the performance of the underlying communication layer, the LogP or LogGP models may be more appropriate [30,31]. For single-node runs where there is no inter-process communication, models like LogCA [32] should be adapted to incorporate the overhead of OpenMP parallelization.

Whereas our tool is nominally geared for analyzing threaded single-process executions, other tools like TAU [33] or HPCToolkit [34] are more adept at integrating and analyzing highly-concurrent, distributed-memory performance characteristics to identify communication or computational load imbalance. Similarly, when running on Cray supercomputers, one may use CrayPat [35] to instrument and analyze performance. In addition to timings, CrayPat provides access (via PAPI) to the underlying performance counters in order to measure cache, memory, and floating-point performance. Nevertheless, neither PAPI, LIKWID, CrayPat, TAU, or HPCToolkit have an underlying performance model that can be used for performance analysis rather than simply performance instrumentation.

6   Summary and Outlook

We have shown in this paper that utility of an "Integrated" Roofline Model approach for evaluating and guiding the optimization of application performance. This novel approach, as implemented in the latest Intel Vector Advisor tool via an included cache simulator, provides simple to understand visual indication of which (if any) level of the cache-memory limits performance and the amount of data-reuse present in each. For example, for a given loop or function, the visual separation of the four plotted points corresponding to AI's from L1, L2, LLC, and DRAM corresponds directly to cache-reuse. We observe that the effect of cache-blocking optimizations can be easily visualized in this manner.

The integration with Intel Advisor enables the automated collection of integrated roofline information, not just for simplistic kernels but for real, large-scale applications with multiple bottlenecks. It effectively combines the process of collecting a profile and analyzing the performance limiters of the hotspots into a single step. The result is the presentation of actionable performance data for all the top hotspots in an application.

At LBNL and LANL, this information is used to inform code teams which viable optimization paths are available to them and which KNL architectures features they should target. For example, if an application bandwidth bound in certain cache or memory layer, it isn't likely very profitable to tackle improved vector code generation — but adding a layer of cache blocking or tiling (e.g. in the KNL MCDRAM) would likely enable greater performance.

In many cases, even with the increased granularity of information provided by all four points in the Integrated Roofline Model, it isn't always immediately clear what the performance limiter of an application is. For example, none of the measure performance points may lie clearly on one of their respective ceilings. In practice what we have found, is the Roofline model, and IRM in particular, are, however, always great tools for starting or framing a conversation with facility users around performance. Asking the question "why are my performance points not on their ceilings" nearly always leads to fruitful investigation whereby the code teams learns something new and deeper about their application — well beyond using walltime to profile an application alone.

In many cases, the answer to the above quoted question is related to the fact that the ceilings for each level of the cache-memory hierarchy are based on streaming (unit-stride) access patterns, but real applications often exhibit strided or random memory access patterns. It is straightforward to empirically compute "effective" ceilings for such access patterns (which are typically lower than unit-stride access patterns) but we leave a detailed discussion of extending the utility of the Roofline model in this way to a future work.

In addition, one may, in principle, add additional levels (and corresponding performance points) to the Integrated Roofline Model corresponding to data accessed from off-node (e.g. via MPI communication), from I/O during execution, or other limiters of in-core performance (e.g. floating-point divides). This is important not only for applications that are communication or I/O bound, but also for applications that depart from the multiply-add idiom that modern architectures are optimized for. This is a fruitful avenue for future work.

References

1. Williams, S., et al.: CACM **52**(4), 65–76 (2009)
2. Ilic, A., et al.: IEEE Comput. Architect. Lett. **12**(1), 21–24 (2013)
3. Marques, D., et al.: Performance analysis with cache-aware roofline model in intel advisor. In: 2017 International Conference on High Performance Computing & Simulation (HPCS), pp. 898–907. IEEE, 17 July 2017
4. Doerfler, D., et al.: Applying the roofline performance model to the intel xeon phi knights landing processor. In: ISC Workshops (2016)
5. Intel Advisor Roofline. https://software.intel.com/en-us/articles/intel-advisor-roofline
6. Intel(r) Advisor Roofline Analysis. CodeProject, February 2017 https://www.codeproject.com/Articles/1169323/Intel-Advisor-Roofline-Analysis
7. How to use Intel Advisor Python. Intel Developer Zone, June 2017. https://software.intel.com/en-us/articles/how-to-use-the-intel-advisor-python-api
8. Koskela, T., et al.: Performance tuning of scientific codes with the roofline model. Tutorial in SC 2017 (2017). http://bit.ly/tut160, https://sc17.supercomputing.org/full-program/
9. Koskela, T., et al.: A practical approach to application performance tuning with the Roofline Model, Tutorial submitted to ISC 2018 (2018)
10. Classical molecular dynamics proxy application, Exascale Co-Design Center for Materials in Extreme Environments. exmatex.org, https://github.com/ECP-copa/CoMD.git
11. Ku, S., et al.: Nuclear Fusion, vol. 49 no. 11, Article 115021 (2009)
12. Koskela, T., Deslippe, J.: Optimizing fusion PIC code performance at scale on cori phase two. In: Kunkel, J.M., Yokota, R., Taufer, M., Shalf, J. (eds.) ISC High Performance 2017. LNCS, vol. 10524, pp. 430–440. Springer, Cham (2017). https://doi.org/10.1007/978-3-319-67630-2_32
13. https://software.intel.com/en-us/articles/intel-xeon-processor-scalable-family-technical-overview
14. Kresse, G., Furthmüller, J.: Efficiency of ab-initio total energy calculations for metals and semiconductors using a plane-wave basis set. Comput. Mat. Sci. **6**, 15 (1996)
15. http://www.vasp.at/
16. Wende, F., Marsman, M., Zhao, Z., Kim, J.: Porting VASP from MPI to MPI+OpenMP [SIMD]. In: de Supinski, B.R., Olivier, S.L., Terboven, C., Chapman, B.M., Müller, M.S. (eds.) IWOMP 2017. LNCS, vol. 10468, pp. 107–122. Springer, Cham (2017). https://doi.org/10.1007/978-3-319-65578-9_8
17. Shan, H., et al.: Parallel implementation and performance optimization of the configuration-interaction method. In: Supercomputing (SC) (2015)
18. Johansen, H., et al.: Toward exascale earthquake ground motion simulations for near-fault engineering analysis. Comput. Sci. Eng. **19**(5), 27 (2017)
19. Mohd-Yusof, J.: CoDesign Molecular Dynamics (CoMD) Proxy App, LA-UR-12-21782, Los Alamos National Lab (2012)
20. Cicotti, P., et al.: An evaluation of threaded models for a classical MD proxy application. In: 2014 Hardware-Software Co-Design for High Performance Computing, New Orleans, LA, pp. 41–48 (2014). https://doi.org/10.1109/Co-HPC.2014.6

21. Adedoyin, A.: A Case Study on Software Modernizationusing CoMD - A Molecular Dynamics Proxy Application, LA-UR-17-22676, Los Alamos National Lab (2017)
22. Gunter, D., Adedoyin, A.: Kokkos Port of CoMD Mini-App, DOE COE Performance Portability Meeting (2017)
23. Germann, T.C., et al.: 369 Tflop-s molecular dynamics simulations on the petaflop hybrid supercomputer 'Roadrunner'. Concurrency Comput. Pract. Experience **21**(17), 2143–2159 (2009)
24. https://berkeleygw.org
25. https://github.com/cyanguwa/BerkeleyGW-GPP
26. Soininen, J.A., et al.: Electron self-energy calculation using a general multi-pole approximation. J. Phys. Condensed Matter **15**(17), 2573 (2003)
27. Treibig, J., Hager, G.: Introducing a performance model for bandwidth-limited loop kernels. In: Wyrzykowski, R., Dongarra, J., Karczewski, K., Wasniewski, J. (eds.) PPAM 2009. LNCS, vol. 6067, pp. 615–624. Springer, Heidelberg (2010). https://doi.org/10.1007/978-3-642-14390-8_64
28. http://icl.cs.utk.edu/papi
29. https://github.com/RRZE-HPC/likwid
30. Culler, D., et al.: LogP: towards a realistic model of parallel computation. In: PPoPP (1993)
31. Alexandrov, A., et al.: LogGP: incorporating long messages into the LogP model. JPDC **44**(1), 71–79 (1997)
32. Altaf, M.B., Wood, D.A.: LogCA: a performance model for hardware accelerators. In: ISCA (2017)
33. Shende, S., Malony, A.: The TAU parallel performance system. IJHPCA **20**(2), 287–311 (2005)
34. Adhianto, L., et al.: HPCToolkit: performance measurement and analysis for supercomputers with node-level parallelism. In: Workshop on Node Level Parallelism for Large Scale Supercomputers (2008)
35. http://docs.cray.com

Hardware Performance Variation:
A Comparative Study Using
Lightweight Kernels

Hannes Weisbach[1]($\boxtimes$), Balazs Gerofi[3], Brian Kocoloski[2], Hermann Härtig[1],
and Yutaka Ishikawa[3]

[1] Operating Systems Chair, TU Dresden, Dresden, Germany
{weisbach,haertig}@os.inf.tu-dresden.de
[2] Washington University in St. Louis, St. Louis, USA
brian.kocoloski@wustl.edu
[3] RIKEN Advanced Institute for Computational Science, Kobe, Japan
{bgerofi,yutaka.ishikawa}@riken.jp

Abstract. Imbalance among components of large scale parallel simulations can adversely affect overall application performance. Software induced imbalance has been extensively studied in the past, however, there is a growing interest in characterizing and understanding another source of variability, the one induced by the hardware itself. This is particularly interesting with the growing diversity of hardware platforms deployed in high-performance computing (HPC) and the increasing complexity of computer architectures in general. Nevertheless, characterizing hardware performance variability is challenging as one needs to ensure a tightly controlled software environment.

In this paper, we propose to use lightweight operating system kernels to provide a high-precision characterization of various aspects of hardware performance variability. Towards this end, we have developed an extensible benchmarking framework and characterized multiple compute platforms (e.g., Intel x86, Cavium ARM64, Fujitsu SPARC64, IBM Power) running on top of lightweight kernel operating systems. Our initial findings show up to six orders of magnitude difference in relative variation among CPU cores across different platforms.

Keywords: Performance variation · Performance characterization
Lightweight kernels

1 Introduction

Since the end of Dennard scaling, performance improvement of supercomputing systems has primarily been driven by increasing parallelism. With no end in sight to this trend, it is projected that exascale systems will reach multi-hundred million-way of thread level parallelism [1], which by itself poses a crucial challenge in efficiently utilizing these platforms. Further complicating things, the majority

© Springer International Publishing AG, part of Springer Nature 2018
R. Yokota et al. (Eds.): ISC High Performance 2018, LNCS 10876, pp. 246–265, 2018.
https://doi.org/10.1007/978-3-319-92040-5_13

of current large-scale parallel applications follow a lock-step execution model, where phases of computation and tight synchronization alternate and imbalance across components can lead to significant performance degradation. Additionally, unpredictable performance also complicates tuning, as it becomes difficult to tell apart performance differences induced by platform variability from the result of the tuning effort.

Although performance variability is a well-studied problem in high-performance computing (HPC), for the most part variability has historically been induced by either operating system or application *software*. For example, it has been shown that interference from the system software (a.k.a., OS jitter or OS noise) can have an adverse impact on performance [2–5]. This has led to several efforts in lightweight operating systems [6–8] that reduce OS jitter, as well as work in parallel runtimes that attempt to balance load dynamically across processors at runtime [9,10]. However, exascale computing is driving a separate trend in *hardware* complexity and diversity that may further complicate the issue. With the increasing complexity of computer architecture and the growing diversity of hardware (HW) used in HPC systems, variability caused by the hardware itself [11] may become as problematic as software induced variability. Examples of causes for hardware induced variability include differences between SKUs of the same model due to process variation [12] during manufacturing, the impact of shared resources in multi/many-core systems such as shared caches and the on-chip network, or performance variability due to thermal effects [13].

While system software induced variability can be addressed by, for instance, lightweight operating system kernels [7,14–16], HW variability is a latent attribute of the system. As of today, there is little understanding of how the degree of hardware induced variability compares to that induced by software, and whether or not this difference varies across different architectures. One of the primary issues with precisely characterizing hardware performance variability is that measurements of hardware variability need to be made in such a fashion that eliminates software induced variability as much as possible, but making this differentiation is challenging on large scale HPC systems due to the presence of commodity operating system kernels. For example, a recent study investigated run-to-run variability on a large scale Intel Xeon Phi based system [11], but because of the Linux software environment, it is currently difficult to attribute all of the variability exclusively to the hardware platform.

In this paper, we provide a solution to this problem by designing a performance evaluation framework that leverages lightweight operating system kernels to eliminate software induced variability. With this technique we systematically characterize hardware performance variability across multiple HPC hardware architectures. We have developed an extensible benchmarking framework that stresses different HW components (e.g., integer units, FPUs, caches, etc.) and measures variability induced by these components. Given that variability is a key measure of how well an architecture will perform for large scale parallel workloads, our work is a key step towards understanding the capabilities of new and emerging architectures for HPC applications and to help HPC architects and programmers to better understand whether or not the magnitude of variability induced by the hardware is an issue for their intended workloads.

This paper focuses on per-core performance variation with limited memory usage, i.e., limiting working set sizes so that they fit into first level caches. The results provided here constitute our first steps towards a more comprehensive characterization of the HW performance variability phenomenon, including measurements that involve simultaneous usage of multiple cores/SMT threads, higher level caches, the memory subsystem, as well as comparison across multiple SKUs of particular CPU models. Specifically, this paper makes the following contributions:

- We propose a benchmarking framework for systematically characterizing different aspects of hardware performance variability running on top of lightweight kernel operating systems.
- Using the framework we provide a comprehensive set of measurements on per-core run-to-run hardware performance variability comparing Intel Xeon, Intel Xeon Phi, Cavium ThunderX (64 bit ARM), Fujitsu FX100 (SPARC-V9) and IBM BlueGene/Q (PowerISA) platforms.
- We use our performance evaluation framework to highlight a number interesting architectural differences. For example, we find that some workloads generate six orders of magnitude difference between variability on the FX100 and the Xeon Phi platforms. We also demonstrate that the fixed work quantum (FWQ) test [17], often used for OS jitter measurements is not a precise instrument for characterizing performance variability.

The rest of this paper is organized as follows. We begin with related work in Sect. 2. We provide background information on lightweight kernels and the architectures we investigated in Sect. 3. We describe our approach in Sect. 4 and provide measurements and performance analysis in Sect. 5. Finally, Sect. 6 concludes the paper.

2   Related Work

Performance variability is an age-old problem in high-performance computing, with a plethora of research efforts over the past several decades detailing its detrimental impacts on tightly coupled BSP applications [18]. There are many diverse sources of variability, ranging from contention for cluster level resources such as interconnects [19] and power, to "interference" from operating system daemons [4,5], or intrinsic application properties that make it challenging to evenly balance data and workload *a priori* – for example, when application workload evolves and changes during runtime.

To mitigate these classes of variability, the HPC community has generally leveraged two strategies: (1) lightweight operating systems that reduce kernel interference by eliminating daemons and other unnecessary system services, and (2) parallel runtimes that provide mechanisms to respond to variability by, for example, balancing load [9,10,13], or by saving energy by throttling power [20,21] on the portions of the system less impacted by the particular source of variability.

Despite these efforts, there are indications that performance variability is poised to increase not only as a function of system software and algorithmic challenges, but also as a function of intrinsic hardware characteristics. With architectures continuing to trend towards thousand-way parallelism with heterogeneous cores and memory technologies, other architectural resources such as buses, interconnects, and caches are shared among a large set of processors that may simultaneously compete for them. While it is possible that parallel runtimes can address the resulting variability to some degree, recent research results indicate that today's runtimes are not particularly well suited to this type of hardware variability [22]. Thus, we believe there is a need for a performance evaluation framework that can precisely quantify the extent to which intrinsic hardware variability exists in an architecture.

As we mentioned earlier, multiple studies have investigated performance variation at the level of an entire distributed machine, however, none of them utilized lightweight kernels to clearly distinguish software and hardware sources [11,18]. It is also worth noting that the hardware community has been aware of some of these issues, for example, Borkar et al. showed the impact of voltage and temperature variations on circuit and microarchitecture [23].

3   Background

3.1   Lightweight Kernels

Lightweight kernels (LWKs) [16] tailored for HPC workloads date back to the early 1990s. These kernels ensure low operating system noise, excellent scalability and predictable application performance for large scale HPC simulations. Design principles of LWKs include simple memory management with pre-populated mappings covering physically contiguous memory, tickless non-preemptive (i.e., co-operative) process scheduling, and the elimination of OS daemon processes that could potentially interfere with applications [15]. One of the first LWKs that has been successfully deployed on a large scale supercomputer was Catamount [14], developed at Sandia National laboratories. IBM's BlueGene line of supercomputers have also been running an HPC-specific LWK called the Compute Node Kernel (CNK) [7]. While Catamount has been developed entirely from scratch, CNK borrows a significant amount of code from Linux so that it can better comply with standard Unix features. The most recent of Sandia National Laboratories' LWKs is Kitten [8], which distinguishes itself from their prior LWKs by providing a more complete Linux-compatible environment. There are also LWKs that start from Linux and modifications are done to meet HPC requirements. Cray's Extreme Scale Linux [24,25] and ZeptoOS [26] follow this path. The usual approach is to eliminate daemon processes, simplify the scheduler, and replace the memory management system. Linux' complex code base, however, can be prohibitive to entirely eliminate all undesired effects. In addition, it is also difficult to maintain Linux modifications with the rapidly evolving Linux source code.

Recently, with the advent of many-core CPUs, a new multi-kernel based approach has been proposed [6, 27–29]. The basic idea of multi-kernels is to run Linux and an LWK side-by-side on different cores of the CPU and to provide OS services in collaboration between the two kernels. This enables the LWK cores to provide LWK scalability, but also to retain Linux compatibility.

As we will see in Sect. 4, from this study's perspective the most important aspect of multi-kernel systems is the LWK's jitterless execution environment, which enables us to perform HW performance variability measurements with high precision. Note that several of the aforementioned studies considering lightweight kernels have investigated the jitter induced by the Linux kernel and thus we intentionally do not include results from Linux measurements in this work.

3.2   Growing Architectural Diversity in HPC

Over the course of the past two decades, the majority of HPC systems have deployed clusters of homogeneous architectures based on the Intel/AMD x86 processor family [30], reflecting the overall dominance and ubiquity of x86 for heavy duty computational processing during this period. Architects and applications programmers have largely been successful at gleaning maximum performance from these processors by extensively tuning and optimizing key mathematical libraries, as well as leveraging low latency, high bandwidth interconnects to allow workloads to scale well with the number of machines. Based on the large body of effort in this space, a critical mass developed around the x86 ecosystem, which fueled further development and productivity for many generations of HPC systems.

However, the exascale era has brought a new set of problems, stemming from the end of Dennard scaling and increasing power and energy concerns, which are driving a shift away from solely commodity x86 servers towards a more diverse set of chip architectures and processors. On the one hand, to continue to provide increasing levels of parallelism, chip architectures have turned to heterogeneous resources. This can be seen with many-core processors, such as Intel Xeon Phi, now deployed on several large supercomputers [30]. Furthermore, the emergence of heterogeneous processors has created a need for other types of heterogeneous resources; for example, high bandwidth memory devices are provided alongside DDR4 on Intel Xeon Phi chips to provide the requisite bandwidth needed by the many cores.

At the same time, a renewed focus on power and energy efficiency has caused the HPC community to consider a wider set of more energy efficient processor architectures. Due to its widespread use in mobile devices where power efficiency has long been a key concern, ARM processors are seen as one candidate architecture, with several research efforts demonstrating energy efficiency benefits for

Table 1. Summary of architectures.

Platform/Property	Intel Ivy Bridge	Intel KNL	Fujitsu FX100	Cavium ThunderX	IBM BG/Q
ISA	x86	x86	SPARC	ARM	PowerISA
Nr. of cores	8	64 + 4	32 + 2	48	16 + 2
Nr. of SMT threads	2	4	N/A	N/A	4
Clock frequency	2.6 GHz	1.4 GHz	2.2 GHz	2.0 GHz	1.6 GHz
L1d size	32 kB	32 kB	64 kB	32 kB	16 kB
L1i size	32 kB	32 kB	64 kB	78 kB	16 kB
L2 size	256 kB	1 MB x 34	24 MB	16 MB	32 MB
L3 size	20480 kB	N/A	N/A	N/A	N/A
On-chip network	?	2D mesh	?	?	Cross-bar
Process technology	22 nm	14 nm	20 nm	28 nm	45 nm

HPC workloads [31,32], as well as indications that ARM chips are on a similar performance trajectory as x86 chips before they started to gain adoption in HPC systems in the early 2000s [33]. Other processors with RISC-based ISAs, such as SPARC's SPARC64 processors used in Fujitsu's K-computer [34], present potential energy-efficient options for HPC.

Whether focusing on diversity in ISAs or heterogeneity of resources within a specific architecture, it is clear that the HPC community is facing a range of architectural diversity that has largely not existed for the past couple of decades. In this paper, we carefully examine some of the key architectural differences across a set of architectures, with a focus on the consistency of their performance characteristics. While others have performed performance comparisons across these architectures for HPC [33] and more general purpose workloads [31], we focus on the extent to which performance variability arises intrinsically from the architecture.

3.3   Architectures

While our framework is configurable to measure both core-specific as well as core-external resources, in this paper we present a detailed analysis of key workloads utilizing only core-local resources. In each of these architectures, this includes L1/L2 caches, as well as the arithmetic and floating point units of the core. We study these resources to understand how and if different processor architectures generate variability in different ways.

Table 1 summarizes the architectures used in our experiments. We went to great lengths to cover as many different architectures as we could, given the condition that we needed to deploy a lightweight kernel. We used two Intel platforms, Intel Xeon E5-2650 v2 (Ivy Bridge) [35] and Intel Xeon Phi Knight's Landing [36]. We also used Fujitsu's SPARC64 XIfx (FX100) [37], which is the next generation Fujitsu chip after the one deployed in the K Computer. ARM has been receiving a great deal of attention for its potential in the supercomputing space during the past couple of years. We used Cavium's ThunderX_CP [38] in this paper to characterize a processor implementing the ARM ISA. Finally, we also used the BlueGene/Q [39] platform from IBM.

Some of these platforms suite multi-kernels by design offering CPU cores separately for OS and application activities. The KNL is equipped with 4 OS CPU cores, leaving 64 CPUs to the application, while the FX100 and BG/Q have 2 OS cores and provide 32 and 16 application cores, respectively. This is indicated by the plus sign in Table 1. Except FX100 and ThunderX, all platforms provide symmetric multithreading. The cache architecture also exhibit visible differences across platforms. For example, the KNL has 1 MB of L2 cache on each tile (i.e., a pair of CPU cores), which makes the overall L2 size 34 MBs. Except Intel's Ivy Bridge, all architectures provide only two levels of caches. We couldn't find publicly available information regarding the on-chip network for all architectures, we left a question mark for those.

4   Our Approach: Lightweight Kernels to Measure HW Performance Variability

To provide a high precision characterization of hardware performance variability we need to ensure that we have absolutely full control over the software environment in which measurements are performed. We assert that Linux is not an adequate environment for this purpose. The Linux kernel is designed with general purpose workloads in mind, where the primary goal is to ensure high utilization of the hardware by providing fairness among applications with respect to access to underlying resources.

4.1   Drawbacks of Linux

While Linux based operating systems are ubiquitous on supercomputing platforms today, the Linux kernel is not built for HPC, and many Linux kernel features have been identified as problematic for HPC workloads, ranging from variability in large page allocation and memory management [40], to untimely preemption by kernel threads and daemons [5], and to unexpected delivery of interrupts from devices [41]. Generally speaking, these issues arise from the Linux design philosophy, which is to highly optimize the common case code paths with "best effort" resource management policies that minimize average case performance but that sacrifice worst-case performance. This is in contrast to the policies used in lightweight kernels that attempt to converge the worst and average case behavior of the kernel so as to eliminate software induced variability.

While the behavior of the Linux kernel can be optimized to some degree for HPC workloads via administrative tools (e.g., `cgroups`, `hugeTLBfs`, IRQ affinities, etc.) and kernel command line options (e.g., the `isolcpus` and `nohz_full` arguments), the excessive number of knobs renders this process error prone and the complexity of the Linux kernel prohibits high-confidence verification even for a well-tuned environment.

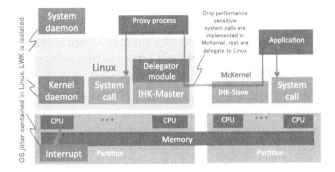

Fig. 1. Overview of the IHK/McKernel architecture.

4.2 IHK/McKernel and CNK

Because of these issues, we instead rely on lightweight operating system kernels introduced in Sect. 3. Specifically, we used the IHK/McKernel [42], [6] lightweight multikernel in this study on all architectures except the BlueGene/Q where we took advantage of IBM's proprietary lightweight kernel [7]. While not the primary contribution of the paper, this work involved significant efforts related to porting IHK/McKernel to multiple platforms, in particular support for the ARM architecture.

The overall architecture of IHK/McKernel is shown in Fig. 1. What makes McKernel suitable for this purpose is that we have full control over OS activities in the LWK. For example, there are no timer interrupts or IRQs from devices, there is no load balancing across CPUs and anonymous memory is mapped by large pages. All daemon processes, device driver and Linux kernel thread activities are restricted to the Linux cores. On the other hand, the multi-kernel structure of McKernel ensures that we can run standard Linux applications and it also makes multi-platform support considerably easier as we can rely on Linux for device drivers. As for BlueGene/Q, CNK provides a similarly controlled environment, although it is a standalone lightweight kernel that runs only on IBM's platform.

5 Performance Analysis

Previous studies on software induced performance variation relied on the FWQ and FTQ benchmarks to capture the influence of the system software stack on application codes. We hypothesize that simple benchmarks kernels like FWQ/FTQ or Selfish are insufficient to capture hardware performance variation. The full extent of hardware performance variation can only be observed when the resources which cause these variations are actually used. For basically empty loops which perform almost no computation this premise is not true. We propose a diverse set of benchmark kernels which exercise different functional units and resources as well as their combinations in an effort to reveal sources of hardware performance variation.

5.1   Benchmark Suite

Our benchmark suite currently consists of eight benchmark kernels and four sub-kernels. We selected our kernels from well-known algorithms such as DGEMM and SHA256, Mini-Apps, and micro benchmarks.

FWQ. To test our hypothesis we have to include FWQ in our benchmark suite to provide a baseline. The FWQ benchmark loops for a pre-determined amount of times. The only computation is the comparison and increment of the loop counter.

DGEMM. Matrix multiplication is a key operation used by many numerical algorithms. While special algorithms have been devised to compute a matrix product, we confine ourselves to naïve matrix multiplication to allow compilers to emit SIMD instructions, if possible. Thus, the DGEMM benchmark kernel is intended to measure hardware performance variation for double-precision floating point and vector operations.

SHA256. We use the SHA256 algorithm to exert integer execution units to determine if hardware performance variation measurably impacts integer processing.

HACCmk. HACCmk from the CORAL benchmark suite is a compute-intensive kernel with regular memory accesses. It uses N-body techniques to approximate forces between neighboring particles. We adjusted the number of iterations for the inner loop to achieve shorter runtimes. We are not interested in absolute performance, but rather the difference of performance for repeated invocations.

HPCCG. HPCCG, or High Performance Computing Conjugate Gradients, is a Mini-App aimed at exhibiting the performance properties of real-world physics codes working on unstructured grid problems. Our HPCCG code is based on Mantevo's HPCCG code. We removed any I/O code, notably printf() statements, and timing code so that only raw computation is performed by the kernel.

MiniFE. MiniFE like HPPCG is a proxy application for unstructured implicit finite element codes from Mantevo's benchmark suite. We also removed or disabled code related to runtime measurement, output, and logfile generation so our measurement is not disturbed by I/O operations.

STREAM. We include John McCalpin's STREAM benchmark to assess variability in the cache and memory subsystems. In addition we also provide the STREAM-Copy, STREAM-Scale, STREAM-Add, and STREAM-Triad as sub-kernels.

Capacity. The Capacity benchmark is intended to measure the performance variation of cache misses themselves. The Capacity benchmarks does so by touching successive cache lines of a buffer that is twice the size of the cache to under measurement.

For most of the benchmarks the input parameters adjust the problem size and thus benchmark runtime. As discussed below, we decouple problem size and benchmark runtime so that we can adjust problem size and benchmark runtime independently. While our benchmarking framework allows to configure benchmarks for arbitrary problem sizes, in this study we focus on problem sizes that fit into the L1 caches of our architectures. The idea is to eliminate or at least minimize the impact of the memory subsystem and shared resources beyond the L1 cache when we attempt to measure the performance variation of execution units. We adjust the working set to 90% of the L1 data cache size, except for the Capacity benchmark, where we set the working set to twice the L1 data cache size.

We repeat a benchmark multiple times to fill a fixed amount of wallclock time with computation. A fixed time goal, in contrast to a fixed amount of work, allows us to dynamically adjust the amount of work to the performance of each platform and keep the total runtime of the benchmarks manageable. This is possible, because we are not interested in the absolute performance of each architecture but rather how performance varies between benchmark runs.

We select a benchmark runtime of 1 s to balance overall runtime and still have a long enough benchmark runtime to have meaningful results. After selecting the wallclock time, the benchmark suite performs a preparation run to estimate the number of times a benchmark has to be repeated to fill the requested amount of runtime with computation, which we call *rounds*.

We use architecture-specific high-resolution tick counters for performance measurement. For x86_64, we use the Time Stamp Counter with the `rdtscp` instruction. On AArch64 we use the `mrs` instruction to read the Virtual Timer Count register, CNTVCT_EL0, which is accessible from userspace. SPARC64 offers a TICK register, which we read with the `rd %%tick`-mnemonic. On the BlueGene/Q we use the `GetTimeBase()` inline function, which internally reads the Time Base register of the Power ISA v.2.06.

Timing measurements using architecture-specific high resolution timers are the lowest-level software-only measurements possible. We have considered employing performance counter data to narrow down sources of variability, but ultimately decided against it for the following reasons: (1) equivalent performance counters are not available on all architectures, (2) performance counters also vary between models of a single architecture, and (3) performance counter are occasionally poorly documented and/or do not work as documented. Nevertheless our framework has performance counter support for selected architectures, which we utilize to verify cache behavior. We plan to extend performance counter support to all architectures in the future.

Our benchmark suite is designed to run benchmarks on physical or SMT cores. Cores can be measured either in isolation by measuring core after core or a group of cores at once. The isolation mode is intended to measure core-local sources of variation, while the group-mode allows to measure variation caused by sharing resources between cores. Examples of interesting groups include all SMT-threads of a physical core, the first SMT-thread of all physical cores, or all SMT-threads of a processor. We restrict ourselves to measurements of all SMT-threads in isolation-mode in this first study of hardware performance variation.

Note that during the measurement of a core in isolation-mode all other cores in the system are idle.

To obtain a measure of performance variation we repeat a benchmark 13 times and discard the first three iterations as warm-up. We use the remaining ten measurements of each SMT thread to determine the performance variation. We use two measures of variation in the study. The first measure normalizes the variation to the median performance of each core, the second to the minimum runtime measured for each core. We use the median-based measure when plotting performance variation for all cores of a machine. Given a vector $\mathbf{x}$, let $\widetilde{\mathbf{x}}$ be the median of $\mathbf{x}$. We visualize the variation by plotting the result of

$$(\mathbf{x} - \widetilde{\mathbf{x}})/\widetilde{\mathbf{x}} * 100.$$

Since this measure is based on the median variation might be positive as well as negative.

To reduce the variation of a single core into a single number, we calculate

$$\max \mathbf{x} / \min \mathbf{x} * 100 - 100$$

which yields the highest observed variation as percentage of the minimal observed runtime. Because the variations we observed between cores exhibited high fluctuation we decided against reducing the result to a single number, for example calculating a mean or average. Instead, we aim to preserve not only the minimal and maximal variation observed for each architecture, but also how the measured variations are distributed. Therefore, we present the measured variations in the form of a violin plot.

5.2   Results

We begin our evaluation by substantiating our claim that "empty loop benchmarks" such as FWQ are not suitable to measure hardware performance variation. In Fig. 2 we plot the measured variation of each SMT core of our 2-socket x86_64 Intel Ivy Bridge E5-2650 v2 platform with FWQ and HPCCG. We set the working set size of HPCCG to 70% of the L1 data cache size (32 KiB). We use the median-based variation, described in the previous paragraph, i.e. for each core we plot ten dots showing the percentage of variation from the median of each core.

The plot shows 30 of 32 SMT threads, because the two SMT threads of the first physical core run Linux, while the rest of the cores execute the benchmark under the McKernel lightweight kernel.

We turned the TurboBoost feature off, selected the performance governor, and set the frequency to the nominal frequency of 2.6 GHz. We additionally sampled the performance counters for L1 data cache and L1 instruction cache misses and confirmed that both benchmarks experience little to no misses.

Nevertheless all cores show significantly more variation under HPCCG than under FWQ. The difference cannot be accounted to cache misses, because even cores that show no data or instruction cache misses exhibit increased variation

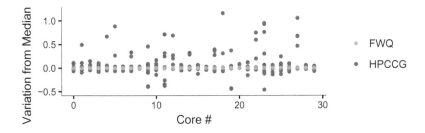

Fig. 2. Performance variation of FWQ and HPPCG on a dual-socket Intel E5-2650 v2.

under HPCCG. In particular cores one to seven and 16 to 29 experience neither instruction cache nor data cache misses under HPCCG.

After motivating the need for a diverse benchmark suite, we begin our comparison of performance variation. Because of the high dynamic range of performance variations within some architectures as well as across architectures we chose to plot the variation on a logarithmic scale. We keep the scale constant for all following plots to ease comparison between benchmarks. Lower values signify lower variation. Within a plot all violins are normalized to have the same area. The width of the violin marks how often different cores exhibited the same or at least a similar amount of variation. The height of the violins is a measure of how variation between cores fluctuates; a tall violin indicates that some cores show little to no variation and other cores exhibit high variation. In contrast a small or flat violin is the result of cores having similar or even equal variation.

We treat CPUs as black boxes because CPU manufacturers and chip designers are not likely to share their intellectual property (i.e., chip designs and architectures), which are required to exactly pinpoint the sources of variability. We have considered using performance counters to narrow down sources of variability but dropped the idea due to the problems with performance counters iterated in the previous subsection.

First we present our results for the FWQ benchmark, plotted in Fig. 3. The small violins in Fig. 3 already indicate very low variation. A lot of measurements, particularly for the FX100 and BlueGene/Q systems, show no variation at all, i.e. we measured the same number of cycles. Because zero values become negative infinity on a logarithmic scale, we clipped the values at $0.5 \times 10^{-7}\%$ to avoid distortion of the plots caused by non-plottable data.

Nevertheless the plot clearly shows KNL with the highest variation of all platforms, while BlueGene/Q and FX100 show the lowest variation. To help the reader to put these variation measurements into perspective we note that the higher end of the ThunderX violin at $10^{-6}\%$ corresponds to a "variation" of a single cycle.

Next we analyze the results of the STREAM benchmark in Fig. 4. STREAM contains memory accesses as well as few arithmetic operations in its instruction mix. Although the working set is small enough to fit in the L1-cache we still see cache misses on architectures where we have support for performance

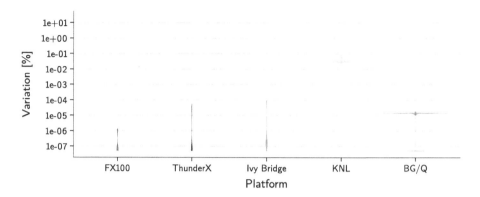

Fig. 3. Hardware performance variation under the FWQ benchmark.

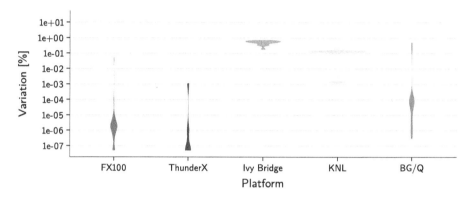

Fig. 4. Hardware performance variation under the STREAM benchmark.

counters. The observed variation increases for all architectures dramatically. The STREAM benchmark seems to have the least impact on variation on the ThunderX platform, where the variation only increases by one order of magnitude.

The Capacity benchmark is similar to the STREAM benchmarks, but here the memory subsystem has to deal only with a single data stream (Fig. 5). No computation is performed on the data, but the working set size is twice the size of the L1 data cache to intentionally and deterministically cause L1 cache misses. While the FX100 experiences little variation, the variation on the ThunderX platform increases substantially. The KNL platform shows very similar results for both the STREAM and Capacity benchmarks (Figs. 4 and 5).

We found that the different architectures exhibited diverse behaviour for the SHA256 benchmark. Despite the same L1 cache size and associativity, we observed no L1 data misses on the ThunderX platform but approximately 150k misses on the Intel Ivy Bridge platform. We decided to include the results as-is because we consider cache implementation details also micro-architecture-specific. Another reason is that the number of L1 misses on Ivy Bridge show

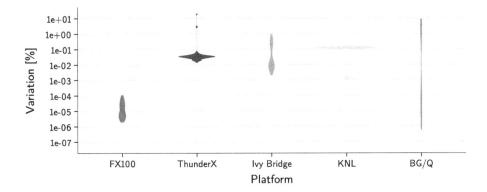

Fig. 5. Hardware performance variation under the Capacity benchmark.

little variation themselves. The wide base of the violins on FX100 and ThunderX already indicate that a lot of cores experience no variation at all, while Ivy Bridge performs significantly worse and KNL shows an order of magnitude more variation still.

We expected the BlueGene/Q to be among the lowest variation platforms but our measurements do not reflect that. At this point we can only speculate that the 16 KiB L1 data cache and the only 4-way set associativity of the L1 instruction cache have influence on the performance variation. We reduced the cache fill level to 80% so that auxiliary data such as stack variables have the same cache space in 32 KiB and 16 KiB caches, but we could not measure lower cache miss number of lower performance variation (Fig. 6).

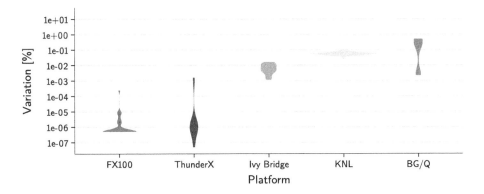

Fig. 6. Hardware performance variation under the SHA256 benchmark.

DGEMM is the first benchmark using floating point operations. This benchmark confirms the low variation of the FX100 and ThunderX platforms and the rather high variation of the Ivy Bridge, KNL and BlueGene/Q platforms. We saw high numbers of cache misses on the Ivy Bridge platforms and therefore reduced the cache pressure to 70% fill level. We saw stable or even zero cache miss numbers for all cores of the Ivy Bridge platform, but variation did not improve (Fig. 7).

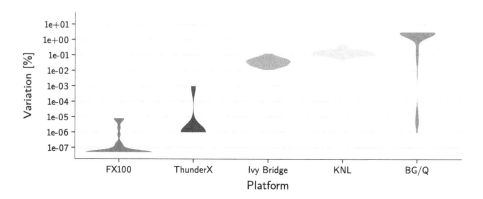

Fig. 7. Hardware performance variation under the DGEMM benchmark.

HACCmk has a call to the math library function `pow`, while Ivy Bridge and KNL instruction sets have `pow` vector instructions, we are not aware of such vector instruction on the FX100 and ThunderX platforms. FX100 and ThunderX show two orders of magnitude higher variation; $10^{-4}\%$ corresponds to 100 cycles on the ThunderX platform. KNL and Ivy Bridge are more deterministic in the variation the exhibit, which results in "flatter" violins (Fig. 8).

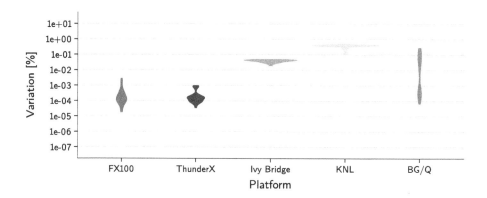

Fig. 8. Hardware performance variation under the HACCmk benchmark.

HPCCG is the only benchmark where the BlueGene/Q shows a variation close to our expectations (Fig. 9). We also highlight that while the variation on the FX100 and ThunderX platforms show a reduction in their variation compared to DGEMM, Ivy Bridge and KNL show increased variation for this benchmark. We confirmed on both the Ivy Bridge and ThunderX platforms that no L1 data cache misses occur (Figs. 7 and 9).

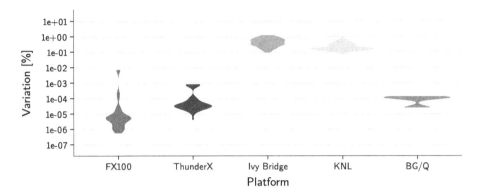

Fig. 9. Hardware performance variation under the HPCCG benchmark.

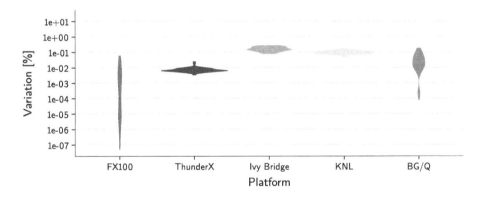

Fig. 10. Hardware performance variation under the MiniFE benchmark.

The MiniFE benchmark solves the same algorithmic problem as HPCCG. We expected similar results to HPCCG but our expectation was not confirmed by our measurements. The FX100 and ThunderX platforms show increased variation compared to HPCCG, while the Ivy Bridge and KNL platforms exhibit slightly lower variation (Figs. 9 and 10).

6   Conclusion and Future Work

With the increasing complexity of computer architecture and the growing diversity of hardware used in HPC systems, variability caused by the hardware has been receiving a great deal of attention. In this paper, we have taken the first steps towards a high-precision, cross-platform characterization of hardware performance variability. To this end, we have developed an extensible benchmarking framework and characterized multiple compute platforms (e.g., Intel x86, Cavium ARM64, Fujitsu SPARC64, IBM Power). In order to provide a tightly controlled software environment we have proposed to utilize lightweight kernel operating systems for our measurements. To the best of our knowledge, this is the first study that clearly distinguishes performance variation of the hardware from its software induced counterparts. Our initial findings focusing on CPU core local resources show up to six orders of magnitude difference in relative variation among CPUs across different platforms.

In the future, we will continue extending our study focusing on higher levels of caches, the on-chip network, the memory subsystem, etc., with the goal of providing a complete characterization of the entire hardware platform.

Acknowledgments. Part of this work has been funded by MEXT's program for the Development and Improvement of Next Generation Ultra High-Speed Computer System, under its Subsidies for Operating the Specific Advanced Large Research Facilities. The research and work presented in this paper has also been supported in part by the German priority program 1648 "Software for Exascale Computing" via the research project FFMK [43]. We acknowledge Kamil Iskra and William Scullin from Argone National Laboratories for their help with the BG/Q experiments. We would also like to thank our shepherd Saday Sadayappan for the useful feedbacks.

References

1. Markidis, S., et al.: The EPiGRAM project: preparing parallel programming models for exascale. In: Taufer, M., Mohr, B., Kunkel, J.M. (eds.) ISC High Performance 2016. LNCS, vol. 9945, pp. 56–68. Springer, Cham (2016). https://doi.org/10.1007/978-3-319-46079-6_5

2. Beckman, P., Iskra, K., Yoshii, K., Coghlan, S.: The influence of operating systems on the performance of collective operations at extreme scale. In: 2006 IEEE International Conference on Cluster Computing, pp. 1–12, September 2006

3. Ferreira, K.B., Bridges, P., Brightwell, R.: Characterizing application sensitivity to OS interference using kernel-level noise injection. In: Proceedings of the 2008 ACM/IEEE Conference on Supercomputing, SC 2008, pp. 19:1–19:12. IEEE Press, Piscataway (2008)

4. Hoefler, T., Schneider, T., Lumsdaine, A.: Characterizing the influence of system noise on large-scale applications by simulation. In: Proceedings of the 2010 ACM/IEEE International Conference for High Performance Computing, Networking, Storage and Analysis, SC 2010, pp. 1–11. IEEE Computer Society, Washington, DC (2010)

5. Petrini, F., Kerbyson, D., Pakin, S.: The case of the missing supercomputer performance: achieving optimal performance on the 8,192 processors of ASCI Q. In: Proceedings of the 15th Annual IEEE/ACM International Conference for High Performance Computing, Networking, Storage and Anaylsis, SC 2003 (2003)

6. Gerofi, B., Takagi, M., Hori, A., Nakamura, G., Shirasawa, T., Ishikawa, Y.: On the scalability, performance isolation and device driver transparency of the IHK/McKernel hybrid lightweight kernel. In: 2016 IEEE International Parallel and Distributed Processing Symposium (IPDPS), pp. 1041–1050, May 2016
7. Giampapa, M., Gooding, T., Inglett, T., Wisniewski, R.W.: Experiences with a lightweight supercomputer kernel: lessons learned from Blue Gene's CNK. In: Proceedings of the 2010 ACM/IEEE International Conference for High Performance Computing, Networking, Storage and Analysis. SC (2010)
8. Pedretti, K.T., Levenhagen, M., Ferreira, K., Brightwell, R., Kelly, S., Bridges, P., Hudson, T.: LDRD final report: a lightweight operating system for multi-core capability class supercomputers. Technical report SAND2010-6232, Sandia National Laboratories, September 2010
9. Kale, L., Zheng, G.: Charm++ and AMPI: adaptive runtime strategies via migratable objects. In: Advanced Computational Infrastructures for Parallel and Distributed Applications. Wiley (2009)
10. Kaiser, H., Brodowicz, M., Sterling, T.: ParalleX: an advanced parallel execution model for scaling-impaired applications. In: Proceedings of the International Conference on Parallel Processing Workshops, ICPPW 2009 (2009)
11. Chunduri, S., Harms, K., Parker, S., Morozov, V., Oshin, S., Cherukuri, N., Kumaran, K.: Run-to-run variability on Xeon Phi based Cray XC systems. In: Proceedings of the International Conference for High Performance Computing, Networking, Storage and Analysis, SC 2017, pp. 52:1–52:13. ACM, New York (2017)
12. Dighe, S., Vangal, S., Aseron, P., Kumar, S., Jacob, T., Bowman, K., Howard, J., Tschanz, J., Erraguntla, V., Borkar, N., De, V., Borkar, S.: Within-die variation-aware dynamic-voltage-frequency-scaling with optimal core allocation and thread hopping for the 80-core TeraFLOPS processor. IEEE J. Solid-State Circuits $46(1)$, 184–193 (2011)
13. Acun, B., Miller, P., Kale, L.V.: Variation among processors under Turbo Boost in HPC systems. In: Proceedings of the 2016 International Conference on Supercomputing, ICS 2016, pp. 6:1–6:12. ACM, New York (2016)
14. Kelly, S.M., Brightwell, R.: Software architecture of the light weight kernel, Catamount. In: Cray User Group, pp. 16–19 (2005)
15. Riesen, R., Brightwell, R., Bridges, P.G., Hudson, T., Maccabe, A.B., Widener, P.M., Ferreira, K.: Designing and implementing lightweight kernels for capability computing. Concurr. Comput. Pract. Exp. $21(6)$, 793–817 (2009)
16. Riesen, R., Maccabe, A.B., Gerofi, B., Lombard, D.N., Lange, J.J., Pedretti, K., Ferreira, K., Lang, M., Keppel, P., Wisniewski, R.W., Brightwell, R., Inglett, T., Park, Y., Ishikawa, Y.: What is a lightweight kernel? In: Proceedings of the 5th International Workshop on Runtime and Operating Systems for Supercomputers. ROSS. ACM, New York (2015)
17. Fixed Time Quantum and Fixed Work Quantum Tests. https://asc.llnl.gov/sequoia/benchmarks. Accessed Dec 2017
18. Kramer, W.T.C., Ryan, C.: Performance variability of highly parallel architectures. In: Sloot, P.M.A., Abramson, D., Bogdanov, A.V., Gorbachev, Y.E., Dongarra, J.J., Zomaya, A.Y. (eds.) ICCS 2003. LNCS, vol. 2659, pp. 560–569. Springer, Heidelberg (2003). https://doi.org/10.1007/3-540-44863-2_55
19. Bhatele, A., Mohror, K., Langer, S., Isaacs, K.: There goes the neighborhood: performance degradation due to nearby jobs. In: Proceedings of the 25th Annual IEEE/ACM International Conference for High Performance Computing, Networking, Storage and Analysis, SC 2013 (2013)

20. Rountree, B., Lowenthal, D., de Supinski, B., Schulz, M., Freeh, V., Bletsch, T.: Adagio: making DVS practical for complex HPC applications. In: Proceedings of the 23rd ACM International Conference on Supercomputing, ICS 2009 (2009)

21. Venkatesh, A., Vishnu, A., Hamidouche, K., Tallent, N., Panda, D., Kerbyson, D., Hoisie, A.: A case for application-oblivious energy-efficient MPI runtime. In: Proceedings of the 27th Annual IEEE/ACM International Conference for High Performance Computing, Networking, Storage and Analysis, SC 2015 (2015)

22. Ganguly, D., Lange, J.: The effect of asymmetric performance on asynchronous task based runtimes. In: Proceedings of the 7th International Workshop on Runtime and Operating Systems for Supercomputers, ROSS 2017 (2017)

23. Borkar, S., Karnik, T., Narendra, S., Tschanz, J., Keshavarzi, A., De, V.: Parameter variations and impact on circuits and microarchitecture. In: Proceedings of the 40th Annual Design Automation Conference, DAC 2003, pp. 338–342. ACM, New York (2003)

24. Oral, S., Wang, F., Dillow, D.A., Miller, R., Shipman, G.M., Maxwell, D., Henseler, D., Becklehimer, J., Larkin, J.: Reducing application runtime variability on Jaguar XT5. In: Proceedings of CUG 2010 (2010)

25. Pritchard, H., Roweth, D., Henseler, D., Cassella, P.: Leveraging the Cray Linux Environment core specialization feature to realize MPI asynchronous progress on Cray XE systems. In: Proceedings of Cray User Group. CUG (2012)

26. Yoshii, K., Iskra, K., Naik, H., Beckmanm, P., Broekema, P.C.: Characterizing the performance of big memory on Blue Gene Linux. In: Proceedings of the 2009 International Conference on Parallel Processing Workshops. ICPPW, pp. 65–72. IEEE Computer Society (2009)

27. Wisniewski, R.W., Inglett, T., Keppel, P., Murty, R., Riesen, R.: mOS: an architecture for extreme-scale operating systems. In: Proceedings of the 4th International Workshop on Runtime and Operating Systems for Supercomputers. ROSS. ACM, New York (2014)

28. Ouyang, J., Kocoloski, B., Lange, J.R., Pedretti, K.: Achieving performance isolation with lightweight co-kernels. In: Proceedings of the 24th International Symposium on High-Performance Parallel and Distributed Computing, HPDC 2015, pp. 149–160. ACM, New York (2015)

29. Lackorzynski, A., Weinhold, C., Härtig, H.: Decoupled: low-effort noise-free execution on commodity systems. In: Proceedings of the 6th International Workshop on Runtime and Operating Systems for Supercomputers, ROSS 2016, pp. 2:1–2:8. ACM, New York (2016)

30. Top500 supercomputer sites. https://www.top500.org/

31. Jarus, M., Varrette, S., Oleksiak, A., Bouvry, P.: Performance evaluation and energy efficiency of high-density HPC platforms based on Intel, AMD and ARM processors. In: Pierson, J.-M., Da Costa, G., Dittmann, L. (eds.) EE-LSDS 2013. LNCS, vol. 8046, pp. 182–200. Springer, Heidelberg (2013). https://doi.org/10.1007/978-3-642-40517-4_16

32. Rajovic, N., Rico, A., Puzovic, N., Adeniyi-Jones, C., Ramirez, A.: Tibidabo: making the case for an ARM-based HPC system. Future Gener. Comput. Syst. **36**(Supplement C), 322–334 (2014)

33. Rajovic, N., Carpenter, P., Gelado, I., Puzovic, N., Ramirez, A., Valero, M.: Supercomputing with commodity CPUs: are mobile SoCs ready for HPC? In: Proceedings of the 2013 ACM/IEEE Conference on Supercomputing. SC (2013)

34. Miyazaki, H., Kusano, Y., Shinjou, N., Shoji, F., Yokokawa, M., Watanabe, T.: Overview of the K computer system. Scitech **48**(3), 255–265 (2012)

35. Intel: Intel Xeon Processor E5–1600/E5-2600/E5-4600 v2 Product Families (2014). https://www.intel.com/content/www/us/en/processors/xeon/xeon-e5-1600-2600-vol-2-datasheet.html
36. Sodani, A.: Knights landing (KNL): 2nd generation Intel Xeon Phi processor. In: 2015 IEEE Hot Chips 27 Symposium (HCS), pp. 1–24, August 2015
37. Yoshida, T., Hondou, M., Tabata, T., Kan, R., Kiyota, N., Kojima, H., Hosoe, K., Okano, H.: Sparc64 XIfx: Fujitsu's next-generation processor for high-performance computing. IEEE Micro **35**(2), 6–14 (2015)
38. Cavium: ThunderX_CP Family of Workload Optimized Compute Processors (2014)
39. IBM: Design of the IBM Blue Gene/Q Compute chip. IBM J. Res. Dev. **57**(1/2), 1:1–1:13 (2013)
40. Kocoloski, B., Lange, J.: HPMMAP: lighweight memory management for commodity operating systems. In: Proceedings of 28th IEEE International Parallel and Distributed Processing Symposium, IPDPS 2014 (2014)
41. Widener, P., Levy, S., Ferreira, K., Hoefler, T.: On noise and the performance benefit of nonblocking collectives. Int. J. High Perform. Comput. Appl. **30**(1), 121–133 (2016)
42. Shimosawa, T., Gerofi, B., Takagi, M., Nakamura, G., Shirasawa, T., Saeki, Y., Shimizu, M., Hori, A., Ishikawa, Y.: Interface for heterogeneous kernels: a framework to enable hybrid OS designs targeting high performance computing on manycore architectures. In: 21th International Conference on High Performance Computing. HiPC, December 2014
43. FFMK Website. https://ffmk.tudos.org

Exascale Networks

The Pitfalls of Provisioning Exascale Networks: A Trace Replay Analysis for Understanding Communication Performance

Joseph P. Kenny[1]([✉]), Khachik Sargsyan[1], Samuel Knight[1],
George Michelogiannakis[2], and Jeremiah J. Wilke[1]

[1] Sandia National Laboratories, 7011 East Ave, Livermore, CA, USA
jpkenny@sandia.gov
[2] Lawrence Berkeley National Laboratory, 1 Cyclotron Rd, Berkeley, CA, USA

Abstract. Data movement is considered the main performance concern for exascale, including both on-node memory and off-node network communication. Indeed, many application traces show significant time spent in MPI calls, potentially indicating that faster networks must be provisioned for scalability. However, equating MPI times with network communication delays ignores synchronization delays and software overheads independent of network hardware. Using point-to-point protocol details, we explore the decomposition of MPI time into communication, synchronization and software stack components using architecture simulation. Detailed validation using Bayesian inference is used to identify the sensitivity of performance to specific latency/bandwidth parameters for different network protocols and to quantify associated uncertainties. The inference combined with trace replay shows that synchronization and MPI software stack overhead are at least as important as the network itself in determining time spent in communication routines.

1 Introduction

As high performance computing (HPC) systems are pushed to greater scales, the compute throughput of nodes has grown rapidly. Bandwidth/throughput ratios for network/compute performance have not been maintained [37], leading to concern that off-node interconnects may become severe bottlenecks [7,30]. Choosing the relative provisioning of network/compute is a critical step in any system procurement. Application traces can be a useful mechanism to understand performance on existing systems and extrapolate performance to next-generation systems [21]. For many HPC systems, message passing (MPI) is the dominant network runtime [1]. Understanding MPI performance is therefore critical to the problem of network design. In order to properly understand MPI application performance, however, it is necessary to disambiguate the effects of the network hardware itself from properties of the application and underlying communication library. If an application spends significant time waiting for message completion,

R. Yokota et al. (Eds.): ISC High Performance 2018, LNCS 10876, pp. 269–288, 2018.
https://doi.org/10.1007/978-3-319-92040-5_14

the cause may be that the network is under-provisioned relative to compute. However, observed delays may also be caused by synchronization mismatches between sender and receiver. MPI delays may also be in the system software rather than the time spent traversing network links and switches.

Full system architecture simulation has proven useful to analyze performance details. System simulation is robustly suited to explore design options that would be too costly or impractical to test on real systems or test beds. These design studies can include scaling system size, tuning system bandwidth/latency parameters, or even implementation of parallel algorithms. A discrete event simulator allows access to arbitrary performance counters or statistics while also imposing a perfectly synchronized global clock across the virtual system. Simulation therefore provides a level of omniscience lacking on physical systems.

In this work, decompositions of communication protocols are defined to allow precise attribution of application delays to network hardware, system software, and synchronization. A trace replay endpoint model and a detailed MPI software stack which was modified for detailed accounting of protocol timing has been used in conjunction with a hierarchy of full scale network models to perform system-scale simulation. Bayesian inference was used to quantify uncertainties and validate the most accurate model against a production software stack running on physical hardware (OpenMPI running over an Intel Omni-Path network). This simulation framework was used to collect communication decompositions for a suite of applications representing typical workloads for HPC systems run by the U.S. Department of Energy. This suite is representative of applications currently being used in codesign activities and system acceptance testing. These simulations demonstrate that performance degradation which would typically be attributed to poor network performance is often dominated by other factors instead. The analysis approach presented here is not necessarily limited to simulation. Adding this capability to real MPI implementations would allow deeper insight into application performance, provided the requisite precision in system clocks can be obtained.

2   Prior Work

2.1   Detailed MPI Performance Analysis

MPI profiling tools collect information about a running MPI application and provide post-mortem, or in some cases, live analysis. The information collected varies with how the application is tooled, and may include MPI call times, parameters, system counters, or hand-flagged portions of code. The MPI standard includes PMPI, which profilers use to intercept MPI calls at the point of invocation and record statistics including the time, communication pattern, and call arguments. Despite PMPI's wide adoption by tracing libraries, it does not provide insight into what the application or the underlying MPI layer does between MPI calls. PERUSE was an early effort to improve trace support in MPI that introduced callbacks for profiling tools to track state changes in the underlying implementation [25]. PERUSE was not accepted into the MPI standard, however, and MPI 3.1 introduced a different API called the MPI Tool Interface

(MPI_T), which exposes internal MPI runtime structures [1]. MPI_T is a recent standard, and is still undergoing adoption by profiling tool developers. The new API has still been used in recent research to profile MPI implementation memory overhead [19], create MPI-oriented software performance counters [13], and perform runtime introspection and application auto-tuning [35].

Of the numerous MPI trace collection tools, ScoreP adoption has grown considerably in recent years. It wraps the MPI compiler to instrument trace collection, and can generate event traces of MPI, OpenMP, CUDA, and PAPI counters [3]. The OTF2 format is compatible with a number of visualization tools [27], including Vampir [6], OpenSpeedShop [2], and Tau [4]. Trace visualization tools for OTF2 have the potential to show the culprits of communication barrier bottlenecks, but they suffer two shortcomings. Firstly, while a trace visualizer can elucidate cases where specific ranks enter into a collective late, they generally cannot visualize operations that occur in an MPI call. Secondly, compute nodes on HPC systems often have clock skews of several hundred milliseconds [24], which may ruin temporal alignment of communication barriers in trace files.

2.2   Network Architecture Simulation

Rather than profiling production runs, simulation of HPC systems is a common tool for performance analysis [10,21,22,29]. For estimating communication time, simulators can model packet or flit arbitration on individual components or they may use a simple delay function. The most popular delay-based model is LogP and its related models, with some variants incorporating congestion effects [17]. There are high levels of detail in Booksim [23], packet-level models in SST/macro [47] and CODES [20], and more coarse-grained models or flow models in BSIM [44] and SMPI [12]. Beyond simply simulating network traffic, many simulators also provide middleware implementing MPI semantics within the simulator, allowing different protocols or collective algorithms to be tested. CODES [20] implements some MPI semantics and has a separate collectives library. SMPI contains a fairly complete MPI implementation with flexible collectives [12]. SST/macro provides a nearly complete MPI 3.0 implementation for 2-sided and collective functions [47]. Most simulators can replay MPI traces, although SMPI and SST/macro emphasize on-line skeleton apps as simulation drivers.

Typically, performance studies have focused on evaluating time to solution for given workloads and network hardware configurations rather than delineating sources of performance degradation in the software stack. Casanova et. al. used piecewise linear regressions to account for MPI point-to-point protocols in a flow-based model [9]. Using an analytical model, Hoefler et al. examined the impact of system noise, an external cause of synchronization issues, on application performance [18]. Likewise, Totoni et al. used packet-level network simulations to examine noise impacts [46]. Yoga and Chabbi have used simulation to prototype communication protocol and hardware extensions that allow source code attribution and detailed tracking of network flows [48]. Their focus was on hardware events rather than application and protocol performance.

2.3   Uncertainty Quantification

While some form of validation is common for network simulators, detailed uncertainty quantification (UQ) is more difficult and therefore less common. In this work, the UQ approach consists of two main ingredients, (a) Forward modeling: Polynomial Chaos machinery for surrogate model construction and global sensitivity analysis, and (b) Inverse modeling: a Bayesian approach for calibrating the simulation model – or its surrogate – given experimental data. Both approaches are fairly well established in the UQ community. Synthetic, surrogate approximations have been employed in various computationally intensive studies, such as design optimization [34], reliability analysis [43] and, more relevantly, global sensitivity analysis [38,43]. Previous work did apply similar UQ methods to an earlier version of the highest-accuracy model used in this study. This work examined collective performance on Cray XE6 architectures [47].

3   MPI Implementations

3.1   Point-to-point Protocols and Synchronization

We wish to disambiguate what portion of observed MPI times is due to network delays and what portion is due to synchronization mismatches between MPI ranks or system software overheads. How to appropriately define synchronization depends on the exact protocol used for messages. Here we use three protocols modeled after those used on Cray Gemini and Aries systems [33] and validated against OpenMPI over OmniPath (see Sect. 5.1). Protocols distinguish small, medium, and large messages. These cutoffs are usually tunable, but the maximum small message is often 1–4 KB while the maximum medium message is 8–64 KB depending on the implementation (e.g. OpenMPI vs MPICH) and the underlying transport. Small messages are sent directly into preallocated mailboxes on the receiver (Fig. 1). The send completes immediately, provided there are sufficient mailbox credits. The receive completes immediately (after a memcopy from mailbox into buffer) if the message has already arrived. Synchronization delays can only occur on the receiver side since the sender completes

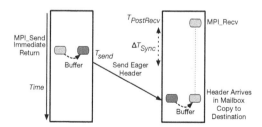

Fig. 1. Illustration of mailbox protocol for small messages. The sender returns immediately after copying into buffer. Receiver completes as soon as payload arrives, copying from mailbox buffer into recv array. T_{Send} and $T_{PostRecv}$ from Eq. (1) are shown. The receiver sees a synchronization delay (ΔT_{sync})

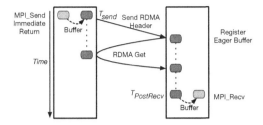

Fig. 2. Illustration of eager RDMA protocol for medium messages. The sender returns immediately after copying into send buffer. Upon receiving RDMA header, receiver selects buffer to receive RDMA get. Receiver completes as soon as RDMA get finishes, copying from buffer into receive array. T_{Send} and $T_{PostRecv}$ from Eq. (1) are shown. The sender completes immediately (eager). The receiver sees only network delays, not synchronization.

immediately. For the receiver, any time gap between posting the receive and the send beginning is due to synchronization, not a network delay - see Eq. (2).

Medium messages also use an eager protocol, but using an intermediate RDMA buffer (Fig. 2). The sender copies into a temporary buffer in pinned memory and sends a coordination header to the receiver. The sender then completes immediately. Once the header is received (regardless of whether a corresponding MPI_Recv was posted), the receiver performs an RDMA get into its own temporary buffer in pinned memory. Upon completion of the RDMA get (and posting of matching receive), the payload is copied from the temporary buffer into the receive buffer. Synchronization is defined the same way as the mailbox protocol, and again can only occur on the receiver.

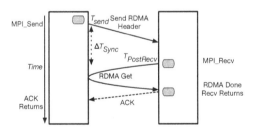

Fig. 3. Illustration of rendezvous RDMA protocol for large messages. The sender must wait for receiver synchronization. Data is transferred via zero-copy RDMA get. Receiver completes as soon as RDMA get finishes. Sender completes as soon as RDMA ack is received. T_{Send} and $T_{PostRecv}$ from Eq. (1) are shown. In this case, the sender sees a synchronization delay (ΔT_{sync}).

Large messages use a zero-copy rendezvous protocol (Fig. 3). The sender pins its buffer and then sends a coordination header to the receiver. After both the receive is posted and the coordination header is received, the receiver pins its buffer and posts an RDMA get directly from the remote buffer into the local buffer. The receiver completes when the RDMA get completes. The sender completes after it receives an ACK from the receiver that the operation is complete. Synchronization for the receiver is the same as in the eager and mailbox protocols. In the rendezvous protocol, the sender can also see synchronization delays. The time gap between the send beginning and posting the receive will contribute to the total observed MPI_Send time, but does not arise from a network delay.

Memcopy operations and RDMA pinning are not included in synchronization and are included as a distinct "MPI Stack" category. In Eq. (1), T_{Send} is the time *after* all local buffer operations have completed. In the same way, $T_{PostRecv}$ is the time *before* all local buffer operations have started.

$$\Delta T_{sync}(sender) = max(0, T_{PostRecv} - T_{Send}) \tag{1}$$

$$\Delta T_{sync}(recver) = max(0, T_{Send} - T_{PostRecv}) \tag{2}$$

These quantities clearly require a precisely synchronized clock between sender and receiver to accurately compute.

For non-blocking calls with deferred waits, the definitions must be amended slightly. Synchronization (and network) delays are not counted until the sender/receiver begins waiting:

$$\Delta T_{sync}(sender) = max(0, T_{PostRecv} - T_{WaitSend}) \tag{3}$$

$$\Delta T_{sync}(recver) = max(0, T_{Send} - T_{WaitRecv}) \tag{4}$$

Synchronization definitions easily generalize for collectives. Each collective is a sequence of point-to-point sends implementing a spanning tree [45]. Synchronization delays for collectives are therefore a sum over individual operations.

4   Methodology

4.1   Experimental Methodology

As the simulation framework and highest accuracy network model used in this study have been previously validated for collective operations on Cray XE6 architectures [47], the validation component of this work focused on improving the accuracy of the software stack component of the model using point-to-point operations. Parameterization and validation of the network model was performed on a cluster utilizing a 24-port Intel Omni-Path 100 Series Edge Switch. The switch was fully populated with one compute node per port, with each node containing two Intel Xeon E5-2683V4 processors with 16 cores each and a base clock rate of 2.10 GHz. An MPI benchmark was run on two nodes within this cluster to generate throughputs for message sizes ranging from 256 to 1,048,576 bytes. After a warmup period, the source node sends messages of increasing size in repeated windows to the same destination node. The total number of repeats for each size decreases from 2,560 messages for the smallest size to 40 messages for the largest size. Each run of the application produces an average throughput value for each of 18 message sizes. 100 runs of the benchmark were completed to gauge runtime variability. These experimental data were then used as input for uncertainty quantification.

4.2 Simulation

The Structural Simulation Toolkit (SST) [36] was used as a discrete event core for combining our simulation components: PISCES, MACRELS, and DUMPI trace replay [5]. The following application traces were generated or obtained from the NERSC DOE mini-app characterization website [31]:

Simulation	MPI Ranks
AMR Boxlib	1728
CESAR Nekbone	1024
Geometric multigrid	10648
GTC	16384
MiniDFT	1920
miniPIC	1024

The long-running DFT and GTC traces were truncated to 33% and 10%, respectively. Simulations were run with a hierarchy of network models in order to analyze various congestion and synchronization effects. The PISCES model (Packet-flow Interconnect Simulation for Congestion at Extreme Scale), is a packet-level model which breaks up network flows into coarse-grained packets. While large packet sizes are typically used to improve simulation efficiency, packets are allowed to share bandwidth when their paths intersect. This bandwidth sharing approximates the interleaving of finer-grained flow control units (FLITs) and reduces the errors associated with coarse-grained packets.

MACRELS (Message passing AnalytiC REally Lightweight Simulation) is an analytic network model with low computational cost. MACRELS approximates communication similarly to the LogP family of analytic network models [17]. Network delays assume an analytic function of the form

$$\Delta t = \alpha + \beta N \tag{5}$$

with communication time Δt, communication latency α, inverse bandwidth β, and message size N. Although network contention is ignored, it is modeled on injection/ejection with messages being constrained to arrive in-order and serializing when two messages depart or arrive at the same time. Since MACRELS is driven by the same fairly detailed endpoint models as PISCES, analysis of low level features such as MPI protocol overheads is still possible. Comparing MACRELS with PISCES for a given workload provides insight into both the importance of congestion in network modeling and into the subtle interplay between network congestion and application synchronization effects.

A third set of simulation results, termed "Compute Only", shows application performance for a theoretical system with zero latency and infinite bandwidth in the network as well as zero MPI software overheads ($\Delta t = 0$ for all messages). This probes the limit of performance as MPI time can only be attributed to inherent application load balance and associated synchronization issues.

Each trace was simulated on a canonical dragonfly topology [26] consisting of 48-switch groups (connected all-to-all) with a concentration of 4 nodes per switch. Up to eight intergroup connections were allowed per switch (with a maximum of one link to each group per switch). Minimal routing was chosen in order to generate worst case network congestion and thereby derive pessimistic values for network delays. PISCES (with minimal routing) and MACRELS should therefore estimate lower and upper bounds on network performance. Using a hierarchy of models rather than a single set of high accuracy simulations should provide both a better understanding of performance issues and more information about the reliability of the simulation data.

One MPI task was simulated per network endpoint (node) simulating a MPI+X execution model. While MPI traces were collected on the NERSC Edison platform with one MPI rank per core, we wish to understand internode MPI performance rather than intranode. Compute times from the DUMPI trace were therefore sped up by a factor of ten to represent the same application executing with thread-level parallelism on a state of the art multi-core processor. Applications run in MPI-only mode with one process per core will obviously have very different network characteristics. The procedure outlined here could be extended to validate and calibrate intranode MPI protocols and simulation models.

The set of parameters used for simulation is detailed later in Sect. 5.1 in Table 1. The latency and bandwidth parameters are separated into those affecting network performance and those affecting performance of the system software stack. Memory bandwidth, although a hardware parameter, is important for CPU operations in the MPI stack (memory copies) as shown in Figs. 1, 2 and 3.

4.3 Uncertainty Quantification

The overall high-level workflow for the UQ analysis is shown in Fig. 4. In the next section, we proceed to demonstrate the results of surrogate-enabled calibration to arrive at a full probabilistic description of input parameters as informed by the collected experimental data. Full mathematical details of the UQ procedure are delayed until the appendix. Here we give a conceptual overview.

The first step is surrogate construction. Running the full inference using the simulator directly is too expensive since >100K samples must be visited in a Monte Carlo procedure. Instead, a polynomial surrogate suitable for fast generation of Monte Carlo samples is constructed. The surrogate is built by collecting simulator results over a multidimensional sparse grid and fitting to a multi-dimensional polynomial.

While the resulting surrogate polynomial has some inaccuracies, previous work has shown that accuracy is sufficient for parameter calibration; in fact the

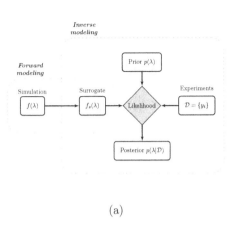
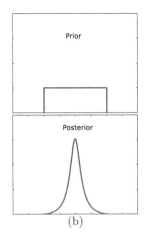

(a)   (b)

Fig. 4. (a) The UQ workflow employs polynomial chaos machinery for surrogate construction and global sensitivity analysis (forward modeling), and Bayesian inference with Markov Chain Monte Carlo (MCMC) for parameter calibration (inverse modeling). (b) Refinement from a prior distribution (all parameter values in a reasonable range equally likely) to a well-defined posterior distribution with small uncertainty.

surrogate-related errors are incorporated in the likelihood function for calibration. In the next step, the space of allowed parameter values (prior ranges) is explored. Each point in parameter space is a set of latencies/bandwidths that produces corresponding simulator output that can be compared to experimental values. The procedure searches for a maximum likelihood set of parameters while also quantifying the associated certainties. This is illustrated schematically in Fig. 4b where the prior distribution is updated into a posterior distribution with a well-defined maximum posterior value (which in the current context coincides with the maximum likelihood value), but also includes corresponding uncertainty information.

5   Results

5.1   Simulator Validation

Before we can accurately partition MPI times into contributions from network, MPI software stack, and synchronization, we must first validate the simulation framework. Validation here focuses on the more detailed PISCES model. The critical simulation parameters are displayed in Table 1. At issue is (1) what calibrated values to use for trace replay and (2) whether the chosen simulation is able to reproduce MPI point-to-point throughputs from OpenMPI over OmniPath (see Sect. 4.1). In particular, we wish to assign uncertainties and sensitivities to individual pieces of the simulation models.

We can improve the efficiency of inference by examining the parameter sensitivities in Fig. 5. The inference procedure is problem-agnostic, but sensitivities

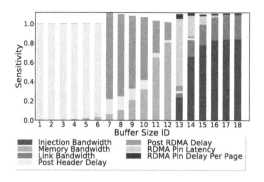

Buffer Sizes/Protocols		
Mailbox	Eager	Rendezvous
1. 256B	7. 6KB	13. 64KB
2. 512B	8. 8KB	14. 96KB
3. 1KB	9. 12KB	15. 128KB
4. 2KB	10. 16KB	16. 256KB
5. 3KB	11. 32KB	17. 512KB
6. 4KB	12. 48KB	18. 1MB

Fig. 5. The sensitivity to model parameters of each simulated point-to-point send (buffer size ID). The table provides the message size and protocol which corresponds to each buffer size ID. Shifts between communication protocols based on buffer sizes are clearly observed in the model parameter sensitivities.

help double-check the physical intuition and make the parameter inference as efficient as possible. Different parameters are more critical for different protocols. For example, some parameters are size-independent (post delays, pin latency) while others are size-dependent (bandwidth). As the size of message sent increases, sensitivity to bandwidth parameters increase. For mailbox protocols (1–6), header post delays are the most critical. RDMA is not performed. Some sensitivity to memory bandwidth appears for larger buffers. For eager RDMA protocols (7–12), RDMA post delays become important. The two memory copies (sender-size and receiver-side) dominate any network delays from injection or link bandwidth. For rendezvous protocols (13–18), zero-copy is used so memory bandwidth is no longer critical. While the eager protocol assumes reusable temporary buffers, rendezvous buffers must be registered for each zero-copy transfer. Thus RDMA pinning parameters appear in 13–18.

Figure 6 shows the prior distribution for the point-to-point send benchmark. Plotted here is the full sweep of simulator outputs if the complete prior range (Table 1) for each parameter is scanned. These are plotted along with the 100 experimental trials for each send buffer size. This demonstrates the inherent experimental variance and *prior uncertainty* in the simulation assuming any combination of parameter values within the prior range is equally likely. The inference procedure refines the prior distributions based on these discrepancies to yield the posterior distribution in Fig. 6. After parameter calibration, the posterior distribution demonstrates the remaining uncertainty and discrepancies between simulation and experimental results.

It is important to distinguish simple parameter fitting from the detailed calibration here. Any single data point can be reproduced by fitting parameters. However, fitting all data points together is only possible if the simulator is accurate. Data point 1 in Fig. 6 will "move" the prior parameters towards one set of posterior parameters that exactly reproduce the experiment. Exactly reproducing data point 8, however, may require different parameters from data point 1.

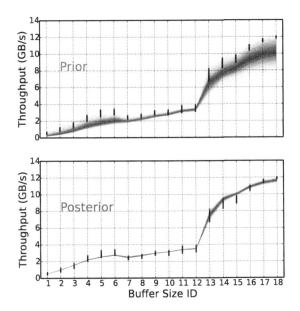

Fig. 6. Prior and posterior distributions of point-to-point send throughputs. The markers indicate output values from experimental trials. Buffer size ID specifies the message size as defined in Fig. 5.

Table 1. Breakdown of parameters used in simulated trace replay showing maximum likelihood parameters derived from inference. The prior range illustrates the "reasonable" values for each parameter visited during the inference. Maximum likelihood parameters are constrained to land within the prior range.

Parameter	Max likelihood[a]	Prior range	Type
Injection bandwidth (GB/s)	13.04	8.0–16.0	Network
Link bandwidth (GB/s)	12.47	10.0–15.0	Network
Memory bandwidth (GB/s)	11.20	8.0–15.0	System software
Post Header Delay (us)	0.36	0.1–1.5	System software
Post RDMA Delay (us)	0.88	0.5–2.0	System software
RDMA Pin Latency (us)	5.43	1.0–7.0	System software
RDMA Pin Delay Per Page (ns)	50.50	1.0–100.0	System software
Hop Latency[b] (ns)	100	n/a	n/a

[a]Maximum likelihood is peak of full 7-dimensional multivariate likelihood function. Values will differ slightly from the peaks in the *marginal* distributions in Fig. 7.
[b]This is an aggregate parameter accounting for the zero-load switch and link latency. In initial calibrations, it had little effect on the final result and was instead fixed at a nominal value.

This conflict in "best fit" amongst the individual data points creates the uncertainty in the posterior distribution. Additional uncertainty comes from the experiment itself.

Despite discontinuities and irregular shape, the simulation is able to almost exactly reproduce the experimental results in Fig. 6 after parameter calibration. The detailed calibration also shows that the simulator is reproducing individual pieces of the protocol, not just total throughputs. After calibration, each parameter has a definitive maximum posterior value (Fig. 7), with the exception of the per page memory pinning delay. This pin delay parameter has little effect on the final results and therefore is unconstrained. This is consistent with the sensitivities in Fig. 5. If a parameter were either not important or not accurately modeled, the posterior distribution would be unconstrained (i.e. have large uncertainties). In trace replay, injection and link bandwidth will contribute to network delays while the remaining parameters measure events in the MPI software stack. The validation therefore supports our assertion that MPI times are accurately decomposed into network, software stack, and synchronization.

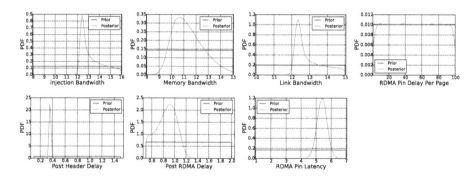

Fig. 7. Marginal Probability Density Functions (PDFs) from the Bayesian inference for each model input parameter. Peaks indicate parameters have well-defined values that accurately reproduce experiment. The flat distribution for pin delay per page indicates the simulation is not sensitive to this parameter.

5.2   Application Analysis

Figure 8 presents the simulated time decompositions for each examined application using the PISCES, MACRELS and Compute Only models. Looking at the most accurate PISCES simulations, the most striking observation is that for four of the six applications the network delay time is largely overwhelmed by the combination of MPI stack and synchronization times. The communication delays are only comparable to these hidden delays for DFT and GTC, yet even in these cases the network delays are smaller. The size of the network delays ranges from 83% of the combined hidden delays for DFT, the application in which communication is most significant, to only 4.1% for Multigrid. Clearly, attributing all

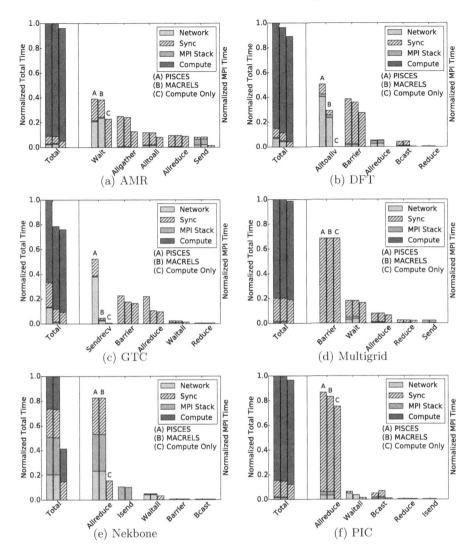

Fig. 8. Decomposition of simulated runtimes for application trace replays. Each trace was simulated with (A) the congestion-aware packet model PISCES, (B) the congestion-free flow-level analytic model MACRELS, and (C) a compute-only simulation with all network delays set to zero. Decompositions demonstrate that the large fraction of time spent performing MPI operations are often due to MPI stack overheads or synchronization due to load/performance imbalance.

time spent in MPI operations to network delays would lead to erroneous understanding of performance bottlenecks. For Multigrid in particular, extra network provisioning would make almost no performance difference.

Comparison of the PISCES and MACRELS decompositions illustrates the significance of network congestion in application performance. For most of the applications, the simulations which take into account network congestion (PISCES) are almost identical to the simulations that don't (MACRELS). GTC is the only application showing a significant amount of network time attributable to congestion; with the MACRELS model network time for Sendrecv operations drops by a factor greater than ten and the corresponding total time drops by 21%. This discrepancy will shrink when adaptive routing (such as UGAL) is used. Here we instead use minimal packet routing (PISCES) and contention-free flow models (MACRELS) to establish lower and upper bounds on network performance. For the rest of the applications, MACRELS total times differ from PISCES by less than four percent. Despite lacking contention, MACRELS can result in *longer* simulation times than PISCES. MACRELS assumes in-order message arrival and exclusive access to injection links by each flow. Because PISCES flow control allows multiple messages to "multiplex" across injection/ejection links, simulation times can be lower when contention is not a major factor.

Compute Only simulations only include application computation time, with MPI stack overhead eliminated and the network parameterized such that network operations are instantaneous. Compute Only simulations were included to rule out any possibility that network effects themselves were prolonging synchronization times in any significant way. This measures the inherent synchronization properties of the parallel algorithm. Some subtle or counterintuitive effects can occur as the model changes from PISCES to MACRELS to compute-only. In MACRELS, e.g., network delays can "hide" synchronization delays between ranks. Suppose Rank 0 and Rank 1 have a 1ms synchronization mismatch in the compute-only case. If Rank 0 is delayed 1ms by other communication before posting the receive from Rank 1, Ranks 0 and 1 will now be synchronized and the 1ms will be perceived as a network delay in Rank 0 instead. This occurs in Multigrid, e.g., where synchronization delays *increase* when communication delays are set to zero.

The majority of the applications do show a decrease in synchronization delays when communication is made instantaneous. GTC and Nekbone are the outliers. Nekbone stands out as the total time drops by 59% between the PISCES and Compute Only models. While the Allreduce operations in Nekbone don't cause any significant congestion in the simulation, they nevertheless generate a great deal of MPI stack overhead and communication delays. Nekbone shows a very poor parallel efficiency on the baseline architecture and would benefit greatly from improvements to the interconnect network and MPI stack overhead.

Though all applications in the examined workload spend at least nine percent of the total time outside of useful computation, the resulting communication delay is not entirely due to the network. The network delay itself is under three percent for AMR, Multigrid and PIC. The overwhelming measure of inefficiency for these applications is due to inherent synchronization issues, and improving the network will have a minimal impact on performance. With total time spent in network delays of seven and thirteen percent, respectively, DFT and GTC occupy a middle ground in which moderate performance improvements could be made by improving the network. Nekbone is unique among these applications in that communication, MPI stack, and synchronization each have significant impacts on performance and represent useful targets for performance improvement.

6 Conclusion

Managing the costs of network design and network provisioning is a serious challenge in any machine procurement. Application traces can support an evidence-based design, allowing the proper provisioning of networks to meet application requirements. Properly attributing application trace data to physical processes in the machine is critical, however, for properly selecting a design. This work demonstrates the utility of combining application trace replay with architecture simulation and Bayesian inference to understand expected application performance. The decomposition of execution time into network delays, software stack overhead, and inherent synchronization shows that not all time spent in MPI operations is equivalent. Even though all applications show significant time spent in MPI routines, this does not necessarily equate to insufficient network throughput.

Under the system conditions assumed in this study, applications such as Multigrid and PIC are almost entirely bound by imbalance (either load imbalance or system noise) leading to poorly synchronized communication. No improvements to the network would yield meaningful performance improvements for such applications. Conversely, applications such as Nekbone show very significant performance degradation due to communication delays, but also communication library overheads. Thus network provisioning alone would not entirely alleviate communication bottlenecks. The combination of detailed network and endpoint models with low-level instrumentation of simulations provides a powerful framework for disambiguating the individual causes of observed MPI times. As such, it provides a useful tool in system design by focusing improvements to have the biggest performance impact.

Acknowledgment. This work was funded by Sandia National Laboratories, which is a multimission laboratory managed and operated by National Technology and Engineering Solutions of Sandia, LLC, a wholly owned subsidiary of Honeywell International, Inc., for the U.S. Department of Energy's (DOE) National Nuclear Security Administration (NNSA) under contract DE-NA-0003525. The views expressed in the article do not necessarily represent the views of the U.S. Department of Energy or the United States Government.

A   Uncertainty Quantification

Consider the experimental data described in Sect. 4.1, collected as $R = 100$ replicas for $N = 18$ message sizes. The data set is denoted as $\mathcal{D} = \{y_i^{(r)}\}_{i=1,\ldots,N}^{r=1,\ldots,R}$. The goal is to tune the $M = 7$ parameters $\lambda = (\lambda_1, \ldots, \lambda_M)$ of the simulation model with vector output $f(\lambda) = (f_1(\lambda), \ldots, f_N(\lambda))$, to match with the data $f_i(\lambda) \approx y_i$. Bayesian inference is employed to arrive at a probabilistic representation of model input parameters. The Bayesian method is well-suited to work with noisy, heterogeneous data, as well as efficiently incorporate prior, expert-based information with experimental data [8, 39].

The parameter calibration relies on Bayes' formula, which in the present context reads as

$$\underbrace{p(\lambda|\mathcal{D})}_{\text{Posterior}} \propto \underbrace{p(\mathcal{D}|\lambda)}_{\text{Likelihood}} \underbrace{p(\lambda)}_{\text{Prior}} \tag{6}$$

The prior probability density function (PDF) encapsulates prior information about the input parameters $\lambda = (\lambda_1, \ldots, \lambda_M)$. In the current setting, we are given the ranges $[a_m, b_m]$ of possible values for each λ_m, for $m = 1, \ldots, M$, and employed uniform priors on $[a_m, b_m]$ accordingly.

The proportionality constant in Eq. (6) is typically difficult to compute and is not necessary if one's goal is to sample from the posterior PDF. Samples from the latter are obtained via Markov chain Monte Carlo (MCMC), which builds a Markov chain that has the posterior PDF as its stationary distribution [14, 16]. The key component of the Bayes' formula is the likelihood function $L_\mathcal{D}(\lambda) = p(\mathcal{D}|\lambda)$ that encodes the fit of the model with parameter settings λ to the observed data $\mathcal{D}$. In order to construct the likelihood function, one needs to assume a noise model of the experiments compared to the simulation outputs as follows. Specifically, an independent Gaussian noise is assumed:

$$L_\mathcal{D}(\lambda) = \prod_{i=1}^{N} \frac{1}{\sigma_i \sqrt{2\pi}} \exp\left(-\frac{(f_i(\lambda) - \mu_i)^2}{2\sigma_i^2}\right), \tag{7}$$

where $\mu_i = \frac{1}{R} \sum_{r=1}^{R} y_i^{(r)}$ and $\sigma_i^2 = \frac{1}{R} \sum_{r=1}^{R} (y_i^{(r)} - \mu_i)^2$ are the sample mean and variance of the experimental data over $R = 100$ replicas, correspondingly.

Besides obtaining samples from the posterior PDF, the maximum a posteriori (MAP) value of λ is of interest. It is defined as $\lambda_{\text{MAP}} = \text{argmax}_\lambda p(\lambda|\mathcal{D})$ and, for the current work coincides with the maximum likelihood (ML) estimate λ_{ML}, since uniform prior PDF $p(\lambda) = \text{const}$ is employed.

Note that in order to achieve a sufficient number of posterior λ-samples, one is required to evaluate the model $f(\lambda)$ many – usually between 10,000 and 100,000 – times. In the current work, model evaluation corresponds to running the simulation benchmark. Even for benchmarks running quickly (5–10s), calibration becomes expensive - particularly if it must be repeated as the model is changed to correct errors. For this purpose, it is common to pre-build a *surrogate model* $f_s(\lambda) \approx f(\lambda)$ that is computationally inexpensive to evaluate. Specifically, we built a surrogate model that has a polynomial form

$$f_s(\lambda) = \sum_{k=0}^{K-1} s_k \Psi_k(\lambda), \tag{8}$$

where $\Psi_k(\lambda) = L_k(\tilde{\lambda})$ are multivariate Legendre orthogonal polynomials, scaled to inputs $\tilde{\lambda} \in [-1, 1]$, and defined as products of univariate Legendre polynomials

$L_k(\tilde{\lambda}) = \prod_{j=1}^{M} L_{k_j}(\tilde{\lambda}_j)$. The polynomial expansion (8) is truncated at total order $K = 4$, i.e. $\sum_{j=1}^{M} k_j \leq K$, leading to $K = (M + P)!/M!/P! = 330$ terms. The form (8) is a special case of Polynomial Chaos expansions, which are convenient for uncertain quantity representations, propagation and moment estimation [15,28]. The surrogate model coefficients are found by a least-squares regression using a set of 2465 simulations of $f(\lambda)$, selected at 4-th order sparse quadrature locations [32,40], for sufficient coverage of the 7-dimensional parameter space. Note that we also extract leave-one-out (LOO) error measure of the surrogate model [11], compared to the simulation $f(\lambda)$, and augment the likelihood variance σ_i^2 in Eq. (7) accordingly.

Due to orthogonality of the basis polynomials in Eq. (8), one can extract sensitivity coefficients, or Sobol indices, analytically [42]. This procedure is also called global sensitivity analysis or variance-based decomposition, since each sensitivity index is interpreted as the fractional reduction of the output variance if one fixed the corresponding parameter [41]. More specifically, we employ the *total* sensitivity index that accounts for total effect of the given parameter including all interactions with other parameters.

As the sensitivity results in Sect. 5.1 suggest, model input parameters and outputs are conveniently divided into sensitivity based subgroups. We took advantage of such structure in order to accelerate MCMC and make the posterior sampling as efficient as possible. Namely, the first six outputs (Mailbox) are dominated by Post Header Delay (λ_4), while the next six (Eager) are most sensitive to Memory Bandwidth (λ_2) and Post RDMA Delay (λ_5), and the last group (Rendezvous) mostly depends on Injection Bandwidth (λ_1), Link Bandwidth (λ_3) and RDMA Pin Latency (λ_6). Note that the last parameter, RDMA Pin Delay Per Page (λ_7) has relatively little effect on any of the outputs, and the corresponding posterior PDF coincides with the prior PDF. In order to take advantage of the group-sensitive structure, we split the data into three subgroups $\mathcal{D} = \{\mathcal{D}_1, \mathcal{D}_2, \mathcal{D}_3\}$, and simplify the likelihood of the Bayes' formula as

$$p(\mathcal{D}|\lambda_1, \dots, \lambda_7) \approx p(\mathcal{D}_1|\lambda_4)\, p(\mathcal{D}_2|\lambda_2, \lambda_5)\, p(\mathcal{D}_3|\lambda_1, \lambda_3, \lambda_6) \qquad (9)$$

With such reformulation and independent uniform priors $p(\lambda) = \prod_{i=1}^{M} p(\lambda_i)$ for $M = 7$, instead of one 7-dimensional MCMC we arrived at three difference MCMC sampling procedures, with 1, 2 and 3 dimensions respectively, and the corresponding MCMC chains were much more efficiently sampled. We note that the missing λ's in each of the three product terms in (9) are set to their nominal values without losing accuracy due to the low sensitivity towards the corresponding group of outputs.

References

1. MPI: A Message-Passing Interface Standard; Version 3.1 (2015). http://mpi-forum. org/docs/mpi-3.1/mpi31-report.pdf
2. Open—speedshop (2017). https://openspeedshop.org/
3. Score-P (2017). http://www.vi-hps.org/projects/score-p/
4. Tau Home Page (2017). https://www.cs.uoregon.edu/research/tau/home.php
5. The DUMPI trace file format (2017). https://github.com/sstsimulator/sst-dumpi/ blob/master/docs/traceformat.dox
6. Vampir - Performance Optimization (2017). https://www.vampir.eu/
7. ASCAC Subcommittee, Lucas, et al.: Top ten exascale research challenges. US Department Of Energy Report (2014)
8. Carlin, B.P., Louis, T.A.: Bayesian Methods for Data Analysis. Chapman and Hall/CRC, Boca Raton (2011)
9. Casanova, H., et al.: Versatile, scalable, and accurate simulation of distributed applications and platforms. J. Parallel Distrib. Comput. **74**(10), 2899–2917 (2014)
10. Chan, C.P., et al.: Topology-aware performance optimization and modeling of adaptive mesh refinement codes for exascale. In: International Workshop on Communication Optimizations in HPC (COMHPC), pp. 17–28. IEEE (2016)
11. Christensen, R.: Plane Answers to Complex Questions: The Theory of Linear Models, 3rd edn. Springer, New York (2002). https://doi.org/10.1007/978-1-4419-9816-3
12. Degomme, A., Legrand, A., Markomanolis, G.S., Quinson, M., Stillwell, M., Suter, F.: Simulating MPI applications: the SMPI approach. IEEE Trans. Parallel Distrib. Syst. **28**, 2387–2400 (2017)
13. Eberius, D., Patinyasakdikul, T., Bosilca, G.: Using software-based performance counters to expose low-level open MPI performance information. In: Proceedings of the 24th European MPI Users' Group Meeting, pp. 7:1–7:8 (2017)
14. Gamerman, D., Lopes, H.F.: Markov Chain Monte Carlo: Stochastic Simulation for Bayesian Inference. Chapman and Hall/CRC, Boca Raton (2006)
15. Ghanem, R., Spanos, P.: Stochastic Finite Elements: A Spectral Approach. Springer Verlag, New York (1991)
16. Haario, H., Saksman, E., Tamminen, J.: An adaptive metropolis algorithm. Bernoulli **7**, 223–242 (2001)
17. Hoefler, T., Schneider, T., Lumsdaine, A.: LogGOPSim: Simulating large-scale applications in the LogGOPS model. In: HPDC 2010: 19th ACM International Symposium on High Performance Distributed Computing, pp. 597–604 (2010)
18. Hoefler, T., Schneider, T., Lumsdaine, A.: Characterizing the influence of system noise on large-scale applications by simulation. In: Proceedings of the 2010 ACM/IEEE International Conference for High Performance Computing, Networking, Storage and Analysis, pp. 1–11. IEEE Computer Society (2010)
19. Islam, T., Mohror, K., Schulz, M.: Exploring the capabilities of the new MPI_T interface. In: Proceedings of the 21st European MPI Users' Group Meeting, pp. 91:91–91:96 (2014)
20. Jain, N., et al.: Evaluating HPC networks via simulation of parallel workloads. In: SC16: International Conference for High Performance Computing, Networking, Storage and Analysis, pp. 154–165 (2016)
21. Jain, N., et al.: Evaluating HPC networks via simulation of parallel workloads. In: SC16: International Conference for High Performance Computing, Networking, Storage and Analysis, pp. 154–165. IEEE (2016)

22. Jain, N., et al.: Predicting the Performance Impact of Different Fat-tree Configurations (2017)
23. Jiang, N., Becker, D.U., Michelogiannakis, G., Balfour, J.D., Towles, B., Shaw, D.E., Kim, J., Dally, W.J.: A detailed and flexible cycle-accurate Network-on-Chip simulator. In: ISPASS, pp. 86–96 (2013)
24. Jones, T., Ostrouchov, G., Koenig, G.A., Mondragon, O.H., Bridges, P.G.: An evaluation of the state of time synchronization on leadership class supercomputers. Concurr. Comput. Pract. Exp. e4341. https://doi.org/10.1002/cpe.4341
25. Keller, R., Bosilca, G., Fagg, G., Resch, M., Dongarra, J.J.: Implementation and usage of the PERUSE-interface in open MPI. In: Mohr, B., Träff, J.L., Worringen, J., Dongarra, J. (eds.) EuroPVM/MPI 2006. LNCS, vol. 4192, pp. 347–355. Springer, Heidelberg (2006). https://doi.org/10.1007/11846802_48
26. Kim, J., Dally, W.J., Scott, S., Abts, D.: Technology-driven, highly-scalable dragonfly topology. In: Proceedings of the 35th Annual International Symposium on Computer Architecture, pp. 77–88. ISCA 2008 (2008)
27. Knüpfer, A., et al.: Score-P: A Joint Performance Measurement Run-Time Infrastructure for Periscope, Scalasca, TAU, and Vampir, January 2012
28. Le Maître, O., Knio, O.: Spectral Methods for Uncertainty Quantification. Springer, New York (2010). https://doi.org/10.1007/978-90-481-3520-2
29. Michelogiannakis, G., et al.: APHiD: hierarchical task placement to enable a tapered fat tree topology for lower power and cost in HPC networks. In: Proceedings of the 17th IEEE/ACM International Symposium on Cluster, Cloud and Grid Computing, pp. 228–237. IEEE Press (2017)
30. Minkenberg, C.: HPC networks: challenges and the role of optics. In: Optical Fiber Communications Conference and Exhibition (OFC), 2015, pp. 1–3. IEEE (2015)
31. National Energy Research Scientific Computing Center: Characterization of the DOE Mini-apps (2017). https://portal.nersc.gov/project/CAL/doe-miniapps.htm
32. Petras, K.: Smolyak cubature of given polynomial degree with few nodes for increasing dimension. Numerische Mathematik **93**, 729–753 (2003)
33. Pritchard, H., Gorodetsky, I., Buntinas, D.: A uGNI-based MPICH2 nemesis network module for the cray XE. In: 18th European MPI Users' Group Conference on Recent Advances in the Message Passing Interface, pp. 110–119 (2011)
34. Queipo, N.V., Haftka, R.T., Shyy, W., Goel, T., Vaidyanathan, R., Tucker, P.K.: Surrogate-based analysis and optimization. Prog. Aerosp. Sci. **41**(1), 1–28 (2005)
35. Ramesh, S., et al.: MPI performance engineering with the MPI tool interface: the integration of MVAPICH and TAU. In: Proceedings of the 24th European MPI Users' Group Meeting, pp. 16:1–16:11. EuroMPI 2017 (2017)
36. Rodrigues, A.F., et al.: The structural simulation toolkit. ACM SIGMETRICS Perform. Eval. Rev. **38**(4), 37–42 (2011)
37. Rumley, S., Bahadori, M., Polster, R., Hammond, S.D., Calhoun, D.M., Wen, K., Rodrigues, A., Bergman, K.: Optical interconnects for extreme scale computing systems. Parallel Comput. **64**, 65–80 (2017)
38. Sargsyan, K., Safta, C., Najm, H., Debusschere, B., Ricciuto, D., Thornton, P.: Dimensionality reduction for complex models via Bayesian compressive sensing. Int. J. Uncertainty Quantification **4**(1), 63–93 (2014)
39. Sivia, D.S., Skilling, J.: Data Analysis: A Bayesian Tutorial, 2nd edn. Oxford University Press, New York (2006)
40. Smolyak, S.A.: Quadrature and interpolation formulas for tensor products of certain classes of functions. Sov. Math. Dokl. **4**, 240–243 (1963)
41. Sobol, I.M.: Sensitivity estimates for nonlinear mathematical models. Math. Modeling Comput. Exper. **1**, 407–414 (1993)

42. Sudret, B.: Global sensitivity analysis using Polynomial Chaos expansions. Reliability Engineering and System Safety (2007). https://doi.org/10.1016/j.ress.2007.04.002

43. Sudret, B.: Meta-models for structural reliability and uncertainty quantification. In: Asian-Pacific Symposium on Structural Reliability and its Applications, pp. 1–24 (2012)

44. Susukita, R., et al.: Performance prediction of large-scale parallel system and application using macro-level simulation. In: SC 2008: International Conference for High Performance Computing, Networking, Storage and Analysis (2008)

45. Thakur, R., Rabenseifner, R., Gropp, W.: Optimization of collective communication operations in MPICH. Int. J. High Perform. Comput. Appl. **19**(1), 49–66 (2005)

46. Totoni, E., et al.: Simulation-based performance analysis and tuning for a two-level directly connected system. In: IEEE 17th International Conference on Parallel and Distributed Systems (ICPADS), 2011, pp. 340–347. IEEE (2011)

47. Wilke, J.J., Sargsyan, K., Kenny, J.P., Debusschere, B., Najm, H.N., Hendry, G.: Validation and uncertainty assessment of extreme-scale HPC simulation through Bayesian inference. In: Wolf, F., Mohr, B., an Mey, D. (eds.) Euro-Par 2013. LNCS, vol. 8097, pp. 41–52. Springer, Heidelberg (2013). https://doi.org/10.1007/978-3-642-40047-6_7

48. Yoga, A., Chabbi, M.: Path-synchronous performance monitoring in HPC interconnection networks with source-code attribution. In: Jarvis, S., Wright, S., Hammond, S. (eds.) PMBS 2017. LNCS, vol. 10724, pp. 221–235. Springer, Cham (2018). https://doi.org/10.1007/978-3-319-72971-8_11

Megafly: A Topology for Exascale Systems

Mario Flajslik[1](✉), Eric Borch[2](✉), and Mike A. Parker[3]

[1] Intel Corporation, Hudson, MA, USA
mario.flajslik@intel.com
[2] Intel Corporation, Fort Collins, CO, USA
eric.borch@intel.com
[3] Intel Corporation, Santa Clara, CA, USA
mike.a.parker@intel.com

Abstract. In this paper we explore network topologies suitable for future exascale systems that need to support over fifty thousand endpoints. With the increased necessity to use optics at higher link speeds, some of the more traditional topologies, such as Tori and Fat-Trees, become prohibitively expensive at such large scale. We identify two cost efficient hierarchical topologies, one a canonical Dragonfly, and one a variant of the Dragonfly topology that we call Megafly. Megafly is an indirect hierarchical topology with high path diversity, flexible tapering options and an abundance of possible system design points. We describe and analyze the Megafly topology to understand its key features and advantages, when compared to the Dragonfly. Additionally, we define a Megafly tapering scheme that enables a good balance of system performance versus cost. Our evaluation shows that the Megafly topology achieves equal or better throughput than the Dragonfly on a variety of traffic patterns, while requiring only half of the virtual channels for deadlock-free routing. Megafly also provides better fairness, which is shown in the evaluation of synchronizing traffic patterns, such as neighbor exchanges. We also showcase the design flexibility and cost vs. performance trade-offs of Megafly in a mini case study that illustrates the challenges of building a high performance fabric topology.

1 Introduction

Interconnection networks are a critical component of system design as they enable communication between discrete endpoints. Large systems often contain tens of thousands of endpoints, with future exascale systems expected to consist of over fifty thousand endpoints. A network topology defines the count and layout of network switches and cables that connect those endpoints. Choosing the topology that maximizes the network performance while staying within the cost and power constraints is a key design challenge.

Recently, the Dragonfly topology [18] has established itself as a cost-effective solution for large scale systems containing tens of thousands of nodes. Dragonfly

R. Yokota et al. (Eds.): ISC High Performance 2018, LNCS 10876, pp. 289–310, 2018.
https://doi.org/10.1007/978-3-319-92040-5_15

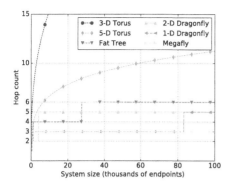

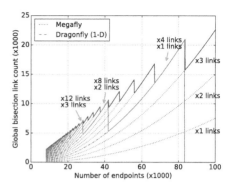

Fig. 1. Hop count for candidate topologies with radix-48 switches.

Fig. 2. Megafly has more possible design points than a canonical 1-D Dragonfly.

draws on its hierarchical design to reduce cabling costs, and it leverages adaptive routing to provide applications with good performance. A design premise for the Dragonfly is that the local group can be constructed using cheaper electrical cables, while optical cables are used for longer global links. The attractiveness of this design has been confirmed by its adoption in PERCS [4] and Cascade [10] systems.

However, with constant increase in link speeds between generations, the reach of copper cables has been reduced, and their price has increased to accommodate the necessary improvements in signal integrity. In the exascale system time frame, we expect to use links with speeds of 50G or 100G per lane, with most of the links being optical. A good example for this constraint is the Tofu2 interconnect [2], a 6-D torus topology that should be suitable for short copper cables, yet 2/3 of the links have to be optical even with 25G per lane speeds. The expected high ratio of optical vs. copper links highlights the network diameter (i.e. the number of network hops) as the key driver of the network cost.

We consider several topologies, with their hop counts (i.e. diameter) shown in Fig. 1 for different system sizes with 48 port switches. The tori are good topologies that fit neighbor exchange problems well, but with increased link speeds, most of their links need to be optical, making them prohibitively expensive at large scale. Dragonflies [18] are typically defined to have a Flattened Butterfly [17] (most often 1-D or 2-D) topology inside each group, with groups globally connected all-to-all. The 1-D Dragonfly is interesting because it can reach our target 50,000 endpoint scale with only 3 hops, while the 2-D Dragonfly would require 5 hops, assuming radix-48 switches. Fat Tree [20] topology is known to perform well for all kinds of traffic patterns, but to reach our desired scale, with same radix-48 switches, it would have to be a 4-level fat tree, which is also prohibitively expensive. Megafly is our name for a derivative of a 1-D Dragonfly, where the group is a butterfly topology (i.e. the group topology has not been flattened). Variants of this topology have previously been used in the Black Widow system [24] and other clusters [22]. This topology has also recently been mentioned under the name of Dragonfly+ in [8], and then published under the same name in [25]. We decided to keep our own, more distinct, Megafly name because Megafly is fundamentally an indirect topology, unlike the canonical Dragonflies, with Flattened Butterfly groups, that are all direct topologies. The indirect nature of Megafly is central to all of its many benefits over the direct Dragonfly topology, which we discuss in detail in this paper.

Topologies that are notably missing from our list of options in Fig. 1 are the diameter-2 topologies such as Slim Fly [5], or Orthogonal Fat Trees [28]. These lower diameter networks are generally cheaper, but the maximum number of ports per switch ASIC (i.e. the switch radix) has not yet reached a point where 2-hop topologies can support large systems with over fifty thousands of endpoints. Additionally, those topologies do not have an obvious building block (such as a Dragonfly/Megafly group) that can be reused across multiple systems of different sizes, making them impractical.

In this paper we identify the direct 1-D Dragonfly and the indirect Megafly topologies as the most likely candidates for an exascale system, since they are both 3-hop topologies, and can be built with the fewest number of optical links per endpoint. Throughout the paper we directly compare the 1-D Dragonfly (with all-to-all group topology) to the Megafly topology in their adaptive routing performance, tapering capabilities, and their cost vs. performance trade-offs.

While the Dragonfly topology has been well studied, the Megafly topology has not yet been extensively analyzed or evaluated, beyond the Dragonfly+ work [25]. We analyze the Megafly topology in Sect. 3 to show why its indirect nature leads to larger scale, and prove that the Megafly topology is the largest and highest path diversity 3-hop hierarchical topology one can build. We also show that the indirect Megafly group topology offers flexible tapering options, beyond the capabilities of a Dragonfly, enabling fine grained cost vs. performance trade-offs. In the Megafly group we can also define "up" and "down" local links that go from and towards the switches with nodes on them. This distinction of up-links and down-links enables deadlock-free routing in Megafly that requires only half of the virtual channels compared to the Dragonfly. Although routing requires fewer virtual channels, the adaptive routing primitives used by a Megafly are largely the same as those used by a Dragonfly. Consequently, a Megafly topology can be built using existing switches that already support a Dragonfly.

Another advantage of Megafly is the increased number of minimal paths between groups, when compared to a 1-D Dragonfly. Increasing path diversity leads to higher average throughput, better fairness, and improved robustness against failures, while also providing additional design flexibility for large systems. Figure 2 shows possible design points for the Megafly and 1-D Dragonfly topologies using radix 48 switches. Each line in the figure corresponds to design points with a different number of links between any two groups. It is common to use multiple links between groups (e.g. x4 links) to achieve good bisection bandwidth when the total number of global ports in a group is several times larger than the total number of groups. We see in Fig. 2, that for a fixed system size between 21k and 42k endpoints, there are only two possible global bisection bandwidths (i.e. design points) one can achieve with a Dragonfly, compared to between 8 and 11 Megafly design points (depending on the exact number of endpoints). In addition, there are critical system sizes at which maximum global bisection drops sharply due to the decrease in the maximum number of global links between groups. This decrease is more pronounced in the 1-D Dragonfly topology, although it is present in the Megafly as well. The number of endpoints is typically a fixed constraint in a large system design, and Megafly's flexibility enables extracting the highest network performance at any budget.

Increased Megafly path diversity also leads to better network fairness. Network fairness is particularly important for applications with synchronizing patterns, where the slowest node can determine the performance of the entire application. We evaluate the fairness of the Megafly and the Dragonfly, as well as their average throughput for several traffic patterns in a mini case study that highlights system design advantages of the Megafly topology in Sect. 6.

2   Background

Throughout the paper we evaluate the throughput of uniform random, random permutation and tornado synthetic patterns. A random permutation, or sometimes called static permutation, is a pattern where each node sends packets to exactly one other randomly chosen node. This is different from uniform random pattern where the target node randomly changes with every new packet. A tornado pattern is a particular permutation instance where each node communicates exclusively with the node that is located at some fixed offset away from it. In hierarchical topologies, such as a Dragonfly or a Megafly, a tornado pattern typically implies an offset that is a multiple of the group size, thus creating the worst case scenario with adverse hot-spots. These synthetic patterns are good first indicators of the topology and the routing algorithm performance. We augment those simple patterns with application proxy patterns in Sect. 6.

Our approach of measuring random permutation performance is similar to the Effective Bisection Bandwidth (EBB) metric previously used in [12]. To compute the EBB metric, authors first select a random bisection cut in the network, then randomly pair up nodes, one from each half, that communicate exclusively with each other. The resulting traffic pattern of such an EBB measurement is a random permutation, and consequently our random permutation results reflect the Effective Bisection Bandwidth metric.

In addition to the topology construction itself, the effectiveness of adaptive routing [18,26] is critical to the overall performance of modern topologies, such as those described later in this section (e.g. Dragonfly [18], Slim Fly [5]), but also Megafly. While not crucial for randomized traffic, adaptive routing is required for good performance on adversarial traffic patterns, such as tornado, where all nodes in a group communicate exclusively with nodes in one other group. Significant work has been devoted to improving the performance of Dragonfly adaptive routing [15,29], and Megafly topology can leverage most of those recent advances just as well.

2.1   Dragonfly

Since the introduction of high-radix switches [19], multiple 3-hop topologies have been proposed [17,18], with Dragonfly [18] generally accepted as the most cost efficient way to build large scale systems. Dragonfly is a hierarchical topology, globally connected all-to-all and locally connected with a Flattened butterfly. Under its broadest definition, Dragonfly could include any hierarchical topology (including Megafly), but we consider the canonical Dragonfly to have a Flattened butterfly group topology. The Flattened butterfly group can be 1-D (equivalent to an all-to-all topology), as first described in the original Dragonfly paper [18], but the group topology can also be a higher dimensional Flattened butterfly, such as a 2-D Flattened butterfly used in the NERSC Cori system [3]. We call these topologies 1-D and 2-D Dragonflies. An example of a 2-D Dragonfly is drawn in Fig. 3.

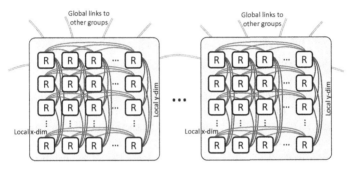

Fig. 3. Example of a 2-D Dragonfly. Only two groups are shown. Each router R also connects to the nodes (not shown in figure).

Furthermore, a balanced canonical 1-D Dragonfly is one where the number of global channels connected to each router is equal to the number of nodes (sometimes referred to as processors), and the number of routers in a group is equal to twice the number of nodes on a router. This is expressed in the Dragonfly paper [18] as $a = 2p = 2h$, with radix of the router adding up to: $r = p+h+(a-1)$. They define p as the number of nodes (processors) connected to each router; h is the number of global links on each router; and a is the number of routers in each group. We can expand this definition to a 2-D Dragonfly with a_1 routers in a row (x-dimension) and a_2 routers in each local group column (y-dimension). The balanced 2-D Dragonfly requires $a_1 = a_2 = 2p = 2h$, with router radix adding up to: $r = p+h+(a_1-1)+(a_2-1)$. While the 2-D Dragonfly generally has larger local groups, we need to reduce the number of nodes and global links connected to each router to stay within the constraints of a given router radix (e.g. 48 or 64 ports). Maintaining the balance is not a necessary requirement, but imbalance generally results in a wasted capacity on some links. As long as the wasted capacity is on the cheap copper links, some imbalance can usually be tolerated.

It is important to note that this imbalance is not a property of the Dragonfly topology, but of all topologies in general, including the Megafly. We generally prefer balanced designs for best performance on arbitrary traffic patterns, but we also often trade off some of that performance for cost reduction by tapering the network, thus introducing some imbalance. Tapering refers to reducing the available bandwidth at different levels of the topology hierarchy, compared to the aggregate injection bandwidth. For example, a Dragonfly group may have $a \cdot p$ units of injection bandwidth, but it may break the $h = p$ balance requirement and instead have only $3/4$ of the global links (i.e. $h = 0.75p$). This is referred to as a 75% global taper.

Throughout the paper we compare the Megafly topology directly to the canonical 1-D Dragonfly (both balanced and tapered variants). We do so under two constraints: (1) copper cable length is limited to about 2 m; and (2) changing the board and rack design between topology variants is prohibitively expensive. These two constraints may be specific to our needs, but we believe they are general enough to apply to most exascale design exercises. The Dragonfly topology itself provides many flexible design options in general, but under our specific constraints we find that only a handful of 1-D Dragonfly variants meet our needs.

In particular, one can taper the Dragonfly quite effectively at local and global level by changing the number of nodes/processors (p) and global links (h) on each router. For example, with radix-48 routers, a canonical balanced topology would likely have 12 nodes and 12 global links per router, and 24 routers in each group ($a = 24; p = 12; h = 12$). An alternative, tapered, 1-D Dragonfly could be built with 16 nodes and 8 global links per router, and 24 routers in each group ($a = 24; p = 16; h = 8$). This alternative Dragonfly has 50% global taper and 67% local taper. Many other configurations can also be constructed to exactly match the design needs. However, this design breaks our rule number two. In particular, changing the number of nodes connected to each router would severely impact the design of the compute board, as well as the rack design because of cooling and power provisioning. Megafly, on the other hand, provides local and global tapering options by simply adding or removing cables, so the tapering decision can be done very late in the design process, possibly when the cost of the optical cables can be much better estimated.

The 2-D Dragonfly enables larger local groups, thus providing more path diversity, and many more design and tapering options. While these topologies have worked well in the past [3], we found that due to our constraint number one, which limits the copper cable length to about 2 m, the added local dimension would have to be connected with optical cables. With that constraint in mind, the additional 2 hops in the 2-D Dragonfly are both optical hops, roughly tripling the number of optical links required, compared to the 1-D Dragonfly. Similar issue arises when analyzing tori, as shown in Fig. 1 with the hop count comparison between topologies. In addition to the increased number of optical links, 2-D Dragonfly generally requires more routers to reach the same number of nodes, because fewer nodes can be connected to each router, so that it can accommodate the links in the additional local dimension. These factors all impact the overall cost of the network. In fact, we found that using our simple cost model (described in Sect. 5), the cost of a full size 2-D Dragonfly would be over 80% higher than the same size 1-D Dragonfly. Again, this is because the number of optical links increases by about 3x, and the number of routers increases by about 50%, depending on the exact arrangement of the 2-D Flattened butterfly group.

Given these constraints, we find the design space of the usable Dragonfly topologies quite limited to a few 1-D canonical Dragonfly options, and we may refer to those simply as Dragonfly in the rest of the paper. This realization motivated our work on the Megafly topology which offers more design points without compromising performance, and it meets our design constraints.

2.2 Diameter Two Topologies

Two-hop topologies promise to be a low cost solution, but they are inherently limited in the scale they can reach. For example, 2-level Fat trees [20] are extremely popular in today's datacenters, but they are limited in the maximum number of nodes they can connect to $r^2/2$, where r is the switch radix. This makes them suitable only for small systems. Prior work has pushed the scale boundaries of diameter two topologies, with a good review given in [16]. Orthogonal Fat trees [28] scale up to approximately $r^3/4$, and Slim Fly [5] scales to approximately $r^3/8$, for radix r switches.

For diameter two topologies to be universally feasible, they require a higher number of ports per router than is available today. Although high-radix switch architectures have been proposed [19] and implemented [24], there are significant design and packaging challenges limiting further scaling. Current trends are to use growing switch bandwidth to increase the port bandwidth in every switch generation rather than increasing the port count. As a result, the highest radix routers available today are in the 48 to 64 port range, which is not enough to support a two-hop topology at the scale of the largest HPC systems (e.g. Sunway TaihuLight with 40,960 nodes [9,27]).

There are other challenges and inflexibilities of two-hop networks that make them unappealing for practical system design. For example, Orthogonal Fat trees are the largest 2-hop topology, but it is yet to be proven they can be built at low cost, given the global nature of all inter-switch cables. As a comparison, the same size Dragonfly or Megafly requires only half of the global cables due to its hierarchical design. In addition to scale and packaging challenges, both Slim Fly and Orthogonal Fat Tree design points depend on the existence of prime numbers in the desired range, and it is unclear if and how they could be tapered to fit into budget constraints.

3 Megafly Topology

In this section we describe the 3-hop Megafly topology and analyze its features. The construction of Megafly has already been given in [25], under the name

Fig. 4. Example Megafly topology.

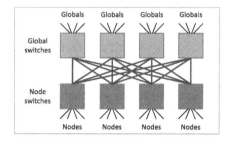

Fig. 5. Single Megafly group diagram.

of Dragonfly+. We summarize the construction and provide a more detailed analysis focused on the underlying reasons that enable Megafly to reach very large scale. All comparisons to a Dragonfly topology also assume a 3-hop 1-D Dragonfly, with all-to-all connections within the groups, and global all-to-all between groups.

3.1   Description

Megafly is a hierarchical topology, and it is constructed out of multiple groups connected by global links. The global links are expected to be formed by long optical cables, and groups are expected to be densely packed, with physical packaging discussed more in Sect. 5. An example Megafly is shown in Fig. 4, with individual groups connected all-to-all at the global level. Each group can have one or more global links connecting it to every other group. We use multiple links between groups to maintain good bisection bandwidth when the total number of global ports in a group is several times larger than the total number of groups. The exact switch pairs connected by global cables have traditionally been left unspecified in hierarchical topology definitions [18,25], with the only requirement being that each group has the same number of global connections to every other group. These global link arrangements have been studied separately in [7,11], and in our simulations we chose to randomize the global connections for both Megafly and Dragonfly to avoid any unintended artifacts introduced by one specific arrangement.

Within each group (shown in Fig. 5), switches are divided into *node switches* that connect directly to nodes, and *global switches* that connect directly to other groups over global links. Global switches do not have any nodes attached to them, thus establishing Megafly as an indirect topology. Within a group, each node switch connects directly to all global switches, and each global switch connects to all node switches. However, there are no connections made between any two node switches or any two global switches. Therefore, the underlying graph of a Megafly group is a complete bipartite graph. Figure 5 shows a balanced complete bipartite graph, but in the general case the number of global and node switches does not need to be the same.

We claim that the described Megafly group is the largest group possible, for a balanced 3-hop hierarchical topology and a fixed switch radix. We consider a topology balanced if it is not tapered, i.e. if aggregate node injection bandwidth can be supported by local and global bandwidth. The benefit of a large group is in the maximum scale the topology can reach, but it also increases the available path diversity. Therefore, maximizing the size of the group also maximizes the path diversity in the topology.

Claim 1. *A Megafly group is the largest possible group for any balanced 3-hop hierarchical topology.*

Proof. To form a 3-hop hierarchical topology, any node in the group must be at most 1 network hop (counting only hops between switches) away from every global link leaving that group. Conversely, each global link must be at most 1 network hop away from reaching every node in the group. Let's assume there is a switch with both node and global links connected to it. Such a switch must also directly connect to all other switches in the group to guarantee 1-hop distance between nodes and globals. If that is the case, however, the maximum number of switches in the group is limited to $r - 1$, where r is the switch radix. This is necessary to accommodate the switch that is connected to all other switches, in addition to at least one global link and at least one node. A balanced complete bipartite graph (i.e. a Megafly group) has r vertices/switches, and is therefore larger than any non-bipartite graph that contains a switch connected to both global and node links. Additionally, a complete bipartite graph of diameter 2 is also a bipartite Moore graph [23], which makes it the largest bipartite graph possible for a given degree and diameter. Therefore, a balanced Megafly group has the most possible switches, and as a corollary the most nodes and global links of all 3-hop hierarchical networks.

The combination of large node count and large global link count in each group yields a large total node count for the Megafly topology. With switch radix r, the number of nodes in a Megafly group is given by $(r/2)^2$, which is two times larger than a Dragonfly group built out of the same radix switches. Additionally, in a balanced topology, the number of global links in a group is the same as the number of nodes, and the maximum group count is one larger than the global link count, given by $((r/2)^2 + 1)$. Therefore, the maximum total number of nodes in a Megafly is $(r/2)^2 \cdot ((r/2)^2 + 1)$, which is about four times larger than a Dragonfly given by $((r/2)(r/4)) \cdot ((r/2)(r/4) + 1)$.

Although theoretically interesting, such high node counts are not yet relevant, even for the largest systems. However, this scale allows smaller systems to be built with more links between any two groups. Since a Megafly group is 2x larger than a Dragonfly group it has 2x more global links leaving each group, and, at the same time, the Megafly topology would have 2x fewer groups to reach the same system size. This multiplies to give Megafly four times as many global links between any two groups in an equal size system, therefore increasing path diversity. Trading off scale for path diversity is not unique to Megafly, but Megafly is better positioned to take advantage of it due to its large inherent scale. In fact, most of the advantages of Megafly arise from the ability to trade its large scale for increased path diversity.

3.2   Analysis

We define a topology graph where vertices are network switches, and edges are links between switches. In a direct topology, all of the switches/vertices also have some number of nodes attached to them, however for simplicity reasons we do not include the nodes in the topology graph. If the topology is balanced, the number of attached nodes is equal to the graph degree divided by graph diameter. Since the nodes are not included in the topology graph, they do not contribute to the graph degree either, but we do have to consider them when calculating the switch radix because they do consume ports on each switch. As a result, the radix of the switches that form the topology is equal to the degree of the underlying graph plus the number of nodes connected to each switch. Direct 3-hop topologies (e.g. Dragonfly, 3-D Flattened butterfly) have topology graphs of diameter 3. There is a known upper bound, called the Moore bound [23], limiting the overall graph size for a given degree and diameter. The Moore bound for 3-hop direct topologies is given in Fig. 6, together with hypothetical topologies derived from the largest known graphs approaching the Moore bound, as found in [23].

Megafly is an indirect topology, and its underlying graph does not need to be a diameter-3 graph for the topology to still be a 3-hop topology. In particular, two global switches can be more than 3 hops away, and indeed, they are 5 hops away in the general case. If one were to route from one global switch to another global switch (see Figs. 4 and 5), the general route would first go "down" to a node switch, then "up" to a global switch with a link to the destination group, then "across" a global link, and finally "down" and "up" local links in the destination group to reach the target global switch. This adds up to 5 hops (2 local + 1 global + 2 local). However, since global switches do not have any nodes attached to them, routes never start or finish at global switches, and Megafly is still a 3-hop topology, because all node switches are at most 3-hops away from each other. This advantage of an indirect topology is shown in Fig. 6, as Megafly is within 60% of the Moore bound for direct topologies, and thus capable of larger scale than any other known 3-hop topologies.

As already mentioned, the large scale of Megafly translates into multiple minimal paths for smaller systems, and this path diversity is critical to achieving high performance and fairness. If we compare equivalent size Dragonfly and Megafly topologies, each Megafly group has four times as many minimal paths to other groups. This is the result of a Megafly group having twice as many global links, along with twice as many nodes. Because there are 2x more nodes, a Megafly topology needs only half of the groups to reach the same size, resulting in

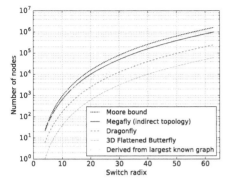

Fig. 6. Comparison of maximum node counts for 3-hop networks.

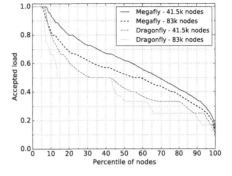

Fig. 7. Minimal routing performance with random permutation traffic.

four times more paths between any pair of groups. While minimal path diversity increases by a factor of four, minimal bandwidth per node increases by a factor of two because the number of nodes per group is doubled.

We perform a simulation study of the impact of increased bandwidth and minimal path diversity on random permutation traffic, with primary focus on throughput fairness of minimal routing. Minimal routing performance is important for traffic that cannot be adaptively routed (e.g. traffic requiring ordering), and it also establishes a lower bound for adaptive routing performance. Adaptive routing and other traffic patterns are studied in Sect. 4. Simulation results for minimal routing on Megafly and Dragonfly topologies built out of 48 port switches are shown in Fig. 7. In particular, we simulate 83k node and 41.5k node topologies. At the larger size, the Dragonfly topology has only one minimal path between any pair of groups, and for the smaller size there are two minimal paths between groups. Equivalent size Megaflies have four and eight minimal paths between groups, respectively.

Results in Fig. 7 show that Megafly significantly outperforms Dragonfly topology at either size. The x-axis shows percentile of nodes that achieve at least the throughput given on the y-axis. For example, median throughput can be read from the graph at the 50th percentile value. The median node in Megafly has about 0.2 higher throughput than the median node in Dragonfly, which is about a 50% increase. Average throughput is difficult to read directly out of the graph, but Megafly reaches about 0.14 higher average throughput than the same size Dragonfly, or about a 30% throughput increase. Another interesting comparison to make is that only about 43% of nodes see more than 0.5 throughput in the 41.5k Dragonfly, while almost 70% of nodes see more than 0.5 throughput in the 41.5k Megafly. Megafly's minimal routing provides higher throughput, which means there is less congestion in the fabric and thus, decreased need for non-minimal adaptive routing. Although not studied here, one can also reason that adaptive routing is more effective at improving fairness when there are fewer poorly performing nodes, as is the case with Megafly.

In conclusion, the increased scale of the indirect Megafly topology translates to more minimal path diversity that provides better throughput and improved fairness.

4 Routing Evaluation

We distinguish between minimal, valiant and adaptive routing in Megafly. Minimal routing traverses the fewest possible links between the source and the destination (up to 3 network hops), but it is susceptible to link congestion with adversarial traffic patterns (e.g. tornado traffic). To alleviate this congestion concern, valiant routing randomizes all traffic by first routing minimally to a randomly chosen intermediate router (called root), then routing minimally from the root to the destination. Performance of valiant routing is consistent across all traffic patterns, but each packet consumes twice as many network resources compared to minimal routing, thus limiting the overall throughput to 50%. Adaptive routing chooses between minimal and valiant algorithms based on some congestion metric so that well behaved traffic is routed minimally and adversarial patterns use valiant routing [15, 26].

Routing principles and adversarial patterns of Megafly are similar to Dragonfly, since they are both hierarchical topologies. In this section we evaluate Megafly performance using existing Dragonfly routing algorithms that are implemented in switches supporting the Dragonfly topology.

Minimal routing in a Megafly takes up to three hops (two local and one global), similar to a Dragonfly, but it can be made deadlock-free with just one virtual channel. Even though two local links are traversed, one of them is always taken in the up direction, and the other in the down direction. Consequently, minimal routing in Megafly is deadlock free without requiring extra virtual channels (VCs) for deadlock avoidance. This is a significant advantage over the Dragonfly topology which requires 2 VCs for deadlock-free minimal routing.

Adaptive routing is used to avoid congestion in Megafly, analogous to how it is used in a Dragonfly. We evaluate a variant of Progressive Adaptive Routing [15] that is similar to an algorithm that has been implemented in practice [10] for Dragonfly topologies. The adaptive routing algorithm uses output queue occupancy to choose between minimal and non-minimal paths, with a 2:1 bias towards the minimal path.

Megafly routing performance was evaluated using a flit based simulator [14], and compared to a similarly sized Dragonfly. Simulated topologies are made of 24 port switches, which results in a 73 group Dragonfly with 72 nodes per group for a total of 5256 nodes, and a 37 group Megafly with 144 nodes per group for a total of 5328 nodes. We did not choose a specific global link arrangement, instead we randomized the order of global links in each group. This global link randomization was applied to both Megafly and Dragonfly topologies, and is intended to remove any performance artifacts resulting form a group pair repeatedly appearing on the same switch in other groups.

Simulation results are shown in Fig. 8. The left column shows results for minimal routing, the middle column for valiant routing, and the right column

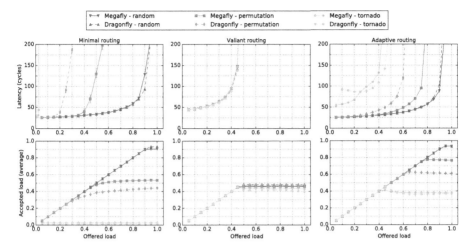

Fig. 8. Simulation results for 5.3k Megafly vs. Dragonfly topologies. Top row: latency vs. offered load; bottom row: accepted load vs. offered load. Left column: minimal routing; middle column: valiant routing; right column: adaptive routing.

for adaptive routing. The top row are latency results and the bottom row shows results for average accepted load. Megafly has 4x more bandwidth between any two groups, but the groups are 2x larger than Dragonfly, resulting in 2x more minimal throughput per node for any Megafly group pair. This directly translates into 2x higher tornado minimal routing throughput, and a significant increase in permutation minimal routing throughput (bottom left subfigure in Fig. 8). The increase in minimal routing throughput carries over into adaptive routing, and simulation results show higher throughput for the permutation traffic pattern (bottom right subfigure in Fig. 8).

Latency results are shown in the top row of Fig. 8. Latency is largely a reflection of when the bandwidth graph saturates, with an interesting pattern appearing in adaptive routing with tornado traffic, where latency initially increases, then stabilizes before finally saturating. This has been observed multiple times in a Dragonfly [15,18], and is an artifact of adaptive routing favoring minimal paths under low congestion. All of the permutation results are averages across multiple permutations with different random seed values. Error bars are also plotted for all permutation pattern plots, but they are generally too small to be visible in Fig. 8, except at a few latency points.

5   System Considerations

In this section we consider practical system implications of the topology, in particular tapering and packaging. Tapering allows us to adjust the amount of bisection bandwidth to balance it against cost or application requirements. At the same time, physical packaging of the system can make or break the budget, with long optical cables being an order of magnitude more expensive than short copper cables. We find that Megafly offers good flexibility and it can be built in a compact and cost efficient way.

5.1 Tapering

To simplify how we reason about tapering, we propose organizing global switches into *slices*, as shown in Fig. 9. Each slice contains one or more global switches and all links (local and global) that are connected to each of those global switches. The set of all switches in each slice connects to all other groups in the system. Consequently, each slice provides full connectivity between all groups. Since each node switch connects to every global switch in a group, each slice provides full connectivity between all node switches, and thus all nodes. Note that a node switch is not a part of a particular slice, and this distinction between node and global switches makes slices, as we define them, incompatible with a Dragonfly.

Global tapering can be used to reduce the number of expensive optical links. For example, if a system is globally tapered to 75%, that implies only 75% of the global cables are required, thus reducing cost and energy requirements. Such a global tapering approach can be equally effective in Dragonfly and Megafly topologies.

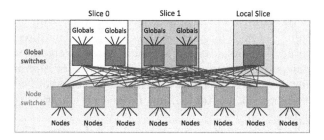

Fig. 9. Tapering Megafly to 50%/75% global/local by using local slices.

In addition to global tapering, Megafly can also be locally tapered by reducing the number of local cables, which we call local tapering. Global and local tapering can be combined in a balanced way by removing entire slices, which tapers both local and global bandwidth evenly. This method of tapering by removing switches is limited to indirect topologies because removed switches can not have any nodes attached to them, and as such is not available on a Dragonfly.

Local level of tapering can be adjusted independently of the global tapering, as long as local bandwidth is same or higher than global available bandwidth. A scheme for local tapering is shown in Fig. 9, where a special local slice is introduced to increase the amount of local bandwidth. This local slice requires only half of the switches of a regular slice, because all of the switch ports are used to connect local cables. Requiring only half of the switches for reclaiming each slice's local bandwidth leads to cost and energy savings.

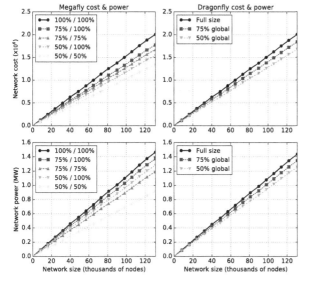

Table 1. Parameters for cost and energy models.

Local link cost	1
Global link cost	10
Switch cost	100
Power per port	2.8W

Fig. 10. Cost and energy models for global/local tapering of Megafly, and global tapering of Dragonfly.

The ability to remove switches, and the attached links, from the topology without reducing the number of endpoints leads to significant savings in cost and power of tapered Megafly topologies. We create a cost model based on rough estimates shown in Table 1. Large systems are custom made and any attempt at estimating exact dollar cost for all topology variants is futile, so we instead focus on representative ratios. We find that global optical links are generally 10x more expensive than local or node links that are either formed using copper cables or even copper traces on a low-loss circuit board. At the same time, a high radix switch ASIC cost is about an order of magnitude more expensive than one global optical link. Our energy model is equally simple, and it only assumes 2.8W of power usage per switch port, which is in line with assumptions used in [1,5].

Even with these simple cost and energy models, Fig. 10 clearly shows the benefits of combined global and local tapering compared to a full size system, or to a Dragonfly-style global tapering. For example, our models show that 75%/75% global/local tapered Megafly costs about the same as the 50% globally tapered Dragonfly, and it also uses less power.

5.2   Packaging

We envision densely packaging Megafly groups to enable some of the node and local links to be formed out of short copper cables, depending on signal integrity requirements. Inter-group connections are formed using long optical global cables that are significantly more expensive.

The main challenge in packaging a Megafly group, compared to a Dragonfly, is that the group size is doubled, and the number of nodes connected to a single node switch is doubled. We alleviate the latter problem by decoupling node packaging from switches completely. Instead, we propose building a Megaswitch, which contains all switches of a single group. A megaswitch is constructed out of two kinds of boards: *node switch boards* containing one or more node switches and *global switch boards* containing one or more global switches. Several of each board kind are stacked together, with node switch boards placed orthogonally to global switch boards. This design enables the butterfly connectivity needed for the Megafly group, as shown in Fig. 5, where each node switch connects to each global switch, and vice versa.

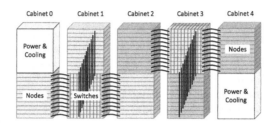

Fig. 11. Example cabinet layout.

We estimate a Megaswitch to fit within half a cabinet, as shown in Fig. 11. All of the node links of Megaswitch are exposed at the front of the cabinet, and the global links are at the back (not shown in Fig. 11). The rest of the cabinet containing the Megaswitch and its neighboring cabinets are packed with node blades. We envision densely packing cabinets together to reduce the cabling cost of connecting node blades with node switches, and to possibly enable the use of copper cables depending on signal integrity constraints. Each of the links shown in Fig. 11 is a bundle of cables connecting all of the nodes in a blade to the corresponding switch. As shown in the same figure, we can stage this "T" design throughout the entire row. At each edge of the row, half of the cabinet is left unpopulated, and this space can be used for power and cooling equipment. While some cooling equipment is necessary in each rack, we envision bringing cooled water from the outside into an intermediate unit which can be shared between several racks to amortize cost and space.

By containing all local links inside a Megaswitch, we expect to limit the length of required cables and enable most cables to be of the same length, further reducing cost. Assuming cabinets are packed closely together, the longest cable needs to reach about half of the cabinet height. This is better than co-locating switches with nodes which forces all-to-all connectivity between blades. In this all-to-all configuration the longest cable needs to reach almost the entire height of the cabinet, and most cables are of different lengths.

6   Case Study

In this mini case study we illustrate the flexibility of the Megafly topology in real system design. Our objective is to build a 8192 node system with radix 32 routers. We chose these parameters to keep our simulation size manageable, but any conclusions we make are directly applicable to larger system sizes with higher radix routers because maximum number of endpoints scales evenly with r^3 for all of the topologies we consider: 1-D Dragonfly, Megafly, 3-level Fat Tree and Slim Fly. We are also on a tight budget, and we are willing to consider up to 50% of bisection bandwidth reduction if that leads to significant cost savings.

We consider building a 3-level Fat Tree as we know it performs well under a variety of traffic patterns, but under our cost model the 3-level Fat Tree is 1.9x more expensive than the fully provisioned Dragonfly or Megafly. Even if we taper the Fat Tree to 50% of bandwidth, it still comes out more expensive than the fully provisioned Dragonfly or Megafly, therefore we abandon the Fat Tree. We also consider building a Slim Fly, which promises to be a cheaper option, but Slim Fly does not scale beyond approximately 4k nodes with radix 32 routers, so we abandon that topology as well. Again, we come to the conclusion that the 1-D Dragonfly and the Megafly are our best options.

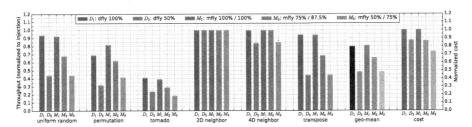

Fig. 12. Performance and cost of tapered Megafly (global/local) and Dragonfly (global) across multiple traffic patterns.

The system size of 8192 nodes is near optimal for both Megafly and Dragonfly topologies. With radix 32 routers, Megafly group size is 256 nodes, and Dragonfly group size is 128 nodes, leading to a system size of 32 Megafly groups or 64 Dragonfly groups, which is only one group shy of optimal for both topologies. We simulate all design points of Dragonfly and Megafly, using a variety of traffic patterns in search of a good cost vs. performance trade-off.

Workloads. Each topology design point is evaluated on six traffic patterns: uniform random, permutation, tornado, 2D neighbor, 4D neighbor and transpose. Uniform random, permutation and tornado are the same synthetic patterns that were used in routing algorithm evaluation. Neighbor and transpose patterns are intended to simulate real application behavior as found in stencil kernels or in distributed 3D FFT implementations.

To ensure fair evaluation, we map the neighbor pattern to nodes using a sub-volume randomization technique, similar to [6,13]. A sub-volume of 32 nodes is always packed together and mapped to a minimum number of switches in the same group, which efficiently uses local bandwidth available within each group. However, different sub-volumes are randomized across the entire topology to efficiently use all of the available global bandwidth. Traffic is generated as a permutation pattern in each dimension of the neighbor exchange, but the ratio of traffic local to the sub-volume vs. traffic leaving the sub-volume is carefully controlled. In the 2D neighbor pattern we set 81% of traffic to be local to the sub-volume, which is intended to closely mimic a 4 point neighbor exchange. Similarly, in the 4D neighbor pattern 56% of traffic is local, resembling an 8 point 4D exchange. The transpose pattern assumes no locality, and it is constructed as 64 superimposed static permutations, which is similar to matrix transpose behavior in 2D pencil decompositions used for 3D FFTs [21].

We implement both synchronizing and non-synchronizing versions of the traffic patterns. The synchronizing versions exchange messages between the neighbors and then wait for those messages to complete, while the non-synchronizing patterns continuously generate traffic. For synchronizing traffic we report run time, while for the non-synchronizing case we measure steady state throughput.

Results. The simulation results for all six workloads are combined into a single performance metric through a geometric mean. Cost for each of the tapered topologies is calculated using the simple model described in Sect. 5. Cost vs. performance for all of the design points is given in Fig. 13.

Figure 13 illustrates the flexibility of the Megafly topology, as it shows 15 possible Megafly design points compared to only 2 possible Dragonfly options. Megafly enables finer grained tapering because of its scalability, but it additionally enables semi-independent tapering at the global and local level. In the same figure we draw the Pareto frontier which connects topologies for which there are no other topologies that are cheaper and higher performing at the same time. Neither of the Dragonfly topologies are on this Pareto frontier, implying that there is always a cheaper and higher performing Megafly. While this is very true for the 50% tapered Dragonfly, we do note the fully provisioned Dragonfly is very close in cost and performance to the fully provisioned Megafly.

We analyze further, in Fig. 12, both Dragonfly topologies, as well as the Megafly topologies with either similar performance or similar cost to the Dragonfly variants. We observe that tapered Megafly topologies perform similarly or better than their Dragonfly counterparts across all workloads. We also notice neighbor patterns perform very well, even with some local taper, because a significant portion of the traffic ends up being local to a single switch, and is thus not affected by taper at any level. Transpose pattern is global bandwidth limited, and behaves very similarly to uniform random.

Overall, we find the Megafly topology to offer much more flexibility in the cost vs. performance trade-off space than Dragonfly, and any design point on the Pareto frontier shown in Fig. 13 is a good choice.

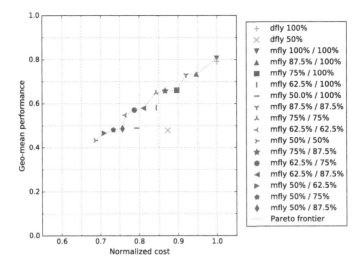

Fig. 13. Pareto frontier of cost vs. geo-mean performance for tapered Megafly (global/local) and 1-D Dragonfly (global) variations. In general, there are more possible Dragonfly variations, but we find that only these two fit our constraints, as discussed in Sect. 2.

Fairness Evaluation. Network fairness is another important metric that impacts application performance. In particular, applications with synchronization patterns are affected when some nodes are slow to complete their communication, because other nodes must wait on them. We implement synchronizing versions of the neighbor exchange and the transpose patterns described earlier in this section. All stencil (i.e. neighbor) patterns exchange 8 kB messages between immediate neighbors before synchronizing, while the Transpose pattern exchanges 1.6 kB messages to keep the simulation runtime manageable. We simulate the synchronizing patterns on a Dragonfly and a Megafly with 8k endpoints and 50% global taper. Global taper does not necessarily mean there is a reduced number of global links, it can also be viewed as an increase in local bandwidth to better support neighbor patterns. A timing diagram of an example 4D stencil is shown in Fig. 14.

In the timing diagram, the three simulated communication phases (shown in red) are broken up by two computation phases (shown in blue). Compute time is fixed to 10,000 cycles. The simulation is run for three iterations, instead of running to convergence like in the earlier bandwidth experiments. The pattern starts with an empty network, and the network is again emptied (or mostly emptied) during the computation phases. This behavior mimics the applications better than measuring bandwidth in the steady state. One can see in Fig. 14 that Megafly performs better on average, but it also has fewer, and smaller outliers, indicating better fairness.

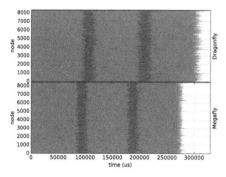
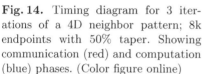

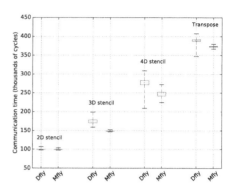

Fig. 14. Timing diagram for 3 iterations of a 4D neighbor pattern; 8k endpoints with 50% taper. Showing communication (red) and computation (blue) phases. (Color figure online)

Fig. 15. Communication times for synchronizing patterns on 8k Dragonfly and Megafly with 50% global taper.

We ran similar experiments for a 2D, 3D, 4D stencil neighbor exchanges and a transpose pattern. All of the results are shown in boxplot format in Fig. 15. We see that for all patterns Megafly has better median times, but also better worst case times (indicated by the max whisker on the boxplot), and better variability (indicated by the height of the boxplot).

7 Conclusion

In this paper we identify two 3-hop network topologies as the most likely candidates for future exascale systems based on their cost advantages over other topologies: a 1-D Dragonfly, and a Megafly. Furthermore, we show that Megafly has better path diversity, compared to a 1-D Dragonfly, leading to better throughput, better fairness, and more possible design points. For cost and power driven designs, Megafly offers global and local tapering options with the ability to trade off bisection bandwidth for cost savings. We show the benefits of tapering flexibility through a mini case study in Sect. 6.

Routing in Megafly, both minimal and adaptive, largely leverages existing routing algorithms developed for the Dragonfly. Therefore, Megafly can be built out of existing switches that already support Dragonfly. However, minimal routing in a Megafly requires only a single virtual channel, compared to two virtual channels needed for deadlock avoidance in a Dragonfly topology.

References

1. Abts, D., Marty, M.R., Wells, P.M., Klausler, P., Liu, H.: Energy proportional datacenter networks. In: ACM SIGARCH Computer Architecture News. ACM (2010)
2. Ajima, Y., Inoue, T., Hiramoto, S., Uno, S., Sumimoto, S., Miura, K., Shida, N., Kawashima, T., Okamoto, T., Moriyama, O., Ikeda, Y., Tabata, T., Yoshikawa, T., Seki, K., Shimizu, T.: Tofu interconnect 2: system-on-chip integration of high-performance interconnect. In: Kunkel, J.M., Ludwig, T., Meuer, H.W. (eds.) ISC 2014. LNCS, vol. 8488, pp. 498–507. Springer, Cham (2014). https://doi.org/10.1007/978-3-319-07518-1_35
3. Antypas, K., Wright, N., Cardo, N.P., Andrews, A., Cordery, M.: Cori: a cray XC pre-exascale system for NERSC. In: Cray User Group Proceedings. Cray (2014)
4. Arimilli, B., Arimilli, R., Chung, V., Clark, S., Denzel, W., Drerup, B., Hoefler, T., Joyner, J., Lewis, J., Li, J., Ni, N., Rajamony, R.: The PERCS high-performance interconnect. In: 2010 18th IEEE Symposium on High Performance Interconnects, pp. 75–82, August 2010
5. Besta, M., Hoefler, T.: Slim Fly: a cost effective low-diameter network topology. In: Proceedings of the International Conference for High Performance Computing, Networking, Storage and Analysis, pp. 348–359. IEEE Press (2014)
6. Bhatele, A., Jain, N., Gropp, W.D., Kale, L.V.: Avoiding hot-spots on two-level direct networks. In: Proceedings of 2011 International Conference for High Performance Computing, Networking, Storage and Analysis, p. 76. ACM (2011)
7. Camarero, C., Vallejo, E., Beivide, R.: Topological characterization of hamming and dragonfly networks and its implications on routing. ACM Trans. Architect. Code Optim. (TACO) **11**(4), 39 (2015)
8. Chen, D., Heidelberger, P., Stunkel, C., Sugawara, Y., Minkenberg, C., Prisacari, B., Rodriguez, G.: An evaluation of network architectures for next generation supercomputers. In: 2016 7th International Workshop on Performance Modeling, Benchmarking and Simulation of High Performance Computer Systems (PMBS), pp. 11–21, November 2016
9. Dongarra, J.: Report on the Sunway TaihuLight system (2016). http://www.netlib.org/utk/people/JackDongarra/PAPERS/sunway-report-2016.pdf
10. Faanes, G., Bataineh, A., Roweth, D., Court, T., Froese, E., Alverson, B., Johnson, T., Kopnick, J., Higgins, M., Reinhard, J.: Cray cascade: a scalable HPC system based on a Dragonfly network. In: Proceedings of the International Conference on High Performance Computing, Networking, Storage and Analysis (2012)
11. Hastings, E., Rincon-Cruz, D., Spehlmann, M., Meyers, S., Xu, A., Bunde, D.P., Leung, V.J.: Comparing global link arrangements for dragonfly networks. In: 2015 IEEE International Conference on Cluster Computing (CLUSTER), pp. 361–370. IEEE (2015)
12. Hoefler, T., Schneider, T., Lumsdaine, A.: Multistage switches are not crossbars: Effects of static routing in high-performance networks. In: 2008 IEEE International Conference on Cluster Computing, pp. 116–125. IEEE (2008)
13. Jain, N., Bhatele, A., Ni, X., Wright, N.J., Kale, L.V.: Maximizing throughput on a Dragonfly network. In: Proceedings of the International Conference for High Performance Computing, Networking, Storage and Analysis, pp. 336–347. IEEE Press (2014)

14. Jiang, N., Balfour, J., Becker, D.U., Towles, B., Dally, W.J., Michelogiannakis, G., Kim, J.: A detailed and flexible cycle-accurate network-on-chip simulator. In: 2013 IEEE International Symposium on Performance Analysis of Systems and Software (ISPASS), April 2013

15. Jiang, N., Kim, J., Dally, W.J.: Indirect adaptive routing on large scale interconnection networks. In: Proceedings of the 36th Annual International Symposium on Computer Architecture, ISCA 2009, pp. 220–231. ACM, New York (2009)

16. Kathareios, G., Minkenberg, C., Prisacari, B., Rodriguez, G., Hoefler, T.: Cost-effective diameter-two topologies: analysis and evaluation. In: Proceedings of the International Conference for High Performance Computing, Networking, Storage and Analysis. ACM (2015)

17. Kim, J., Balfour, J., Dally, W.: Flattened butterfly topology for on-chip networks. In: Proceedings of the 40th Annual IEEE/ACM International Symposium on Microarchitecture, pp. 172–182. IEEE Computer Society (2007)

18. Kim, J., Dally, W.J., Scott, S., Abts, D.: Technology-driven, highly-scalable Dragonfly topology. In: Proceedings of the 35th Annual International Symposium on Computer Architecture, ISCA 2008, pp. 77–88. IEEE Computer Society, Washington, DC (2008)

19. Kim, J., Dally, W.J., Towles, B., Gupta, A.K.: Microarchitecture of a high-radix router. In: Proceedings of the 32nd Annual International Symposium on Computer Architecture, ISCA 2005, pp. 420–431. IEEE Computer Society, Washington, DC (2005)

20. Leiserson, C.E.: Fat-trees: universal networks for hardware-efficient supercomputing. IEEE Trans. Comput. **100**(10), 892–901 (1985)

21. Li, N., Laizet, S.: 2DECOMP & FFT-a highly scalable 2d decomposition library and FFT interface. In: Cray User Group 2010 conference, pp. 1–13 (2010)

22. Matsuoka, S., et al.: You don't really need big fat switches anymore-almost. ARC 2003(84 (2003-ARC-154)), pp. 157–162 (2003)

23. Miller, M., Širáň, J.: Moore graphs and beyond: a survey of the degree/diameter problem. Electron. J. Comb. (2013). 1000, DS14-May, second Edition. http://www.combinatorics.org/ojs/index.php/eljc/article/view/DS14

24. Scott, S., Abts, D., Kim, J., Dally, W.J.: The BlackWidow high-radix clos network. In: Proceedings of the 33rd Annual International Symposium on Computer Architecture, ISCA 2006, pp. 16–28. IEEE Computer Society, Washington, DC (2006)

25. Shpiner, A., Haramaty, Z., Eliad, S., Zdornov, V., Gafni, B., Zahavi, E.: Dragonfly+: low cost topology for scaling datacenters. In: 2017 IEEE 3rd International Workshop on High-Performance Interconnection Networks in the Exascale and Big-Data Era (2017)

26. Singh, A.: Load-balanced routing in interconnection networks. Ph.D. thesis, Stanford University (2005)

27. Top500: Top 500 supercomputers, June 2016. http://www.top500.org

28. Valerio, M., Moser, L., Melliar-Smith, P.: Recursively scalable fat-trees as interconnection networks. In: Phoenix Conference on Computers and Communications, vol. 13 (1994)

29. Won, J., Kim, G., Kim, J., Jiang, T., Parker, M., Scott, S.: Overcoming far-end congestion in large-scale networks. In: 2015 IEEE 21st International Symposium on High Performance Computer Architecture (HPCA), pp. 415–427, February 2015

Packetization of Shared-Memory Traces for Message Passing Oriented NoC Simulation

Vincenzo Catania, Monteleone Salvatore, Maurizio Palesi, and Davide Patti[✉]

Department of Electric, Electronic and Computer Engineering,
University of Catania, Catania, Italy
{vcatania,smontele,mpalesi,dpatti}@dieei.unict.it

Abstract. Several benchmark suites, which provide a wide spectrum of applications in relevant domains, have been proposed and widely used in the computer architecture community. In the majority of them, a shared-memory based communication model is assumed for communication among tasks/threads of an application. Yet, most of the works in the context of Network-on-Chip (NoC) architectures use these benchmarks as a basis for their experiments. Nevertheless, NoC architectures enable message passing communication that is not exploited by the applications in current benchmark suites. In this paper, we propose a technique for converting the trace of memory references generated by the execution of a shared memory based multi-threaded program to the trace of communication messages that would be obtained if the same program would have been designed to use message passing. The proposed technique is applied to a set of representative benchmarks belonging to SPLASH-2 and PARSEC benchmark suites.

Keywords: Simulation · Message passing · NoC
Trace transformation

1 Introduction

The Network-on-Chip (NoC) design paradigm [3,11], based on a modular packet-switched mechanism, is currently seen as the most effective solution to address the scalability limitation of manycore architectures. The design of NoC based systems involves several aspects, such as the partitioning and mapping of the application to the cores, the selection of an appropriate interconnection topology, together with an appropriate routing scheme for dispatching the packets among the nodes, and an optimized allocation of the limited hardware resources (*e.g.*, buffer sizes, and flit width).

The assessment of NoC based systems, which integrate tens if not hundreds of cores, by performing a low-level (*e.g.*, RTL) simulation evaluation and/or a full system simulation [5,18] of the whole NoC architecture, is an extremely time-consuming approach that makes unfeasible an exhaustive exploration of all the

© Springer International Publishing AG, part of Springer Nature 2018
R. Yokota et al. (Eds.): ISC High Performance 2018, LNCS 10876, pp. 311–325, 2018.
https://doi.org/10.1007/978-3-319-92040-5_16

design alternatives. Thus, the evaluation, test, and verification of different design choices is often achieved by means of techniques operating at a higher level of abstraction, where the different components and functionalities are characterized in terms of area, timing, and power. In this regard, high level cycle-accurate NoC simulators [6,13,16] are widely used to quickly get an estimation of the target requirements/objectives, such as power and energy consumption, communication delay, and throughput [12]. When using this kind of simulators, a fundamental role is played by the workload, both in terms of application tasks being run and input data fed into the network. While several studies in literature rely on the use of synthetic traffic patterns, these are often characterized by specific statistical properties only (*e.g.*, packet injection rate) and do not accurately model other important aspects of real traffic scenarios, including, communications bursts,, dynamically changing hotspots, data-dependency, irregular packet generation rates, *etc.*

To overcome such limitations, different benchmark suites [4,24] were proposed with the aim of including a set of applications representative of new emerging workloads for massively parallel architectures. These include several areas which are gaining attraction in the field, such as financial analysis, computer vision, pattern recognition, data mining, and synthesis. An key aspect of the source code implementing all these application benchmarks is that they all assume a traditional shared memory mechanism in order to exchange data among the different processing elements. NoC architectures can implement such shared memory communication mechanism, *e.g.*, using node-specific private cache and coherence protocols. Nevertheless, especially in the perspective of thousands-nodes sized networks, a message passing mechanism based on the direct exchange of data packets between nodes would probably be a more appropriate and scalable choice [23,26]. Unfortunately, modifying the huge amount of benchmarks sources would be a not worthy effort, especially because it would involve a new whole cycle of testing/debugging of the applications which took years to stabilize and consolidate.

In this paper, we propose a technique to transform execution traces of the shared memory accesses into a set of corresponding message passing data flows, together with a statistical characterization of the packets that would be required to implement the exchange of those messages. The basic idea is that, starting from a sequence of shared memory based traces, where the exchange of data is not expressed explicitly, a spatial and temporal analysis can be performed to detect matching read/writes that semantically correspond to an information exchange. Further, the detected data exchanges are clustered in order to "packetize data", obtaining the sequence of packets that would be needed according to actual NoC parameters, such as packets length and flit size. The whole process results in two fundamental advantages as compared to the original traces:

- All the implicit communications based on shared memory are transformed into corresponding set of messages, packetized with the appropriate source destination pairs, amount of data and timing.

– Time-consuming and resource-hungry real traces simulations are replaced by simulation of traffic patterns that, although synthetic, are still realistic in terms of statistical properties, having been characterized from the packetization of real traces.

The conversion of a shared memory based trace into a message passing based trace is realized by means of a set of Perl scripts integrated into the Graphite Multicore Simulator platform [18] and are publicly available as open source software.

The paper is organized as follows: Sect. 2 summarizes some similar/previous efforts in literature, highlighting the main differences when compared to the proposed one. In Sect. 3 a formal description of the proposed technique is presented, together with a complete overview of the design flow into which we imagine the use of trace transformation approach. Finally, in Sect. 4 we concretely apply the technique to two of the most representative benchmark suites for multi-core processing, evaluating the level of message passing orientation detected by transforming the traces of each application.

2   Related Work

Several works in literature address the problem of generating more realistic NoC traffic scenarios by processing and augmenting simulation traces. In particular, some works focus their attention on the removal of prefixed timings of traditional trace-driven simulations by adding information about temporal dependencies. Authors of Netrace [9], propose a tool and a methodology for processing traces of caches and memory accesses in order to capture dependencies between network messages. In [19] authors introduce an abstract model of a "transmission event" to discover dependencies using a temporal ordering of the same events. While embedding dependencies into traces certainly improves accuracy, on the other side it makes traces a lot more complex, both in terms of storage and processing required while performing the trace-driven simulation. To tackle this problem, authors of Attackboard [10] propose the use of bloom filters to create tables for storing dependency patterns at each router, avoiding the storage of cyclic/recurrent dependencies. Other works aim at modifying existing full system simulators in order to achieve a time affordable trace-driven simulation. For example, authors of [14] propose an extension of the Garnet [1] that generates approximate dependencies dynamically.

Several approach propose the use of traffic generators to avoid the simulation of IP cores and obtain a significant speedup in simulation time. Deterministic traffic generators, such as [17], are essentially a replay of the original traffic where events are annotated in order to be replicated in future simulation. While accurate, they have a prefixed length and do not allow input-dependent traffic generation.

On the other side, stochastic traffic generators use traces to build a model of the traffic. Authors of [15] present a framework to process traces generated by message passing applications modeled as acyclic task graphs: the resulting task generators are then used to feed NoC architectures emulated on a FPGA. Task generators are also proposed in [21], where traffic phases are automatically detected in order to replicate the stochastic behaviour of a specific parallel application.

While the approach proposed in this work belongs to the field of the stochastic traffic generators, it still differentiates from the previous proposal for some features we consider quite relevant. A first difference is that multiple memory accesses are not considered as multiple events, but they are temporally ordered and then aggregated so that the appropriate number of packetized messages is considered: this allows to generate a packet injection rate that realistically synthesizes the traffic for a specific time range and a given data flow. Another notable difference is that the proposed approach does not generate packets related to communications between traditional elements of a shared memory paradigm, $e.g.$, interaction between L1 cache and memory controllers, shared L2 caches, packets sent for applying coherence protocols, read/writes to shared area in main memory, and so on. Instead, what is generated is a set packets that would be exchanged between source/destination pairs, according to a message passing mechanism where nodes cooperate to the computational effort by explicitly sending each other the required data, without relying on some underlying shared repository of values. Finally, concerning the detection of dependencies, in our approach they are only taken into account when imply a temporal data-dependency between a couple of cores. On the other side, functional dependencies are not being considered, since the final aim is not to provide a faster full-system functional simulation, but to generate traces suitable for a higher level simulation.

3   Memory Trace Transformation

In this section, we describe the procedure for converting the trace of memory accesses generated during the execution of parallel shared memory based applications to a correspondent trace of messages that would be generated if a message passing communication model is used. Several design space exploration strategies [2, 22] use a communication graph as main input for modeling the communication characteristics of an application. Thus, in this section, we show how to derive the communication graph starting from the message passing based trace file.

3.1   Converting a Shared Memory Trace to a Message Passing Trace

The basic idea for converting a shared memory based transaction to a message passing transaction is shown in Fig. 1. Let us consider the case shown in Fig. 1(a). At time t_s, core s stores v_s bytes of information to memory address a of the shared memory. At time t_d, core d loads v_d bytes of information from memory address a of the shared memory. We convert such shared memory based

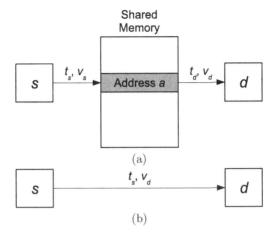

Fig. 1. Converting subsequent store and load transactions at the same memory address (a) to a core-to-core communication (b).

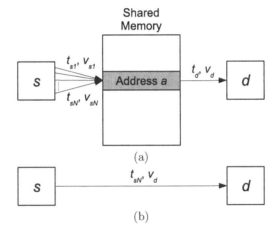

Fig. 2. Converting subsequent multiple store and load transactions at the same memory address (a) to core-to-core communication (b).

transaction to a message passing based transaction like shown in Fig. 1(b) in which core s sends v_d bytes of information to core d at time t_s.

Figure 2 shows the case of multiple stores in which the same core s stores $v_{s1}, v_{s2}, \ldots, v_{sN}$, bytes of information to the same memory address a at times $t_{s1}, t_{s2}, \ldots, t_{sN}$, respectively. Then, at time t_d, core d loads v_d bytes of information from memory address a. In this case, we convert such shared memory based transaction to a message passing based transaction like shown in Fig. 2(b) in which core s sends v_d bytes of information to core d at time t_{sN}.

Formally, the translation of a shared memory trace to a message passing trace can be defined as follows. Let $T^{(SM)} = \{T_i^{(SM)}, i = 1, 2, \ldots, N\}$ be the trace of memory references generated by the execution of a program. A generic pattern of a shared memory based trace is a 5-tuple

$$T_i^{(SM)} ::= \left\langle t_i^{(SM)}, c_i^{(SM)}, a_i^{(SM)}, o_i^{(SM)}, v_i^{(SM)} \right\rangle$$

where $t_i^{(SM)}$ is the starting time of the transaction, $c_i^{(SM)}$ is the core that generates the transaction, $a_i^{(SM)}$ is the memory address, $o_i^{(SM)}$ is the transaction type, and $v_i^{(SM)}$ is the data volume of the transaction. The transaction type can be either store (s) or load (l).

Starting from the shared memory based trace $T^{(SM)}$ we can generate a message passing based trace $T^{(MP)} = \{T_i^{(MP)}, i = 1, 2, \ldots, M\}$ where $T_i^{(MP)}$ is a 4-tuple

$$T_i^{(MP)} ::= \left\langle t_i^{(MP)}, s_i^{(MP)}, d_i^{(MP)}, v_i^{(MP)} \right\rangle$$

where $t_i^{(MP)}$ is the starting time of the communication, $s_i^{(MP)}$ and $d_i^{(MP)}$ are the source and destination cores of the communication, respectively, and $v_i^{(MP)}$ is the data volume of the communication.

Specifically, let $T_i^{(SM)}$ be a generic pattern of the shared memory based trace. If exists a $j > i$ such that:

$$o_i^{(SM)} = \text{s} \wedge o_j^{(SM)} = \text{l} \wedge \tag{1}$$
$$a_i^{(SM)} = a_j^{(SM)} \wedge \tag{2}$$
$$c_i^{(SM)} \neq c_j^{(SM)}. \tag{3}$$

then, a communication $T_k^{(MP)}$ can be generated as follows:

$$t_k^{(MP)} ::= t_i^{(SM)} \tag{4}$$
$$s_k^{(MP)} ::= c_i^{(SM)}, \quad d_k^{(MP)} ::= c_j^{(SM)} \tag{5}$$
$$v_k^{(MP)} ::= v_j^{(SM)} \tag{6}$$

Conditions (1) and (2) assure the spatial and temporal dependency between the i-th and j-th transactions. That is, both the store and load transactions must act to the same memory address and the store transaction must precede the load transaction. Condition (3) dicates that the cores involved in the load and store transactions must be different. If all the aforementioned conditions are satisfied, the resulting communication $T_k^{(MP)}$ is such that its starting time corresponds to the time of the store transaction $t_i^{(SM)}$ [Relation (4)], its source and destination cores correspond to the core of the store transaction and the core of the load transaction, respectively [Relation (5)], and its data volume corresponds to the data volume of the load transaction [Relation (6)].

The above formulation does not cover the case of multiple stores as illustrated in Fig. 2. The extension to this case can be operated by selecting the greatest j that satisfies Conditions (1–3). That is, let

$$j_{max} = \max\{j : \text{conditions } (1\text{--}3)\}$$

then,

$$T_k^{(MP)} = \left\langle t_i^{(SM)}, c_i^{(SM)}, c_{j_{max}}^{(SM)}, v_{j_{max}}^{(SM)} \right\rangle$$

Based on Condition (2), a communication is generated when the address of the store and the load transactions correspond. Actually, a communication can also be generated when the address of the load and store transaction differ by a certain amount. A store transaction at address $a_i^{(SM)}$ of $v_i^{(SM)}$ bytes, involves all the memory locations from address $a_i^{(SM)}$ to address $a_i^{(SM)} + v_i^{(SM)} - 1$. Thus, if the address of a load transaction falls into that memory address range, a communication should be generated. Based on this, the above formulation is updated by replacing Condition (2) with Condition (7)

$$a_j^{(SM)} \in MR_i \tag{7}$$

where $MR_i = \{a_i^{(SM)}, a_i^{(SM)} + 1, \ldots, a_i^{(SM)} + v_i^{(SM)} - 1\}$.

3.2 Generating the Communication Graph

Most of application specific optimization techniques proposed in literature in the different contexts, including, design space exploration [2], routing algorithms [20], mapping techniques [22], *etc.*, require a communication graph rather than a communication trace as input. A communication graph $CG = G(V, E)$ is a direct graph where V is the set of nodes of the network (*e.g.*, cores), and E is the set of communications among nodes. A communication graph is usually annotated with traffic volume information. For each communication $comm_i = (v_s, v_d) \in E$, $v_s, v_d \in V$, the function $vol(comm_i)$ returns the total amount of information transferred from node v_s to node v_d.

It is straightforward obtaining the communication graph starting from the message passing based trace, $T^{(MP)}$. In fact, V corresponds to the set of cores that appear in $T^{(MP)}$ as source or destination core:

$$V = \{c : \exists \langle \cdot, c, \cdot, \cdot \rangle \in T^{(MP)} \vee \exists \langle \cdot, \cdot, c, \cdot \rangle \in T^{(MP)}\}$$

E corresponds to the set of communications in $T^{(MP)}$:

$$E = \{(c_s, c_d) : \exists \langle \cdot, c_s, c_d, \cdot \rangle \in T^{(MP)}\}$$

and the volume function vol for a communication (c_s, c_d) is built by summing up the volume information for each communication (c_s, c_d) in $T^{(MP)}$:

$$vol\left((c_s, c_d)\right) = \sum_{\langle \cdot, c_s, c_d, v \rangle} v$$

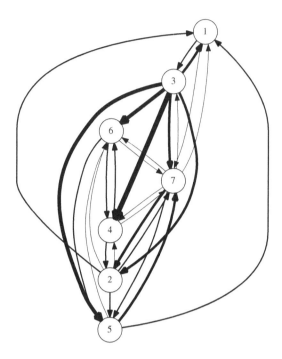

Fig. 3. Communications among cores in `freqmine` application

An example of communication graph for PARSEC's `freqmine` application is shown in Fig. 3. Since there are only a few cores sharing data among themselves during the whole simulation, this application is particularly useful for giving a clear example of communication graph. In particular, only 7 out of 64 cores communicate each other with communications from node 3 to nodes 4, 5, and 6 dominating in terms of traffic volume. Please also notice how the traffic volume information has been pictorially represented by varying the thickness of the edges of the communication graph.

3.3   Proposed Design Flow

The proposed design flow is illustrated in Fig. 4. Overall, it is divided into two main phases, namely, system-level simulation and network simulation. System-level simulation is performed by means of a multicore simulator (*e.g.*, Graphite [18]) on shared memory based applications like those collected in widespread benchmark suites, including, SPLASH-2 [24] and PARSEC [4]. This phase is a time consuming part of the design flow, especially as the number of cores of the multi/manycore architectures to be simulated increases. However, it is a one-time-effort and the generated shared memory trace file is the input of the second phase of the design flow. In the second phase, the proposed technique (highlighted in gray in the figure) is used for generating the message passing

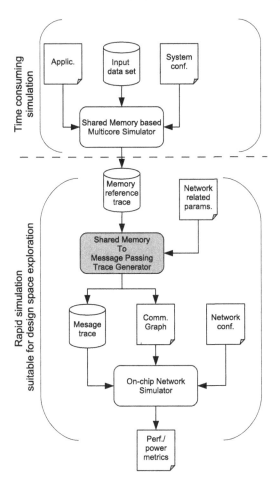

Fig. 4. The proposed design flow.

based trace file along with a communication graph which summarizes the topological and statistical characteristics of the application. The outcome of this step depends on some network related parameters, namely, packet size and flit size, which are inputs for the proposed technique. Finally, either the message passing based trace file or the communication graph can be used as stimulus for the NoC simulator (*e.g.*, Noxim [6]) used for obtaining communication performance and power figures in different scenarios [7,8]. It should be noted that, the second phase of the design flow can be seen as the core of a design space exploration loop in which the network related parameters are made to vary for generating the different NoC configurations to be assessed without the need of performing a time consuming system level simulation.

4   Experimental Results

We selected 19 applications from PARSEC [4] and SPLASH-2 [24] multithreaded benchmark suites as shown in Table 2. Each of them has been simulated in Graphite Multicore Simulator [18] with simsmall input set. The simulated system is a 64-core chip-multiprocessors (CMP), where each core has its own private two-level caches and the memory coherence is achieved using a limitLESS directory scheme. Table 1 shows the parameters chosen for carrying out the collection of traces. Please notice that all the parameters not mentioned in the table have been left to their default values: these include, for example, physical parameters only affecting energy/power figures, or low-level micro-architectural aspects which are not in the current scope of investigation (*e.g.*, assembly instruction delays, pipeline).

Table 1. Configuration parameter used for the multi-core simulation with Graphite.

Parameter	Value
L1I (size, block, assoc)	64 B, 16 KB, 4
L1D (size, block, assoc)	64 B, 32 KB, 4
L2U (size, block, assoc)	64 B, 512 KB, 8
Flit width	64
No.m of flits/port buffer	4

4.1   Message Passing Orientation

The shared memory trace file generated by the execution of the applications in Table 2 has been converted to a message passing trace file as described in Sect. 3 and the percentage of communication among cores has been computed and plotted in Fig. 5.

The percentage of communication among cores measures the fraction of communications that can be realized by means of message passing rather than sharing memory. Thus, an high percentage value is an indication that the application would benefit of message passing as it would drastically reduce the pressure on the memory subsystem. As it can be seen, the variance among the different applications is quite relevant, depending on characteristics such as parallelization model, data sharing, synchronization, *etc.* Let us consider, for example, the application *radiosity* for computing the light distribution in a scene containing polygonal patches. Since the radiosity of each polygon is computed as a function of all the other polygons radiosities, there is a computational interdependency among the application threads which eventually translates into a good opportunity for adopting message passing mechanisms, as shown in Fig. 5. On the other side, a counterexample is represented by *blacksholes*, a well known financial application for computing the prices of a portfolio of options. In this case

Table 2. Overview of applications used in the experimental analysis.

Program	Application domain	Suite
barnes	High-performance computing	SPLASH-2
blackscholes	Financial analysis	PARSEC
canneal	Engineering	PARSEC
cholesky	High-performance computing	SPLASH-2
dedup	Enterprise storage	PARSEC
ferret	Similarity search	PARSEC
fft	Signal processing	SPLASH-2
fluidanimate	Animation	PARSEC
fmm	High-performance computing	SPLASH-2
freqmine	Data mining	PARSEC
lu_contiguous	High-performance computing	SPLASH-2
lu_non_contiguous	High-performance computing	SPLASH-2
ocean_contiguous	High-performance computing	SPLASH-2
ocean_non_contiguous	High-performance computing	SPLASH-2
radiosity	Graphics	SPLASH-2
radix	General	SPLASH-2
raytrace	Graphics	SPLASH-2
streamcluster	Data mining	PARSEC
vips	Media processing	PARSEC
volrend	Graphics	SPLASH-2
water-nsquared	High-performance computing	SPLASH-2

the portfolio is split into a number of work units equal to the number of threads, and then such units are processed concurrently, without any requirement for cooperation among cores.

4.2 Validation

For the sake of validation, we considered a JPEG encoder [25], from which we derived two multithread implementations, namely, a shared memory based implementation (JPEGsm) and a message passing based implementation (JPEGmp). We apply the proposed technique to the memory reference trace file generated by the execution of JPEGsm to obtain the trace of messages. Then, we compare the trace of messages with the actual messages generated by JPEGmp. We consider a 4×4 mesh based NoC and input images of 512×512 pixels. The image is divided into 4 regions of 128×128 pixels where each of them is assigned to 4 parallel threads implementing the level shift, DCT, quantization, and entropy encoding tasks, respectively. Both in JPEGsm and JPEGmp, the aforementioned tasks are executed in a pipeline fashion at a macro-block

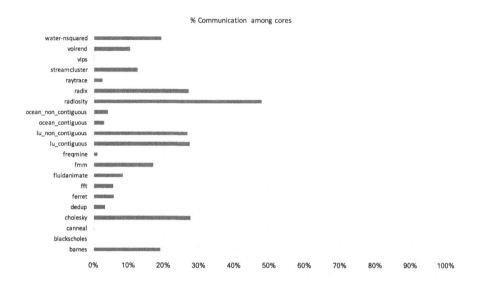

Fig. 5. Percentage of communications among cores.

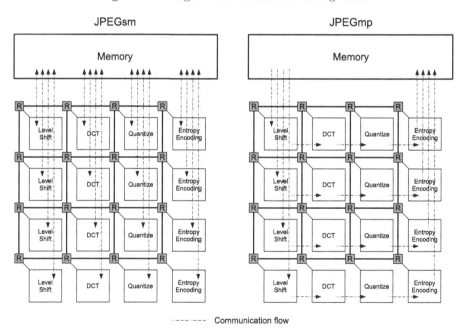

Fig. 6. Communication flows for JPEGsm and JPEGmp.

granularity and based on a the producer-consumer model. In JPEGsm, the four threads fetch a macro-block from the memory, perform their specific task, and write back the modified macro-block into memory. In JPEGmp, the macro-block is manipulated by a core and then sent to the next core implementing the subsequent pipeline stage by means of send communication primitive. Figure 6 shows the communication flows for JPEGsm and JPEGmp. We have instrumented the Graphite Multicore Simulator to trace NoC messages generated during the execution of the application (JPEGmp). Then, the trace has been used to derive the communication graph of the application. Then, this communication graph has been compared with the one generated by the proposed technique applied to the memory reference trace file generated by the execution of JPEGsm. The two communication graphs resulted equivalent in terms of communication topology (*i.e.*, they feature the same communicating pairs) but slight differ in terms of the total number of exchanged packets (about 3%). This difference is due to the mechanism, adopted by Graphite to initialize and allocate resources in the bootstrap phase, which implies further memory accesses that are not shown in Fig. 6.

5 Conclusions

In this paper, we have presented a technique for generating a trace of communication messages starting from the trace of memory references obtained by the simulation of a multi/many core architecture executing shared memory based applications. The proposed technique is based on detecting whether a specific memory transaction might be translated into a message that can be exploited by a message based communication model. The paper formally provides all the conditions that a memory transaction must adhere to be translated into a correspondent communication message among with the specific attributes of the message, including, message generation time and message size. A tool implementing the proposed technique is released and publicly available as open source software. Such tool, tailored to be used in tandem among with Graphite and Noxim simulation platforms, is useful for predicting the expected communication performance and power metrics of current applications implemented with traditional shared-memory based communication model in the case in which they would be converted for exploiting the native message based communication model of NoC based architectures.

References

1. Agarwal, N., Krishna, T., Peh, L.S., Jha, N.K.: Garnet: a detailed on-chip network model inside a full-system simulator. In: IEEE International Symposium on Performance Analysis of Systems and Software, 2009, ISPASS 2009, pp. 33–42. IEEE (2009)
2. Ascia, G., Catania, V., Di Nuovo, A.G., Palesi, M., Patti, D.: Performance evaluation of efficient multi-objective evolutionary algorithms for design space exploration of embedded computer systems. Appl. Soft Comput. J. **11**(1), 382–398 (2011). https://doi.org/10.1016/j.asoc.2009.11.029
3. Benini, L., Micheli, G.D.: Networks on chips: a new SoC paradigm. IEEE Comput. **35**(1), 70–78 (2002)

4. Bienia, C., Li, K.: PARSEC 2.0: a new benchmark suite for chip-multiprocessors. In: Proceedings of the 5th Annual Workshop on Modeling, Benchmarking and Simulation, June 2009

5. Binkert, N., Beckmann, B., Black, G., Reinhardt, S.K., Saidi, A., Basu, A., Hestness, J., Hower, D.R., Krishna, T., Sardashti, S., Sen, R., Sewell, K., Shoaib, M., Vaish, N., Hill, M.D., Wood, D.A.: The gem5 simulator. SIGARCH Comput. Archit. News **39**(2), 1–7 (2011). https://doi.org/10.1145/2024716.2024718

6. Catania, V., Mineo, A., Monteleone, S., Palesi, M., Patti, D.: Cycle-accurate network on chip simulation with noxim. ACM Trans. Model. Comput. Simul. **27**(1), 4:1–4:25 (2016)

7. Catania, V., Mineo, A., Monteleone, S., Palesi, M., Patti, D.: Improving energy efficiency in wireless network-on-chip architectures. ACM J. Emerg. Technol. Comput. Syst. **14**(1) (2017). https://doi.org/10.1145/3138807

8. Catania, V., Mineo, A., Monteleone, S., Patti, D.: Distributed topology discovery in self-assembled nano network-on-chip. Comput. Electr. Eng. **40**(8), 292–306 (2014). https://doi.org/10.1016/j.compeleceng.2014.09.003

9. Hestness, J., Grot, B., Keckler, S.W.: Netrace: dependency-driven trace-based network-on-chip simulation. In: Proceedings of the Third International Workshop on Network on Chip Architectures, NoCArc 2010, pp. 31–36. ACM, New York (2010). https://doi.org/10.1145/1921249.1921258

10. Huang, Y.S.C., Chang, Y.C., Tsai, T.C., Chang, Y.Y., King, C.T.: Attackboard: a novel dependency-aware traffic generator for exploring NoC design space. In: Proceedings of the 49th Annual Design Automation Conference, DAC 2012, pp. 376–381. ACM, New York (2012). https://doi.org/10.1145/2228360.2228428

11. Ivanov, A., Micheli, G.D.: The network-on-chip paradigm in practice and research. IEEE Des. Test Comput. **22**(5), 399–403 (2005)

12. Jafarzadeh, N., Palesi, M., Khademzadeh, A., Afzali-Kusha, A.: Data encoding techniques for reducing energy consumption in network-on-chip. IEEE Trans. Very Large Scale Integr. VLSI Syst. **22**(3), 675–685 (2014). https://doi.org/10.1109/TVLSI.2013.2251020

13. Jiang, N., Becker, D.U., Michelogiannakis, G., Balfour, J., Towles, B., Shaw, D.E., Kim, J., Dally, W.J.: A detailed and flexible cycle-accurate network-on-chip simulator. In: 2013 IEEE International Symposium on Performance Analysis of Systems and Software (ISPASS), pp. 86–96 (2013)

14. Li, R.M., King, C.T., Das, B.: Extending gem5-garnet for efficient and accurate trace-driven NoC simulation. In: Proceedings of the 9th International Workshop on Network on Chip Architectures, NoCArc 2016, pp. 3–8. ACM, New York (2016). https://doi.org/10.1145/2994133.2994140

15. de Lima, O.A., Fresse, V., Rousseau, F., Sheibanyrad, H.: Synthesis of dependency-aware traffic generators from NoC simulation traces. J. Syst. Archit. **71**, 102–113 (2016). https://doi.org/10.1016/j.sysarc.2016.10.004. http://www.sciencedirect.com/science/article/pii/S1383762116301813

16. Lis, M., Shim, K.S., Cho, M.H., Ren, P., Khan, O., Devadas, S.: Darsim: a parallel cycle-level NoC simulator. In: MoBS 2010-Sixth Annual Workshop on Modeling, Benchmarking and Simulation (2010)

17. Mahadevan, S., Angiolini, F., Storoaard, M., Olsen, R.G., Sparso, J., Madsen, J.: Network traffic generator model for fast network-on-chip simulation. In: Design, Automation and Test in Europe, vol. 2, pp. 780–785, March 2005. https://doi.org/10.1109/DATE.2005.22

18. Miller, J.E., Kasture, H., Kurian, G., Gruenwald, C., Beckmann, N., Celio, C., Eastep, J., Agarwal, A.: Graphite: a distributed parallel simulator for multicores. In: 2010 IEEE 16th International Symposium on High Performance Computer Architecture (HPCA), pp. 1–12. IEEE (2010)
19. Nitta, C., Farrens, M., Macdonald, K., Akella, V.: Inferring packet dependencies to improve trace based simulation of on-chip networks. In: Proceedings of the Fifth ACM/IEEE International Symposium on Networks-on-Chip, NOCS 2011, pp. 153–160. ACM, New York (2011). https://doi.org/10.1145/1999946.1999971
20. Palesi, M., Kumar, S., Catania, V.: Bandwidth aware routing algorithms for networks-on-chip platforms. IET Comput. Digit. Tech. **3**(11), 413–429 (2009)
21. Scherrer, A., Fraboulet, A., Risset, T.: Automatic phase detection for stochastic on-chip traffic generation. In: Proceedings of the 4th International Conference on Hardware/Software Codesign and System Synthesis, CODES+ISSS 2006, pp. 88–93. ACM, New York (2006). https://doi.org/10.1145/1176254.1176277
22. Tornero, R., Orduña, J.M., Palesi, M., Duato, J.: A communication-aware topological mapping technique for NoCs. In: Luque, E., Margalef, T., Benítez, D. (eds.) Euro-Par 2008. LNCS, vol. 5168, pp. 910–919. Springer, Heidelberg (2008). https://doi.org/10.1007/978-3-540-85451-7_98
23. Valero-Lara, P., Krishnasamy, E., Jansson, J.: Towards HPC-embedded. Case study: Kalray and message-passing on NoC. Scalable Comput. Pract. Exp. **18**(2), 151–160 (2017)
24. Woo, S.C., Ohara, M., Torrie, E., Singh, J.P., Gupta, A.: The SPLASH-2 programs: characterization and methodological considerations. In: Proceedings of the 22nd Annual International Symposium on Computer Architecture, ISCA 1995, pp. 24–36. ACM, New York (1995). https://doi.org/10.1145/223982.223990
25. Yazdanbakhsh, A., Mahajan, D., Esmaeilzadeh, H., Lotfi-Kamran, P.: AxBench: a multiplatform benchmark suite for approximate computing. IEEE Des. Test **34**(2), 60–68 (2017)
26. Zimmer, C., Mueller, F.: NoCMsg: scalable NoC-based message passing. In: 2014 14th IEEE/ACM International Symposium on Cluster, Cloud and Grid Computing, pp. 186–195, May 2014. https://doi.org/10.1109/CCGrid.2014.19

Parallel Algorithms

Chebyshev Filter Diagonalization on Modern Manycore Processors and GPGPUs

Moritz Kreutzer[1], Dominik Ernst[1], Alan R. Bishop[2], Holger Fehske[3], Georg Hager[1(✉)], Kengo Nakajima[4], and Gerhard Wellein[1]

[1] Erlangen Regional Computing Center (RRZE),
Friedrich-Alexander University of Erlangen-Nuremberg, Erlangen, Germany
georg.hager@fau.de
[2] Theory, Simulation and Computation Directorate,
Los Alamos National Laboratory, Los Alamos, USA
[3] Institut für Physik, Ernst Moritz Arndt University Greifswald,
Greifswald, Germany
[4] Information Technology Center, The University of Tokyo, Tokyo, Japan

Abstract. Chebyshev filter diagonalization is well established in quantum chemistry and quantum physics to compute bulks of eigenvalues of large sparse matrices. Choosing a block vector implementation, we investigate optimization opportunities on the new class of high-performance compute devices featuring both high-bandwidth and low-bandwidth memory. We focus on the transparent access to the full address space supported by both architectures under consideration: Intel Xeon Phi "Knights Landing" and Nvidia "Pascal"/"Volta." After a thorough performance analysis of the single-device implementations using the roofline model we propose two optimizations: (1) Subspace blocking is applied for improved performance and data access efficiency. We also show that it allows transparently handling problems much larger than the high-bandwidth memory without significant performance penalties. (2) Pipelining of communication and computation phases of successive subspaces is implemented to hide communication costs without extra memory traffic. As an application scenario we perform filter diagonalization studies for topological quantum matter. Performance numbers on up to 2048 nodes of the Oakforest-PACS and Piz Daint supercomputers are presented, achieving beyond $500\,\mathrm{Tflop/s}$ for computing 10^2 inner eigenvalues of sparse matrices of dimension $4 \cdot 10^9$.

1 Introduction and Related Work

Stacked memory technologies such as HBM2 and MCDRAM have boosted the attainable main memory bandwidth by a factor of five to six compared to conventional multicore systems. Soon after the commercial availability of these technologies, four out of the ten most powerful supercomputers were equipped with

© Springer International Publishing AG, part of Springer Nature 2018
R. Yokota et al. (Eds.): ISC High Performance 2018, LNCS 10876, pp. 329–349, 2018.
https://doi.org/10.1007/978-3-319-92040-5_17

the new fast memories (see the TOP500 [2] list as of November 2017). Typically holding 16 GiB of data, the size of stacked memories is still very limited and hierarchical concepts have been implemented, offering additional large DDR4 memory spaces. The two major players as of today, Intel with its "self-hosted" Xeon Phi "Knights Landing" (KNL) series and Nvidia with its "Pascal" (P100) and "Volta" (V100) GPGPUs, implement these hierarchical concepts in different ways. While the KNL is directly connected to the DDR4 partition, the Nvidia GPGPUs access the large host node memory through the PCIe interface. However, both architectures are capable of transparently addressing the complete (slow and large) memory on a node, thereby offering easy access to large data sets.

The computation of bulks of eigenvalues of large sparse matrices is very data intensive, both in terms of bandwidth demands (i.e., low computational intensity) and data set sizes. Subspace projection using polynomial filters based on the Chebyshev iteration is an efficient approach for the computation of extremal and interior eigenvalues in quantum physics and quantum chemistry. Application areas include inner eigenvalue problems in the context of modeling graphene or topological insulator materials [22,23] or electronic structure calculations based on density functional theory [5,29]. Beyond eigenvalue computations, Chebyshev polynomials can be used as acceleration techniques for linear solvers (see, e.g., [6,21]) in various application areas (e.g., power flow modeling [11,16,17]). Moreover, the closely related kernel polynomial method (KPM) (see [27] for a review on KPM and its relation to Chebyshev polynomials) also relies on evaluating those polynomials to calculate spectral properties of sparse matrices, such as the density of states [7,9].

From a computational perspective, the evaluation of Chebyshev polynomials is a simple series of vector operations and sparse matrix-vector multiplications (SpMV). It allows for kernel fusion to increase the computational intensity [13]. Global communication can be avoided or limited to a single invocation for the full-degree polynomial. In the above application scenarios the polynomial is usually evaluated for multiple vectors and the algorithm can be reformulated to use blocks of vectors. This further increases the computational intensity and pushes the corresponding sparse matrix-multiple-vector multiplication (SpMMV) towards regular data access [13]. We emphasize that the benefits of SpMMV have been known for a long time [10] but have only recently gained renewed interest (see, e.g., [3,4,18]).

Performance modeling, code optimization strategies, and parallel scalability studies have been presented for KPM [13] and Chebyshev filter diagonalization [20]. These investigations were performed on two Pflop/s-class supercomputers: the SuperMUC-Phase2 system[1], which is based on the Intel Xeon Haswell, and the first phase of the Piz Daint supercomputer[2] (Cray XC30), using Intel Xeon Sandy Bridge processors and Nvidia K20 GPGPUs.

---

[1] https://www.lrz.de/services/compute/supermuc/systemdescription/.
[2] http://www.cscs.ch/computers/piz_daint.

1.1   Contribution

This paper extends existing work towards the new class of supercomputers using compute nodes that feature both high- and low-bandwidth memory and transparent access to the full memory address space of a node. The systems under consideration are phase two of Piz Daint and the Oakforest-PACS[3] system, representing the Nvidia P100-based accelerator and the standalone Intel Xeon Phi approach, respectively. As of November 2017 these supercomputers were ranked in positions 3 and 9 of the TOP500 list.

Table 1. Key architectural features of the two compute devices. The slow memory partition uses DDR4 memory technology on both systems. FP64 CUDA units are counted as cores on the GPGPUs.

	KNL	Tesla P100	Tesla V100
Vendor	Intel	Nvidia	Nvidia
Model	Xeon Phi 7250	P100 PCIe 16 GB	V100 PCIe 16 GB
Codename	Knights Landing	Pascal	Volta
Cores	68 (66 used)	1792	2560
Clock frequency [MHz]	1400	1328	1380
Peak performance [Tflop/s]	3	4.7	7
L2 cache capacity [MiB]	34	4	6
Fast memory technology	MCDRAM	HBM2	HBM2
Fast memory capacity [GiB]	16	16	16
Slow memory capacity [GiB]	96	64	64

We first investigate the attainable bandwidth within the compute nodes, focusing on the usage modes for accessing the low-bandwidth partitions. Concerning the transparent use of the low-bandwidth memory, the tighter hardware integration allows much faster access to large data sets on the KNL. Then we report on efforts porting and optimizing the code for the new compute device architectures and analyze the attainable performance levels and hardware bottlenecks if the working set data fits into the high-bandwidth memory. Our block vector implementation (i.e., storing all n_s vectors in a consecutive array) and the simplicity of the algorithm allow for a straightforward implementation of subspace blocking strategies. We perform these in three directions: (1) We block for optimal compute performance, i.e., the computation of the Chebyshev filter polynomial is restricted to a subset of n_b vectors at a time. (2) We show that the subspace blocking is adequate to enable the efficient use of transparent DRAM data access for large problems. (3) We interchange the original order of polynomial evaluation in combination with a pipeline strategy and demonstrate that overlapping of communication and computation between successive subblocks of size n_b can be realized, avoiding the redundant memory transfers of

---

[3] http://www.cc.u-tokyo.ac.jp/system/ofp/index-e.html.

standard communication hiding mechanisms in SpMMV. We investigate these approaches using scalable test cases (sparse matrices) from eigenvalue computations for topological insulator simulations together with realistic parameter settings for the filter diagonalization algorithm. We also show that these kinds of computations fit very well to this new class of supercomputers.

As our library is available as open-source software, our implementations and approaches can be easily adapted by the large community using numerical methods that involve the evaluation of Chebyshev polynomials of large sparse matrices.

1.2   Hardware Testbed

The two supercomputers considered in the present work harness non-standard compute devices to bring forth their massive computational power. The Piz Daint system consists of 5,320 nodes, each equipped with an Intel Xeon E5-2690v3 compute node hosting one Nvidia Tesla "Pascal" (P100) GPGPU. Oakforest-PACS features 8,208 compute nodes, each with a self-hosted Intel Xeon Phi 7250 "Knights Landing" manycore CPU. In addition we present single-device performance data for a Nvidia V100 GPGPU in order to demonstrate a potential shift of hardware bottlenecks and the general performance benefits of the architectural update.

In Table 1 we summarize the key features of the KNL, the P100, and the V100. From a high-level point of view, these architectures have similar memory organization and key performance figures. However, technical implementations (e.g., SIMD vs. SIMT execution, slow memory organization) and programming approaches (e.g., access to slow memory) are substantially different. As we focus in this work on large data sets and ways to use the slow memory, a more extensive evaluation of the different memory modes and the respective attainable data access rates is provided in the next section. Finally, the network structure of both supercomputers is briefly discussed in Sect. 4.

Memory Subsystems and Operating Modes. A crucial difference between both architectures is their basic operating mode. KNL is self-hosted, i.e., everything, including the operating system and management processes, runs on the compute device. The processor features a large partition of slow DDR4 memory and a small partition of fast MCDRAM memory. It can be configured such that each of them is visible to the programmer as a separate ccNUMA domain ("flat mode"). If both domains should be used, the programmer explicitly needs to specify the data location and, if required, copy data between the domains. Another operating mode uses MCDRAM as a transparent cache for the DDR4 memory ("cache mode"). In this case all memory requests go to the MCDRAM; if data is not available there it will be loaded from DDR4 memory transparently to the MCDRAM and delivered to the processing units. No explicit data management is required by the programmer.

The P100/V100 GPGPU is installed as an accelerator via PCI-Express. The device itself only contains the fast HBM2 memory. In case the data sets exceed

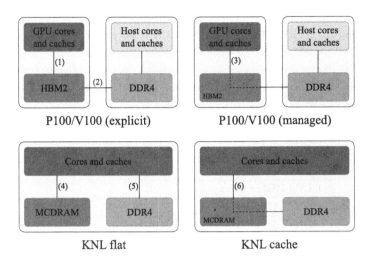

Fig. 1. Memory access modes on P100/V100 (top) and KNL (bottom): Explicit management (left) of the full memory vs. transparent access (right) to the full memory.

its capacity, the host memory has to be used. This can be done via explicit CUDA calls that copy data between host and GPGPU. The Pascal architecture is the first to support a transparent view to device memory and full host memory. Similar to the cache mode on KNL, this "Unified Memory" feature enables transparent data transfers between the host and the device ("managed mode"). Programmers need to allocate data with a special function (`cudaMallocManaged()`). Data transfers between host and GPGPU is then managed automatically by the Page Migration Engine (PME).

The memory subsystems and operating modes are illustrated in Fig. 1. For data sets fitting into the fast memory partitions, the operating modes on the left are preferred and data should be transferred via path (1) or (4). If the data set exceeds 16 GiB, KNL offers the cache mode which corresponds to path (6). Explicit transfers via path (1) + (2) can be used on P100/V100 but require explicit coding of the data transfers by the programmer. This can be avoided using the managed mode, i.e., data path (3), which provides a transparent view of the complete address space of the host and the GPGPU.

In order to get estimates for achievable performance we investigate attainable bandwidth numbers for accessing large consecutive data sets, which is the typical memory access scenario for the application considered in this work. We use the STREAM benchmark [19] and adapt it to the different memory access modes. Appropriate data set sizes are chosen to measure the different bandwidth paths shown in Fig. 1, i.e., for transparent access to the slow memory we use data sets larger than the fast memories. The measurements for all relevant data path combinations are shown in Table 2. On all three architectures the highest bandwidth is naturally attained when using the fast memory only. Access speed to the slow memory component is substantially higher on the KNL owing to its on-chip

Table 2. Memory bandwidth in Gbyte/s for different operating modes as illustrated in Fig. 1 using the STREAM benchmark. On the P100 pinned memory was used for the explicit data access ("DDR4-HBM2 explicit").

	Mode	Copy	Scale	Add	Triad
KNL	MCDRAM (4)	466	468	481	489
	DDR4 (5)	81	81	85	85
	DDR4-MCDRAM cache (6)	60	60	60	59
P100	HBM2 (1)	542	542	556	557
	DDR4-HBM2 explicit (1) + (2)	13	13	12	12
	DDR4-HBM2 managed (3)	3	2	3	3
V100	HBM2 (1)	788	792	832	831
	DDR4-HBM2 explicit (1) + (2)	13	13	12	12
	DDR4-HBM2 managed (3)	5	5	5	5

DDR4 memory controllers, while host memory access on P100/V100 is limited by the capabilities of the PCIe 3.0×16 interfaces. For explicit slow memory access approximately 75% of the maximum uni-directional PCIe bandwidth can be attained on the P100/V100. However, the bandwidth for transparent access ("managed mode"; path (3) in Fig. 1) breaks down to 2–3 Gbyte/s (5 Gbyte/s) on P100 (V100) in our benchmarks, which may severely restrict the use of this mode in real world applications. The PCIe models of P100 and V100 use the same PCIe 3.0×16 interface, and have the same explicit transfer bandwidth. However, V100 does improve the on-demand paging mechanism and improves the transparent access bandwidth significantly. The overall low transfer rates may be caused by the PME, which handles all remote page faults generated by the GPGPU and tries to consolidate them into consecutive PCIe data transfers. An analysis of the "Host to Device Transfers" using the Nvidia profiler shows that the average transfer size granularity even for simple kernels like STREAM is in the order of 40 KiB.

In summary, the transparent access to large consecutive data sets in the slow memory on the P100 (V100) is ten to twenty times slower, while the access to the fast memory is 25% (80%) faster than on the KNL. In absolute numbers, the V100 improves on P100 in both fast memory and transparent system memory bandwidth by about 50%.

1.3   Software Testbed

All computations were carried out using (real or complex) double precision data. Index values are 4-byte integers. The CUDA toolkit in version 8.0.44 was used for P100 and in version 9.1.85 for V100.[4] The respective cuBLAS version was

---

[4] No relevant performance differences were observed between CUDAv8 and CUDAv9 on V100.

employed as a baseline implementation. The benchmark code for the bandwidth baseline tests on Nvidia GPGPUs is available at https://github.com/te42kyfo/cuda-benches. All in-cache and unified memory GPGPU bandwidth benchmark numbers reported in this paper were measured using this code. The Intel C Compiler (ICC) version 17.0.1 was used for KNL with the corresponding MKL and MPI versions. On Piz Daint we used Cray MPICH 7.5.0.

The performance numbers we present for the Chebyshev Filter Diagonalization kernel are median values from ten consecutive runs applying the full filter polynomial. Before the actual measurements, one additional warmup run was performed on the assigned set of nodes. No error bars are given for the performance results because the variations were small ($\leq 5\%$). In order to limit the impact of OS noise, only 66 out of 68 cores were used on the KNL nodes. This is recommended practice on Oakforest-PACS.

2   Chebyshev Filter Diagonalization

We investigate Chebyshev Filter Diagonalization (ChebFD) as a representative algorithm for large-scale and efficient eigenvalue computations. Filter diagonalization is frequently used to find a set of inner eigenstates of a sparse matrix H in a given search interval of eigenvalues. It uses a window function approximated by a polynomial filter of degree n_p to project a subspace of n_s search vectors to a given search interval of eigenvalues. A comprehensive description of this method is given in [20]. The computational core of ChebFD is the application of the polynomial filter together with the computation of the Chebyshev moments. This is shown in Algorithm 1 for a formulation with block vectors. Basic numerical operations involved in the filter application kernel (lines 7–13) are a SpMV involving a large sparse matrix H and a series of scaled vector addition kernels (i.e., BLAS1 kernels). These kernels can be formulated as a single SpMMV operation involving special scaling factors and offset computations (line 9). In lines 10/11 the Chebyshev moments are computed; they are used to monitor the number of eigenstates in the search interval, which is not known a priori. Finally, in line 12 the "filtered vector" is updated. As the polynomial filter of degree n_p is applied independently to n_s search vectors, a block formulation as indicated in Algorithm 1 can be used. In particular, the block variant of SpMV, i.e., the SpMMV kernel, is favorable in terms of computational intensity since the matrix data (H) has to be loaded only n_p times instead of $n_p \times n_s$ times if the full filter polynomial is applied separately to each vector in the SpMV. Note that the block formulation of the vector kernels does not impact their computational efficiency as n_s BLAS1 type operations are still involved, e.g., in line 10 n_s independent dot products are computed.

The full filter diagonalization algorithm requires orthogonalization of the n_s "filtered vectors" in the block vector X after applying the filter above and before restarting the procedure. A rank-revealing technique such as SVQB [25] or TSQR [8] is used in the orthogonalization step, but as its contribution to the overall runtime is typically small for reasonably large filter polynomial degrees n_p we do not include it in the performance analysis.

Algorithm 1. Application of the ChebFD polynomial filter to block vectors.

```
 1: U := u_1, ..., u_{n_s}                              ▷ define block vector
 2: W := w_1, ..., w_{n_s}                              ▷ define block vector
 3: X := x_1, ..., x_{n_s}                              ▷ define block vector
 4: U  ← (αH + β𝟙)X                                            ▷ spmmv()
 5: W  ← 2(αH + β𝟙)U − X                                       ▷ spmmv()
 6: X  ← g_0c_0X + g_1c_1U + g_2c_2W               ▷ baxpy()+bscal()
 7: for  p = 3 to n_p  do
 8:     swap(W, U)
 9:     W  ← 2(αH + β𝟙)U − W
10:     η_p ← ⟨W, U⟩                                  ▷ CHEBFD_OP(H, U, W, X)
11:     μ_p ← ⟨U, U⟩
12:     X  ← X + g_pc_pW
13: end for
```

At this point we must emphasize that performance numbers presented in [20] use the ChebFD formulation presented here, while in [13] only the Chebyshev moments have been computed, i.e., Algorithm 1 without line 12.

2.1 Physical Application and Problem Setting

We have chosen the computation of a bulk of central eigenstates of a topological insulator as a test case for our performance study. Such applications are of current interest in quantum physics research. The model Hamiltonian [24] describing the topological insulator acts on a discrete 3D lattice of size $N_x \times N_y \times N_z$ carrying four degrees of freedom per site. The matrix formulation leads to a sparse matrix of size $n = 4 \times N_x \times N_y \times N_z$ with an average of $n_{zr} = 13$ complex double precision non-zero elements per matrix row (denoted by "Topi-N_x-N_y-N_z"). The matrices have several subdiagonals leading to a structure similar to 3D stencil. Please see [13,20] for more details on the model Hamiltonian and its mapping to a sparse matrix. Relevant problem parameter settings in topological insulator research are matrix dimensions of $n = 10^6, \ldots, 10^8$ and search spaces of $n = 10^2, \ldots, 10^3$. In terms of algorithmic efficiency it has been shown in [20] that high polynomial degrees ($n_p \approx 10^3$) deliver best results.

3 Node-Level Implementation and Performance Analysis

The compute kernels and implementation alternatives discussed in the following are available for download at https://bitbucket.org/essex/ghost. As parallelization approaches we use OpenMP for KNL (and CPU architectures) and CUDA for Nvidia GPGPUs. Best performance on the KNL for our application is typically achieved with four OpenMP threads per core.

3.1   Implementation

The structure of the ChebFD algorithm presented in Algorithm 1 can easily be mapped to a series of vector operations (of BLAS1 type) and a SpMMV. All vendors provide highly optimized library routines for these. However, calling those routines results in redundant data transfers for the involved block vectors. As discussed in [13, 20] it is possible to fuse all operations in the p-loop of Algorithm 1 to a single algorithm-specific kernel (CHEBFD_OP(H, U, W, X))and perform all computations on the three block vectors (U, W, X) once they are in the cache or register. While this strategy allows for minimum data transfer, the tailored kernels become very bulky and complex. In particular, for GPU architectures the resulting CUDA kernel requires manual architecture-specific tuning as demonstrated in [13] for the Nvidia K20.

Another important issue to consider is the storage format of the block vectors. Here, a row-major approach is beneficial which drives the irregular access pattern of the SpMV towards streaming access as n_s consecutive block vector elements are loaded for a single matrix element. Moreover row-major storage also enables SIMD/SIMT vectorization along the block vector elements and a simple compressed row storage (CRS) format can be used to store the matrix on all architectures.

On KNL, the implementation is done via AVX512 compiler intrinsics. The rather bulky nature of the kernel, together with the use of complex arithmetic, prevents efficient vectorization of high-level code from the compiler and necessitates the use of compiler intrinsics.

On the P100 we started with the KPM implementation for the K20m presented in [13]. Extending this kernel by the update of the "filtered" block vector (line 12 in Algorithm 1) is straightforward but does not change the computational bottlenecks, which were the reductions required in the dot products. Here a new feature of the Pascal architecture is employed: atomic additions using double precision numbers can increase the performance of the reduction operation for Chebyshev moments (η_p, μ_p).

3.2   Performance Measurement

In Fig. 2, we present the performance levels which can be achieved on the KNL and P100/V100 architectures and demonstrate the need for optimized algorithm-specific kernels. For these tests we used working sets that completely fit into the high-bandwidth memory. We find that a tuned implementation of the CHEBFD_OP() kernel (labeled "GHOST") outperforms implementations based on a minimum set of standard library calls (SpMMV and BLAS1) typically by 50%. It is interesting to note that our manual implementation of those standard calls ("GHOST-nofuse") can even outperform the latest vendor-tuned implementations (MKL and cuBLAS/cuSPARSE), the reason being that GHOST provides highly optimized row-major variants of all block vector kernels used. Achieving approximately 10% of their peak performance, the three compute devices outperform a standard CPU-based compute node by factors of up to 4–7.

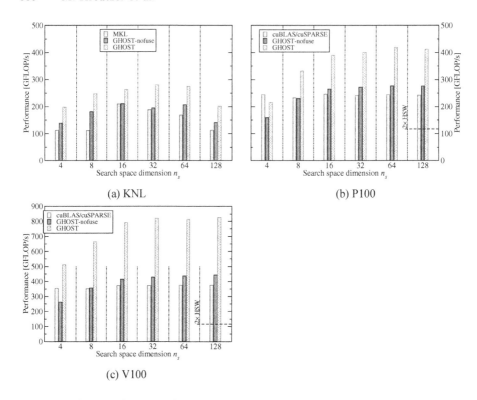

Fig. 2. ChebFD performance for the Topi-128-64-64 matrix with $n_p = 500$ using different implementations. Maximum performance of a compute node with two Intel Xeon E5-2697v3 processors (Haswell) is shown for reference (data taken from [20]). Note the different y axis scaling of the V100 results.

3.3 ChebFD Polynomial Filter Application Subspace Blocking

In agreement with published results for CPUs and previous-generation Nvidia GPGPUs [13,20] we find that performance saturates (P100/V100) or even decreases (KNL) at an intermediate block vector size of $n_s = 32$. To enable optimal performance levels for the large values of n_s required by the above application scenario, subspace blocking for the block vectors needs to be employed. Introducing a factor n_b ($\leq n_s$), the application of the filter can be restricted to a sufficiently small vector block (holding n_b vectors) to achieve optimal performance. The corresponding implementation is shown in Algorithm 2. Though simple, this code transformation has strong implications for the row-major data layout of the block vectors. Row-major ordering now must also be restricted to blocks containing n_b vectors while the blocks are stored column-wise (see Fig. 3). We are now free to choose the vector block size independently of our baseline application, thus we will restrict the following performance analysis to vector blocks of size n_b.

Algorithm 2. ChebFD polynomial filter application blocking. Here, n_s is assumed to be a multiple of n_b for simplicity.

1: **for** $b = 0$ to $n_s/n_b - 1$ **do**
2:     $U_b := u_{bn_b}, \ldots, u_{(b+1)n_b}$
3:     $W_b := w_{bn_b}, \ldots, w_{(b+1)n_b}$
4:     $X_b := x_{bn_b}, \ldots, x_{(b+1)n_b}$
5:     **for** $n = 3$ to n_p **do**
6:         swap(W_b, U_b)
7:         CHEBFD_OP(H, U_b, W_b, X_b)
8:     **end for**
9: **end for**

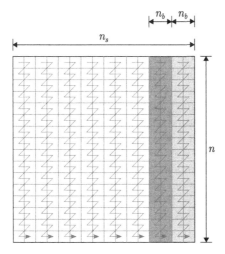

Fig. 3. Block vector layout for $n_s = 16$, choosing $n_b = 2$ for filter application (subspace) blocking. Pairs of blocks of width n_b will later be used for subspace pipelining (see Sect. 4.2). The zigzag arrows indicate the storage order of the vector elements in memory.

3.4   Performance Analysis

We choose the Roofline performance model [28] to investigate the quality of our implementations and to detect the current hardware bottlenecks:

$$P^* = \min\left(P^{\max}; I(n_b) \times b\right) . \tag{1}$$

This model assumes that the attainable performance is either limited by in-core execution ($P^{\max}$) or by data transfer ($I(n_b) \times b$), where b is the main memory bandwidth (see Table 2 for typical values) if data comes from main memory. The arithmetic intensity of the ChebFD scheme for the Topi test case as a function of n_b is given by [20]:

$$I(n_b) = \frac{146}{260/n_b + 80} \frac{\text{Flops}}{\text{Byte}} \stackrel{n_b \to \infty}{\approx} 1.83 \frac{\text{Flops}}{\text{Byte}} . \tag{2}$$

This intensity value is calculated as the average numerical workload and minimum data traffic for applying one matrix row. The first term in the denominator ($260/n_b$ Byte) represents the matrix data traffic: As we have double complex entries, 20 Byte per matrix entry (using 4 Byte indices) are required. In average one row has 13 entries and we expect to reuse the row entries for each of the n_b block vector entries. The minimum data traffic for the three vectors involved in CHEBFD_OP(H, U, W, X) accounts for 80 Byte of data traffic, as U is read only (see lines 9–12 in Algorithm 1).

Combining (1) and (2), and assuming the attainable main memory bandwidths as given by the STREAM Scale benchmarks (see Table 2), we expect a performance increase when going from $n_b = 4$ to $n_b = 128$ as follows: 540 Gflop/s to 960 Gflop/s on P100, 797 Gflop/s to 1410 Gflop/s on V100, and 470 Gflop/s to 836 Gflop/s on KNL. The measurements fall short of this expectation by a factor of 2–3 as seen in Sect. 3.2. Two possible reasons can account for this effect: Either there is an on-chip bottleneck or the memory bandwidth is saturated but the actual memory traffic is larger than the assumed minimum.

Choosing an intermediate value of $n_b = 32$, we investigate the actual data transfer volumes and attained data transfer rates in more detail. In Table 3 we present data volumes measured with the Nvidia profiler [1] and likwid-perfctr [26] for the P100/V100 and the KNL[5], respectively. For P100 and KNL we find that the actual memory memory bandwidth rates using MCDRAM and HBM2 are far off the maximum attainable numbers presented in Table 2. Moreover, the write data volume matches our assumption underlying (2) very well (two vector blocks each of size $n \times n_s \times 16$ Byte need to be written to main memory). On the other hand, the measured read data volume is substantially higher than our model assumption, indicating that the right hand vector block involved in the spMMV is reloaded on the P100/V100 (KNL) approximately four (five) times (see [14] for modeling right hand vector access). Since the block vector chunks are always loaded consecutively, latency effects are not expected to be the reason for the low memory bandwidth utilization on P100 and KNL.

P100. The Nvidia profiler identifies the high L1/TEX cache utilization as primary hardware bottleneck which operates at more than 3 TB/s bandwidth. Caching right hand side vector elements and warp broadcasts for reusing the matrix elements across n_s threads may cause this pressure. This is different from previous results for the K20 presented in [20], where the TEX cache utilization was also high, but performance was limited by the reduction operations required in lines 10 and 11 of Algorithm 1. This bottleneck has been removed using the new atomic additions (see above).

V100. Contrary to the P100 and KNL results, the measured HBM bandwidth in Table 3 of V100 matches its STREAM benchmark value. The V100's L1/TEX

---

[5] Due to the absence of suitable tools, measurements were not conducted on the Oakforest-PACS system but on an Intel Xeon Phi 7210 with 64 cores and the same amount of L2 cache.

Table 3. Transferred data volume for memory subsystem components and a single ChebFD iteration with the Topi-128-64-64 matrix ($n = 2.1 \times 10^6$) and $n_b = 32$. The second row shows minimum data transfers as assumed in the calculation of $I(n_b)$.

	Read (GB)	Write(GB)	Bandwidth (GB/s)
Minimum	3.77	2.15	-
KNL2 MCDRAM	8.09	2.26	205.81
P100 HBM2	7.02	2.28	412.17
P100 L2	14.82	2.42	764.18
P100 TEX	38.23	-	}3129.36
P100 L1	29.96	2.42	
V100 HBM2	7.10	2.31	787.30
V100 L2	10.20	2.44	1061.97
V100 TEX	46.21	-	}5871.93
V100 L1	21.25	2.44	

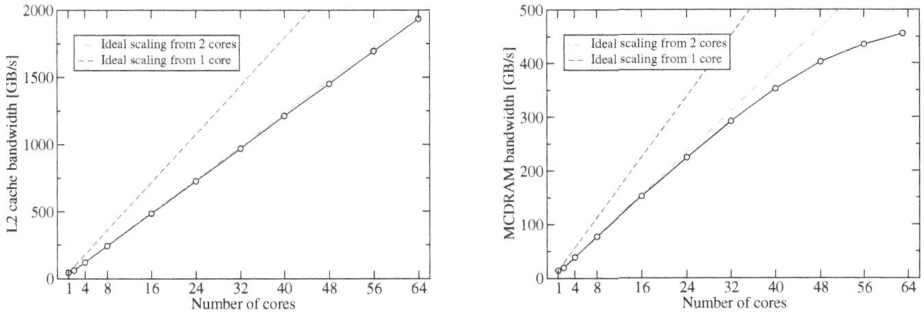

(a) L2 cache bandwidth

(b) MCDRAM bandwidth

Fig. 4. Bandwidth scaling of L2 cache and MCDRAM on KNL using vector update benchmark explained in the text. L2 measurements were run in throughput mode using data sets fitting into the thread-local L2 cache.

cache bandwidth has been increased by a factor of four (13.6 Tbyte/s according to the in-cache benchmarks referenced in Sect. 1.3), thereby shifting the bottleneck to the HBM interface. Indeed, according to the Nvidia profiler, the L1/TEX cache has only medium utilization. Consequently we find a performance gain of $2\times$ from P100 to V100, which is higher than the boost in attainable main memory bandwidth. Considering the increased data traffic from the right-hand sides (comparing minimum and measured data volume numbers in Table 3) in (1) we expect a performance of 823 Gflop/s, which is actually achieved.

KNL. Reliable in-cache data traffic volume measurements were not available for the KNL architecture at the time of writing. Therefore we substantiate our expectation that the performance bottleneck is in-core by a brief scalability analysis of the device architecture and of our code on one KNL.

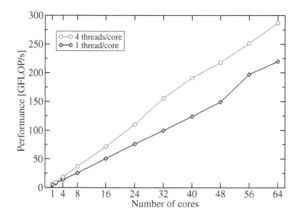

Fig. 5. OpenMP scaling of ChebFD performance for Topi-128-64-64 matrix with $n_p = 10/100/500$ for 1–4/8–24/32–64 cores and $n_b = 16$ on one KNL.

In Fig. 4 we show attainable bandwidth values and scalability of MCDRAM and L2 when running a simple DAXPY kernel. As the L2 cache segments are shared by two cores and we only perform local L2 cache accesses we find perfect scalability across the segments. On contrary, the MCDRAM bandwidth shows the typical saturation behavior even if only one thread per core is run. However, our ChebFD implementation scales well across the device and also benefits substantially from using all SMT threads (see Fig. 5), indicating that neither MCDRAM nor L2 access are the limiting factor. Thus, we identify the in-core execution of the code to be the bottleneck.[6]

In summary, we find that all three architectures can achieve approximately 10% of their theoretical peak performance, but only the V100 is able to fully leverage its available memory bandwidth. On KNL and P100, in-cache and in-core bottlenecks prevent full memory bus utilization despite manually optimized kernels.

3.5   Subspace Blocking and Large Problems

Often in real world filter diagonalization applications the available main memory is the limiting factor as one typically aims at large physical problem sizes (n) and a large number of inner eigenstates (n_s) at the same time. Thus, the size of the high bandwidth memory can easily restrict the accessible problem space and may require (massive) parallelization to provide the required main memory space. As described in Sect. 1.2, the two architectures under consideration in this work address this problem and allow for a transparent access to large but slow memory regions located in the host node (P100/V100) or in a separate DDR4 domain (KNL). We now investigate the transparent memory access mechanisms

---

[6] The identification of the respective bottleneck is ongoing but probably pointless as this architecture line will not be continued by Intel.

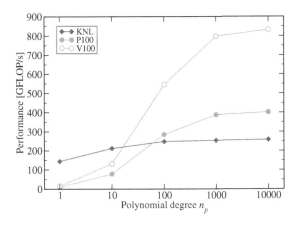

Fig. 6. ChebFD performance versus polynomial degree n_p for the Topi-128-64-64 matrix with $n_s = 512$ and $n_b = 64$ (128) on KNL (P100/V100).

provided on both architectures, i.e., the "managed mode" on P100/V100 and the "cache mode" on KNL, to use those large memory spaces implicitly.

As we have demonstrated in Table 2, the transfer rates of transparent data accesses to the slow memories are very low. In our case, the time (i.e., the work to be done on the device) between two accesses to the slow memory is determined by the polynomial filter degree n_p: As shown in Algorithm 2, a local working set of n_b vectors is loaded to the high-bandwidth memory and then reused $n_p - 3$ times. Thus the data access to slow memory may be amortized if n_p is large enough. Indeed we observe no significant impact of the low-bandwidth memory access for an overall working set of ≈ 60 GiB beyond $n_p \gtrsim 500$ on P100/V100 and $n_p \gtrsim 100$ on KNL (see Fig. 6). The different behavior is expected due to the much lower transparent access bandwidth on the P100/V100 (see Table 2). At small n_p, the performance advantage of V100 over P100 can be attributed to the higher transparent access bandwidth on V100 (see Table 2).

As discussed in Sect. 2.1, algorithmic efficiency requires high polynomial degrees $n_p \gg 100$, which matches the demands of both architectures to achieve high single device performance for large data sets on the two architectures under consideration.

4   Large-Scale Performance

In this section we present scaling results on both supercomputers using data sets fitting into the fast memory of both devices. The Oakforest-PACS nodes are operated in "flat" mode. Distributed-memory parallelization is done using the GHOST library [15], which supports heterogeneous parallel execution using an MPI+X approach (currently, X $\in$ {OpenMP, CUDA}). On Piz Daint we run one MPI process per host node and on Oakforest-PACS we use one MPI process and 264 OpenMP threads per KNL node (66 cores). We employ the standard data-level parallelization approach for ChebFD: Matrix elements and vector data are distributed across the MPI processes, each process working with a contiguous set of matrix rows and the corresponding part of the block vectors. The communication pattern is determined by the sparsity pattern of the matrix, and communication of remote block vector elements to local buffers must be performed before the process-local CHEBFD_OP is applied As the matrix structure is reminiscent of a 3D stencil, nearest-neighbor communication dominates and leads to easy load balancing and a well-controlled communication volume.

The Cray-proprietary interconnect of Piz Daint uses a dragonfly network topology. Oakforest-PACS is based on Intel Omni-Path with a full fat-tree network built on 48-port leaf switches and 768-port spine switches. As these networks should provide sufficient bandwidth for nearest-neighbor communication, no optimized mapping of MPI ranks to the topology was done.

4.1 Weak Scaling

The weak scaling experiments are based on the problem scaling used in [20]. A subdomain of $128 \times 64 \times 64$ is assigned to each process, corresponding to the Topi-128-64-64 problem considered so far. For scaling out we run $2 \times n_{\text{scal}}^2$ processes ($n_{\text{scal}} = 1, 2, 4, 8, 16$) on a lattice with fixed z dimension that is quadratic in x and y, i.e., Topi-$(128 \times n_{\text{scal}})$-$(64 \times 2 \times n_{\text{scal}})$-64 for a given n_{scal}. As long as the communication time is small compared to the actual computation, which is the case for our choice of parameters, a simple communication scheme ("vector mode," see Algorithm 3), can be used: Data exchange using non-blocking MPI (lines 4 and 5) is separated from the process-local computation (CHEBFD_OP(H, U_b, W_b, X_b)). The weak scaling performance results for both systems are shown in Fig. 7 for up to 2048 nodes. The communication overhead introduced by the vector mode is visible for two and eight nodes because communication sets in first in the y direction at $n_{\text{scal}} = 1$ and then additionally in the x direction at $n_{\text{scal}} = 2$. From eight nodes onward we see perfect scaling since per-node communication and computation times stay constant. Based on the single-node performance the systems achieve a parallel efficiency of 85% (Oakforest-PACS) and 60% (Piz Daint) at 2048 nodes, which compares to 73% obtained on the SuperMUC-Phase2 system on 512 nodes in a previous publication [20]. The lower efficiency of Piz Daint can be attributed to the transfer of vector data over the PCIe bus (even though our implementation uses GPUdirect communication avoiding an intermediate copy of communication data in the host memory) and the high single-node performance. Still Piz Daint provides best absolute performance, achieving 514 Tflop/s at 2048 nodes. The underlying numerical problem considered here is the computation of approximately 100 inner eigenvalues ($\leq n_s$) of a matrix of dimension $n = 4 \cdot 10^9$.

4.2 Strong Scaling and Subspace Pipelining

Sparse linear algebra problems often show limited strong scalability because the computation time per process decreases faster than the corresponding communication time. Our vector mode implementation, which was acceptable with

Algorithm 3. Blocked application of the ChebFD polynomial filter with explicit and non-overlapping data exchange ("vector mode").

1: **for** $b = 0$ to $n_s/n_b - 1$ **do**
2:     **for** $p = 3$ to n_p **do**
3:         swap(W_b, U_b)
4:         INIT_COMMUNICATION(U_b)
5:         FINALIZE_COMMUNICATION(U_b)
6:         CHEBFD_OP(H, U_b, W_b, X_b)
7:     **end for**
8: **end for**

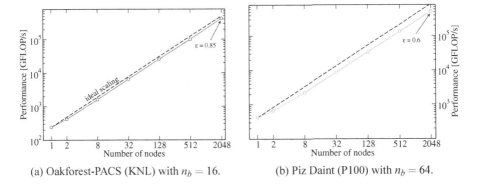

(a) Oakforest-PACS (KNL) with $n_b = 16$.   (b) Piz Daint (P100) with $n_b = 64$.

Fig. 7. Weak scaling of ChebFD in "vector mode" with matrices ranging from Topi-128-128-64 (two nodes) to Topi-2048-2048-64 (2048 nodes). The parallel efficiency at 2048 nodes is indicated (see the text for details on problem scaling). ($n_s = 128$, $n_p = 500$)

weak scaling and rather large per-node problem sizes, must thus be improved by explicitly overlapping communication with computation. A typical approach to this problem is to do local computations (i.e., handle matrix elements which only access local vector elements) while communicating the non-local vector elements and then doing the remaining work with the just-received data, updating the partial results [12]. This implementation needs to update the local result vector twice and thus increases the main memory data traffic. Modifying the subspace blocking scheme introduced in Sect. 3.3 towards pipelining of computation and communication steps of successive filter applications as presented in Algorithm 4 offers an interesting alternative.

Instead of calculating the full polynomial for a given block of n_s vectors, the polynomial degree for the full block vector is increased step by step. The inner loop runs over the full block vector and the computation on the current sub-block can be overlapped with the communication required for the next subblock. This strategy avoids the overhead of writing the result vector twice, maintaining the same computational intensity as the non-MPI code. As long as n_b/n_s is sufficiently large and asynchronous communication is supported by the MPI implementation, the communication should be effectively hidden. A comparison

Algorithm 4. Blocked application of the ChebFD polynomial filter with pipelined communication and computation ("pipelined mode").

1: **for** $p = 3$ to n_p **do**
2:    swap(W, U)
3:    INIT_COMMUNICATION(U_0)
4:    FINALIZE_COMMUNICATION(U_0)
5:    **for** $b = 0$ to $n_s/n_b - 2$ **do**
6:        INIT_COMMUNICATION(U_{b+1})
7:        CHEBFD_OP(H, U_b, W_b, X_b)
8:        FINALIZE_COMMUNICATION(U_{b+1})
9:    **end for**
10:    CHEBFD_OP$(H, U_{n_s/n_b-1}, W_{n_s/n_b-1}, X_{n_s/n_b-1})$
11: **end for**

---

of vector mode and subspace pipelining for strong scaling on Oakforest-PACS is given in Fig. 8 for the Topi-128-128-64 problem ($n = 4 \times 10^6$). As expected, the benefit of subspace pipelining increases as the number of processes goes up because the communication becomes more relevant. A maximum speed-up with respect to vector mode of 50% could be observed in this test. Note that the speed-up of communication-hiding approaches in SpMV is limited to a factor of two. Further increasing the processor count will diminish the benefit of subspace pipelining as we reach the completely communication-bound regime.

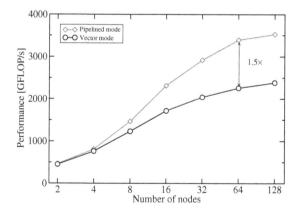

Fig. 8. Strong scaling ChebFD performance for the Topi-128-128-64 matrix with $n_s = 128$, $n_p = 500$ and $n_b = 16$ on Oakforest-PACS, comparing pipelined and vector communication modes.

On Piz Daint subspace pipelining did not show any benefits. With low-level experiments we have checked that non-blocking MPI communication using GPUdirect does not overlap with GPU computation (Cray is currently investigating this problem).

Summary

This work has investigated performance properties and subspace blocking optimization techniques for a Chebyshev filter diagonalization (ChebFD) algorithm on the Intel Xeon Phi ("Knights Landing"), the Nvidia P100 ("Pascal"), and the Nvidia V100 ("Volta") architectures. Our block vector implementation achieves approximately 10% of the theoretical peak performance and is not memory bound on the former two architectures, while it exhausts the high-bandwidth memory interface on the V100. We have demonstrated that subspace blocking with a sufficiently large polynomial filter degree enables efficient use of the complete node-level address space (i.e., high-bandwidth and low-bandwidth memory) transparently without impacting the node performance even if the working set exceeds the high-bandwidth memory size by far. Subspace blocking can be further extended towards a pipelining of the communication and computation phase in the filter application, which allows for simple communication hiding. All these optimizations enabled a scaled performance of more than $0.5\,\text{Pflop/s}$ on 2048 nodes of Piz Daint for computing approximately 100 inner eigenvalues of a large sparse matrix (dimension $4 \cdot 10^9$) originating from a quantum mechanical model of a topological insulator material.

Though this study has focused on using ChebFD in the context of inner eigenvalue computations for highly relevant topological quantum matter, the basic strategies presented can be applied to many applications evaluating Chebyshev polynomials of large sparse matrices and should be of interest for block formulations of iterative solvers in sparse linear algebra.

Acknowledgments. This work was funded by DFG SPP1648 through the ESSEX-II project and by a grant from the Swiss National Supercomputing Centre (CSCS) under project ID d35. We gratefully acknowledge the access to the Oakforest-PACS supercomputers at JCAHPC (University of Tokyo) and inspiring discussions with Andreas Alvermann, Bruno Lang, and Jonas Thies. H.F. and G.W. are thankful for the hospitality of Los Alamos National Laboratory.

References

1. NVIDIA Profiler. http://docs.nvidia.com/cuda/profiler-users-guide
2. TOP500 Supercomputer Sites, June 2017. http://www.top500.org
3. Aktulga, H.M., Buluç, A., Williams, S., Yang, C.: Optimizing sparse matrix-multiple vectors multiplication for nuclear configuration interaction calculations. In: Proceedings of the 2014 IEEE International Parallel and Distributed Processing Symposium, May 2012. IEEE Computer Society (2014)
4. Anzt, H., Tomov, S., Dongarra, J.: Accelerating the LOBPCG method on GPUs using a blocked sparse matrix vector product. In: Proceedings of the Symposium on High Performance Computing, HPC 2015, pp. 75–82. Society for Computer Simulation International, San Diego (2015). http://dl.acm.org/citation.cfm?id=2872599.2872609

5. Banerjee, A.S., Lin, L., Hu, W., Yang, C., Pask, J.E.: Chebyshev polynomial filtered subspace iteration in the discontinuous Galerkin method for large-scale electronic structure calculations. J. Chem. Phys. **145**(15), 154101 (2016). https://doi.org/10.1063/1.4964861
6. Basermann, A., Reichel, B., Schelthoff, C.: Preconditioned CG methods for sparse matrices on massively parallel machines. Parallel Comput. **23**(3), 381–398 (1997). http://www.sciencedirect.com/science/article/pii/S0167819197000057
7. Bhardwaj, O., Ineichen, Y., Bekas, C., Curioni, A.: Highly scalable linear time estimation of spectrograms – a tool for very large scale data analysis. Poster at 2013 ACM/IEEE International Conference on High Performance Computing Networking, Storage and Analysis (2013)
8. Demmel, J., Grigori, L., Hoemmen, M., Langou, J.: Communication-optimal parallel and sequential QR and LU factorizations. SIAM J. Sci. Comput. **34**, 206–239 (2012)
9. Di Napoli, E., Polizzi, E., Saad, Y.: Efficient estimation of eigenvalue counts in an interval. Numer. Linear Algebra Appl. **23**(4), 674–692 (2016)
10. Gropp, W.D., Kaushik, D.K., Keyes, D.E., Smith, B.F.: Towards realistic performance bounds for implicit CFD codes. In: Proceedings of Parallel CFD 1999, pp. 233–240. Elsevier (1999)
11. Kamiabad, A.A., Tate, J.E.: Polynomial preconditioning of power system matrices with graphics processing units. In: Khaitan, S., Gupta, A. (eds.) High Performance Computing in Power and Energy Systems, pp. 229–246. Springer, Heidelberg (2013). https://doi.org/10.1007/978-3-642-32683-7_8
12. Kreutzer, M., Hager, G., Wellein, G., Fehske, H., Basermann, A., Bishop, A.R.: Sparse matrix-vector multiplication on GPGPU clusters: A new storage format and a scalable implementation. In: 2012 IEEE 26th International Parallel and Distributed Processing Symposium Workshops PhD Forum, pp. 1696–1702, May 2012
13. Kreutzer, M., Pieper, A., Hager, G., Wellein, G., Alvermann, A., Fehske, H.: Performance engineering of the Kernel Polynomal Method on large-scale CPU-GPU systems. In: 2015 IEEE International Parallel and Distributed Processing Symposium (IPDPS), pp. 417–426, May 2015
14. Kreutzer, M., Hager, G., Wellein, G., Fehske, H., Bishop, A.R.: A unified sparse matrix data format for efficient general sparse matrix-vector multiplication on modern processors with wide SIMD units. SIAM J. Sci. Comput. **36**(5), C401–C423 (2014). https://doi.org/10.1137/130930352
15. Kreutzer, M., Thies, J., Röhrig-Zöllner, M., Pieper, A., Shahzad, F., Galgon, M., Basermann, A., Fehske, H., Hager, G., Wellein, G.: GHOST: building blocks for high performance sparse linear algebra on heterogeneous systems. In: International Journal of Parallel Programming, pp. 1–27 (2016)
16. Li, X., Li, F.: Estimation of the largest eigenvalue in Chebyshev preconditioner for parallel conjugate gradient method-based power flow computation. IET Gener. Transm. Distrib. **10**(1), 123–130 (2016)
17. Li, X., Li, F.: GPU-based power flow analysis with Chebyshev preconditioner and conjugate gradient method. Electr. Power Syst. Res. **116**(Suppl. C), 87–93 (2014). http://www.sciencedirect.com/science/article/pii/S0378779614001850
18. Liu, X., Chow, E., Vaidyanathan, K., Smelyanskiy, M.: Improving the performance of dynamical simulations via multiple right-hand sides. In: Proceedings of the 2012 IEEE International Parallel and Distributed Processing Symposium, May 2012, pp. 36–47. IEEE Computer Society (2012)

19. McCalpin, J.D.: Memory bandwidth and machine balance in current high performance computers. In: IEEE Computer Society Technical Committee on Computer Architecture (TCCA) Newsletter, pp. 19–25, December 1995
20. Pieper, A., Kreutzer, M., Alvermann, A., Galgon, M., Fehske, H., Hager, G., Lang, B., Wellein, G.: High-performance implementation of Chebyshev filter diagonalization for interior eigenvalue computations. J. Comput. Phys. **325**, 226–243 (2016). http://www.sciencedirect.com/science/article/pii/S0021999116303837
21. Saad, Y.: Chebyshev acceleration techniques for solving nonsymmetric eigenvalue problems. Math. Comput. **42**, 567–588 (1984)
22. Schubert, G., Fehske, H.: Metal-to-insulator transition and electron-hole puddle formation in disordered graphene nanoribbons. Phys. Rev. Lett. **108**, 066402 (2012)
23. Schubert, G., Fehske, H., Fritz, L., Vojta, M.: Fate of topological-insulator surface states under strong disorder. Phys. Rev. B **85**, 201105 (2012)
24. Sitte, M., Rosch, A., Altman, E., Fritz, L.: Topological insulators in magnetic fields: Quantum Hall effect and edge channels with a nonquantized θ term. Phys. Rev. Lett. **108**, 126807 (2012)
25. Stathopoulos, A., Wu, K.: A block orthogonalization procedure with constant synchronization requirements. SIAM J. Sci. Comput. **23**, 2165–2182 (2002)
26. Treibig, J., Hager, G., Wellein, G.: LIKWID: A lightweight performance-oriented tool suite for x86 multicore environments. In: Proceedings of PSTI2010, the First International Workshop on Parallel Software Tools and Tool Infrastructures, San Diego, CA (2010)
27. Weiße, A., Wellein, G., Alvermann, A., Fehske, H.: The kernel polynomial method. Rev. Mod. Phys. **78**, 275–306 (2006). https://link.aps.org/doi/10.1103/RevModPhys.78.275
28. Williams, S., Waterman, A., Patterson, D.: Roofline: An insightful visual performance model for multicore architectures. Commun. ACM **52**(4), 65–76 (2009). https://doi.org/10.1145/1498765.1498785
29. Zhou, Y., Saad, Y., Tiago, M.L., Chelikowsky, J.R.: Self-consistent-field calculations using Chebyshev-filtered subspace iteration. J. Comput. Phys. **219**(1), 172–184 (2006). http://www.sciencedirect.com/science/article/pii/S002199910600146X

Combining HTM with RCU to Speed Up Graph Coloring on Multicore Platforms

Christina Giannoula$^{(\boxtimes)}$, Georgios Goumas, and Nectarios Koziris

School of Electrical and Computer Engineering,
National Technical University of Athens, Athens, Greece
{cgiannoula,goumas,nkoziris}@cslab.ece.ntua.gr

Abstract. Graph algorithms are hard to parallelize, as they exhibit varying degrees of parallelism and perform irregular memory accesses. Graph coloring is a well studied problem, that colors the vertices of a graph, such that no adjacent vertices have the same color. This is a necessity for a large number of applications that require a coloring with few colors in near-linear time. In this work, we propose a simple and fast parallel graph coloring algorithm, well suited for shared memory architectures. Our algorithm employs Hardware Transactional Memory (HTM) to detect coloring inconsistencies between adjacent vertices, and exploits Read-Copy-Update (RCU) to enable high performance and ensure correctness.

We evaluate our algorithm on an Intel Haswell server using large-scale synthetic and real-world graphs, chosen to vary in terms of density and structure. With 14 threads, we achieved a geometric-mean speedup of 4.35 and a maximum speedup of 11.44.

1 Introduction

Graph coloring assigns colors to vertices such that each vertex has a different color from its neighbors. The algorithm is used in many real world applications such as scheduling of conflicting jobs [1,2], register allocation [3], sparse-matrix computations [4,5], machine learning (to select non-similar samples that form an effective training set), chromatic scheduling [6] of data graph computations. The case of chromatic scheduling is illustrative: It colors the data graph and then schedules the vertices of the same color in parallel (independent vertices). The PageRank algorithm is a good real-life example of a data graph computation. In this example, chromatic scheduling processes the colors serially, but updates all PageRanks of vertices of the same color in parallel. Hence, it is vital to compute a coloring with few colors (high coloring quality), as it enables more parallelism. However, minimizing the number of colors is a NP-complete problem [7].

A greedy coloring algorithm (GREEDY) [1] is a typical graph algorithm that records the colors of the neighborhood of a vertex v and assigns the minimum legal color to v. With a straightforward parallelization of GREEDY, coloring conflicts may arise when two parallel threads assign the same color to adjacent

R. Yokota et al. (Eds.): ISC High Performance 2018, LNCS 10876, pp. 350–369, 2018.
https://doi.org/10.1007/978-3-319-92040-5_18

vertices. To deal with this problematic case, recent works [8–10] proposed two additional phases: a conflict detection phase, which detects coloring inconsistencies between adjacent vertices, and a conflict resolution phase, which resolves the detected coloring inconsistencies. Nevertheless, these two additional phases may introduce significant performance overhead, since they result in traversing the graph more than once.

In this work, we parallelize GREEDY by combining Read-Copy-Update (RCU) [11] with Hardware Transactional Memory (HTM). The RCU technique, a technique used to implement scalable concurrent data structures, is here to ensure correctness and enable high performance, while the HTM mechanism detects and resolves coloring inconsistencies between adjacent vertices. HTM seems a promising approach to provide performance gains, if the processing threads access the same memory location rarely. Graph coloring, and generally several graph algorithms have complex data dependencies and perform irregular memory accesses. When parallelizing them, multiple threads access different cache lines without interfering with each other too many times. Therefore, we argue that HTM is a good candidate support mechanism to design parallel algorithms for irregular problems.

To summarize, in this paper, we make the following contributions:

- We leverage HTM on graph coloring to detect and resolve coloring inconsistencies between adjacent vertices.
- We exploit RCU to reduce the transaction footprint (consequently achieve high performance), and ensure correctness. To the best of our knowledge, this is the first work that applies a technique proposed for concurrent data structures to a graph algorithm.
- We compare our algorithm with state-of-the-art graph coloring algorithms using large scale (both synthetic and real-world) graphs. Our evaluation reveals that by combining HTM with RCU, we are able to successfully expose high levels of parallelism in graph coloring.

2   Background

2.1   Hardware Transactional Memory (HTM)

Transactional Memory (TM) is a synchronization mechanism that allows a transaction, namely a group of instructions, to be executed atomically. The system tracks the read memory locations in the transaction's read-set and the written ones in the write-set. If the read- and write-sets do not conflict with memory accesses from other threads, the transaction commits. Otherwise, the transaction aborts and none of its memory writes becomes visible to other threads.

Hardware Transactional Memory (HTM) is an implementation of TM in hardware. Nowadays, HTM is available on many modern processors such as Intel Haswell [12] (and successors) and IBM Power8 [13]. Besides conflict aborts due to concurrent memory accesses, an HTM transaction may suffer from capacity aborts, due to the bounded size of the hardware buffers that store the read- and write-sets, or it may fail due to other reasons such as cache line evictions, interrupts and/or unsupported instructions. Finally, the current HTM implementations are best-effort HTMs and provide no guarantees that any transaction will eventually commit inside the transactional path. It is thus the programmer's responsibility to provide an alternative path of execution that uses no transactions, i.e., a non-transactional fallback path.

2.2 Read-Copy-Update (RCU)

Read-Copy-Update [11] is a synchronization technique that is used to implement scalable concurrent data structures [14–16] by providing asynchronized traversals. In RCU, threads first read and copy parts of the data structure they intend to update, modify their local copy and replace the old version of the data structure with their new modified version. This replacement is performed in a single atomic step, such that other threads observe either the old or the new version of the data. However, while a thread modifies its private copy, the affected parts of the data structure copied privately may be modified by other threads. Therefore, before installing its new modified version of the data structure, the thread has to validate that all the affected parts have remained unchanged since they were read. If this validation succeeds, the thread then installs the copy in the data structure. The validation and the installation of the private copy also need to be performed atomically, to guarantee that the structure remains consistent.

2.3 The GREEDY Algorithm

The Algorithm

Algorithm 1 presents the pseudocode of a sequential, greedy coloring algorithm [1] (GREEDY). Considering an undirected graph $G = (V, E)$, the neighborhood $N(v)$ of a vertex $v \in V$ is defined as: $N(v) = \{u \in V : (v, u) \in E\}$ and the degree of a vertex is defined as the number of its neighbors: $deg(v) = |N(v)|$. In each step, GREEDY selects an uncolored vertex v, records the colors of $v's$ neighbors in a forbidden set of colors, and colors the vertex v with the minimum legal color. This scheme will produce at most $\Delta + 1$ colors, where Δ is the degree of the graph G that can be denoted as: $\Delta = max_{v \in V}\{deg(v)\}$.

Algorithm 1. GREEDY(G)

```
1 Input: Graph G=(V,E)
2 for v ∈ V
3   for u ∈ N(v)
4     forbidden = forbidden ∪ {u.color}
5   v.color = minColor(forbidden)
```

Parallelizing GREEDY

A straightforward parallel version of GREEDY can be achieved by distributing the vertices of the graph to the processing threads. However, due to crossing edges, the coloring subproblems assigned to threads are not independent and the algorithm may terminate with an invalid coloring. Specifically, a race condition arises when two threads that examine adjacent vertices, assign them the same color. The algorithm implies that when a thread updates the color of a vertex, the forbidden set of colors has not changed. As a result, the nature of this algorithm imposes that the reads to the colors of the neighborhood of a vertex v have to be executed *atomically* with the write-update to v's color.

Algorithms 2 and 3 describe two parallelization schemes for GREEDY proposed in [8] and [9,10], respectively. The processing threads first speculatively color the vertices, then they detect coloring inconsistencies and resolve them either serially, Sequential-Solve (SS), or in an iterative way, Iterative-Solve (IS). IS is widely used in shared memory architectures [9], as well as in distributed systems [10]. However, both of these algorithms perform two additional steps: the conflict detection and the conflict resolution phases.

Algorithm 2. Sequential-Solve(G)

```
 1 Input: Graph G=(V,E)
 2 //speculative coloring
 3 //(Phase 1)
 4 for v ∈ V do in parallel
 5   assign the min legal
 6     color to v
 7 //detect conflicts (Phase 2)
 8 for v ∈ V do in parallel
 9   for u ∈ N(v)
10     if v.color==u.color and v<u
11       store{v}
12 //resolve conflicts (Phase 3)
13 color vertices sequentially
```

Algorithm 3. Iterative-Solve(G)

```
 1 Input: Graph G=(V,E)
 2 U = V
 3 while U ≠ ∅
 4   //speculative coloring
 5   //(Phase 1)
 6   for v ∈ U do in parallel
 7     assign the min legal color to v
 8   //R: set of vertices
 9   //to be re-colored
10   R = ∅
11   //detect conflicts (Phase 2)
12   for v ∈ U do in parallel
13     for u ∈ N(v)
14       if v.color==u.color and v<u
15         R = R ∪ v
16   U = R
```

In SS, Algorithm 2, the speculative coloring (Phase 1) and the conflict detection phase (Phase 2) are parallelized, while the conflict resolution phase (Phase 3) is serial. There are two implicit barriers, one after Phase 1 and one after Phase 2. In case that a coloring conflict arises, only one of the involved neighbors needs to be recolored (line 10). When the number of conflicts is low, the algorithm scales well. However, as the number of threads increases and the graph becomes more dense, more conflicts arise, which will be resolved in a serial way. Finally, the SS algorithm traverses the graph at least two times (Phase 1 and Phase 2) and, as we show later in the evaluation part, these traversals introduce significant performance overhead.

The IS algorithm, Algorithm 3, resolves the coloring inconsistencies in an iterative way. Similarly to SS, IS has two implicit barriers (Phase 1 and Phase 2), and it also traverses the graph at least two times. In IS, when two vertices u and v obtain the same color, the programmer has to explicitly define only one of them to be recolored (line 14), by choosing the vertex with the smaller vertex_id, to ensure forward progress. Otherwise, these adjacent vertices may always obtain the same color, if they are processed by different threads. The programmer has to explicitly define forward progress in the code, so that the algorithm terminates. Furthermore, the iterative process of fixing coloring conflicts may introduce new conflicts, and thus, IS may need additional iterations to fix them. The authors in [9] notice empirically that only a few iterations of the algorithm are required to produce a valid coloring. However, the more iterations needed, the more synchronization barriers are introduced in the execution and the more traversals on the vertices of the graph are performed, which remarkably degrade scalability.

3   Our Approach

3.1   General Concept and Design

Our approach parallelizes GREEDY by employing HTM as a synchronization mechanism to deal with the race condition that arises when two threads examine two adjacent vertices. Compared to SS and IS, our algorithm traverses the graph only once, since it omits the conflict detection and conflict resolution phases by employing HTM. The motivation to introduce HTM in this algorithm comes from three observations:

- **HTM is aligned with the nature of the algorithm:** GREEDY requires atomicity between the reads to the colors of the neighborhood of a vertex v and the write to v's color. Since the aim of HTM is to allow a block of code to be executed atomically, the mechanism employed for synchronization will fit with the nature of the algorithm.
- **HTM can detect conflicts:** HTM can detect coloring conflicts that arise due to crossing edges. Supposing that we enclose the reads to the colors of the neighborhood of a vertex v and the write to v's color within a single transaction. When two threads attempt to update (write) the colors of two adjacent vertices using two different transactions, the HTM mechanism will detect a read-write conflict, since a running transaction attempts to write the read-set of another running transaction. Figure 1 explains how HTM detects coloring conflicts. When a thread T_1 attempts to color the vertex v, the running transaction has the vertex v in its write-set and the adjacent vertices u, z in its read-set. Similarly, when a thread T_2 attempts to color the vertex u, the transaction's write-set includes the vertex u and read-set includes the vertex v. HTM will detect a read-write conflict either on vertex v or on u, since T_1 attempts to write the read-set of T_2, and visa versa. As a result, it will abort one of these transactions, while the other will commit.
- **HTM can resolve conflicts:** In case of n conflicting transactions, HTM will abort $n\text{-}1$ running transactions and will commit only one of them. Therefore, in contrast to IS, when a coloring conflict arises between two running transactions, there is no need to explicitly define a resolution policy for it. HTM will commit one of the two running transactions and will abort the other. Thus, HTM chooses the vertex to be recolored according to its conflict resolution policy.

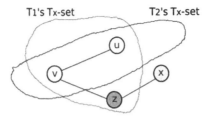

Fig. 1. HTM detects coloring inconsistencies.

However, the current best-effort HTM implementations do not guarantee forward progress, and need a non-transactional fallback path. The most common practice is to retry a transaction for a given amount of times (threshold), and if it fails to commit, it fall backs to the acquisition of a lock that allows only a single thread to enter the critical section in a coarse-grained manner. To achieve this, the lock has to be added to the transaction's read set so that, when the lock is acquired by a thread (write to the lock variable), the remaining threads will be aborted and wait until the lock is released.

The straightforward approach to parallelize GREEDY would be to enclose within a single transaction the whole block of code of each iteration of the main for loop (lines 3–5 in Algorithm 1). However, this implementation results to a large transaction footprint causing two main problems: (a) the transaction sets are large, increasing the probability of capacity abort and (b) the duration of the transaction is too long, increasing the probability of abort due to time interrupt. Note that, when the duration of a transaction exceeds the scheduling quantum, the scheduler schedules out the processing thread and the transaction aborts. Moreover, the longer the transactions last and the larger their sets are, the probability for a conflict abort between running transactions becomes higher. As a result, in this work, we exploit the RCU technique [11] to reduce the transaction footprint, by enclosing within the transaction only the necessary data and computations, and ensure correctness at the same time. Our solution is described in more detail in the next paragraph.

3.2 Implementation Details

In an attempt to reduce the transaction footprint, we noticed that, in the straightforward parallelization of GREEDY, there is no need to include inside the transaction all the neighbors of the considered vertex v. Therefore, we can omit from the transaction the following groups of v's neighbors:

1. **The colored neighbors:** The race condition in the algorithm arises when two threads attempt to color two adjacent vertices concurrently. Therefore, coloring conflicts may arise between **uncolored** neighbors. In our approach, once a vertex obtains color, its color will be included at the forbidden set of colors of its neighboring uncolored vertices and will not cause any conflict in later rounds. Hence, we safely omit the colored vertices from the transaction.

2. **The neighbors assigned to the same thread as v:** Since each thread colors the vertices assigned to it sequentially, coloring conflicts cannot arise between adjacent vertices assigned to the same thread. Therefore, we can omit from the transaction the neighbors assigned to the same thread as the considered vertex. Given that a set of vertices (assigned to a thread) can be represented as a range of vertex_ids, it is straightforward to implement this optimization in the code.

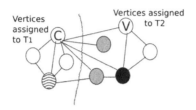

Fig. 2. The graph is partitioned between threads T1 and T2. When T1 attempts to color the vertex C, the only necessary neighbor that has to be included in the transaction is the vertex V.

To summarize, we only include in the transaction the uncolored vertices assigned to another thread. For instance, in Fig. 2, the white vertices represent uncolored vertices, while the graph is partitioned between threads T_1 and T_2. In this scenario, thread T_1 attempts to color the vertex C. According to our optimizations, we omit from the transaction the neighboring vertices assigned to T_1 as well as the colored vertices assigned to T_2. Thus, the transaction will only contain the neighboring vertex V.

As a result, to achieve a smaller transaction footprint, we enclose within the transaction only the necessary neighbors, and we also omit the calculations needed to compute the minimum legal color. Each loop iteration of GREEDY is separated in two phases. In the first phase, we read the forbidden colors of the neighbors, and compute a speculative color for the considered vertex. In the second phase, we execute the transaction, which includes only the necessary neighbors described previously, and assigns the speculative color to the considered vertex. However, while a thread computes a speculative color for a vertex v, one of its neighbors may have changed color, and a conflict may arise. Therefore, as RCU imposes, before updating v's color (installation part), a validation step is needed to be executed in an atomic way with the installation part.

Our approach, htm_rcu, is described in Algorithm 4. Each thread, for each vertex v, reads and copies locally the colors (READ-COPY, line 6) of v's neighbors, and computes a speculative color for the vertex v. It also records in a *check_list* (lines 8–9) the necessary neighbors to be validated. If *check_list* is empty (there are no neighbors to be validated), the transaction can be omitted. Otherwise, both the validation step and the update-store to v's color are enclosed within a single HTM transaction (VALIDATE-UPDATE, lines 16–28). The validation step ensures that the speculative color computed is valid to be assigned to vertex v. If the validation step fails, the current thread re-attempts to find another color for the considered vertex (lines 27–30).

In concurrent data structures [11], to ensure consistency, the validation step in RCU checks if the affected parts of the structure have remained unchanged, such that modifications performed by other threads are not discarded. We modify the RCU validation step and adapt it to our specific graph algorithm. Htm_rcu does not check if the affected neighboring vertices have remained unchanged (have not changed their coloring state). In the meantime, another thread may have colored a neighboring vertex with a different color from the speculative computed and in this case, the validation step should succeed. Therefore, we only need to validate, if the coloring state of the affected neighbors conflicts with the speculative color computed (line 19). In this way, we extract more parallelism, since concurrent threads that assign different colors to neighboring vertices, will not cause validation failure. We also reduce the number of retries to color a specific vertex (the validation step fails fewer times).

Algorithm 4. htm_rcu(G)

```
 1 Input: Graph G=(V,E)
 2 for v ∈ U do in parallel
 3 RETRY:
 4    forbidden = ∅
 5    for u ∈ N(v) do
 6       forbidden = forbidden ∪ u.color // track forbidden colors
 7       // the uncolored neighbors assigned to another thread
 8       if(isUncolored(u) && belongs(u) != thread_id)
 9          check_list = check_list ∪ u
10    end_for
11    spec_color=compute_color(forbidden) // the min legal color
12    // if check_list is empty, we omit the validation step
13    if check_list == ∅
14       v.color = spec_color
15    else
16     BEGIN_TM
17       check = 1
18       for u ∈ check_list do // validate neighbors
19          if u.color == spec_color
20             check = 0
21             break
22          end_if
23       if check == 1   //validation succeeds
24          v.color = spec_color // update the speculative color
25        END_TM
26       end_if
27       else                // validation fails
28        END_TM
29          goTo RETRY       // find another color
30       end_else
31    end_else
32 end_for
```

Finally, to record the forbidden colors efficiently, we implement a bitwise representation for the color set (*forbidden*), as proposed in [17]. Generally, this approach provides a trade-off between memory and execution time. It may require multiple traversals of the neighboring list, but it has very low memory cost for the representation of the forbidden set of colors, a trade-off that is clearly relevant for a memory bound graph algorithm.

3.3   Progress and Correctness

Htm_rcu has progress and finally terminates, since each thread attempts to color a specific vertex a limited number of retries. A thread re-attempts to find another color for its vertex v, when validation fails. However, this can only happen a bounded number of times. The validation step fails when a neighbor has obtained the same color as the speculative computed for v. In the worst case, validation will fail $deg(v)$ times, where $deg(v)$ is the degree of the vertex v. When all v's neighbors are colored, the validation step will be omitted (lines 13–14). Therefore, each thread attempts to color a specific vertex at most $(deg(v) + 1)$ times.

Secondly, the computed coloring of htm_rcu is valid. There are two race conditions under which a coloring conflict may arise. First, while a thread computes the speculative color k for its vertex v, another thread has just colored a neighbor u with the same color k. In this case, the validation step of the first thread will fail, since the neighbor u has just obtained color k. Then, the first thread will retry to find another color for vertex v. The second race condition arises when two threads attempt to color (write) two neighbors with the same color k within two different transactions. In that case, since the read-set of the transaction includes the colors of the neighbors, HTM will notice a read-write conflict and one of these transactions will abort, while the other will commit. When the aborted transaction retries, its validation step fails, since now there is a neighbor colored with color k (committed transaction). The current thread will retry to find another color for its vertex. Consequently, our algorithm handles correctly these two race conditions and it will eventually terminate with a valid coloring.

4   Evaluation

4.1   Experimental Setup

For our experiments we used a 2-socket Intel Haswell server with an Intel Xeon E5-2697 v3 processor with 28 physical cores and 56 hardware threads. The processor runs at 2.6 GHz and each physical core has its own L1 and L2 caches of sizes 32 KB and 256 KB, respectively. Each socket includes a shared 35 MB L3 cache. We statically pin software threads to hardware threads and enable hyperthreading only on 56-threaded executions, unless otherwise stated.

Our evaluation includes the following implementations:

- **GREEDY:** The serial GREEDY algorithm.
- **SS:** The algorithm presented in Algorithm 2 parallelized with OpenMP 4.0.

- **IS:** The algorithm presented in Algorithm 3 parallelized with OpenMP 4.0.
- **lock_naive:** A fine grained locking implementation. Each vertex is associated with a lock and when updating a vertex all its neighbors are locked. To avoid deadlocks, the locks of the vertex's neighborhood are acquired from the lowest to the highest vertex_id, to impose a global order of locks. Lock_naive is used as a baseline for our evaluation.
- **lock_rcu:** A variant of our algorithm using locks instead of transactional memory. Specifically, prior to the validation step, the current thread acquires only the locks of the neighboring vertices in the check_list and validates their colors. If the validation succeeds, the thread assigns the speculative color, releases the locks and proceeds to another vertex. If the validation fails, the thread releases the locks and re-attempts to find another color for the vertex. Similarly with lock_naive, we avoid deadlocks by locking vertices ordered by their unique ids.
- **htm_rcu:** Our scheme employing HTM. Each transaction can be retried up to 50 times, before resorting to the non-transactional fallback path. The non-transactional path is a coarse-grain lock solution for the critical section (lines 16–28 in Algorithm 4).

All implementations color the vertices in the order they appear in the input graph. Our graph suite includes large-scale graphs, both synthetic and real-

Table 1. Our graph suite. The parameters for the generation of R-MAT graphs are: (i) RMAT1 (A = 0.45, B = C = 0.15, D = 0.25) and (ii) RMAT2 (A = 0.57, B = C = 0.19, D = 0.05). deg_{max} and deg_{avg} are the maximum and the average degree ($|E|/|V|$) of the graph respectively, while the last column shows the ratio of the standard deviation of the vertex degrees to the average degree.

Graph	Source	GraphID	V	E	deg_{max}	deg_{avg}	$\frac{std(deg(v))}{deg_{avg}}$
Random-5M × 100M	Generated	Rnd-1	5M	100M	79	20	1.01
Random-5M × 200M	Generated	Rnd-2	5M	200M	137	40	1.02
Random-5M × 500M	Generated	Rnd-3	5M	500M	274	100	1.10
RMAT1-5M × 100M	Generated	Rmt1-1	5M	100M	3558	20	2.84
RMAT1-5M × 200M	Generated	Rmt1-2	5M	200M	7062	40	2.93
RMAT1-5M × 500M	Generated	Rmt1-3	5M	500M	17707	100	3.60
RMAT2-5M × 100M	Generated	Rmt2-1	5M	100M	441585	20	26.80
RMAT2-5M × 200M	Generated	Rmt2-2	5M	200M	884287	40	30.26
RMAT2-5M × 500M	Generated	Rmt2-3	5M	500M	2210899	100	43.43
com-Orkut	[18]	Real-1	3M	117M	33313	38.14	12.51
soc-Live-Journal1	[18]	Real-2	4M	68M	22889	14.24	12.01
sx-stackoverflow	[18]	Real-3	2M	63M	194806	24.41	54.57
dbpedia-link	[19]	Real-4	18M	172M	632558	9.43	38.99
youtube-u-growth	[19]	Real-5	3M	9M	91751	2.91	120.25
USA-road.D	[20]	Real-6	23M	58M	18	2.44	1.27

world graphs, chosen to cover a wide range of density and structure (working sets ranging from 120 MB to 3.89 GB). We use the term irregular graphs for those graphs in which vertices have highly varying degrees (e.g. RMAT2 graph family), while those with similar degrees are qualitatively referred to as regular graphs. Their characteristics are presented in Table 1.

4.2   Scalability

Figures 3, 4, 5 and 7 present the time elapsed by all implementations in our synthetic and real world graphs. The single-threaded execution of htm_rcu is close to the serial GREEDY execution. When only one thread is used, htm_rcu does not perform any additional work from the serial solution.

Overall, all implementations scale well on regular graphs, but exhibit limited scalability on irregular ones. On irregular graphs, the lock-based implementations acquire too many locks in high degree vertices, while htm_rcu exhibits many capacity aborts. In SS and IS algorithms, irregular graphs result to an increased number of coloring conflicts, which in the former, are resolved serially, and in the latter, introduce many synchronization points.

Htm_rcu outperforms all other implementations and has the lowest overhead. The single-threaded executions of the lock-based implementations, lock_naive and lock_rcu, exhibit high overhead due to per vertex locks. On the other hand, SS and IS traverse the graph at least two times and thus, their single-threaded executions have increased performance overhead compared to GREEDY. In some graphs like Real-5 and Real-6, the single-threaded executions of SS and htm_rcu are approximately the same. We believe this is due to the memory footprint of these graphs which may fit in the cache hierarchy. Therefore, the speedups achieved in those two schemes are quite similar.

Table 2 presents the geometric mean of execution times and the number of colors (lower is better) on our graph suite for all implementations in single-threaded and multiple-threaded executions. Htm_rcu exhibits the lowest execution time, being 1.56 times faster than SS, and 1.76 times faster than IS, in case of the maximum capacity of our machine (56 threads). However, when passing

Table 2. The geometric mean of execution times in seconds (T) and the number of colors (C) on our graph suite using one thread, all cores of one socket, two sockets and the maximum capacity of our machine (hyperthreading enabled).

	T1	C1	T14	C14	T28	C28	T56	C56
GREEDY	3.82	85.81	-	-	-	-	-	-
SS	6.06	85.81	1.28	89.71	0.87	91.37	0.74	94.33
IS	5.79	85.81	1.40	89.53	0.99	91.70	0.84	93.84
lock_naive	7.65	85.81	3.13	88.17	2.43	88.39	2.33	89.34
lock_rcu	5.47	85.81	1.53	88.27	1.14	89.28	1.09	90.53
htm_rcu	4.08	85.81	0.88	89.38	0.57	90.41	0.48	90.83

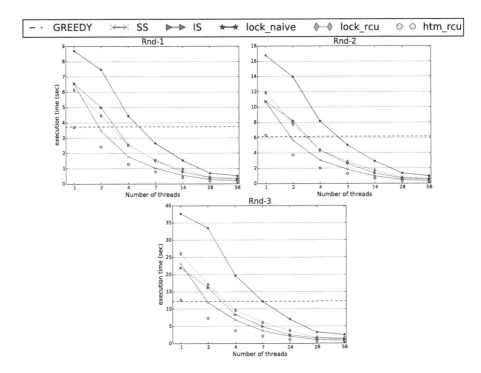

Fig. 3. The scalability achieved of all implementations in Random graphs. The horizontal line represents the serial GREEDY execution. Notice the differences in the y-axis range between the figures.

from one to two sockets of our machine, htm_rcu has little performance improvement due to hyperthreading and NUMA effects. We further comment on these effects in the next paragraph. Concerning the coloring quality, the results do not change significantly among different parallelization schemes of GREEDY, while the coloring quality becomes slightly worse as the number of threads increases.

Overall, Fig. 6 summarizes the speedup achieved by htm_rcu over the serial GREEDY algorithm when using all cores of one socket, two sockets, and all the available hardware threads of the system (i.e. employing hyperthreading). In case of the maximum capacity of our machine (hyperthreading enabled), the geometric mean of the speedup achieved on our graph suite is 8.03. In Random graphs, which are the most regular graph family, htm_rcu achieves a near linear speedup. Increasing the irregularity of the graph, i.e. RMAT family, results in less speedup. Specifically, on RMAT2 graphs, htm_rcu performs poorly due to excessive capacity aborts. Generally, high degree vertices will always cause capacity aborts (full hardware buffers) and cannot be validated inside the transactional path. We intend to further experiment with these graphs in future work. Finally, the real world graphs have low serial execution times (Fig. 7), apart from Real-4, and thus, there is not enough space to achieve high speedup.

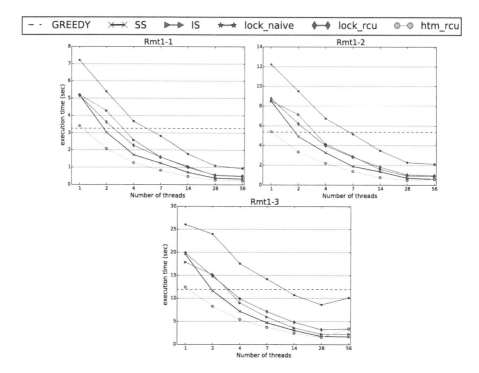

Fig. 4. The scalability achieved of all implementations in our Rmat1 graphs. The horizontal line represents the serial GREEDY execution. Notice the differences in the y-axis range between the figures.

4.3   Analysis of Execution Behavior

We further investigate the scalability of htm_rcu by analyzing its HTM behavior. Figure 8 presents the abort ratio (the number of aborts divided by the number of attempted transactions), and Fig. 9 presents the type of aborts for a synthetic and a real world graph. In $14 + 14$ threaded execution, we have pinned all threads on the same socket enabling hyperthreading, while in 28-threaded execution, threads are pinned on both sockets of our machine (hyperthreading disabled).

In one-socket executions (up to 14 threads), htm_rcu exhibits a low number of capacity aborts, apart from the highly irregular graphs like RMAT2. In 14-threaded execution, the geometric mean of the capacity abort ratio on our graph suite is 0.81%. Secondly, in one-socket executions, the number of conflict aborts is also quite low. When using 14 threads, the geometric mean of the conflict abort ratio in all our graphs is 0.13%. Threads work concurrently without interfering with each other frequently, and causing conflict aborts. We believe this is due to the complex data dependencies and irregular memory access patterns of this graph algorithm. Consequently, the HTM mechanism seems to expose high levels of parallelism in GREEDY.

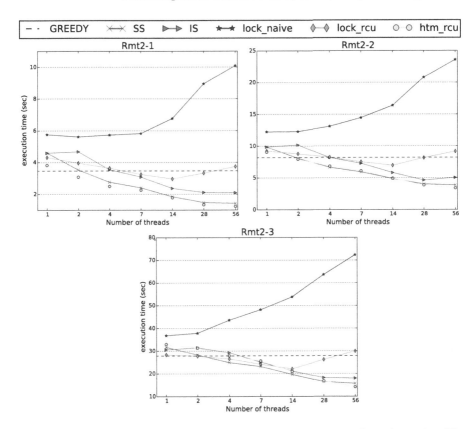

Fig. 5. The scalability achieved of all implementations in our Rmat2 graphs. The horizontal line represents the serial GREEDY execution. Notice the differences in the y-axis range between the figures.

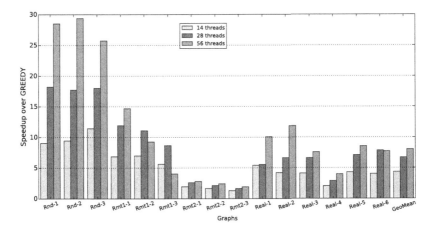

Fig. 6. The speedup achieved by htm_rcu over GREEDY on our graph suite when using all cores of one socket, two sockets, and all the available hardware threads of the system.

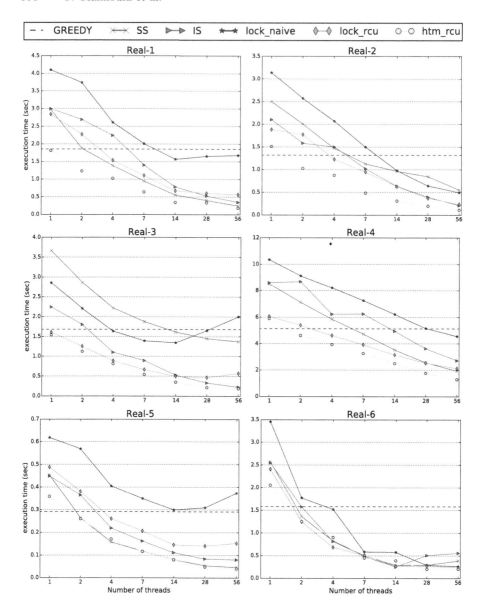

Fig. 7. The scalability achieved of all implementations in our real graphs. The horizontal line represents the serial GREEDY execution. Notice the differences in the y-axis range between the figures.

As shown in Fig. 9, when a specific type of aborts increases, lock aborts (aborts due to lock acquired) increase, too. When the execution exhibits a high number of conflict or capacity aborts, the predefined limit of retrying a transaction is exceeded frequently. Then, the corresponding thread falls back to the non-transactional path, acquiring the lock and provoking lock aborts to all other threads. Moreover, since the lock is just a variable in the code, some conflict aborts are caused by writes in this lock variable. Thus, a part of lock aborts is counted as conflict aborts in our measurements.

When using both sockets of our machine (28-threads in Fig. 9), we notice that the number of conflicts aborts increases due to the NUMA effect. The NUMA effect extends the duration of the transaction and thus, the probability of conflict abort between running transactions becomes too strong. The HTM mechanism is not NUMA friendly, as also discussed in [21]. On the other hand, when we pin the software threads on the same socket enabling hyperthreading (14 + 14 threads in Fig. 9), the number of capacity aborts increases excessively. The hyperthreading pair of threads shares the HTM resources (buffers, memory, etc.). Each thread can now access less data within its transaction. As a result, capacity aborts arise more frequently. Finally, in case of the maximum capacity of our machine (hyperthreading enabled), conflict aborts increase due to the NUMA effect, capacity aborts due to limitations to the shared HTM resources between the hyperthreading pair of threads, and lock aborts due to the raise of conflict and capacity aborts. Therefore, in all graphs, htm_rcu exhibits high abort ratio in 56-threaded execution (Fig. 8).

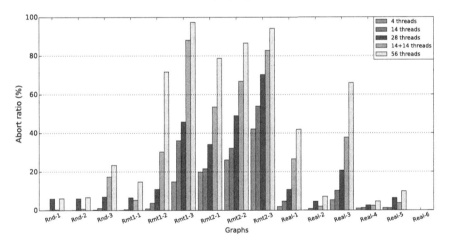

Fig. 8. Abort ratio exhibited by htm_rcu on our graph suite.

To summarize, htm_rcu achieves high performance in one-socket executions, since it exhibits a low number of capacity and conflict aborts. We successfully reduce the transaction footprint significantly, and extract high levels of parallelism employing HTM. However, the scalability degrades due to NUMA and hyperthreading effects. The NUMA effect results to a significant increase in the number of conflict aborts, while hyperthreading to an increase in the number of capacity aborts. We aim to further explore this behavior in future work.

Finally, we measured the number of failures in the validation step (due to coloring conflicts) as well as the number of neighbors included in the transaction for each vertex. The validation step fails very few times (less than 0.01%) for all

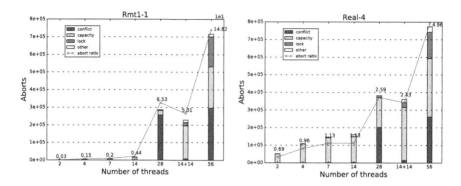

Fig. 9. The number of each type of aborts as well as the abort ratio of each n-thread execution for (a) a synthetic graph and (b) a real world graph.

of our graphs and executions. The worst case was the 56-threaded execution on Rmt1-3 graph, where it failed 485 times on 5 million vertices (0.0097%). On the other hand, the neighbors included in the transaction in case of using all cores of one socket (14 threads) is on average 56% on our graph suite. Generally, our transaction includes 20%–70% of neighboring vertices. This percentage increases as the number of threads increases, since partitioning a graph to more threads results to more crossing edges.

5   Related Work

Researchers have explored parallel graph coloring algorithms in both shared memory and distributed systems. Gebremedhin and Manne [8] proposed a parallelization of GREEDY for shared memory architectures (SS algorithm). Similarly, Boman et al. [10] proposed the iterative IS algorithm and adapted it to distributed systems, while Catalyurek et al. [9] evaluated IS in shared memory systems. Rokos et al. [22] improved the IS algorithm, devising a more optimistic algorithm with less thread synchronization. We intend to compare htm_rcu with this improved version of IS in future work. Finally, Deveci et al. [17] presented an edge-based approach for graph coloring that is better suited to GPUs.

Jones and Plassmann [23] proposed a parallel algorithm (JP) which is based on independent sets. In each iteration, an independent set of vertices is selected and can be colored concurrently. JP often takes longer to run than GREEDY, as it does more work, and may need a large number of synchronization points. In this work, we mainly focus on parallelizing the GREEDY algorithm to evaluate the applicability of HTM on a typical and well studied graph algorithm. Htm_rcu employs HTM to extract parallelism and runs with a low thread synchronization overhead (no barriers needed). On the other hand, the main advantage of JP is that it can support different vertex orderings. A vertex ordering defines the order in which the algorithm has to color the vertices to improve the coloring quality of the graph (fewer colors). Hasenplaugh et al. [24] implemented JP for multicore architectures and proposed new vertex orderings (largest-log-degree-first and smallest-log-degree-last).

Recent works also employ TM for synchronization purposes to parallelize efficiently graph algorithms. Nikas et al. [25] exploit it to parallelize Dijkstra's algorithm implementing a helper threading scheme to extract parallelism, Kang and Bader [26] to compute minimum spanning forests of sparse graphs. We also incorporate the RCU technique on a graph algorithm. So far, RCU has only been applied to concurrent Binary Search Trees, either balanced [27] or unbalanced [14,15], to provide asynchronized traversals, while Siakavaras et al. [16] combined RCU with HTM to allow multiple updaters to modify different parts of the data structure concurrently. In this work, we exploit RCU to reduce the transaction footprint and thus, design a scalable graph algorithm.

6   Conclusions and Future Work

In this paper, we employ HTM to efficiently parallelize GREEDY, a typical graph coloring algorithm. HTM detects coloring conflicts and resolves them without demanding any effort by the programmer. However, the HTM mechanism restricts the size of the transaction sets (read- and write-set), as well as the duration of the transaction. To reduce the transaction footprint, we pair HTM with RCU, a technique proposed for concurrent data structures. We exploit RCU to enclose within the transaction only the necessary data and computations. To the best of our knowledge, this is the first work that adopts a technique proposed for concurrent data structures to implement a scalable and efficient graph algorithm.

Our experimental results show that: (a) we successfully reduce the transaction footprint, since htm_rcu exhibits a low number of capacity aborts and (b) we extract high levels of parallelism, since htm_rcu exhibits a low number of conflict aborts. Considering the low number of conflict aborts, we conclude that threads do not interfere with each other frequently and thus, HTM exposes high levels of parallelism in GREEDY. Given that graph algorithms generally have similar characteristics (i.e. complex data dependencies and irregular memory access patterns), we argue that several graph algorithms can scale efficiently on multiple threads with the aid of HTM. As future work, we will investigate the applicability of HTM on other graph algorithms and irregular applications.

Moreover, we aim to further experiment with the NUMA effect, as well as with hyperthreading, and attempt to implement a NUMA-aware policy in our algorithm, which will be based on judicious partitioning of our data structures. We also intend to incorporate different vertex orderings on htm_rcu to improve the produced coloring quality, as well as to design hybrid approaches to address the highly irregular graphs. In a hybrid approach, the high degree vertices will be colored within a non-transactional path, since they always cause capacity aborts. Finally, to show the importance of coloring on a real application, we will exploit graph coloring as a part of a more complex workflow, as for example implementing chromatic scheduling to speed up the PageRank algorithm.

Acknowledgments. Christina Giannoula is funded by PhD fellowship from the General Secretariat for Research and Technology (GSRT) and the Hellenic Foundation for Research and Innovation (HFRI). The authors thank their anonymous reviewers and their colleagues Nikela Papadopoulou, Konstantinos Nikas, Vasileios Karakostas and Dimitrios Siakavaras for their insightful comments and valuable feedback.

References

1. Welsh, D.J.A., Powell, M.B.: An upper bound for the chromatic number of a graph and its application to timetabling problems. Comput. J. **10**, 85–86 (1967)
2. Marx, D.: Graph coloring problems and their applications in scheduling. In: Proceedings of John Von Neumann PhD Students Conference, pp. 1–2 (2004)
3. Chaitin, G.J., Auslander, M.A., Chandra, A.K., Cocke, J., Hopkins, M.E., Markstein, P.W.: Register allocation via coloring. Comput. Lang. **6**, 47–57 (1981)
4. Coleman, T.F., Moré, J.J.: Estimation of sparse Jacobian matrices and graph coloring problems. SIAM J. Numer. Anal. **20**, 187–209 (1983)
5. Saad, Y.: Sparskit: a basic tool kit for sparse matrix computations (1994)
6. Kaler, T., Hasenplaugh, W., Schardl, T.B., Leiserson, C.E.: Executing dynamic data-graph computations deterministically using chromatic scheduling. In: Proceedings of the 26th ACM Symposium on Parallelism in Algorithms and Architectures, SPAA 2014, pp. 154–165 (2014)
7. Garey, M.R., Johnson, D.S., Stockmeyer, L.: Some simplified NP-complete graph problems. Theor. Comput. Sci. **1**, 237–267 (1976)
8. Gebremedhin, A.H., Manne, F.: Scalable parallel graph coloring algorithms. Pract. Exp. Concurr. **12**, 1131–1146 (2000)
9. Çatalyürek, Ü.V., Feo, J., Gebremedhin, A.H., Halappanavar, M., Pothen, A.: Graph coloring algorithms for muti-core and massively multithreaded architectures. CoRR (2012)
10. Boman, E.G., Bozdağ, D., Catalyurek, U., Gebremedhin, A.H., Manne, F.: A scalable parallel graph coloring algorithm for distributed memory computers. In: Cunha, J.C., Medeiros, P.D. (eds.) Euro-Par 2005. LNCS, vol. 3648, pp. 241–251. Springer, Heidelberg (2005). https://doi.org/10.1007/11549468_29
11. McKenney, P.E., Slingwine, J.D.: Read-copy update: using execution history to solve concurrency problems (1998)
12. Yoo, R.M., Hughes, C.J., Lai, K., Rajwar, R.: Performance evaluation of Intel transactional synchronization extensions for high-performance computing. In: Proceedings of the International Conference on High Performance Computing, Networking, Storage and Analysis, SC 2013 (2013)
13. Cain, H.W., Michael, M.M., Frey, B., May, C., Williams, D., Le, H.: Robust architectural support for transactional memory in the power architecture. SIGARCH Comput. Archit. News **41**, 225–236 (2013)
14. Arbel, M., Attiya, H.: Concurrent updates with RCU: search tree as an example. In: Proceedings of the 2014 ACM Symposium on Principles of Distributed Computing, PODC 2014 (2014)
15. Matveev, A., Shavit, N., Felber, P., Marlier, P.: Read-log-update: a lightweight synchronization mechanism for concurrent programming. In: Proceedings of the 25th Symposium on Operating Systems Principles, SOSP 2015 (2015)

16. Siakavaras, D., Nikas, K., Goumas, G.I., Koziris, N.: RCU-HTM: combining RCU with HTM to implement highly efficient concurrent binary search trees. In: 26th International Conference on Parallel Architectures and Compilation Techniques, PACT 2017 (2017)
17. Deveci, M., Boman, E., Devine, K.D., Rajamanickam, S.: Parallel graph coloring for manycore architectures. In: IPDPS 2016 (2016)
18. Leskovec, J., Krevl, A.: SNAP datasets: Stanford large network dataset collection, June 2014. http://snap.stanford.edu/data
19. Kunegis, J.: KONECT: the Koblenz network collection (2013)
20. Demetrescu, C., Goldberg, A., Johnson,, D.: 9th DIMACS implementation challenge - shortest paths (2006). http://www.dis.uniroma1.it/challenge9/
21. Brown, T., Kogan, A., Lev, Y., Luchangco, V.: Investigating the performance of hardware transactions on a multi-socket machine. In: Proceedings of the 28th ACM Symposium on Parallelism in Algorithms and Architectures, SPAA 2016 (2016)
22. Rokos, G., Gorman, G., Kelly, P.H.J.: A fast and scalable graph coloring algorithm for multi-core and many-core architectures. In: Träff, J.L., Hunold, S., Versaci, F. (eds.) Euro-Par 2015. LNCS, vol. 9233, pp. 414–425. Springer, Heidelberg (2015). https://doi.org/10.1007/978-3-662-48096-0_32
23. Jones, M.T., Plassmann, P.: A parallel graph coloring heuristic. SIAM J. Sci. Comput. **14**, 654–669 (1993)
24. Hasenplaugh, W., Kaler, T., Schardl, T.B., Leiserson, C.E.: Ordering heuristics for parallel graph coloring. In: Proceedings of the 26th ACM Symposium on Parallelism in Algorithms and Architectures, SPAA 2014 (2014)
25. Nikas, K., Anastopoulos, N., Goumas, G.I., Koziris, N.: Employing transactional memory and helper threads to speedup Dijkstra's algorithm. In: International Conference on Parallel Processing, ICPP 2009, pp. 388–395 (2009)
26. Kang, S., Bader, D.A.: An efficient transactional memory algorithm for computing minimum spanning forest of sparse graphs. In: Proceedings of the 14th ACM Symposium on Principles and Practice of Parallel Programming, PPoPP 2009 (2009)
27. Clements, A.T., Kaashoek, M.F., Zeldovich, N.: Scalable address spaces using RCU balanced trees. In: Proceedings of the Seventeenth International Conference on Architectural Support for Programming Languages and Operating Systems, ASPLOS XVII, pp. 199–210 (2012)

Distributed Deep Reinforcement Learning: Learn How to Play Atari Games in 21 minutes

Igor Adamski[1], Robert Adamski[2,3], Tomasz Grel[1(✉)], Adam Jędrych[1], Kamil Kaczmarek[1], and Henryk Michalewski[1,4]

[1] deepsense.ai, Warsaw, Poland
tomasz.grel@deepsense.ai
[2] Intel, Warsaw, Poland
[3] Biz On Sp. z o.o.,, Warsaw, Poland
[4] Polish Academy of Sciences, Warsaw, Poland

Abstract. We present a study in Distributed Deep Reinforcement Learning (DDRL) focused on scalability of a state-of-the-art Deep Reinforcement Learning algorithm known as Batch Asynchronous Advantage Actor-Critic (BA3C). We show that using the Adam optimization algorithm with a batch size of up to 2048 is a viable choice for carrying out large scale machine learning computations. This, combined with careful reexamination of the optimizer's hyperparameters, using synchronous training on the node level (while keeping the local, single node part of the algorithm asynchronous) and minimizing the model's memory footprint, allowed us to achieve linear scaling for up to 64 CPU nodes. This corresponds to a training time of 21 min on 768 CPU cores, as opposed to the 10 h required when using a single node with 24 cores achieved by a baseline single-node implementation.

Keywords: Distributed computing · Reinforcement learning
Deep learning · Atari games · Asynchronous computations

1 Introduction

Gradient descent optimization is an indispensable element of solving many real-world problems including but not limited to training deep neural networks [14, 19]. Because of its inherent sequentiality it is also particularly difficult to parallelize [17]. Recently a number of advances in developing distributed versions of gradient descent algorithms have been made [11, 15, 36, 38, 39]. However, most of them deal with relatively simple variants of the algorithm, for which using larger batch sizes and increasing the learning rate (step size) often yield satisfactory results.

This research was supported in part by PL-Grid Infrastructure, grant identifier rl2algos.
All authors contributed equally to this work.

In the case of tasks encountered in Deep Reinforcement Learning these simple optimization procedures are often insufficient and so more advanced algorithms such as RMSProp [34] and Adam [18] are used more often [2,6,20,22,26]. However, these have not yet been subject to extensive formal analysis or even tests in largely distributed settings. This is crucial since the usual tasks of training models for reinforcement learning are often extremely computationally expensive [22]. Therefore distributed training is gaining more and more traction in the supervised learning community. Devising efficient ways of distributing advanced variants of SGD has the potential to speed up the progress of the entire field.

As our benchmarking task we chose the Atari 2600 emulator [8] provided by the OpenAI Gym framework [10] and the wide variety of games it offers. Atari games are considered a viable benchmark for testing deep reinforcement learning algorithms [2,6,26]. The early attempts to develop agents that would efficiently play Atari games were presented in [21]. This algorithm required as much as 8 days of training on a GPU [20] to reach a level that surpassed a casual human player. Later developments of the Asynchronous Advantage Actor-Critic (A3C) algorithm [20] reduced the learning time to several hours. Because of the work presented in [2] a version of this algorithm optimized for Intel® CPUs was already publicly available. A brief discussion of the single-node version of the algorithm is presented in Sect. 2.1.

In this work we present a distributed version of this algorithm that achieves linear scaling for the tested games for configurations of up to 64 nodes (see Fig. 8). This allowed us to reduce the training time from roughly 10 h to around 20 min while preserving the original accuracy of the models obtained. For a comparison with other similar implementations we refer the reader to Table 3.

Our contribution applies and extends the recent advances [11,15] in distributed supervised learning to the field of reinforcement learning. Sections 2.2, 2.3, 2.4 and 2.5 report on the design choices we made and the results they yielded. We also make our source code available for anyone who would like to reproduce or improve upon our results. Detailed instructions about running the experiments are also provided[1].

1.1 Related Work

While distributed machine learning has recently been a topic of extensive research, it has mainly focused on supervised learning. For an in-depth review of scalability of modern supervised learning approaches, we refer the reader to [17]. This work also lists common problems with various approaches to distributing various gradient descent optimization procedures. The pitfalls identified include the communication overhead arising from the necessity to share the weight updates between the nodes. The authors concluded that using larger batches and step sizes had the potential to solve this problem but resulted in less accurate models.

---

[1] The source code along with game-play videos can be found at: https://github.com/deepsense-ai/Distributed-BA3C.

Relation to [11]. Research done in [11] delves more into the architectural aspects of distributed learning, by proposing to abandon the asynchronous design in favor of a synchronous one. It also makes detailed arguments about the problem of "stale gradients", which prevents the asynchronous paradigm from scaling beyond several nodes. We set out to verify these claims by performing our reinforcement learning experiments using both synchronous and asynchronous training in Sect. 2.3. For a survey of the various asynchronous gradient descent procedures we refer the reader to [9,16].

Relation to [15]. Work done in [15] focuses on large-scale supervised learning. It showed that a setup with many machines working concurrently can effectively speed up the training by a large margin. As a result of parallelizing multiple GPUs and using appropriate learning rates for effectively larger batches, training Resnet-50 on Imagenet was completed in 1 h. The work [15] also showed that using very large batch sizes requires rethinking the optimization algorithms used. In [15] authors focused on the SGD with momentum optimizer which often works very well in supervised learning [33]. Our work attempts to apply similar principles to the Adam optimizer which we found more suitable for reinforcement learning tasks. The details can be found in Sect. 2.4.

The authors of [38] recognized the need to modify the optimization procedures in order to better utilize the distributed settings. The modification proposed a novel procedure called "Layer-wise Adaptive Rate Scaling", which enabled efficient training of supervised learning models with batch size of up to 32768. Deploying this algorithm to the task of training large convolutional nets in [39] yielded extremely competitive training times of 24 min, as opposed to 1 h achieved without these modifications in [15].

An interesting approach to reducing the communication overhead by ternarizing the gradients was recently proposed in [36]. This is a part of larger research aiming at gradient quantization i.e., reducing the precision of the communicated values [4,27]). A related approach is gradient sparsification, i.e. refraining from the exchange of small gradients, see e.g., [3,32]). However, both quantization and sparsification drastically change the flow of training of a neural model. Since Reinforcement Learning training is already quite complex, we refrained from employing these methods. Still, they certainly should be considered in future DDRL experiments.

To date, only limited formal research has been done in optimizing and parallelizing targeted strictly at reinforcement learning procedures. Notable works in this domain include [23], which focused on reducing the long training times observed in [22]. A significant speedup (by an order of magnitude [23]) and higher game scores were achieved. This was done using large resources of up to 130 nodes, by applying the Asynchronous SGD paradigm to the model developed in [22] in a manner similar to the work focusing on supervised learning presented in [12].

Further work in [20] applied the asynchronous paradigm to the policy optimization methods, resulting in the Asynchronous Advantage Actor-Critic algorithm (A3C). These experiments used the relatively low computing power of a

16-core CPU. The work in [2] sought to optimize a more efficient batched variant of this algorithm for use with commodity Intel® Xeon CPUs by employing the Math Kernel Library. A GPU-based version of this algorithm has also been presented in [6]. None of these works explicitly dealt with communication overheads in distributed policy optimization.

Significant computing resources were used in the work presented in [28] to develop AlphaGo – a program for playing the game of Go. This work was based on a combination of reinforcement learning, supervised learning and tree search methods. The authors reported using configurations of up to 1920 CPUs and 280 GPUs for testing the algorithm which provided a significant improvement in the quality of the results achieved. It is also mentioned that the training of the policy network was done using 50 GPUs for one day [28].

Further work in [30] focused on achieving better results without using supervised learning and handcrafted features. Computationally, the training utilized the synchronous paradigm with 64 GPU workers and 19 parameter servers, using a total batch size of 2048. For optimization the Momentum SGD optimizer with learning rate annealing was used. Recently this work has been further extended in [29] where the authors presented a general algorithm able to achieve expert level also in chess and shogi. Notably the training was completed in 24 h and a relatively large batch size of 4096 was used.

Recently a novel algorithm called Proximal Policy Optimization (PPO) was proposed in [26]. Notably it also uses the Adam optimizer on which we focused in this work and achieved promising scores in Atari games. A distributed version of this algorithm was used in [7], where the authors used 4 GPUs, Adam optimizer and batch size of 5120. Further examination of PPO in a distributed setup appears as a promising area of future research.

A different approach to distributing reinforcement learning has recently been presented in [24]. In this work the parallelization was applied to an evolution strategy (ES), which is a direct search method. This property enables efficient exchange of information between the workers since they only have to communicate scalar values. Because of that the algorithm is especially easy to distribute since the communication costs of sharing the gradient updates don't apply to this scheme. When training a 3D humanoid to walk the authors reported linear scaling for up to 1440 CPU cores [24, p. 8]. After 1 h of training agents for Atari games on 720 CPUs evolution strategies were able to achieve scores comparable to the ones achieved by A3C (which was trained for 24 h with a single CPU) [24, p. 7].

Detailed analysis of Deep Reinforcement Learning on a single machine with multiple GPUs was recently published in [31]. The authors reported using a batch size of up to 2048 and utilizing 8 GPUs for various Deep RL algorithms. Impressive training times (under 10 min) are also reported.

2   Distributed BA3C Implementation

For all our experiments we used the Batch Asynchronous Advantage Actor-Critic algorithm implemented in [37] and later modified in [2]. A similar algorithm was also described in [6]. We will not elaborate on its properties here but rather focus on explaining the details behind implementing it on multiple parallel machines. A good description of the single-node version of this algorithm can be found in [2]. Here we are using multiple clustered CPUs and each of them individually performs the BA3C algorithm. The individual nodes maintain a shared copy of the model through the use of special nodes called parameter servers, which store the model weights. Table 1 presents the hyperparameters of the algorithms, which were specifically tuned to achieve lowest training times during our research. Some of the hyperparameters are omitted and for those we assume the default values used in [2]. Detailed description of the hyperparameters describing the Adam optimizer is presented in Sect. 2.4.

Table 1. Hyperparameters of the distributed BA3C implementation

Symbol	Default value	Description
n	64	Number of CPU nodes used for the distributed training
c	12	Number of cores in each worker CPU
η	0.001	Learning rate (step-size)
bs	32	Number of data-points in each training batch (on each node)
ps	4	Number of nodes responsible for holding the model parameters
n_sim	10	Number of atari simulators used simultaneously on one worker
ϵ	10^{-8}	Constant used for numerical stability in the Adam optimizer
β_1, β_2	0.8, 0.75	Decay rates of the running averages used in Adam optimizer

2.1   BA3C Background

The BA3C design on a single node focuses on parallel interactions of multiple agents with game environments, that produce experience data later aggregated into mini-batches used for training. We call an "agent" an instance of the model interacting with the outside environment, in our context the Atari 2600 emulator.

The interaction with an Atari game is attained via OpenAI Gym [10] providing the model with input of RGB image pixels and enabling the agents to act upon any state of the game. On a single machine, n_sim simulators of the Atari environment are running concurrently and an agent plays one game on each of them. Each consecutive frame_hist frames from the game count as one state. For each state of the game a policy query is sent to the prediction thread, which then feeds the input image to the neural net, outputting a respective behavioral guideline. The action performed is then gathered together with the state it was acted on and the reward it received from that action. This tuple creates a data-point. Then, bs data-points are assembled into a mini-batch, that is back-propagated through the neural net giving gradients, later used to perform gradient descent on a cost function.

2.2   Architecture

Let us suppose that we are using n workers. Each of the n workers possesses a copy of the BA3C algorithm, which will parallelize the training among its c cores. As aforementioned, a tuple of state, action and reward constitutes a single data-point, and a mini-batch of **bs** of those data-points is then used to compute the gradients which are synchronously gathered from all the workers, averaged and applied to the weights through the Adam optimizer. All the weights are located in **ps** different parameter servers, each of which stores $1/\mathbf{ps}$ of the model's parameters (4 convolution layers and 3 fully connected layers). The parameter servers then send the updated parameters back to the workers, which then again play the games and the process goes on until a satisfactory model is achieved.

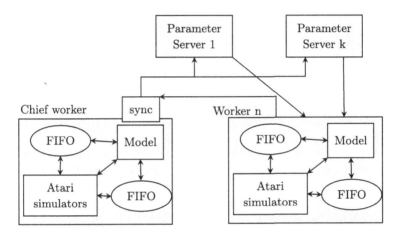

Fig. 1. Our approach to distributed learning. The figure shows the synchronous training architecture which was our final choice.

2.3   Synchronous vs Asynchronous Training

Background on Gradient Descent Optimization. Training deep neural networks usually involves gradient descent optimization. This is convenient since the gradient of the model with respect to some chosen loss function can be easily obtained by backpropagation [19]. Gradient descent is an iterative algorithm that in each iteration attempts to modify the model's parameters $\boldsymbol{\theta}$ in order to achieve a lower value of the cost function $J(\boldsymbol{\theta}, \boldsymbol{x})$ for some training data $\boldsymbol{x}$. Given the gradient $\boldsymbol{g}_t$ of the cost function w.r.t. the model parameters $\boldsymbol{\theta}$ (which can be obtained from the backpropagation procedure) the basic update rule for obtaining the new values of parameters at time step t given the old values $\boldsymbol{\theta}_{t-1}$ can be written as:

$$\boldsymbol{\theta}_t = \boldsymbol{\theta}_{t-1} - \lambda \boldsymbol{g}_t, \tag{1}$$

where the λ parameter controls the learning rate (step size).

Numerous improvements to this scheme have been proposed. For a broad overview of different approaches we refer the reader to [19]. Of the recent improvements the RMSProp [34] and Adam [18] procedures are widely used in Reinforcement Learning [2,6,20,22,26]. In the course of our experiments we found that Adam performs better on our task and therefore we will not elaborate on RMSProp further. A brief description of Adam optimizer is given in Sect. 2.4.

An important decision that largely influences the outcome of the model's performance is the way of parallelizing the work of multiple nodes. Data parallelism in gradient descent algorithms can be done in two ways: synchronously or asynchronously. We have found that when using a large number of distributed nodes, these two approaches produce completely different results.

Asynchronous Training. In the asynchronous approach, each of the workers, after collecting a mini-batch of data points, computes gradients and then uses them to perform weight updates. The weights of the model reside in parameter servers, which receive gradients from the workers and send the updated copy of the current model to each training instance. Therefore each individual worker updates the commonly shared parameters of the model without delay as soon as it completes computing its gradient. This has several advantages, one is that compared to a single machine implementation our model is guaranteed to perform k times as many updates, if we are using k workers. Another is that because workers do not need to wait for others to finish but rather apply updates continuously, we are utilizing a lock-free paradigm that helps make the most of the processing power at our disposal.

However, the pure asynchronous approach possesses also other characteristics that could impede the learning and prevent convergence. One such disadvantage is called stale gradients [11]. It arises when a worker updates the weights using gradients that are outdated with regard to the current model. This is guaranteed to happen because during the time that the worker was processing the data and computing the gradients, the model has been updated several times by other nodes and now, when the worker applies the gradients, it will do so with respect to the model that is out-of-date. This is shown in the Fig. 2.

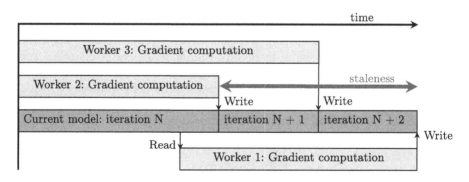

Fig. 2. A diagram representing gradient staleness - a systematic flaw related to asynchronous training with many workers.

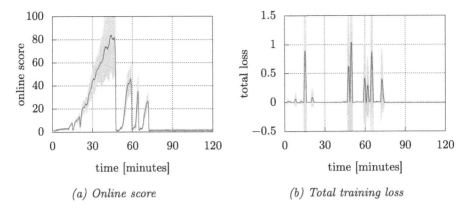

Fig. 3. Typical asynchronous training attempt, 64 workers.

Synchronous Training. The synchronous training architecture is visualized in Fig. 1. One of the workers (called a *chief worker*) is special in a sense that it's responsible for aggregating the gradients from all the others. A "regular" worker no longer posseses the power to update the model on its own – it can only compute its gradient estimate and send it to the chief worker. Once enough gradients from the workers are accumulated, the chief worker updates the weights and sends the new them to the parameter servers. The new weights are then sent to other workers and a new training iteration begins. This ensures that all the workers always have an up-to-date copy of the model weights, which solves the stale gradients problem.

The side effect of this procedure is the increase of the effective batch size used for performing a single update. Although we are not able to linearly increase the speed of model updates with the number of workers as in the asynchronous design, we expect the updates that are made to be more accurate since the gradient estimate is done using a larger batch size. This might in turn allow for larger step sizes to be used, which can hopefully compensate for the updates being less frequent and provide speed up. Importantly, synchronous training removes the problem of gradient staleness, as no worker computes gradients on an obsolete model, because updates are performed only after all of the workers compute their individual gradients.

The fact that we need to wait for all the workers can cause delays. This arises whenever, for various reasons, some of the workers may be lagging behind others in assembling their batches and computing gradients. We call this the *slow stragglers problem*. Since the synchronous design imposes waiting for all the workers' gradients to perform a weight update, the effective time it takes for an update to occur is the time it takes the slowest worker to assemble his batch and compute the gradients. Therefore, reducing the number of gradients that we need to wait for to make an update could significantly reduce the influence of the slow stragglers. Detailed analysis of this phenomenon presented in [11] confirms that waiting for around 90% of gradients as opposed to all of them significantly improves the training times.

Another key fact that needs to be addressed when discussing synchronous training is the large effective batch size[2] it tends to create. Since we are using n mini-batches of data-points from every worker and then averaging them, we arc virtually using a single batch of size $n \times$ bs to perform a single update. This may indicate the need to adjust other hyperparameters of the algorithm such as the learning rate. We revisit this issue in Sect. 2.4.

With the slow stragglers problem removed, the synchronous approach is much more intuitive and reasonable – it does not risk gradient staleness and the weight updates that are made are much more accurate and less noisy. Making just one update for all the workers working on a model assures that the nodes are working collectively and efficiently upon a goal, whereas the asynchronous learning strategy seems rather chaotic and unstructured.

We performed a series of experiments to determine which paradigm is better in our use case. We found that asynchronous training causes large instabilities in the learning process. One of such experiments is shown in the Figs. 3a and b. In this experiment the learning was proceeding correctly until after about 50 min the online score[3] dropped suddenly to zero. This coincided with a large spike in the total training loss visible in the Fig. 3b. We suspect it is caused by the stale gradients. We did not encounter this phenomenon when using synchronous training, therefore we have chosen to work with the synchronous architecture.

2.4   Optimizer Changes

Background on Adam Optimizer. Adam optimizer was first described in [18] and can be thought of as extension of the works presented in [13,34]. It maintains the exponentially decaying running averages m_t and v_t of all the previous gradients and squared gradients:

$$m_t = \beta_1 m_{t-1} + (1 - \beta_1) g_t, \tag{2}$$

$$v_t = \beta_2 v_{t-1} + (1 - \beta_1) g_t^2 \tag{3}$$

---

[2] We use the term *effective batch size* to denote the number of training samples participating in a single weight update. In synchronous training this is equal to the local batch size on each node multiplied by the number of workers required to perform an update. In asynchronous training effective batch size is equal to the local batch size.

[3] By *online score* we refer to the scores obtained by the agent during training. By contrast an *evaluation score* would be a score obtained during the test phase. These scores can differ substantially, because while training the actions are sampled from the distribution returned by the policy network (this ensures more exploration). On the other hand, during test time the agent always chooses the action that gives the highest expected reward. This usually yields higher scores, but using it while training would prevent exploration.

It then perform bias correction to define $\hat{m}_t = m_t/(1 - \beta_1^t)$ and $\hat{v}_t = v_t/(1 - \beta_2^t)$ and gives the final weight update for parameter θ at timestep t as:

$$\theta_t = \theta_{t-1} - \eta \frac{\hat{m}_t}{\sqrt{\hat{v}_t} + \epsilon} \tag{4}$$

Instead, many implementations (including TensorFlow [1]) use less clear but more efficient formulation:

$$\eta_t = \eta \frac{\sqrt{1 - \beta_2^t}}{1 - \beta_1^t}, \tag{5}$$

$$\theta_t = \theta_{t-1} - \eta_t \frac{m_t}{\sqrt{v_t} + \hat{\epsilon}} \tag{6}$$

The $\hat{\epsilon}$ in the Eq. 6 and ϵ in Eq. 4 are added for numerical stability, not to divide by 0 in the first timestep.

This means that the algorithm in this formulation has 4 hyperparameters that need tuning: the learning rate η, the decay factors for the running averages: β_1 and β_2 and $\hat{\epsilon}$. Next section provides insight into how these might need to be modified when transitioning from a single-node to a multi-node configuration.

Increasing the Learning Rate. Using very large batches that result from utilizing a large number of workers in the synchronous paradigm poses some challenges on the selection of optimizer hyperparameters. This problem is especially severe when distributing an algorithm that already had its hyperparameters chosen carefully.

Research on large scale distributed SGD by [15] has addressed this problem by deploying the linear scaling rule: when multiplying the mini-batch size by k, multiply the learning rate by k. However this was done using much simpler SGD with momentum optimizer. We on the other hand have experimented with multiple optimizers and have found that only Adam [18] and occasionally RMSProp [34] have brought about positive results in the asynchronous design.

With Adam optimizer, using the linear scaling rule did not yield any positive results. We found that increasing the learning rate made the training highly unstable and often resulted in the model learning how to play well only to later abruptly forget and score 0 until the end (see Fig. 4). We settled on using $\eta = 0.001$ (the same as in the single-node version), as it was the largest value for which we did not experience large instabilities.

Apart from the learning rate some of the other default optimizer parameters also needed examination. Moving to a synchronous distributed setup requires a re-thinking of how exactly momentum accumulation and learning rate adaptivity are impacted by the batch size.

Modifying the ϵ parameter. Curiously enough, some implementations can be found that manipulate this variable so that it no longer serves the mere purpose of avoiding numerical instability (see e.g. the implementation of BA3C in [37]).

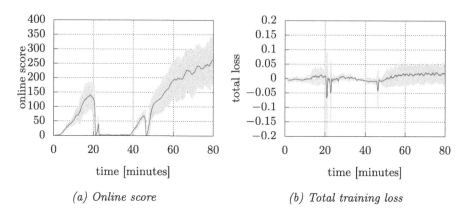

(a) Online score   (b) Total training loss

Fig. 4. Experiment with a learning rate $\eta = 0.002$. 64 nodes, synchronous training, local batch size of 64, total batch size of 4096. Increasing the learning rate for the Adam optimizer from 0.001 to 0.002 causes large instabilities clearly visible on the online score plot (Fig. a) and the total training loss plot (Fig. b)

Through experiments we found that for some tasks setting the ϵ parameter of the optimizer to much lower values (e.g. 10^{-8} instead of 10^{-3}) can yield much better training times. A comparison of online scores for two similar experiments with different epsilon values is shown in the Fig. 5. It is important to note that this positive effect when using smaller ϵ was observable only when using large effective batch sizes (i.e., 512 and more). For smaller effective batch sizes using a lower ϵ did not produce positive results.

This is understandable since a high ϵ value significantly constrains the ability of the Adam optimizer to automatically adapt the learning rate to the variance of the gradients. We suspected that averaging more data points through the use of synchronous data parallelism reduced the variance of the gradient estimate to the point that the algorithm could be allowed more freedom in automatically adapting the learning rate based on the noise estimations.

Based on these experiments we decided to change the default value of the ϵ hyperparameter from 10^{-3} to 10^{-8}. This significantly sped up the training for some games (such as Breakout and Boxing). However, we cannot claim this effect is universal, e.g., it made training for Atari Pong slower. The results cited for this game in Sect. 3 were obtained with $\epsilon = 10^{-3}$.

Table 2. Number of network parameters when considering different number of neurons in the fully connected layer.

Hidden neurons	Network weights	% of initial setup
256	538 119	100%
128	332 295	61%
64	229 383	43%
32	177 927	33%
16	152 199	28%

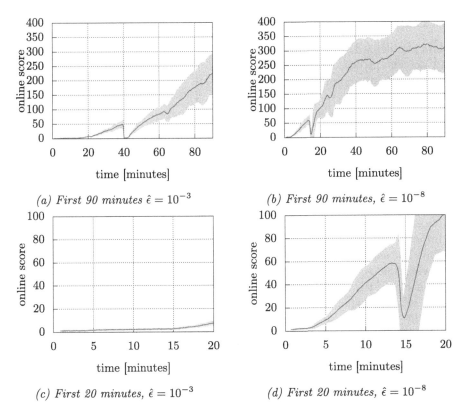

(a) First 90 minutes $\hat{\epsilon} = 10^{-3}$

(b) First 90 minutes, $\hat{\epsilon} = 10^{-8}$

(c) First 20 minutes, $\hat{\epsilon} = 10^{-3}$

(d) First 20 minutes, $\hat{\epsilon} = 10^{-8}$

Fig. 5. Two experiments of training agents for Breakout on 64 nodes with different ϵ parameter values. Figure a and c show an experiment where $\epsilon = 10^{-3}$ was used. Figure b and d show training with $\epsilon = 10^{-8}$. The most important difference lies at the beginning of the training. This is visible in the closer views presented in the bottom row. Lower values of ϵ seem to give a significant speedup at this stage. Note that the vertical axis shows online score.

Other Hyperparameters. Motivated by the research in [15] we decided that we should optimize Adam's decay factors β_1, β_2 to the very large batch that we are using. This did not turn out to be an easy task - with the Adam optimizer update policy being quite complicated, choosing β_1 and β_2 for the effective batch-size analytically was difficult. The results of our experiments do not support any gains from using different values of these parameters; however we are leaving it to the community to try and find the factors that work best for a distributed setup.

2.5   Communication Overhead

In data parallelized synchronous gradient descent procedures the nodes have to transmit roughly $2n$ multiplicities of the size of the model (where n is the number of workers) during a single training step [17]. Our initial model architecture consisted of approximately half a million weights stored as 32-bit floats. Thus, when using 64 workers we needed to send ≈ 263 MB of data during every iteration.

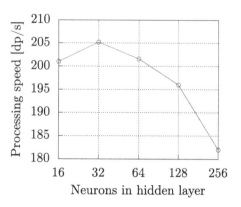

Fig. 6. Data points per second for models with different number of hidden neurons in the fully connected layer. Each experiment was repeated 5 times and results were averaged. Experiments were run with 32 workers and 4 parameter servers.

Importantly, if all nodes have roughly the same processing speed and synchronous training is being used then all this communication occurs at approximately the same time. This is because in a gradient descent training the communication cannot be easily overlaid with computation to maximally utilize both network bandwidth and compute power (see [17] for details). This further reduces the scaling capabilities.

In our experiments we measured the speed of our algorithm by calculating the number of training examples backpropagated through our model every second. In next section we will refer to this speed as data points per second.

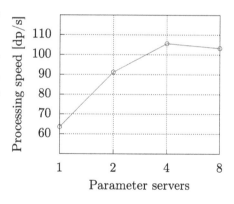

Fig. 7. Data points per second for different numbers of parameter servers. Each experiment was repeated 5 times and the results were averaged. 32 workers, 332 k parameters, local; batch size set to 4. The conclusion is that after some point there's no more gains to be achieved by adding more parameter servers.

Changing the Model. One way to reduce network communication is to shrink the model. In the initial architecture most weights ($\approx 76\%$) were in a single fully connected layer that follows the last convolution layer (see [2] for the details about the exact neural model used). The relation between number of neurons in this layer and the processing speed is shown in Fig. 6. Although all of the tested architectures were able to achieve decent results, we decided to use 128 neurons since this setup was able to learn as fast and stable as the initial architecture, while having only $\approx 61\%$ of its weights (see Table 2). Despite the fact that further reduction of the model size accelerated data processing, smaller networks were taking more time to reach corresponding scores.

Adding More Parameter Servers. Adding more parameter servers, each storing only fraction of model weights, causes data sent through the network to be distributed into more nodes. This leads to more optimized network usage (see Fig. 7 for details).

3   Results

Synchronous training allowed us to use more workers and avoid instabilities common in the asynchronous paradigm. By reducing model size and adding more parameter servers we could better utilize network communication which led to the possibility of further increase in the number of workers. As a result we were able to train models to reach 300 points in Breakout in 21 ± 2 min using 64 workers (each consisting of 12 physical cores, i.e. using 768 cores in total).

3.1   Scaling

We compared times it took to reach a predetermined score in Atari Breakout for different number of workers. The reference was reaching a mean score of 300 points or higher for 50 consecutive games played. This is considered vastly better than a human tester (see [22] for data on detailed human performance for this game). The results are shown in Fig. 8.

Experiment settings: Each of the 64 workers had 12 CPU cores. We used 4 parameter servers for storing model weights. Model trained had 128 hidden neurons in the fully connected layer described in Sect. 2.3. Every experiment was repeated 10 times and results were averaged. Additionally we have plotted a theoretical linear speedup. This line represents the theoretical time that should be achieved when using n times more computing power in reference to a single node experiment.

Learning rate: All experiments used the learning rate of 10^{-3}.

Optimizer's hyperparameters: In all experiments optimizer's hyperparameters were: $\epsilon = 10^{-8}$, $\beta_1 = 0.8$, $\beta_2 = 0.75$.

Batch size: In experiments with 32 and 64 workers batch size was set to 32, because smaller batches caused too much network communication overhead. For the rest of experiments the per-worker batch size was set, so that the effective batch size equaled $n \times \mathsf{bs} = 512$.

Evaluation: Every 1000 steps the model played 50 games and the mean score was saved. During the games the model parameters were frozen. By step we mean single global update performed by the chief worker.

Baseline: As a baseline we have chosen the single node setup (i.e. using a single 12-core CPU). To be comparable with effective batch sizes on multiple nodes, a relatively large batch size of 512 was chosen. This baseline achieves the solving score in mean time of 14.2 h.

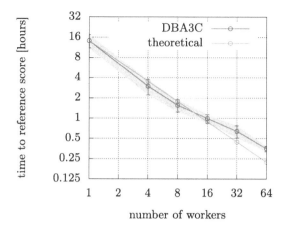

Fig. 8. Red plot shows mean time to reference score of 300 points ± standard deviation for Breakout. Green plot shows theoretical linear speedup in reference to 1 node experiment. Notice that the real performance of our configuration is consistent with the expected values for a wide number of workers. For 64 workers the communication overheads start to inhibit further scaling. Notice that the mean time to achieve a mean score of 300 in Atari breakout is 21 min when using 64 workers. (Color figure online)

3.2 Training Times

In this section we present example learning curves for various Atari games. The plots show mean and max scores from evaluation games. Each game was played on the 64 worker setup (Fig. 9).

3.3 Comparison with Other Solutions

The most notable similar work in optimizing Atari games training for speed is presented in [6]. The results presented there were achieved by a hybrid GPU-CPU algorithm called GA3C which is a flavor of A3C focusing on batching the data points in order to better utilize the massively parallel nature of GPU computations. This is similar to the single node algorithm called BA3C [2] which we used as a starting point for this work.

Comparing the training curves included in [6] for 3 common games tested in both works (Boxing, Breakout, SpaceInvaders) shows that our implementation is much faster and achieves as good or better scores[4] (see Table 3). Importantly our experiments used 64 CPU nodes of 12 cores each, while the experiments

---

[4] It is important to note that the scores achieved by different implementations are not directly comparable and should interpreted cautiously. For future comparisons we'd like to state that the evaluation scores presented by us in this work are always mean scores of 50 consecutive games played by the agent. Unless otherwise stated they're evaluation scores achieved by choosing the action giving the highest future expected reward.

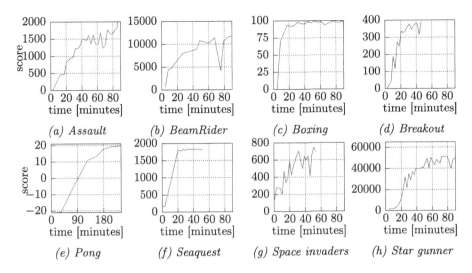

Fig. 9. Score vs time plots for different games in the final setup.

presented in [5] were all single node. However the results show that using distributed computations on CPU clusters is a viable alternative for using GPUs, even when training convolutional neural networks.

Table 3. Algorithm performance in 6 selected games. Best stable score and time (in hours) to achieve it are given. The data are based on the best reported results found in the training plots in [2,6,20].

Game	DDRL A3C	GA3C [6]	BA3C [2]	A3C [20]
BeamRider	14900 (2.7 h)	3000 (24 h)	–	15000 (15 h)
Breakout	350 (0.5 h)	350 (21 h)	400 (15h)	500 (11 h)
Boxing	98 (0.5 h)	92 (2h)	–	–
Pong	20 (4 h)	18 (1h)	17 (24 h)	20 (8h)
Seaquest	1832 (0.5 h)	1706 (24 h)	1840 (24 h)	2300 (24 h)
SpaceInvaders	650 (0.5 h)	600 (24 h)	700 (24 h)	1400 (15 h)

4   Conclusions and Future Work

We presented a detailed description of our experiments with large scale Distributed Deep Reinforcement Learning (DDRL). Detailed motivation behind all the important design choices was given in Sects. 2.2, 2.3, 2.4 and 2.5. We also provided some empirical information about tuning the Adam optimizer to perform well when using large training batches that arise in synchronous data parallelism. Our key experimental results described in Sect. 3 involve being able to train agents for playing Atari games in minutes rather than hours on clusters of commodity CPUs.

Extending this work to other RL algorithms, most notably those presented in [25, 26, 35] would provide a natural extension to this work. Also developing a framework for distributed RL training that is independent of the algorithm itself would certainly be a valuable contribution.

Given the results reported in [39] testing the Intel® Xeon Phi™ architecture on distributed RL training would also be an interesting experiment.

On a wider scale, further research on adaptive optimization algorithms, most notably those presented in [13, 18, 34] in the context of training with large batch sizes seems to be necessary to further reduce training times both in supervised and reinforcement learning.

Acknowledgments. The work presented in this paper would not have been possible without the computational power of Prometheus supercomputer, provided by the PL-Grid infrastructure.

We would also like to thank the four anonymous reviewers who provided us with valuable insights and suggestions about our work.

This work was supported by the LABEX MILYON (ANR-10-LABX-0070) of Université de Lyon, within the program "Investissements d'Avenir" (ANR-11-IDEX- 0007) operated by the French National Research Agency (ANR).

References

1. Abadi, M., Agarwal, A., Barham, P., Brevdo, E., Chen, Z., Citro, C., Corrado, G.S., Davis, A., Dean, J., Devin, M., Ghemawat, S., Goodfellow, I., Harp, A., Irving, G., Isard, M., Jia, Y., Jozefowicz, R., Kaiser, L., Kudlur, M., Levenberg, J., Mané, D., Monga, R., Moore, S., Murray, D., Olah, C., Schuster, M., Shlens, J., Steiner, B., Sutskever, I., Talwar, K., Tucker, P., Vanhoucke, V., Vasudevan, V., Viégas, F., Vinyals, O., Warden, P., Wattenberg, M., Wicke, M., Yu, Y., Zheng, X.: TensorFlow: Large-scale machine learning on heterogeneous systems (2015). Software available from https://www.tensorflow.org/
2. Adamski, R., Grel, T., Klimek, M., Michalewski, H.: Atari games and intel processors. CoRR abs/1705.06936 (2017)
3. Aji, A.F., Heafield, K.: Sparse communication for distributed gradient descent. CoRR abs/1704.05021 (2017)
4. Alistarh, D., Li, J., Tomioka, R., Vojnovic, M.: QSGD: Randomized quantization for communication-optimal stochastic gradient descent. CoRR abs/1610.02132 (2016)
5. Babaeizadeh, M., Frosio, I., Tyree, S., Clemons, J., Kautz, J.: GA3C: GPU-based A3C for deep reinforcement learning. CoRR abs/1611.06256 (2016)
6. Babaeizadeh, M., Frosio, I., Tyree, S., Clemons, J., Kautz, J.: Reinforcement learning through asynchronous advantage actor-critic on a GPU. In: ICLR (2017)
7. Bansal, T., Pachocki, J., Sidor, S., Sutskever, I., Mordatch, I.: Emergent complexity via multi-agent competition. CoRR abs/1710.03748 (2017)

8. Bellemare, M.G., Naddaf, Y., Veness, J., Bowling, M.: The arcade learning environment: an evaluation platform for general agents. CoRR abs/1207.4708 (2012)
9. Bhardwaj, O., Cong, G.: Practical efficiency of asynchronous stochastic gradient descent. In: 2016 2nd Workshop on Machine Learning in HPC Environments (MLHPC), pp. 56–62, November 2016
10. Brockman, G., Cheung, V., Pettersson, L., Schneider, J., Schulman, J., Tang, J., Zaremba, W.: OpenAI Gym. CoRR abs/1606.01540 (2016)
11. Chen, J., Monga, R., Bengio, S., Jozefowicz, R.: Revisiting distributed synchronous SGD. In: International Conference on Learning Representations Workshop Track (2016)
12. Dean, J., Corrado, G.S., Monga, R., Chen, K., Devin, M., Le, Q.V., Mao, M.Z., Ranzato, M., Senior, A., Tucker, P., Yang, K., Ng, A.Y.: Large scale distributed deep networks. In: Proceedings of the 25th International Conference on Neural Information Processing Systems, NIPS 2012, vol. 1, pp. 1223–1231. Curran Associates Inc., USA (2012)
13. Duchi, J., Hazan, E., Singer, Y.: Adaptive subgradient methods for online learning and stochastic optimization. J. Mach. Learn. Res. **12**, 2121–2159 (2011)
14. Goodfellow, I., Bengio, Y., Courville, A.: Deep Learning. MIT Press (2016). http://www.deeplearningbook.org
15. Goyal, P., Dollár, P., Girshick, R.B., Noordhuis, P., Wesolowski, L., Kyrola, A., Tulloch, A., Jia, Y., He, K.: Accurate, large minibatch SGD: training ImageNet in 1 hour. CoRR abs/1706.02677 (2017)
16. Keuper, J., Pfreundt, F.: Asynchronous parallel stochastic gradient descent - A numeric core for scalable distributed machine learning algorithms. CoRR abs/1505.04956 (2015)
17. Keuper, J., Preundt, F.J.: Distributed training of deep neural networks: Theoretical and practical limits of parallel scalability. In: Proceedings of the Workshop on Machine Learning in High Performance Computing Environments, MLHPC 2016, pp. 19–26. IEEE Press, Piscataway (2016)
18. Kingma, D.P., Ba, J.: Adam: A method for stochastic optimization. CoRR abs/1412.6980 (2014)
19. Le, Q.V., Ngiam, J., Coates, A., Lahiri, A., Prochnow, B., Ng, A.Y.: On optimization methods for deep learning. In: Proceedings of the 28th International Conference on International Conference on Machine Learning, ICML 2011, pp. 265–272. Omnipress, USA (2011)
20. Mnih, V., Badia, A.P., Mirza, M., Graves, A., Lillicrap, T.P., Harley, T., Silver, D., Kavukcuoglu, K.: Asynchronous methods for deep reinforcement learning. CoRR abs/1602.01783 (2016)
21. Mnih, V., Kavukcuoglu, K., Silver, D., Graves, A., Antonoglou, I., Wierstra, D., Riedmiller, M.: Playing atari with deep reinforcement learning. In: NIPS Deep Learning Workshop (2013)
22. Mnih, V., Kavukcuoglu, K., Silver, D., Rusu, A.A., Veness, J., Bellemare, M.G., Graves, A., Riedmiller, M., Fidjeland, A.K., Ostrovski, G., Petersen, S., Beattie, C., Sadik, A., Antonoglou, I., King, H., Kumaran, D., Wierstra, D., Legg, S., Hassabis, D.: Human-level control through deep reinforcement learning. Nature **518**(7540), 529–533 (2015)
23. Nair, A., Srinivasan, P., Blackwell, S., Alcicek, C., Fearon, R., Maria, A.D., Panneershelvam, V., Suleyman, M., Beattie, C., Petersen, S., Legg, S., Mnih, V., Kavukcuoglu, K., Silver, D.: Massively parallel methods for deep reinforcement learning. CoRR abs/1507.04296 (2015)

24. Salimans, T., Ho, J., Chen, X., Sutskever, I.: Evolution strategies as a scalable alternative to reinforcement learning. CoRR abs/1703.03864 (2017)
25. Schulman, J., Levine, S., Moritz, P., Jordan, M.I., Abbeel, P.: Trust region policy optimization. CoRR abs/1502.05477 (2015)
26. Schulman, J., Wolski, F., Dhariwal, P., Radford, A., Klimov, O.: Proximal policy optimization algorithms. CoRR abs/1707.06347 (2017)
27. Seide, F., Fu, H., Droppo, J., Li, G., Yu, D.: 1-bit stochastic gradient descent and application to data-parallel distributed training of speech DNNs. In: Interspeech 2014, September 2014
28. Silver, D., Huang, A., Maddison, C.J., Guez, A., Sifre, L., van den Driessche, G., Schrittwieser, J., Antonoglou, I., Panneershelvam, V., Lanctot, M., Dieleman, S., Grewe, D., Nham, J., Kalchbrenner, N., Sutskever, I., Lillicrap, T., Leach, M., Kavukcuoglu, K., Graepel, T., Hassabis, D.: Mastering the game of go with deep neural networks and tree search. Nature **529**(7587), 484–489 (2016)
29. Silver, D., Hubert, T., Schrittwieser, J., Antonoglou, I., Lai, M., Guez, A., Lanctot, M., Sifre, L., Kumaran, D., Graepel, T., Lillicrap, T., Simonyan, K., Hassabis, D.: Mastering Chess and Shogi by Self-Play with a General Reinforcement Learning Algorithm, December 2017
30. Silver, D., Schrittwieser, J., Simonyan, K., Antonoglou, I., Huang, A., Guez, A., Hubert, T., Baker, L., Lai, M., Bolton, A., Chen, Y., Lillicrap, T., Hui, F., Sifre, L., van den Driessche, G., Graepel, T., Hassabis, D.: Mastering the game of go without human knowledge. Nature **550**, 354–359 (2017)
31. Stooke, A., Abbeel, P.: Accelerated methods for deep reinforcement learning. CoRR abs/1803.02811, March 2018
32. Strom, N.: Scalable distributed DNN training using commodity GPU cloud computing. In: INTERSPEECH, ISCA, pp. 1488–1492 (2015)
33. Sutskever, I., Martens, J., Dahl, G., Hinton, G.: On the importance of initialization and momentum in deep learning. In: Proceedings of the 30th International Conference on International Conference on Machine Learning, ICML 2013, vol. 28, pp. III-1139–III-1147 (2013). JMLR.org
34. Tieleman, T., Hinton, G.: Lecture 6.5–RmsProp: Divide the gradient by a running average of its recent magnitude. In: COURSERA: Neural Networks for Machine Learning (2012)
35. Wang, Z., Bapst, V., Heess, N., Mnih, V., Munos, R., Kavukcuoglu, K., de Freitas, N.: Sample efficient actor-critic with experience replay. CoRR abs/1611.01224 (2016)
36. Wen, W., Xu, C., Yan, F., Wu, C., Wang, Y., Chen, Y., Li, H.: TernGrad: Ternary gradients to reduce communication in distributed deep learning. CoRR abs/1705.07878 (2017)
37. Wu, Y.: Tensorpack (2016). https://github.com/ppwwyyxx/tensorpack
38. You, Y., Gitman, I., Ginsburg, B.: Scaling SGD batch size to 32K for ImageNet training. CoRR abs/1708.03888 (2017)
39. You, Y., Zhang, Z., Hsieh, C.J., Demmel, J.: 100-epoch ImageNet training with AlexNet in 24 minutes (2017). arXiv preprint arXiv:1709.05011

TaskGenX: A Hardware-Software Proposal for Accelerating Task Parallelism

Kallia Chronaki[1,2(✉)], Marc Casas[1(✉)], Miquel Moreto[1,2(✉)], Jaume Bosch[1], and Rosa M. Badia[1,3]

[1] Barcelona Supercomputig Center (BSC), Barcelona, Spain
{kallia.chronaki,marc.casas,miquel.moreto,
jaume.bosch,rosa.m.badia}@bsc.es
[2] Universitat Politècnica de Catalunya (UPC), Barcelona, Spain
[3] Spanish National Research Council (CSIC), Bellaterra, Spain

Abstract. As chip multi-processors (CMPs) are becoming more and more complex, software solutions such as parallel programming models are attracting a lot of attention. Task-based parallel programming models offer an appealing approach to utilize complex CMPs. However, the increasing number of cores on modern CMPs is pushing research towards the use of fine grained parallelism. Task-based programming models need to be able to handle such workloads and offer performance and scalability. Using specialized hardware for boosting performance of task-based programming models is a common practice in the research community.

Our paper makes the observation that task creation becomes a bottleneck when we execute fine grained parallel applications with many task-based programming models. As the number of cores increases the time spent generating the tasks of the application is becoming more critical to the entire execution. To overcome this issue, we propose TaskGenX. TaskGenX offers a solution for minimizing task creation overheads and relies both on the runtime system and a dedicated hardware. On the runtime system side, TaskGenX decouples the task creation from the other runtime activities. It then transfers this part of the runtime to a specialized hardware. We draw the requirements for this hardware in order to boost execution of highly parallel applications. From our evaluation using 11 parallel workloads on both symmetric and asymmetric multicore systems, we obtain performance improvements up to 15×, averaging to 3.1× over the baseline.

1 Introduction

Since the end of Dennard scaling [13] and the subsequent stagnation of CPU clock frequencies, computer architects and programmers rely on multicore designs to achieve the desired performance levels. While multicore architectures constitute a solution to the CPU clock stagnation problem, they bring important challenges both from the hardware and software perspectives. On the hardware side,

R. Yokota et al. (Eds.): ISC High Performance 2018, LNCS 10876, pp. 389–409, 2018.
https://doi.org/10.1007/978-3-319-92040-5_20

multicore architectures require sophisticated mechanisms in terms of coherence protocols, consistency models or deep memory hierarchies. Such requirements complicate the hardware design process. On the software side, multicore designs significantly complicate the programming burden compared to their single-core predecessors. The different CPUs are exposed to the programmer, who has to make sure to use all of them efficiently, as well as using the memory hierarchy properly by exploiting both temporal and spatial locality. This increasing programming complexity, also known as the Programmability Wall [9], has motivated the advent of sophisticated programming paradigms and runtime system software to support them.

Task-based parallelism [3,6,7,22] has been proposed as a solution to the Programmability Wall and, indeed, the most relevant shared memory programming standards, like OpenMP, support tasking constructs. The task based model requires the programmer to split the code into several sequential pieces, called tasks, as well as explicitly specifying their input and output dependencies. The task-based execution model (or runtime system) consists of a master thread and several worker threads. The master thread goes over the code of the application and creates tasks once it encounters source code annotations identifying them. The runtime system manages the pool of all created tasks and schedules them across the threads once their input dependencies are satisfied. To carry out the task management process, the parallel runtime system creates and maintains a Task Dependency Graph (TDG). In this graph nodes represent tasks and edges are dependencies between them. Once a new task is created, a new node is added to the TDG. The connectivity of this new node is defined by the data dependencies of the task it represents, which are explicitly specified in the application's source code. When the execution of a task finalizes, its corresponding node is removed from the TDG, as well as its data dependencies.

This task-based runtime system constitutes of a software layer that enables parallel programmers to decouple the parallel code from the underlying parallel architecture where it is supposed to run on. As long as the application can be decomposed into tasks, the task-based execution model is able to properly manage it across homogeneous many-core architectures or heterogeneous designs with different core types. A common practice in the high performance domain is to map a single thread per core, which enables the tasks running on that thread to fully use the core capacity. Finally, another important asset of task-based parallelism is the possibility of automatically managing executions on accelerators with different address spaces. Since the input and output dependencies of tasks are specified, the runtime system can automatically offload a task and its dependencies to an accelerator device (e.g., GPU) without the need for specific programmer intervention [8]. Additional optimizations in terms of software prefetching [21] or more efficient coherence protocols [20] can also be enabled by the task-based paradigm.

Despite their advantages, task-based programming models also induce computational costs. For example, the process of task creation requires the traversal of several indexed tables to update the status of the parallel run by adding the

```
1      ...
2    //task_clause
3    memalloc(&task, args, size);
4    createTask(deps, task, parent, taskData);
5      ...
```

Listing 1.1. Compiler generated pseudo-code equivalence for task annotation.

```
1   void createTask(DepList dList, Task t,
2                   Task parent, Data args) {
3     initAndSetupTask(task1, parent, args);
4     insertToTDG(dList, task1);
5   }
```

Listing 1.2. Pseudo-code for task creation.

new dependencies the recently created tasks bring, which produces a certain overhead. Such overhead constitutes a significant burden, especially on architectures with several 10's or 100's of cores where tasks need to be created at a very fast rate to feed all of them. This paper proposes the Task Generation Express (TaskGenX) approach. Our proposal suggests that the software and hardware are designed to eliminate the most important bottlenecks of task-based parallelism without hurting their multiple advantages. This paper focuses on the software part of this proposal and draws the requirements of the hardware design to achieve significant results. In particular, this paper makes the following contributions beyond the state-of-the-art:

– A new parallel task-based runtime system that decouples the most costly routines from the other runtime activities and thus enables them to be offloaded to specific-purpose helper cores.
– A detailed study of the requirements of a specific-purpose helper core able to accelerate the most time consuming runtime system activities.
– A complete evaluation via trace-driven simulation considering 11 parallel OpenMP codes and 25 different system configurations, including homogeneous and heterogeneous systems. Our evaluation demonstrates how TaskGenX achieves average speedups of 3.1× when compared against currently use state-of-the-art approaches.

The rest of this document is organized as follows: Sect. 2 describes the task-based execution model and its main bottlenecks. Section 3 describes the new task-based runtime system this paper proposes as well as the specialized hardware that accelerates the most time-consuming runtime routines. Section 4 contains the experimental set-up of this paper. Section 5 describes the evaluation of TaskGenX via trace-driven simulation. Finally, Sect. 6 discusses related work and Sect. 7 concludes this work.

2   Background and Motivation

2.1   Task-Based Programming Models

Task-based parallel programming models [3,6,7,22], are widely used to facilitate the programming of parallel codes for multicore systems. These programming models offer annotations that the programmer can add to the application's sequential code. One type of these annotations is the task annotations with dependency tracking which OpenMP [1] supports since its 4.0 release. By adding these annotations, the programmer decomposes the application into *tasks* and specifies the input and output data dependencies between them. A compiler is responsible to translate the annotations into code by adding calls to the programming model's runtime system. The runtime system consists of software threads and is responsible for the efficient execution of the tasks with respect to the data dependencies as well as the availability of resources.

When the compiler encounters a task annotation in the code, it transforms it to the pseudo-code shown in Listing 1.1. `Memalloc` is performing the memory allocation for the task and its arguments. Next is a runtime call, which is the `createTask`, responsible for the linking of the task with the runtime system. At this point a task is considered *created* and below are the three possible states of a task inside the runtime system:

– *Created:* A task is initialized with the appropriate data and function pointers and it is inserted in the Task Dependency Graph (TDG). The insertion of a task in the TDG implies that the data dependencies of the tasks have been identified and the appropriate data structures have been created and initialized.
– *Ready:* When all the data dependencies of a created task have been satisfied, the task is ready and it is inserted in the *ready queue* where it waits for execution.
– *Finished:* When a task has finished execution and has not been deleted yet.

The runtime system creates and manages the software threads for the execution of the tasks. Typically one software thread is being bound to each core. One of the threads is the *master thread*, and the rest are the *worker threads*. The master thread starts executing the code of Listing 1.1 sequentially. The allocation of the task takes place first. What follows is the task creation, that includes the analysis of the dependencies of the created task and the connection to the rest of the existing dependencies. Then, if there are no task dependencies, which means that the task is *ready*, the task is also inserted in the ready queue and waits for execution.

Listing 1.2 shows the pseudo-code for the task creation step within the runtime. The `createTask` function is first initializing the task by copying the corresponding data to the allocated memory as well as connecting the task to its parent task (`initAndSetupTask`). After this step, the task is ready to be inserted in the TDG. The TDG is a distributed and dynamic graph structure that the runtime uses to keep the information about the current tasks of the application.

```
1  void insertToTDG(DepList dList, Task t) {
2    if( dList is empty ) {
3      readyQ->push(t);
4      return;
5    }
6    Dependency entry;
7    for( d in dList ) {
8      entry = depMap[d.address()];
9      if(entry==NULL) depMap.add(entry, t);
10     if(d.accessType() == "write")
11       entry.addLastWriter(t);
12     if(d.accessType() == "read") {
13       entry.addReader(t);
14       entry.lastWriter()->addSuccessor(t);
15     }
16   }
17 }
```

Listing 1.3. Pseudo-code for TDG insertion

The insertion of a task in the TDG is done by the `insertToTDG` function. This function takes as arguments a list with all the memory addresses that are to be written or read by the task (`dList`), and the task itself. Listing 1.3 shows the pseudo-code for the TDG insertion. If for a task the `dList` is empty (line 2), this means that there are no memory addresses that need to be tracked during the execution; thus, the task is marked as *ready* by pushing it to the *ready queue* (line 3). Each entry of `dList` contains the actual memory address as well as the access type (read, write or read-write). The runtime keeps a distributed unified dependency tracking structure, the `depMap` where it stores all the tracked memory addresses together with their writer and reader tasks. For each item in the `dList` the runtime checks if there is an existing representation inside the `depMap` (line 8). If the memory address of an entry of the `dList` is not represented in the `depMap`, it is being added as shown in line 9. If the address of a `dList` item exists in the `depMap`, this means that a prior task has already referred to this memory location, exhibiting a data dependency. According to the access type of d, the readers and the writers of the specific address are updated in the `depMap` (lines 10–15).

To reduce the lookup into the `depMap` calls, every time the contents of a memory address are modified, the tasks keep track of their *successors* as well as the number of *predecessors*. The *successors* of a task are all the tasks with inputs depending on the output of the current task. The *predecessors* of a task are the tasks whose output is used as input for the current task. When a `read` access is identified, the task that is being created is added to the list of successors of the last writer task, as shown on line 20 of Listing 1.2.

As tasks are executed, the dependencies between them and their successors are satisfied. So the successor tasks that are waiting for input, eventually become *ready* and are inserted to the ready queue. When a task goes to the *finished*

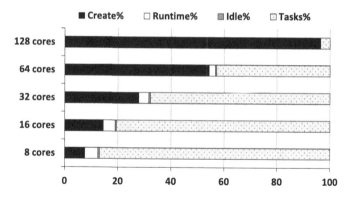

Fig. 1. Master thread activity for Cholesky as we increase the number of cores.

state, the runtime has to perform some actions in order to prepare the successor tasks for execution. These actions are described in Listing 1.4. The runtime first updates the `depMap` to remove the possible references of the task as reader or writer (line 2). Then, if the task does not have any successors, it can safely be deleted (line 3). If the task has successors, the runtime traverses the successor list and for each successor task it decreases its predecessor counter (lines 5–6). If for a successor task its predecessor counter reaches zero, then this task becomes *ready* and it is inserted in the *ready queue* (lines 7–8). The runtime activity takes place at the task state changes. One state change corresponds to the task creation, so a task from being just allocated it becomes *created*. At this point the runtime prepares all the appropriate task and dependency tracking data structures as well as inserts the task into the TDG. The second change occurs when a task from being *created* it becomes *ready*; this implies that the input dependencies of this task are satisfied so the runtime schedules and inserts the task into the ready queue. The third change occurs when a running task finishes execution. In this case, following our task states, the task from being *ready* it becomes *finished*; this is followed by the runtime updating the dependency tracking data structures and scheduling possible successor tasks that become ready. For the rest of the paper we will refer to the first state change runtime activity as the task creation overheads (*Create*). For the runtime activity that takes place for the following two state changes (and includes scheduling and dependence analysis) we will use the term runtime overheads (*Runtime*).

2.2   Motivation

Figure 1 shows the runtime activity of the master thread during the execution of the Cholesky[1] benchmark on 8, 16, 32, 64 and 128 cores[2]. The execution time represented here is the wall clock time during the parallel region of the benchmark. Each one of the series represents a different runtime overhead from the

---

[1] Details about the benchmarks used are in Sect. 4.
[2] The experimental set-up is explained in Sect. 4.

```
1   void task_finish(Task *t) {
2     depMap.removeReaderWriter(t);
3     if(t->successors.empty()) delete t;
4     else {
5       for( succ in t->successors ) {
6         succ.decreasePredecessors();
7         if(succ.numPredecessors == 0)
8           readyQ->push(succ);
9       }
10    }
11  }
```

Listing 1.4. Pseudo-code for task_finish runtime activity.

ones described above. The percentage of time spent on task creation is increasing as we increase the number of cores. This is because the creation overhead is invariant of core count: the more we reduce the application's execution time by adding resources the more important this step becomes in terms of execution time. In contrast, the task execution time percentage is decreased as we increase the number of cores because the computational activity is being shared among more resources. One way to reduce the task creation overhead is by introducing nested parallelism. In this programming technique, every worker thread is able to generate tasks thus the task creation is spread among cores and its overhead is reduced. However, not all applications can be implemented with this parallelization technique and there are very few applications using this scheme. *Runtime* decreases as we increase the number of cores because this activity is also shared among the resources. This is because this part of the runtime takes place once the tasks finish execution and new tasks are being scheduled. So the more the resources, the less the runtime activity per thread, therefore less activity for the master thread.

Our motivation for this work is the bottleneck introduced by task creation as shown in Fig. 1. Our runtime proposal decouples this piece of the runtime and accelerates it on a specialized hardware resulting in higher performance.

3   Task Generation Express

In this paper we propose a semi-centralized runtime system that dynamically separates the most computationally intensive parts of the runtime system and accelerates them on specialized hardware. To develop the TaskGenX we use the OpenMP programming model [1]. The base of our implementation is the Nanos++ runtime system responsible for the parallel execution and it is used in this paper as a replacement of the entire OpenMP's default runtime.

Nanos++ [5] is a distributed runtime system that uses dynamic scheduling. As most task-based programming models, Nanos++ consists of the master and the worker threads. The master thread is launching the parallel region and

creates the tasks that have been defined by the programmer[3]. The scheduler of
Nanos++ consists of a *ready queue* (*TaskQ*) that is shared for reading and writing among threads and is used to keep the tasks that are ready for execution.
All threads have access to the *TaskQ* and once they become available they try
to pop a task from the *TaskQ*. When a thread finishes a task, it performs all
the essential steps described in Sect. 2.1 to keep the data dependency structures
consistent. Moreover, it pushes the tasks that become ready to the *TaskQ*.

3.1   Implementation

TaskGenX relieves the master and worker threads from the intensive work of
task creation by offloading it on the specialized hardware. Our runtime, apart
from the master and the worker threads, introduces the Special Runtime Thread
(SRT). When the runtime system starts, it creates the SRT and binds it to the
task creation accelerator, keeping its thread identifier in order to manage the
usage of it. During runtime, the master and worker threads look for ready tasks
in the task ready queue and execute them along with the runtime. Instead of
querying the ready queue for tasks, the SRT looks for runtime activity requests
in the Runtime Requests Queue (*RRQ*) and if there are requests, it executes
them.

Figure 2 shows the communication infrastructure between threads within
TaskGenX. Our system maintains two queues; the Ready Task Queue (*TaskQ*)
and the Runtime Requests Queue (*RRQ*). The *TaskQ* is used to keep the tasks
that are ready for execution. The *RRQ* is used to keep the pending runtime
activity requests. The master and the worker threads can push and pop tasks to
and from the *TaskQ* and they can also add runtime activity to the *RRQ*. The
special runtime thread (SRT) pops runtime requests from the *RRQ* and executes
them on the accelerator.

```
1  void SRTloop() {
2    while( true ) {
3      while(RRQ is not empty)
4        executeRequest( RRQ.pop() );
5      if( runtime.SRTstop() ) break;
6    }
7    return;
8  }
```

Listing 1.5. Pseudo-code for the SRT loop.

When the master thread encounters a task clause in the application's code,
after allocating the memory needed, it calls the `createTask` as shown in

---

[3] Nanos++ also supports nested parallelism so any of the worker threads can potentially create tasks. However the majority of the existing parallel applications are not
implemented using nested parallelism.

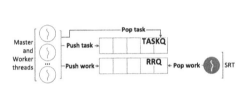

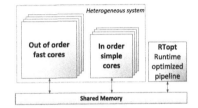

Fig. 2. Communication mechanism between master/workers and SRT threads.

Fig. 3. SoC architecture including three types of cores: out of order, in-order and RTopt.

Listing 1.2 and described in Sect. 2.1. TaskGenX decouples the execution of `createTask` from the master thread. To do so, TaskGenX implements a wrapper function that is invoked instead of `createTask`. In this function, the runtime system checks if the SRT is enabled; if not then the default behaviour takes place, that is, to perform the creation of the task. If the SRT is enabled, a *Create* request is generated and inserted in the *RRQ*. The *Create* runtime request includes the appropriate info to execute the code described in Listing 1.2. That is, the dependence analysis data, the address of the allocated task, its parent and its arguments.

While the master and worker threads are executing tasks, the SRT is looking for *Create* requests in the *RRQ* to execute. Listing 1.5 shows the code that the SRT is executing until the end of the parallel execution. The special runtime thread continuously checks whether there are requests in the *RRQ* (line 3). If there is a pending creation request, the SRT calls the `executeRequest` (line 4), which extracts the appropriate task creation data from the creation request and performs the task creation by calling the `createTask` described in Listing 1.2. When the parallel region is over, the runtime system informs the SRT to stop execution. This is when the SRT exits and the execution finishes (line 5).

3.2 Hardware Requirements

As described in the previous section, TaskGenX assumes the existence of specialized hardware that accelerates the task creation step. The goal of this paper is not to propose a detailed micro-architecture of the specialized hardware; instead we sketch the high-level hardware requirements for the TaskGenX set-up, in the hope to be an insightful and useful influence for hardware designers. The SRT is bound to the task creation accelerator and executes the requests in the RRQ. Previous studies have proposed custom accelerators for the runtime activity [12,15,18,19,25,26]. These proposals significantly accelerate (up to three orders of magnitude) different bottlenecks of the runtime system[4]. These special purpose designs can only execute runtime system activity.

---

[4] Section 6 further describes these proposals.

Table 1. Evaluated benchmarks and relevant characteristics

Application	Problem size	#Tasks	Avg task CPU cycles (thousands)	Per task overheads (CPU cycles)			Measured perf. ratio	r	Parallel model
				Create	All	Deps + Sched			
Cholesky factorization	32K 256	357 762	753	15221	73286	58065	3.5	10.34	Dependencies
	32K 128	2829058	110	17992	58820	40828		83.74	
QR factorization	16K 512	11 442	518 570	17595	63008	45413	6.8	0.01	Dependencies
	16K 128	707 265	3 558	21642	60777	39135		3.11	
Blackscholes	Native	488 202	348	29141	85438	56297	2.3	42.87	Data-parallel
Bodytrack	Native	329 123	383	9 505	18979	9474	4.2	12.70	Pipeline
Canneal	Native	3 072 002	67	25781	50094	24313	2.0	197.01	Unstructured
Dedup	Native	20 248	1 532	1294	9647	8353	2.7	0.43	Pipeline
Ferret	Native × 2	84 002	29 088	38913	98457	59544	3.6	0.68	Pipeline
Fluidanimate	Native	128 502	16 734	30210	94079	64079	3.3	0.91	Data-parallel
Streamcluster	Native	3 184 654	161	6892	13693	6801	3.5	21.91	Data-parallel

As an alternative, in our envisioned architecture we propose to have a general purpose core that has been optimized to run the runtime system activity more efficiently. The runtime optimized (RTopt) core can be combined with both homogeneous or heterogeneous systems and accelerate the runtime activity. Figure 3 shows the envisioned architecture when RTopt is combined with an asymmetric heterogeneous system. This architecture has three core types that consist of simple in-order cores, fast out-of-order cores and an RTopt core for the SRT. RTopt can optimize its architecture, having a different cache hierarchy, pipeline configuration and specialized hardware structures to hold and process the SRT. As a result, the RTopt executes the SRT much faster than the other cores. The RTopt can also execute tasks, but will achieve limited performance compared to the other cores as its hardware structures have been optimized for a specific software (the SRT).

To evaluate our approach we study the requirements of the RTopt in order to provide enough performance for TaskGenX. Based on the analysis by Etsion et al. [15], there is a certain *task decode rate* that leads to optimal utilization of the multicore system. This rule can be applied in the case of TaskGenX for the *task creation rate*, i.e., the frequency of task generation of the runtime system. If the *task creation rate* is higher than the *task execution rate*, then for a highly parallel application the resources will always have tasks to execute and they will not remain idle. To achieve a high *task creation rate*, we can accelerate the task creation cost. Equation 1 shows the maximum optimal task creation cost, $C_{opt}(x)$ in order to keep x cores busy, without starving due to task creation.

$$C_{opt}(x) = avg.\ task\ duration/x \qquad (1)$$

If C_{gp} is the cost of task creation when it is performed on a general purpose core, then the RTopt has to achieve a speedup of $r = C_{gp}/C_{opt}(x)$ to achieve full utilization of the system. Section 4.2 performs an analysis based on these requirements for the evaluated applications. As we will see in Sect. 4.2, a modest and implementable value of $r = 16\times$ is enough to significantly accelerate execution on a 512-core system.

Finally, if TaskGenX executes on a regular processor without the RTopt core, the SRT is bound to a regular core without any further modification. In this scenario, applications will not significantly benefit from having a separate SRT.

4 Experimental Methodology

4.1 Applications

Table 1 shows the evaluated applications, the input sizes used, and their characteristics. All applications are implemented using the OpenMP programming model. We obtain Cholesky and QR from the BAR repository [4] and we use the implementations of the rest of the benchmarks from the PARSECSs suite [10]. More information about these applications can be found in [10,11]. As the number of cores in SoCs is increasing, so does the need of available task parallelism [24]. We choose the input sizes of the applications so that they create enough fine-grained tasks to feed up to 512 cores. The number of tasks per application and input as well as the average per-task CPU cycles can be found on Table 1.

4.2 Simulation

To evaluate TaskGenX we make use of the TaskSim simulator [16,23]. TaskSim is a trace driven simulator, that supports the specification of homogeneous or heterogeneous systems with many cores. The tracing overhead of the simulator is less than 10% and the simulation is accurate as long as there is no contention in the shared memory resources on a real system [16]. By default, TaskSim allows the specification of the amount of cores and supports up to two core types in the case of heterogeneous asymmetric systems. This is done by specifying the number of cores of each type and their difference in performance between the different types (performance ratio) in the TaskSim configuration file.

Our evaluation consists of experiments on both symmetric and asymmetric platforms with the number of cores varying from 8 to 512. In the case of asymmetric systems, we simulate the behaviour of an ARM big.LITTLE architecture [17]. To set the correct performance ratio between big and little cores, we measure the sequential execution time of each application on a real ARM big.LITTLE platform when running on a little and on a big core. We use the Hardkernel Odroid XU3 board that includes a Samsung Exynos 5422 chip with ARM big.LITTLE. The big cores run at 1.6 GHz and the little cores at 800 MHz. Table 1 shows the measured performance ratio for each case. The average performance ratio among our 11 workloads is 3.8. Thus in the specification of the asymmetric systems we use as performance ratio the value 4.

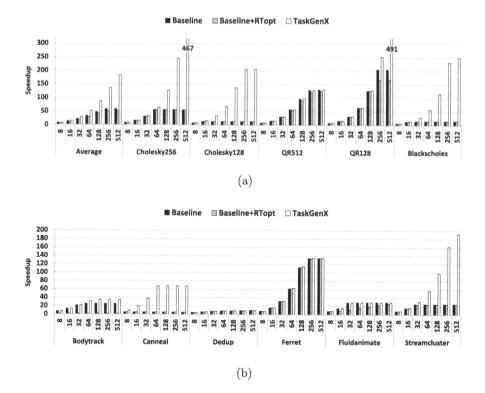

Fig. 4. Speedup of TaskGenX compared to the speedup of Baseline and Baseline+RTopt for each application for systems with 8 up to 512 cores. The average results of (a) show the average among all workloads shown on (a) and (b)

To simulate our approaches using TaskSim we first run each application/input in the TaskSim trace generation mode. This mode enables the online tracking of task duration and synchronization overheads and stores them in a trace file. To perform the simulation, TaskSim uses the information stored in the trace file and executes the application by providing this information to the runtime system. For our experiments we generate three trace files for each application/input combination on a Genuine Intel 16-core machine running at 2.60 GHz.

We modify TaskSim so that it features one extra hardware accelerator (per multicore) responsible for the fast task creation (the RTopt). Apart from the task duration time, our modified simulator tracks the duration of the runtime overheads. These overheads include: (a) task creation, (b) dependencies resolution, and (c) scheduling. The RTopt core is optimized to execute task creation faster than the general purpose cores; to determine how much faster a task creation job is executed we use the analysis performed in Sect. 3.2.

Using Eq. 1, we compute the $C_{opt}(x)$ for each application according to their average task CPU cycles from Table 1 for $x = 512$ cores. C_{gp} is the cost of task creation when it is performed on a general purpose core, namely the *Create* column shown on Table 1. To have optimal results for each application on systems up to 512 cores, C_{gp} needs to be reduced to $C_{opt}(512)$. Thus the specialized hardware accelerator needs to perform task creation with a ratio $r = C_{gp}/C_{opt}(512)\times$ faster than a general purpose core.

We compute r for each application shown on Table 1. We observe that for the applications with a large number of per-task CPU cycles and relatively small *Create* cycles (QR512, Dedup, Ferret, Fluidanimate), r is very close to zero, meaning that the task creation cost (C_{gp}) is already small enough for optimal task creation without the need of a faster hardware accelerator. For the rest of the applications, more powerful hardware is needed. For these applications r ranges from 3× to 197×. Comparing r to the measured performance ratio of each application we can see that in most cases accelerating the task creation on a big core would not be sufficient for achieving higher task creation rate. In our experimental evaluation we accelerate task creation in the RTopt and we use the ratio of 16× which is a relatively small value within this range that we consider realistic to implement in hardware. The results obtained show the average results among three different traces for each application-input.

5   Evaluation

5.1   Homogeneous Multicore Systems

Figures 4a and b show the speedup over one core of three different scenarios:

- *Basel ine*: the Nanos++ runtime system, which is the default runtime without using any external hardware support
- *Baseline+RTopt*: the Nanos++ runtime system that uses the external hardware as if it is a general purpose core
- *TaskGenX*: our proposed runtime system that takes advantage of the optimized hardware

We evaluate these approaches with the TaskSim simulator for systems of 8 up to 512 cores. In the case of Baseline+RTopt the specialized hardware acts as a slow general purpose core that is additional to the number of cores shown on the x axis. If this core executes a task creation job, it executes it 16× faster, but as it is specialized for this, we assume that when a task is executed on this core it is executed 4× slower than in a general purpose core. The runtime system in this case does not include our modifications that automatically decouple the task creation step for each task. The comparison against the Baseline+RTopt is used only to show that the baseline runtime is not capable of effectively utilizing the accelerator. In most of the cases having this additional hardware without the appropriate runtime support results in slowdown as the tasks are being executed slower on the special hardware.

Focusing on the average results first, we can observe that TaskGenX constantly improves the baseline and the improvement is increasing as the number of cores is increased, reaching up to 3.1× improved performance on 512 cores.

This is because as we increase the number of cores, the task creation overhead becomes more critical part of the execution time and affects performance even more. So, this becomes the main bottleneck due to which the performance of many applications saturates. TaskGenX overcomes it by automatically detecting and moving task creation on the specialized hardware.

Looking in more detail, we can see that for all applications the baseline has a saturation point in speedup. For example Cholesky256 saturates on 64 cores, while QR512 on 256 cores. In most cases this saturation in performance comes due to the sequential task creation that is taking place for an important percentage of the execution time (as shown in Fig. 1). TaskGenX solves this as it efficiently decouples the task creation code and accelerates it leading to higher speedups.

TaskGenX is effective as it either improves performance or it performs as fast as the baseline (there are no slowdowns). The applications that do not benefit (QR512, Ferret, Fluidanimate) are the ones with the highest average per task CPU cycles as shown on Table 1. Dedup also does not benefit as the per task creation cycles are very low compared to its average task size. Even if these applications consist of many tasks, the task creation overhead is considered negligible compared to the task cost, so accelerating it does not help much.

This can be verified by the results shown for QR128 workload. In this case, we use the same input size as QR512 (which is 16K) but we modify the block size, which results in more and smaller tasks. This not only increases the speedup of the baseline, but also shows even higher speedup when running with TaskGenX reaching very close to the ideal speedup and improving the baseline by 2.3×.

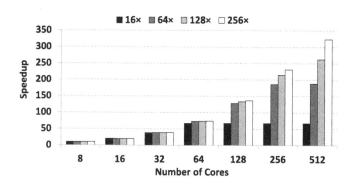

Fig. 5. Canneal performance as we modify r; x-axis shows the number of cores.

Modifying the block size for Cholesky, shows the same effect in terms of TaskGenX over baseline improvement. However, for this application, using the bigger block size of 256 is more efficient as a whole. Nevertheless, TaskGenX improves the cases that performance saturates and reaches up to 8.5× improvement for the 256 block-size, and up to 16× for the 128 block-size.

Blackscholes and Canneal, are applications with very high task creation overheads compared to the task size as shown on Table 1. This makes them very sensitive to performance degradation due to task creation. As a result their performance saturates even with limited core counts of 8 or 16 cores. These are the ideal cases for using TaskGenX as such bottlenecks are eliminated and performance is improved by 15.9× and 13.9× respectively. However, for Canneal for which the task creation lasts a bit less than half of the task execution time, accelerating it by 16 times is not enough and soon performance saturates at 64 cores. In this case, a more powerful hardware would improve things even more. Figure 5 shows how the performance of Canneal is affected when modifying the task creation performance ratio, r between the specialized hardware and general purpose. Using hardware that performs task creation close to 256× faster than the general purpose core leads to higher improvements.

Streamcluster has also relatively high task creation overhead compared to the average task cost so improvements are increased as the number of cores is increasing. TaskGenX reaches up to 7.6× improvement in this case.

The performance of Bodytrack saturates on 64 cores for the baseline. However, it does not approach the ideal speedup as its pipelined parallelization technique introduces significant task dependencies that limit parallelism. TaskGenX still improves the baseline by up to 37%. This improvement is low compared to other benchmarks, firstly because of the nature of the application and secondly because Bodytrack introduces nested parallelism. With nested parallelism task creation is being spread among cores so it is not becoming a sequential overhead as happens in most of the cases. Thus, in this case task creation is not as critical to achieve better results.

5.2   Heterogeneous Multicore Systems

At this stage of the evaluation our system supports two types of general purpose processors, simulating an asymmetric multicore processor. The asymmetric system is influenced by the ARM big.LITTLE architecture [17] that consists of big and little cores. In our simulations, we consider that the big cores are four times faster than the little cores of the system. This is based on the average measured performance ratio, shown on Table 1, among the 11 workloads used in this evaluation.

In this set-up there are two different ways of executing a task-based application. The first way is to start the application's execution on a big core of the system and the second way is to start the execution on a little core of the system If we use a big core to load the application, then this implies that the master thread of the runtime system (the thread that performs the task creation when running with the baseline) runs on a fast core, thus tasks are created faster than when using a slow core as a starting point. We evaluate both approaches and compare the results of the baseline runtime and TaskGenX.

Figure 6 plots the average speedup over one little core obtained among all 11 workloads for the Baseline, Baseline+RTopt and TaskGenX. The chart shows two categories of results on the x axis, separating the cases of the master thread's execution. The numbers at the bottom of x axis show the total number of cores and the numbers above show the number of big cores.

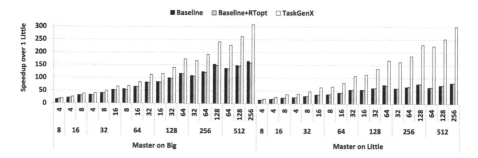

Fig. 6. Average speedup among all 11 workloads on heterogeneous simulated systems. The numbers at the bottom of x axis show the total number of cores and the numbers above them show the number of big cores. Results are separated depending on the type of core that executes the master thread: a big or little core.

The results show that moving the master thread from a big to a little core degrades performance of the baseline. This is because the task creation becomes even slower so the rest of the cores spend more idle time waiting for the tasks to become ready. TaskGenX improves performance in both cases. Specifically when master runs on big, the average improvement of TaskGenX reaches 86%. When the master thread runs on a little core, TaskGenX improves performance by up to 3.7×. This is mainly due to the slowdown caused by the migration of master thread on a little core. Using TaskGenX on asymmetric systems achieves approximately similar performance regardless of the type of core that the master thread is running. This makes our proposal more portable for asymmetric systems as the programmer does not have to be concerned about the type of core that the master thread migrates.

5.3   Comparison to Other Approaches

As we saw earlier, TaskGenX improves the baseline scheduler by up to 6.3× for 512 cores. In this section we compare TaskGenX with other approaches. To do so, we consider the proposals of Carbon [19], Task Superscalar [15], Picos++ [26] and Nexus# [12]. We group these proposals based on the part of the runtime activity they are offloading from the CPU. Carbon and Task Superscalar are runtime-driven meaning that they both accelerate all the runtime and scheduling parts. The task creation, dependence analysis as well as the scheduling, namely the ready queue manipulation, are transferred to the RTopt with these approaches. These overheads are represented on Table 1 under ALL. For the evaluation of these approaches one RTopt is used optimized to accelerate all the runtime activities. The second group of related designs that we compare against is the dependencies-driven, which includes approaches like Picos++ and Nexus#. These approaches aim to accelerate only the dependence analysis part of the runtime as well as the scheduling that occurs when a dependency is satisfied. The RTopt in this case is optimized to accelerate these activities. For example, when a task finishes execution, and it has produced input for another task, the dependency tracking mechanism is updating the appropriate counters of the reader task and if the task becomes ready, the task is inserted in the ready queue. The insertion into the ready queue is the scheduling that occurs with the dependence analysis. These overheads are represented on Table 1 under *Deps+Sched*.

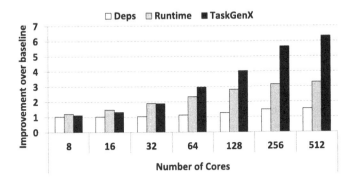

Fig. 7. Average improvement over baseline; x-axis shows the number of cores.

Figure 7 shows the average improvement in performance for each core count over the performance of the baseline scheduler on the same core count. *Runtime* represents the runtime driven approaches and the *Deps* represents the dependencies driven approaches as described above. X-axis shows the number of general purpose cores; for every core count one additional RTopt core is used.

Accelerating the scheduling with *Runtime*-driven is as efficient as TaskGenX for a limited number of cores, up to 32. This is because they both accelerate task creation which is an important bottleneck. *Deps*-driven approaches on the other hand are not as efficient since in this case the task creation step takes place on the master thread.

Increasing the number of cores, we observe that the improvement of the *Runtime*-driven over the baseline is reduced and stabilized close to 3.2× while TaskGenX continues to speedup the execution. Transferring all parts of the runtime to RTopt with the *Runtime*-driven approaches, leads to the serialization of the runtime. Therefore, all scheduling operations (such as enqueue, dequeue of tasks, dependence analysis etc.) that typically occur in parallel during runtime are executed sequentially on the RTopt. Even if RTopt executes these operations faster than a general purpose core, serializing them potentially creates a bottleneck as we increase the number of cores. TaskGenX does not transfer other runtime activities than the task creation, so it allows scheduling and dependence analysis operations to be performed in a distributed manner.

Deps driven approaches go through the same issue of the serialization of the dependency tracking and the scheduling that occurs at the dependence analysis stage. The reason for the limited performance of *Deps* compared to *Runtime* is that *Deps* does not accelerate any part of the task creation. Improvement over the baseline is still significant as performance with *Deps* is improved by up to 1.5×.

TaskGenX is the most efficient software-hardware co-design approach when it comes to highly parallel applications. On average, it improves the baseline by up to 3.1× for homogeneous systems and up to 3.7× for heterogeneous systems. Compared to other state of the art approaches, TaskGenX is more effective on a large number of cores showing higher performance by 54% over *Runtime* driven approaches and by 70% over *Deps* driven approaches.

6   Related Work

Our approach is a new task-based runtime system design that enables the acceleration of task creation to overcome important bottlenecks in performance. Task-based runtime systems have intensively been studied. State of the art task-based runtime systems include the OpenMP [1], OmpSs [14], StarPU [2] and Swan [27]. All these models support tasks and maintain a TDG specifying the inter-task dependencies. This means that the runtime system is responsible for the task creation, the dependence analysis as well as the scheduling of the tasks. However, none of these runtime systems offers automatic offloading of task creation.

The fact that task-based programming models are so widely spread makes approaches like ours very important and also gives importance to studies that focus on adding hardware support to boost performance of task-based runtime systems. Even if their work focuses more on the hardware part of the design, their contributions are very relative to our study as we can distinguish which parts of the hardware is more beneficial to be accelerated.

Carbon [19] accelerates the scheduling of tasks by implementing hardware ready queues. Carbon maintains one hardware queue per core and accelerates all possible scheduling overheads by using these queues. Nexus# [12] is also a distributed hardware accelerator capable of executing the *in, out, inout, taskwait* and *taskwait on* pragmas, namely the task dependencies. Unlike Carbon and Nexus, TaskGenX accelerates only task creation. Moreover, ADM [24] is another distributed approach that proposes hardware support for the inter-thread communication to avoid going through the memory hierarchy. This aims to provide a more flexible design as the scheduling policy can be freely implemented in software. These designs require the implementation of a hardware component for each core of an SoC [28]. Our proposal assumes a centralized hardware unit that is capable of operating without the need to change the SoC.

Task Superscalar [15] and Picos++ [26] use a single hardware component to accelerate parts of the runtime system. In the case of Task superscalar, all the parts of the runtime system are transferred to the accelerator. Picos++ [26] is a hardware-software co-design that supports nested tasks. This design enables the acceleration of the inter-task dependencies on a special hardware. Swarm [18] performs speculative task execution. Instead of accelerating parts of the runtime system, Swarm uses hardware support to accelerate speculation. This is different than our design that decouples only task creation.

Our work diverges to prior studies for two main reasons:

- The implementation of prior studies requires changes in hardware of the SoC. This means that they need an expensive design where each core of the chip has an extra component. Our proposal offers a much cheaper solution by requiring only a single specialized core that, according to our experiments, can manage the task creation for 512-core SoCs.
- None of the previous studies is aiming at accelerating exclusively task creation overheads. According to our study task creation becomes the main bottleneck as we increase the number of cores and our study is the first that takes this into account.

7 Conclusions

This paper presented TaskGenX, the first software-hardware co-design that decouples task creation and accelerates it on a runtime optimized hardware. In contrast to previous studies, our paper makes the observation that task creation is a significant bottleneck in parallel runtimes. Based on this we implemented TaskGenX on top of the OpenMP programming model. On the hardware side, our paper sets the requirements for the RTopt in order to achieve optimal results and proposes an asymmetric architecture that combines it with general purpose cores.

Based on this analysis we evaluate the performance of 11 real workloads using our approach with TaskSim simulator. Accelerating task creation, TaskGenX achieves up to 15.8× improvement (Cholesky128) over the baseline for homogeneous systems and up to 16× (Blackscholes) on asymmetric systems when the application is launched on a little core. Using TaskGenX on asymmetric systems offers a portable solution, as the task creation is not affected by the type of core that the master thread is bound to.

We further showed that for some cases like Canneal where task creation needs to be accelerated as much as 197× in order to steadily provide enough created tasks for execution. However, even by using a realistic and implementable hardware approach that offers 16× speedup of task creation, achieves satisfactory results as it improves the baseline up to 14×.

Comparing TaskGenX against other approaches such as Carbon, Nexus, Picos++ or TaskSuperscalar that manage to transfer different parts of the runtime to the RTopt proves that TaskGenX is the most minimalistic and effective approach. Even if TaskGenX transfers the least possible runtime activity to the RTopt hardware it achieves better results. This implies that TaskGenX requires a less complicated hardware accelerator, as it is specialized for only a small part of the runtime, unlike the other approaches that need specialization for task creation, dependency tracking and scheduling.

We expect that combining TaskGenX with an asymmetry-aware task scheduler will achieve even better results, as asymmetry introduces load imbalance.

Acknowledgements. This work has been supported by the RoMoL ERC Advanced Grant (GA 321253), by the European HiPEAC Network of Excellence, by the Spanish Ministry of Science and Innovation (contracts TIN2015-65316-P), by the Generalitat de Catalunya (contracts 2014-SGR-1051 and 2014-SGR-1272), and by the European Union's Horizon 2020 research and innovation programme under grant agreement No. 671697 and No. 779877. M. Moretó has been partially supported by the Ministry of Economy and Competitiveness under Ramon y Cajal fellowship number RYC-2016-21104. Finally, the authors would like to thank Thomas Grass for his valuable help with the simulator.

References

1. OpenMP architecture review board. OpenMP Specification. 4.5 (2015)
2. Augonnet, C., Thibault, S., Namyst, R., Wacrenier, P.-A.: StarPU: a unified platform for task scheduling on heterogeneous multicore architectures. Concurr. Comput. Pract. Exper. **23**(2), 187–198 (2011)
3. Ayguadé, E., Badia, R., Bellens, P., Cabrera, D., Duran, A., Ferrer, R., Gonzàlez, M., Igual, F., Jiménez-González, D., Labarta, J., Martinell, L., Martorell, X., Mayo, R., Pérez, J., Planas, J., Quintana-Ortí, E.: Extending OpenMP to survive the heterogeneous multicore era. Int. J. Parallel Prog. **38**(5–6), 440–459 (2010)
4. Barcelona Supercomputing Center. BSC Application Repository, 18 April 2014. https://pm.bsc.es/projects/bar
5. Barcelona Supercomputing Center. Nanos++
6. Bauer, M., Treichler, S., Slaughter, E., Aiken, A.: Legion: expressing locality and independence with logical regions. In: SC, pp. 66:1–66:11 (2012)
7. Blumofe, R.D., Joerg, C.F., Kuszmaul, B.C., Leiserson, C.E., Randall, K.H., Zhou,Y.: Cilk: an efficient multithreaded runtime system. In: PPoPP, pp. 207–216 (1995)
8. Bueno, J., Planas, J., Duran, A., Badia, R.M., Martorell, X., Ayguadé, E., Labarta, J.: Productive programming of GPU clusters with OmpSs. In: IPDPS, pp. 557–568 (2012)
9. Chapman, B.: The multicore programming challenge. In: Xu, M., Zhan, Y., Cao, J., Liu, Y. (eds.) APPT 2007. LNCS, vol. 4847, p. 3. Springer, Heidelberg (2007). https://doi.org/10.1007/978-3-540-76837-1_3
10. Chasapis, D., Casas, M., Moreto, M., Vidal, R., Ayguade, E., Labarta, J., Valero, M.: PARSECSs: evaluating the impact of task parallelism in the PARSEC benchmark suite. Trans. Archit. Code Optim. **12**, 41:1–41:22 (2015)
11. Chronaki, K., Rico, A., Badia, R.M., Ayguadé, E., Labarta, J., Valero, M.: Criticality-aware dynamic task scheduling for heterogeneous architectures. In: ICS, pp. 329–338 (2015)
12. Dallou, T., Engelhardt, N., Elhossini, A., Juurlink, B.: Nexus#: a distributed hardware task manager for task-based programming models. In: IPDPS, pp. 1129–1138 (2015)
13. Dennard, R., Gaensslen, F., Rideout, V., Bassous, E., LeBlanc, A.: Design of ion-implanted MOSFET's with very small physical dimensions. IEEE J. Solid-State Circuits **9**, 256–268 (1974)
14. Duran, A., Ayguadé, E., Badia, R.M., Labarta, J., Martinell, L., Martorell, X., Planas, J.: OmpSs: a proposal for programming heterogeneous multicore architectures. Parallel Process. Lett. **21**, 173–193 (2011)

15. Etsion, Y., Cabarcas, F., Rico, A., Ramirez, A., Badia, R.M., Ayguade, E., Labarta, J., Valero, M.: Task superscalar: an out-of-order task pipeline. In: MICRO, pp. 89–100 (2010)
16. Grass, T., Allande, C., Armejach, A., Rico, A., Ayguadé, E., Labarta, J., Valero, M., Casas, M., Moreto, M.: MUSA: a multi-level simulation approach for next-generation HPC machines. In: SC 2016, pp. 526–537, November 2016
17. Jeff, B.: big.LITTLE technology moves towards fully heterogeneous global task scheduling. ARM White Paper (2013)
18. Jeffrey, M.C., Subramanian, S., Yan, C., Emer, J., Sanchez, D.: A scalable architecture for ordered parallelism. In: MICRO, pp. 228–241 (2015)
19. Kumar, S., Hughes, C.J., Nguyen, A.: Carbon: architectural support for fine-grained parallelism on chip multiprocessors. In: ISCA, pp. 162–173 (2007)
20. Manivannan, M., Stenström, P.: Runtime-guided cache coherence optimizations in multicore architectures. In: IPDPS (2014)
21. Papaefstathiou, V., Katevenis, M.G., Nikolopoulos, D.S., Pnevmatikatos, D.: Prefetching and cache management using task lifetimes. In: ICS 2013, pp. 325–334 (2013)
22. Reinders, J.: Intel Threading Building Blocks - Outfitting C++ for Multicore Processor Parallelism. O'Reilly, Sebastopol (2007)
23. Rico, A., Cabarcas, F., Villavieja, C., Pavlovic, M., Vega, A., Etsion, Y., Ramirez, A., Valero, M.: On the simulation of large-scale architectures using multiple application abstraction levels. ACM Trans. Archit. Code Optim. 8(4), 36:1–36:20 (2012)
24. Sanchez, D., Yoo, R.M., Kozyrakis, C.: Flexible architectural support for fine-grain scheduling. In: ASPLOS, pp. 311–322 (2010)
25. Själander, M., Terechko, A., Duranton, M.: A look-ahead task management unit for embedded multicore architectures. In: EUROMICRO DSD, pp. 149–157 (2008)
26. Tan, X., Bosch, J., Vidal, M., Álvarez, C., Jiménez-González, D., Ayguadé, E., Valero, M.: General purpose task-dependence management hardware for task-based dataflow programming models. In: IPDPS, pp. 244–253 (2017)
27. Vandierendonck, H., Tzenakis, G., Nikolopoulos, D.S.: A unified scheduler for recursive and task dataflow parallelism. In: PACT, pp. 1–11 (2011)
28. Castillo, E., Alvarez, L., Moretó, M., Casas, M., Vallejo, E., Bosque, J.L., Beivide, R., Valero, M.: Architectural support for task dependence management with flexible software scheduling. In: HPCA, pp. 283–295 (2018)

Author Index